MOON HANDBOOKS

PUERTO VALLARTA

D0048843

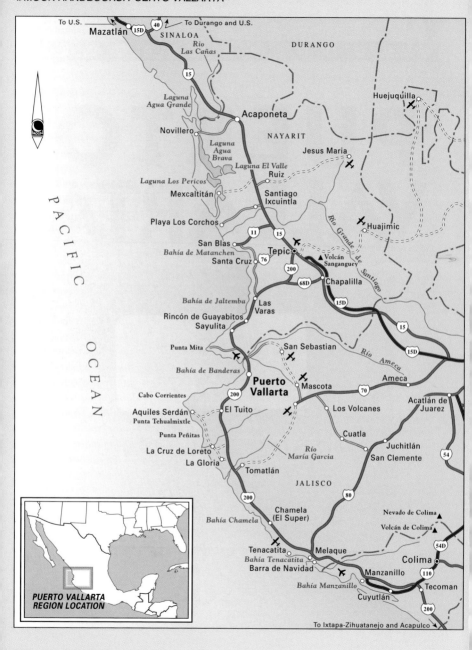

PUERTO VALLARTA
REGION LOCATION

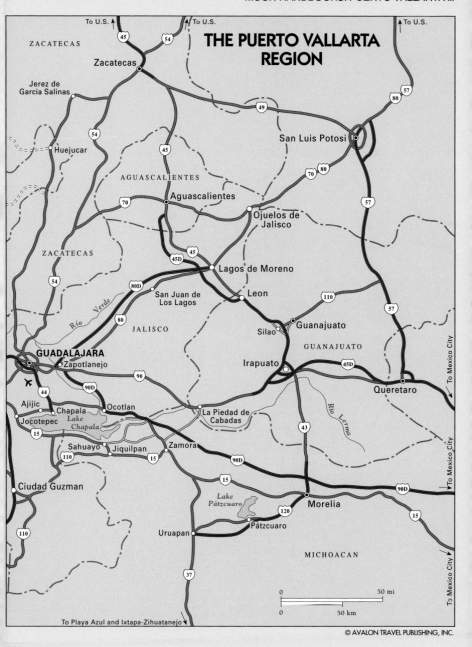

THE PUERTO VALLARTA REGION

MOON HANDBOOKS

PUERTO VALLARTA

INCLUDING 300 MILES OF COASTAL COVERAGE AND SIDE TRIPS TO GUADALAJARA AND LAKE CHAPALA

FOURTH EDITION

BRUCE WHIPPERMAN

AVALON
TRAVEL

MOON HANDBOOKS: PUERTO VALLARTA
FOURTH EDITION
Bruce Whipperman

Published by
    Avalon Travel Publishing
    5855 Beaudry St.
    Emeryville, CA 94608, USA

Please send all comments,
corrections, additions,
amendments, and critiques to:

**MOON HANDBOOKS:
PUERTO VALLARTA
Avalon Travel Publishing
5855 Beaudry St.
Emeryville, CA 94608, USA
e-mail:
atpfeedback@avalonpub.com
www.travelmatters.com**

Printing History
  1st edition—1995
  4th edition—October 2001
  5 4 3 2

ISBN: 1-56691-330-6
ISSN: 1533-4198

Editors: Valerie Sellers Blanton, Erin Van Rheenen
Series Manager: Erin Van Rheenen
Graphics Coordinator: Melissa Sherowski
Production: Alvaro Villanueva
Map Editor: Naomi Dancis
Cartography: Mike Morgenfeld, Chris Folks, Kat Kalamaras, Ben Pease
Index: Karen Bleske

Front cover photo: Robert Fried

Distributed by Publishers Group West

Printed in the United States by R.R. Donnelley.

Although every effort was made to ensure that the information was correct at the time of going to press, the author and publisher do not assume and hereby disclaim any liability to any party for any loss or damage caused by errors, omissions, or any potential travel disruption due to labor or financial difficulty, whether such errors or omissions result from negligence, accident, or any other cause.

To the people of Mexico

CONTENTS

PUERTO VALLARTA: TOWN, BAY, AND MOUNTAINS . . . . 88~158

SPECIAL TOPICS

THE NAYARIT COAST . . . . 159~212

SPECIAL TOPICS

ABBREVIATIONS

a/c—air-conditioned
Av.—*avenida*
Blv.—*bulevar* (boulevard)
C—Celsius
Calz.—*calzada* (thoroughfare, main road)
d—double occupancy

Fco.—Francisco (proper name, as in "Fco. Villa")
Fracc.—*Fraccionamiento* (subdivision)
Hwy.—Highway
Km—kilometer marker
kph—kilometers per hour
km—kilometers

Nte.—*norte* (north)
Ote.—*oriente* (east)
Pte.—*poniente* (west)
s—single occupancy
s/n—*sin número* (no street number)
t—triple occupancy
tel.—telephone number

MAPS

HANDBOOK DIVISIONS

THE NAYARIT COAST

NAYARIT

INLAND TO GUADALAJARA AND LAKE CHAPALA

Puerto Vallarta

Guadalajara

PUERTO VALLARTA: TOWN, BAY, AND MOUNTAINS

JALISCO

THE COAST OF JALISCO

PACIFIC OCEAN

COLIMA

© AVALON TRAVEL PUBLISHING, INC.

MAP SYMBOLS

═══ Divided Highway	○ City/Town	ⓉⓅ Trailer Park
═══ Primary Road	★ Point of Interest	▲ Mountain
═══ Secondary Road	• Accommodation	⋔ Waterfall
---------- Unpaved Road	▼ Restaurant/Bar	▲ Campground
·············· Ferry	▪ Other Location	▮ Gas Station
- - - - - - Trail	⛪ Church	⌟ Golf
├──┼──┤ Railroad	⬗ Archaeological Site	〰 Swamp
═══ Pedestrian Walkway	✕ Airport	〰 Mangrove

ACKNOWLEDGMENTS

Kindness, in major part, was responsible for this book. I gratefully thank the host of Mexican people—at roadside, at their front doors, and behind store, hotel, and turismo counters—who patiently answered my requests for information and directions. At times, their help was vital—such as when two young men extracted my car from a creek, or when a pair of road workers helped me dig it out of a sandy embankment.

To others I owe a unique debt for their continuous generosity. In Puerto Vallarta, thanks to Nancy Adams, who made my work so much more pleasant by gracefully allowing me to set up shop in a corner of her lovely Cafe Sierra. I also owe much to Gary Thompson, of Galería Pacífico, who introduced me to both Puerto Vallarta art and his many gracious friends and associates. For their helpful kindness, I also specially thank John and Nancy Erickson, Kathy von Rohr, Diana Turn, and María Elena Zermeño.

Outside of Puerto Vallarta, on the Nayarit coast, I owe a debt for the kind help and hospitality of Mina and Carlos González in Bucerías; Professor and Mrs. Charles Sacamano, and Adrienne Adams, in Sayulita; Jorge Castuera and his family in Rincón de Guayabitos; Laura del Valle and Emily Spielman at Mar de Jade; Josefina Vásquez and her family in San Blas; Mariano, Susana, and Angelica Valadez at the Huichol Center in Santiago Ixcuintla; and Mr. and Mrs. Tony Burton in Jocotepec. This book is much richer because of them.

Likewise, in Puerto Vallarta's mountain country, thanks to Bud Acord at Hacienda Jalisco for his warm hospitality and sharing his reminiscences of old times in Puerto Vallarta with me. Thanks are also due to Cuca Díaz and her daughter Ana, at Posada Corona in Mascota for their equally kind hospitality.

Back in California, thanks to Avalon Travel Publishing publisher Bill Newlin and his acquisitions committee for their vote of confidence in this project. Thanks, furthermore, to everyone else at ATP for their super-fine editing, graphics, and layout work.

I owe a special debt to Richard Paoli, former editor of the *San Francisco Examiner* travel section, who, in 1983, selected my story about the Raffles Hotel in Singapore, which became my first published work. Thanks also to the others who have encouraged me since then, especially Patricia Lee, president of Bay Area Travel Writers, and many of my fellow members. Singular among them was the late Rebecca Bruns, whose excellent guidebook, Hidden Mexico, was a major inspiration for my present work.

Back home in Berkeley, thanks for the sympathetic cooperation of the friendly staff at my office-away-from-home, Cafe Espresso Roma. Special acknowledgement is due to espresso maestro Miguel, whose delicious, individually decorated, early morning lattes made this book possible.

Thanks also to my friend and business partner, Halcea Valdes, who generously managed without me while I was away in Mexico.

I owe a debt beyond counting to my mother Joan Casebier, my late father and stepmother Bob and Hilda Whipperman, and my sister Doris Davis, for their help in making me who I am.

Finally, I owe a load of thanks to my wife Linda, who cheerfully kept our home together during my absence and lovingly welcomed me back when I returned.

LET US HEAR FROM YOU

We're especially interested in hearing from female travelers, handicapped travelers, people who've traveled with children, RVers, hikers, campers, and residents, both foreign and Mexican. We welcome the comments of business and professional people—hotel and restaurant owners, travel agents, government tourism staff—who serve Puerto Vallarta travelers.

We welcome submissions of unusually good photos and drawings for possible use in future editions. If photos, send duplicate slides or slides-from-negatives; if drawings, send clear photocopies. Please include a self-addressed stamped envelope if you'd like your material returned. If we use it, we'll cite your contribution and give you a free new edition. Please address your responses to:

Moon Handbooks: Puerto Vallarta
Avalon Travel Publishing
5855 Beaudry Street
Emeryville, CA 94608, U.S.A
email: info@travelmatters.com

PREFACE

Many longtime lovers of tropical Mexico know Puerto Vallarta is much more than a beautiful beach. Puerto Vallarta is really two towns: the shiny north-end hotel zone and the stucco-and-tile old town, which nestles between jungle hillsides and the cobbled streets beside the Río Cuale.

Scarcely a generation ago, the old town was all there was to Puerto Vallarta. Bad or nonexistent roads made travel north or south along the coast a bone-jangling ordeal.

Now a network of all-weather highways has made Puerto Vallarta the center of a fascinating region for touring. For those willing to stray an hour or two from their hotel doors, the delights are manifold: lush tropical forests, idyllic palm-shaded beaches, hidden jungle cascades, wildlife-rich mangrove wetlands, and colorful beachside villages. Farther afield, but readily accessible, are Guadalajara's colonial monuments, museums, colorful crafts markets, and the cloud-tipped expanse of Chapala, Mexico's largest lake.

The choices seem endless. More and more visitors opt to stay at out-of-town hotels and small resorts while enjoying Puerto Vallarta's fine food and lively nightlife. Such plumy havens dot the entire Puerto Vallarta regional coast from San Blas in the north to Barra de Navidad in the south. Some are glittering and luxurious, others drowsy and local. Tranquil retreats attract RVers and campers, who linger for a week or a season on palm-dotted, pearly strands where the fishing is good and the living easy.

In short, the Puerto Vallarta region is an unhurried, sun-blessed refuge for lovers of the tropics, simple to visit and easy to appreciate, whether you prefer fashionable luxury, strenuous adventure, or something in between. This book will help you find the way.

INTRODUCTION

THE LAND AND SEA

The sun-drenched resort of Puerto Vallarta (pop. 300,000) and its surrounding region owe their prosperity to their most fortunate location, where gentle Pacific breezes meet the parade of majestic volcanic peaks marching west from central Mexico. Breeze-borne moisture, trickling down mineral-rich volcanic slopes, has nurtured civilizations for millennia in the highland valleys around Tepic and Guadalajara, the state capitals of Nayarit and Jalisco. Running from Lake Chapala, just south of Guadalajara, the waters plunge into the mile-deep canyon of Mexico's longest river, the Río Grande de Santiago. They finally return to the ocean, nourishing the teeming aquatic life of the grand estuary just north of San Blas, Nayarit, two hours' drive north of Puerto Vallarta.

Within sight of Puerto Vallarta rise the jagged mountain ranges of the Sierra Vallejo and the

Sierra Cuale. The runoff from these peaks becomes the Ameca River, which sustains a lush patchwork of fruit, corn, and sugarcane that decorates the broad valley bottom. The Ameca meets the ocean just north of Puerto Vallarta town limits. There, myriad sea creatures seek the river's nourishment at the Puerto Vallarta shoreline, the innermost recess of the Bay of Banderas, Mexico's broadest and deepest bay.

On the map of the Puerto Vallarta region, the Bay of Banderas appears gouged from the coast by some vengeful Aztec god (perhaps in retribution for the Spanish conquest) with a single 20-mile-wide swipe of his giant hand, just sparing the city of Puerto Vallarta.

Time, however, appears to have healed that great imaginary cataclysm. The rugged Sierra Vallejo to the north and Sierra Cuale to the south have acquired green coats of jungly forest on their slopes, and sand has accumulated on the great arc of the Bay of Banderas. There, a diadem of palmy fishing villages—Punta Mita, Cruz de Huanacaxtle, Bucerías, Mismaloya, Boca de Tomatlán, and Yelapa—decorate the bay to the north and south of the town. In the mountains which rise literally from Puerto Vallarta's city streets, the idyllic colonial-era villages of San Sebastián, Mascota, and Talpa nestle in verdant valleys only 20 minutes away by light plane.

Farther afield, smaller bays dotted with pearly strands, sleepy villages, and small resorts adorn the coastline north and south of the Bay of Banderas. To the south, beyond the pine- and oak-studded Sierra Lagunillas summit, stretch the blue reaches of the bays of Chamela, Tenacatita, and, finally, Navidad, at the Jalisco-Colima state border. There, the downscale little resort of Barra de Navidad drowses beside its wildlife-rich lagoon.

To the north of the Bay of Banderas stretches the vine-strewn Nayarit coast, where the broad inlets of Jaltemba and Matanchén curve past the sleepy winter havens of Sayulita, Rincón de Guayabitos, and San Blas. From there, a mangrove marshland extends past the historic Mexcaltitán island-village to the jungly Río Cañas at the Nayarit-Sinaloa border.

A trove of sleepy tropical havens, such as Boca de Tomatlán, shown, dot the lush shores of the Bay of Banderas.

Climate

Nature has graced the Puerto Vallarta region with a microclimate tapestry. Although rainfall, winds, and mountains introduce pleasant local variations, elevation provides the broad brush. The entire coastal strip where frost never bites (including the mountain slopes and plateaus up to 4,000 or 5,000 feet) luxuriates in the tropics.

The seashore is a land of perpetual summer. Winter days are typically warm and rainless, peaking at 80–85° F (27–30° C) and dropping to 55–65° F (16–18° C) by midnight.

Increasing elevation gradually decreases both heat and humidity. In the valley of Tepic (elev. 3,000 feet), you can expect warm, dry winter days 75–80° F, (24–27° C) and cooler nights around 50–60° F (10–15° C). Similar but sometimes cooler winter weather prevails in higher, 5,000-foot (1,600-meter) Guadalajara. Days will usually be balmy and springlike, climbing to around 75° F (24° C) by noon, with nights dropping to a temperate 40–50° F (5–10° C); pack a sweater or light jacket. During occasional winter cold snaps, Guadalajara nighttime temperatures can drop to freezing.

May, before the rains, is often the warmest month in the entire Puerto Vallarta region. Summer days on Puerto Vallarta beaches are very warm, humid, and sometimes rainy. July, August, and September forenoons are typically bright, warming to the high 80s (around 32° C). By afternoon, however, clouds often gather and bring short, sometimes heavy, showers. By late afternoon the clouds part, the sun dries the pavements, and the tropical breeze is just right for enjoying a sparkling Puerto Vallarta sunset.

Tepic and Guadalajara summers are delightful, with afternoons in the 80s (27–32° C) and balmy evenings in the 70s (21–26° C), perfect for strolling.

Many Guadalajara residents enjoy the best of all possible worlds: balmy summers at home and similarly balmy winters in vacation homes on the Bay of Banderas.

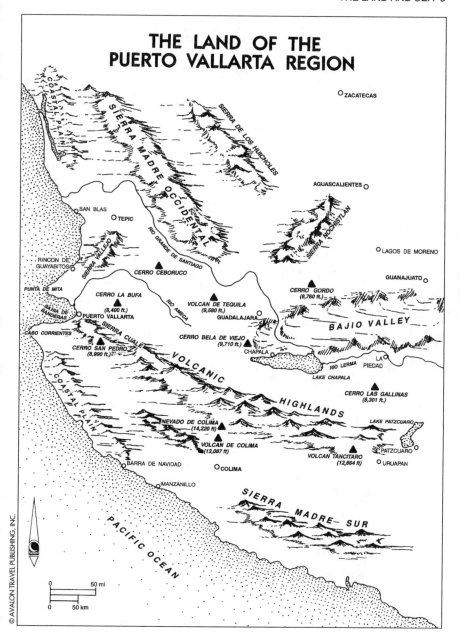

THE LAND OF THE PUERTO VALLARTA REGION

ZACATECAS

COASTAL PLAIN

SIERRA MADRE OCCIDENTAL

SIERRA DE LOS HUICHOLES

AGUASCALIENTES

SAN BLAS

TEPIC

RIO GRANDE DE SANTIAGO

SIERRA NOCHISTLAN

LAGOS DE MORENO

RINCON DE GUAYABITOS

SIERRA VALLEJO

PUNTA DE MITA

CERRO CEBORUCO

GUANAJUATO

CERRO GORDO
(8,760 ft.)

CERRO LA BUFA
(8,400 ft.)

BAHIA DE BANDERAS

RIO AMECA

VOLCAN DE TEQUILA
(9,580 ft.)

GUADALAJARA

BAJIO VALLEY

PUERTO VALLARTA

CABO CORRIENTES

SIERRA CUALE

CERRO SAN PEDRO
(8,990 ft.)

CERRO BELA DE VIEJO
(9,710 ft.)

CHAPALA

RIO LERMA

LA PIEDAD

VOLCANIC

LAKE CHAPALA

CERRO LAS GALLINAS
(8,301 ft.)

COASTAL PLAIN

HIGHLANDS

LAKE PATZCUARO

NEVADO DE COLIMA
(14,220 ft)

VOLCAN DE COLIMA
(13,087 ft)

VOLCAN TANCITARO
(12,664 ft)

PATZCUARO

URUAPAN

BARRA DE NAVIDAD

COLIMA

MANZANILLO

SIERRA MADRE SUR

PACIFIC OCEAN

0   50 mi

0   50 km

FLORA AND FAUNA

Abundant sun and summer rains nurture the vegetation of the Puerto Vallarta region. At roadside spots, spiny bromeliads, pendulous passion fruits, and giant serpentine vines luxuriate, beckoning to admirers. Now and then visitors may stop, attracted by something remarkable, such as a riot of flowers blooming from apparently dead branches or what looks like grapefruit sprouting from the trunk of a roadside tree. More often, travelers pass by the long stretches of thickets, jungles, and marshes without stopping; however, a little advance knowledge of what to expect can blossom into recognition and discovery, transforming the humdrum into the extraordinary.

VEGETATION ZONES

Mexico's diverse landscape and fickle rainfall have sculpted its wide range of plant forms. Botanists recognize at least 14 major Mexican vegetation zones, seven of which occur in the Puerto Vallarta region.

Directly along the coastal highway, you often pass long sections of three of these zones: savanna, thorn forest, and tropical deciduous forest.

Savanna
Great swaths of pasturelike savanna stretch along Hwy. 15 in Nayarit north of Tepic. In its natural state, savanna often appears as a palm-dotted sea of grass—green and marshy during the rainy summer, dry and brown by late winter.

Although grass rules the savanna, palms give it character. Most familiar is the **coconut,** the *cocotero (Cocos nucifera)*—the world's most useful tree—used for everything from lumber to candy. Coconut palms line the beaches and climb the hillsides—drooping, slanting, rustling, and swaying in the breeze like troupes of hula dancers. Less familiar, but with as much personality, is the Mexican **fan palm,** or *palma real (Sabal mexicana),* festooned with black fruit and spread flat like a señorita's fan.

The savanna's list goes on: the grapefruit-like fruit on the trunk and branches identify the **gourd tree,** or *calabaza (Crescentia alata).* The mature gourds, brown and hard, have been carved into *jícaros* (cups for drinking chocolate) for millennia.

Orange-size, pumpkinlike gourds mark the **sand box tree,** or *jabillo (Hura polyandra),* so-named because they once served as desktop boxes full of sand for drying ink. The Aztecs, however, called it the exploding tree, because the ripe gourds burst their seeds forth with a bang like a firecracker.

The waterlogged seaward edge of the savanna nurtures forests of the **red mangrove,** or *mangle colorado (Rhizophora mangle),* short trees that seem to stand in the water on stilts. Their new roots grow downward from above; a time-lapse photo would show them marching, as if on stilts, into the lagoon.

Thorn Forest
Lower rainfall leads to the hardier growth of the thorn forest—domain of the pea family—the **legumes,** marked by bursts of red, yellow, pink, and white flowers. Look closely at the blossoms and you will see they resemble the familiar wild sweet pea of North America. Even when the blossoms are gone, you can identify them by pea pods that hang from the branches. Local folks call them by many names. Other even more colorful plants are the **tabachín,** the scarlet Mexican bird of paradise; and its close relative the *flamboyán,* or **royal poinciana,** an import from Africa, where it's called the "flame tree."

Other spectacular members of the pea family (called "shower trees" in Hawaii) include the bright yellow *abejón,* which blooms nearly year-round; and the *coapinol,* marked by hosts of white blooms (March–July) and large, dark-brown pods. Not only colorful but useful is the **fishfuddle,** with pink flowers and long pods, from which fisherfolk derive a fish-stunning poison.

More abundant (although not so noticeable) are the legumes' cousins, the **acacias** and **mimosas.** Long swaths of thorn forest grow right to the coastal highway and side-road pavements, so that the road appears tunnel-like through a tangle of brushy acacia trees. Pull completely off the road for a look and you will spot the small yellow flower balls, ferny leaves, and long, narrow pods of the **boat spine acacia,** or *quisache tempamo (Acacia cochliacantha).* Take care, however, around the acacias; some of the long-thorned varieties harbor nectar-feeding, biting ants.

Perhaps the most dramatic member of the thorn community is the **morning glory tree,** or *palo blanco (Ipomoea aborescens),* which announces the winter dry season by a festoon of white trumpets atop its crown of seemingly dead branches.

The Mexican penchant for making fun of death shows in the alternate name for *palo del muerto,* or the tree of the dead. It is also called *palo bobo* (fool tree) in some locales because folks believe if you take a drink from a stream near its foot, you will go crazy.

The cactus are among the thorn forest's sturdiest and most spectacular inhabitants. Occasional specimens of the spectacular **candelabra cactus,** or *candelabro (Stenocereus weberi),* spread as much as 40 feet tall and wide.

Tropical Deciduous Forest

In rainier areas, the thorn forest grades into tropical deciduous forest. This is the "friendly" or "short-tree" forest, blanketed by a tangle of summer-green leaves that fall in the dry winter to reveal thickets of branches. Some trees show bright fall reds and yellows, later blossoming with brilliant flowers—spider lily, cardinal sage, pink trumpet, poppylike yellowsilk *(pomposhuti),* and mouse-killer *(mala ratón),* which swirl in the spring wind like cherry-blossom blizzards.

The tropical deciduous forest is a lush jungle coat swathing much of the coastal Puerto Vallarta region. It is especially lush in the mountains above San Blas and along the low summit of Hwy. 200 over the Sierra Vallejo north of Puerto Vallarta. Where the mountains rush directly down to the sea, the forest appears to spill right over the headland into the ocean. Vine-strewn thickets overhang the highway like the edges of a lost prehistoric world, where at any moment you expect a dinosaur to rear up.

The biological realities here are nearly as exotic. A four-foot-long green iguana, looking every bit as primitive as a dinosaur, slithers across the pavement. Beside the road, a spreading, solitary **strangler fig** *(Ficus padifolia)* stands, draped with hairy, hanging air roots (which, in time, plant themselves in the ground and support the branches). Its Mexican name, *matapalo* (killer tree), is gruesomely accurate, for strangler figs often entwine themselves in death embraces with less aggressive tree-victims.

Much more benign is my favorite in the tropical deciduous forest: the **Colima palm** *(Orbygna guacuyule), guaycoyul,* or *cohune,* which means "magnificent." Capped by a proud cock-plume, it presides over the forest singly or in great, graceful swaying groves atop seacliffs. Its nuts, harvested like small coconuts, yield oil and animal fodder.

Excursions by jeep or foot along shaded, off-highway tracks through the tropical deciduous forest can bestow delightful jungle scenes; however, unwary travelers must watch out for the poison-oak-like *mala mujer,* the "evil woman" tree. The oil on its large five-fingered leaves can cause an itchy rash.

Pine-Oak Forest

Along the upland highways (notably at the Sierra Cuale summit of Hwy. 200 south from Puerto Vallarta, and at high stretches of National Hwy. 80 between Barra de Navidad and Guadalajara), the tropical forest gives way to temperate pine-oak forest, the Puerto Vallarta region's most extensive vegetation zone. Here, many of Mexico's 112 oak and 39 pine species thrive. Oval two-inch cones and foot-long drooping needles (three to a cluster) make the **pino triste,** or sad pine *(Pinus lumholtzii),* appear in severe need of water. Unlike many of Mexico's pines, it produces neither good lumber nor much turpentine, although it *is* prized by guitar makers for its wood.

Much more regal in bearing and commercially important are the tall pines, **Chihuahua pine** *(Pinus chihuahuana)* and **Chinese pine** *(Pinus leiophylla).* Both reddish-barked with yellow wood, they resemble the ponderosa pine of the western United States. You can tell them apart by their needles: the Chihuahua pine *(pino prieto)* has three to a cluster, while the Chinese pine *(pino Chino)* has five.

Pines often grow in stands mixed with **oaks,**

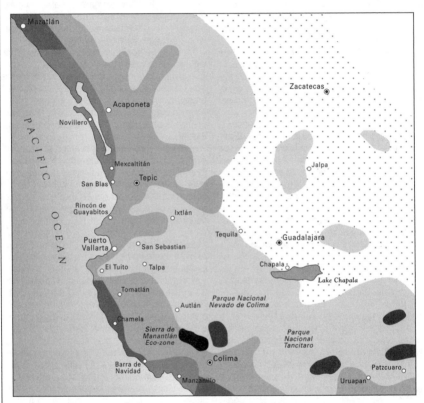

VEGETATION ZONES OF THE PUERTO VALLARTA REGION

Mazatlán
Acaponeta
Noviliero
PACIFIC OCEAN
Mexcaltitán
San Blas
Tepic
Rincón de Guayabitos
Ixtlán
Puerto Vallarta
San Sebastian
El Tuito
Talpa
Tomatlán
Autlán
Chamela
Sierra de Manantlán Eco-zone
Barra de Navidad
Colima
Manzanillo
Zacatecas
Jalpa
Tequila
Guadalajara
Chapala
Lake Chapala
Parque Nacional Nevado de Colima
Parque Nacional Tancitaro
Patzcuaro
Uruapan

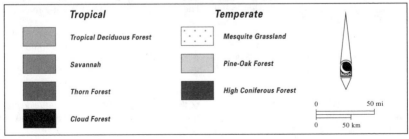

Tropical

- Tropical Deciduous Forest
- Savannah
- Thorn Forest
- Cloud Forest

Temperate

- Mesquite Grassland
- Pine-Oak Forest
- High Coniferous Forest

0   50 mi
0   50 km

which occur in two broad classifications—*encino* (evergreen, small-leafed) and *roble* (deciduous, large-leafed)—both much like the oaks that dot California hills and valleys. Clustered on their branches and scattered in the shade, *bellota* (acorns) distinctly mark them as oaks.

Mesquite Grassland

Although highland valleys have been largely tamed into farmland, outlying districts around Guadalajara still exhibit the landscape of the mesquite grassland vegetation zone, similar to the semi-arid plateauland of the U.S. Southwest.

Despite its oft-monotonous roadside aspect, the mesquite grassland nurtures surprisingly exotic and unusual plants. Among the most interesting is the **maguey** (mah-GAY), or century plant, so-called because it's said to bloom once, then die, after 100 years of growth—although its lifetime is usually closer to 50 years. The maguey and its cactuslike relatives (such as the very useful **mescal, lechugilla,** and **sisal,** all of the genus *Agave*) each grow as a roselike cluster of leathery, long, pointed, gray-green leaves, from which a single flower stalk eventually blooms.

Century plants themselves, which can grow as large as several feet tall and wide, thrive either wild or in cultivated fields in ranks and files like a botanical army on parade. These fields, prominently visible from National Hwy. 15 west of Guadalajara, are eventually harvested, crushed, fermented, and distilled into fiery 80-proof tequila, the most renowned of which comes from the town of Tequila near Hwy. 15.

Watch for the mesquite grassland's *candelilla* (Euphorbia antisyphillitica), an odd cousin of the poinsettia, also a Mexico native. In contrast to the poinsettia, the *candelilla* resembles a tall (two- to three-foot) candle, with small white flowers scattered upward along its single vertical stem. Abundant wax on the many pencil-sized stalks that curve upward from the base is useful for anything from polishing your shoes to lubricating your car's distributor.

Equally exotic is the ***sangre de drago,*** "blood of the dragon" *(Jatropha dioica),* which also grows in a single meaty stem, but with two-inch-long lobed leaves with small white flowers. Break off a stem and out oozes a clear sap, which soon turns blood-red.

Cloud Forest

Adventurous visitors who travel to certain remote, dewy mountainsides above 7,000 feet can explore the plant and wildlife community of the cloud forest. The Sierra Manantlán, a roadless de facto wilderness, southeast of Autlán, Jalisco, preserves such a habitat. There, abundant cool fog nourishes forests of glacial-epoch remnant flora: tree ferns and lichen-draped pines and oaks, above a mossy carpet of orchids, bromeliads, and begonias.

High Coniferous Forest

The Puerto Vallarta region's rarest, least accessible vegetation zone is the high coniferous forest, which swathes the slopes of lofty peaks, notably, the Nevado de Colima, elev. 14,220 feet (4,325 meters), on the Jalisco-Colima border. This pristine green alpine island, accessible only on horseback or by foot, nurtures stands of magnificent pines and spruce, laced by grassy meadows, similar to the higher Rocky Mountain slopes in the U.S. and Canada. Reigning over the lesser species is the regal **Montezuma pine,** *Pinus montezumae,* distinguished by its long, pendulous cones and rough, ruddy bark, reminiscent of the sugar pine of the western United States.

For many more details of Mexico's feast of roadside plants, see M. Walter Pesman's delightful *Meet Flora Mexicana* (unfortunately out of print, but major libraries have copies). Also informative is the popular paperback *Handbook of Mexican Roadside Flora,* by Charles T. Mason Jr. and Patricia B. Mason.

WILDLIFE

Despite continued habitat destruction—forests are logged, wetlands filled, and savannas plowed—great swaths of the Puerto Vallarta region still abound with wildlife. Common in the temperate pine-oak forest highlands are mammals familiar to U.S. residents—such as mountain lion *(puma),* coyote, fox *(zorro),* rabbit *(conejo),* and quail *(codorniz).*

However, the tropical coastal forests and savannas are home to fascinating species seen only in zoos north of the border. The reality of this dawns on travelers when they glimpse something exotic, such as raucous, screeching swarms of small green parrots rising from the roadside, or an armadillo or coati nosing in the sand just a few feet away from them at the forested edge of an isolated beach.

Population pressures have nevertheless decreased wild habitats, endangering many previously abundant animal species. If you are lucky, you may find a tracker who can lead you to a band of now-rare reddish-brown **spider monkeys** *(monos)* raiding a wild fruit tree. And deep in the mountain vastness, you may be led to a view of the endangered striped cat, the **ocelot** *(tigrillo)* or its smaller relative, the **margay.** On such an excursion, if you are really fortunate, you may hear the "chesty" roar or catch a glimpse of a jaguar, fabled *el tigre.*

El Tigre

"Each hill has its own *tigre,*" a Mexican proverb says. With black spots spread over a yellow-tan coat, stretching five feet (1.5 meters) and weighing 200 pounds (90 kg), the typical jaguar resembles a muscular spotted leopard. Although hunted since prehistory, and now endangered, the jaguar lives on in the Puerto Vallarta region, where it hunts along thickly forested stream bottoms and foothills. Unlike the mountain lion, the jaguar will eat any game. Jaguars have even been known to wait patiently for fish in rivers and to stalk beaches for turtle and egg dinners. If they have a favorite food, it is probably the piglike wild peccary, *jabalí.* Experienced hunters agree that no two jaguars will have the same prey in their stomachs.

Although humans have died of wounds inflicted by cornered jaguars, there is little or no hard evidence that they eat humans, despite legends to the contrary.

Armadillos, Coatis, and Bats

Armadillos are cat-size mammals that act and look like opossums, but carry reptilianlike shells. If you see one, remain still, and it may walk right up and sniff your foot before it recognizes you and scuttles back into the woods.

A common inhabitant of the tropics is the raccoonlike coati *(tejón, pisote).* In the wild, coatis like shady stream banks, often congre-

gating in large troops of 15–30 individuals. They are identified by their short brown or tan fur, small round ears, long nose, and straight, vertically held tail. They make endearing pets; the first coati you see may be one on a string offered for sale at a local market.

Mexican bats *(murciélagos)* are widespread, with at least 126 species compared to 37 in the United States. In Mexico, as everywhere, bats are feared and misunderstood. As sunset approaches, many species come out of their hiding places and flit through the air in search of insects. Most people, sitting outside enjoying the early evening, will mistake their darting silhouettes for those of birds, who, except for owls, do not generally fly at night.

Bats are often locally called *vampiros,* even though only three relatively rare Mexican species actually feed on the blood of mammals—nearly always cattle—and of birds.

The many nonvampire Mexican bats carry their vampire cousins' odious reputation with forbearance. They go about their good works, pollinating flowers, clearing the air of pesky gnats and mosquitoes, ridding cornfields of mice, and dropping seeds, thereby restoring forests.

BIRDS

The coastal lagoons of the Puerto Vallarta region lie astride the Pacific Flyway, one of the Americas' major north-south paths for migrating waterfowl. Many of the familiar American and Canadian species, including pintail, gadwall, baldpate, shoveler, redhead, and scaup, arrive Oct.–Jan., when

KAREN McKINLEY

jaguar

their numbers will have swollen into the millions. They settle near food and cover—even at the borders of cornfields, to the frustration of farmers.

Besides the migrants, swarms of resident species—herons and egrets *(garzas),* cormorantlike anhingas, lily-walkers *(jacanas),* and hundreds more—stalk, nest, and preen in the same lagoons.

Few spots are better for observing seabirds than the beaches of the Puerto Vallarta region. Brown pelicans and black-and-white frigate birds are among the prime actors. When a flock of pelicans spots a school of favorite fish, they go about their routine deliberately. Singly or in pairs, they circle and plummet into the waves to come up, more often than not, with fish in their gullets. Each bird then bobs and floats over the swells for a minute or two, seeming to wait for its dozen or so fellow pelicans to take their turns. This continues until they've bagged a dinner of 10–15 fish apiece.

Frigate birds, the scavengers par excellence of the Puerto Vallarta region, often profit by the labor of the teams of fishermen who haul in nets of fish on village beaches. After the fishermen auction off the choice morsels of perch, tuna, red snapper, octopus, or shrimp to merchants, and the local villagers have scavenged everything else edible, the motley residue of small fish, sea snakes, skates, squid, slugs, and sharks is thrown to a screeching flock of frigate birds.

The sprawling, wild mangrove wetland near San Blas, 100 miles north of Puerto Vallarta, nurtures a trove of wildlife, especially birds, ripe for viewing on foot near the town, or by guided boat tours.

For more details on Mexico's mammals and birds in general, check out A. Starker Leopold's very readable classic, *Wildlife of Mexico,* and other works in Suggested Reading.

REPTILES AND AMPHIBIANS

Snakes, Gila Monsters, and Crocodiles

Mexico has 460-odd snake species, the vast majority shy and nonpoisonous; they will get out of your way if you give plenty of warning. In Mexico, as everywhere, poisonous snakes have been largely eradicated in city and tourist areas.

In brush or jungle areas, carry a stick or a machete and beat the bushes ahead of you while watching where you put your feet. When hiking or rock-climbing in the country, don't put your hand in niches you can't see.

You might even see a snake underwater while swimming offshore at an isolated Bay of Banderas beach. The **yellow-bellied sea snake,** *Pelamis platurus* (to about two feet), although rare and shy, can inflict fatal bites. If you see a yellow-and-black snake underwater, get away, pronto.

Some eels, which resemble snakes but have gills like fish and inhabit rocky crevices, can inflict nonpoisonous bites and should also be avoided.

The Mexican land counterpart of the *Pelamis platurus* is the **coral snake** *(coralillo),* which occurs as about two dozen species, all with multicolored bright bands that always include red. Although relatively rare, small, and shy, coral snakes occasionally inflict serious, sometimes fatal bites.

More aggressive and generally more dangerous is the Mexican **rattlesnake** *(cascabel)* and its viper relative, the **fer-de-lance** *(Bothrops atrox).* About the same in size (to six feet) and appearance as the rattlesnake, the fer-de-lance is known by various local names, such as *nauyaca, cuatro narices, palanca,* and *barba amarilla.* It is potentially more hazardous than the rattlesnake because it lacks a warning rattle.

The Gila monster (confined in Mexico to northern Sonora) and its southern tropical relative, the yellow-spotted, black *escorpión (Heloderma horridum),* are the world's only poisonous lizards. Despite its beaded skin and menacing, fleshy appearance, the *escorpión* only bites when severely provoked; and, even then, its venom is rarely, if ever, fatal.

The crocodile *(cocodrilo, caimán),* once prized for its meat and hide, came close to vanishing in Mexican Pacific lagoons until the government took steps to ensure its survival; it's now officially protected. A few isolated breeding populations live on in the wild, while government and private hatcheries are breeding more for the eventual repopulation of lagoons where crocodiles once were common.

Two crocodile species occur in the Puerto Vallarta region. The true crocodile *Crocodilus acutus* has a narrower snout than its local cousin,

Caiman crocodilus fuscus, a type of alligator *(lagarto).* Although past individuals have been recorded at up to 15 feet long (see the stuffed specimen upstairs at the Tepic anthropology and history museum, or in the Hotel Bucanero lobby in San Blas), wild native crocodiles are usually young and two feet or less in length.

Turtles

The story of Mexican sea turtles is similar: they once swarmed ashore on Puerto Vallarta regional beaches to lay their eggs. Prized for their meat, eggs, hide, and shell, the turtles were severely devastated. Now officially protected, sea turtles come ashore in numbers only at a few isolated locations. Of the three locally occurring species, the green turtle, *tortuga negra,* (black turtle, as it's known in Mexico) is by far the most common. From tour boats, it can often be seen grazing on sea grass offshore in the Bay of Banderas. (For many more sea turtle details, see the special topic "Saving Turtles.")

FISH AND MARINE MAMMALS

Shoals of fish abound in Puerto Vallarta's waters. Four billfish species are found in deep-sea grounds several miles offshore: **swordfish, sailfish,** and **blue** and **black marlin.** All are spirited fighters, though the sailfish and marlin are generally the toughest to bring in. The blue marlin is the biggest of the four; in the past, 10-foot specimens weighing more than a thousand pounds were brought in at Pacific-coast marinas. Lately, four feet and 200 pounds for a marlin, and 100 pounds for a sailfish, are more typical. Progressive captains now encourage victorious anglers to return these magnificent "tigers of the sea" (especially the sinewy sailfish and blue marlin, which make for poor eating) to the deep after they've won the battle.

Billfish are not the only prizes of the sea, however. Serious fish lovers also seek varieties of tunalike **jack,** such as **yellowtail, Pacific amberjack, pompano, jack crevalle,** and the tenacious **roosterfish,** named for the "comb" atop its head. These, and the **yellowfin tuna, mackerel,** and *dorado,* which Hawaiians call mahimahi, are among the delicacies sought in Puerto Vallarta waters.

Accessible from small boats offshore and by casting from shoreline rocks are varieties of **snapper** *(huachinango, pargo)* and **sea bass** *(cabrilla).* Closer to shore, **croaker, mullet,** and **jewfish** can be found foraging along sandy bottoms and in rocky crevices.

Sharks and **rays** inhabit nearly all depths, with smaller fry venturing into beach shallows and lagoons. Huge **Pacific manta rays** appear to be frolicking, their great wings flapping like birds, not far off Puerto Vallarta shores. Just beyond the waves, local fisherfolk bring in **hammerhead, thresher,** and **leopard sharks.**

Also common is the **stingray,** which can inflict a painful wound with its barbed tail. Experienced swimmers and waders avoid injury by both shuffling (rather than stepping) and watching their feet in shallow waters with sandy bottoms. (For more fish talk and a chart of species encountered in Puerto Vallarta waters, turn ahead to "Fishing" under "Sports and Recreation" in the On the Road chapter.)

Sea Lions, Porpoises, and Whales

Although seen in much greater numbers in Baja California's colder waters, fur-bearing species, such as seals and sea lions, do occasionally hunt in the tropical waters and bask on the sands of island beaches off the Puerto Vallarta coast. With the rigid government protections that have been enforced for a generation, their numbers appear to be increasing.

The **California Gulf porpoise**—*delfín,* or *vaquita* (little cow)—is much more numerous. The smallest member of the whale family, it rarely exceeds five feet. Its playful diving and jumping antics can occasionally be observed from Puerto Vallarta–based tour and fishing boats, and even sometimes right from Bay of Banderas beaches.

Although the **California gray whale** has a migration pattern extending only to the southern tip of Baja California, occasional pods stray farther south, where deep-sea fishermen and cruise and tour boat passengers see them in deep waters offshore.

Larger whale *(ballena)* species, such as the **humpback** and **blue** whale, appear to enjoy tropical waters even more, ranging the north Pacific tropics, from Puerto Vallarta west to Hawaii and beyond.

Offshore islands, such as the nearby Marietas and María Isabel (accessible from San Blas), and the Revillagigedo (ray-vee-yah-hee-HAY-doh) Islands 300 miles due west of Puerto Vallarta, offer prime viewing grounds for Mexico's aquatic fauna.

HISTORY

Once upon a time, about 50,000 years ago, the first bands of hunters, perhaps following great game herds, crossed from Siberia to the American continent. They drifted southward, many of them eventually settling in the lush highland valleys of Mexico.

Much later, perhaps around 5000 B.C., these early people began gathering and grinding the seeds of a hardy grass that required only the summer rains to thrive. After generations of selective breeding, this grain, called *teocentli,* the sacred seed (which we call maize or corn), led to prosperity.

Quetzalcoatl the Feathered Serpent, the most powerful of all gods

EARLY MEXICAN CIVILIZATIONS

With abundant food, settlements grew and leisure classes arose—artists, architects, warriors, and ruler-priests—who had time to think and create. With a calendar, they harnessed the constant wheel of the firmament to life on earth, defining the days to plant, harvest, feast, travel, and trade. Eventually grand cities arose.

Teotihuacán
Teotihuacán, with a population of perhaps 250,000 around the time of Christ, was one of the world's great metropolises. Its epic monuments, built centuries later on the same site by Aztecs, still stand not far north of Mexico City: the towering Pyramid of the Sun at the terminal of a grand, 150-foot-wide ceremonial avenue facing a great Pyramid of the Moon. Along the avenue sprawls a monumental temple-court surrounded by scowling, ruby-eyed effigies of Quetzalcoatl, the feathered serpent god of gods.

Teotihuacán crumbled mysteriously around A.D. 650, leaving a host of former vassal states to tussle among themselves. These included Xochicalco, not far south of present-day Mexico City. Freed from tribute to Teotihuacán, Xochicalco flourished.

The Living Quetzalcoatl
Xochicalco's wise men tutored a young noble who was to become a living legend. In A.D. 947, Topiltzín (literally, "Our Prince") was born. Records recite Topiltzín's achievements. He advanced astronomy, agriculture, and architecture and founded the city-state of Tula in A.D. 968, north of old Teotihuacán.

Contrary to the times, Topiltzín opposed human sacrifice; he taught that tortillas and butterflies, not human hearts, were the food of Quetzalcoatl. After his benign rule for a generation, Topiltzín's name became so revered the people knew him as the living Quetzalcoatl, the plumed serpent god incarnate.

Bloodthirsty local priests, lusting for human victims, tricked him with alcohol, however; Topiltzín awoke groggily one morning, in bed with his sister. Devastated with shame, Quetzalcoatl banished himself. He headed east from Tula with a band of retainers in A.D. 987, vowing that he would return during the anniversary of his birth year, Ce Acatl. Legends say he sailed across the eastern sea and rose to heaven as the morning star.

The Aztecs

The civilization that Topiltzín founded, known to historians as the Toltec ("People of Tula"), was eventually eclipsed by others. These included the Aztecs, a collection of seven aggressive immigrant sub-tribes. Migrating around 1350 from a mysterious western land of Aztlán (Place of the Herons, see special topic "Aztlán") into the lake-filled valley that Mexico City now occupies, the Aztecs survived by being forced to fight for every piece of ground they occupied. Within a century, the Aztecs' dominant tribe, whose members called themselves the "México," had clawed its way to dominion over the Valley of Mexico. With the tribute labor that their emperors ex-

Pre-Columbian Mexicans, who never domesticated draft animals, relied upon humans, called cargadores, to carry everything.

tracted from local vassal tribes, the México built a magnificent capital, Tenochtitlán, on an island in the middle of the valley-lake. From there, Aztec armies, not unlike Roman legions, marched out and subdued kingdoms for hundreds of miles in all directions. They returned with the spoils of conquest: gold, brilliant feathers, precious jewels, and captives, whom they sacrificed by the thousands as food for their gods.

Among those gods they feared was Quetzalcoatl, who, legends said, was bearded and fair-skinned. It was a remarkable coincidence, therefore, that the bearded, fair-skinned Castilian Hernán Cortés landed on Mexico's eastern coast on April 22, 1519, during the year of Ce Acatl, exactly when Topiltzín, the Living Quetzalcoatl, had vowed he would return.

THE CONQUEST

Although a generation had elapsed since Columbus founded Spain's West Indian colonies, returns had been meager. Scarcity of gold and of native workers, most of whom had fallen victim to European diseases, turned adventurous Spanish eyes westward once again, toward rumored riches beyond the setting sun.

Preliminary excursions piqued Spanish interest, and Hernán Cortés was commissioned by the Spanish governor, Diego Velázquez, to explore further.

Cortés, then only 34, had left his base of Cuba in February 1519 with an expedition of 11 small ships, 550 men, 16 horses, and a few small cannon. By the time he landed in Mexico, he was burdened by a murderous crew. His men, mostly soldiers of fortune hearing stories of the great Aztec empire west beyond the mountains, had realized the impossible odds they faced and became restive.

Cortés, however, cut short any thoughts of mutiny by burning his ships. As he led his grumbling but resigned band of adventurers toward the Aztec capital of Tenochtitlán, Cortés played Quetzalcoatl to the hilt, awing local chiefs. Coaxed by Doña Marina, Cortés's native translator-mistress, local chiefs began to add their warrior-armies to Cortés's march against their Aztec overlords.

Moctezuma, Lord of Tenochtitlán

Once inside the walls of Tenochtitlán, the Aztecs' Venice-like island-city, the Spaniards were dazzled by gardens of animals, gold and palaces, and a great pyramid-enclosed square where tens of thousands of people bartered goods gathered from all over the empire. Tenochtitlán, with perhaps a quarter of a million people, was the grand capital of an empire more than equal to any in Europe at the time.

However, Moctezuma, the lord of that empire, was frozen by fear and foreboding, unsure if these figures truly represented the return of Quetzalcoatl. He quickly found himself hostage to Cortés, then died a few months later, during a riot against Spanish greed and brutality. On July 1, 1520, or what came to be called *noche triste,* the sad night, the besieged Cortés and his men broke out, fleeing for their lives along a lake causeway from Tenochtitlán, carrying Moctezuma's treasure. Many of them drowned beneath their burdens of gold booty, while the survivors hacked a bloody retreat through thousands of screaming Aztec warriors to safety on the lakeshore.

A year later, reinforced by a small fleet of armed sailboats and 100,000 Indian warrior-allies, Cortés retook Tenochtitlán. The stubborn defenders, led by Cuauhtémoc, Moctezuma's nephew, fell by the tens of thousands beneath a smoking hail of Spanish grapeshot. The Indians refused to surrender, forcing Cortés to destroy the city in order to take it.

The triumphant conquistador soon rebuilt the city in the Spanish image; Cortés's cathedral and main public buildings—the present *zócalo* or central square of Mexico City—still rest upon the foundations of Moctezuma's pyramids.

NEW SPAIN

With the Valley of Mexico firmly in his grip, Cortés sent his lieutenants south, north, and west to extend the limits of his domain, which eventually expanded to more than a dozenfold the size of old Spain. In a letter to his king, Charles V, Cortés christened his empire "New Spain of the Ocean Sea."

MALINCHE

If it hadn't been for Doña Marina (whom he received as a gift from a local chief), Cortés may have become a mere historical footnote. Doña Marina, speaking both Spanish and native tongues, soon became Cortés's interpreter, go-between, and negotiator. She persuaded a number of important chiefs to ally themselves with Cortés against the Aztecs. Clever and opportunistic, Doña Marina was a crucial strategist in Cortés's deadly game of divide and conquer. She eventually bore Cortés a son and lived in honor and riches for many years, profiting greatly from the Spaniards' exploitation of the Mexicans.

Latter-day Mexicans do not honor her by the gentle title of Doña Marina, however. They call her Malinche, after the volcano—the ugly, treacherous scar on the Mexican landscape—and curse her as the female Judas who betrayed her country to the Spanish. *Malinchismo* has become known as the tendency to love things foreign and hate things Mexican.

The Missionaries

While the conquistadores subjugated the Indians, missionaries began arriving to teach, heal, and baptize them. A dozen Franciscan brothers impressed Indians and conquistadores alike by trekking the entire 300-mile stony path from Veracruz to Mexico City in 1523. Missionary authorities generally enjoyed a sympathetic ear from Charles V and his successors, who earnestly pursued Spain's Christian mission, especially when it dovetailed with its political and economic goals.

The King Takes Control

Increasingly after 1525, the crown, through the Council of the Indies, began to wrest power away from Cortés and his conquistador lieutenants, many of whom had been granted rights of *encomienda:* taxes and labor of an Indian district. From the king's point of view, tribute pesos collected by *encomenderos* from their Indian serfs reduced the gold that would otherwise flow to the crown. Moreover, many *encomenderos* callously enslaved and sold their Indian wards for quick profit. Such abuses, coupled with Euro-

AZTLÁN

During their first meeting in imperial Tenochtitlán, the Aztec Emperor Moctezuma informed Hernán Cortés that "from the records which we have long possessed and which are handed down from our ancestors, it is known that no one, neither I nor the others who inhabit this land of Anahuac, are native to it. We are strangers and we came from far outer parts."

Although the Aztecs had forgotten exactly where it was, they agreed on the name and nature of the place from which they came: Aztlán, a magical island with seven allegorical caves, each representing an Aztec subtribe—of which the México, last to complete the migration, had clawed its way to dominion. Aztlán, the Aztecs also knew, lay somewhere vaguely to the northwest, and their migration to Anahuac, the present-day Valley of Mexico, had taken many generations.

For centuries, historians puzzled and argued over the precise location of Aztlán, placing it as far away as Alaska and as near as Lake Chapala. This is curious, for there was an actual Aztlán, a chiefdom, well known at the time of the Spanish Conquest. Renegade conquistador Nuño de Guzmán immediately determined its location and three days before Christmas, in 1529, headed out with a small army of followers, driven by dreams of an Aztec empire in western Mexico. However, when Guzmán arrived at Aztlán—present-day San Felipe Aztatlán village, near Tuxpan in Nayarit—he found no golden city. Others who followed, such as Vásquez de Coronado and Francisco de Ibarra, vainly continued to scour northwestern Mexico, seeking the mythical "Seven Cities of Cíbola," which they confused with the legend of Aztlán's seven caves.

Guzmán probably came closest to the original site. Scarcely a dozen miles due west of his trail through San Felipe Aztatlán is the small island-town of Mexcaltitán, which a number of experts now believe to be the original Aztlán. Many circumstances compel their argument. The spelling common to Mexcaltitán and México is no coincidence, they say.

The name Aztlán, furthermore, is probably a contraction of Aztatlán, which translates as "Place of the Herons"—the birds flock in abundance around Mexcaltitán. Moreover, a 1579 map of New Spain by renowned cartographer Ortelius shows an "Aztlán" exactly where Mexcaltitán is today.

The argument goes on: The Codex Boturini, a 16th-century reconstruction of previous Aztec records, reveals a pictogram of Aztecs leaving Aztlán, punting a canoe with an oar. Both the peculiar shape of the canoe and the manner of punting are common to both old Tenochtitlán and present-day Mexcaltitán.

Most compelling, perhaps, is the layout of Mexcaltitán itself. As in a pocket-sized Tenochtitlán, north-south and east-west avenues radiate from a central plaza, dividing the island into four quadrant neighborhoods. A singular, exactly circular plaza-centered street arcs through the avenues, joining the neighborhoods.

If you visit Mexcaltitán, you'll find it's easy to imagine Aztec life as it must have been in Tenochtitlán of old, where many people depended on fishing, rarely left their island, and, especially during the rainy season, navigated their city streets in canoes.

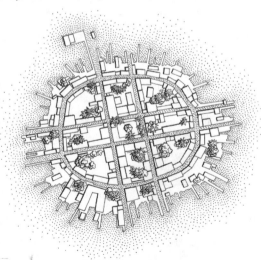

plan view of present-day Mexcaltitán

pean-introduced diseases, began to reduce the Indian population at an alarming rate.

The king and his councillors, realizing that without the Indians' labor New Spain would vanish, acted decisively, instituting new laws and a powerful viceroy to enforce them.

Don Antonio de Mendoza, the new viceroy, arrived in 1535. He wasted no time, first getting rid of the renegade opportunist and Cortés's enemy Nuño de Guzmán, whose private army, under the banner of conquest, had been laying waste to a broad belt of western Mexico, including the modern Puerto Vallarta region states of Nayarit and Jalisco. During his five-year rampage, Guzmán nevertheless managed to found the Puerto Vallarta region towns of Guadalajara, Tepic, and Compostela.

Hernán Cortés,
the Marqués del Valle Oaxaca

Cortés, meanwhile, had done very well for himself. He was one of Spain's richest men, with the title of Marqués del Valle Oaxaca. He received 80,000 gold pesos a year from hundreds of thousands of Indian subjects on 25,000 square miles from the Valley of Mexico through Morelos, Guerrero, and Oaxaca.

Cortés continued tirelessly on a dozen projects: an expedition to Honduras; a young wife whom he brought back from Spain; a palace (which still stands) in Cuernavaca; sugar mills; and dozens of churches, city halls, and presidios. He supervised the exploits of his conquistador-lieutenants: Francisco Orozco and Pedro de Alvarado went south to subdue the Zapotecs and Mixtecs in Oaxaca, while Cortés's nephew, Francisco de Cortés de Buenaventura, explored and christened the valley—"Valle de las Banderas"—where Puerto Vallarta stands today. Meanwhile, Cortés was in Acapulco building ships to explore the Pacific. In 1535, Cortés led an expedition to the Gulf of California (hence the Sea of Cortez) in a dreary six-month search for treasure around La Paz.

Cortés's Monument

Disheartened by his failures and discouraged with Mendoza's interference, Cortés returned to Spain. Mired down by lawsuits, a small war, and his daughter's marital troubles, he fell ill and died in 1547. Cortés's remains, according to his will, were eventually laid to rest in a vault at the Hospital de Jesús, which he had founded in Mexico City.

Since latter-day Mexican politics preclude memorials to the Spanish conquest, no monument anywhere in Mexico commemorates Cortés's remarkable achievements. His single monument, historians note, is Mexico itself.

COLONIAL MEXICO

In 1542, the Council of the Indies, through Viceroy Mendoza, promulgated its liberal New Laws of the Indies. They rested on high moral ground: the only Christian justification for New Spain was the souls and welfare of the Indians. Slavery was outlawed and the colonists' *encomienda* rights over land and the Indians were to eventually revert to the crown.

Despite near-rebellion by the colonists, Mendoza and his successors kept the lid on New Spain. Although some *encomenderos* held their

Guadalajara's cathedral

POPULATION CHANGES IN NEW SPAIN

	Early Colonial (1570)	Late Colonial (1810)
peninsulares	6,600	15,000
criollos	11,000	1,100,000
mestizos	2,400	704,000
indígenas	3,340,000	3,700,000
negros	22,000	630,000

privileges into the 18th century, chattel slavery of native Mexicans was abolished in New Spain 300 years before Lincoln's Emancipation Proclamation.

Peace reigned in Mexico for 10 generations. Viceroys came, served, and went; settlers put down roots; friars built country churches; and the conquistadores' rich heirs played while the Indians worked.

The Church

The church, however, moderated the Indians' toil. On feast days, Indians would dress up, parade their patron saint, drink *pulque,* and ooh and aah at the fireworks.

The church nevertheless profited from the status quo. The biblical tithe—one-tenth of everything earned—filled clerical coffers. By 1800, the church owned half of Mexico.

Moreover, both the clergy and the military were doubly privileged. They enjoyed the right of *fuero* (exemption from civil law) and could only be prosecuted by ecclesiastical or military courts.

Trade and Commerce

In trade and commerce, New Spain existed for the benefit of the mother country. Foreign trade through Mexico was completely prohibited. As a result, colonists had to pay dearly for often-shoddy Spanish manufactures. The Casa de Contratación (the royal trade regulators) always ensured the colony's yearly payment deficit would be made up by bullion shipments from Mexican mines, from which the crown raked 10 percent off the top.

Despite its faults, New Spain, by most contemporary measures, was prospering in 1800.

The Indian labor force was both docile and growing, and the galleons carried increasing tonnages of silver and gold to Spain. The authorities, however, failed to recognize that Mexico had changed in 300 years.

Criollos, the New Mexicans

Nearly three centuries of colonial rule gave rise to a burgeoning population of more than a million criollos—Mexican-born, pure European descendants of Spanish colonists, many rich and educated—to whom power was denied.

High government, church, and military office had always been the preserve of a tiny minority of *peninsulares*—whites born in Spain. Criollos could only watch in disgust as unlettered, unskilled *peninsulares,* derisively called *gachupines,* "wearers of spurs," were boosted to authority over them.

Mestizo, *Indígena,* and *Negro* Classes

Upper-class luxury existed by virtue of the sweat of Mexico's mestizo, *indígena,* and *negro* laborers and servants. African slaves were imported in large numbers during the 17th century after typhus, smallpox, and measles epidemics had wiped out most of the *indígena* population. Although the Afro-Mexicans contributed significantly (crafts, healing arts, dance, music, drums, and marimba), they had arrived last and experienced discrimination from everyone.

INDEPENDENCE

Although the criollos stood high above the mestizo, *indígena,* and *negro* underclasses, that seemed little compensation for the false smiles, deep bows, and costly bribes that *gachupines* demanded.

The chance for change came during the aftermath of the French invasion of Spain in 1808, when Napoléon Bonaparte replaced King Ferdinand VII with his brother Joseph on the Spanish throne. Most *peninsulares* backed the king; most criollos, however, inspired by the example of the recent American and French revolutions, talked and dreamed of independence. One such group, urged on by a firebrand parish priest, acted.

El Grito de Dolores

¡Viva México! Death to the gachupines! **Father Miguel Hidalgo** cried passionately from the church balcony in the Guanajuato town of Dolores on September 16, 1810, igniting action. A mostly *indígena,* machete-wielding army of 20,000 coalesced around Hidalgo and his compatriots, Ignacio Allende and Juan Aldama. Their ragtag force raged out of control through the Bajío, massacring hated *gachupines* and pillaging their homes.

Hidalgo advanced on Mexico City but, unnerved by stiff royalist resistance, retreated and regrouped around Guadalajara. His rebels, whose numbers had swollen to 80,000, were no match for a disciplined, 6,000-strong royalist force. On January 17, 1811, Hidalgo (now "Generalisimo") fled north toward the U.S. but was soon apprehended, defrocked, and executed. His head and those of his comrades hung from the walls of the Guanajuato granary for 10 years in compensation for the slaughter of 138 *gachupines* by Hidalgo's army.

The 10 Year Struggle

Others carried on, however. A mestizo former

Miguel Hidalgo

student of Hidalgo, **José María Morelos,** led a revolutionary shadow government in the present states of Guerrero and Oaxaca for four years until he was apprehended and executed in December 1815.

Morelos's compatriot, **Vicente Guerrero,** continued the fight, joining forces with criollo royalist Brigadier Agustín de Iturbide. Their Plan de Iguala promised "Three Guarantees"—the renowned Trigarantes: Independence, Catholicism, and Equality—which their army would enforce. On September 21, 1821, Iturbide rode triumphantly into Mexico City at the head of his army of Trigarantes. Mexico was independent at last.

Independence, however, solved little except to expel the *peninsulares.* With an illiterate populace and no experience in self-government, Mexicans began a tragic 40-year love affair with a fantasy: the general on the white horse, the gold-braided hero who could save them from themselves.

The Rise and Fall of Agustín I

Iturbide, crowned Emperor Agustín I by the bishop of Guadalajara on July 21, 1822, soon lost his charisma. In a pattern that became sadly predictable for generations of topsy-turvy Mexican politics, an ambitious garrison commander issued a *pronunciamiento* or declaration of rebellion against him; old revolutionary heroes endorsed a plan to install a republic. Iturbide, his braid tattered and brass tarnished, abdicated in February 1823.

Antonio López de Santa Anna, the eager 28-year-old military commander of Veracruz, whose *pronunciamiento* had pushed Iturbide from his white horse, maneuvered to gradually replace him. Meanwhile, throughout the late 1820s the government teetered on the edge of disaster as the presidency bounced between liberal and conservative hands six times in three years. During the last of these upheavals, Santa Anna jumped to prominence by defeating an abortive Spanish attempt at counterrevolution at Tampico in 1829. "The Victor of Tampico," people called Santa Anna.

The Disastrous Era of Santa Anna

In 1833, the government was bankrupt; mobs demanded the ouster of conservative President

Anastasio Bustamante, who had executed the rebellious old revolutionary hero, Vicente Guerrero. Santa Anna issued a *pronunciamiento* against Bustamante; Congress obliged, elevating Santa Anna to "Liberator of the Republic" and naming him president in March 1833.

Santa Anna would pop in and out of the presidency like a jack-in-the-box 10 more times before 1855. First, he foolishly lost Texas to rebellious Anglo settlers in 1836; then he lost his leg (which was buried with full military honors) fighting the emperor of France.

Santa Anna's greatest debacle, however, was to declare war on the United States with just 1,839 pesos in the treasury. With his forces poised to defend Mexico City against a relatively small 10,000-man American invasion force, Santa Anna inexplicably withdrew. United States Marines surged into the "Halls of Montezuma," Chapultepec Castle, where Mexico's six beloved Niños Héroes cadets fell in the losing cause on September 13, 1847.

In the subsequent treaty of Guadalupe Hidalgo, Mexico lost two-fifths of its territory—the present states of New Mexico, Arizona, California, Nevada, Utah, and Colorado—to the United States. Mexicans have never forgotten; they have looked upon gringos with a combination of awe, envy, admiration, and disgust ever since.

For Santa Anna, however, enough was not enough. Called back as president for the last and 11th time in 1853, Santa Anna financed his final extravagances by selling off a part of southern New Mexico and Arizona for $10 million, in what was known as the Gadsden Purchase.

REFORM, CIVIL WAR, AND INTERVENTION

Mexican leaders finally saw the light and exiled Santa Anna forever. While conservatives searched for a king to replace Santa Anna, liberals plunged ahead with three controversial reform laws: the Ley Juárez, Ley Lerdo, and Ley Iglesias. These *reformas,* augmented by a new Constitution of 1857, directly attacked the privilege and power of Mexico's landlords, clergy, and generals. They abolished *fueros* (the separate military and church courts), reduced huge landed estates, and stripped the church of its excess property and power.

Conservative generals, priests, *hacendados* (landholders), and their mestizo and *indígena* followers revolted. The resulting War of the Reform (not unlike the U.S. Civil War) ravaged the countryside for three long years until the victorious liberal army paraded triumphantly in Mexico City on New Year's Day 1861.

Juárez and Maximilian

Benito Juárez, the leading *reformista,* had won the day. Like his contemporary, Abraham Lincoln, Juárez, of pure Zapotec Indian blood, overcame his humble origins to become a lawyer, a champion of justice, and the president who held his country together during a terrible civil war. Like Lincoln, Juárez had little time to savor his triumph.

Imperial France invaded Mexico in January 1862. After two costly years, the French pushed Juárez's liberal army into the hills and installed the king whom Mexican conservatives thought the country needed. Austrian Archduke Maximilian and his wife Carlota, the very models of modern Catholic monarchs, were crowned emperor and empress of Mexico in June 1864.

The naive Emperor Maximilian I was surprised that some of his subjects resented his presence. Meanwhile, Juárez refused to yield, stubbornly performing his constitutional duties in a somber black carriage one jump ahead of the French occupying army. The climax came in May 1867, when the liberal forces besieged and defeated Maximilian's army at Querétaro. Juárez, giving no quarter, sternly ordered Maximilian's execution by firing squad on June 19, 1867.

THE PORFIRIATO, REVOLUTION, AND STABILIZATION

Juárez worked day and night at the double task of reconstruction and reform. He won reelection but died, exhausted, in 1871.

The death of Juárez, the stoic partisan of reform, signaled hope to Mexico's conservatives. They soon got their wish: General **Don Porfirio Díaz,** the "Coming Man," was elected president in 1876.

Pax Porfiriana

Don Porfirio is often remembered wistfully, as old Italians remember Mussolini: "He was a bit rough, but, dammit, at least he made the trains run on time."

Although Porfirio Díaz's humble Oaxaca mestizo origins were not unlike Juárez's, Díaz was not a democrat: when he was a general, his officers took no captives; when he was president, his country police, the *rurales,* shot prisoners in the act of "trying to escape."

Order and Progress, in that sequence, ruled Mexico for 34 years. Foreign investment flowed into the country; new railroads brought the products of shiny factories, mines, and farms to modernized Gulf and Pacific ports. Mexico balanced its budget, repaid foreign debt, and became a respected member of the family of nations.

The human price was high. Don Porfirio allowed more than a hundred million acres—one-fifth of Mexico's land area (including most of the arable land)—to fall into the hands of his friends and foreigners. Poor Mexicans suffered the most. By 1910, 90 percent of the *indígenas* had lost their traditional communal land. In the spring of 1910, a smug, now-cultured, and elderly Don Porfirio anticipated with relish the centennial of Hidalgo's Grito de Dolores.

¡No Reelección!

Porfirio Díaz himself had first campaigned on the slogan. It expressed the idea the president should step down after one term. Although Díaz had stepped down once in 1880, he had gotten himself re-elected for 26 consecutive years. In 1910, Francisco I. Madero, a short, squeaky-voiced son of rich landowners opposed Díaz under the same banner.

Although Díaz had jailed him before the election, Madero refused to quit campaigning. From a safe platform in the U.S., he called for a revolution to begin on November 20, 1910.

Villa and Zapata

Not much happened, but soon the millions of poor Mexicans who had been going to bed hungry began to stir. In Chihuahua, followers of Francisco (Pancho) Villa, an erstwhile ranch hand, miner, peddler, and cattle rustler, began attacking the *rurales,* dynamiting railroads, and

raiding towns. Meanwhile, in the south, horse trader, farmer, and minor official Emiliano Zapata and his *indígena* guerrillas were terrorizing rich *hacendados* and forcibly recovering stolen ancestral village lands. Zapata's movement gained steam and by May had taken the Morelos state capital, Cuernavaca. Meanwhile, Madero crossed the Río Grande and joined with Villa's forces, who took Ciudad Juárez.

The *federales,* government army troops, began deserting in droves, and on May 25, 1911, Díaz submitted his resignation.

As Madero's deputy, General Victoriano Huerta, put Díaz on his ship of exile in Veracruz, Díaz confided, "Madero has unleashed a tiger. Now let's see if he can control it."

The Fighting Continues

Emiliano Zapata, it turned out, was the tiger Madero had unleashed. Meeting with Madero in Mexico City, Zapata fumed over Madero's go-slow approach to the "agrarian problem," as Madero termed it. By November, Zapata had denounced Madero. *"¡Tierra y Libertad!"* (Land and Liberty!) the Zapatistas cried, as Madero's support faded. The army in Mexico City rebelled; Huerta forced Madero to resign on February 18, 1913, then murdered him four days later.

The rum-swilling Huerta ruled like a Chicago mobster; general rebellion, led by the "Big Four"—Villa, Alvaro Obregón, and Venustiano Carranza in the north, and Zapata in the south—soon broke out. Pressed by the rebels and refused U.S. recognition, Huerta fled into exile in July 1914.

Fighting sputtered on for three years as authority see-sawed between revolutionary factions. Finally Carranza, who ended up controlling most of the country by 1917, got a convention together in Querétaro to formulate political and social goals. The resulting Constitution of 1917, while restating most ideas of the Reformistas' 1857 constitution, additionally prescribed a single four-year presidential term, labor reform, and subordinated private ownership to public interest. Every village had a right to communal *ejido* land, and subsoil wealth could never be sold away to the highest bidder.

The Constitution of 1917 was a revolutionary expression of national aspirations and, in retrospect, represented a social and political agenda for the entire 20th century. In modified form, it has lasted to the present day.

Obregón Stabilizes Mexico

On December 1, 1920, General Alvaro Obregón legally assumed the presidency of a Mexico still bleeding from 10 years of civil war. Although a seasoned revolutionary, Obregón was also a negotiator who recognized peace was necessary to implement the goals of the revolution. In four years, his government pacified local uprisings, disarmed a swarm of warlords, executed hundreds of *bandidos,* obtained U.S. diplomatic recognition, assuaged the worst fears of the clergy and landowners, and began land reform.

All this set the stage for the work of **Plutarco Elías Calles,** Obregón's Minister of Gobernación (Interior) and handpicked successor, who won the 1924 election. Aided by peace, Mexico returned to a semblance of prosperity. Calles brought the army under civilian control, balanced the budget, and shifted Mexico's revolution into high gear. New clinics vaccinated millions against smallpox, new dams irrigated thousands of previously dry acres, and campesinos received millions of acres of redistributed land.

By single-mindedly enforcing the pro-agrarian, pro-labor, and anti-clerical articles of the 1917 constitution, Calles made many influential enemies. Infuriated by the government's confiscation of church property, closing of monasteries, and deportation of hundreds of foreign priests and nuns, the clergy refused to perform marriages, baptisms, and last rites. As members of the Cristero movement, militant Catholics crying *"¡Viva Cristo Rey!"* armed themselves, torching public schools and government property and murdering hundreds of innocent bystanders.

Simultaneously, Calles threatened foreign oil companies, demanding they exchange their titles for 50-year leases. A moderate Mexican supreme court decision over the oil issue and the skillful arbitration of American Ambassador Dwight Morrow smoothed over both the oil and church troubles by the end of Calles's term.

Calles, who started out brimming with revolutionary fervor and populist zeal, became increasingly conservative and dictatorial. Although he bowed out peaceably in favor of Obregón (the constitution had been amended to allow one six-year nonsuccessive term), Obregón was assassinated two weeks after his election in 1928. Calles continued to rule for six more years through three puppet-presidents: Emilio Portes Gil (1928–30), Pascual Ortíz Rubio (1930–32), and Abelardo Rodríguez (1932–34).

For the 14 years since 1920, the revolution had first waxed, then waned. With a cash surplus in 1930, Mexico skidded into debt as the Great Depression deepened and Calles and his cronies lined their pockets. In blessing his minister of war, General Lázaro Cárdenas, for the 1934 presidential election, Calles expected more of the same.

Lázaro Cárdenas, President of the People

The 40-year-old Cárdenas, former governor of Michoacán, immediately set his own agenda, however. He worked tirelessly to fulfill the social prescriptions of the revolution. As morning-coated diplomats fretted, waiting in his outer office, Cárdenas ushered in delegations of campesinos and factory workers and sympathetically listened to their petitions.

In his six years of rule, Cárdenas moved public education and health forward on a broad front, supported strong labor unions, and redistributed 49 million acres of farmland, more than any president before or since.

Cárdenas's resolute enforcement of the constitution's Artículo 123 brought him the most renown. Under this pro-labor law, the government turned over a host of private companies to employee ownership and, on March 18, 1938, expropriated all foreign oil corporations.

In retrospect the oil corporations, most of which were British, were not blameless. They had sorely neglected the wages, health, and welfare of their workers while ruthlessly taking the law into their own hands with private police forces. Although Standard Oil cried foul, U.S. President Franklin Roosevelt did not intervene. Through negotiation and due process, the U.S. companies eventually were compensated with $24 million, plus interest. In the wake of the expropriation, President Cárdenas created Petróleos Mexicanos (Pemex), the national oil corporation that continues to run all Mexican oil and gas operations.

Manuel Avila Camacho

Manuel Avila Camacho, elected in 1940, was the last general to be president of Mexico. His administration ushered in a gradual shift of Mexican politics, government, and foreign policy as Mexico allied itself with the U.S. cause during World War II. Foreign tourism, initially promoted by the Cárdenas administration, ballooned. Good feelings surged as Franklin Roosevelt became the first U.S. president to officially cross the Río Grande when he met with Camacho in Monterrey in April 1943.

In both word and deed, moderation and evolution guided President Camacho's policies. *"Soy creente"* ("I am a believer"), he declared to the Catholics of Mexico as he worked earnestly to bridge Mexico's serious church-state schism. Land policy emphasis shifted from redistribution to utilization as new dams and canals irrigated hundreds of thousands of previously arid acres. On one hand, Camacho established IMSS (Instituto Mexicano de Seguro Social) and on the other, trimmed the power of labor unions.

As World War II moved toward its 1945 conclusion, both the U.S. and Mexico were enjoying the benefits of four years of governmental and military cooperation and mutual trade in the form of a mountain of strategic minerals which had moved north in exchange for a similar mountain of U.S. manufactures that moved south.

CONTEMPORARY MEXICO

The Mature Revolution

During the decades after World War II, beginning with moderate President **Miguel Alemán** (1946–52), Mexican politicians gradually honed their skills of consensus and compromise as their middle-aged revolution bubbled along under liberal presidents and sputtered haltingly under conservatives. Doctrine required of all politicians, regardless of stripe, that they be "revolutionary" enough to be included beneath the banner of the PRI (Partido Revolucionario Institucional), Mexico's dominant political party.

Mexico's revolution hasn't been very revolutionary about women's rights, however. The PRI didn't get around to giving Mexican women, millions of whom fought and died during the revolution, the right to vote until 1953.

Adolfo Ruíz Cortínes, Alemán's secretary of the interior, was elected overwhelmingly in 1952. He fought the corruption that had crept into government under his predecessor, continued land reform, increased agricultural production, built new ports, eradicated malaria, and opened a dozen automobile assembly plants.

Women, voting for the first time in a national election, kept the PRI in power by electing liberal **Adolfo López Mateos** in 1958. Resembling Lázaro Cárdenas in social policy, López Mateos redistributed 40 million acres of farmland, forced automakers to use 60 percent domestic components, built thousands of new schools, and distributed hundreds of millions of new textbooks. *"La electricidad es nuestra"* ("Electricity is ours"), Mateos declared as he nationalized foreign power companies in 1962.

Despite his left-leaning social agenda, unions were restive under López Mateos. Protesting inflation, workers struck; the government retaliated, arresting Demetrios Vallejo, the railway union head, and renowned muralist David Siqueiros, former communist party secretary.

Despite the troubles, López Mateos climaxed his presidency gracefully in 1964 as he opened the celebrated National Museum of Anthropology, appropriately located in Chapultepec Park, where the Aztecs had first settled 20 generations earlier.

In 1964, as several times before, the outgoing president's interior secretary succeeded his former chief. Dour, conservative **Gustavo Díaz Ordaz** immediately clashed with liberals, labor, and students. The pot boiled over just before the 1968 Mexico City Olympics. Reacting to a student rebellion, the army occupied the National University; shortly afterwards, on October 2, government forces opened fire with machine guns on a downtown protest, killing and wounding hundreds of demonstrators.

Maquiladoras

Despite its serious internal troubles, Mexico's relations with the U.S. were cordial. President Lyndon Johnson visited and unveiled a statue of Abraham Lincoln in Mexico City. Later, Díaz Ordaz met with President Richard Nixon in Puerto Vallarta.

Meanwhile, bilateral negotiations produced the **Border Industrialization Program.** Within a 12-mile strip south of the U.S.-Mexico border, foreign companies could assemble duty-free parts into finished goods and export them without any duties on either side. Within a dozen years, a swarm of such plants, called *maquiladoras*, were humming as hundreds of thousands of Mexican workers assembled and exported billions of dollars worth of shiny consumer goods—electronics, clothes, furniture, pharmaceuticals, and toys—worldwide.

Concurrently, in Mexico's interior, Díaz Ordaz pushed Mexico's industrialization ahead full steam. Foreign money financed hundreds of new plants and factories. Primary among these was the giant Las Truchas steel plant at the new industrial port and town of Lázaro Cárdenas at the Pacific mouth of the Río Balsas.

Discovery, in 1974, of gigantic new oil and gas reserves along Mexico's Gulf coast added fuel to Mexico's already rapid industrial expansion. During the late 1970s and early 1980s billions in foreign investment, lured by Mexico's oil earnings, financed other major developments—factories, hotels, power plants, roads, airports—all over the country.

Economic Trouble of the 1980s

The negative side to these expensive projects was the huge dollar debt required to finance them. President **Luis Echeverría Alvarez** (1970–76), diverted by his interest in international affairs, passed Mexico's burgeoning financial deficit to his successor, **José López Portillo.** As feared by some experts, a world petroleum glut during the early 1980s burst Mexico's ballooning oil bubble and plunged the country into financial crisis. When the 1982 interest came due on its foreign debt, Mexico's largest holding company couldn't pay the $2.3 billion owed. The peso plummeted more than fivefold, to 150 per U.S. dollar. At the same time, prices doubled every year.

But by the mid-1980s, President **Miguel de la Madrid** (1982–88) was straining to get Mexico's economic house in order. He sliced government and raised taxes, asking rich and poor alike to tighten their belts. Despite getting foreign bankers to reschedule Mexico's debt, de la Madrid couldn't stop inflation. Prices skyrocketed as the peso deflated to 2,500 per U.S. dollar, becoming one of the world's most devalued currencies by 1988.

Salinas de Gortari and NAFTA

Public disgust led to significant opposition during the 1988 presidential election. Billionaire PAN candidate Michael Clothier and liberal National Democratic Front candidate Cuauhtémoc Cárdenas ran against the PRI's Harvard-educated technocrat Carlos Salinas de Gortari. The vote was split so evenly that all three candidates claimed victory. Although Salinas eventually won the election, his showing, barely half of the vote, was the worst ever for a PRI president.

Salinas, however, became Mexico's "Coming Man" of the 1990s. He seemed serious about democracy, sympathetic to the *indígenas* and the poor, and sensitive to women's issues. His major achievement, despite significant national opposition, was the North American Free Trade Agreement (NAFTA), which he, U.S. President George Bush, and Canadian Prime Minister Brian Mulrooney negotiated in 1992.

Incoming U.S. President Bill Clinton continued the drama by pushing NAFTA through the U.S. Congress in November 1993, and the Mexican legislature followed suit two weeks later. However, on the very day in January 1994 that NAFTA took effect, rebellion broke out in the poor, remote state of Chiapas. A small but well-disciplined campesino force, calling itself **Ejército Zapatista Liberación Nacional** (Zapatista National Liberation Army or EZLN), or "Zapatistas," captured a number of provincial towns and held the former governor of Chiapas hostage. Although PRI officials minimized the uprising, and President Clinton expressed confidence in the Mexican government, many thoughtful observers wondered if Mexico was ready for NAFTA.

To further complicate matters, Mexico's already tense drama veered into tragedy. While Salinas de Gortari's chief negotiator, Manuel Camacho Solis, was attempting to iron out a settlement with the Zapatista rebels, Luis Donaldo Colosio, Salinas's handpicked successor, was gunned down just months before the August balloting. However, instead of disintegrating, the nation united in grief; opposition candidates eulogized their fallen former opponent and later earnestly endorsed his replacement, stolid technocrat Ernesto

Zedillo, in Mexico's first presidential election debate.

In a closely watched election relatively unmarred by irregularities, Zedillo piled up a solid plurality against his PAN and PRD opponents. By perpetuating the PRI's 65-year hold on the presidency, the electorate had again opted for the PRI's familiar although imperfect middle-aged revolution.

New Crisis, New Recovery
Zedillo, however, had little time to savor his victory. Right away he had to face the consequences of his predecessor's shabby fiscal policies. The peso, after having been pumped up a thousand-fold to a value of three per dollar as the "new" peso in 1993, continued to be artificially propped up for a year, until it crashed, losing a third of its value just before Christmas 1994. A month later, the new peso was trading at about six per dollar, and Mexican financial institutions, their dollar debt having nearly doubled in a month, were in danger of defaulting on their obligations to international investors. To stave off a worldwide financial panic, U.S. President Clinton, in February 1995, secured an unprecedented multibillion dollar loan package for Mexico, guaranteed by U.S. and international institutions.

Although disaster was temporarily averted and Mexico became an overnight bargain for dollar-spending travelers, the cure for the country's ills was another painful round of inflation and belt-tightening for poor Mexicans. During 1995, inflation soared by 52 percent, pushing already-meager wages down an additional 20 percent. More and more families became unable to purchase staple foods and basic medicines. Malnutrition soared sixfold, and a resurgence of Third-World diseases, such as cholera and dengue fever, occurred in the countryside.

Meanwhile, as negotiations with the rebel Zapatistas sputtered on and off in Chiapas, popular discontent erupted in Guerrero, leading to the massacre of 17 unarmed campesinos at Aguas Blancas, in the hills west of Acapulco, by state police in June 1995. One year later, at a demonstration protesting the massacre, a new, well-armed revolutionary group, **Ejército Popular Revolucionario** (People's Revo-

lutionary Army, or EPR), appeared. A few months later, EPR guerrillas killed two dozen police and soldiers at several locations, mostly in southwestern Mexico. Although President Zedillo's immediate reaction was moderate, platoons of soldiers were soon scouring rural Guerrero, Oaxaca, Michoacán and other states, searching homes and arresting suspected dissidents. Public response was mostly negative, though some locals felt that they were far better off in the hands of the army rather than state or federal police.

Mexican democracy got a much-needed boost when notorious Guerrero governor Ruben Figueroa, who had tried to cover up the Aguas Blancas massacre with a bogus videotape, was forced from office. At the same time, the Zedillo government gained momentum in addressing the Zapatistas' grievances in Chiapas, even as it decreased federal military presence, built new rural electrification networks, and refurbished health clinics. Moreover, Mexico's economy began to improve. By mid-1996, inflation had slowed to a 20 percent annual rate, investment dollars were flowing back into Mexico, the peso had stabilized at about 7.5 to the U.S. dollar, and Mexico had paid back half the borrowed U.S. bailout money.

The Political Cauldron Bubbles On
Unfortunately, however, the improving economy had little effect on Mexico's political ills. Raul Salinas de Gortari, an important PRI party official and the former president's brother, was arrested for money laundering and political assassination. As popular sentiment began to implicate Carlos Salinas de Gortari himself, the former president fled Mexico to an undisclosed location.

Moreover, continued federal military presence, especially in the poor southern states of Guerrero, Oaxaca, and Chiapas, seemed to trigger violent incidents. Worst was the massacre of 45 indigenous *campesinos,* including women and children, at Acteal, Chiapas, in late December 1997 by paramilitary gunmen. Federal investigators later linked the perpetrators to local PRI officials. In mid-1998, the EPR appeared in Ayutla, Guerrero, leafleting villagers and giving impromptu speeches. Government soldiers responded with repression, violent searches, and physical abuse. Finally, federal troops cornered and killed 11 suspected EPR members in a schoolhouse 50 miles east of Acapulco.

Fortunately, foreign visitors have been unaffected by such disputes. In tourist resort towns and along well-traveled highways, and sites of tourist interest, foreign visitors are generally safer than in their home cities in the United States, Canada, or Europe.

Economic Recovery and Political Reforms

The best news for which the government could justly claim credit was the dramatically improving national economy. By mid-1998, annual inflation had dropped below 15 percent, investment dollars continued to pour into Mexico, the peso was stable at about 8 to the U.S. dollar, and Mexico had paid back every penny of the money from the 1995 U.S. bailout.

Moreover, in the political arena, although the justice system generally left much to be desired, a pair of unprecedented events signaled an increasingly open political system. In the 1997 congressional elections, voters elected a host of opposition candidates, depriving the PRI of an absolute congressional majority for the first time since 1929. A year later, in early 1998, Mexicans were participating in their country's first primary elections—in which voters, instead of politicians, chose party candidates.

Although President Zedillo had had a rough ride, he entered the twilight of his 1994–2000 term able to take credit for an improved economy, some genuine political reforms, and relative peace in the countryside. The election of 2000 revealed, however, that the Mexican people were not satisfied.

End of an Era: Vicente Fox Unseats the PRI

During 1998 and 1999 the focal point of opposition to the PRI's three-generation rule had been shifting from lackluster left-of-center Cuauhtémoc Cárdenas to relative newcomer Vicente Fox, former President of Coca Cola Mexico and clean former PAN governor of Guanajuato.

Fox, who had announced his candidacy for President two years before the election, seemed an unlikely challenger. After all, the

minority PAN had always been the party of wealthy businessmen and the conservative Catholic right. But blunt-talking, six-foot-five Fox, who sometimes campaigned in *vaquero* boots and a ten-gallon cowboy hat, preached populist themes of coalition building and "inclusion." He backed up his talk by carrying his campaign to hardscrabble city *barrios,* dirt-poor country villages, and traditional outsider groups, such as Jews.

Meanwhile, as the campaign heated up in early 2000, PRI candidate Francisco Labastida, suave, ex-Interior Secretary and governor of the drug-plagued state of Sinaloa, sounded the usual PRI themes to gatherings of party loyalists. At the same time, dour PRD liberal Cuauhtémoc Cárdenas, resigning from a mediocre term as mayor of Mexico City, faded to a weak third place. On the eve of the election, polls predicted a dead heat of about 40 percent of the vote each for Fox and Labastida.

In a closely monitored election, on July 2, 2000, Fox decisively defeated Labastida, 42 percent to 38 percent, while Cárdenas received only 17 percent. Fox's win also swept a PAN plurality (223/209/57) into the 500-seat Chamber of Deputies lower house (although the senate remained PRI-dominated).

Nevertheless, in removing the PRI from the all-powerful presidency after 71 consecutive years of domination, Fox had ushered Mexico into a new, much more Democratic era.

Despite stinging criticism from his own ranks, President Zedillo, whom historians were already judging as the real hero behind the new democratic era, made an unprecedented, early appeal, less than a week after the election, for all Mexicans to unite behind Fox.

On the eve of his December 1 inauguration, Mexicans awaited Fox's speech with hopeful anticipation. He did not disappoint them. Although acknowledging that he can't reverse 71 years of PRI entrenchment in one six-year term, he vowed to ride the crest of reform, revamping the tax system, and reduce poverty by 30 percent, by creating a million new jobs a year through new private investment in electricity and oil production and a forming a new common market with Latin America, the United States, and Canada.

He promised, moreover, to secure justice for all by a much-needed reform of police, the federal attorney general, and the army. Perhaps most difficult of all, Fox called for the formation of an unprecedented congressional "Transparency Commission" to investigate a generation of past grievances, including the 1968 massacre of student demonstrators and assassinations of, among others, a Roman Catholic cardinal in 1993 and a presidential candidate in 1994.

Regardless of whether Vicente Fox can accomplish such an earnestly ambitious agenda during his single term, it's clear that a legion of Mexican people, including many former opponents, doubters, and cynics, are loudly cheering him on.

ECONOMY AND GOVERNMENT

THE MEXICAN ECONOMY

Post-Revolutionary Gains

By many measures, Mexico's 20th-century revolution appears to have succeeded. Since 1910, illiteracy has plunged from 80 percent to 10 percent, life expectancy has risen from 30 years to nearly 70, infant mortality has dropped from a whopping 40 percent to about two percent, and, in terms of caloric intake, Mexicans are eating about twice as much as their forebears at the turn of the 20th century.

Decades of near-continuous economic growth account for rising Mexican living standards. The Mexican economy has rebounded from its last two recessions due to plentiful natural resources, notably oil and metals; diversified manufacturing, such as cars, steel, and petrochemicals; steadily increasing tourism; exports of fruits, vegetables, and cattle; and its large, willing, low-wage workforce.

Recent Mexican governments, moreover, have skillfully exploited Mexico's economic strengths. The Border Industrialization Program has led to millions of jobs in thousands of border *maquiladora* factories, from Tijuana to the mouth of the Rio Grande. Dependency on oil exports, which led to the 1980s peso collapse, has been reduced from 75 percent in 1982 to only 12 percent in 1994. Foreign trade, a strong source for new Mexican jobs, has burgeoned since the 1980s, due to liberalized tariffs as Mexico joined General Agreement on Tariffs and Trade (GATT) in 1986 and NAFTA in 1994. As a result, Mexico has become a net exporter of goods and services to the United States, its largest trading partner. Although Mexico suffered a peso collapse of about 50 percent (in relation to the U.S. dollar) in 1995, the Zedillo administration acted quickly. Belt-tightening measures brought inflation, which had initially surged, down to 20 percent per year, and foreign investment flowed back into Mexico by mid-1996. Although some factory and business closures led to increased unemployment in 1995, benefits from the devalued peso such as increased tourism and burgeoning exports have contributed to an improving economy since 1997.

Late 20th-Century Economic Challenges

Despite huge gains, Mexico's Revolution of 1910 is nevertheless incomplete. Improved public health, education, income, and opportunity have barely outdistanced Mexico's population, which has increased nearly seven-fold—from 15 million to 100 million—between 1910 and 2000. For example, although the illiteracy rate has decreased, the actual number of Mexican people who can't read, some 10 million, has remained about constant since 1910.

Moreover, the land reform program, once thought to be a Mexican cure-all, has long been a disappointment. The *ejidos* of which Emiliano Zapata dreamed have become mostly symbolic. The communal fields are typically small and unirrigated. *Ejido* land, constitutionally prohibited from being sold, cannot serve as collateral for bank loans. Capital for irrigation networks, fertilizers, and harvesting machines is consequently lacking. Communal farms are typically inefficient; the average Mexican field produces about *one-quarter* as much corn per acre as a U.S. farm. Mexico must accordingly use its precious oil dollar surplus to import millions of tons of corn—originally indigenous to Mexico—annually.

The triple scourge of overpopulation, lack of

Most Puerto Vallarta-region farmers do not own tractors; they mostly rely on horses and oxen to do the heavy work.

arable land, and low farm income has driven millions of campesino families to seek better lives in Mexico's cities. Since 1910, Mexico has evolved from a largely rural country, where 70 percent of the population lived on farms, to an urban nation where 70 percent of the population lives in cities. Fully one-fifth of Mexico's people now live in Mexico City.

Nevertheless, the future appears bright for many privately owned and managed Mexican farms, concentrated largely in the northern border states. Exceptionally productive, they typically work hundreds or thousands of irrigated acres of crops, such as tomatoes, lettuce, chiles, wheat, corn, tobacco, cotton, fruits, alfalfa, chickens, and cattle, just like their counterparts across the border in California, New Mexico, Arizona, and Texas.

Staples—wheat for bread, corn for tortillas, milk, and cooking oil—are all imported and consequently expensive for the typical working-class Mexican family, which must spend half or more of its income (typically $500 per month) for food. Recent inflation has compounded the problem, particularly for the millions of families on the bottom half of Mexico's economic ladder.

Although average gross domestic product figures for Mexico—about $8,000 per capita compared to more than $30,000 for the U.S.—place it above nearly all other Third-World countries, averages, when applied to Mexico, mean little. A primary socioeconomic reality of Mexican history remains: the richest one-fifth of Mexican families earns about 10 times the income of the poorest one-fifth. A relative handful of people own a large hunk of Mexico, and they don't seem inclined to share any of it with the less fortunate. As for the poor, the typical Mexican family in the bottom one-third income bracket often owns neither car nor refrigerator; the children do not finish elementary school, nor do their parents practice birth control.

GOVERNMENT AND POLITICS

The Constitution of 1917

Mexico's governmental system is rooted in the Constitution of 1917, which incorporated many of the features of its reformist predecessor of 1857. The 1917 document, with amendments, remains in force. Although drafted at the behest of conservative revolutionary Venustiano Carranza by his handpicked Querétaro "Constitucionalista" congress, it was greatly influenced by Alvaro Obregón and generally ignored by Carranza during his subsequent three-year presidential term.

Although many articles resemble those of its United States model, the Constitution of 1917 contains provisions developed directly from Mexican experience. Article 27 addresses the question of land. Private property rights are qualified by societal need; subsoil rights are public property, and foreigners and corporations are severely restricted in land ownership. Although the 1917 constitution declared *ejido* (communal) land inviolate, 1994 amendments allow, under certain circumstances, the sale or use of communal land as loan security.

Article 23 severely restricts church powers. In declaring that "places of worship are the property of the nation," it stripped churches of all title to real estate, without compensation. Article 5 and Article 130 banned religious orders, expelled foreign clergy, and denied priests and ministers all political rights, including voting, holding office, and even criticizing the government.

Article 123 establishes the rights of labor: to organize, bargain collectively, strike, work a maximum eight-hour day, and receive a minimum wage. Women are to receive equal pay for equal work and be given a month's paid leave for childbearing. Article 123 also establishes social security plans for sickness, unemployment, pensions, and death.

On paper, Mexico's constitutional government structures appear much like their U.S. prototypes: a federal presidency, a two-house congress, and a supreme court, with their counterparts in each of the 32 states. Political parties field candidates, and all citizens vote by secret ballot.

Mexico's presidents, however, enjoy greater powers than their U.S. counterparts. They need not seek legislative approval for cabinet appointments, can suspend constitutional rights under a state of siege, can initiate legislation, veto all or parts of bills, refuse to execute laws, and replace state officers. The federal government, moreover, retains nearly all taxing authority, relegating the states to a role of merely administering federal programs.

Although ideally providing for separation of powers, the Constitution of 1917 subordinates both the legislative and judicial branches, with the courts being the weakest of all. The supreme court, for example, can only, with repeated deliberation, decide upon the constitutionality of legislation. Five separate individuals must file successful petitions for writs *amparo* ("protection") on a single point of law in order to affect constitutional precedent.

Strong President; Strong PRI

Mexican presidents have successively built upon their potent constitutional mandate for three generations. The **Institutional Revolutionary Party (PRI),** whose handpicked candidates held the presidency continuously for 71 years, became an extra-legal parallel government, as or more powerful than the formal constitutional government. The PRI has been organized hierarchically, in three separate labor, farmer, and "popular" (this last mostly government, business, and professional workers) columns, which sent delegates from local committees to state and, ultimately, national-level conventions.

Past Mexican presidents, as heads of the PRI, traditionally reigned at the top of the party apparatus, sending orders through the national PRI delegates, who in turn looked after their respective state delegations. The delegates reported on the performance of the state and local PRI committees to get out the vote and carry out party mandates. If the local committee's performance was satisfactory, then federal subsi-

dies, public works projects, election funds, and federal jobs flowed from government coffers to the state and local level through PRI organizations. In your hometown, if you were not in the PRI or didn't know someone who was, you might have found it difficult to get a small business loan, crop subsidy, government apartment, teaching job, road-repair contract, or government scholarship.

Democratizing Mexican Politics

Reforms in Mexico's stable but top-heavy "Institutional Revolution" came only gradually. Characteristically, street protests were brutally put down at first, with officials only later working to address grievances. Dominance by the PRI led to widespread cynicism and citizen apathy. Regardless of who gets elected, the typical person on the street would tell you that the officeholder was bound to retire with his or her pockets full.

Nevertheless, by 1985, movement toward more justice and pluralism seemed be in store for Mexico. During the subsequent dozen years, minority parties increasingly elected candidates to state and federal office. Although none captured a majority of any state legislature, the strongest non-PRI parties, such as the conservative pro-Catholic **Partido Acción Nacional (PAN)** or National Action Party and the liberal-left **Partido Revolucionario Democratico (PRD),** elected governors. In 1986, minority parties were given federal legislative seats, up to a maximum of 20, for winning a minimum of 2.5 percent of the national presidential vote. In the 1994 election, minority parties received public campaign financing, depending upon their fraction of the vote.

Following his 1994 inaugural address, in which he called loudly and clearly for more reforms, President Zedillo quickly began to produce results. He immediately appointed a respected member of the PAN opposition party as attorney general—the first non-PRI cabinet appointment in Mexican history. Other Zedillo firsts were federal senate confirmation of both supreme court nominees and the attorney general, multiparty participation in the Chiapas peace negotiations, and congressional approval of the 1995 financial assistance package received from the United States. Zedillo, moreover, organized a series of precedent-setting meetings with opposition leaders that led to a written pact for political reform and the establishment of permanent working groups to discuss political and economic questions.

Perhaps most important was Zedillo's campaign and inaugural vow to separate both his government and himself from PRI decision-making. He kept his promise, becoming the first Mexican president, in as long as anyone could remember, who did not choose his successor.

A New Mexican Revolution

Finally, in 2000, like a Mexican Gorbachev, Ernesto Zedillo, the man most responsible for Mexico's recent democratic reforms, watched as PAN opposition reformer Vicente Fox swept Zedillo's PRI from the presidency after a 71-year rule. Moreover, despite severe criticism from his own party, Zedillo quickly called for the country to close ranks behind Fox. Millions of Mexicans, still dazed but buoyed by Zedillo's

statesmanship and Fox's epoch-making victory, eagerly awaited Fox's inauguration address on December 1, 2000.

He promised nothing less than a new revolution for Mexico and backed it up with concrete proposals: Reduce poverty by 30 percent with a million new jobs a year from revitalized new electricity and oil production, a Mexican Silicon Valley, and free trade between Mexico, all of Latin America, and the United States and Canada. He promised justice for all, through a reformed police, army, and the judiciary. He promised conciliation and an agreement with the Zapatista rebel movement in the south, including a bill of rights for Mexico's native peoples. With all of Mexico listening, Fox brought his speech to a hopeful conclusion: "If I had to summarize my message today in one sentence, I would say: Today Mexico has a future, but we have lost much time and wasted many resources. Mexico has a future, and we must build that future starting today."

PEOPLE

Let a broad wooden chopping block represent Mexico; imagine hacking it with a sharp cleaver until it is grooved and pocked. That fractured surface resembles Mexico's central highlands, where most Mexicans, divided from each other by high mountains and yawning *barrancas,* have lived since before history.

The Mexicans' deep divisions, in large measure, led to their downfall at the hands of the Spanish conquistadores. The Aztec empire that Hernán Cortés conquered was a vast but fragmented collection of tribes. Speaking more than a hundred mutually alien languages, those original Mexicans viewed each other suspiciously, as barely human barbarians from strange lands beyond the mountains. And even today the lines Mexicans draw between themselves—of caste, class, race, wealth—are the result, to a significant degree, of the realities of their mutual isolation.

POPULATION

The Spanish colonial government and the Roman Catholic religion provided the glue that

over 400 years has welded Mexico's fragmented people into a burgeoning nation-state. Mexico's population, more than 100 million by the year 2000, is exploding. This was not always so. Historians estimate that European diseases, largely measles and smallpox, wiped out as many as 25 million—perhaps 95 percent—of the *indígena* population within a few generations after Cortés stepped ashore in 1519. The Mexican population dwindled to a mere one million inhabitants by 1600. It wasn't until 1950, four centuries after Cortés, that Mexico's population recovered to its pre-conquest level of 20 million.

Mestizos, *Indígenas,* Criollos, and *Negros*

Although by 1950 Mexico's population had recovered, it was completely transformed. The mestizo, a Spanish-speaking person of mixed blood, had replaced the pure Native American, the *indígena* (een-DEE-hay-nah), as the typical Mexican.

The trend continues. Perhaps three of four Mexicans would identify themselves as mestizo: that class whose part-European blood ele-

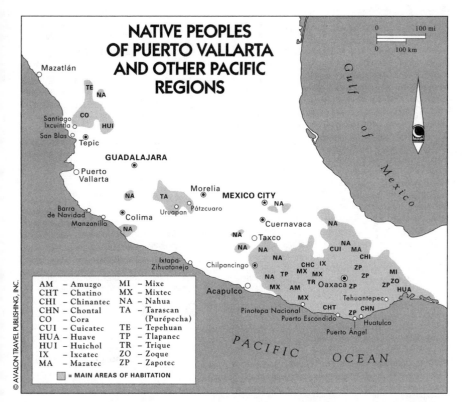

NATIVE PEOPLES
OF PUERTO VALLARTA
AND OTHER PACIFIC
REGIONS

AM – Amuzgo
CHT – Chatino
CHI – Chinantec
CHN – Chontal
CO – Cora
CUI – Cuicatec
HUA – Huave
HUI – Huichol
IX – Ixcatec
MA – Mazatec
MI – Mixe
MX – Mixtec
NA – Nahua
TA – Tarascan
   (Purépecha)
TE – Tepehuan
TP – Tlapanec
TR – Trique
ZO – Zoque
ZP – Zapotec

☐ = MAIN AREAS OF HABITATION

© AVALON TRAVEL PUBLISHING, INC.

vates them, in the Mexican mind, to the level of *gente de razón*—people of "reason" or "right." And there's the rub. The *indígenas* (or, mistakenly but much more commonly, Indians), by the usual measurements of income, health, or education, squat at the bottom of the Mexican social ladder.

The typical *indígena* family lives in a small adobe house in a remote valley, subsisting on corn, beans, and vegetables from their small, unirrigated *milpa* (cornfield). They usually have chickens, a few pigs, and sometimes a cow, but no electricity; their few hundred dollars a year in cash income isn't enough to buy even a small refrigerator, much less a truck.

The usual mestizo family, on the other hand, enjoys most of the benefits of the 20th century. They typically own a modest concrete house in

town. Their furnishings, simple by developed-world standards, will often include an electric refrigerator, washing machine, propane stove, television, and car or truck. The children go to school every day, and the eldest son sometimes looks forward to college.

Sizable *negro* communities, descendants of 18th-century African slaves, live in the Gulf states and along the Guerrero-Oaxaca Pacific coastline. Last to arrive, the *negros* experience discrimination at the hands of everyone else and are integrating very slowly into the mestizo mainstream.

Above the mestizos, a tiny criollo (Mexican-born white) minority, a few percent of the total population, inherits the privileges—wealth, education, and political power—of their colonial Spanish ancestors.

INDIGENOUS POPULATIONS OF PUERTO VALLARTA AND OTHER IMPORTANT PACIFIC REGIONS

For the Puerto Vallarta region states of Nayarit and Jalisco and the significant Pacific states (from north to south) of Sinaloa, Colima, Michoacán, Guerrero, and Oaxaca, the 1990 government census totals were:

INDIGENOUS POPULATION (OVER FIVE YEARS OF AGE),
TOTAL POPULATION (OVER FIVE YEARS OF AGE), PERCENT OF TOTAL

PUERTO VALLARTA REGION:			
Nayarit	24,000	712,000	3.4%
Jalisco	25,000	4,585,000	0.5%

OTHER PACIFIC STATES AND REGIONS:			
Sinaloa	31,000	1,924,000	1.6%
Colima	1,500	372,000	0.4%
Michoacán	106,000	3,037,000	3.4%
Guerrero	299,000	2,228,000	13.4%
Oaxaca	1,307,000	2,603,000	50.2%

The same government sources tabulate indigenous peoples by language groupings. Although such figures are probably low, the 1990 figures revealed significant populations in many areas:

LANGUAGE GROUP, POPULATION (1990), AND IMPORTANT CENTERS

PUERTO VALLARTA REGION:		
Cora	12,000	Nayarit (Acaponeta)
Huichol	20,000	Nayarit-Jalisco (Santiago Ixcuintla, Huejuqilla)
Nahua	5,000	Jalisco (Ciudad Guzmán)

NEIGHBORING STATES AND REGIONS (FROM NORTH TO SOUTH):		
Tepuan	5,000	Sinaloa
Tarasco	95,000	Michoacán (Pátzcuaro)
Nahua	100,000	Guerrero (Taxco and Chilpancingo)
Mixtec	387,000	Western Oaxaca (Huajuapan, Tlaxicao, and Santiago Jamiltepec)
Tlapanec	69,000	East Guerrero (Tlapa de Comonfort)
Amusgo	28,000	Oaxaca-Guerrero (San Pedro Amusgos and Xochistlahuaca)
Chinantec	104,000	Northern Oaxaca (Valle Nacional)
Chatino	29,000	Southern Oaxaca (Santos Reyes Nopala)
Zapotec	402,000	Central, East, and South Oaxaca (Tlacolula, Ocotlán, Tehuántepec)
Chontal	24,000	Southeast Oaxaca (Santiago Astata)
Trique	15,000	West Oaxaca (Juxtlahuaca)
Chocho	13,000	Northwest Oaxaca (Coixtlahuaca)
Cuicatec	13,000	Northern Oaxaca (Cuicatlán)
Huave	12,000	Southeast Oaxaca (San Mateo del Mar)
Mazatec	168,000	North Oaxaca (Huatla de Jiménez)
Mixe	95,000	Northeast Oaxaca (Ayutla)
Zoque	5,000	Southeast Oaxaca (San Miguel Chimalapa)
Ixcatec	1,000	Northwest Oaxaca (Ixcatlán)

THE *INDÍGENAS*

Although anthropologists and census takers classify them according to language groups (such as Nahuatl, Mixtec, and Zapotec), *indígenas* identify themselves as residents of a particular locality rather than by language or ethnic grouping. And although, as a group, they are referred to as *indígenas* (native, or aboriginal), individuals are generally uncomfortable at being labeled as such.

While the mestizos are the emergent self-conscious majority class, the *indígenas,* as during colonial times, remain the invisible people of Mexico. They are politically conservative, socially traditional, and tied to the land. On market day, the typical *indígena* family might make the trip into town. They bag tomatoes, squash, or peppers, and tie up a few chickens or a pig. The rickety country bus will often be full and the mestizo driver may wave them away, giving preference to his friends, leaving them to trudge stoically along the road.

Their lot, nevertheless, has been slowly improving. *Indígena* families now almost always have access to a local school and a clinic. Improved health has led to a large increase in their population. Official census figures, however, are probably low. *Indígenas* are traditionally suspicious of government people, and census takers, however conscientious, seldom speak the local language.

Recent figures, however, indicate 8 percent of Mexicans are *indígenas*—that is, they speak one of Mexico's 50-odd native languages. Of these, a quarter speak no Spanish at all. These fractions are changing only slowly. Many *indígenas* prefer the old ways. If present trends continue, the year 2019 will mark the return of the Mexican indigenous population to the pre-conquest level of 20 million.

Indígena Language Groups

The Maya speakers of Yucatán and the aggregate of the Nahuatl (Aztec language) speakers of the central plateau are Mexico's most numerous *indígena* groups, totaling three million (one million Maya, two million Nahua).

Official figures, which show that the Puerto Vallarta region's indigenous population amounts

The cotton huipil, *a native woman's costume embroidered with animal and floral designs, remains popular in rural areas of southwestern Mexico.*

to a mere 1 percent of the total, are misleading. Official counts do not measure the droves of transient folks—migrants and new arrivals—who sleep in vehicles, shanty towns, behind their crafts stalls, and with friends and relatives. Although they are officially invisible, you will see them in Puerto Vallarta, walking along the beach, for example, laden with their for-sale fruit or handicrafts—men in sombreros and scruffy jeans, women in homemade full-skirted dresses with aprons much like your great-great-grandmother may have worn.

Immigrants in their own country, they flock to cities and tourist resorts from hardscrabble rural areas of the poorest states, often Michoacán, Guerrero, and Oaxaca. Although of pure native blood, they will not acknowledge it or will even be insulted if you ask them if they are *indígenas*. It would be more polite to ask them where they're from. If from Michoacán, they'll often speak Tarasco (more courteously, say Purépecha: poo-

RAY-pay-chah); if from Guerrero, the answer will usually be Nahuatl. Oaxaca folks, on the other hand, will probably be fluent in a dialect of either Zapotec or Mixtec. If not one of these, then it might be Amuzgo, Chatino, Trique, Chontal, or any one of a dozen others from Oaxaca's crazy-quilt of language.

As immigrants always have, they come seeking opportunity. If you're interested in what they're selling, bargain with humor. And if you err, let it be on the generous side. They are proud, honorable people who prefer to walk away from a sale rather than to lose their dignity.

The Huichol and Cora

In contrast to the migrants from the south, the Huichol and their northerly neighbors, the Cora, are native to the Puerto Vallarta region. Isolated and resistant to Mexicanization, about 20,000 Huichol (and half as many Cora) farm, raise cattle, and hunt high in their Sierra Madre mountain homeland, which extends northerly and easterly from the foothills north of Tepic. Although the Cora's traditional territory intermixes with the Huichol's at its southern limit, it also spreads northward, between the foothills and the 6,000-foot-high Sierra Occidental valleys, to the Nayarit-Durango border.

The Huichol, more than all *indígena* groups, have preserved their colorful dress and religious practices. Huichol religious use of hallucinogenic peyote and the men's rainbow-tinted feathered hats and clothes are renowned. Tepic, San Blas, and especially Santiago Ixcuintla north of Puerto Vallarta are the most important and easily accessible Huichol centers. In both Puerto Vallarta and Tepic, several stores specialize in the Huichol's colorful religious crafts. Santiago Ixcuintla (eeks-WEEN-tlah) has a Huichol handicrafts store and community center, and San Blas is an important pilgrimage site where Huichol gather, especially around Easter, for weddings and to pay homage to the sea goddess, Aramara. (See the Nayarit Coast chapter for more Huichol information.)

While not so well known as the Huichol's, the Cora's traditions also remain essentially preserved. These include use of peyote in the worship of pre-Christian deities, such as the fertility gods Grandfather Sun and Grandmother Moon, Earth-mother Tatí, and the heroic monster-killer Brother Morning Star. Although many Cora have migrated to the Nayarit lowland towns, such as Acaponeta, Rosamorada, Tuxpan, and Ruíz along Hwy. 15, they return for festivals to their mountain homeland villages that center around remote Jesús María, about 128 rough mountain kilometers from Ruíz. The most notable festivals occur January 1–5 (inauguration of the Cora governor) and Semana Santa (the week before Easter).

Dress

Country markets are where you're most likely to see people in traditional dress. There, many men still wear the white cottons that blend Spanish and native styles. Absolutely necessary for men is the Spanish-origin straw sombrero (literally, "shade-maker") on their heads, loose white cotton shirt and pants, and leather huaraches on their feet.

Women's dress, by contrast, is more colorful. It can include a *huipil* (long, sleeveless dress) embroidered in bright floral and animal motifs and a handwoven *enredo* (wraparound skirt that identifies the wearer with a locality). A *faja* (waist sash) and, in winter, a *quechquemitl* (shoulder cape) complete the ensemble.

RELIGION

"God and Gold" was the two-pronged mission of the conquistadores. Most of them concentrated on gold, while missionaries tried to shift the emphasis to God. They were famously successful; more than 90 percent of Mexicans profess to be Catholics.

Catholicism, spreading its doctrine of equality of all persons before God and incorporating native gods into the church rituals, eventually brought the *indígenas* into the fold. Within a hundred years, nearly all native Mexicans had accepted the new religion, which raised the universal God of humankind over local tribal deities.

The Virgin of Guadalupe

Conversion of the *indígenas* was sparked by the vision of Juan Diego, a humble farmer. On the hill of Tepayac north of Mexico City in 1531, Juan Diego saw a brown-skinned version of the Virgin Mary enclosed in a dazzling aura of light. She told him to build a shrine in her memory on that spot, where the Aztecs had long worshipped their "earth mother," Tonantzín. Juan Diego's brown virgin told him to go to the cathedral and relay her instruction to Archbishop Zumárraga.

The archbishop, as expected, turned his nose up at Juan Diego's story. The vision returned, however, and this time Juan Diego's brown virgin realized that a miracle was necessary. She ordered him to pick some roses at the spot where she had first appeared to him (a true miracle, since roses had been previously unknown in the vicinity) and take them to the archbishop. Juan Diego wrapped the roses in his rude fiber cape, returned to the cathedral, and placed the wrapped roses at the archbishop's feet. When he opened the offering, Zumárraga gasped: imprinted on the cape was an image of the brown virgin herself—proof positive of a genuine miracle.

In the centuries since Juan Diego, the brown virgin—La Virgen Morena, or Nuestra Señora La Virgen de Guadalupe—has blended native and Catholic elements into something uniquely Mexican. In doing so, she has become the virtual patroness of Mexico, the beloved symbol of Mexico for *indígenas,* mestizos, *negros,* and criollos alike.

Every Puerto Vallarta regional town and village celebrates the cherished memory of their Virgin of Guadalupe on December 12. This celebration, however joyful, is but one of the many fiestas that Mexicans, especially the *indígenas,* live for. Each village holds its local fiesta in honor of their patron saint, who is often a thinly veiled sit-in for a local pre-conquest deity. Themes appear Spanish—Christian vs. Moors, devils vs. priests—but the native element is strong, sometimes dominant.

ON THE ROAD

SPORTS AND RECREATION

BEACHES

It's easy to understand why most vacationers come to Puerto Vallarta to stay on the beach. And these days, they don't simply confine themselves to Playa de Oro, the golden Puerto Vallarta luxury hotel strand. Increasing numbers are venturing out and discovering the entire Puerto Vallarta region's quieter resorts. Beginning in the north, on the lush Nayarit coast, are sleepy San Blas and Rincón de Guayabitos; farther south, the crystal sands of Bucerías decorate the northern arc of the Bay of Banderas, while south past Puerto Vallarta town are tiny Boca de Tomatlán and Yelapa, nestling at the Bay of Banderas's jungly southern edge. Beyond that, south of the pine-clad Sierra Cuale crest, are the gemlike bays of Chamela and Careyes; and past that, the homey country re-

sorts of Melaque and Barra de Navidad bask on the Costa Alegre (Happy Coast) of southern Jalisco.

The shoreline offers more than resorts, however. Visitors are increasingly seeking rustic paradises where they can lay out a picnic or even set up camp and enjoy the solitude, wildlife, and fishing opportunities of a score of breezy little beach hideaways.

The 300-odd miles of the Puerto Vallarta coastal region offer visitors their pick of shorelines, which vary from mangrove-edged lagoons and algae-adorned tidepools to shoals of pebbles and sands of many shades and consistencies.

Sand makes the beach—and the Puerto Vallarta region has plenty—from dark, warm mica to cool, velvety, white coral. Some beaches drop steeply to turbulent, close-in surf, fine for fishing. Others are level, with gentle, rolling breakers, made for surfing and swimming.

Beaches are fascinating for the surprises they yield. Puerto Vallarta-area beaches, especially the hidden strands near resorts and the dozens of miles of wilderness beaches and tidepools, yield troves of shells and treasures of flotsam and jetsam for those who enjoy looking for them. **Beachcombing** is more rewarding during the summer storm season, when big waves deposit acres of shells—conch, scallop, clams, comb of Venus, whelks, limpets, olives, cowries, starfish, and sand dollars. It's illegal to remove seashells, however, so remember to leave them for others to enjoy.

During the rainy season, beaches near river-mouths (notably Río Santiago north of San Blas) are outdoor galleries of fantastic wind and water-sculpted snags and giant logs deposited by the downstream flood.

Viewing Wildlife

Wildlife watchers should keep quiet and always be on the alert. Animal survival depends on them seeing you before you see them. Occasional spectacular offshore sights, such as whales, porpoises, and manta rays, or an onshore giant constrictor, beached squid, crocodile *(caimán),* or even jaguar looking for turtle eggs, are the reward of those prepared to recognize them. Don't forget your binoculars and your Peterson's *Field Guide to Mexican Birds.* (See Suggested Reading.)

Although wildlife-viewing is likely to be rewarding for the prepared everywhere in the Puerto Vallarta region, the lush mangrove lagoons around San Blas are special. For even casual nature enthusiasts, the La Tovara jungle river trip is a must. (See "Sights and Activities" under "San Blas and Vicinity" for details.)

For extensive notes on good hiking, tidepooling, wildlife-viewing, and shell-browsing spots, see each destination chapter's "Sights" section.

WATER SPORTS

Swimming, surfing, windsurfing, snorkeling, scuba diving, kayaking, sailing, and jet skiing are the Puerto Vallarta region's water sports of choice.

Safety First

Viewed from Puerto Vallarta beaches, the Pacific Ocean usually lives up to its name. Many protected inlets, safe for child's play, dot the coastline. Unsheltered shorelines, on the other hand, can be deceiving. Smooth water in the calm morning often changes to choppy in the afternoon; calm ripples that lap the shore in March can grow to hurricane-driven walls of water in November. Such storms can wash away sand, temporarily changing a wide, gently sloping beach into a steep one plagued by turbulent waves and treacherous currents.

Undertow, whirlpools, cross-currents, and occasional oversized waves can make ocean swimming a fast-lane adventure. Getting unexpectedly swept out to sea or hammered onto the beach bottom by a surprise breaker are potential hazards.

Never attempt serious swimming when tipsy or full of food; never swim alone where someone can't see you. Always swim beyond big breakers (which come in sets of several, climaxed by a huge one, which breaks highest and farthest from the beach). If you happen to get caught in the path of such a wave, avoid it by *diving directly toward and under it,* letting it roll harmlessly over

During the fall hurricane season, surfing is the main event at Las Islitas, on Matanchén, near San Blas.

you. If you are unavoidably swept up in a whirling, crashing breaker, try to roll and tumble with it, as football players tumble, to avoid injury.

Look out for other irritations and hazards. Now and then swimmers get a nettlelike (but usually harmless) jellyfish sting. Be careful around coral reefs and beds of sea urchins; corals can sting (like jellyfish) and you can additionally get infections from coral cuts and sea-urchin spines. *Shuffle* along sandy bottoms to scare away stingrays before stepping on one. If you're unlucky, its venomous tail-spines may inflict a painful wound. (See "Staying Healthy" under "Other Practicalities" for first-aid measures.)

Snorkeling and Scuba Diving

A number of clear-water sites await snorkelers and scuba divers. North of the Bay of Banderas, snorkelers enjoy **Isla Islote** just offshore from Rincón de Guayabitos. Accessible from Banderas Bay itself are **Islas Marietas,** off northshore Punta Mita; and the famous **Los Arcos** arch rocks off Mismaloya. Additionally, tour boats regularly take snorkelers to small coves near **Playa Las Animas** and **Playa Quimixto** on the Bay of Banderas's verdant southern shore. Farther afield, adventurous snorkelers and divers explore the wreck at **Tehualmixtle** on the pristine Cabo Corrientes coast past the Bay of Banderas's southern lip. Beyond that, rock-studded bays, such as gemlike **Bahía Careyes** and **Tenacatita,** invite snorkelers and divers to explore their clear waters.

Veteran divers usually arrive during the dry winter and early spring when river outflows are mere trickles, leaving offshore waters clear. In Puerto Vallarta, a number of professional dive shops rent equipment, provide lessons and guides, and transport divers to choice sites.

While beginners can usually do well with rented equipment, serious snorkelers and divers bring their own gear. This should include wetsuits in winter, when many swimmers feel cold after more than an unprotected half-hour in the water.

Sailing, Surfing, Windsurfing, and Kayaking

The surf everywhere is highest and best during the July–Nov. hurricane season, when big swells from storms far out at sea attract surfers to the favored beaches.

During the fall, veterans regularly spend weeks at San Blas waiting for the legendary Big Wave. Their hoped-for reward is one of the giant breakers that can carry them more than a mile toward the soft sands of Playa Matanchén. Although not nearly as renowned, the breaks off Punta Mita also attract advanced surfers.

For intermediates and beginners, the Puerto Vallarta vicinity offers a number of good spots. These include La Peñita (near Rincón de Guayabitos), the mouth of the Río Ameca just north of the Puerto Vallarta airport, and the breakwater at the entrance to the Laguna de Navidad at Barra de Navidad.

Windsurfers, sailboaters, and kayakers who, by contrast, require more tranquil waters, do best in the winter or early spring. It is then they gather to enjoy the ideal conditions in the many coves and inlets along the Puerto Vallarta coast.

While beginners can have fun with the equipment available from beach rental shops, serious surfers, windsurfers, sailboaters, and kayakers should pack their own gear.

POWER SPORTS

The Puerto Vallarta hotel beachfronts of northside Playa de Oro and, to a lesser extent, Playa los Muertos, on the south side, have long been centers for water-skiing, parasailing, and jet skiing. In parasailing, a motorboat pulls while a parachute lifts you, like a soaring gull, high over the ocean. After five or 10 minutes they deposit you—usually gently—back on the sand.

Jet Ski boats ("wave-runners" or personal watercraft) are like snowmobiles except that they operate on water, where, with a little practice, beginners can quickly learn to whiz over the waves.

Although the luxury resort hotels generally provide experienced crews and equipment, crowded conditions increase the hazard to both participants and swimmers. You, as the patron, are paying plenty for the privilege; you have a right to expect that your providers and crew are well-equipped, sober, and cautious.

Beach Buggies and ATVs

Some visitors enjoy racing along the beach and rolling over dunes in beach buggies and ATVs (all-terrain vehicles, called *motos* in Mexico)—

balloon-tired, three-wheeled motor scooters. While certain resort rental agencies cater to the growing use of such vehicles, limits are in order. Of all the proliferating high-horsepower beach pastimes, these are the most intrusive. Noise and gasoline pollution, injuries to operators and bystanders, and the scattering of wildlife and destruction of their habitats have led to the restriction of dune buggies and ATVs on Puerto Vallarta region beaches.

TENNIS AND GOLF

Puerto Vallarta visitors can enjoy a number of excellent private courts and courses. In Puerto Vallarta itself, golfers have their pick of the Marina course in town (available only to guests of certain hotels) and the Los Flamingos course several miles north of the airport. In Guadalajara, visitors can enjoy golf at three good courses, notably the Burgos del Bosque golf course (on the southside Chapala highway) and the San Isidro club (10 miles north of town on the Saltillo highway). Likewise, the big new Isla Navidad resort near Barra de Navidad (on the south, Colima side of the lagoon) has a breezy, beautiful seaside golf course.

As for tennis, many resort hotels in Puerto Vallarta, Nuevo Vallarta, and Guadalajara have tennis courts. Other smaller hotels in Rincón de Guayabitos, Cruz de Huanacaxtle, Mismaloya, Careyes, El Tecuán, Tenacatita (Blue Bay), Melaque, and Barra de Navidad also have courts.

No public golf or tennis courts exist in the Puerto Vallarta region, but many hotels and private clubs allow for-fee use by the general public. If you plan on playing a lot of golf or tennis, best stay at one of the many hotels with access to these facilities.

Use of hotel tennis courts is sometimes, but not always, included in your hotel tariff. If not, fees will run about $5 per hour or more. Golf greens fees, which begin at about $50 for 18 holes, are always extra.

FISHING

The Puerto Vallarta region offers many excellent fishing opportunities. Anglers routinely bring in dozens of species from among the more than 600 that abound in Mexican Pacific waters.

Surf Fishing

Good fishing beaches away from the immediate resort areas will be typically uncrowded, with only a few local folks (mostly fishing with nets) and fewer visitors. Mexicans do little rod-and-reel sportfishing. Most either make their living from fishing or do none at all. Consequently, sportfishing equipment is both expensive and hard to get. Plan to bring your own, including hooks, lures, line, and weights.

A good general information source before you leave home is a local bait-and-tackle shop. Tell them where you're going, and they'll often know the best lures and bait to use and what fish you can expect to catch with them.

In any case, the cleaner the water, the more interesting your catch. On a good day, your reward might be one or more *sierras, cabrillas,* porgies, or pompanos pulled from the Puerto Vallarta surf.

You can't have everything, however. Foreigners cannot legally take Mexican abalone, coral, lobster, pismo clams, rock bass, sea fans, seashells, shrimp, or turtles. Neither are they supposed to buy them directly from fishermen.

Deep-Sea Fishing

Puerto Vallarta captains operate dozens of excellent big charter boats. Rental generally includes a 30- to 40-foot boat and crew for a full or half day, plus equipment and bait for 2–6 persons, not including food or drinks. The charter price depends upon the season. During the high Christmas–New Year and before-Easter seasons, advance reservations are mandatory and a Puerto Vallarta boat can run $400 per day. Off-season rates, which depend strongly on your bargaining ability, can cost as little as half the high-season rate. For high-season charter boat reservations, contact an experienced agency, such as Miller's Travel Agency, or American Express several weeks before departure.

Those who arrive without a reservation (or who prefer dealing directly with local people) can contact the local fishing-boat cooperative, **Sociedad Cooperativa Progreso Turístico,** on the seafront walkway in downtown Puerto Vallarta.

FISH

A bounty of fish darts, swarms, jumps, and wriggles in the Puerto Vallarta region's surf, reefs, lagoons, and offshore depths. While many make delicious dinners (albacore, red snapper, pompano), others are tough (sailfish), bony (bonefish), and even poisonous (puffers). Some grow to half-ton giants (marlin, jewfish), while others are diminutive reef-grazers (parrot fish, damselfish, angelfish) whose bright colors delight snorkelers and divers. Here's a sampling of what you might find underwater or on your dinner plate.

albacore *(albacora, atún):* two to four feet in size; blue; found in deep waters; excellent taste

angelfish *(ángel):* one foot; yellow, orange, blue; reef fish*

barracuda *(barracuda, picuda):* two feet; brown; deep waters; good taste

barracuda

black marlin *(marlin negro):* six feet; blue-black; deep waters; good taste

blue marlin *(marlin azul):* eight feet; blue; deep waters; poor taste

bobo *(barbudo):* one foot; blue, yellow; found in surf; fair taste

bonefish *(macabi):* one foot; blue or silver; found inshore; poor taste

bonito *(bonito):* two feet; black; deep waters; good taste

butterfly fish *(muñeca):* six inches; black, yellow; reef fish*

chub *(chopa):* one foot; gray; reef fish; good taste

croaker *(corvina):* two feet; brownish; found along inshore bottoms; rare and protected

damselfish *(castañeta):* four inches; brown, blue, orange; reef fish*

dolphinfish, mahimahi *(dorado):* three feet; green, gold; deep waters; good taste

grouper *(garropa):* three feet; brown, rust; found offshore and in reefs; good taste

grunt *(burro):* eight inches; black, gray; found in rocks, reefs*

jack *(toro):* one to two feet; bluish-gray; offshore; good taste

mackerel *(sierra):* two feet; gray with gold spots; offshore; good taste

mullet *(lisa):* two feet; gray; found in sandy bays; good taste

needlefish *(agujón):* three feet; blue-black; deep waters; good taste

Pacific porgy *(pez de pluma):* one to two feet; tan; found along sandy shores; good taste

parrot fish *(perico, pez loro):* one foot; green, pink, blue, orange; reef fish*

pompano *(pómpano):* one foot; gray; inshore bottoms; excellent taste

puffer *(botete):* eight inches; brown; inshore; poisonous

red snapper *(huachinango, pargo):* one to two feet; reddish pink; deep waters; excellent taste

roosterfish *(pez gallo):* three feet; black, blue; deep waters; excellent taste

sailfish *(pez vela):* five feet; blue-black; deep waters; poor taste

sardine *(sardina):* eight inches; blue-black; offshore; good taste

bonito

sea bass *(cabrilla):* one to two feet; brown, ruddy; reef and rock crevices; good taste

shark *(tiburón):* 2–10 feet; black to blue; in- and offshore; good taste

snook *(robalo):* two to three feet; black-brown; found in brackish lagoons; excellent taste

spadefish *(chambo):* one foot; black-silver; found along sandy bottoms; reef fish*

swordfish *(pez espada):* five feet; black to blue; deep waters; good taste

triggerfish *(pez puerco):* one to two feet; blue, rust, brown, black; reef fish; excellent taste

damselfish

wahoo *(peto, guahu):* two to five feet; green to blue; deep waters; excellent taste

yellowfin tuna *(atún amarilla):* two to five feet; blue, yellow; deep waters; excellent taste

yellowtail *(jurel):* two to four feet; blue, yellow; off-shore; excellent taste

*generally too small to be considered edible

sailfish

A few big tourist fishing boats also operate from the San Blas and Barra de Navidad marinas. For many more details, see the destination chapters.

Other Boat-Rental Options

Renting an entire big boat is not your only choice. High-season business is sometimes so brisk at Puerto Vallarta that agencies can fill up boats by booking individuals, who typically pay $70 per person.

Pangas, outboard launches seating four to six, are available on the beaches for as little $50, depending on the season. Once in Barra de Navidad four of my friends went out in a *panga* all day, had a great time, and came back with a boatload of big tuna, jack, and mackerel. A restaurant cooked them up as a banquet for a dozen of us in exchange for the extra fish. I discovered for the first time how heavenly fresh *sierra veracruzana* can taste.

If you or a friend speaks a bit of Spanish, you can bargain for a *panga* right on the beach in Puerto Vallarta or at a dozen other seaside villages such as San Blas, Rincón de Guayabitos, Sayulita, Punta Mita, Cruz de Huanacaxtle, Bucerías, Mismaloya, Boca de Tomatlán, Chamela, Careyes, Tenacatita, La Manzanilla, Melaque, and Barra de Navidad.

Bringing Your Own Boat

If you're going to do lots of fishing, your own boat may be your most flexible and economical option. One big advantage is you can go to the many excellent fishing grounds that the charter boats do not frequent. Keep your boat license (see below) up to date, equipment simple, and keep your eyes peeled and ears open for local regulations and customs, plus tide, wind, and fishing information. See the individual destination chapters for boat-launching ramps and sites.

Fishing Licenses and Boat Permits

Anyone 16 or older who is either fishing or riding in a fishing boat in Mexico is required to have a fishing license. Although Mexican fishing licenses are obtainable from certain travel and insurance agents or at government fishing offices in Puerto Vallarta, San Blas, and Barra de Navidad, save yourself time and trouble by getting both your fishing licenses and boat permits by mail ahead of time from the Mexican Department of Fisheries. Call at least a month before departure (tel. 619/233-6956, fax 619/233-0344) and ask for applications. Fees are reasonable but depend upon the period of validity and the fluctuating exchange rate. On the application, fill in the names (exactly as they appear on passports) of the persons requesting licenses. Include a cashier's check or a money order for the exact amount, along with a stamped, self-addressed envelope. Address the application to the Mexican Department of Fisheries, 2550 Fifth Ave., Suite 101, San Diego, CA 92103-6622.

HUNTING AND FRESHWATER FISHING

Considerable game, especially winter-season waterfowl and doves, is customarily hunted in freshwater reservoirs and coastal marshes in the neighboring state of Sinaloa north of the Puerto Vallarta region. Visitors driving or flying south to Puerto Vallarta can arrange to hunt or fish for freshwater bass along the way. Some of the most popular hunting and fishing reservoirs are Domínguez and Hidalgo, near colonial El Fuerte town (an hour northeast of Los Mochis). Farther south, just north of Culiacán, is López Mateos reservoir, while farther south still, Lake Comedero lies two road hours north of Mazatlán or six hours north of Tepic. Near Puerto Vallarta itself, anglers report rewarding catches of freshwater bass at **Cajon de Peñas Reservoir,** about an hour's drive south of town. (See the Coast of Jalisco chapter.)

Bag limits and seasons for game are carefully controlled by the government's Secretary of Social Development (Secretaría de Desarrollo Social), SEDESOL. It and the Mexican consular service jointly issue the required permits through a time-consuming and costly procedure which, at minimum, runs for months and costs hundreds of dollars. For more details on Mexican hunting regulations and permits, consult the AAA (American Automobile Association) *Mexico Travel-Book.* (See Suggested Reading.)

Private fee agencies are a must to complete the mountain of required paperwork. Among the most experienced is the **Wildlife Advisory Service,** P.O. Box 76132, Los Angeles, CA 90076, tel. 213/385-9311, fax 213/385-0782.

For many useful hunting and fishing details, including many sites and lodges throughout Northern Mexico, get a copy of Sanborn's *Mexico Recreational Guide to Mexico* published by Sanborn's insurance agency. Order ($15.95, plus postage and handling) with credit card by phoning 800/222-0158 or by writing P.O. Box 310, McAllen, TX 78502.

BULLFIGHTING

It is said there are two occasions for which Mexicans arrive on time: funerals and bullfights.

Bullfighting is a recreation, not a sport. The bull is outnumbered seven to one, and the outcome is never in doubt. Even if the matador (literally, "killer") fails in his duty, his assistants will entice the bull away and slaughter it in private beneath the stands.

La Corrida de Toros

Moreover, Mexicans don't call it a "bullfight"; it's the *corrida de toros,* during which six bulls are customarily slaughtered, beginning at 5 P.M. (4 in the winter). After the beginning parade, featuring the matador and his helpers, the *picadores* and the *bandilleras,* the first bull rushes into the ring in a cloud of dust. Clockwork *tercios* (thirds) define the ritual: the first, the *puyazos,* or "stabs," requires that two *picadores* on horseback thrust lances into the bull's shoulders, weakening it. During the second *tercio,* the *bandilleras* dodge the bull's horns to stick three long, streamered darts into its shoulders.

Trumpets announce the third *tercio* and the appearance of the matador. The bull—weak, confused, and angry—is ready for the finish. The matador struts, holding the red cape, daring the bull to charge. Form now becomes everything. The expert matador takes complete control of the bull, which rushes at the cape, past its ramrod-erect opponent. For charge after charge, the matador works the bull to exactly the right spot in the ring—in front of the judges, a lovely señorita, or perhaps the governor—where the matador mercifully delivers the precision *estocada* (killing sword thrust) deep into the drooping neck of the defeated bull.

Benito Juárez, as governor during the 1850s, outlawed bullfights in Oaxaca. In his honor, they remain so, making Oaxaca unique among Mexican states.

FESTIVALS AND EVENTS

Mexicans love a party. Urban families watch the calendar for midweek national holidays that create a *puente* or "bridge" to the weekend and allow them to squeeze in a three- to five-day mini-vacation. Visitors should likewise watch the calendar. Such holidays (especially Christmas and Semana Santa, pre-Easter week) mean packed buses, roads, and hotels, especially around the Puerto Vallarta region's beach resorts.

Campesinos, on the other hand, await their local saint's or holy day. The name of the locality often provides the clue: For example, in Santa Cruz del Miramar near San Blas, expect a celebration on May 3, El Día de la Santa Cruz (Day of the Holy Cross). People dress up in their traditional best, sell their wares and produce in a street fair, join a procession, get tipsy, and dance in the plaza.

ARTS AND CRAFTS

Mexico is so stuffed with lovely, reasonably priced handicrafts or *artesanias* (pronounced ar-tay-say-NEE-ahs) that many crafts devotees, if given the option, might choose Mexico over heaven. A sizable fraction of Mexican families still depend upon the sale of homespun items—clothing, utensils, furniture, forest herbs, religious offerings, adornments, toys, musical instruments—which either they or their neighbors make at home. Many craft traditions reach back thousands of years, to the beginnings of Mexican civilization. The work of generations of artisans has, in many instances, resulted in finery so prized that whole villages devote themselves to the manufacture of a single class of goods.

BASKETRY AND WOVEN CRAFTS

Weaving straw, palm fronds, and reeds is among the oldest of Mexican handicraft traditions. Five-thousand-year-old mat- and basketweaving methods and designs survive to the present day. All over Mexico, people weave *petates* (palm-frond mats) that vacationers use to stretch out on the beach and that locals use for everything, from keeping tortillas warm to shielding babies from the sun. Along the coast, you might see a woman or child waiting for a bus or even walking down the street weaving white palm leaf strands into a coiled basket. Later, you may see a similar basket, embellished with a bright animal—parrot, burro, or even Snoopy—for sale in the market.

Like the origami paper-folders of Japan, folks who live around Lake Pátzcuaro have taken basketweaving to its ultimate form by crafting virtually everything—from toy turtles and Christmas bells to butterfly mobiles and serving spoons—from the reeds they gather along the lakeshore.

Hatmaking has likewise attained high refinement in Mexico. Workers in Sahuayo, Michoacán, near the southeast shore of Lake Chapala, make especially fine sombreros. Due east across Mexico, in Becal, Campeche, workers fashion Panama hats, *jipis* (pronounced HEE-pees), so fine, soft, and flexible you can stuff one into your pants pocket without damage.

Although Huichol men (from the Puerto Vallarta region states of Nayarit and Jalisco) do not actually manufacture their headwear, they do decorate them. They take ordinary sombreros and embellish them into Mexico's most flamboyant hats, flowing with bright ribbons, feathers, and fringes of colorful wool balls.

CLOTHING AND EMBROIDERY

Although *traje* (ancestral tribal dress) has nearly vanished in Mexico's large cities, significant numbers of Mexican women make and wear *traje.* Such traditional styles are still common in remote districts of the Puerto Vallarta region and in the states of Michoacán, Guerrero, Oaxaca, Chiapas, and Yucatán. Most favored is the *huipil,* a long, square-shouldered, short- to-mid-sleeved full dress, often hand-embroidered with animal and floral designs. The most treasured are *huipiles* from Oaxaca, especially from San Pedro de Amusgos (Amusgo tribe; white cotton, embroidered with abstract colored animal and floral motifs), San Andrés Chicahuatxtla (Trique tribe; white cotton,

FIESTAS

The following calendar lists national and notable Puerto Vallarta region holidays and festivals. If you happen to be where one of these is going on, get out of your car or bus and join in!

Jan. 1: **¡Feliz Año Nuevo!** Happy New Year! (national holiday)

Jan. 1–5: **Inauguration** of the Cora governor in Jesús María, Nayarit (Cora indigenous dances and ceremonies)

Jan. 6: **Día de los Reyes** (Day of the Kings; traditional gift exchange)

Jan. 12: **Día de Nuestra Señora de Guadalupe** in El Tuito, Jalisco, an hour's drive south of Puerto Vallarta (Festival of the Virgin of Guadalupe: parade, music, evening mass, and carnival)

Jan. 17: **Día de San Antonio Abad** (decorating and blessing animals)

Jan. 20–Feb. 2: **Fiesta of the Virgin of Candlemas,** in San Juan de los Lagos, Jalisco (Millions, from all over Mexico, honor the Virgin with parades, dances depicting Christians vs. Moors, rodeos, cockfights, fireworks, and much more.)

Feb. 1–3: **Festival of the Sea** in San Blas, Nayarit (dancing, horse races, and competitions)

Feb. 2: **Día de Candelaria** (plants, seeds, and candles blessed; procession, and bullfights)

Feb. 5: **Constitution Day** (national holiday commemorating the constitutions of 1857 and 1917)

Feb. 24: **Flag Day** (national holiday)

February: The week before Ash Wednesday, usually in late February, many towns stage **Carnaval**—Mardi Gras—extravaganzas.

March 11–19: Week before the **Day of St. Joseph,** in Talpa, Jalisco (food, edible crafts made of colored *chicle* (chewing gum), dancing, bands, and mariachi serenades to the Virgin)

March 18–April 4: **Ceramics and handicrafts fair,** in Tonalá (Guadalajara), Jalisco

March 19: **Día de San José** (Day of St. Joseph)

March 21: **Birthday of Benito Juárez,** the revered "Lincoln of Mexico" (national holiday)

April 1–19: **Fiesta de Ramos,** in Sayula, Jalisco (on Hwy. 54 south of Guadalajara; local area crafts fair, food, dancing, mariachis)

April 18–30: Big **country fair,** in Tepatitlán, Jalisco (on Highway 80 east of Guadalajara; many livestock and agricultural displays and competitions; regional food, rodeos, and traditional dances)

April: **Semana Santa** (pre-Easter Holy Week, culminating in Domingo Gloria, Easter Sunday national holiday)

May 1: **Labor Day** (national holiday)

May (first and third Wednesday): **Fiesta of the Virgin of Ocotlán,** in Ocotlán, Jalisco (on Lake Chapala, religious processions, dancing, fireworks, regional food)

May 3: **Día de la Santa Cruz** (Day of the Holy Cross, especially in Santa Cruz de Miramar, Nay., and Mascota, Jal.)

May 3–15: **Fiesta of St. Isador the Farmer,** in Tepic, Nayarit (blessing of seeds, animals, and water; agricultural displays, competitions, and dancing)

May 5: **Cinco de Mayo** (defeat of the French at Puebla in 1862; national holiday)

May 10: **Mothers' Day** (national holiday)

May 10–12: **Fiesta of the Coronation of the Virgin of the Rosary,** in Talpa, Jalisco (processions, fireworks, regional food, crafts, and dances)

May 10–24: **Book fair** in Guadalajara (readings, concerts, and international book exposition)

June 24: **Día de San Juan Bautista** (Day of St. John the Baptist, fairs and religious festivals, playful dunking of people in water)

June 15–July 2: **National Ceramics Fair** in the Tlaquepaque district, Guadalajara (huge crafts fair; exhibits, competitions, and market of crafts from all over the country)

June 28–29: **Regatta** in Mexcaltitán, Nayarit (friendly rivalry between boats carrying images of St. Peter and St. Paul to celebrate opening of the shrimp season)

June 29: **Día de San Pablo y San Pedro** (Day of St. Peter and St. Paul)

Sept. 14: **Charro Day** (Cowboy Day, all over Mexico; rodeos, or *charreadas*)

Sept. 16: **Independence Day** (national holiday; mayors everywhere reenact Father Hidalgo's 1810 Grito de Dolores from city hall balconies on the night of September 15)

Oct. 4: **Día de San Francisco** (Day of St. Francis)

Oct. 12: **Día de la Raza** (Columbus Day, national holiday that commemorates the union of the races)

Oct. 12: **Fiesta of the Virgin of Zapopan,** in Guadalajara (procession carries the Virgin home to Guadalajara cathedral; regional food, crafts fair, mariachis, and dancing)

October (last Sunday): **Día de Cristo Rey** in Ixtlán del Río, Nayarit (Day of Christ the King, with "Quetzal y Azteca" and "La Pluma" *indígena* dances, horse races, processions, and food)

Nov. 1: **Día de Todos Santos** (All Souls' Day, in honor of the souls of children. The departed descend from heaven to eat sugar skeletons, skulls, and treats on family altars.)

Nov. 2: **Día de los Muertos** (Day of the Dead; in honor of ancestors. Families visit cemeteries and decorate graves with flowers and favorite food of the deceased.)

Nov. 20: **Revolution Day** (anniversary of the revolution of 1910–17; national holiday)

Dec. 1: **Inauguration Day** (National government changes hands every six years: 1994, 2000, 2006, etc.)

Dec. 8: **Día de la Purísima Concepción** (Day of the Immaculate Conception)

Dec. 12: **Día de Nuestra Señora de Guadalupe** (Festival of the Virgin of Guadalupe, patroness of Mexico; processions, music, and dancing nationwide, especially celebrated around the church in downtown Puerto Vallarta)

Dec. 16–24: **Christmas Week** (week of *posadas* and piñatas; midnight mass on Christmas Eve)

Dec. 25: **Christmas Day** (*¡Feliz Navidad!;* Christmas trees and gift exchange; national holiday)

Dec. 31: **New Year's Eve**

Children are the main actors in the Virgin of Guadalupe festival, held in December.

richly embroidered red stripes, interwoven with greens, blues, and yellows, and hung with colored ribbons), and Yalalag (Zapotec tribe; white cotton, with bright flowers embroidered along two or four vertical seams and distinctive colored tassels hanging down the back). Beyond Oaxaca, Maya *huipiles* are also highly desired. They are usually made of white cotton and embellished with brilliant machine-embroidered flowers around the neck and shoulders, front and back.

Shoppers sometimes can buy other, less-common types of *traje* accessories, such as a **quechquémitl** (shoulder cape), often made of wool and worn as an overgarment in winter. The **enredo** (literally, "tangled") wraparound skirt, by contrast, enfolds the waist and legs, like a Hawaiian sarong. Mixtec women in Oaxaca's warm south coastal region around Pinotepa Nacional (west of Puerto Escondido) commonly wear the *enredo,* known locally as the **pozahuanco** (poh-sah-oo-AHN-koh), below the waist, and when at home, go bare-breasted. When wearing her *pozahuanco* in public, a Mixtec woman usually ties a **mandil,** a wide calico apron, around her front side. Women weave the best *pozahuancos* at home, using cotton thread, dyed a light purple with secretions of tidepool-harvested snails, *Purpura patula pansa,* and silk, dyed deep red with cochineal, extracted from the dried bodies of a locally cultivated beetle, *Dactylopius coccus.*

Colonial Spanish styles have blended with native *traje* to produce a wider class of dress, known generally as **ropa típica.** Fetching embroidered blouses *(blusas),* shawls *(rebozos),* and dresses *(vestidos)* fill boutique racks and market stalls throughout the Mexican Pacific. Among the most handsome is the so-called **Oaxaca wedding dress,** in white cotton with a crochet-trimmed riot of diminutive flowers, hand-stitched about the neck and yoke. Some of the finest examples are made in Antonino Castillo Velasco village, in the Valley of Oaxaca.

In contrast to women, only a very small population of Mexican men—members of remote groups, such as Huichol, Cora, Tepehuan, and Tarahumara in the northwest, and Maya and Lacandon in the southeast—wear *traje.* Nevertheless, shops offer some fine men's *ropa típica,* such as serapes, decorated wool blankets with a hole or slit for the head, worn during northern or highland winters, or *guayaberas,* hip-length, pleated tropical dress shirts.

Fine embroidery *(bordado)* embellishes much traditional Mexican clothing, tablecloths *(manteles),* and napkins *(servilletas).* As everywhere, women define the art of embroidery. Although some still work by hand at home, cheaper machine-made factory lace needlework is more commonly available in shops.

Leather

The Puerto Vallarta region abounds in for-sale leather goods that, if not manufactured locally, are shipped from the renowned leather centers. These include Guadalajara, Mazatlán, and Oaxaca (sandals and huaraches), and León and Guanajuato (shoes, boots, and saddles). For unique and custom-designed articles you'll probably have to confine your shopping to the pricier stores; for more usual though still attractive leather items such as purses, wallets, belts, coats, and boots, veteran shoppers find bargains at the Municipal Crafts market in Puerto Vallarta and Guadalajara's Libertad Market, where an acre of stalls offers the broadest selection at the most reasonable prices (after bargaining) in Mexico.

FURNITURE

Although furniture is usually too bulky to carry back home with your airline luggage, low Mexican prices make it possible for you to ship your purchases home and enjoy beautiful, unusual pieces for half the price, including transport, you would pay—even if you could find them—outside Mexico.

A number of classes of furniture (*muebles,* moo-AY-blays) are crafted in villages near the sources of raw materials: notably, wood, rattan, bamboo, or wrought iron.

Sometimes it seems as if every house in Mexico is furnished with **colonial-style furniture,** the basic design for much of it dating at least to the middle ages. Although many variations exist, most colonial-style furniture is heavily built. Table and chair legs are massive, usually lathe-turned; chair backs are customarily arrow-straight and often vertical. Although usually brown-varnished, colonial-style tables, chairs, and chests sometimes shine with inlaid wood or tile, or animal and flower designs. Family shops turn out good furniture, usually in the country highlands, where suitable wood is available. Products from shops in and around Guadalajara, Lake Pátzcuaro (especially Tzintzuntzán), and Taxco and Olinalá, Guerrero, are among the most renowned.

Equipal, a very distinctive and widespread class of Mexican furniture, is made of leather, usually brownish pigskin or cowhide, stretched over wood frames. Factories center mostly in Guadalajara and nearby villages.

It is interesting that **lacquered furniture,** in both process and design, has much in common with lacquerware produced half a world away in China. The origin of Mexican lacquerware tradition presents an intriguing mystery. What is certain, however, is that it predated the Conquest and was originally practiced only in the Pacific states of Guerrero and Michoacán. Persistent legends of pre-Columbian coastal contact with Chinese traders give weight to the speculation, shared by a number of experts, that the Chinese may have taught the lacquerware art to the Mexicans many centuries before the Conquest.

Today, artisan families in and around Pátzcuaro, Michoacán, and Olinalá, Guerrero, carry on the tradition. The process, which at its finest resembles cloisonné manufacture, involves carving and painting intricate floral and animal designs, followed by repeated layerings of lacquer, clay, and sometimes gold and silver to produce satiny, jewel-like surfaces.

A sprinkling of villages produce furniture made of plant fiber, such as reeds, raffia, and bamboo. In some cases, entire communities, such as Ihuatzio (near Pátzcuaro), and Villa Victoria (west of Toluca) have long harvested the bounty of local lakes and marshes as the basis for their products.

Wrought iron, produced and worked according to Spanish tradition, is used to produce tables, chairs, and benches. Ruggedly fashioned in a riot of baroque scrollwork, they often decorate garden and patio settings. Several colonial cities, notably San Miguel de Allende, Toluca, and Guanajuato, are wrought iron-manufacturing centers.

GLASS AND STONEWORK

Glass manufacture, unknown in pre-Columbian times, was introduced by the Spanish. Today, the tradition continues in factories throughout Mexico that turn out mountains of *burbuja* (boor-BOO-hah) bubbled glass tumblers, goblets, plates, and pitchers, usually in blue or green. Finer glass is manufactured, notably, in Guadalajara; in suburban Tlaquepaque village, you can watch artisans blow glass into a number of shapes—often paper-thin balls—in red, green, and blue.

Mexican artisans work stone, usually near sources of supply. Puebla, Mexico's major onyx *(onix)* source, is the manufacturing center for the galaxy of mostly rough-hewn, cream-colored items, from animal charms and chess pieces to beads and desk sets, which crowd curio shop shelves all over the country. *Cantera,* a pinkish stone, quarried near Pátzcuaro, is used similarly.

For a keepsake from a truly ancient Mexican tradition, don't forget the hollowed-out stone *metate* (may-TAH-tay), corn-grinding basin, or the three-legged *molcajete* (mohl-kah-HAY-tay), mortar for grinding chiles.

HUICHOL ART

Huichol art evolved from the charms that Huichol shamans (see special topic Huichol) crafted to empower them during their hazardous pilgrimages to their peyote-rich sacred land of Wirikuta. Although the Huichol's original commercial outlets in Tepic still market their goods, many shops, especially in Puerto Vallarta (and even commercial Christmas catalogs in the U.S.) now offer Huichol goods. To the original items—mostly devotional arrows, yarn *cicuri* (God's eyes), and decorated gourds for collecting peyote—have been added colorful *cuadras* (yarn paintings) and bead masks.

Cuadras, made of synthetic yarns pressed into beeswax on a plywood backing, traditionally depict plant and animal spirits, the main actors of the Huichol cosmos. Bead masks likewise blend the major elements of the Huichol worldview into an eerie human likeness, usually of Grandmother Earth (Tatei Nakawe).

Although inferior made-for-tourist Huichol curios are the most common, fine examples can be found at the Huichol Cultural Center in Santiago Ixcuintla and in better shops. (Look under "Shopping" in the Tepic and Puerto Vallarta destination sections.)

JEWELRY

Gold and silver were once the basis for Mexico's wealth. Her Spanish conquerors plundered a mountain of gold—religious offerings, necklaces, pendants, rings, bracelets—masterfully crafted by a legion of native metalsmiths and jewelers. Unfortunately, much of that indigenous tradition was lost because the Spanish denied access to precious metals to the Mexicans for generations while they introduced Spanish methods. Nevertheless, a small goldworking tradition survived the dislocations of the 1810–21 War of Independence and the 1910–17 revolution. Silvercrafting, moribund during the 1800s, was revived in Taxco, Guerrero, principally through the efforts of architect-artist William Spratling and the local community.

Today, spurred by the tourist boom, jewelry-making thrives in Mexico. Taxco, where dozens of enterprises—guilds, families, cooperatives—produce sparkling silver and gold adornments, is the acknowledged center. Many Puerto Vallarta regional shops sell fine Taxco products—shimmering butterflies, birds, jaguars, serpents, turtles, fish—reflecting pre-Columbian tradition. Taxco-made pieces, mostly in silver, vary from humble but good-looking trinkets to candelabras and place settings for a dozen, sometimes embellished with turquoise, garnet, coral, lapis, jade, and, in exceptional cases, emeralds, rubies, and diamonds.

WOODCARVING AND MUSICAL INSTRUMENTS

Masks
Spanish and Native Mexican traditions have blended to produce a multitude of masks—some strange, some lovely, some scary, some endearing, all interesting. The tradition flourishes in the strongly indigenous southern Pacific states of Michoacán, Guerrero, Oaxaca, and Chiapas, where campesinos gear up all year for the village festivals—especially Semana Santa (Easter week), early December (Virgin of Guadalupe), and the festival of the local patron, whether it be San José, San Pedro, San Pablo, Santa María, Santa Barbara, or one of a host of others. Every local fair has its favored dances, such as the Dance of the Conquest, the Christians and Moors, the Old Men, or the Tiger, in which masked villagers act out age-old allegories of fidelity, sacrifice, faith, struggle, sin, and redemption.

Although masks are made of many materials—from stone and ebony to coconut husks and paper—wood, where available, is the medium of choice. For the entire year, carvers cut, carve, sand, and paint to ensure that each participant will be properly disguised for the festival.

The popularity of masks has led to an entire made-for-tourist mask industry of mass-produced duplicates, many cleverly antiqued. Examine the goods carefully; if the price is high, don't buy unless you're convinced it's a real antique.

Alebrijes
Tourist demand has made zany wooden animals *(alebrijes)* (ah-lay-BREE-hays) a Oaxaca growth industry. Virtually every family in the Valley of Oaxaca villages of Arrazola and San Martin Tilcajete runs a factory studio. There, piles of soft *copal* wood, which men carve and women finish and intricately paint, become whimsical giraffes, dogs, cats, iguanas, gargoyles, dragons, and most of the possible permutations in between. The farther from the source you get, the higher the *alebrije* price becomes; what costs $5 in Arrazola will probably run about $10 in Puerto Vallarta and $30 in the U.S. or Canada.

Also commonly available wooden items are the charming colorfully painted fish carved mainly in the Pacific coastal state of Guerrero, and the burnished, dark hardwood animal and fish sculptures of desert ironwood from the state of Sonora.

Musical Instruments
Virtually all of Mexico's guitars are made in Paracho, Michoacán (southeast of Lake Chapala, 50 miles north of Uruapan). There, scores of cottage factories turn out guitars, violins, mandolins,

viruelas, ukuleles, and a dozen more variations every day. They vary widely in quality, so look carefully before you buy. Make sure that the wood is well cured and dry; damp, unripe wood instruments are more susceptible to warping and cracking.

METALWORK

Bright copper, brass, and tinware; sturdy iron-work; and razor-sharp knives and machetes are made in a number of regional centers. **Copper-ware,** from jugs, cups, and plates to candle-sticks—and even the town lampposts and band-stand—all come from Santa Clara del Cobre, a few miles south of Pátzcuaro, Michoacán.

Although not the source of brass itself, **Tonalá,** in the Guadalajara eastern suburb, is the place where brass is most abundant and beautiful, appearing as menageries of brilliant, fetching birds and animals, sometimes embellished with shiny nickel highlights.

A host of Oaxaca family factories turn out fine knives and machetes, scrolled cast-iron grill-work, and a swarm of bright tinware mirror frames, masks, and glittering Christmas deco-rations.

Be sure not to miss the tiny *milagros,* one of Mexico's most charming forms of metalwork. Usually of brass, they are of homely shapes—a horse, dog, or baby, or an arm, head, or foot—which, accompanied by a prayer, the faithful pin to the garment of their favorite saint whom they hope will intercede to cure an ailment or ful-fill a wish.

PAPER AND PAPIER-MÂCHÉ

Papier-mâché has become a high art in Tonalá, Jalisco, where a swarm of birds, cats, frogs, gi-raffes, and other animal figurines are meticu-lously crafted by building up repeated layers of glued paper. The result—sanded, brilliantly var-nished, and polished—resemble fine sculptures rather than the humble newspaper from which they were fashioned.

Other paper goods you shouldn't overlook in-clude **piñatas** (durable, inexpensive, and as Mexican as you can get) available in every town

market; also colorful decorative cutout banners (string overhead at your home fiesta) from San Salvador Huixcolotla, Puebla; and *amate,* wild fig tree bark paintings in animal and flower motifs, from Xalitla and Ameyaltepec, Guerrero.

POTTERY AND CERAMICS

Although Mexican pottery tradition is as diverse as the country itself, some varieties stand out. Among the most prized is the so-called Talavera (or Ma-jolica), the best of which is made by a few family-run shops in Puebla. The names Talavera and Majolica derive from Talavera, the Spanish town from which the tradition migrated to Mexico; prior to that it originated on the Spanish Mediterranean island of Mayorca, from a combination of still older Arabic, Chinese, and African ceramic styles. Shapes include plates, bowls, jugs, and pitchers, hand-painted and hard-fired in intricate bright yel-low, orange, blue, and green floral designs. So few shops make true Talavera these days that other, cheaper, look-alike grades, made around Gua-najuato, are more common, selling for one-half to one-third the price of genuine article.

More practical and nearly as prized is hand-painted **stoneware** from Tlaquepaque and Tonalá in Guadalajara's eastern suburbs. Al-though made in many shapes and sizes, such stoneware is often sold as complete dinner place settings. Decorations are usually in abstract flo-ral and animal designs, hand-painted over a red-dish clay base.

From the same tradition come the famous *bruñido* pottery animals of Tonalá. Round, smooth, and cuddly as ceramic can be, the Tonala animals—very commonly doves and ducks, but also cats and dogs and sometimes even armadillos, frogs, and snakes—each seem to embody the essence of its species.

Some of the most charming Mexican pottery, made from a ruddy low-fired clay and crafted following pre-Columbian traditions, comes from western Mexico, especially Colima. Charming figurines in timeless human poses—flute-playing musicians, dozing grandmothers, fidgeting ba-bies, loving couples—and animals, especially Colima's famous playful dogs, decorate the shelves of a sprinkling of shops.

The southern states of Guerrero and Oaxaca

are both centers of a vibrant pottery tradition. Humble but very attractive are the unglazed brightly painted animals—cats, ducks, fish, and many others—that folks bring to Puerto Vallarta centers from their family village workshops.

Much more acclaimed are certain types of pottery from the valley surrounding the city of Oaxaca. The village of Atzompa is famous for its tan, green-glazed clay pots, dishes, and bowls. Nearby San Bártolo Coyotepec village has acquired even more renown for its **black pottery,** sold all over the world. Doña Rosa, now deceased, pioneered the crafting of big round pots without using a potter's wheel. Now made in many more shapes by Doña Rosa's descendants, the pottery's exquisite silvery black sheen is produced by the reduction (reduced air) method of firing, which removes oxygen from the clay's red (ferric) iron oxide, converting it to black ferrous oxide.

Although most latter-day Mexican potters have become aware of the health dangers of lead pigments, some for-sale pottery may still contain lead. The hazard comes from low-fired pottery in which the lead has not been firmly melted into the glaze. Acids in foods such as lemons, vinegar, and tomatoes dissolve the lead pigments, which, when ingested, eventually result in lead poisoning. In general, the hardest, shiniest pottery, which has been twice fired—such as the high-quality Tlaquepaque stoneware used for dishes—is the safest.

WOOLEN WOVEN GOODS

Mexico's finest wool weavings come from Teotitlán del Valle, in the Valley of Oaxaca, less than an hour's drive east of Oaxaca city. The tradition, carried on by Teotitlán's Zapotec-speaking families, dates back at least 2,000 years. Most families still carry on the arduous process, making everything from scratch. They gather the dyes from wild plants and the bodies of insects and sea snails. They hand-wash, card, spin, and dye the wool and even travel to remote mountain springs to gather water. The results, they say, *vale la pena,* "are worth the pain": intensely colored, tightly woven carpets, rugs, and wall-hangings that retain their brilliance for generations.

Rougher, more loosely woven, blankets, jackets, and serapes come from other parts, notably mountain regions, especially around San Cristobal Las Casas, in Chiapas, and Lake Pátzcuaro in Michoacán.

ACCOMMODATIONS

The Puerto Vallarta region has hundreds of lodgings to suit every style and pocketbook: world-class resorts, small beachside hotels, comfortable apartments and condos, homey *casas de huéspedes* (guesthouses), palmy trailer parks, and dozens of miles of pristine camping beaches. The high seasons, when reservations are generally required, run from mid-December through March, during Easter week, and during the month of August.

The dozens of accommodations described in the destination chapters of this book are positive recommendations—checked out in detail—solid options from which you can pick according to your taste and purse.

Hotel Rates

The rates listed in this book are U.S. dollar equivalents of peso prices, taxes included, as quoted by the hotel management at the time of writing. They are intended as a general guide only and probably will only approximate the asking rate when you arrive. Some readers, unfortunately, try to bargain by telling desk clerks that, for example, the rate should be $20 because they read it in this book. This is unwise, because it makes hotel clerks and managers reluctant to quote rates, for fear readers might, years later, hold their hotel responsible for such quotes.

In Puerto Vallarta, hotel rates depend strongly upon inflation and season. To cancel the effect of relatively steep Mexican inflation, rates are reported in U.S. dollars (although, when settling your hotel bill, *you will nearly always save money by insisting on paying in pesos*). To further increase accuracy, estimated low- and high-season rates are quoted whenever possible.

RESORT TOLL-FREE NUMBERS AND WEBSITES

These hotel chains have branches (** = outstanding, * = recommended) at Puerto Vallarta (PV), Nuevo Vallarta (NV), Guadalajara (GD), and other Puerto Vallarta region locations:

Great Hotels of Mexico (Playa Carecitos**, Tamarindo*)	tel. 01-800/021-7526, dialable only within Mexico	www.ghm.com
Blue Bay , (PV*, Los Angeles Locos* Punta Serena*)	tel. 800/BLUEBAY (800/258-3229)	www.bluebayresort.com
Camino Real (PV**, GD**)	tel. 800/7CAMINO (800/722-6466)	www.caminoreal.com
Club Med, (Playa Blanca*)	tel. 800/CLUBMED (800/258-2633)	www.clubmed.com
Club Maeva, (PV)	tel. 800/GOMAEVA (800/466-2382)	——
Las Alamandas (Chamela)	tel. 888/882-9616	www.las-alamandas.com
Fiesta Americana (GD*, PV**)	tel. 800/FIESTA1 (800/343-7821)	www.fiestaamericana.com.mx
Holiday Inn, (GD*, PV)	tel. 800/465-4329	www.basshotels.com
Krystal (PV**)	tel. 800/231-9860	www.krystal.com.mx
Marriott (PV)	tel. 800/228-9290	www.marriot.com
Sheraton (PV)	tel. 800/325-3535	www.sheraton.com
Sierra Hotels (NV*)	tel. 800/515-4321	——
Westin (PV)	tel. 800/228-3000	www.westin.com

Saving Money

The listed hotel prices are rack rates, the maximum tariff, exclusive of packages and promotions, that you would pay if you walked in and rented an unreserved room for one day. Savvy travelers seldom pay the maximum. Always inquire if there are any discounts or packages *(descuentos o paquetes)* (des-koo-AYN-tohs OH pah-KAY-tays). At any time other than the super-high Christmas and Easter seasons, you can often get at least one or two free days with a one-week stay. Promotional packages available during slack seasons usually include free extras such as breakfast, a car rental, a boat tour, or a sports rental. A travel agent can be of great help in shopping around for such bargains.

For stays of more than two weeks, you'll save money and add comfort with an apartment or condominium rental. Monthly rates range $500–1,500 (less than half the comparable hotel per diem rate) for comfortable one-bedroom furnished kitchenette units, often including resort amenities such as pool and sundeck, beach club, and private-view balcony.

Airlines regularly offer air/hotel packages that may save you lots of pesos. These deals require that you depart for Puerto Vallarta through certain gateway cities, which depend on the airline. Accommodations are usually (but not exclusively) in luxury resorts. If you live near one of these gateways, it may pay to contact the airlines for more information.

GUESTHOUSES AND LOCAL HOTELS

Puerto Vallarta, as many coastal resorts, began as an old town that expanded into a new *zona hotelera* (hotel strip), where big hotels rise along a golden strand of beach. In the old town, surrounded by the piquant smells, sights, and charms of old Mexico, are the family-managed *casas de huéspedes* (guesthouses) and smaller hotels, often arranged around sunny, plant-festooned inner patios.

Such lodgings vary from scruffy to spic and span, and humble to distinguished. At minimum, you can expect a plain room, a shared toilet and hot-water shower, and plenty of atmosphere for your money. Rates typically run between $10 and $20, depending upon season and amenities. Discounts for long-term stays are often available. Such family-run, small hostelries are rarely near the beach, unlike many of the medium and larger older hotels.

Medium and Larger Older-Style Hotels

These hotels make up a large fraction of the recommendations of this book. Many veteran travelers find it hard to understand why people come to Mexico and spend $200 or more a day for a hotel room when good alternatives are available for as little as $25.

Many such hostelries are the once-grand first-class hotels established long before their towering international-class neighbors mushroomed along the beach. You can generally expect a clean, large (but not deluxe) room with bath and toilet and even sometimes a private beach-view balcony. Although they often share the same velvety sand and golden sunsets as their more expensive neighbors, such hotels usually lack the costly international-standard amenities—a/c, cable TV, direct-dial phones, tennis courts, exercise gyms, and golf access—of the big resorts. Their guests, however, enjoy surprisingly good service, good food, and a native ambience more charming and personal than that of many of their five-star neighbors.

Booking these hotels is straightforward. All of them may be dialed direct (dial 011-52, then the local area code and number) and, like the big resorts, may even have U.S. and Canada toll-free information and reservation numbers.

INTERNATIONAL-CLASS RESORT HOTELS

The Puerto Vallarta region offers many beautiful, well-managed, international-class resort hotels in Puerto Vallarta, Nuevo Vallarta, and Guadalajara. A number of others dot the pristine southern coastline between Puerto Vallarta and Barra de Navidad. Most are in Puerto Vallarta, however, where they line the Bay of Banderas's crystal strand north of the old town.

The resorts' super-plush amenities, moreover, need not be overly expensive. During the right time of year you can vacation at many of the big-name spots—Sheraton, Camino Real, Westin, Fiesta Americana, Holiday Inn—for surprisingly little. While high-season tariffs ordinarily run $100–300, low-season (May–Nov., and to a lesser degree, Jan.–Feb.) packages and promotions can cut these prices significantly. Shop around for savings via your Sunday newspaper travel section, through travel agents, and by calling the hotels directly at their toll-free 800 numbers. (See the chart Resort 800 Numbers and Websites.)

APARTMENTS, BUNGALOWS, CONDOMINIUMS, AND VILLAS

For longer stays, many Puerto Vallarta visitors prefer the convenience and economy of an apartment or condominium or the luxurious comfort of a villa vacation rental. Choices vary, from spartan studios to deluxe beachfront suites and rambling homes big enough for entire extended families. Prices depend strongly upon season and amenities, ranging from about $500 per month for the cheapest, to at least 10 times that for the most luxurious.

At the low end, you can expect a clean, furnished apartment within a block or two of the beach, with kitchen and regular maid service. More luxurious condos, which rent for about $500 per week, are typically high-rise oceanview suites with hotel-style desk services and resort amenities such as pool, hot tub, sundeck, and beach-level restaurant. Villas vary from moderately upscale homes to sky's-the-limit beach-view mansions blooming with built-in designer luxuries, private pools and beaches, tennis courts, gardeners, cooks, and maids.

In contrast to Puerto Vallarta town, owners in country beach resorts such as Bucerías, Rincón de Guayabitos, and Barra de Navidad call their apartment-style accommodations **"bungalows."** This generally implies a motel-type kitchenette-suite with less service, though more spacious and more suitable for families than a hotel room. For long stays by the beach, where you want to save money by cooking your own meals, such an accommodation might be ideal.

Back in town, most of Puerto Vallarta's best-buy *apartamentos* (ah-par-ta-MAYN-tohs) and *condominios* (cohn-doh-MEE-nee-ohs) are in the colorful Olas Altas old town district. They are generally rented on the spot or reserved in advance by writing or phoning the individual owners or local managers.

More expensive Puerto Vallarta condo and villa rentals are even easier to find. They're located everywhere, from the marina on the north side to the Conchas Chinas ocean-view hillside on the southern edge of town. A number of U.S.-based agencies rent them through toll-free information and reservations numbers: Villa de Oro Vacation Rentals, 638 Scotland Dr., Santa Rosa, CA 95409, tel. 800/638-4552; Villas of Mexico, P.O. Box 3730, Chico, CA 95927, tel. 800/456-3133; and Condo and Villa World, 4230 Orchard Lake Rd., Suite 3, Orchard Lake, MI 48323, tel. 800/521-2980 from the U.S. or 800/453-8714 from Canada. (For many more condo and villa rental details, see "Apartments and Condominiums" under "Accommodations" in the Puerto Vallarta town chapter.)

Another good vacation rental source is the Sunday travel section of a major metropolitan daily, such as the *Los Angeles Times,* which routinely lists Puerto Vallarta vacation rentals. National real estate networks, such as Century 21, also rent (or can recommend someone who does) Puerto Vallarta properties.

You may also want to consider using the services of a home exchange agency, whereby you swap homes with someone in Puerto Vallarta for a contracted time period.

Closing the Deal
Prudence should guide your vacation rental decision-making. Before paying a deposit on a sight-unseen rental, ask for satisfied customer testimonials and photographs of the property you are considering. As with all rentals, don't pay anything until you have approved a written contract describing the rental and what's included (such as inclusive dates, linens, towels, dishes and utensils, maid service, view, pool,

taxes, and transportation from airport) for the specified sum. Put down as little advance payment as possible, preferably with a credit card, to secure your reservation.

CAMPING

Although few, if any, good campsites are available in the Puerto Vallarta resort city itself, camping is customary at many favored sites in the Puerto Vallarta region. Mexican middle-class families crowd certain choice strands—those with soft sand and gentle, child-friendly waves— only during the Christmas–New Year week and during Semana Santa, the week before Easter. Most other times, tenters and RV campers find beaches uncrowded.

The best spots typically have a shady palm grove for camping and a *palapa* (palm-thatched)

Choice beach campsites in Mexico are customarily crowded only twice a year; the week after Christmas and the week before Easter, known as Semana Santa.

PUERTO VALLARTA REGION TRAILER PARKS AND CAMPING

To Mazatlán and U.S.

Acaponeta

Novillero

Laguna Agua Brava

Laguna El Valle

Laguna Los Pericos

Mexcaltitán

NAYARIT

Jesus Maria

Ruiz

Santiago Ixcuintla

Playa Los Corchos

San Blas

Bahía de Matanchen

Santa Cruz

Tepic

Laguna Santa Maria

Chapalilla

JALISCO

ZACATECAS

To Zacatecas and U.S.

Río Grande de Santiago

Bahía de Jaltemba

Chacala

Las Varas

La Penita

Rincón de Guayabitos

Lo de Marco

Sayulita

San Sebastian

SAUCILLO CREEK

Punta Mita

Cruz de Huanacaxtle

Bucerias

Laguna Juanacatlan

Navidad

Río Ameca

Bahía de Banderas

Puerto Vallarta

Mascota

Ameca

GUADALAJARA

Playa Las Animas

Playa Quimixto

Cabo Corrientes

Yelapa

El Tuito

CORINCHES RESERVOIR

Los Volcanes

Ajijic

Jocotepec

Lake Chapala

Tehualmixtle

Ipala

Talpa

Cajon de Peñas Reservoir

Río María García

Tomatlán

Ayutla

Juchitlán

JALISCO

Autlán

Ciudad Guzman

PACIFIC

Playa Chalacatepec

Perula

Chamela

Nevado de Colima

Volcán de Colima

Playa Careyes

Playa Las Brisas

Tenacatita

Boca de Iguana

Barra de Navidad

Playa de Cocos

Melaque

Colima

OCEAN

Manzanillo

Bahía Manzanillo

Tecoman

Cuyutlán

To Ixtapa-Zihuatanejo

0   25 mi

0   25 km

© AVALON TRAVEL PUBLISHING, INC.

restaurant that serves drinks and fresh seafood. Heads up for falling coconuts, especially in the wind. Costs for parking and tenting are minimal—usually only the price of food at the restaurant.

Days are often perfect for swimming, strolling, and fishing, and nights are balmy—too warm for a sleeping bag, but fine for a hammock (which allows the air circulation that a tent does not.) However, good tents keep out mosquitoes and other pesties, which may be further discouraged by a good bug repellent. Tents can get hot, requiring only a sheet or very light blanket for sleeping cover.

As for camping on isolated beaches, opinions vary, from dire warnings of *bandidos* to bland assurances that all is peaceful along the coast. The truth is somewhere in between. Trouble is most likely to occur in the vicinity of towns, where a few local thugs sometimes harass isolated campers.

When scouting out an isolated place to camp, a good rule is to arrive early enough in the day to get a feel for the place. Buy a soda at the *palapa* or store and take a stroll along the beach. Say *"Buenos días"* to the people along the way; ask if the fishing is good *("¿Pesca buena?").* Above all, use your common sense and intuition. If the people seem friendly, ask if it's *seguro* (safe). If so, ask permission: *"¿Es bueno acampar acá?"* ("Is it okay to camp around here?"). You'll rarely be refused.

TRAILER PARKS

Campers who prefer company to isolation stay in trailer parks. About 20 of them dot the Puerto Vallarta region beaches from San Blas to Barra de Navidad. The most luxurious have all hookups and dozens of amenities, including restaurants, recreation rooms, and swimming pools; the humblest are simple palm-edged lots beside the beach. Virtually all of them have good swimming, fishing, and beachcombing. Prices run from a few dollars for a tent space to about $18 per night including air-conditioning power. Significant discounts are available for weekly and monthly rentals.

Although there are no official government-maintained campgrounds in the area, private RV parks and informal RV parking and tent camping spots are sprinkled throughout the Puerto Vallarta region. Private trailer parks typically charge around $15 per day or $350 per month with all hookups and are located in San Blas, Matanchén Bay, Tepic, Laguna Santa María, Guadalajara, Lake Chapala, La Peñita, Rincón de Guayabitos, Lo de Marco, Sayulita, Cruz de Huanacaxtle, Bucerías, Puerto Vallarta, Chamela Bay, Boca de Iguana, and Melaque.

Tenting and RV parking are permitted for a fee at most trailer parks. A number of other informal spots, mostly at pretty beaches with no facilities, await those travelers prepared to venture from the well-worn path. Likely spots include Novillero, Matanchén Bay, Chacala, Lo de Marco, Saucillo Creek, Laguna Juanacatlán, Corinches Reservoir (all three in the mountains near Mascota), Playa las Animas, Playa Quimixto, Yelapa, Chico's Paradise, Tehualmixtle, Ipala, Cajón de Peñas reservoir, Playa Chalacatepec, Chamela Bay, Playa Careyes, Playa Las Brisas, Playa Tenacatita, Playa Boca de Iguana, Barra de Navidad-Melaque, and Playa de Cocos.

FOOD

Some travel to Puerto Vallarta for the food. True Mexican-style food is old-fashioned, home-style fare requiring many hours of loving preparation. Such food is short on meat and long on corn, beans, rice, tomatoes, onions, eggs, and cheese.

Mexican food is the unique product of thousands of years of native tradition. It is based on corn—*teocentli*, the Aztec "holy food"—called *maíz* (mah-EES) by present-day Mexicans. In the past, a Mexican woman spent much of her time grinding and preparing corn: soaking the grain in lime water, which swells the kernels and removes the tough seed-coat, and grinding the bloated seeds into meal on a stone *metate*. Finally, she patted the meal into tortillas and cooked them on a hot, baked mud griddle.

Sages (men, no doubt) wistfully imagined that gentle pat-pat-pat of women all over Mexico to be the heartbeat of Mexico, which they feared would cease when women stopped making tortillas.

Fewer women these days make tortillas by hand. The gentle pat-pat-pat has been replaced by the whir and rattle of the automatic tortilla-making machine in myriad *tortillerías,* where women and girls line up for their family's daily kilo-stack of tortillas.

A TROVE OF FRUITS AND NUTS

Besides carrying the usual temperate fruits, *jugerías* and especially markets are seasonal sources of a number of exotic (followed by an *) varieties:

avocado (*aguacate,* pronouced "ah-wah-KAH-tay"): Aztec aphrodisiac

banana (*platano*): many kinds—big and small, red and yellow

chirimoya* (*chirimoya*): green scales, white pulp; sometimes called an anona

coconut (*coco*): coconut "milk" is called *agua coco*

grapes (*uvas*): Aug.–Nov. season

guanabana* (*guanabana*): looks, but doesn't taste, like a green mango

guava (*guava*): delicious juice, widely available canned

lemon (*limón,* pronounced "lee-MOHN"): uncommon and expensive; use lime instead

lime (*lima* pronounced "LEE-mah"): douse salads with it

mamey* (*mamey,* pronounced "mah-MAY"): yellow, juicy fruit; excellent for jellies and preserves

mango (*mango*): king of fruit, in a hundred varieties June–Nov.

orange (*naranja,* pronounced "nah-RAHN-ha"): greenish skin but sweet and juicy

papaya (*papaya*): said to aid digestion and healing

peach (*durazno,* pronounced "doo-RAHS-noh"): delicious and widely available as canned juice

peanut (*cacahuate,* pronounced "kah-kah-WAH-tay"): home roasted and cheap

pear (*pera*): fall season

pecan (*nuez*): for a treat, try freshly ground pecan butter

piña anona* (*piña anona*): looks like a thin ear of corn without the husk; tastes like pineapple

pineapple (*piña*): huge, luscious, and cheap

strawberry (*fresa,* pronounced "FRAY-sah"): local favorite

tangerine (*mandarina*): common around Christmas

watermelon (*sandía,* pronounced "sahn-DEE-ah"): perfect on a hot day

zapote* (*zapote,* pronounced "sah-POH-tay"): yellow, fleshy fruit; said to induce sleep

zapote colorado* (*zapote colorado*): brown skin, red, puckery fruit, like persimmon; incorrectly called *mamey*

CATCH OF THE DAY

Ceviche (say-VEE-chay): A chopped raw fish appetizer as popular on Puerto Vallarta beaches as sushi is on Tokyo sidestreets. Although it can contain anything from conch to octopus, the best ceviche consists of diced young shark *(tiburón)* or mackerel *(sierra)* fillet and plenty of fresh tomatoes, onions, garlic, and chiles, all doused with lime juice.

Filete de pescado (fish fillet): sautéed *al mojo* (ahl-MOH-hoh)—with butter and garlic.

Pescado frito (pays-KAH-doh FREE-toh): Fish, pan-fried whole; if you don't specify that it be cooked lightly *(a medio)*, the fish may arrive well done, like a big, crunchy French fry.

Pescado veracruzana: A favorite everywhere. Best with red snapper *(huachinango)*, smothered in a savory tomato, onion, chile, and garlic sauce. *Pargo* (snapper), *mero* (grouper), and *cabrilla* (sea bass) are also popularly used in this and other specialties.

Shellfish abound: *ostiones* (oysters) and *almejas* (clams) by the dozen; *langosta* (lobster) and *langostina* (crayfish) *asado* (broiled), *al vapor* (steamed), or fried. Pots of fresh-boiled *camarones* (shrimp) are sold on the street by the kilo; cafes will make them into *cóctel,* or prepare them *en gabardinas* (breaded) at your request.

Tortillas are to the Mexicans as rice is to the Chinese and bread to the French. Mexican food is invariably some mixture of sauce, meat, beans, cheese, and vegetables wrapped in a tortilla, which becomes the culinary be-all: the food, the dish, and the utensil wrapped into one.

If a Mexican man has nothing to wrap in his lunchtime tortilla, he will content himself by rolling a thin filling of salsa (chile sauce) in it.

Hot or Not?

Much food served in Mexico is not "Mexican." Eating habits, as most other customs, depend upon social class. Upwardly mobile Mexicans typically shun the corn-based *indígena* fare in favor of the European-style food of the Spanish colonial elite: chops, steaks, cutlets, fish, clams, omelettes, soups, pasta, rice, and potatoes.

Such fare is often as bland as Des Moines on a summer Sunday afternoon. *No picante*—not spicy—is how the Mexicans describe bland food. *Caliente,* the Spanish adjective for "hot" (as in hot water), does not, in contrast to English usage, imply spicy, or *picante.*

Strictly vegetarian cooking is rare in Mexico, as are macrobiotic restaurants, health-food stores, and organic produce. Meat is such a delicacy for most Mexicans that they can't understand why people would give it up voluntarily. If vegetable-lovers can manage with corn,

MEXICAN FOOD

Chiles rellenos: Fresh roasted green chiles, stuffed usually with cheese but sometimes with fish or meat, coated with batter, and fried. They provide a piquant, tantalizing contrast to tortillas.

Enchiladas and **tostadas:** variations on the filled-tortilla theme. Enchiladas are stuffed with meat, cheese, olives, or beans and covered with sauce and baked, while tostadas consist of toppings served on crisp, open-faced tortillas.

Guacamole: This luscious avocado, onion, tomato, lime, and salsa mixture remains the delight it must have seemed to its Aztec inventors centuries ago. In Mexico, it's served sparingly as a garnish, rather than in appetizer bowls as is common in the U.S. Southwest.

Moles (MOH-lays): uniquely Mexican specialties. *Mole poblano,* a spicy-sweet mixture of chocolate, chiles, and a dozen other ingredients, is cooked to a smooth sauce, then baked with chicken (or turkey, a combination called *mole de pavo*). So *típica* it's widely regarded as the national dish.

Quesadillas: made from soft flour tortillas, rather than corn, quesadillas resemble tostadas and always contain melted cheese

Sopas: Soups consist of vegetables in a savory chicken broth and are an important part of both *comida* (afternoon) and *cena* (evening) Mexican meals. *Pozole,* a rich steaming stew of hominy, vegetables, and pork or chicken, often constitutes the prime evening offering of small side-street shops. *Sopa de taco,* an ever-popular country favorite, is a medium-spicy cheese-topped thick chile broth served with crisp corn tortillas.

Tacos or **taquitos:** tortillas served open or wrapped around any ingredient

Tamales: as Mexican as apple pie is American. This savory mixture of meat and sauce imbedded in a shell of corn dough and baked in a wrapping of corn husks is rarely known by the singular, however. They're so yummy that one tamal invariably leads to more tamales.

Tortas: the Mexican sandwich, usually hot meat with fresh tomato and avocado, stuffed between two halves of a crisp *bolillo* (boh-LEE-yoh) or Mexican bun

Tortillas y frijoles refritos: cooked brown or black beans, mashed and fried in pork fat, and rolled into tortillas with a dash of vitamin C-rich salsa to form a near-complete combination of carbohydrate, fat, and balanced protein

beans, cheese, eggs, *legumbres* (vegetables), and fruit, and not be bothered by a bit of pork fat *(manteca de cerdo),* Mexican cooking will suit you fine.

Seafood

Early chroniclers wrote that Moctezuma employed a platoon of runners to bring fresh fish 300 miles from the sea every day to his court. Around Puerto Vallarta, fresh seafood is fortunately much more available from dozens of shoreline establishments, ranging from humble beach *palapas* to luxury hotel restaurants.

Seafood is literally here for the taking. When strolling certain beaches, I have seen well-fed, middle-class local vacationers breaking and eating oysters and mussels right off the rocks. In the summer on the beach at Puerto Vallarta, fish and squid can swarm so thickly in the surf that

tourists pull them out bare handed. Villagers up and down the coast use small nets (or bare hands) to retrieve a few fish for supper, while communal teams haul in big netfuls of silvery, wriggling fry for sale right on the beach.

Despite the plenty, Puerto Vallarta seafood prices reflect high worldwide demand, even at the lowliest seaside *palapa.* The freshness and variety, however, make the typical dishes bargains at any price.

Fruits and Juices

Squeezed vegetable and fruit juices called *jugos* (HOO-gohs), are among the widely available thousand delights of Puerto Vallarta. Among the many establishments—restaurants, cafes, and *loncherías*—willing to supply you with your favorite *jugo,* the juice bars *(jugerías)* are the most fun. Colorful fruit piles mark *jugerías.* If you don't immediately spot your favorite fruit, ask; it might be hidden in the refrigerator.

Besides your choice of pure juice, a *jugería* will often serve *licuados*. Into the juice, they whip powdered milk, your favorite flavoring, and sugar to taste, for a creamy afternoon pick-me-up or evening dessert. One big favorite is a cool banana-chocolate *licuado*, which comes out tasting like a milk shake (minus the calories).

Alcoholic Drinks

The Aztecs sacrificed anyone caught drinking alcohol without permission. The later, more lenient, Spanish attitude toward getting *borracho* (soused) has led to a thriving Mexican renaissance of native alcoholic beverages: tequila, mescal, Kahlúa, pulque, and *aguardiente*. Tequila and mescal, distilled from the fermented juice of the maguey, originated in Oaxaca, where the best are still made. Quality tequila (named after the Guadalajara-area distillery town) and mescal come 76 proof (38% alcohol) and up. A small white worm, endemic to the maguey, is customarily added to each bottle of factory mescal for authenticity.

Pulque, although also made from the sap of the maguey, is locally brewed to a small alcohol content between that of beer and wine. The brewing houses are sacrosanct preserves, circumscribed by traditions that exclude women and outsiders. The brew, said to be full of nutrients, is sold to local *pulquerías* and drunk immediately. If you are ever invited into a *pulqería*, it is an honor you cannot refuse.

Aguardiente, by contrast, is the notorious fiery Mexican "white lightning," a locally distilled, dirt-cheap ticket to oblivion for poor Mexican men.

While pulque comes from age-old Indian tradition, beer is the beverage of modern mestizo Mexico. Full-bodied and tastier than "light" U.S. counterparts, Mexican beer enjoys an enviable reputation.

Those visitors who indulge usually know their favorite among the many brands, from light to dark: Superior, Corona, Pacífico, Tecate (served with lime), Carta Blanca, Modelo, Dos Equis, Bohemia, Tres Equis, and Negro Modelo. Nochebuena, a hearty dark brew, becomes available only around Christmas.

Mexicans have yet to develop much of a taste for *vino tinto* or *vino blanco* (red or white table

wine), although some domestic wines (such as the Baja California labels Cetto and Domecq) are quite drinkable.

Bread and Pastries

Excellent locally baked bread is a delightful surprise to many first-time Puerto Vallarta visitors. Small bakeries everywhere put out trays of hot, crispy-crusted *bolillos* (rolls) and sweet *panes dulces* (pastries). The pastries range from simple cakes, muffins, cookies, and donuts to fancy fruit-filled turnovers and puffs. Half the fun occurs before the eating: perusing the goodies, tongs in hand, and picking out the most scrumptious. With your favorite dozen or two finally selected, you take your tray to the cashier, who deftly bags everything up and collects a few pesos

---

CHOCOLATL

The refreshing drink *chocolatl* enjoyed by Aztec nobility is a remote but distinct relative of the chocolate consumed today by hundreds of millions of people. It was once so precious chocolate beans were a common medium of exchange in pre-Conquest Mexico. In those days a mere dozen cacao beans could command a present value of upwards of $100 in goods or services. Counterfeiting was rife—entrepreneurs tried to create *chocolatl* from anything, including avocado seeds. Moreover, *chocolatl* was thought to be so potent an aphrodisiac and hallucinogen that its use was denied, under penalty of death, to commoners.

Although intrigued, Europeans were put off by the bitter taste of *chocolatl*. Around 1600, a whole shipload of chocolate beans was jettisoned at sea by English privateers who, having captured a Spanish galleon, mistook its cargo for goat dung.

The French soon made *chocolatl* easier to stomach by powdering it; the British added milk; and finally the Swiss, of Nestlé fame, cashed in with chocolate candy. The world hasn't been the same since.

Though *chocolatl* found its way to Europe, it never left Mexico, where hot chocolate, whipped frothy with a wooden-ringed *molinillo* (little mill), is more common now than in Aztec times. In Mexico chocolate is more than mere dessert; used to spice the tangy *moles* of southern Mexico, it's virtually a national food.

Picnics are easy at the beach, where the main course is free for the catching.

(two or three dollars) for your entire mouthwatering selection.

Restaurant Price Key
In the destination chapters, restaurants that serve dinner are described as budget, moderate, expensive, or a combination thereof, at the end of some restaurant descriptions. Budget means that the entreés cost under $7; moderate, $7–14; expensive, over $14.

GETTING THERE

BY AIR

From the U.S. and Canada
The vast majority of travelers reach Puerto Vallarta by air. Flights are frequent and reasonably priced. Competition sometimes shaves tariffs down as low as $250 or less for a Puerto Vallarta roundtrip from the departure gateways of San Francisco, Los Angeles, Denver, Dallas, or Houston.

Air travelers can save lots of money by shopping around. Don't be bashful about asking for the cheapest price. Make it clear to the airline or travel agent you're interested in a bargain. Ask the right questions: Are there special-incentive, advance-payment, night, midweek, tour package, or charter fares? Peruse the ads in the Sunday newspaper travel section for bargain-oriented travel agencies. Although some agents charge booking fees and don't like discounted tickets because their fee depends on a percentage of ticket price, many will nevertheless work hard to get you a bargain, especially if you book an entire air-hotel package with them.

Although few airlines fly directly to Puerto Vallarta from the northern U.S. and Canada, many charters do. In locales near Vancouver, Calgary, Ottawa, Toronto, Montreal, Minneapolis, Chicago, Detroit, Cleveland, and New York, consult a travel agent for charter flight options. Be aware that charter reservations, which often require fixed departure and return dates and provide minimal cancellation refunds, decrease your flexibility. If available charter choices are unsatisfactory, then you might choose to begin your vacation with a connecting flight to one of the Puerto Vallarta gateways of San Francisco, Los Angeles, San Diego, Denver, Phoenix, Dallas, or Houston.

You may be able to save money by booking an air/hotel package through one of the airlines that routinely offer them from certain Puerto Vallarta gateway cities:

Mexicana: from Los Angeles, Denver, and Chicago; tel. 800/531-9321

Alaska: from Seattle, San Francisco, Los Angeles, and Phoenix; tel. 800/468-2248

America West: from Phoenix; tel. 800/356-6611

American: from Dallas; tel. 800/321-2121

Aeroméxico: from Los Angeles and San Diego; tel. 800/245-8585

Continental: from Houston; tel. 888/898-9255

Canadian World of Vacations (charter): from Toronto, Winnepeg, Regina, Saskatoon, Calgary-Edmonton, and Vancouver; tel. 800/661-8881

Delta: from Los Angeles; tel. 800/872-7786

Trans-World Airlines: from St. Louis; tel. 800/275-6495

From Europe, Australasia, and Latin America

Few airlines fly across the Atlantic or Pacific directly to Mexico. Travelers from Australasia and Europe transfer at New York, Chicago, Dallas, San Francisco, or Los Angeles for Puerto Vallarta.

A number of Latin American flag carriers fly directly to Mexico City. From there, easy connections are available via Mexicana, Aeroméxico, or Aerocalifornia airlines to Puerto Vallarta.

Baggage, Insurance, "Bumping," and In-Flight Meals

Tropical Puerto Vallarta makes it easy to pack light. See the "Packing Checklist" at the end of this chapter. Veteran tropical travelers condense their luggage to carry-ons only. Airlines routinely allow a carry-on (not exceeding 45 inches in combined length, width, and girth), small book bag, and purse. Thus relieved of heavy burdens, your trip will become much simpler. You'll avoid possible luggage loss and long baggage-check-in lines by being able to check in directly at the boarding gate.

Even if you can't avoid checking luggage, loss of it needn't ruin your vacation. Always carry your irreplaceable items in the cabin with you. These should include all money, credit cards, traveler's checks, keys, tickets, cameras, passport, prescription drugs, and eyeglasses.

At the X-ray security check, insist that your film and cameras be hand-inspected. Regardless of what attendants claim, repeated X-ray scanning will fog any undeveloped film, especially the sensitive ASA 400 and 1,000 high-speed varieties.

Travelers packing lots of expensive baggage, or who (because of illness, for example) may have to cancel a nonrefundable flight or tour, might consider buying **travel insurance.** Travel agents routinely sell packages that include baggage, trip cancellation, and default insurance. Baggage insurance covers you beyond the conventional $1,250 domestic, $400 international baggage liability limits, but check with your carrier. **Trip cancellation insurance** pays if you must cancel your prepaid trip, while **default insurance** protects you if your carrier or tour agent does not perform as agreed. Travel insurance, however, can be expensive. Traveler's Insurance Company, for example, offers $1,000 of baggage insurance per person for two weeks for about $50. Weigh your options and the cost against benefits carefully before putting your money down.

It's wise to reconfirm both departure and return flight reservations, especially during the busy Christmas and Easter seasons. This is a useful strategy, as is prompt arrival at check-in, against getting "bumped" (losing your seat) by the tendency of airlines to overbook the rush of high-season vacationers. For further protection, always get your seat assignment and boarding pass included with your ticket.

Airlines generally try hard to accommodate travelers with dietary or other special needs. When booking your flight, inform your travel agent or carrier of the necessity of a low-sodium, low-cholesterol, vegetarian, or lactose-reduced meal, or other requirements. Seniors, handicapped persons, and parents traveling with children, see "Specialty Travel" under "Other Practicalities" near the end of this chapter for more information.

BY BUS

As air travel rules in the U.S., bus travel rules in Mexico. Hundreds of sleek, first-class buses lines with names such as Elite, Turistar, Futura, Transportes Pacífico, and White Star (Estrella Blanca) depart the border daily, headed for the Puerto Vallarta region.

Since North American bus lines ordinarily terminate just north of the Mexican border, you must usually disembark, collect your things, and, after having filled out the necessary but very simple paperwork at the immigration booth, proceed on foot across the border to Mexico, where you can bargain with one of the local taxis to drive you the few miles to the *camionera central* (central bus station).

First-class bus service in Mexico is much cheaper and better than in the United States. Tickets for comparable trips in Mexico cost a fraction (as little as $50 for a thousand-mile trip, compared to $100 in the U.S.).

In Mexico, as on United States buses, you often have to take it like you find it. *Asientos reservados* (seat reservations), *boletos* (tickets), and information must generally be obtained in person at the bus station, and credit cards and traveler's checks are not often accepted. Neither are reserved bus tickets typically refundable, so don't miss the bus. On the other hand, plenty of buses roll south almost continuously.

Bus Routes to Puerto Vallarta

From California and the West, cross the border to Tijuana, Mexicali, or Nogales, where you can ride one of at least three bus lines along the Pacific coast route (National Hwy. 15) south to Puerto Vallarta by Estrella Blanca (via its subsidiaries, Elite, Transportes Norte de Sonora, or Turistar) or independent Transportes del Pacífico.

A few Estrella Blanca and Transportes del Pacifico departures go all the way from the border to Puerto Vallarta. Otherwise, you will have to change buses at Mazatlán or Tepic, depending on your connection. Allow a full day and a bit more (about 30 hours), depending upon connections, for the trip. Carry liquids and food (which might only be minimally available en route) with you.

From the Midwest, cross the border from El Paso to Juárez and head for Mazatlán by way of Chihuahua and Durango by either Estrella Blanca (via subsidiaries Turistar, Transportes Chihuahuenses, or super first-class Turistar) or independent Omnibus de Mexico. Both Transportes Chihuahuenses and Turistar usually offer a few daily departures direct to Mazatlán. Oth-

erwise, transfer at Durango to a Mazatlán-bound bus and continue south to Puerto Vallarta as described above. Similarly, from the U.S. Southeast and East, cross the border at Laredo to Nuevo Laredo and ride Transportes del Norte or Turistar direct to Mazatlán, or to Durango. At Durango, transfer to a Mazatlán bus, where you can continue south to Puerto Vallarta, as described above.

BY CAR OR RV

If you're adventurous, like going to out-of-the way places, but still want to have all the comforts of home, you may enjoy driving your car or RV to Puerto Vallarta. On the other hand, consideration of cost, risk, wear on both you and your vehicle, and the congestion hassles in towns may change your mind.

Mexican Car Insurance

Mexico does not recognize foreign insurance. When you drive into Mexico, Mexican auto insurance is at least as important as your passport. At the busier crossings, you can get it at insurance "drive-ins" just south of the border. The many Mexican auto insurance companies (AAA and National Automobile Club agents recommend La Provincial and Tepeyac insurance, respectively) are government-regulated; their numbers keep prices and services competitive.

Sanborn's Mexico insurance, one of the best known agencies, certainly seems to be trying hardest. It offers a number of books and services, including a guide to RV campgrounds, road map, *Travel With Health* book, "smile-by-mile" *Travelog* guide to "every highway in Mexico," hotel discounts, and more. All of the above is available to members of Sanborn's "Sombrero" Club. You can buy insurance, sign up for membership, or order books through its toll-free number, 800/222-0158. For other queries, call 956/682-7433 or write Sanborn's Mexico, P.O. Box 310, McAllen, TX 78502.

Mexican car insurance runs from a bare-bones rate of about $5 a day to a more typical $10 a day for more complete coverage ($50,000/$40,000/$80,000 public liability/property damage/medical payments) on a vehicle worth $10,000–15,000. On the same scale, insurance

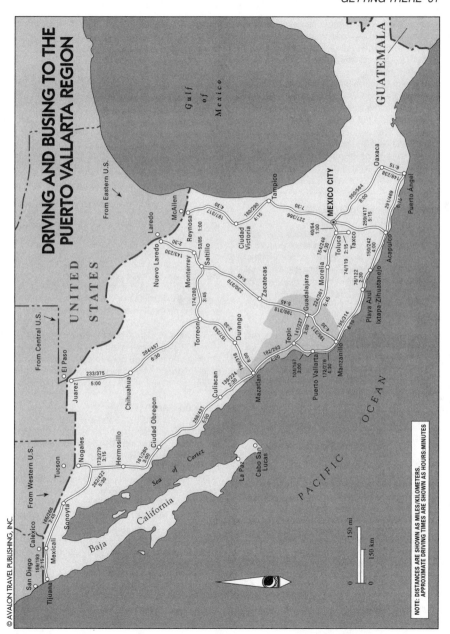

DRIVING AND BUSING TO THE
PUERTO VALLARTA REGION

© AVALON TRAVEL PUBLISHING, INC.

NOTE: DISTANCES ARE SHOWN AS MILES/KILOMETERS.
APPROXIMATE DRIVING TIMES ARE SHOWN AS HOURS:MINUTES.

for a $50,000 RV and equipment runs about $30 a day. These daily rates decrease sharply for six-month or one-year policies, which run from about $200 for the minimum to $400–1,600 for complete coverage.

If you get broken glass, personal effects, and legal expenses coverage with these rates, you're lucky. Mexican policies don't usually cover them.

You should get something for your money, however. The deductibles should be no more than $300–500, the public liability/medical payments should be about double the ($25,000 /$25,000/$50,000) legal minimum, and you should be able to get your car fixed in the U.S.

ROAD SAFETY

Hundreds of thousands of visitors enjoy safe Mexican auto vacations every year. Their success is due in large part to their frame of mind: drive defensively, anticipate and adjust to danger before it happens, and watch everything—side roads, shoulders, the car in front, and cars far down the road. The following tips will help ensure a safe and enjoyable trip:

Don't drive at night. Range animals, unmarked sand piles, pedestrians, one-lane bridges, cars without lights, and drunk drivers are doubly hazardous at night.

Although **speed limits** are rarely enforced, *don't break them.* Mexican roads are often narrow and shoulderless. Poor markings and macho drivers who pass on curves are best faced at a speed of 40 mph (64 kph) rather than 75 (120).

Don't drive on sand. Even with four-wheel-drive, you'll eventually get stuck if you drive often or casually on beaches. When the tide comes in, who'll pull your car out?

Slow down at the *topes* (speed bumps) at the edges of towns and for *vados* (dips), which can be dangerously bumpy and full of water.

Extending the **courtesy of the road** goes hand-in-hand with safe driving. Both courtesy and machismo are more infectious in Mexico; on the highway, it's much safer to spread the former than the latter.

---

and receive payment in U.S. dollars for losses. If not, shop around.

A Sinaloa Note of Caution

Although *bandidos* no longer menace Mexican roads (but loose burros, horses, and cattle still do), be cautious in the infamous marijuana- and opium-growing region of Sinaloa state north of Mazatlán. Best not stray from Hwy. 15 between Culiacán and Mazatlán or from Hwy. 40 between Mazatlán and Durango. Curious tourists have been assaulted in the hinterlands adjacent to these roads.

The Green Angels

The Green Angels have answered many motoring tourists' prayers in Mexico. Bilingual teams of two, trained in auto repair and first aid, help distressed tourists along main highways. They patrol fixed stretches of road twice daily by truck. To make sure they stop to help, pull completely off the highway and raise your hood. You may want to hail a passing trucker to call them for you (toll-free tel. 01–800/903-9200 for the tourism hotline, who might alert the Green Angels for you).

If, for some reason, you have to leave your vehicle on the roadside, don't leave it unattended. Hire a local teenager or adult to watch it for you. Unattended vehicles on Mexican highways are quickly stricken by a mysterious disease, the symptoms of which are rapid loss of vital parts.

Mexican Gasoline

Pemex, short for Petróleos Mexicanos, the government oil monopoly, markets diesel fuel and two grades of gasoline: 92-octane premium and 89-octane **Magna Sin plomo** ("without lead"). Magna Sin ("MAHG-nah seen") is good gas, yielding performance similar to that of U.S.-style "regular or super-unleaded" gasoline. (My car, whose manufacturer recommended 91-octane, ran well on Magna.) It runs about 55 cents per liter (or about $2 per gallon.)

On main highways, Pemex makes sure that major stations (spaced typically about 30 miles apart) stock Magna.

Gas Station Thievery

Although the problem has abated considerably in recent years, boys who hang around gas stations to wash windows are notoriously light-fin-

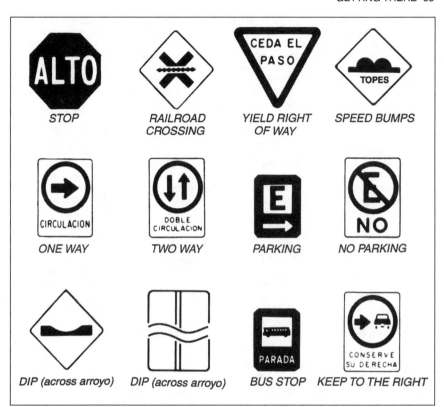

STOP RAILROAD CROSSING YIELD RIGHT OF WAY SPEED BUMPS

ONE WAY TWO WAY PARKING NO PARKING

DIP (across arroyo) DIP (across arroyo) BUS STOP KEEP TO THE RIGHT

gered. When stopping at the *gasolinera,* make sure that your cameras, purses, and other movable items are out of reach. Also, make sure that your car has a lockable gas cap. If not, insist on pumping the gas yourself, or be super-watchful as you pull up to the gas pump. Make certain that the pump reads zero before the attendant pumps the gas.

A Healthy Car
Preventative measures spell good health for both you and your car. Get that tune-up (or that long-delayed overhaul) *before,* rather than after, you leave.

Carry a stock of spare parts, which will be more difficult to get and more expensive in Mexico than at home. Carry an extra tire or two, a few cans of motor oil and octane enhancer, oil and gas filters, fan belts, spark plugs, tune-up kit, points, and fuses. Be prepared with basic tools and supplies, such as screwdrivers, pliers including Vice-Grip, lug wrench, jack, adjustable wrenches, tire pump and patches, tire pressure gauge, steel wire, and electrical tape. For breakdowns and emergencies, carry a folding shovel, a husky rope or chain, a gasoline can, and flares.

Car Repairs in Mexico
The American big three—General Motors, Ford, and Chrysler—as well as Nissan and Volkswagen are well represented by extensive dealer networks in Mexico. Getting your car or truck serviced at such agencies is straightforward. While parts will probably be higher in price, shop rates run about half U.S. prices, so repairs will generally come out cheaper than back home.

The same is not true for repairing other makes, however. Mexico has few, if any, Toyota or other Japanese car or truck dealers; and other than Mercedes-Benz, which has some truck agencies, it is difficult to find officially certified mechanics for Japanese, British, and European makes other than Volkswagen.

Many clever Mexican independent mechanics, however, can fix any car that comes their way. Their humble *talleres mecánicos* (tah-YER-ays may-KAH-nee-kohs) or repair shops dot town and village roadsides everywhere.

Although most mechanics are honest, beware of unscrupulous operators who try to collect double or triple their original estimate. If you don't speak Spanish, find someone who can assist you in negotiations. *Always* get a cost estimate, including needed parts and labor, in writing, even if you have to write it yourself. Make sure the mechanic understands, then ask him to sign it before he starts work. Although this may be a hassle, it might save you a much nastier hassle later. Shop labor at small, independent repair shops should run $10–20 per hour. For much more information, and for entertaining anecdotes of car and RV travel in Mexico, consult Carl Franz's *The People's Guide to Mexico*.

Bribes *(Mordidas)*

The usual meeting ground of the visitor and Mexican police is in the visitor's car on a highway or downtown street. To the tourists, such an encounter may seem mild harassment by the police, accompanied by vague threats of going to the police station or impounding the car for such-and-such a violation. The tourist often goes on to say, "It was all right, though . . . we paid him $10 and he went away. . . . Mexican cops sure are crooked, aren't they?"

And, I suppose, if people want to go bribing their way through Mexico, that's their business. But calling Mexican cops crooked isn't exactly fair. Police, like most everyone else in Mexico, have to scratch for a living, and they have found that many tourists are willing to slip them a $10 bill for nothing. Rather than crooked, I would call them hungry and opportunistic.

Instead of paying a bribe, do what I've done a dozen times: Remain cool, and if you're really guilty of an infraction, calmly say, "Ticket, please." *("Boleto, por favor.")* After a minute or

two of stalling, and no cash appearing, the officer most likely will not bother with a ticket, but will wave you on with only a warning. If, on the other hand, the officer does write you a ticket, he will probably keep your driver's license, which you will be able to retrieve at the *presidencia municipal* (city hall) the next day in exchange for paying your fine.

Highway Routes from the U.S.

If you've decided to drive to Puerto Vallarta, you have your choice of four general routes. At safe highway speeds, each of these routes requires about 24 hours of driving time. For comfort and safety, many folks allow three full south-of-the-border driving days to Puerto Vallarta.

From the U.S. Pacific coast and west, follow National Hwy. 15 from the border at Nogales, Sonora, an hour's drive south of Tucson, Arizona. Highway 15 continues southward smoothly, leading you through cactus-studded mountains and valleys, which turn into green to lush farmland and tropical coastal plain and forest by the time you arrive in Mazatlán. Watch for the peripheral bypasses *(periféricos)* and truck routes that route you past the congested downtowns of Hermosillo, Guaymas, Ciudad Obregón, Los Mochis, and Culiacán. Between these centers, you speed along, via *cuota* (toll) expressways virtually all the way to Mazatlán. If you prefer not to pay the high tolls (around $50 total for a passenger car, about double that for big, multiple-wheeled RVs) you should stick to the old *libre* (free) highway. Hazards, bumps, and slow going might force you to reconsider, however.

From Mazatlán, continue along the narrow (but soon to be replaced) two-lane route to Tepic, where Hwy. 15 forks left (east) to Guadalajara and Hwy. 200 heads south a smooth 100 miles to Puerto Vallarta.

If, however, you're driving to Puerto Vallarta from the central U.S., cross the border at El Paso to Ciudad Juárez, Chihuahua. There, National Highway 45, via the new *cuota* multilane expressway, leads you southward through high dry plains past the cities of Chihuahua and Jiménez where you continue by expressway Hwy. 49, to Gómez Palacio-Torreón. There, proceed southwest toward Durango, via expressway Hwy. 40. At Durango, head west along the winding but spectacular two-lane trans-Sierra National Hwy. 40, which intersects National Hwy. 15 just south of Mazatlán. From there, continue south as described above.

Folks heading to Puerto Vallarta from the eastern and southeastern U.S. should cross the border from Laredo, Texas, to Nuevo Laredo. From there, you can follow either the National Hwy. 85 non-toll *(libre)* route or the new toll *(cuota)* road, which continues, bypassing Monterrey, where you proceed via expressway Hwy. 40 all the way to Saltillo. At Saltillo, keep going westward on Hwy. 40, via either the two-lane old highway or the new toll expressway, through Torreón to Durango. Continue, via the two-lane Hwy. 40 over the Pacific crest all the way to National Hwy. 15, just south of Mazatlán. Continue southward, as described above.

BY TRAIN

Privatization is rapidly putting an end to most passenger train service in Mexico, with the exception of the **Copper Canyon** tourist route.

One of the few remaining passenger train rides in Mexico begins with a bus trip or flight south to Chihuahua, where you board the Chihuahua-Pacific Railway train and ride west along the renowned Copper Canyon (Barranca del Cobre) route to the Pacific. Only finished during the early 1960s, this route traverses the spectacular canyonland home of the Tarahumara people. At times along the winding, 406-mile (654-km) route, your rail car seems to teeter at the very edge of the labyrinthine Barranca del Cobre, a canyon so deep that its climate varies from Canadian at the top to tropical jungle at the bottom. The railway-stop village of Creel, with a few stores and hotels and a Tarahumara mission, is the major jumping-off point for trips into the canyon. For a treat, reserve a stay en route to Puerto Vallarta at the Copper Canyon Lodge in Creel. From there, the canyon beckons: explore the village, enjoy panoramic views, observe mountain wildlife, and breathe pine-scented mountain air. Farther afield, you can hike to a hot spring or spend a few days exploring the canyon-bottom itself. For more information, call 800/776-3942 or 248/340-7230; write Copper Canyon Hiking Lodges, 2741 Paldan St., Auburn Hills, MI 48326; or check the website: www.coppercanyonlodges.com.

Copper Canyon Tours

Some agencies arrange unusually good Copper Canyon rail tours. Among the best is **Columbus Travel,** 900 Ridge Creek Lane, Bulverde, TX 78163-2872, tel. 800/843-1060, website: www.canyontravel.com, which employs its own resident, ecologically sensitive guides. Trips range from small-group, rail-based sightseeing and birding-natural history tours to customized wilderness rail-jeep-backpacking adventures.

Elderhostel has long provided some of the best-buy Copper Canyon options, designed for seniors. Participants customarily fly to Los Mochis on the Pacific coast, then transfer to the first-class Mexican Chihuahua-Pacific train for a four-day canyonland adventure. Highlights include nature walks, visits to native missions, and cultural sites in Cerrocahui village and Creel, the frontier outpost in the Tarahumara heartland. The return includes a comfortable overnight at Posada Barranca, at the canyon's dizzying edge. For more information and reservations, contact 75 Federal St., Boston MA 02110-1941, tel. 877/426-8056, or website: www.elderhostel.org.

Another noteworthy tour provider is the **Mexican American Railway Company,** which specializes in luxury Copper Canyon rail sightseeing tours. Trips begin at either Chihuahua or Los Mochis, at opposite ends of the Copper Canyon Line. Participants can enjoy the amenities of either restored 1940s-era first-class cars or the "South Orient Express," super-deluxe European-class cars that are added to the regular train. In addition to onboard sightseeing, the four- to six-day itineraries include short tours to points of interest such as Creel and the Tarahumara Mission, Mennonite settlements at Cuauhtémoc, and the colonial town of El Fuerte.

The South Orient Express service features gourmet fare in opulent dining cars and expansive mountain vistas from deluxe-view dome rail coaches. Evenings, participants enjoy meals and comfortable accommodations in first-class hotels and mountain lodges. Tariffs run roughly $1,600 per person double occupancy, all-inclusive, for the usual super-deluxe five-day tour. For details, call 800/659-7602 or write the Mexican American Railway Company, 14359-A Torrey Chase Blvd., Houston TX 77014, email: info@thetraincollection.com. For additional details, visit the website www.thetraincollection .com. In Mexico, contact the company at Cortés de Monroy 2514, Colonia San Felipe, Chihuahua, Chih. 31240, tel. 14/107-570.

BY FERRY

The ferries *(transbordadores)* from La Paz at the tip of Baja California across the Gulf of California to Mazatlán or Topolobampo in Sinaloa provide a tempting route to Puerto Vallarta, especially for travelers without cars. However, if you try to take your car during busy times, especially Christmas and Easter holidays, you may get "bumped" by the large volume of commercial traffic, despite your reservation.

The ferry system, privatized in the early 1990s, has greatly improved service, at the expense of steeply increased fares. Tickets and reservations (apply early) are available at the terminals and may be available through certain travel agents in La Paz, Los Mochis, and Mazatlán.

Passengers are not allowed to remain in their vehicles during the crossing but must purchase a passenger ticket. Options include *salón* (reclining coach seats), *turista* (shared cabin with bunks), *cabina* (private cabin with toilet), and *especial* (deluxe private cabin). La Paz-Mazatlán tariffs range from about $15 to $60 per person. Additional vehicle fees run about $60 for a motorcycle, about $270 for an automobile or light RV, and more for a large motor home. Charges for the shorter La Paz-Topolobampo run are about half these.

The La Paz-Mazatlán ferries usually depart in the mid-afternoon daily, arriving at the opposite shores the following morning. The La Paz-Topolobampo crossing is shorter; ferries depart from either end at around 10 A.M. daily and arrive on the opposite shores around 6 P.M.

For more information and reservations, usually available in either English or Spanish, contact the ferry headquarters direct from outside Mexico by dialing La Paz: 112/538-33; Mazatlán: 011-52 (69) 817-020; and Topolobambo: 011-52 686/201-41. Within Mexico, dial these numbers, (substitute 01 for the 011-52), or, better yet, toll-free 01 800/696-9600.

BY TOUR, CRUISE, AND SAILBOAT

For travelers on a tight time budget, pre-arranged tour packages can provide a hassle-free option for sampling the attractions of Puerto Vallarta, Guadalajara, and other regional spots. If, however, you prefer a self-paced vacation, or desire thrift over convenience, you should probably defer tour arrangements until after arrival. Many Puerto Vallarta agencies are as close as your hotel telephone or front lobby tour desk and can customize a tour for you. Options range from city highlight tours and bay snorkeling adventures to Guadalajara shopping and sightseeing overnights to safaris through San Blas's wildlife-rich mangrove jungle. For a number of in-town Puerto Vallarta bay cruise and adventure tour options, see the "Puerto Vallarta: Town, Bay, and Mountains" chapter.

By Cruise or Sailboat

Travel agents will typically have a stack of cruise brochures that include Puerto Vallarta on their itineraries. People who enjoy being pampered with lots of food and ready-made entertainment (and who don't mind paying for it) can have great fun on cruises. Accommodations on a typical 10-day winter cruise (which would include a day or two in Puerto Vallarta) can run as little as $100 per day per person, double occupancy, to as much as $1,000 or more.

If, however, you want to get to know Mexico and the local people, a cruise is not for you. Onboard food and entertainment is the main event of a cruise; shore sightseeing excursions, which generally cost extra, are a sideshow.

Sailboats, on the other hand, offer an entirely different kind of sea route to Puerto Vallarta. Ocean Voyages, a California-based agency, arranges passage on a number of sail and motor vessels that regularly depart to the Puerto Vallarta region from Pacific ports such as San Diego, Los Angeles, San Francisco, and Vancouver, British Columbia. They offer customized itineraries and flexible arrangements that can vary from complete Puerto Vallarta roundtrip voyages to weeklong coastal idylls between Puerto Vallarta and other Pacific ports of call. Some captains allow passengers to save money by signing on as crew. For more information, contact Ocean Voyages, 1709 Bridgeway, Sausalito, CA 94965, tel. 800/299-4444 or 415/332-4681, fax 415/332-7460, email: sail@oceanvoyages.com, website www.oceanvoyages.com.

Special Tours and Study Options
Some tour and work-study programs include in-depth activities centered around arts and crafts, language and culture, wildlife-viewing, ecology, or off-the-beaten-track adventuring.

A number of agencies arrange excellent cultural and nature tours. Outstanding among them are programs by the San Diego Museum of Natural History, Mexi-Maya Academic Travel, Inc., Elderhostel, Mar de Jade, Outland Adventures, Rancho El Charro, Field Guides, and the Oceanic Society.

The naturalist-guided San Diego Museum of Natural History Copper Canyon tour begins at Los Mochis, the western terminus of the Copper Canyon railroad. Highlights include the colonial town of El Fuerte (1564), the Sinaloan thorn forest, the Jesuit Tarahumara Indian mission at the Copper Canyon village of Cerrocahui, the Cusarare "Place of Eagles" waterfall, and folkloric dances in the colonial city of Chihuahua. For details, contact Betchart Expeditions, Inc., 17050 Montebello Road, Cupertino, CA 95014-5435, tel. 800/252-4910, fax 408/252-1444, email: bx@aol.com.

The nine-day **Mexi-Maya** trip includes visits to Chihuahua Mennonite colonies and the Tarahumara Indian mission in Creel, and climaxes with a Mayo Indian fiesta (or an Easter pageant) near Los Mochis. For details, contact Mexi-Maya Academic Travel, Inc., at 12 South 675 Knoebel Drive, Lemont, IL 60439, tel. 630/972-9090, fax 630/972-9393. (For Copper Canyon route details and more tours, see "By Train," preceding.)

Elderhostel's rich offering includes a pair of cultural programs in Guadalajara. One of them focuses on the arts and crafts of colonial Mexico and includes visits to the venerable monuments of downtown Guadalajara, especially Hospicio Cabañas for viewing and discussions of the Diego Rivera murals. The tour continues on to Uruapan and Pátzcuaro, in Michoacán, where the focus shifts to native and colonial arts and crafts traditions. Another Guadalajara program includes intensive intermediate-level Spanish language instruction, combined with cultural experiences. For details, request the international catalog: Elderhostel, 75 Federal St., Boston, MA 02110-1941, tel. 877/426-8056, website: www.elderhostel.org.

Mar de Jade, a holistic-style living center at Playa Chacala, about 50 miles (80 km) north of Puerto Vallarta, offers unique people-to-people work-study opportunities. These include Spanish language study at Mar de Jade's rustic beach study-center and assisting at its health clinic in Las Varas town nearby. It also offers accommodations and macrobiotic meals for travelers who would want to do nothing more than stay a few days and enjoy Mar de Jade's lovely tropical ambience.

For more details of the Mar de Jade area and accommodations and fees, see "The Road to San Blas" section in The Nayarit Coast chapter. For additional information, contact Mar de Jade from the U.S. by dialing its local Puerto Vallarta numbers direct: tel./fax 011-52 (3) 222-1171 or 011-52 (3) 222-3524, emailing: info @mardejade.com, or visiting the website: www.mardejade.com.

Adventurous, physically fit travelers might enjoy the off-the-beaten-path biking, snorkeling, fishing, kayaking, hiking, and sightseeing tours of Seattle-based **Outland Adventures.** Its itineraries (typically about $100 per day) run three to 10 days and include lots of local color and food, accommodations in small hotels, and sightseeing in the Jalisco coast hinterland of beaches, forest trails, mangrove lagoons, and country roads. For more information, contact Outland Adventures, P.O. Box 16343, Seattle, WA 98116, tel./fax 206/932-7012, website: www.choice1.com.

A Puerto Vallarta ranch, **Rancho El Charro,** Francisco Villa 895, Fracc. Las Gaviotas, Puerto Vallarta, Jalisco 48300, tel. (3) 224-0114, email: aguirre@pvnet.com.mx, organizes naturalist-led **horseback treks** in the mountains near Puerto Vallarta. Tours run several days and include guided backcountry horseback riding, exploring antique colonial villages, camping out on the trail, swimming, hearty dinners, and cozy evenings at a rustic hacienda. Tariffs begin at about $1,000 per person. For more information, take a look at its website: www.puerto_vallarta .com\ranchocharro\.

Naturalists should consider the excellent **Field Guides** birding tour, centered in wildlife-rich Jalisco and Colima backcountry. For more information, call toll-free 800/728-4953, fax 512/263-0117, email: fieldguides@field-guides.com, or visit the website: www.field-guides.com.

The remote lagoons and islands of Baja California, about 200 miles (300 km) due west of Mazatlán, nurture a trove of marine and onshore wildlife. Such sanctuaries are ongoing destinations of winter **Oceanic Society** expedition-tours from La Paz, Baja Califor-

nia. Tours customarily cost about $1,400, cover several islands, and include a week of marine mammal watching, snorkeling, birding, and eco-exploring, both on- and offshore. For details, contact the Oceanic Society, Fort Mason Center, Building E, San Francisco, CA 94123, tel. 800/326-7491 or 415/441-1106, fax 474-3395, website: www.oceanic-society.org.

This trip might make an exciting overture or finale to your Puerto Vallarta vacation. You can connect with the Oceanic Society's Baja California (La Paz-Los Cabos) jumping-off-points via Mexican Airlines' (Mexicana, Aéromexico, or Aerocalifornia) mainland (Mazatlán/Guadalajara/Puerto Vallarta) destinations.

GETTING AROUND

BY AIR

The Puerto Vallarta region's four major jet airports are in Puerto Vallarta, Guadalajara, Manzanillo, and Tepic. Both scheduled and non-scheduled airlines connect these points with a number of national destinations, such as Mexico City, Mazatlán, Acapulco, La Paz, and Los Cabos. Although much pricier than first-class bus tickets, Mexican domestic airfares are on a par with U.S. prices. See the destination chapters of this book for specific flight information and reservations details.

Local Flying Tips
If you're planning on lots of in-Mexico flying, upon arrival get the airlines' handy (although rapidly changeable) *itinerarios de vuelo* (flight schedules) at the airport.

Mexican airlines have operating peculiarities that result from their tight budgets. Don't miss a flight; you will likely lose half the ticket price. Adjusting your flight date may cost 25% of the ticket price. Get to the airport an hour ahead of time. Last-minute passengers are often "bumped" in favor of early-bird waiting-listers. Conversely, go to the airport and get in line if you must catch a flight that the airlines claim is full. You might get on anyway. Keep your lug-

gage small so you can carry it on. Lost-luggage victims receive scant compensation in Mexico.

Although the Puerto Vallarta-Guadalajara air connection is both convenient and frequent, flying between most other Puerto Vallarta regional destinations is much less convenient than riding the bus.

BY BUS

The passenger bus is the king of the Mexican road. Several lines connect major destinations in the Puerto Vallarta region, both with each other and with the rest of Mexico.

Classes of Buses
Three distinct levels of intercity service—super first-class, first-class, and second-class—are generally available. **Luxury-class** (called something like "Primera Plus," depending upon the line) is express coaches speeding between the major destinations of Puerto Vallarta, Tepic, Guadalajara, and Barra de Navidad, seldom stopping en route. In exchange for relatively high fares (about $50 for Puerto Vallarta-Guadalajara, for example), passengers enjoy rapid passage and airline-style amenities: plush reclining seats, a (usually) clean toilet,

air-conditioning, onboard video, and an aisle attendant.

Although less luxurious, for about two-thirds the price **first-class** service is frequent and always includes reserved seating. Additionally, passengers enjoy soft reclining seats and air-conditioning (if it is working). Besides their regular stops at or near most towns and villages en route, first-class bus drivers, if requested, will usually stop and let you off anywhere along the road. For information on routes and bus station locations, refer to the destination chapters.

Second-class bus seating is unreserved. In outlying parts of the Puerto Vallarta region, there is even a class of bus beneath second-class, but given the condition of many second-class buses, it seems as if third-class buses wouldn't run at all. Such buses are the stuff of travelers' legends: the recycled old GMC, Ford, and Dodge schoolbuses that stop everywhere and carry everyone and everything to even the smallest villages tucked away in the far mountains. As long as there is any kind of a road, the bus will most likely go there.

Now and then you'll read a newspaper story of a country bus that went over a cliff somewhere in Mexico, killing the driver and a dozen unfortunate souls. The same newspapers, however, never bother to mention the half-million safe passengers for whom the same bus provided trips during its 15 years of service prior to the accident.

Second-class buses are not for travelers with weak knees or stomachs. Often, you will initially have to stand, cramped in the aisle, in a crowd of campesinos. They are warm-hearted but poor people, so don't tempt them with open, dangling purses or wallets bulging in back pockets. Stow your money safely away. After a while, you will be able to sit down. Such privilege, however, comes with obligation, such as holding an old woman's bulging bag of carrots or a toddler on your lap. But if you accept your burden with humor and equanimity, who knows what favors and blessings may flow to you in return.

WHICH BUSES GO WHERE

DESTINATIONS

Barra de Navidad-Melaque, Jal.	AC, ACP, EL, ETN, PP, TCN
Colima, Col.	AO, EL, ETN, OM, PP
Guadalajara (new terminal)	ACP, ATM, AO, EL, ETN, FU, OM, PPm, TC, TN, TP
Guadalajara (old terminal)	AGC, AMT
Chapala, Jal.	AGC
Manzanillo, Col.	AC, AO, ACP, EL, ETN, FA, GA, PP, TNS
Mazatlán, Sin.	EL, TC, TN, TNS, TP
Puerto Vallarta, Jal.	AC, EL, ETN, PP, TCN, TNS, TP
Rincón de Guayabitos-La Peñita, Nay.	EL, PP, TNS, TP
San Blas, Nay.	TNS, TNN
Las Varas, Nay.	EL, TNS, TP, TNN
Santiago Ixcuintla, Nay.	TNN
Tepic, Nay.	EL, FU, OM, TC, TNS, TNN, TP

BUS KEY:

AC	Autobuses Costa Alegre (subsidiary of FA)
ACP	Autocamiones del Pacifico
AGC	Autotransportes Guadalajara-Chapala
ATM	Autotransportes Guadalajara-Talpa-Mascota (red)
AMT	Autobuses Mascota Talpa Guadaljara (blue)
AO	Autobuses del Occidente
EB	Estrella Blanca
EL	Elite (subsidiary of EB)
ETN	Enlaces Transportes Nacionales
FA	Flecha Amarilla
FU	Futura (subsidiary of EB)
GA	Galeana (subsidiary of FA)
OM	Omnibus de Mexico
PP	Primera Plus (subsidiary of FA)
TC	Transportes Chihuahuenses (subsidiary of EB)
TCN	Transportes Cihuatlán
TN	Transportes del Norte (subsidiary of EB)
TNN	Transportes Noroeste de Nayarit
TNS	Transportes Norte de Sonora (subsidiary of EB)
TP	Transportes del Pacífico

Tickets, Seating, and Baggage

Mexican bus lines do not usually publish schedules or fares. You have to ask someone who knows (such as your hotel desk clerk), or call the bus station. Few travel agents handle bus tickets. If you don't want to spend the time to get a reserved ticket yourself, hire someone trustworthy to do it for you. Another option is to get to the bus station early enough on your traveling day to ensure that you'll get a bus to your destination.

Although some lines accept credit cards and issue computer-printed tickets at their major stations, most reserved bus tickets are sold for cash and handwritten, with a specific seat number, *número de asiento,* on the back. If you miss the bus, you lose your money. Furthermore, airlines-style automated reservations systems have not yet arrived at many Mexican bus stations. Consequently, you can generally buy reserved tickets only at the local departure *(salida local)* station. (An agent in Puerto Vallarta, for example, cannot ordinarily reserve you a ticket on a bus that originates in Tepic, 100 miles up the road.)

Request a reserved seat, if possible, with numbers 1–25 in the front *(delante)* to middle *(medio)* of the bus. The rear seats are often occupied by smokers, drunks, and rowdies. At night, you will sleep better on the right side *(lado derecho)* away from the glare of oncoming traffic lights.

Baggage is generally secure on Mexican buses. Label it, however. Overhead racks are generally too cramped to accommodate airline-sized carry-ons. Carry a small bag with your money and irreplaceables on your person; pack clothes and less-essentials in your checked luggage. For peace of mind, watch the handler put your checked baggage on the bus and watch to make sure it is not mistakenly taken off the bus at intermediate stops.

If your baggage gets misplaced, remain calm. Bus employees are generally competent and

	U.S.	CANADA
CAR RENTAL AGENCY **TOLL-FREE NUMBERS AND WEBSITES**		
Avis www.avis.com	800/831-2847	800/831-2847
Alamo www.alamo.com	800/522-9696	800/522-9696
Budget www.drivebudget.com	800/472-3325	800/472-3325
Dollar www.dollar.com	800/800-4000	800/800-4000
Hertz www.hertz.com	800/654-3001	476/620-9620
National www.national.com	800/227-3876	800/227-3876
Thrifty www.thrifty.com	800/367-2277	800/367-2277

conscientious. If you are patient, recovering your luggage will become a matter of honor for many of them. Baggage handlers are at the bottom of the pay scale; a tip for their mostly thankless job is very much appreciated.

On long trips, carry food, beverages, and toilet paper. Station food may be dubious, and the sanitary facilities may be ill-maintained.

If you are waiting for a first-class bus at an intermediate *salida de paso* (passing station), you have to trust to luck that there will be an empty seat. If not, your best option may be to ride a more frequent second-class bus.

BY TRAIN OR CAR

The Puerto Vallarta region's only rail line, the Pacific route, has been privatized and does not now provide passenger service; go by bus or airplane (see previous) or car instead.

Driving your own car in Mexico may or may not be for you. See "By Car or RV" under "Getting There," preceding.

Rental Car

Car and jeep rentals are an increasingly popular transportation option in Puerto Vallarta. They

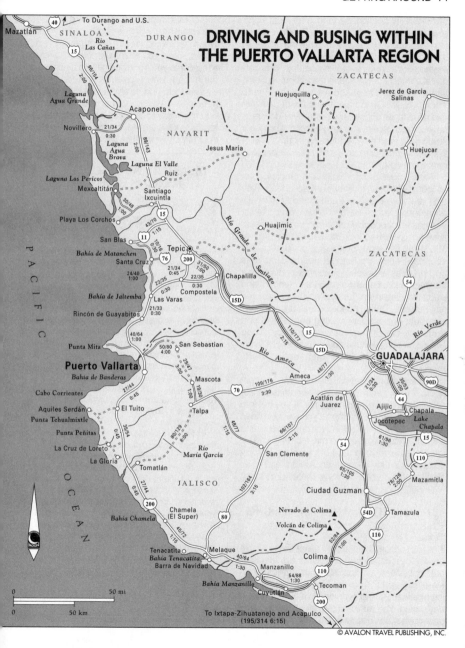

DRIVING AND BUSING WITHIN THE PUERTO VALLARTA REGION

To Durango and U.S.

Mazatlán

SINALOA

DURANGO

ZACATECAS

Río Las Cañas

Huejuquilla

Jerez de Garcia Salinas

Laguna Agua Grande

Acaponeta

NAYARIT

Novillero 21/34 0:30

Laguna Agua Brava

Jesus Maria

Huejucar

Laguna El Valle

Ruiz

Laguna Los Pericos

Mexcaltitán

Santiago Ixcuintla

Huajimic

Playa Los Corchos

ZACATECAS

San Blas 11

Tepic 200

Bahía de Matanchen 76

Santa Cruz 21/34 0:45 31/50 1:00

Chapalilla

54

24/40 1:00

22/35 0:30

22/35

Bahía de Jaltemba

Las Varas Compostela 15D

Rincón de Guayabitos 21/33 0:30

Río Grande de Santiago

110/177 2:15

Río Verde

Punta Mita 40/64 1:00

San Sebastián 50/80 4:00

15

15D

GUADALAJARA

Puerto Vallarta

Bahía de Banderas

29/47 3:00

Mascota 19/30 1:00

Río Ameca

Ameca 48/77 1:30

21/34 0:30

35/23 0:30

90D

Cabo Corrientes 27/44 0:45

109/176 3:30

70

Acatlán de Juarez

44

Ajijic

Chapala

Aquiles Serdán El Tuito

Talpa

66/107 2:15

Jocotepec Lake Chapala

54

15

Punta Tehualmixtle 39/54 0:45

80/129 8:00

48/77 1:15

61/96 1:30

110

Punta Peñitas

Río Maria Garcia

San Clemente

La Cruz de Loreto

La Gloria

Tomatlán 27/44 0:45

JALISCO

54

65/105 1:30

78/126 2:00

Mazamitla

O C E A N

102/164 3:15

Ciudad Guzman

200

Chamela (El Super) 80

Nevado de Colima

54D

Tamazula

Bahía Chamela 45/72

Volcán de Colima

110

Tenacatita Melaque 40/64

52/84 1:00

Bahía Tenacatita

1:30

Barra de Navidad

Manzanillo

Colima 110

54/88 1:30

Bahía Manzanilla

Cuyutlán

Tecoman

200

To Ixtapa-Zihuatanejo and Acapulco
(195/314 6:15)

0   50 mi

0   50 km

© AVALON TRAVEL PUBLISHING, INC.

offer mobility and independence for local sightseeing and beach excursions. In Puerto Vallarta, Guadalajara, Tepic, and Manzanillo the gang's all there: Hertz, National, Avis, Budget, Thrifty, Alamo, Dollar, and several local outfits. (For car-rental contact specifics, see the airport sections, under "Getting There and Away" in the Puerto Vallarta town, Guadalajara, and Barra de Navidad destination chapters.) They require drivers to have a valid driver's license, passport, and major credit card, and may require a minimum age of 25. Some local companies do not accept credit cards, but do offer lower rates in return.

Base prices of international agencies such as Hertz, National, and Avis are not cheap. With a 17% value-added tax and mandatory insurance, rentals run more than in the United States. The cheapest possible rental car, usually a used, stick-shift VW beetle, runs $40–60 per day or $250–450 per week, depending on location and season. Prices are highest during Christmas and pre-Easter weeks. Before departure, use the international agencies' toll-free numbers and websites (see chart) for availability, prices, and reservations. During nonpeak seasons, you may save lots of pesos by waiting until arrival and renting a car through a local agency. Shop around, starting with the agent in your hotel lobby or with the local Yellow Pages (under *"Automoviles, renta de"*).

Car insurance that covers property damage, public liability, and medical payments is an absolute "must" with your rental car. If you get into an accident without insurance, you will be in deep trouble, probably jail. Narrow, rough roads and animals grazing at roadside make driving in Mexico more hazardous than back home. For important car safety and insurance information, see "By Car or RV" under "Getting There," preceding.

BY TAXI, TOUR, AND HITCHHIKING

Taxis

The high prices of rental cars make taxis a viable option for local excursions. Cars are luxuries, not necessities, for most Mexican families. Travelers might profit from the Mexican money-saving practice of piling everyone in a taxi for a Sunday outing. You may find that an all-day taxi and driver, who, besides relieving you of driving, will become your impromptu guide, will cost less than a rental car.

The magic word for saving money by taxi is *colectivo:* a taxi you share with other travelers. The first place you'll practice getting a taxi will be at the airport, where *colectivo* tickets are routinely sold from booths at the terminal door.

If, however, you want your own private taxi, ask for a *taxi especial,* which will run about three or four times the individual tariff for a *colectivo.*

Your airport experience will prepare you for in-

DISASTER AND RESCUE ON A MEXICAN HIGHWAY

My litany of Mexican driving experiences came to a climax one night when, heading north from Tepic, I hit a cow at 50 mph head on. The cow was knocked about 150 feet down the road, while I and my two friends endured a scary impromptu roller-coaster ride. When the dust settled, we, although in shock, were grateful that we hadn't suffered the fate of the poor cow, which had died instantly from the collision.

From that low point, our fortunes soon began to improve. Two buses stopped and about 40 men got out to move my severely wounded van to the shoulder. The cow's owner, a rancher, arrived to cart off the cow's remains in a jeep. Then the police—a man and his wife in a VW bug—pulled up. *"Pobrecita camioneta,"* "Poor little van," the woman said, gazing at my vehicle, which now resembled an oversized, crumpled accordion. They gave us a ride to Mazatlán, found us a hotel room, and generally made sure we were okay.

If I hadn't had Mexican auto insurance I would have been in deep trouble. Mexican law—based on the Napoleonic Code—presumes guilt and does not bother with juries. It would have kept me in jail until all damages were settled. The insurance agent I saw in the morning took care of everything. He called the police station, where I was excused from paying damages when the cow's owner failed to show. He had my car towed to a repair shop, where the mechanics banged it into good enough shape so I could drive it home a week later. Forced to stay in one place, my friends and I enjoyed the most relaxed time of our entire three months in Mexico. The *pobrecita camioneta,* all fixed up a few months later, lasted 14 more years.

town taxis, which rarely have meters. You must establish the price before getting in. Bargaining comes with the territory in Mexico, so don't shrink from it, even though it seems a hassle. If you get into a taxi without an agreed-upon price, you are letting yourself in for a more serious and potentially nasty hassle later. If your driver's price is too high, he'll probably come to his senses as soon as you hail another taxi.

After a few days, getting taxis around town will be a cinch. You'll find that you don't have to take the more expensive taxis lined up in your hotel driveway. If the price isn't right, walk toward the street and hail a regular taxi.

In town, if you can't find a taxi, it may be because they are waiting for riders at the local stand, called a taxi *sitio*. Ask someone to direct you to it: *"Excúseme. ¿Dónde está el sitio taxi, por favor?"* ("Excuse me. Where is the taxi stand, please?")

Tours and Guides

For many Puerto Vallarta region visitors, locally arranged tours offer a hassle-free alternative to sightseeing by rental car or taxi. Hotels and travel agencies, many of whom maintain front-lobby travel and tour desks, offer a bounty of sightseeing, water sports, bay cruise, fishing, and wildlife-viewing tour opportunities.

Hitchhiking

Most everyone agrees hitchhiking is not the safest mode of transport. If you're unsure, don't do it. Continual hitchhiking does not make for a healthy travel diet, nor should you hitchhike at night.

The recipe for trouble-free hitchhiking requires equal measures of luck, savvy, and technique. The best places to catch rides are where people are arriving and leaving anyway, such as bus stops, highway intersections, gas stations, RV parks, and the highway out of town.

Male-female hitchhiking partnerships seem to net the most rides, although it is technically illegal for women to ride in commercial trucks. The more gear you and your partner have, the fewer rides you will get. Pickup and flatbed truck owners often pick up passengers for pay. Before hopping onto the truck bed, ask how much the ride will cost.

OTHER PRACTICALITIES

TOURIST CARDS AND VISAS

For U.S. and Canadian citizens, entry by air into Mexico for a few weeks could hardly be easier. Airline attendants hand out tourist cards *(tarjetas turísticas)* en route and officers make them official by glancing at passports and stamping the cards at the immigration gate. Business travel permits for 30 days or less are handled by the same simple procedures.

Entry is not entirely painless, however. The Mexican government currently charges an approximate $15 fee per person for a tourist card. For air and bus travelers, this is no problem, since the fee is automatically included in the fare. The fee can be a bit of a hassle for drivers, however. At this writing the government does not allow collection of the fee by border immigration officers. Instead, the officers issue a form that you must take to a bank, where you pay the fee. For multiple entries this can get complicated and time-consuming.

In addition to the entry fee, Mexican immigration officials require that all entering U.S. citizens 15 years old or over must present proper identification—either a valid U.S. passport, original birth certificate, or military ID, while naturalized citizens must show naturalization papers or a valid U.S. passport.

Canadian citizens must show a valid passport or original birth certificate. Nationals of other countries (especially those such as Hong Kong, which issue more than one type of passport) may be subject to different or additional regulations. For advice, consult your regional Mexico Tourism Board office or consulate. For more Mexico-entry details, visit the Mexico Tourism Board's **website: www.visitmexico.com** or call toll-free 800/44-MEXICO.

More Options

For more complicated cases, get your tourist card early enough to allow you to consider the options. Tourist cards can be issued for multiple entries and a maximum validity of 180 days;

MEXICO TOURISM BOARD OFFICES

More than a dozen Mexico Tourism Board offices and scores of Mexican government consulates operate in the United States. Consulates generally handle questions of Mexican nationals in the U.S., while Mexico Tourism Boards serve travelers heading for Mexico. For simple questions and Mexico regional information brochures, dial 800/44MEXICO (800/446-3942) from the U.S. or Canada or visit the website www.visit-mexico.com.

Otherwise, contact one of the North American regional or European Mexico Tourism Boards for guidance:

IN NORTH AMERICA

From Arizona, California, Colorado, Hawaii, Idaho, Montana, Nevada, New Mexico, and Utah, contact **Los Angeles:** 2401 W. 6th Street, Fifth Floor, Los Angeles, CA 90057, tel. 213/351-2069, fax 213/351-2074.

From Alaska, Washington, Oregon, Idaho, Wyoming and Montana and the Canadian Provinces of British Columbia, Alberta, Yukon, Northwest Territories, and Saskatchewan, contact **Vancouver:** 999 W. Hastings St., Suite 1110, Vancouver, B.C. V6C 2W2, tel. 604/669-2845, fax 604/669-3498.

From Texas, Oklahoma, and Louisiana, contact **Houston:** 4507 San Jacinto, Suite 308, Houston TX 77004, tel. 713/772-2581, fax 713/772-6058.

From Alabama, Arkansas, Florida, Georgia, Mississippi, Tennessee, North Carolina, and South Carolina, contact **Miami:** 1200 NW 78th Ave. #203, Miami FL 33126-1817; tel. 305/718-4091, fax 305/718-4098.

From Illinois, Indiana, Iowa, Kansas, Michigan, Minnesota, Missouri, Nebraska, North Dakota, Ohio, South Dakota, and Wisconsin, contact **Chicago:** 300 North Michigan Ave., 4th Floor, Chicago, IL 60601, tel. 312/606-9252, fax 312/606-9012.

From Connecticut, Delaware, Kentucky, Maine, Maryland, Massachusetts, New Hampshire, New Jersey, New York, Pennsylvania, Rhode Island, Vermont, Virginia, Washington D.C., and West Virginia, contact **New York:** 21 E. 63rd Street, 3rd Floor, New York, NY 10021, tel. 212/821-0313 or 212/821-0314, fax 212/821-3067.

From Ontario and Manitoba, contact **Toronto:** 2 Bloor St. West, Suite 1502, Toronto, Ontario M4W 3E2, tel. 416/925-2753, fax 416/925-6061.

From New Brunswick, Newfoundland, Nova Scotia, Prince Edward Island, and Quebec, contact **Montreal:** 1 Place Ville Marie, Suite 1931, Montreal, Quebec H3B2C3, tel. 514/871-1052 or 514/871-1103, fax 514/871-3825.

IN EUROPE

Mexico also maintains Mexico Tourism Boards throughout Western Europe:

London: Wakefield House, 41 Trinity Square, London EC3N 4DT, England, UK, tel. 207/488-9392, fax 207/265-0704.

Frankfurt: Weisenhuttenplatz 26, 60329 Frankfurt-am-Main, Deutschland, tel. 69/25-3509, fax 69/25-3755.

Paris: 4, Rue Notre-Dame des Victoires, 75002 Paris, France, tel. 1/426-15180, fax 1/428-60580.

Madrid: Calle Velázquez 126, 28006 Madrid, España, tel. 91/561-1827, fax 91/411-0759,

Rome: Via Barbarini 3-piso 7, 00187 Roma, Italia, tel. 6/487-2182, fax 6/487-3630.

photos are often required. If you don't request multiple entry or the maximum time, your card will probably be stamped single entry, valid for some shorter period, such as 90 days. If you are not sure how long you'll stay in Mexico, request the maximum.(One hundred eighty days is the absolute maximum for a tourist card; long-term foreign residents routinely make semiannual "border runs" for new tourist cards.)

Student and Business Visas

A visa is a notation stamped and signed on your passport showing the number of days and entries allowable for your trip. Apply for a student visa at the consulate nearest your home well in advance of your departure; the same is true if you require a business visa of longer than 30 days. One-year renewable student visas are available (sometimes with considerable red tape). An ordinary 180-day tourist card may be the easiest option, if you can manage it.

Your Passport

Your passport (or birth or naturalization certificate) is your positive proof of national identity; without it, your status in any foreign country is in doubt. Don't leave home without one. United States citizens may obtain passports (allow four to six weeks) at local post offices.

Entry for Children

Children under 15 can be included on their parents' tourist cards, but complications occur if the children (by reason of illness, for example) cannot leave Mexico with both parents. Parents can avoid such red tape by getting a passport and a Mexican tourist card for each of their children.

In addition to passport or birth certificate, minors (under age 18) entering Mexico without parents or legal guardians must present a notarized letter of permission signed by both parents or legal guardians. Even if accompanied by one parent, a notarized letter from the other must be presented. Divorce or death certificates must also be presented, when applicable.

Puerto Vallarta travelers should hurdle all such possible delays far ahead of time in the cool calm of their local Mexican consulate rather than the hot, hurried atmosphere of a border or airport immigration station.

Entry for Pets

A pile of red tape stalls the entry of many dogs, cats, and other pets into Mexico. Veterinary health and rabies certificates must be stamped by a Mexican consul responsible for a specific locality. Contact your regional Mexico Tourism Board, call 800/44-MEXICO, or visit the website www.visitmexico.com for assistance.

Don't Lose Your Tourist Card

If you do, present your passport at the police station and get an official police report detailing your loss. Take the report to the nearest federal *oficina de turismo* (in Puerto Vallarta, Guadalajara, Tepic, San Blas, Rincón de Guayabitos, and Barra de Navidad; see destination chapters for locations) and ask for a duplicate tourist card. Savvy travelers carry copies of their passports, tourist cards, car permits, and Mexican auto insurance policies, while leaving the originals in a hotel safe-deposit box.

Car Permits

If you drive to Mexico, you will need a permit for your car. Upon entry into Mexico, be ready with originals and copies of your proof-of-ownership or registration papers (state title certificate, registration, or notarized bill of sale), current license plates, and current driver's license. The auto permit fee runs about $12, payable only by non-Mexican bank MasterCard, Visa, or American Express credit cards. (The credit-card-only requirement discourages those who sell or abandon U.S.-registered cars in Mexico without paying customs duties.) Credit cards must bear the same name as the vehicle proof-of-ownership papers.

The resulting car permit becomes part of the owner's tourist card and receives the same length of validity. Vehicles registered in the name of an organization or person other than the driver must be accompanied by a notarized affidavit authorizing the driver to use the car in Mexico for a specific time.

Border officials generally allow you to carry or tow additional motorized vehicles (motorcycle, another car, large boat) into Mexico but will probably require separate documentation and fee for each vehicle. If a Mexican official desires to inspect your trailer or RV, go through it with him.

Accessories, such as a small trailer, boat less than six feet, CB radio, or outboard motor, may be noted on the car permit and must leave Mexico with the car.

For updates and details on documentation required for taking your car into Mexico, call the toll-free Mexican government number in the U.S., 800/446-3942. For many more details on motor vehicle entry and what you may bring in your baggage to Mexico, consult the AAA (American Automobile Association) *Mexico TravelBook.*

Since Mexico does not recognize foreign automobile insurance, you must purchase Mexican automobile insurance. (For more information on this and other details of driving in Mexico, see "Getting There" above.)

Crossing the Border and Returning Home
Squeezing through border bottlenecks during peak holidays and rush hours can be time-consuming. Avoid crossing 7–9 A.M. and 4:30–6:30 P.M.

Just before returning across the border with your car, park and have a customs *(aduana)* official **remove and cancel the holographic identity sticker that you received on entry.** If possible, get a receipt *(recibo)* or some kind of verification that it's been canceled *(cancelado).* Tourists have been fined hundreds of dollars for inadvertently carrying uncanceled car entry stickers on their windshields. At the same time, return all other Mexican permits, such as tourist cards and hunting and fishing licenses. Also, be prepared for Mexico exit inspection, especially for cultural artifacts and works of art, which may require exit permits. Certain religious and pre-Columbian artifacts, legally the property of the Mexican government, cannot be taken from the country.

If you entered Mexico with your car, you cannot legally leave without it except by permission from local customs authorities, usually the Aduana (Customs House) or the Oficina Federal de Hacienda (Federal Treasury Office). For local details, see under "Services and Information" in the destination chapters.

All returnees are subject to U.S. customs inspection. United States law allows a fixed value (presently $400) of duty-free goods per returnee. This may include no more than one liter of alcoholic spirits, 200 cigarettes, and 100 cigars. A flat 10% duty will be applied to the first $1,000 (fair retail value, save your receipts) in excess of your $400 exemption. You may, however, mail packages (up to $50 value each) of gifts duty-free to friends and relatives in the United States. Make sure to clearly write "unsolicited gift" and a list of the value and contents on the outside of the package. Perfumes (over $5), alcoholic beverages, and tobacco may not be included in such packages.

Improve the security of such mailed packages by sending them by **Mexpost** class, similar to U.S. Express Mail service. Even better (but much more expensive), send them by **Federal Express** or **DHL** international couriers, which maintain offices in Puerto Vallarta, Tepic, and Guadalajara. For more information on customs regulations important to travelers abroad, write for a copy of the useful pamphlet *Know Before You Go,* from the U.S. Customs Service, P.O. Box 7047, Washington, D.C. 20044, tel. 877/287-8667.

Additional U.S. rules prohibit importation of certain fruits, vegetables, and domestic animal and endangered wildlife products. Certain live animal species, such as parrots, may be brought into the U.S., subject to 30-day agricultural quarantine upon arrival, at the owner's expense. For more details on agricultural product and live animal importation, write for the free booklet *Travelers' Tips,* by the U.S. Department of Agriculture, Washington, D.C. 20250, tel. 202/720-2791. For more information on the importation of endangered wildlife products, contact the Wildlife Permit Office, U.S. Department of the Interior, Washington, D.C. 20240, tel. 202/208-4662.

MONEY

The Peso: Down and Up
Overnight in early 1993, the Mexican government shifted its monetary decimal point three places and created the "new" peso, which, subsequently, has deflated to about one-third of its initial value of three per dollar. Since the peso value sometimes changes rapidly, U.S. dollars have become a much more stable indicator of Mexican prices; for this reason they are used in this book to report prices. You should, nevertheless, always use pesos to pay for everything in Mexico.

Since the introduction of the new peso, the centavo (one-hundredth of a new peso) has appeared, in coins of 10, 20, and 50 centavos. Incidentally, the dollar sign, "$," also marks Mexican pesos. Peso bills, in denominations of 5, 10, 20, 100, and 200 pesos, are common. Since banks like to exchange your traveler's checks for a few crisp large bills rather than the often-tattered smaller denominations, ask for some of your change in 20- and 50-peso notes. A 200-peso note, while common at the bank, looks awfully big to a small shopkeeper, who might be hard-pressed to change it.

Banks, ATMs, and Money Exchange Offices
Mexican banks, like their North American counterparts, have lengthened their business hours. Banco Internacional (BITAL), maintains the longest hours: as long as Mon.–Sat. 8 A.M.–7 P.M. Banamex (Banco Nacional de Mexico), generally the most popular with local people, usually posts the best in-town dollar exchange rate in its lobbies; for example: *Tipo de cambio: venta 9.615, compra 9.720,* which means they will sell pesos to you at the rate of 9.615 per dollar and buy them back for 9.720 per dollar.

ATMs (Automated Teller Machines) *("Cajeros Automáticos,"* kah-HAY-rohs ahoo-toh-MAH-tee-kohs) are rapidly becoming the money source of choice in Mexico. Virtually every bank has a 24-hour ATM, accessible (with proper PIN identification code) by a swarm of U.S. and Canadian credit and ATM cards.

Although one-time bank charges, typically about $2 per $100, for ATM cash remain small, the money you can usually get from a single card is limited to about $200 or less per day.

Even without an ATM card, you don't have to go to the trouble of waiting in long bank service lines. Opt for a less-crowded bank, such as Bancomer, Banco Serfín, Banco Internacional, or a private money-exchange office *(casa de cambio).* Often most convenient, such offices often offer long hours and faster service than the banks for a fee (as little as $.50 or as much as $3 per $100).

Keeping Your Money Safe
Traveler's checks, the universal prescription for safe money abroad, are widely accepted in the Puerto Vallarta region. Even if you plan to use your ATM card, purchase some U.S. dollar traveler's checks (a well-known brand such as American Express or Visa) at least as an emergency reserve. Canadian traveler's checks and cur-

rency are not as widely accepted as U.S. traveler's checks. European and Asian checks are even less acceptable. Unless you like signing your name or paying lots of per-check commissions, buy denominations of $50 or more.

In Puerto Vallarta, as everywhere, **thieves** circulate among the tourists. Keep valuables in your hotel *caja de seguridad* (security box). If you don't particularly trust the desk clerk, carry what you cannot afford to lose in a money belt. Pickpockets love crowded markets, buses, and airport terminals where they can slip a wallet out of a back pocket or dangling purse in a blink. Guard against this by carrying your wallet in your front pocket, and your purse, waist pouch, and daypack (which clever crooks can sometimes slit open) on your front side.

Don't attract thieves by displaying wads of money or flashy jewelry. Don't get sloppy drunk; if so, you may become a pushover for a determined thief.

Don't leave valuables unattended on the beach; share security duties with trustworthy-looking neighbors, or leave a bag with a shopkeeper nearby.

Tipping
Without their droves of visitors, Mexican people would be even poorer. Deflation of the peso, while it makes prices low for outsiders, makes it rough for Mexican families to get by. The help at your hotel typically get paid only a few dollars a day. They depend on tips to make the difference between dire and bearable poverty. Give the *camarista* (chambermaid) and floor attendant 20 pesos every day or two. And whenever uncertain of what to tip, it will probably mean a lot to someone—maybe a whole family—if you err on the generous side.

In restaurants and bars, Mexican tipping customs are similar to those in the U.S. and Europe: tip waiters, waitresses, and bartenders about 15% for satisfactory service.

SHOPPING

What to Buy
Although bargains abound in Mexico, savvy shoppers are selective. Steep import and luxury

Many indigenous artisans and their families have migrated to Puerto Vallarta from their rural homes to sell their handiwork to visitors.

taxes drive up the prices of foreign-made goods such as cameras, computers, sports equipment, and English-language books. Instead, concentrate your shopping on locally made items: leather, jewelry, cotton resort wear, Mexican-made designer clothes, and the galaxy of handicrafts for which Mexico is renowned.

Handicrafts
A number of Puerto Vallarta regional centers are havens for crafts shoppers. Guadalajara (including its suburban villages of Tlaquepaque and Tonalá) and Tepic nurture vibrant traditions with roots in the pre-Columbian past. This rich cornucopia spills over to Puerto Vallarta, where shoppers enjoy a rich selection from both regional and national Mexican sources. These, along with a kaleidoscope of offerings from the local art colony, fill sidewalks, stalls, and shops all over town. (See "Arts and Crafts," earlier in this chapter, and destination-chapter "Shopping" sections for details.)

How to Buy
Credit cards, such as Visa, MasterCard, and, to a lesser extent, American Express, are widely honored in the hotels, crafts shops, and boutiques that cater to foreign tourists. Although convenient, such shops' offerings will be generally higher-priced than those of stores in the older downtown districts that depend more on local trade. Local shops sometimes offer discounts for cash purchases.

Bargaining will stretch your money even farther. It comes with the territory in Mexico and needn't be a hassle. On the contrary, if done with humor and moderation, bargaining can be an enjoyable way to meet Mexican people and gain their respect, even friendship.

The local crafts market is where bargaining is most intense. For starters, try offering half the asking price. From there on, it's all psychology: you have to content yourself with not having to have the item. Otherwise, you're sunk; the vendor will sense your need and stand fast. After a few minutes of good-humored bantering, ask for *el último precio* ("the final price"), which, if it's close, just may be a bargain.

Buying Silver and Gold Jewelry
Silver and gold jewelry, the finest of which is crafted in Taxco, Guerrero, and Guanajuato, fills many Puerto Vallarta region shops. One hundred percent pure silver is rarely sold because it's too soft. Silver (sent from processing mills in the north of Mexico to be worked in Taxco shops) is nearly always alloyed with 7.5% copper to increase its durability. Such pieces, identical in composition to sterling silver, should have ".925," together with the initials of the manufacturer, stamped on their back sides. Other, less common grades, such as "800 fine" (80% silver), should also be stamped.

If silver is not stamped with the degree of purity, it probably contains no silver at all and is an alloy of copper, zinc, and nickel, known by the generic label "alpaca," or "German" silver. Once, after haggling over the purity and prices of his offerings, a street vendor handed me a shiny handful and said, "Go to a jeweler and have them tested. If they're not real, keep them." Calling his bluff, I took them to a jeweler, who applied a dab of hydrochloric acid to each piece. Tiny, telltale bubbles of hydrogen revealed the cheapness of the merchandise, which I returned the next day to the vendor.

Some shops price sterling silver jewelry simply by weighing, which typically translates to about $1 per gram. If you want to find out if the price is fair, ask the shopkeeper to weigh it for you.

People prize pure gold partly because, unlike silver, it does not tarnish. Gold, nevertheless, is rarely sold pure (24 karat); for durability, it is alloyed with copper. Typical purities, such as 18 karat (75%) or 14 karat (58%), should be stamped on the pieces. If not, chances are they contain no gold at all.

COMMUNICATIONS

Using Mexican Telephones

Although Mexican phone service is improving, it's still sometimes hit-or-miss. If a number doesn't get through, you may have to redial it more than once. When someone answers (usually *"Bueno"*) be especially courteous. If your Spanish is rusty, say, *"¿Por favor, habla inglés?"* (¿POR fah-VOR, AH-blah een-GLAYS?). If you want to speak to a particular person (such as María), ask, *"¿María se encuentra?"* ("¿mah-REE-ah SAY ayn-koo-AYN-trah?").

Mexican phones operate more or less the same as in the U.S. and Canada. Mexican phone numbers are always in a state of flux because the system is rapidly growing, but a complete telephone number (in Puerto Vallarta town, for example) is generally written like this: 3/222-4709. As in the U.S., the "3" denotes the telephone area code *(lada)* ("LAH-dah") and the 222-4709 is the number that you dial locally. If you want to dial this number long-distance *(larga distancia)* first dial "01" then 3/222-4709. *Ladas* may be one, two, or three digits; local phone numbers may contain anywhere from four to seven digits. As a general guideline, the largest cities have one-digit *ladas,* medium-sized towns have two-digit *ladas,* and the smallest towns have three-digit *ladas.* In this book, the *lada* is included with each phone number listed.

In Puerto Vallarta region towns and cities, direct long-distance dialing is the rule—from hotels, public phone booths, and efficient private Computel telephone offices. The cheapest, often most convenient way to call is by purchasing

and using a **public telephone *Ladatel* card.** Buy them in 20-, 30-, 50-, and 100-peso denominations at the many outlets—mini-markets, pharmacies, liquor stores—that display the blue and yellow *Ladatel* sign.

For station-to-station calls to the U.S., dial 001 plus the area code and the local number. For calls to other countries, ask your hotel desk clerk or see the easy-to-follow directions in the local Mexican telephone directory.

To reach Mexican long-distance numbers, dial 01, followed by the *lada* (Mexican area code) and the local number.

Another convenient way (although a more expensive one) to call home is via your personal telephone credit card. Contact your U.S. long-distance operator by dialing 001-800-462-4240 for AT&T; 001-800-674-6000 for MCI; or 001-800-877-8000 for Sprint.

Another convenient (although expensive) way of calling home is collect. You can do this in one of two ways. Simply dial 09 for the local English-speaking international operator; or dial the AT&T, MCI and Sprint numbers listed in the previous paragraph.

Beware of certain private "call the U.S. with your Visa or MasterCard" telephones installed prominently in airports, tourist hotels, and shops. Tariffs on these phones can run as high as $10 a minute. If you do use such a phone, always ask the operator for the rate, and if it's too high, take your business elsewhere.

In smaller towns, you must often do your long-distance phoning in the *larga distancia* (local phone office). Typically staffed by a young woman and often connected to a cafe, the *larga distancia* becomes an informal community social center as people pass the time waiting for their phone connections.

Calling Mexico

To call Mexico direct from the U.S., first dial 011 (for international access), then 52 (for Mexico), followed by the area code and local number. Some Puerto Vallarta regional *ladas* (area codes) are: Puerto Vallarta (3), Guadalajara (3), (although you can't dial locally between Puerto Vallarta and Guadalajara), Tepic (32), Nuevo Vallarta-Bucerías 329/, San Blas 328/, Sayulita and Rincón de Guayabitos 327/, and Barra de Navidad-Melaque 335/.

Post and Telegraph

Mexican *correos* (post offices) operate similarly, but more slowly and less securely, than their counterparts all over the world. Mail services usually include *lista de correo* (general delivery, address letters *"a/c lista de correo,"*), *servicios filatelicas* (philatelic services), *por avión* (airmail), *giros* (postal money orders), and Mexpost secure and fast delivery service, usually from separate Mexpost offices.

Mexican ordinary mail is sadly unreliable and pathetically slow. If, for mailings within Mexico, you must have security, use the efficient, reformed government **Mexpost** (like U.S. Express Mail) service. For international mailings, check the local yellow pages for widely available **DHL** or **Federal Express** courier service.

Telégrafos (telegraph offices), usually near the post office, send and receive *telegramas* (telegrams) and *giros*. *Telecomunicaciones* (Telecom), the new high-tech telegraph offices, add telephone and public fax to the available services.

Electricity and Time

Mexican electric power is supplied at U.S.-standard 110 volts, 60 cycles. Plugs and sockets are generally two-pronged, nonpolar (like the pre-1970s U.S. ones). Bring adapters if you're going to use appliances with polar two-pronged or three-pronged plugs. A two-pronged polar plug has different-sized prongs, one of which is too large to plug into an old-fashioned nonpolar socket.

The Puerto Vallarta region is split between two time zones. The state of Jalisco portion, which includes Puerto Vallarta, Barra de Navidad, and Guadalajara, operates on central time, while the state of Nayarit portion, which includes Rincón de Guayabitos, Tepic, and San Blas, operates on mountain time. The Ameca River and bridge, just north of the Puerto Vallarta airport, mark the Nayarit-Jalisco border. When traveling by highway south into Puerto Vallarta from Nayarit, set your watch ahead one hour; conversely, when you cross the Ameca River traveling north set your watch back an hour.

Mexican businesses and government offices sometimes use the 24-hour system to tell time. Thus, a business who posts its hours as 0800–1700 is open 8 A.M.–5 P.M. When speaking, however, people customarily use the 12-hour system.

STAYING HEALTHY

In Puerto Vallarta, as everywhere, prevention is the best remedy for illness. For visitors who confine their travel to the beaten path, a few common sense precautions will ensure vacation enjoyment.

Resist the temptation to dive headlong into Mexico. It's no wonder that people get sick—broiling in the sun, gobbling peppery food, guzzling beer and margaritas, then discoing half the night—all in their first 24 hours. An alternative is to give your body time to adjust. Travelers often arrive tired and dehydrated from travel and heat. During the first few days, drink plenty of bottled water and juice, and take siestas.

Traveler's Diarrhea

Traveler's diarrhea (known in Southeast Asia as "Bali Belly" and in Mexico as turista or "Montezuma's Revenge") sometimes persists, even among prudent vacationers. You can suffer turista for a week after simply traveling from California to Philadelphia or New York. Doctors say the familiar symptoms of runny bowels, nausea, and sour stomach result from normal local bacterial strains to which newcomers' systems need time to adjust. Unfortunately, the dehydration and fatigue from heat and travel reduce your body's natural defenses and sometimes lead to a persistent cycle of sickness at a time when you least want it.

Time-tested protective measures can help your body either prevent or break this cycle. Many doctors and veteran travelers swear by Pepto-Bismol for soothing sore stomachs and stopping diarrhea. Acidophilus, the bacteria found in yogurt, is widely available in the U.S. in tablets and aids digestion. Warm *manzanilla* (chamomile) tea, used widely in Mexico (and by Peter Rabbit's mother), provides liquid and calms upset stomachs. Temporarily avoid coffee and alcohol, drink plenty of *manzanilla* tea, and eat bananas and rice for a few meals until your tummy can take regular food.

Although powerful antibiotics and antidiarrhea medications such as Lomotil and Imodium are readily available over *farmacia* counters, they may involve serious side effects and should not be taken in the absence of medical advice. If in doubt, consult a doctor. (See "Mexican Doctors," following.)

Safe Water and Food

Although municipalities have made great strides in sanitation, food and water are still potential sources of germs in the Puerto Vallarta region. Do not drink local tap water. Drink bottled water only. Hotels, whose success depends vitally on their customers' health, generally provide *agua purificada* (purified bottled water). If, for any reason, the water quality is doubtful, add a water purifier, such as "Potable Aqua" brand (get it at a camping goods stores before departure) or a few drops per quart of water of *blanqueador* (household chlorine bleach) or *yodo* (tincture of iodine) from the pharmacy.

Pure bottled water, soft drinks, beer, and fresh fruit juices are so widely available it is easy to avoid tap water, especially in restaurants. Ice and *paletas* (iced juice-on-a-stick) may be risky, especially in small towns.

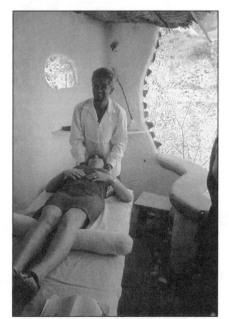
enjoying a massage at Terra Noble

Washing hands before eating in a restaurant is a time-honored Mexican ritual that visitors should religiously follow. The humblest Mexican eatery will generally provide a basin to *lavar las manos* (wash the hands). If it doesn't, don't eat there.

Hot, cooked food is generally safe, as are peeled fruits and vegetables. Milk and cheese these days in Mexico are generally processed under sanitary conditions and sold pasteurized (ask, "¿*Pasteurizado?*") and are typically safe. Mexican ice cream used to be both bad-tasting and of dubious safety, but national brands available in supermarkets are so much improved that it's no longer necessary to resist ice cream while in town.

In recent years, much cleaner public water and increased hygiene awareness has made salads—once shunned by Mexico travelers—generally safe to eat in tourist-frequented cafes and restaurants in the Puerto Vallarta region. Nevertheless, lettuce and cabbage, particularly in country villages, is more likely to be contaminated than tomatoes, carrots, cucumbers, onions, and green peppers. In any case, whenever in doubt, douse your salad in vinegar *(vinagre)* or plenty of sliced lime *(limón)* juice, the acidity of which kills bacteria.

Afflictions, Medications, and Immunizations

A good physician can recommend the proper preventatives for your Puerto Vallarta trip. If you are going to stay in town, your doctor may suggest little more than updating your basic typhoid, diphtheria-tetanus, and polio shots.

For sunburn protection, use a good sunscreen with a sun protection factor (SPF) of 15 or more, which will reduce burning rays to one-fifteenth or less of direct sunlight. Better still, take a shady siesta-break from the sun during the most hazardous midday hours. If you do get burned, applying your sunburn lotion (or one of the "caine" creams) after the fact usually decreases the pain and speeds healing.

For camping or trekking in remote tropical areas—below 4,000 feet or 1,200 meters—doctors often recommend a gamma-globulin shot against hepatitis A and a schedule of chloroquine pills against malaria. While in backcountry areas, use other measures to discourage mosquitoes—and fleas, flies, ticks, no-see-ums, "kissing bugs" (see below), and other tropical pesties—from biting you. Common precautions include sleeping under mosquito netting, burning *espirales mosquito* (mosquito coils), and rubbing on plenty of pure DEET (n,n dimethyl-meta-toluamide) "jungle juice," mixed in equal parts with rubbing (70% isopropyl) alcohol. Although supereffective, 100% DEET dries and irritates the skin.

Chagas' disease, spread by the "kissing" (or, more appropriately, "assassin") bug, is a potential hazard in the Mexican tropics. Known locally as a *vinchuca,* the triangular-headed, three-quarter-inch (two centimeter) brown insect, identifiable by its yellow-striped abdomen, often drops upon its sleeping victims from the thatched ceiling of a rural house at night. Its bite is followed by swelling, fever, and weakness and can lead to heart failure if left untreated. Application of drugs at an early stage can, however, clear the patient of the trypanosome parasites that infect victims' bloodstreams and vital organs. See a doctor immediately if you believe you're infected.

Also while camping or staying in a *palapa* or other rustic accommodation, watch for scorpions, especially in your shoes, which you should shake out every morning. Scorpion stings and snakebites are rarely fatal to an adult but are potentially very serious for a child. Get the victim to a doctor calmly but quickly. For more snakebite details, see "Reptiles and Amphibians" under "Flora and Fauna" in the general Introduction.

Injuries from Sea Creatures

While snorkeling or surfing, you may suffer a coral scratch or jellyfish sting. Experts advise you to wash the afflicted area with ocean water and pour alcohol (rubbing alcohol or tequila) over the wound, then apply hydrocortisone cream available from the *farmacia.*

Injuries from sea urchin spines and stingray barbs are painful and can be serious. Physicians recommend similar first aid for both: remove the spines or barbs by hand or with tweezers, then soak the injury in as-hot-as-possible fresh water to weaken the toxins and provide relief. Another method is to rinse the area with an antibacterial solution—rubbing alcohol, vinegar, wine, or ammonia diluted with water. If none are available, the same effect may be achieved with urine, either your own or someone else's in your party. Get medical help immediately.

First-Aid Kit

In the tropics, ordinary cuts and insect bites are more prone to infection and should receive immediate first aid. A first-aid kit with aspirin, rubbing alcohol, hydrogen peroxide, water-purifying tablets, household chlorine bleach or iodine for water purifying, swabs, Band-Aids, gauze, adhesive tape, Ace bandage, chamomile *("manzanilla")* tea bags for upset stomachs, Pepto-Bismol, acidophilus tablets, antibiotic ointment, hydrocortisone cream, mosquito repellent, knife, and good tweezers is a good precaution for any traveler and mandatory for campers.

Mexican Doctors

For medical advice and treatment, let your hotel, or if you're camping, the closest *farmacia,* refer you to a good doctor, clinic, or hospital. Mexican doctors, especially in medium-to-small towns, practice like private doctors in the U.S. and Canada once did before the onset of HMOs, liability, and group practice. They will come to you if you request; they often keep their doors open even after regular hours and charge very reasonable fees.

You will receive good treatment at the local hospitals in the Puerto Vallarta region's tourist

---

MEDICAL TAGS AND AIR EVACUATION

Travelers with special medical problems might consider wearing a medical identification tag. For a reasonable fee, **Medic Alert** (P.O. Box 1009, Turlock, CA 95381, tel. 800/344-3226) provides such tags, as well as an information hotline that will provide doctors with your vital medical background information.

For life-threatening emergencies, **Critical Air Medicine** (Montgomery Field, 4141 Kearny Villa Rd., San Diego, CA 92123, tel. 619/571-0482; from the U.S. toll-free 800/247-8326, from Mexico 24 hours toll-free 001-800/010-0268) provides high-tech jet ambulance service from any Mexican locale to the United States. For a fee averaging about $10,000, they promise to fly you to the right U.S. hospital in a hurry.

centers. If, however, you must have an English-speaking doctor, **IAMAT** (International Association for Medical Assistance to Travelers, 417 Center Street, Lewiston, NY 14092, tel. 716/754-4483, email: iamat@sentex.net; website: www.sentex.net/~iamat) maintains a worldwide network of English-speaking doctors. Some IAMAT medical groups practice in the Puerto Vallarta region. In Puerto Vallarta, contact Alfonso Rodríguez L., M.D., Hospital CMQ, at Av. B. Badillo 365, tel. 3/223-0011 or 222-5119; or John H. Mabrey, M.D., Rio Nilo 132, #8, Colonia Mariano Otero, cell phone 044 329/221-88. In Guadalajara, contact J. Jaime Rodríguez Parra, M.D., Tarascos 3514-14, Rinconada Santa Rita, tel. 3/813-0440, 813-0700, or 813-1025; or Robert A. Dumois, M.D., Francisco Zarco 2345, Colonia Ladron de Guevara, tel. 3/616-9616,

fax 615-9542, email: rdumois@infosel.net.mx.

For many more useful details of health and safety in Mexico, consult Dr. William Forgey's *Traveler's Medical Alert, Series 5, Mexico* (Merrillville, IN: ICS Books); or Dirk Schroeder's *Staying Healthy in Asia, Africa, and Latin America* (Emeryville, CA: Moon Travel Handbooks of Avalon Travel Publishing, 1999).

CONDUCT AND CUSTOMS

Safe Conduct

Behind its modern glitz, Mexico is an old-fashioned country where people value traditional ideals of honesty, fidelity, and piety. Violent crime rates are low; visitors are often safer in Mexico than in their home cities.

Even though four generations have elapsed

MACHISMO

I once met an Acapulco man who wore five gold wristwatches and became angry when I quietly refused his repeated invitations to get drunk with him. Another time, on the beach near San Blas, two drunk campesinos nearly attacked me because I was helping my girlfriend cook a picnic dinner. Outside Taxco I once spent an endless hour in the seat behind a bus driver who insisted on speeding down the middle of the two-lane highway, honking aside oncoming automobiles.

Despite their wide differences (the first was a rich criollo, the campesinos were *indígenas,* and the bus driver, mestizo), the common affliction shared by all four men was machismo, a disease that seems to possess many Mexican men. Machismo is a sometimes reckless obsession to prove one's masculinity, to show how macho you are. Men of many nationalities share the instinct to prove themselves. Japan's *bushido* samurai code is one example. Mexican men, however, often seem to try the hardest.

When confronted by a Mexican braggart, male visitors should remain careful and controlled. If your opponent is yelling, stay cool, speak softly, and withdraw as soon as possible. On the highway, be courteous and unprovocative; don't use your car to spar with a macho driver. Drinking often leads to problems. It's best to stay out of bars or cantinas unless you're prepared to deal with the macho consequences. Polite refusal of a drink may be taken as a

challenge. If you visit a bar with Mexican friends or acquaintances, you may be heading for a no-win choice of a drunken all-night *borrachera* (binge) or an insult to the honor of your friends by refusing.

For women, machismo requires even more cautious behavior. In Mexico, women's liberation is long in coming. Few women hold positions of power in business or politics. One woman, Rosa Luz Alegría, did attain the rank of minister of tourism during the former Portillo administration; she was the president's mistress.

Machismo requires that female visitors obey the rules or suffer the consequences. Keep a low profile; wear bathing suits and brief shorts only at the beach. Follow the example of your Mexican sisters: make a habit of going out, especially at night, in the company of friends or acquaintances. Mexican men believe an unaccompanied woman wants to be picked up. Ignore such offers; any response, even refusal, might be taken as a "maybe." If, on the other hand, there is a Mexican man whom you'd genuinely like to meet, the traditional way is an arranged introduction through family or friends.

Mexican families, as a source of protection and friendship, should not be overlooked—especially on the beach or in the park, where, among the gaggle of kids, grandparents, aunts, and cousins, there's room for one more.

since Pancho Villa raided the U.S. border, the image of a Mexico bristling with *bandidos* persists. And similarly for Mexicans: despite the century and a half since the *yanquis* invaded Mexico City and took half their country, the communal Mexican psyche still views gringos (and by association all white foreigners) with a combination of revulsion, envy, and awe.

Fortunately, the Mexican love-hate affair with foreigners in general does not necessarily apply to individual visitors. Your friendly *"Buenos días"* or courteous *"por favor"* are always appreciated. The shy smile you receive in return will be your not insignificant reward.

Women

Your own behavior, despite low crime statistics, largely determines your safety in Mexico. For women traveling solo, it is important to realize that the double standard is alive and well in Mexico. Dress and behave modestly and you will most likely avoid embarrassment. Whenever possible, stay in the company of friends or acquaintances; find companions for beach, sightseeing, and shopping excursions. Ignore strange men's solicitations and overtures. A Mexican man on the prowl will invent the sappiest romantic overtures to snare a gringa. He will often interpret anything but a firm "no" as a "maybe," and a "maybe" as a yes.

Men

For male visitors, alcohol often leads to trouble. Avoid bars and cantinas; and if, given Mexico's excellent beers, you can't abstain completely, at least maintain soft-spoken self-control in the face of challenges from macho drunks.

The Law and Police

While Mexican authorities are tolerant of alcohol, they are decidedly intolerant of other substances such as marijuana, psychedelics, cocaine, and heroin. Getting caught with such drugs in Mexico usually leads to swift and severe results.

Equally swift is the punishment for nude sunbathing, which is both illegal in public and offensive to Mexicans. Confine your nudist colony to very private locations.

Traffic police around the Puerto Vallarta resorts watch foreign cars with eagle eyes. Officers seem to inhabit busy intersections and

one-way streets, waiting for confused tourists to make a wrong move. If they whistle you over, stop immediately or you will really get into hot water. If guilty, say *"Lo siento"* ("I'm sorry") and be cooperative. Although he probably won't mention it, the officer is usually hoping that you'll cough up a $20 *mordida* (bribe) for the privilege of driving away.

Don't do it. Although he may hint at confiscating your car, calmly ask for an official *boleto* (written traffic ticket, if you're guilty) in exchange for your driver's license (have a copy), which the officer will probably keep if he writes a ticket. If after a few minutes no money appears, the officer will most likely give you back your driver's license rather than go to the trouble of writing the ticket. If not, the worst that will usually happen is you will have to go to the *presidencia municipal* (city hall) the next morning and pay the $20 to a clerk in exchange for your driver's license.

Pedestrian and Driving Hazards

Although the Puerto Vallarta region's many rutted pavements and "holey" sidewalks won't land you in jail, one of them might send you to the hospital if you don't watch your step, especially at night. "Pedestrian beware" is especially good advice on Mexican streets, where it is rumored that some drivers speed up rather than slow down when they spot a tourist stepping off the curb. Falling coconuts, especially frequent on windy days, constitute an additional hazard to unwary campers and beachgoers.

Driving Mexican country roads, where slow trucks and carts block lanes, campesinos stroll the shoulders, and horses, burros, and cattle wander at will, is hazardous—doubly so at night.

Socially Responsible Travel

Latter-day jet travel has brought droves of vacationing tourists to developing countries largely unprepared for the consequences. As the visitors' numbers swell, power grids black out, sewers overflow, and roads crack under the strain of accommodating more and larger hotels, restaurants, cars, buses, and airports.

Worse yet, armies of vacationers drive up local prices and begin to change native customs. While visions of tourists as sources of fast money replace traditions of hospitality, television wipes out folk entertainments, Coke and Pepsi substitute for fruit drinks, and prostitution and drugs flourish.

Some travelers have said enough is enough and are forming organizations to encourage visitors to travel with increased sensitivity to native people and customs. They have developed travelers' codes of ethics and guidelines that encourage visitors to stay at local-style accommodations, use local transportation, and seek alternative vacations and tours, such as language-study and cultural programs and people-to-people work projects.

SPECIALTY TRAVEL

Bringing the Kids

Children are treasured like gifts from heaven in Mexico. Traveling with kids will ensure your welcome most everywhere. On the beach, take extra precautions to make sure they are protected from the sun.

A sick child is no fun for anyone. Fortunately, clinics and good doctors are available even in small towns. When in need, ask a storekeeper or a pharmacist, *¿Dónde hay un doctor, por favor?"* (¿DOHN-day eye oon doc-TOHR por fah-VOHR?"). In most cases, within five minutes you will be in the waiting room of the local physician or hospital.

Children who do not favor typical Mexican fare can easily be fed with always available eggs, cheese, *hamburguesas,* milk, oatmeal, corn flakes, bananas, cakes, and cookies.

Your children will generally have more fun if they have a little previous knowledge of Mexico and a stake in the trip. For example, help them select some library picture books and magazines so they'll know where they're going and what to expect; or give them responsibility for packing and carrying their own small travel bag.

Be sure to mention your children's ages when making air reservations; child discounts of 50 percent or more are often available. Also, if you can arrange to go on an uncrowded flight, you can stretch out and rest on the empty seats.

For more details on traveling with children, check out *Adventuring With Children* by Nan Jeffries. (See Suggested Reading.)

Travel for the Handicapped

Mexican airlines and hotels are becoming increasingly aware of the needs of handicapped travelers. Open, street-level lobbies and large, wheelchair-accessible elevators and rooms are available in most Puerto Vallarta resort hotels.

U.S. law forbids travel discrimination against otherwise qualified handicapped persons. As long as your handicap is stable and not liable to deteriorate during passage, you can expect to be treated like any passenger with special needs.

Make reservations far ahead of departure and ask your agent to inform your airline of your needs, such as boarding wheelchair or in-flight oxygen. Be early at the gate in order to take advantage of the pre-boarding call.

For many helpful details to smooth your trip, get a copy of *Traveling Like Everyone Else: A Practical Guide for Disabled Travelers* by Jacqueline Freeman and Susan Gerstein. It's now out of print but hopefully will soon be available at bookstores or from the publisher (Lambda Publishing, Inc., 3709 13th Ave., Brooklyn, NY 11218, tel. 718/972-5449.) Also useful is the book *The Wheelchair Traveler,* by Douglas R. Annand. Yet another helpful publication is the *The Air Carrier Access Act: Make it Work For You,* by the Paralyzed Veterans of America; call toll-free 888/860-7244.

Certain organizations both encourage and provide information about handicapped travel. One with many Mexican connections is **Mobility International USA** (P.O. Box 10767, Eugene, OR 97440, tel. 541/343-1284 voice/TDD, fax 541/343-6812, website: www.miusa.org). A $35 membership gets you a semi-annual newsletter and referrals for international exchanges and homestays.

Similarly, **Partners of the Americas** (1424 K St. NW, Suite 700, Washington, D.C. 20005, tel. 800/322-7844 and 202/628-3300), with chapters in 45 U.S. states, works to improve handicapped understanding and facilities in Mexico and Latin America. They maintain lists of local organizations and individuals whom handicapped travelers may contact at their destinations.

Travel for Senior Citizens

Age, according to Mark Twain, is a question of mind over matter: If you don't mind, it doesn't matter. Mexico is a country where whole extended families, from babies to great-grandparents, live together. Elderly travelers will benefit from the respect and understanding Mexicans accord to older people. Besides these encouragements, consider the number of retirees already in havens in Puerto Vallarta, Guadalajara, Lake Chapala, and other regional centers.

Certain organizations support senior travel. Leading the field is **Elderhostel** (75 Federal St., 3rd Fl., Boston, MA 02110-1941, tel. 877/426-8056. website: www.elderhostel.org), which publishes extensive U.S. and international catalogs of special tours, study, homestays, and people-to-people travel programs.

A number of newsletters publicize Puerto Vallarta region vacation and retirement opportunities. Among the best is *Adventures in Mexico,* published six times yearly and filled with pithy hotel, restaurant, touring, and real estate information for independent travelers and retirees seeking the "real" Mexico. For information, address Adventures in Mexico, P.O. Box 31–70, Guadalajara, Jalisco 45050, Mexico. Back issues are $2; one-year subscription $16, Canadian $19.

Several books and newsletters publicize senior travel opportunities in general. *Mature Traveler* is a lively, professional-quality newsletter featuring money-saving tips, discounts, and tours for over-50 active senior and handicapped travelers. Individual copies are $3, a one-year subscription $31.95. Editor Adele Mallot has compiled years of past newsletters and experience into the *Book of Deals,* a 150-page travel tip and opportunity book, which sells for $7.95, plus postage and handling. Order, with a credit card, by calling toll-free 800/460-6676, local number 916/923-6346, or writing John Stickler Publishing Group, P.O. Box 15791, Sacramento, CA 95852. Another good buy is the pamphlet *Complete Guide to Discounts for Travellers 50 and Beyond* and the book *Special Report for Discount Travelers,* which list a plethora of hotel, travel club, cruise, air, credit card, single, and off-season discounts. (Order them for $6 and $17 respectively, from Vacation Publications, Inc., 1502 Augusta, Suite 415, Houston, TX 77057, tel. 713/974-6903, www.vacationsmagazine.com).

WHAT TO TAKE

"Men wear pants, ladies be beautiful," once the dress code of one of the Puerto Vallarta region's classiest hotels, is still good advice. Men in casual Puerto Vallarta can get by easily without a jacket, women with simple skirts and blouses.

Loose-fitting, hand-washable, easy-to-dry clothes make for trouble-free tropical vacationing. Synthetic or cotton-synthetic-blend shirts, blouses, pants, socks, and underwear will fit the bill everywhere in the coastal Puerto Vallarta region. For breezy nights, bring a lightweight windbreaker. If you're going to the highlands (Guadalajara, San Sebastián-Mascota-Talpa, or Tepic), add a medium-weight jacket.

In all cases, leave showy, expensive clothes and jewelry at home. Stow items that you cannot lose in your hotel safe or carry them with you in a sturdy zipped purse or a waist pouch on your front side.

Packing

What you pack depends on how mobile you want to be. If you're staying the whole time at a self-contained resort you can take the two suitcases and one carry-on allowed by airlines. If, on the other hand, you're going to be moving around a lot, best condense everything down to one easily carried bag with wheels that doubles as luggage and soft backpack. Experienced travelers accomplish this by packing prudently and tightly, choosing items that will do double or triple duty (such as a Swiss army knife with scissors).

Campers will have to be super-careful to accomplish this. Fortunately, camping along the tropical coast requires no sleeping bag. Simply use a hammock (buy it in Mexico) or, if sleeping on the ground, a sleeping pad and a sheet for cover. In the winter, at most, you may have to buy a light blanket. A compact tent that you and your partner can share is a must against bugs, as is mosquito repellent. A first-aid kit is absolutely necessary (see "Staying Healthy," earlier in the chapter).

PACKING CHECKLIST

Necessary Items

- ☐ camera, film (expensive in Mexico)
- ☐ clothes, hat
- ☐ comb
- ☐ guidebook, reading books
- ☐ inexpensive watch, clock
- ☐ keys, tickets
- ☐ mosquito repellent
- ☐ passport
- ☐ prescription eyeglasses
- ☐ prescription medicines and drugs
- ☐ purse, waist-belt carrying pouch
- ☐ sunglasses
- ☐ sunscreen
- ☐ swimsuit
- ☐ toothbrush, toothpaste
- ☐ tourist card, visa
- ☐ traveler's checks, money
- ☐ windbreaker

Useful Items

- ☐ address book
- ☐ birth control
- ☐ checkbook, credit cards
- ☐ contact lenses
- ☐ dental floss
- ☐ earplugs
- ☐ first-aid kit
- ☐ flashlight, batteries
- ☐ immersion heater
- ☐ lightweight binoculars
- ☐ portable radio/cassette player
- ☐ razor
- ☐ travel booklight
- ☐ vaccination certificate

Necessary Items for Campers

- ☐ collapsible gallon plastic bottle
- ☐ dish soap
- ☐ first-aid kit
- ☐ hammock (buy in Mexico)
- ☐ insect repellent
- ☐ lightweight hiking shoes
- ☐ lightweight tent
- ☐ matches in waterproof case
- ☐ nylon cord
- ☐ plastic bottle, quart
- ☐ pot scrubber/sponge
- ☐ sheet or light blanket
- ☐ Sierra Club cup, fork, and spoon
- ☐ single-burner stove with fuel
- ☐ Swiss army knife
- ☐ tarp
- ☐ toilet paper
- ☐ towel, soap
- ☐ two nesting cooking pots
- ☐ water-purifying tablets or iodine

Useful Items for Campers

- ☐ compass
- ☐ dishcloths
- ☐ hot pad
- ☐ instant coffee, tea, sugar, powdered milk
- ☐ moleskin (Dr. Scholl's)
- ☐ plastic plate
- ☐ poncho
- ☐ short candles
- ☐ whistle

PUERTO VALLARTA: TOWN, BAY, AND MOUNTAINS

PUERTO VALLARTA

The town of Puerto Vallarta (pop. 300,000) perches at the most tranquil recess of one of the Pacific Ocean's largest, deepest bays, the Bay of Banderas. The bay's many blessings—golden beaches, sparkling sunshine, blue waters, and the seafood that they nurture—are magnets for a million seasonal visitors.

Visitors find that Puerto Vallarta is really two cities in one—a new town strung along the hotel strip on its northern beaches, and an old town nestled beneath jungly hills on both sides of a small river, the Río Cuale. Travelers arriving from the north, whether by plane, bus, or car, see the new Puerto Vallarta first—a parade of luxury hotels, condominiums, apartments, and shopping centers. Visitors can stay for a month in a slick new Vallarta hotel, sun on the beach every day, disco every night, and return home, never having experienced the old Puerto Vallarta.

HISTORY

Before Columbus
For centuries prior to the arrival of the Spanish, the coastal region that includes present-day Puerto Vallarta was subject to the indigenous kingdom of Xalisco, centered near the modern Nayarit city of Xalisco. Founded around A.D. 600, the Xalisco civilization was ruled by chiefs who worshipped a trinity of gods: foremost, Naye, a legendary former chief elevated to a fierce god of war, followed by the more benign Teopiltzin, god of rain and fertility, and finally by wise Heri, the god of knowledge.

Recent archaeological evidence indicates another influence: the Aztecs, who probably left Nahuatl-speaking colonies along the southern Nayarit coastal valleys during their centuries-

PUERTO VALLARTA

HOTEL VELA VALLARTA

↑ To Airport, Punta Mita, Tepic, and Guadalajara

BOAT LAUNCHING RAMP

MARINA OFFICE
HOTEL PLAZA IGUANA
CLUB DE YATES
TACHO'S
AV. AMAPA
TP

HOTEL MARRIOTT
LOS PEINES
HOTEL ROYAL MAEVA
MOORING
HOTEL MELIA
HOTEL VIDAFEL
BULL RING LA PALOMA
HOTEL WESTIN REGINA
BASE NAVAL

Marina Vallarta

200

ADUANA
TERMINAL MARITIMA
PEMEX
MIGRACION

Río Pitillal

Playa de Oro
DISCO CHRISTINE
HOTEL HACIENDA BUENAVENTURA

HOTEL KRYSTAL

VILLA DEL PALMAR

QUALTON CLUB

BLV. FCO. M. ASCENCIO

HOTEL FIESTA AMERICANA PUERTO VALLARTA
RESTAURANT L' PETIT FRANCE
GIGANTE

Playa Los Tules
HOTEL PELICANOS
FRANCIA
AV. FCO. VILLA

HOTEL LAS PALMAS
HOTEL PLAZA LAS GLORIAS
TP
PUERTO VALLARTA
Playa Las Glorias
LUCERNA
HOTEL CONTINENTAL PLAZA

CAMARA DE COMERCIO
COMERCIAL MEXICANA

Bahía de Banderas

AV. DE LAS AMÉRICAS

HOTEL SHERATON

Playa Camarones
MEXICO
UNIDAD DEPORTIVA

HOTEL BUENAVENTURA
CINE LUZ MARIA
TERRA NOBLE

LIBRAMIENTO (BYPASS)
TUNNEL

SANATORIO VALLARTA
CINE LUZ MARÍA
HOTEL ROSITA

AV.

To Cuale Mine (20 mi, 32 km)

MALECON
Parque Hidalgo

PASEO DIAZ ORDAZ
PLAZA DE ARMAS
Isla Río Cuale

LAZARO CARDENAS

PLAZA L. CÁRDENAS
Playa los Muertos

VALLARTA
INSURGENTES

OLAS ALTAS

VENUSTIANO CARRANZA

Río Cuale

SEE "PUERTO VALLARTA DOWNTOWN" MAP

0   1 mi
0   1 km

Playa Conchas Chinas
HOTEL PLAYA CONCHAS CHINAS
200
↓ To Mismaloya and Manzanillo

long migration to the Valley of Mexico.

Conquest and Colonization

Some of those villages still remained when the Spanish conquistador Francisco Cortés de Buenaventura, nephew of Hernán Cortés, arrived on the Jalisco-Nayarit coast in 1524.

In a broad mountain-rimmed green valley, an army of 20,000 warriors, their bows decorated by myriad colored cotton banners, temporarily blocked the conquistador's path. So impressive was the assemblage that Cortés called the fertile vale of the Ameca River north of present Puerto Vallarta the Valle de las Banderas (Valley of the Banners), and thus the great bay later became known as the Bahía de Banderas.

The first certain record of the Bay of Banderas itself came from the log of conquistador Don Pedro de Alvarado, who sailed into the bay in 1541 and disembarked (probably at Mismaloya) near some massive sea rocks. He named these Las Peñas, undoubtedly the same as the present "Los Arcos" rocks that draw daily boatloads of snorkelers and divers.

For 300 years the Bay of Banderas slept under the sun. Galleons occasionally watered there; a few pirates hid in wait for them in its jungle-fringed coves.

Independence

The rebellion of 1810–21 freed Mexico, and finally, a generation later, the lure of gold and silver led, as with many of Mexico's cities, to the settlement of Puerto Vallarta. Enterprising merchant Don Guadalupe Sanchez made a fortune (ironically, not

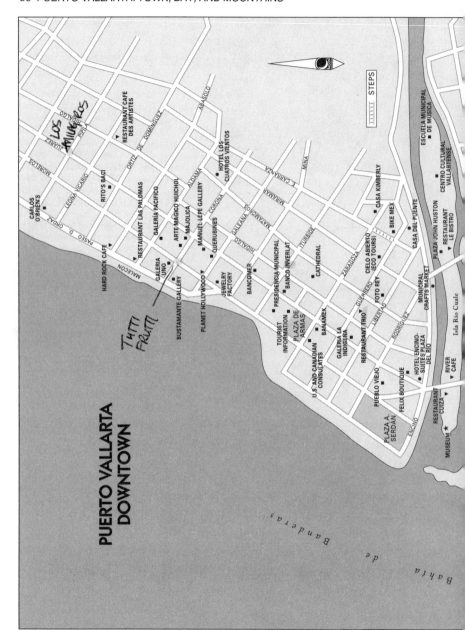

**PUERTO VALLARTA
DOWNTOWN**

Bahía de Banderas

RESTAURANT CAFE
DES ARTISTES

Los Muertos

HOTEL LOS
CUATROS VIENTOS

CARLOS
O'BRIEN'S

RITO'S BACI

GALERIA PACIFICO

ARTE MAGICO HUICHOL

MAJOLICA

MANUEL LEPE GALLERY

QUERUBINES

RESTAURANT LAS PALOMAS

HARD ROCK CAFE

GALERIA
UNO

CASA KIMBERLY

BIKE MEX

BUSTAMANTE GALLERY

Tutti Frutti

JEWELRY
FACTORY

BANCOMER

PLANET HOLLYWOOD

PRESIDENCIA MUNICIPAL

BANCO INVERLAT

CATHEDRAL

CASA DEL PUENTE

PLAZA JOHN HUSTON

RESTAURANT
LE BISTRO

TOURIST
INFORMATION

PLAZA DE
ARMAS

BANAMEX

CIELO ABIERTO
(ECO TOURS)

FOTO REY

MUNICIPAL
CRAFTS MARKET

U.S. AND CANADIAN
CONSULATES

GALERIA LA
INDIGENA

RESTAURANT TRIO

HOTEL ENCINO-
SUITES PLAZA
DEL RIO

Isla Río Cuale

PUEBLO VIEJO

FELIX BOUTIQUE

RIVER
CAFE

PLAZA A.
SERDAN

RESTAURANT
COIZA

MUSEUM

ESCUELA MUNICIPAL
DE MUSICA

CENTRO CULTURAL
VALLARTENSE

STEPS

ESCLA MUNICIPAL

CATRA

HIDALGO

GUERRERO

ZARAGOZA

MATAMOROS

CORONA

ALDAMA

ORTIZ

DE. DOMÍNGUEZ

ABASOLO

MINA

E. CARRANZA

MIRAMAR

GALEANA

ITURBIDE

LIBERTAD

RODRIGUEZ

MORELOS

JUAREZ

HIDALGO

PIPILA

LEONA VICARIO

PASEO D. OROZO

MALECON

ENCINO

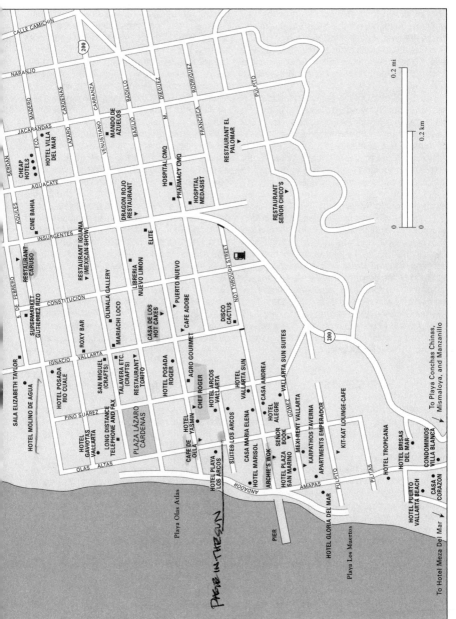

from gold, but from salt, for ore processing), which he hauled from the beach to the mines above the headwaters of the Río Cuale. In 1851 Don Guadalupe built a hut and brought his wife and children. Their tiny trading station grew into a little town, Puerto de Las Peñas, at the mouth of the river.

Later, the local government founded the present municipality, which, on May 31, 1918, officially became Puerto Vallarta, in honor of the celebrated jurist and former governor of Jalisco, Ignacio L. Vallarta.

However, the mines eventually petered out, and Puerto Vallarta, isolated, with no road to the outside world, slumbered again.

Modern Puerto Vallarta

But not for long. Passenger planes began arriving sporadically from Tepic and Guadalajara in the 1950s; a gravel road was pushed through from Tepic in the 1960s. The international airport was built, the highway was paved, and tourist hotels sprouted on the beaches. Meanwhile, in 1963, director John Huston, at the peak of his creative genius, arrived with Richard Burton, Elizabeth Taylor, Ava Gardner, and Deborah Kerr to film *Night of the Iguana*. Huston, Burton, and Taylor stayed on for years, waking Puerto Vallarta from its long slumber. It hasn't slept since.

SIGHTS

Getting Oriented

Puerto Vallarta is a long beach town, stretching about five miles from the Riviera-like Conchas Chinas condo headland at the south end. Next, heading north, comes the popular Playa Los Muertos beach and the intimate old Río Cuale neighborhood, which join, across the river, with the busy central *malecón* (seawall) shopping and restaurant (but beachless) bayfront. North of there, the beaches resume again at Playa Camarones and continue past the Zona Hotelera string of big resorts to the Marina complex, where tour boats and cruise liners depart from the Terminal Maritima dock. In the Marina's northern basin lie the Peines (pay-EE-nays) sportfishing and Club de Yates docks. A mile farther north, the city ends at the bustling International Airport.

One basic thoroughfare serves the entire beachfront. Officially, Búlevar Francisco Medina Ascencio, but commonly called the **Carretera Aeropuerto** (Airport Highway) as it conducts express traffic south past the Zona Hotelera, it changes names three times. Narrowing, it becomes the cobbled Av. México, then Paseo Díaz Ordaz along the seafront *malecón* with tourist restaurants, clubs, and shops, changing finally to Av. Morelos before it passes the Presidencia Municipal (city hall) and central plaza.

When southbound traffic reaches Isla Río Cuale, the tree-shaded, midstream island where the city's pioneers built their huts, traffic slows to a crawl and finally dissipates in the colorful old neighborhood on the south side of the river.

There being little traffic south of the Cuale, people walk everywhere, and slowly, because of the heat. Every morning men in sombreros lead burros down to the mouth of the river to gather sand. Little *papelerías, miscelaneas,* and streetside *taquerías* serve the local folks while small restaurants, hotels, and clubs serve the visitors.

Getting Around

Since nearly all through traffic flows along one thoroughfare, Puerto Vallarta transportation is a snap. Simply hop on one of the frequent (but usually crowded) city buses (fare 15–30 cents), virtually all of which end up at Plaza Lázaro Cárdenas on Av. Olas Altas a few blocks south of the river. Northbound, the same buses retrace the route through the Zona Hotelera to one of several destinations scrawled across their windows. Taxis, while much more convenient, are all individual and rather expensive (about $3–4 per trip within the city limits; don't get in until the price is settled).

Drivers who want to quickly travel between the north and the south ends of town often take the *libramiento* bypass (see the map "Puerto Vallarta") and avoid the crowded downtown traffic.

Car rentals, while expensive, are an efficient way of getting around locally, especially for independent out-of-town excursions north and south. Expect to pay about $40–50 a day for the cheapest rental, including legally required liability insurance. Cut the cost by sharing with others.

In Puerto Vallarta, the gang's all there: contact Avis, tel. 3/221-1112 or 221-1657, fax 3/221-1656; Budget, tel. 3/222-2980, fax 3/223-1120; Dollar, tel. 3/223-1354, fax 3/223-1434; Nation-

NIGHT OF THE IGUANA:
THE MAKING OF PUERTO VALLARTA

The idea to film Tennessee Williams's play *Night of the Iguana* in Puerto Vallarta was born in the bar of the Beverly Hills Hotel. In mid-1963, director John Huston, whose movies had earned a raft of Academy Awards, met with Guillermo Wulff, a Mexican architect and engineer. For the film's location Wulff proposed Mismaloya, an isolated cove south of Puerto Vallarta. On leased land, Wulff would build the movie set and cottages for staff housing, which he, Huston, and producer Ray Stark would later sell for a profit as tourist accommodations.

Most directors would have been scared away by the Mismaloya jungle, where they would find no roads, phones, or electricity. But, according to Alex Masden, one of Huston's biographers, Huston loved Mismaloya: "To me, *Night of the Iguana* was a picnic, a gathering of friends, a real vacation."

A "gathering of friends," indeed. The script required most of the cast to be dissolute, mentally ill, or both: A blonde nymphet tries to seduce an alcoholic defrocked minister while his dead friend's love-starved, hard-drinking widow keeps a clutch of vulturous biddies from destroying his last bit of self-respect—all while an iguana roped to a post passively awaits its slaughter.

Huston's casting was perfect. The actors simply played themselves. Richard Burton (the minister) came supplied with plenty of booze. Burton's lover, Elizabeth Taylor, who was not part of the cast and still married to singer Eddie Fisher, accompanied him. Sue Lyon (the nymphet) came with her lovesick boyfriend, whose wife was rooming with Sue's mother; Ava Gardner (the widow) became the toast of Puerto Vallarta while romping with her local beach paramour; Tennessee Williams, who was advising the director, came with his lover Freddy; while Deborah Kerr, who acted the only prim lead role, jokingly complained that she was the only one not having an affair.

With so many mercurial personalities isolated together in Mismaloya, the international press flew to Puerto Vallarta in droves to record the expected fireworks. Huston gave each of the six stars, as well as Elizabeth Taylor, a velvet-lined case containing a gold derringer with five bullets, each engraved with the names of the others. Unexpectedly, and partly due to Huston's considerable charm, none of the bullets were used. Bored by the lack of major explosions, the press corps discovered Puerto Vallarta instead.

As Huston explained later to writer Lawrence Grobel: "That was the beginning of its popularity, which was a mixed blessing." Huston nevertheless returned to the area and built a home on the Bay of Banderas, where he lived the last 11 years of his life. Burton and Taylor bought Puerto Vallarta houses, got married, and also stayed for years. Although his Mismaloya tourist accommodations scheme never panned out, Guillermo Wulff became wealthy building for the rich and famous many of the houses and condominiums that now dot Puerto Vallarta's jungly hillsides and golden beaches.

---

al, tel. 3/209-0356, fax 3/209-0337; and Advantage, tel. 3/221-1809 or 3/221-1499, fax 3/221-1849. You might also save money with an air-car package or by reserving a discount (ask for AARP, AAA, senior, airline, credit card, or other) rental car before you leave for Mexico.

A Walk along Isla Cuale
Start at the **Museo Río Cuale,** a joint government-volunteer effort near the very downstream tip of Isla Río Cuale. Inside is a small but fine collection of paintings by local artists as well as locally excavated pre-Columbian artifacts (open Tues.–Sun. 10 A.M.–2 P.M. and 4–7 P.M., no phone).

Head upstream beneath the bridge and enjoy the shady *paseo* of shops and restaurants. For fun, stroll out on one of the two quaint suspension bridges over the river. Evenings, these are the coolest spots in Puerto Vallarta. A river of cool night air often funnels down the Cuale valley, creating a refreshing breeze along the length of the clear, tree-draped stream.

The **Río Cuale** was not always so clean. Once upon a time, a few dozen foreign residents, tired of looking down upon the littered riverbank, came out one Sunday and began hauling trash from the riverbed. Embarrassed by the example, a neighborhood crowd pitched in. The river has been clean ever since.

Farther upstream, on the adjacent riverbank, stands the **Mercado Municipal Río Cuale,** a honeycomb of stalls stuffed with crafts from all over Mexico. Continue past the upriver (Av. Insurgentes) bridge to **Plaza John Huston,** marked by a smiling bronze likeness of the renowned Hollywood director who helped put Puerto Vallarta on the map with his filming of Tennessee Williams's *Night of the Iguana* in 1963.

About 50 yards farther on, stop in at the small gallery of the **Centro Cultural Vallartense,** a volunteer organization that conducts art classes, sponsors shows of promising artists, and sometimes invites local artists to meet the public and interested amateurs for informal instruction and idea exchange. Ask the volunteer on duty for more information or see the community events listings in *Vallarta Today,* the local English-language community newspaper.

A few more steps upstream, at a small plaza, stands the round stucco headquarters and practice room of the **Escuela Municipal de Musica.** On the left side are the classrooms of the **Instituto de Allende.** They, along with the Centro Cultural Vallartense, offer courses to the general public. See "Arts and Music Courses," following.

At the boulder-strewn far upstream point of the island, a cadre of women wash clothes. Many of them are professionals who practice their craft on special rocks, perfectly positioned for a day of productive washing. Their clean handiwork stretches out to dry—on rocks, on grass, on bushes—in rainbow arrays beneath the sun.

Gringo Gulch

The steep, villa-dotted hillside above the island's upper end is called Gringo Gulch, for the colony of rich *norteamericanos* who own big homes there. It's an interesting place for a stroll.

Get there by heading downstream, back over the Insurgentes bridge. Turn north, toward the center of town. After the bridge, bear right to the end of one-block Calle Emilio Carranza and continue up a steep, bougainvillea-festooned staircase to Calle Zaragoza one block above.

At the corner of Zaragoza and the upper level of Emilio Carranza, you are at the gateway to Gringo Gulch. Wander through the winding, hillside lanes and enjoy the picturesque scenes that seem to appear around each rickety-chic corner. For example, note the luxurious *palapas* perched atop the tall villa on Carranza, half a block above Zaragoza.

During your meanderings, don't miss the Gringo Gulch centerpiece mansion at Zaragoza 446, once owned by Elizabeth Taylor. (You'll scarcely be able to miss it, for it has a pink passageway arching over the street.) The house was a gift to Taylor from Richard Burton. After they were married, they also bought the house on the other side of Zaragoza, renovated it, and built a pool; thus the passageway became nec-

A bronze likeness of John Huston, the celebrated director of Night of the Iguana, *presides benignly over Huston's namesake plaza on Isla Río Cuale.*

essary. The house across the street, no. 446, is now the **Casa Kimberly,** a private Elizabeth Taylor-Richard Burton museum, which offers public tours for about $6 per person. Call 3/222-1336 for details.

The **Club Internacional de la Amistad** (Friendship Club) conducts seasonal tours through some of Puerto Vallarta's showplace homes, beginning at the central plaza around 11 A.M. Look for announcement posters or community events listings in *Vallarta Today* or call 3/222-1336. (See "Volunteer Work" under "Information," later in this chapter.)

On the *Malecón*

Head back down Zaragoza, and let the church belfry be your guide. Named **La Parroquia de Nuestra Señora de Guadalupe,** for the city's patron saint, the church is relatively new (1951) and undistinguished except for the very unusual huge crown atop the tower. Curiously, it was modeled after the crown of the tragic 19th-century Empress Carlota, who went insane after her husband was executed. On the church steps, a native woman frequently sells textiles, which she weaves on the spot with a traditional backstrap loom (in Spanish, *tela de otate,* loom of bamboo, from the Nahuatl *otlatl,* bamboo).

Continue down Zaragoza past the Presidencia Municipal at one side of the central Plaza de Armas, straight toward Los Arcos (The Arches), right at the water's edge. They form a backdrop for frequent free weekend evening music and dance performances. From there, the *malecón* seawall-walkway stretches north toward the Zona Hotelera hotels, which you can see along the curving northern beachfront.

The *malecón* marks the bay's innermost point. From there the shoreline stretches and curves westerly many miles on both sides, adorned by dozens of sandy beaches until it reaches its wave-washed extremities at Punta Mita (on the distant horizon, at the bay's northwest extremity) and Punta La Iglesia to the far southwest.

Terra Noble

The dreamchild of owner Jorge Rubio, Terra Noble, on a vista hilltop above the middle of town, is at least unique and at best exhilarating. It's a New-Age style retreat, spreading downhill over a breathtakingly scenic tropical deciduous forested hillside, at the western edge of the big Agua Azul Nature Reserve hinterland. The headquarters building is a latter-day interpretation of a traditional Mexican stick-and-mud wattle house. The inside view, of curving ceilings and passageways dotted with round window-holes, leaves the impression of the interior of a huge hunk of Swiss cheese. For more architectural details, see the Terra Noble feature story in *Architectural Digest,* July 1996.

Besides its singular building and park-like grounds, Terra Noble is a serious healing center, featuring massage ($50 per hour), or an all-day treatment ($150), including massage, a sauna-like *temascal* sweat bath and shamanistic ceremony, tarot reading, and more. It also offers day sculpture and painting workshops.

Regardless of whether you get the full treatment or not, Terra Noble would be worth a visit, if for nothing more than a look around and a picnic. (Bring your own food.) It's generally open daily 8 A.M.–3 P.M.; admission is about $5. Contact Terra Noble ahead of time, tel. 3/223-3530 or 3/222-5400, fax 3/222-4058, email: shanti-hc@prodigy.com, to verify hours. Get there by car, taxi, or any local bus that follows the bypass *(libramiento)* through the hills east of town. Follow the side road, signed "Par Vial Zona Centro," about 100 yards south of the summit tunnel (not the tunnel at the south end), on the west (ocean) side of the *libramiento.* After about a half mile, curving uphill, you'll see the Terra Noble entrance sign on the view side of the road.

BEACHES

Playa los Muertos

Generations ago, when Puerto Vallarta was a small, isolated town, there was only one beach, Playa los Muertos, the strand of yellow sand that stretches for a mile south of the Cuale River. Old-timers still remember the Sundays and holidays when it seemed as if half the families in Puerto Vallarta had come south of the Río Cuale, to Los Muertos Beach especially, to play in the surf and sand.

This is still largely true, although now droves of winter-season North American vacationers and residents have joined them. Fortunately, Playa los Muertos is much cleaner than during the polluted 1980s. The fish are coming back, as evidenced by the flocks of diving pelicans and the crowd of folks who drop lines every day from the **New Pier** (foot of Francisca Rodriguez).

Fishing is even better off the rocks on the south end of the beach. *Lisa* (mullet), *sierra* (mackerel), *pargo* (snapper), and *torito* are commonly caught anywhere along close-in beaches. On certain unpredictable occasions, fish (and one memorable time even giant 30-pound squids) swarm offshore in such abundance that anyone can pick them out of the water barehanded.

Gentle waves and lack of undertow make Playa Los Muertos generally safe for wading and good for swimming beyond the close-in breakers. The same breakers, however, eliminate Los Muertos for bodysurfing, boogie boarding, or surfing (except occasionally at the far south end).

Playas Conchas Chinas

Playa Conchas Chinas (Chinese, or "Curly," Shells Beach) is not one beach but a series of small sandy coves dotted by rocky outcroppings beneath the condo-clogged hillside that extends for about a mile south of Playa los Muertos. A number of streets and driveways lead to the beach from the Manzanillo Hwy. 200 (the extension of Insurgentes) south of town. Drive, taxi, or ride one of the many the minibuses marked "Mismaloya" or "Boca" that leave from Calle Basilio Badillo, just below Insurgentes, or hike along the tidepools from Los Muertos Beach.

Fishing off the rocks is good here; the water is even clear enough for some snorkeling. Bring your gear, however, as there's none for rent. The usually gentle waves, however, make any kind of surfing very doubtful.

Beach Exploring

Beach lovers can spend many enjoyable days poking around the many little beaches south of town. Drive, taxi, or take a Mismaloya- or Boca-marked minibus from Plaza Lázaro Cárdenas.

Just watch out the window, and when you see a likely spot, ask the driver to stop. Say *"Pare* (PAH-ray) *por favor."* The location will most likely be one of several lovely *playas:* **El Gato** (Cat), **Los Venados** (Deers), **Los Carrizos** (Reeds), **Punta Negra** (Black Point), **Garza Blanca** (White Heron), or **Gemelas** (Twins).

Although many of these little sand crescents have big hotels and condos, it doesn't matter because beaches are public in Mexico up to the high-tide line. There is always some path to the beach used by local folks. Just ask *"¿Donde está el camino* (road, path) *a la playa?"* and someone will probably point the way.

Mismaloya and Los Arcos

If you ride all the way to Playa Mismaloya, you will not be disappointed, despite the oversized

Los Arcos rocks, south of town at Mismaloya, became Puerto Vallarta's first recorded landmarks when conquistador Pedro Alvarado entered them into his log in 1541.

Hotel Mismaloya crowding the beach. Follow the dirt road just past the hotel to the intimate little curve of sand and lagoon where the cool, clear Mismaloya stream meets the sea. A rainbow array of fishing *lanchas* lie beached around the lagoon's edges, in front of a line of beachside *palapa* restaurants.

Continue a few hundred yards past the *palapas* to the ruins of the movie set of the *Night of the Iguana*. Besides being built for the actual filming, the rooms behind those now-crumbling stucco walls served as lodging, dining, and working quarters for the dozens of crew members who camped here for those eight busy months in 1963.

North, offshore beyond the Mismaloya cove, rise the green-brushed **Los Arcos** sea rocks, a federal underwater park and eco-preserve. The name comes from the arching grottoes that channel completely through the bases of some of the rocks. Los Arcos is one of the best snorkeling grounds around Puerto Vallarta. Get there by hiring a glass-bottomed boat in the lagoon.

Snorkeling near the wave-washed Los Arcos is a Puerto Vallarta "must do." Swirling bunches of green algae and branching ruddy corals attract schools of grazing parrot, angel, butterfly, and goat fish. Curious pencil-thin cornet fish may sniff you out as they pass, while big croakers and sturgeon will slowly drift, scavenging along the coral-littered depths.

Fishing, especially casting from the rocks beneath the movie set, and every other kind of beach activity are good at Mismaloya, except surfing and boogie boarding, for which the waves are generally too gentle.

Stop for food (big fish fillet plate, any style, with all the trimmings, $6, or breakfast eggs from their own hens) or a drink at the **Restaurant Las Gaviotas** *palapas* across the river.

Alternatively, for food and nostalgia, go to the viewpoint **John Huston Cafe** or the neighboring showplace **Night of the Iguana Restaurant,** off the highway, ocean side, on Mismaloya Bay's south headland. Both are open daily—the restaurant for breakfast, lunch, and dinner, the cafe for lunch and dinner. Both are designed around the Night of the Iguana legend, replete with old Hollywood photos and mementos and a daily video screening of the original *Night of the Iguana* film at the restaurant.

For still another treat, visit ne[...]
Paradise. Follow the riverside l[...] forks upstream at the north end of the [...] across the road from the hotel. Arrive in the late morning (around 11) or late afternoon (around 3) to avoid the tour-bus rush. Chino's streamside *palapas* nestle like big mushrooms on a jungle hillside above a cool, cascading creek. Adventurous guests enjoy sliding down the cascades (be careful—some have injured themselves seriously), while others content themselves with lying in the sun or lolling in sandy-bottomed, clear pools. Beneath the *palapas,* they serve respectable but uninspired seafood and steak plates and Mexican *antojitos.* Open daily 11 A.M.–5 P.M.

For a more rustic alternative, follow the road another mile uphill to **El Eden,** a jungle swimming hole, complete with food *palapas,* a natural pool, and Tarzan-style rope swing; open daily until about 5 P.M.

Beaches Farther South

Three miles south of Mismaloya is **Boca de Tomatlán,** a tranquil country village, overlooking a broad strip of yellow sand bordering a petite, blue bay. *Palapa* restaurants supply enough food and shade for days of easy relaxation.

If you decide to linger, contact **Agustín Bas,** a personable, English-speaking Argentinian expatriate who provides lodging in his gorgeous two-bedroom, three-bath jungle hillside **Casa Tango.** Tariffs run about $450 weekly for four, including airport pickup. Contact him at his Puerto Vallarta office, tel. 3/228-0057, email: vallarta@casatango.com, website: www.casatango.com.

You can continue by *colectivo* water taxi (about $3 per person) to the pristine paradises of Las Animas, Quimixto, and Yelapa farther south. **Las Animas** has seafood *palapas,* an idyllic beach, and snorkeling; the same is true for **Quimixto,** which also has a waterfall nearby for splashing.

Yelapa, a settlement nestled beneath verdant, palm-crowned hills beside an aquamarine cove, is home for perhaps a hundred local families and a small colony of foreign expatriates. For visitors, it offers a glimpse of South Seas life as it was before the automobile. Accessible only by sea, Yelapa's residents get around on foot norseback. A waterfall cascades through the tropical forest above the village, and a string of *palapa* restaurants lines the beach. Lodging is available in the *palapa*-roofed cabanas of the rustic **Hotel Lagunita**. Rooms run about $35 d low season, $65 high, and, although generally not necessary, you can reserve by calling its agent at 329/805-54, email: hotellagunita@prodigy.com.mx, website: www.hotellagunita.com.mx.

North-End (Zona Hotelera) Beaches

These are Puerto Vallarta's cleanest, least-crowded in-town beaches, despite the many hotels that line them. Beginning at the Hotel Rosita at the north end of the *malecón,* **Playas Camarones, Las Glorias, Los Tules,** and **de Oro** form a continuous three-mile strand to the Marina. Stubby rock jetties about every quarter-mile have succeeded in retaining a 50-yard-wide strip of golden-cream sand most of the way.

The sand is midway between coarse and fine; the waves are gentle, breaking right at the water's edge; and the ocean past the breakers is relatively clear (10- or 20-feet visibility) and blue. Stormy weather occasionally dredges up clam, cockle, limpet, oyster, and other shells from the offshore depths.

Fishing by pole, net, or simply line is common along here. Surfing, bodysurfing, and boogie boarding, however, are not. All other beach sports, especially the high-powered variety, are available at nearly every hotel along the strand (see "Sports and Recreation," later in this chapter).

Farther north, along the shore past the Maritime Terminal-Marina Harbor entrance, the beach narrows to a seasonally rocky strip at the oceanfronts of a row of big resort hotels.

Beach Hikes

A pair of good close-in hikes are possible. For either of them, don't forget a sun hat, sunscreen, bug repellent, a shirt, and some light shoes. On the south side, walk from Playa los Muertos about a mile and a half along the little beaches and tidepools to Playa Conchas Chinas. Start at either end and take half a day swimming, snorkeling, sunning, and poking among the rocks.

More ambitiously, you can hike the entire three-mile beach strip from the northern end of the *malecón* to the Marina. If you start by nine

you'll enjoy the cool of the morning with the sun at your back. Stop along the way at the show-place pools and beach restaurants of hotels such as the Sheraton, the Plaza Las Glorias, the Fiesta Americana Vallarta, and Krystal. Walk back, or opt for a return by taxi or city bus.

WATER TAXIS AND DAY CRUISES

Puerto Vallarta visitors can also reach the little southern beaches of Quimixto, Las Animas and Yelapa from Puerto Vallarta itself. You have two options: fast water taxis or one of several all-day tourist cruises. The water taxis, which allow you more time at your destination, customarily leave the Playa los Muertos New Pier twice in the morning, usually at about 10:30 and 11 A.M., (returning at 4 P.M.) and once in the afternoon, at about 4 P.M., for those staying overnight. The morning departures allow about three hours for lunch and swimming at either the Quimixto or Yelapa waterfalls. The roundtrip tariff runs about $17.

The more leisurely tourist cruises leave around 9 A.M. (return by 4 P.M.) from the dock at the Puerto Vallarta Maritime Terminal. They also customarily pick up additional passengers at the New Pier on Playa los Muertos downtown.

One of the most popular of these excursions is aboard the big *Princess Yelapa,* a tripled-decked white steel tub with room for hundreds. The route follows the coastline, stopping at Los Arcos for snorkeling, and continues for Las Animas and Quimixto. At Quimixto, passengers disembark for a few hours, just long enough for the short waterfall hike (or by horseback, if desired) and lunch at a beach *palapa.* The package includes breakfast, lunch, and no-host bar for about $40 per person.

Princess Cruises also runs the *Sarape,* a sailboat accommodating around 30, for snorkeling at Los Arcos, continuing to Yelapa for a hike (or horseback ride) and swimming at the waterfall. Open bar, live music, and lunch are included, for about $40 per person.

For romantics, the *Princess Vallarta,* a scaled-down version of the *Princess Yelapa,* offers a 6:30–9 P.M. sunset cruise, with snacks, open bar, and live music for dancing, for about $30 per person.

For information and reservations for all of the above cruises and more, contact a travel agent, your hotel tour desk, or the Princess Cruises directly at 3/224-4777 or email: crucerosprincesa@pvnet.com.mx.

If you tend toward seasickness, fortify yourself with Dramamine before these cruises. Destination disembarkation at Las Animas, Quimixto, and Yelapa is by motor launch and can be difficult for the physically handicapped.

ACCOMMODATIONS

In Puerto Vallarta you can get any type of lodging you want at nearly any price. The location sets the tone, however. The relaxed, relatively tranquil but interesting neighborhood south of the Río Cuale (especially around Av. Olas Altas) has many budget and moderately priced hotels, apartments, and condos within easy walking distance of restaurants, shopping, and services. Many of them are very close, if not right on, lively Playa los Muertos. While no strict dividing line separates the types of available lodgings, hotels (listed first, below) generally offer rooms with maximum service (desk, daily cleaning, restaurant, pool) without kitchens for shorter-term guests, while apartments and condos virtually always offer multiple-room furnished kitchen units for greatly reduced per diem rates for longer term rentals. If you're staying more than two weeks, you'll save money and also enjoy more of the comforts of home in a good apartment or condo rental.

Hotels—Río Cuale and South

Although landmark **Hotel Molino de Agua** (Water Mill), located at the corner of Ignacio Vallarta and Aquiles Serdán, Puerto Vallarta 48380, tel. 3/222-1957, fax 3/222-6056, email: molino@acnet.net, occupies two riverfront blocks right on the beach, many visitors miss it completely. Its very tranquil colony of rustic-chic cabanas hides in a jungle-garden of cackling parrots, giant-leafed vines, and gigantic, spreading trees. Most of the cabanas are at ground level and unfortunately don't feel very private inside unless you close the shutters—which seems a shame in a tropical garden. The very popular beachside upstairs units remedy this dilemma.

The hotel's 40 garden rooms rent for about $75 d low season, $108 high, while the upstairs beachside rooms go for about $125 d low season, $170 high season; amenities include two pools, restaurant, a/c, credit cards accepted.

Adjacent to the Hotel Molino de Agua, as you head south, away from the river, at the corner of I. Vallarta and A. Serdán, the diminutive **Hotel Posada Río Cuale** packs a lot of hotel into a small space. Find it at Av. Aquiles Serdán 242, P.O. Box 146, Puerto Vallarta 48300, tel./fax 3/222-0450, 3/222-1148, or 3/222-0914, email: legourmet@go2mexico.com. Good management is the key to this picturesque warren of rooms that clusters beside its good restaurant/bar and a small but pleasant pool and patio. Tasteful brown and brick decor makes the rooms somewhat dark, especially on the ground floor. Artful lighting, however, improves this. Unless you like diesel-bus noise, try to avoid getting a room on the busy Av. Vallarta side of the hotel. The 41 a/c rooms rent for about $38 d low season, about $46 high season; credit cards are accepted.

Nearby, the high-rise but moderately priced **Hotel Gaviotas Vallarta** is curiously hidden, though nearly right on the beach at Fco. I. Madero 154, P.O. Box 497, Puerto Vallarta, Jalisco 48300, tel. 3/222-1500 or 3/222-5518, fax 3/222-5516. Clean, well managed, and newly decorated, the hotel rises in eight tile-and-brick tiers around an inviting, plant-decorated interior pool/patio. A small restaurant and snack bar serves guests downstairs, while, upstairs, guests enjoy ocean vistas directly from their room windows or from arch-framed breezeways just outside their doorways. The 84 semi-deluxe, clean and comfortable rooms rent for about $50 s, $56 d low season, $60 and $68 high; with TV and a/c.

In the opposite direction, north, just across the river bridge from the Molino de Agua, stands the renovated old **Hotel Encino-Suites Plaza del Río** at Av. Juárez 122, Puerto Vallarta, Jalisco 48300, tel. 3/222-0051 or 3/222-0280, fax 3/222-2573, email: encino@prodigy.net.mx. The entrance lobby opens into a pleasant, tropical fountain-patio, enfolded by tiers of rooms. Inside, the rooms are tastefully decorated in blue and white, many with ocean or city-hill views. Many large, similarly appointed kitchenette suites are available in an adjoining building. The hotel climaxes at the rooftop pool and sundeck, where

PUERTO VALLARTA ACCOMMODATIONS

Accommodations (telephone area code 3; postal code 48300 unless otherwise noted), are listed in increasing order of approximate high-season, double-room rates. Toll-free numbers are for reservations from the U.S. and Canada; "all inclusive" means all in-house food, drinks, and entertainment are included in the lodging price, quoted for two, double-occupancy.

HOTELS—RIO CUALE AND SOUTH

Hotel Villa del Mar, Fco. I. Madero 440, postal code 48380, tel.222-0785, $21

Hotel Yasmin, Basilio Badillo 168, postal code 48380, tel. 222-0087, $28

Casa del Puente, sobre Puente Av. Insurgentes, postal code 48380, tel. 222-0749 or U.S. (415) 648-7245, email: casadelpuente@yahoo.com, $35

Hotel Posada Río Cuale, A. Serdán 242, P.O. Box 146, tel./fax 222-0450 or 222-1148, email: legourmet@go2mexico.com, $46

Hotel Gloria del Mar, Amapas 114, postal code 48380, tel. 222-5143, fax 222-4689, $48

Hotel Alegre, F. Rodríguez 168, postal code 48380, tel./fax 222-4793, $48

Hotel Posada Roger, Basilio Badillo 237, postal code 48380, tel. 222-0836, fax 223-0482, email: pvroger@pvnet.com.mx, $48

Casa Corazón, Amapas 326, P.O. Box 66, tel. 222-6364, tel./fax 222-2738 or U.S. tel./fax (505) 523-4666, $50

Hotel Tropicana, Amapas 214, postal code 48380, tel. 222-0912, fax 222-6737, $50

Hotel Encino-Suites Plaza del Río Juárez 122, tel. 222-0051 or 222-0280, fax 222-2573, email: encino@prodigy.net.mx, $50

Hotel Gaviotas Vallarta, Fco. I. Madero 154, P.O. Box 497, tel. 222-1500 or 222-5518, fax 222-5516, $68

Hotel Brisas del Mar, Privada Abedul 10, tel./fax 222-1800 or 222-1821, $70

Hotel Playa Los Arcos, Olas Altas 380, postal code 48380, tel. 222-0583 or 222-1583 or 800/648-2403, fax 222-2418, email: reservaciones@playalosarcos.com, $72

Hotel San Marino Plaza, Rudolfo Gómez 111, postal code 48380, tel. 222-1555 or 222-3050, fax 222-2431, $80

Hotel Arcos Vallarta, M. Diéguez 171, postal code 48380, tel. 222-0712, or 800/648-2403, email: reservaciones@playalosarcos.com, $80

Hotel Puerto Vallarta Beach, Calle Malecón s/n, P.O. Box 329, tel. 222-5040, fax 222-2176, $85

Hotel Playa Conchas Chinas, P.O. Box 346, postal code 48390, tel./fax 221-5770, tel. 221-5733, $85

Suites Los Arcos, M. Diéguez s/n, postal code 48380, tel. 222-0717 or 800/648-2403, fax 222-2418, , email: reservaciones@playalosarcos.com, $100

Hotel Molino de Agua, I. Vallarta at A. Serdán, postal code 48380, tel. 222-1957, fax 222-6056, email: molino@acnet.net, $108

Hotel Meza del Mar, Amapas 380, tel. 222-4888 or U.S. toll-free 888/694-0010, fax 222-2308, $174 all-inclusive

---

guests enjoy a panoramic view of the surrounding green jungly hills above the white-stucco-and-tile old town, spreading to the blue, mountain-rimmed bay. The 75 rooms and suites rent from about $32 s, $40 d low season, $40 and $50 high season; one- and two-bedroom kitchenette suites begin at about $45 low season, $50 high season; amenities include a/c, phones,

security boxes, restaurant/bar.

Head directly upstream, to the upper (Av. Insurgentes) river bridge, and you'll find **Casa del Puente** tucked uphill behind the sidewalk cafe by the bridge. The elegant villa-home of Molly Stokes, grand-niece of celebrated naturalist John Muir, Casa del Puente is a lovely home-away-from-home. Antiques and art adorn the

Hotel Blue Bay Club Vallarta, Km 4 Carretera a Barra de Navidad, P.O. Box 385, tel. 221-5500 or 800/BLUEBAY (800/258-3229), fax 221-5105, email: reservpvr@bluebayresorts.com, $190 all-inclusive

Hotel Camino Real, P.O. Box 95, Playa de las Estacas, tel./fax 221-5000 or 800/7CAMINO (800/722-6466), email: pvr@caminoreal.com, $230

HOTELS—NORTH OF THE RIO CUALE

Hotel Rosita, Díaz Ordaz 901, P.O. Box 32, tel./fax 223-2000, 223-2177, 223-2151, or 223-2185, $48

Hotel Los Cuatro Vientos, Matamoros 520, P.O. Box 520, tel./fax 222-0161, tel. 222-2831, email: fourwinds@pvnet.com.mx, $65

Hotel Hacienda Buenaventura, Paseo de la Marina, P.O. Box 95B, postal code 48310, tel. 224-6667, fax 224-6242, email: buenavista@pvnet.com.mx, $95

Hotel Plaza Las Glorias, Km 2.5 Plaza Las Glorias, tel./fax 224-4444 or 800/515-4321, email: hcpvl@sidek.com.mx, $108

Hotel Buenaventura, México 1301, P.O. Box 8B, postal code 48350, tel. 222-3737, fax 222-3546, $110

Hotel Las Palmas Beach, Blv. Fco. Ascencio, Km 2.5, tel./fax 224-0650 or 800/876-5278, email: laspalmas@omegaresort.com, $140 all-inclusive

Hotel Pelicanos Av. Fco. Ascencio Km 2.5, tel./fax 224-1010 or 800/515-4321, email: hcpvl@sidek.com.mx, $160 all inclusive

Hotel Fiesta Americana, P.O. Box 270, tel. 224-2010 or 800/FIESTA1 (800/343-7821), fax 224-2108, email: favsale@pvnet.com.mx, $170

Hotel Krystal, Av. de las Garzas s/n, tel. 224-0202 or 800/231-9860, fax 224-0111, www.krystal.com.mx, $180

Hotel Continental Plaza, Blv. Fco. Ascencio Km 2.5 Plaza Las Glorias, tel. 224-0123 or 800/515-4321, fax 224-5236, email: hcpvl@sidek.com.mx, $196 all-inclusive

Hotel Qualton Club and Spa, Blv. Fco. Ascencio, Km 2.5 , tel. 224-4446 or 800/661-9174, fax 224-4447, email: qualton@pvnet.com.mx, $240 all-inclusive

APARTMENTS AND CONDOMINIUMS

Prices listed are the approximate high-season monthly rental rate for a studio or one-bedroom unit.

Hotel Villa del Mar, Fco. I. Madero 440, postal code 48380, tel. 222-0785, $500

Suites Plaza del Río, Juárez 122, tel. 222-0051 or 222-0820, fax 222-2573, email: encino@prodigy.net.mx, $1,000

Casa María Elena, F. Rodríguez 163, tel. 222-0113, fax 223-1380, email: mariazs@prodigy.net.mx, $1,000

Hotel Brisas del Mar, Privada Abedul 10, tel./fax 222-1800 or 222-1821, $1,000

Vallarta Sun Suites, R. Gómez 169, tel. 222-2262, fax. 222-1626, $1,100

Emperador, Amapas 114, postal code 48380, tel./fax 222-5143 or 222-4689, $1,100

Condominios Villa Blanca, Amapas 349, tel./fax 222-6190, $1,500

Casa Andrea, F. Rodríguez 174, tel./fax 222-1213, email: casaandrea@aol.com, $1,600

spacious, high-beamed-ceiling rooms, while outside its windows and around the decks great trees spread, tropical birds flit and chatter, jungle hills rise, and the river gurgles, hidden from the city hubbub nearby. Molly offers three lodging options: an upstairs river-view room with big bath and double bed for around $25 low season, $35 high, and a pair of spacious apartments (a one-bedroom/one-bath, and a two-bedroom/two-bath) for around $40 low season, $50 high, and $45 low, $70 high, respectively. Discounts may be negotiated, depending upon season and length of stay. Reserve early for the winter season. For more information contact Molly Stokes, Casa del Puente, Av. Insurgentes, Puerto Vallarta, Jalisco 48380, tel.

3/222-0749, website: www.casadelpuente.com. In the U.S. or Canada, reserve through Molly's daughter, María, at tel. 415/648-7245, or email casadelpuente@yahoo.com.

Nearby, across the river and two more blocks upstream, along Avenidas Aquiles Serdán and Fco. I. Madero, are a number of super-economy hotels. These bare-bulb lodgings, with rates averaging around $10 d, offer tiers of interior rooms with few amenities other than four walls, a bath (check for hot water), and a bed.

One notable exception is the **Hotel Villa del Mar,** whose longtime loyal patrons swear by it as the one remnant of Puerto Vallarta "like it used to be," located at Fco. I. Madero 440, corner of Jacarandas, Puerto Vallarta, Jalisco 48300, tel. 3/222-0785. The austere dark-wood, street corner lobby leads to a double warren of clean upstairs rooms, arranged in a pair of separate "A" and "B" wings. (Above that is a top-floor cluster of attractive studio kitchenette apartments; for details, see "Apartments and Condominiums—Río Cuale and South," below.) The "A" wing rooms are generally the best, with nondeluxe but comfortable amenities, including queen-size beds, traditional-style dark wood decor, ceiling fans, and, in some cases even private street-view balconies. Section "A," with exterior-facing windows, has the triple advantage of more privacy, light, and quiet. "B" rooms, by contrast, have windows that line walkways around a sound-reflective, and therefore oft-noisy, interior tiled atrium, where guests must draw curtains for quiet and privacy. Year-round rates for the approximately 30 "A" rooms run about $16 s, $21 d, $24 t. "B" rooms rent, year-round, for about $10 s, $12 d, $14 t. Rooms vary, so inspect a few before you decide. No TV, phones, or pool are available, and credit cards are not accepted.

Head three blocks farther away from the river and back downstream to Av. I. Vallarta (corner Basilio Badillo) to the longtime favorite **Hotel Posada Roger,** Basilio Badillo 237, Puerto Vallarta, Jalisco 48380, tel. 3/222-0836, fax 3/223-0482, email: pvroger@pvnet.com.mx. Although not the budget bargain it once was, the Hotel Posada Roger's three stories of rooms still enclose an inviting vine-decorated courtyard with plenty of quiet nooks for reading and relaxing. Freddy's Tucan, the hotel's breakfast cafe (open daily 8 A.M.–2 P.M.), provides yet another setting for relaxed exchanges with other travelers. A small pool/patio on the roof adds a bit of class to compensate for the increased price of the many smallish rooms that Roger offers. The 50 rooms run about $32 s, $48 d high season, $30 s, $42 d low. It's three blocks from the beach, with TV and a/c; credit cards are accepted.

The **Hotel Yasmin,** nearby at Basilio Badillo 168, at Pino Suárez, Puerto Vallarta, Jalisco 48380, tel. 3/222-0087, offers a viable budget-lodging alternative. The Yasmin's main attractions are its two short blocks to the beach; its verdant, plant-festooned inner patio; and Cafe de Olla, a good restaurant next door. The three tiers of fan-only rooms are clean, but small and mostly dreary. Inspect before you pay. You can compensate by renting one of the lighter, more secluded sunny-side upper rooms. Rates for all 30 rooms run about $28 d year-round.

Head downhill toward the beach and left around the Av. Olas Altas corner and you are in the popular Olas Altas neighborhood. At the hub of activity is the **Hotel Playa Los Arcos** (middle of the block between Calles Basilio Badillo and M. Dieguez), a best-buy favorite of a generation of savvy American and Canadian winter vacationers. The Playa Los Arcos is the flagship of a triad that includes the nearby Hotel Arcos Vallarta and the apartments Suites Los Arcos, both of whose guests are welcome to enjoy all of the Playa Los Arcos's leisurely beachfront facilities.

All three of these lodgings have swimming pools and comfortable, tastefully decorated, air-conditioned rooms with TV, phones, and small refrigerators in many rooms. The mecca, however, is the bustling Playa Los Arcos, with its palm- and vine-decorated inner pool/patio sundeck, restaurant with salad bar, live music every night, and beach chairs in the sand beneath shady palms or golden sun. The Hotel Playa Los Arcos is at Olas Altas 380, Puerto Vallarta, Jalisco 48380, reservations tel. 3/222-0583 or 3/222-1583, fax 3/222-2418, or from U.S. and Canada toll-free 800/648-2403, email: reservaciones@playalosarcos.com, website www.playalosarcos.com. The 183 rooms rent from about $60 d low season, approximately $72 high season, for standard grade rooms. More spacious, some with ocean views, superior-grade rooms run about $80 d low season, $95 high season, with credit cards accepted.

The **Hotel Arcos Vallarta** (formerly Hotel Fontana) is half a block away, around the corner, on a quiet cul-de-sac, at M. Dieguez 171, Puerto Vallarta, Jalisco 48380, tel. 3/222-0712, same reservations numbers and email as Playa Los Arcos, above. Its amenities include a rooftop pool/patio with a city and hill view. The Arcos Vallarta's 42 thoughtfully furnished pastel rooms, built around a soaring interior atrium, rent from about $65 d low season, $80 d high season; credit cards are accepted.

Right across the street, on M. Dieguez (contact information is the same as the Hotel Arcos Vallarta), are the apartment-style **Suites Los Arcos,** with a long blue pool/patio and an airy sitting area to one side of the lobby. Upstairs are 15 studio apartments, simply but attractively furnished in tile, wood furniture, and pastel-blue sofas and bedspreads. All have baths (some with tub-shower), king-size beds, furnished kitchenette, a/c, TV, and private balcony. The apartments rent (daily rate only) for about $75 d, $80 t low season, and $100 d, $110 t high.

The Hotels Playa Los Arcos, Arcos Vallarta, and Suites Los Arcos all accept bookings through travel agents. During times of low occupancy (May, June, July, September, and October, and sometimes even January), all three may offer special promotions, such as two kids under 12 free when sharing a room with parents, long-term discounts, or fourth night free. Be sure to ask when you book.

A block farther up Olas Altas, on a quiet uphill side street, at Francisca Rodríguez 168, Puerto Vallarta, Jalisco 48380, tel./fax 3/222-4793, stands the modest but well-managed **Hotel Alegre** (formerly Hotel Costa Alegre). The small lobby leads to an intimate, leafy pool/patio, enclosed by three tiers of rooms simply decorated in rustic wood, tile, and stucco, with TV, a/c, and shower bath. Rates are about $33 s or d, $38 d (with two beds) low season, $43 and $48 high, add $5 for kitchenette; credit cards are accepted. During times of low occupancy, the Alegre sometimes offers promotions, such as kids free with parents or fourth day free. Ask before you reserve.

Another good choice, three doors uphill and across the street from the Alegre, is the new **Hotel Vallarta Sun,** at Francisca Rodríguez 169, tel./fax 3/222-1626. Here, about 20 spacious rooms with balconies overlook a sunny pool patio. Inside, rooms are clean, attractive, and comfortable, with modern-standard bathrooms and queen-size beds. Rentals run about $46 d, $950/month low season, $60 and $1,100 high.

Vacationers who need more beachside ambience often pick the Playa Los Arcos's neighbor, the **Hotel San Marino Plaza,** at Rudolfo Gómez 111, Puerto Vallarta, Jalisco 48380, tel. 3/222-1555 or 3/222-3050, fax 3/222-2431. The San Marino's soaring *palapa* restaurant patio opens to an oceanfront pool and courtyard with a sundeck. Occupants of all of the marble-floored, pastel-and-white rooms enjoy city, mountain, or ocean views. The 160 rooms and suites rent for about $50 d low season, about $120 (all food, drinks, and entertainment included) high season; ocean-view suites $65 d low season and $130 high season; with a/c, TV, phones, and access to the bar and two restaurants. (Inspect two or three rooms and make sure that everything, such as the a/c, is operating before you pay your money.)

Farther south on Playa los Muertos, the Hotel Tropicana and its nearby brother, condo-style Hotel Gloria del Mar, offer ocean-view lodgings at moderate prices. Although the seven-story beachfront apartment **Hotel Gloria del Mar** at Amapas 114, Puerto Vallarta, Jalisco 48380, tel. 3/222-5143, fax 3/222-4689, has no pool or beach facilities, its prices are certainly right; The Gloria del Mar has 50 bright kitchenette suites, with either ocean or hill views. For the cheaper hill-view suites, expect to pay $32 low season, $48 high; for ocean view, $52 and $64, with a/c, phones, TV, and credit cards accepted. If you want cheaper monthly rates, they're available at the Apartments Emperador across the street. (See "Apartments and Condominiums—Río Cuale and South," following.)

The **Hotel Tropicana,** Amapas 214, Puerto Vallarta, Jalisco 48380, tel. 3/222-0912, fax 3/222-6737, although large, is easy to miss because the beach-level lobby is street-accessible only by an unobtrusive downward staircase. From there, the hotel's popular beachfront amenities—pool, sundeck, restaurant, volleyball court, and shady *palapas*—spread all the way to the surf. Upstairs, nearly all of the comfortable rooms enjoy private balconies and ocean vistas. Asking prices for the 160 rooms run about $50 d year-round, with a/c, security boxes, and credit cards accepted. Bargain for a better low-season rate.

About a block south along Amapas, the breezy, plant-decorated room tiers of **Casa Corazón** spread down its beachfront hillside at Amapas 326, P.O. Box 66, Puerto Vallarta, Jalisco 48300, tel./fax 3/222-6364 or 3/222-2738. Tucked on one of the middle levels, a homey open-air restaurant and adjacent soft-couch lobby with a shelf of used paperbacks invite relaxing, reading, and socializing with fellow guests. No TVs, ringing phones, or buzzing air-conditioners disturb the tranquility; the people and the natural setting—the adjacent lush garden and the boom and swish of the beach waves—set the tone. The 14 rooms, while not deluxe, are varied and comfortably decorated with tile, brick, and colorful native arts and crafts. Guests in some of the most popular rooms enjoy spacious, sunny beach-view patios. Tariffs for smaller rooms run about $25 s, $35 d low season, $50 s or d high; larger run $35 and $40 low season, $60 high. You may book directly by contacting either the hotel above, or owner George Tune, P.O. Box 937, Las Cruces, NM 88004, tel./fax 505/523-4666.

Nearby, on the short beachfront Calle Malecón, stands the neighboring condo-style **Hotel Puerto Vallarta Beach,** P.O. Box 329, Puerto Vallarta, Jalisco 48300, tel. 3/222-5040, fax 3/222-2176. Aptly named for its location right on popular Los Muertos Beach, the hotel's five stories of attractively furnished, tile-and-stucco studios offer all the ingredients for a restful beach vacation: queen-size bed, private ocean-view balconies, restaurant, and rooftop pool/sundeck with panoramic beach and bay view. The spacious rooms with ocean view rent for $75 low season, $85 high; with hill view, $53 and $63; with no view, $45 and $55.Depending upon occupancy, longer term and low-season discounts may be available; amenities are cable TV, a/c, phones, and elevator.

The all-inclusive **Hotel Meza del Mar,** Amapas 380, Puerto Vallarta 48300, tel./fax 3/222-4888, fax 3/222-2308, a block farther south, offers a contrasting alternative. A host of longtime returnees swear by the hotel's food, service, and friendly company of fellow guests, who, during the winter, seem to be divided equally between Americans, and English- and French-speaking Canadians. The Meza del Mar's 127 rooms and suites are distributed among two adjacent buildings: the Main Tower, a view high-rise overlooking the pool deck, and the Ocean Building, a three-story tier with views right over the beach. Guests in the preferred rooms, most of which are in the Ocean Building, enjoy private balconies and the sound of the waves outside their window. Other guests are quite happy with the expansive ocean view from the top floors of the Main Tower.

The rooms themselves, while not super-deluxe, are comfortably furnished in the Mexican *equipal* style of handcrafted leather furniture. Although all rooms are clean, details, especially in the cheaper rooms, sometimes appear makeshift. Ask for another room if your assignment isn't satisfactory.

Rates vary sharply according to season and grade of room and include all food (not gourmet, but good), drinks, and entertainment in the hotel's restaurants, bars, pools, and beachfront club. Rates, quoted per person double occupancy, for a minimum three-night stay, run from about $43 low season, $56 high, for a bare-bones no-view room to $70 low season, $87 high for a choice view suite. All rooms have a/c, but no TV nor phones, and only limited wheelchair access. Add $7 per person in lieu of tipping. Although the hotel does accept walk-in guests, individual reservations outside of Mexico must be through its Denver-based reservations office. For information and reservations from the U.S. and Canada, call 888/694-0010; or from the Denver metropolitan area, tel. 303/321-7779, fax 303/322-1939, website: www.clubmeza.com.

Hotels South of Town

Follow the Manzanillo Hwy. 200 (the southward extension of Insurgentes) about a mile south of town and your reward will be the **Hotel Playa Conchas Chinas,** which offers a bit of charm at moderate rates, P.O. Box 346, Puerto Vallarta, Jalisco 48390, tel./fax 3/221-5770 or 3/221-5733. The stucco and brick complex rambles down a palm-shaded hillside (with dozens of stairs to climb) several levels to an intimate cove on Conchas Chinas beach. Here, sandy crescents nestle between tidepool-dotted sandstone outcroppings.

The lodgings themselves come in three grades. Standard rooms are spacious, decorated in Mexican traditional tile-brick and furnished in brown wood with kitchenette and tub bath; most have an ocean view. Deluxe grade adds a bedroom and ocean-view patio/balconies; plushest superior grade comes with all of the above, plus a small private pool with hot tub. It's very popular, so reserve early, especially during high season. Of the 39 rooms, the standard rooms begin at about $60 d low season, $85 high; deluxe, $70 low, $96 high. Amenities include a/c, phones, and the romantic El Set sunset restaurant above and a beachfront breakfast cafe below; there is no pool, elevator, or wheelchair access, but credit cards are accepted. Low-season discounts, such as one day free for a four-day stay or two days free for a one-week stay, are sometimes offered.

Another mile south, you can enjoy the extravagant isolation of the **Hotel Camino Real**, at correspondingly extravagant prices. Reserve at P.O. Box 95, Playa de las Estacas, Puerto Vallarta, Jalisco 48300, tel. 3/221-5000, fax 3/221-6000, email: pvr@caminoreal.com, website: www.caminoreal.com. From the U.S. and Canada, dial 800/7-CAMINO (800/722-6466).

Puerto Vallarta's first world-class hotel, the Camino Real has aged gracefully. It is luxuriously set in a lush tropical valley, with polished wooden walkways that wind along a beachside garden intermingled with blue swimming pools.

A totally self-contained resort on a secluded, sometimes seasonally narrow, strip of golden-white sand, the twin-towered Camino Real offers every delight: luxury view rooms, all water sports, restaurants, bars, and live music every night. The 250 rooms of the main tower begin at about $175 d low season, $230 high, while the 150 hot tub-equipped rooms of the Royal Beach Club tower go for about $230 d low season, $350 high, with everything, including wheelchair access.

On the other hand, for folks who prefer activity over serenity, the all-inclusive **Hotel Blue Bay Club Puerto Vallarta** (formerly Casa Grande) another mile south may be the right choice for a hassle-free tropical vacation. Find it at Km 4, Carretera a Barra de Navidad, P.O. Box 385, Puerto Vallarta, Jalisco 48300, tel. 3/221-5500, fax 3/221-5105, from the U.S. and Canada, tel. 800/BLUEBAY (800-258-3229), email: reservpvr@bluebayresorts.com, website: www.bluebayresort.com.

Although the hotel's tower rises like a giant space-age beehive sandwiched between the highway and the sea, the beach-level pool deck reveals an entirely different scene: Platoons of guests—reclining, socializing, snoozing, frolicking, and eating—enjoy at no extra charge the hotel's generous menu of activities. These vary from paddleboard, Ping-Pong, scuba lessons, and exercise machines for the athletic, to Spanish lessons, bingo, and pool-soaking in the airy

feeding the birds at Playa los Muertos

SPLENDID ISOLATION

A sprinkling of luxuriously secluded upscale mini-resorts, perfect for a few days of quiet tropical relaxation, have opened in some remote corners corners of the Puerto Vallarta region. Being hideaways, they are not easily accessible. But for those willing to make an extra effort, the rewards are rustically luxurious accommodations in lovely natural settings.

In order of accessibility, first comes the mini-haven **Majahuitas Resort,** tucked into a diminutive palm-shaded golden strand on the bay between Quimixto and and Yelapa. Here, guests have their choice of seven uniquely decorated cabañas, including a honeymoon suite. Solar panels supply electricity, and a luxuriously appointed central house serves as dining room and common area. A spring-fed pool, sunning, snorkeling, and horseback and hiking excursions into the surrounding tropical forest provide diversions for guests. Rates run about $200 for two, including all meals. Call 3/22158-08, email: relax@cruzio.com, or visit the website: www2.cruzio.com/~relax/ for reservations and information; in the U.S. and Canada, call 831/336-5036. Get there by water taxi, from the beach at Boca de Tomatlán, accessible by car or the Boca-marked buses, from the south-of-Cuale corner of Basilio Badillo, one block downhill from Insurgentes.

Farther afield but nevertheless car-accessible, **Hotelito Desconocido** ("Undiscovered Little Hotel") basks in luxurious isolation on a pristine lagoon and beach two hours south of Puerto Vallarta. Here, builders have created a colony of thatched designer houses on stilts. From a distance, it looks like a native fishing village. However, inside the houses (called "palafitos" by their Italian creator), elegantly simple furnishings—antiques, plush bath towels, and artfully draped mosquito nets—set the tone. Lighting is by candle and oil lantern only. Roof solar panels power ceiling fans and warm showers. Outside, nature blooms, from squadrons of pelicans wheeling above the waves by day to a brilliant overhead carpet of southern stars by night. In the morning, roll over in bed and pull a rope that raises a flag, and your morning coffee soon arrives. For the active, a full menu, including volleyball, billiards, bird-watching, kayaking, and mountain biking, can fill the day. Rates, which include all food and activities, begin at about $200 per person during the April 15–Dec. 20 low season, and rise to about $300 during the winter-spring high season. For reservations and more information, call 3/222-2546, 3/222-2526,

---

solarium spa for the more sedentary. With so much going on, the hotel beach hardly seems necessary for an enjoyable week in the sun. A luxurious room with private sea-view balcony, cable TV, a/c, and phone runs about $90 s, $150 d low season, $110 s, $190 d high, including all in-house food, drinks, and activities. Kids under five free; kids 6–12,$30 low season, $45 high.

Hotels North of Río Cuale

Hotels generally get more luxurious and expensive the farther north of the Río Cuale you look. The far northern section, on the Marina's ocean side, the site of several huge international chain hotels, is both isolated several miles from downtown (and Mexico) and has only a rocky beach, usually with little, if any, sand. Most of the central part of town, which stretches for a mile along the *malecón,* has no good beach either and is too noisy and congested for comfortable lodgings.

A notable exception, however, is the **Hotel Los Cuatros Vientos,** Matamoros 520, P.O.

Box 83, Puerto Vallarta, Jalisco 48300, tel./fax 3/222-0161 or 3/222-2831, email: fourwinds @pvnet.com.mx, perched in the quiet, picturesque hillside neighborhood above and behind the main town church. The 16 rooms and suites are tucked in tiers above a flowery patio and restaurant Chez Elena, and beneath a rooftop panoramic view bar-sundeck. The fan-only units are simply but attractively decorated in colonial style, with tile, brick, and traditional furniture and crafts. Rates (excluding Dec. 15–Jan. 5) run about $65 s or d from Oct. 15 to June 15, lower other times, with continental breakfast and a small pool; credit cards are accepted.

Near the north end of the downtown *malecón,* where the good beach resumes at Playa Camarones, so do the hotels. They continue, dotting the tranquil, golden strands of Playa las Glorias, Playa los Tules, and Playa de Oro. On these beaches are the plush hotels (actually, self-contained resorts) from which you must have wheels to escape to the shopping, restau-

or 800/851-1143 from the U.S. and Canada, fax 3/223-0293, email: hotelito@pvnet.com, or visit the website: www.hotelito.com. Get there, at the side road, to El Gargantino and Cruz de Loreto, at Km 131, via Hwy 200 south of Puerto Vallarta. Continue west several miles via good gravel road to Cruz de Loreto village. Follow the signs to Hotel Desconocido from there.

About 30 miles farther south, the small sign at Km 83 gives no hint of the pleasant surprises that **Las Alamandas** conceals behind its guarded gate. Solitude and elegant simplicity seem to have been the driving concepts in the mind of Isabel Goldsmith, daughter of the late British tycoon Sir James Goldsmith, when she acquired control of the property in the latter 1980s. Although born into wealth, Isabel has not been idle. She converted her dream of paradise—a small, luxuriously isolated resort on an idyllic beach in Puerto Vallarta's sylvan coastal hinterland—into reality. Now, her guests (22 maximum) enjoy accommodations that range from luxuriously simple studios to entire villas that sleep six. Activities include a health club, tennis, horseback riding, bicycling, fishing, and lagoon and river excursions. Daily rates begin at about $350 low season, $450 high for garden-view studios, to beachfront villas for about $900 low, $1,400 high; all with full breakfast. Three meals, prepared to your order, cost about $200 additional per day per person. For more information and reservations, call the hotel's agents: from U.S. and Canada, tel. (888) 882-9616, or contact Las Alamandas in Mexico directly, at Quémaro, Km. 83 Carretera Puerto Vallarta-Barra de Navidad, Jalisco 48854, tel. 328/555-00, fax 328/550-27, email info@las-alamandas.com, website: www.las-alamandas.com. Don't arrive unannounced; the guard will not let you through the gate unless you have reservation in hand or have made a prior appointment.

Alternatively, about three hours south of Puerto Vallarta, you can choose the holistic retreat **Punta Serena,** perching on a hill overlooking the blue Bay of Tenacatita. Here, guests soak it all in—enjoying meditation, massage, hot tub, traditional *temascal* hot room, and healthy food. Expect to pay about $115 low season, $155 high, per person per day, all included. For more information, call 335/150-13 or 800/BLUEBAY in the U.S. and Canada (Punta Serena is part of the Blue Bay Hotel chain), fax 0, email: info@puntaserena.com, or website: www.puntaserena.com. Get there via the side road signed Hotel Blue Bay, at Km 20 (120 miles south of Puerto Vallarta, 15 miles north of Barra de Navidad). Be sure to call ahead for a reservation or an appointment; otherwise the guard at the gate will, most likely, not let you pass.

rants, and the piquant sights and sounds of old Puerto Vallarta.

At the north end of the *malecón* (at 31 de Octubre) stands one of Puerto Vallarta's popular old mainstays, the friendly, beachfront **Hotel Rosita,** Díaz Ordaz 901, P.O. Box 32, Puerto Vallarta, Jalisco 48300, tel./fax 3/223-2185, 223-2000, 3/223-2151, or 3/223-2177. The Rosita centers on a grassy, palm-shadowed ocean-view pool, patio, and restaurant, with plenty of space for relaxing and socializing. About half of the spacious rooms, of *típica* Mexican tile, white stucco, and wood, look down upon the tranquil patio scene, while others, to be avoided if possible, border the noisy, smoggy main street. An unfortunate wire security fence mars the ocean view from the patio. Egress to the beach, Playa Camarón, is through a side door. The Rosita's 90 rooms range, depending on location, between $32 and $55 d low season, $48–75 high, including fans or a/c, security boxes, and a bar; credit cards are accepted.

The **Hotel Buenaventura,** Av. México 1301, P.O. Box 8B, Puerto Vallarta, Jalisco 48350, tel. 3/222-3737, fax 3/222-3546, email ventas@buenaventurahoteles.com, on the beach several blocks farther north, where the airport boulevard narrows as it enters old town, is one of Puerto Vallarta's few close-in deluxe hotels. The lobby rises to an airy wood-beamed atrium then opens toward the beach through a jungle walkway festooned with giant hanging leafy philodendrons and exotic palms. At the beachfront Los Tucanes Beach Club, a wide, palm-silhouetted pool/patio borders a line of shade *palapas* along the whitish-yellow sand beach. Most of the small rooms, decorated in wood, tile, and earth-tone drapes and bedspreads, open to small, private, ocean-facing balconies. The 206 rooms go for about $80 d low season, $110 high, including a/c, phones, buffet breakfast, restaurant, bar, live music nightly in season, and credit cards accepted.

Zona Hotelera Luxury Hotels

Puerto Vallarta's plush hostelries vary widely, and higher tariffs do not guarantee quality. Nevertheless, some of Pacific Mexico's best-buy luxury gems glitter among the 20-odd hotels lining Puerto Vallarta's north-end Zona Hotelera beaches. The prices listed are "rack rates"—the highest prices paid by walk-in customers. Much cheaper—as much as a 50 percent discount—airfare/lodging packages are often available, especially during low seasons, which are January, May–July, and Sept.–November. Get yourself a good buy by shopping around among travel agents at least several weeks before departure.

Heading north, about two miles from downtown, you'll find the **Hotel Continental Plaza,** Av. de Ingreso Km 2.5 Blv. Fco. Ascencio, Plaza Las Glorias, Puerto Vallarta, Jalisco 48300, tel. 3/224-0123, tel. 800/515-4321 from the U.S. and Canada, fax 3/224-5236, email: hcpv @sidek.com.mx. New management is operating the Continental Plaza and the nearby Hotel Pelicanos (see below) on an all-inclusive plan, and the Hotel Plaza Las Glorias next door on a conventional room-only basis.

Of the three hotels, the activity focuses on the Continental Plaza, which buzzes all day with tennis in the adjacent eight-court John Newcombe Tennis Club next door, aerobics, water polo, and volleyball in the big pool, and parasailing, jetboating, and windsurfing from the golden Playa las Glorias beach. Happy hours brighten every afternoon, and live music fills every balmy evening. The luxurious but not large rooms, decorated in soothing pastels, open to balconies overlooking the broad, palmy patio. The Continental Plaza's 434 room tariffs run about $142 for two, low season, $196 high, all inclusive (all in-house food, drinks, and entertainment included) with a/c, some sports, restaurants, bars, sauna, hot tub, exercise room, wheelchair access, and parking.

Next door, the **Hotel Plaza Las Glorias,** Km 2.5, Blv. Fco. Medina Ascencio, Puerto Vallarta, Jalisco 48300, tel./fax 3/224-4444 (same information and reservation numbers as Hotel Continental Plaza), once a Mexican-oriented hotel, now caters to a majority of North American clientele, except during Mexican national holidays, pre-Easter week, and August. At the Plaza Las Glorias, a blue swimming pool meanders beneath a manicured patio/grove of rustling palms. The rooms, behind the Spanish-style stucco, brick, and tile facade, overlook the patio and ocean from small view balconies. The South-Seas ambience ends, however, in an adjacent jogging track. Inside, the luxurious rooms are tile-floored, in dark wood, white stucco, and blue and pastels. The 237 rooms rent for about $108 d high season, $68 low. All rooms have a/c, cable TV, phone, and use of two pools, bars, restaurants, and easy access to the tennis courts next door at John Newcombe Tennis Club, parking, and wheelchair access. Credit cards are accepted.

The Hotel Plaza Las Glorias' "villa" section, the semi-deluxe **Hotel Pelicanos,** tel./fax 3/224-1010, fax 3/224-1414 (same information and reservation numbers as Hotel Continental Plaza) has no ocean view but offers studios for about $160 for two high season, $124 low, all inclusive, with a/c, TV, phones, and access to all the luxurious beachfront facilities of the Hotels Plaza Las Glorias next door.

A quarter-mile farther north, the recently enlarged **Hotel Las Palmas Beach,** Km 2.5, Blv. Fco. Medina Ascencio, Puerto Vallarta, Jalisco 48300, tel. 3/224-0650, fax 3/224-0543, an older, scaled-down, less luxurious version of the Plaza Las Glorias. An airy, rustic *palapa* shelters the lobby, which continues to a palm-adorned beachside pool/patio. Here, on the wide, sparkling Playa las Glorias, opportunities for aquatic sports are at their best, with the hotel's sport shop (snorkeling, fishing, Hobie Cat sailboats, parasailing) located right on the beachfront. The 240 rooms, most with private ocean-view balconies, are comfortable but not luxurious. Rates run about $70 per person low season, $140 per person high, all inclusive, with a/c phones, TV, restaurant, snack bar, bars, pool, and parking; credit cards are accepted. For information and reservations from the U.S. and Canada, dial 800/876-5278, or email: laspalmas@omegaresort.com.

Another quarter-mile north, the **Hotel Fiesta Americana Puerto Vallarta,** P.O. Box 270, Puerto Vallarto, Jalisco 48300, tel. 3/224-2010, tel. 800/FIESTA-1 (800-343-7821) from the U.S. and Canada, fax 3/224-2108, email: favsale @pvnet.com.mx, website: www.fiestaamericana.com.mx, is, for many, the best hotel in town. The lobby-*palapa,* the world's largest, is an attraction unto itself. Its 10-story palm-thatch chimney draws air upward, creating a continuously cool breeze through the open-air reception. Outside, the high-rise rampart of ocean-view rooms overlooks a pool and garden of earthly delights, complete with a gushing pool fountain, water volleyball, swim-up bar, and in-pool recliners. Beyond spreads a 150-foot-wide strip of wave-washed yellow sand. The 291 superdeluxe view rooms run about $105 d low season, rising to $170 high, with a/c, TV, phones, all sports, three restaurants, huge pool, three bars, wheelchair access, and parking.

Next door, the all-inclusive **Hotel Qualton Club and Spa,** Km 2.5, Av. de las Palmas s/n, Puerto Vallarta, Jalisco 48300, tel. 3/224-4446, tel. 800/446-2747 from the U.S. and Canada, fax 3/224-4447, email: qualton@pvnet.com.mx, offers an attractive all-inclusive option for vacationers who enjoy lots of food, fun, and company. On a typical day, hundreds of fellow sunbathing guests line the rather cramped poolside, while, a few steps away, dozens more relax beneath shady beachfront *palapas.* Nights glow with beach buffet theme dinners—Italian, Mexican, Chinese, and more—for hundreds, followed by shows where guests often become part of the entertainment. The list goes on—continuous food, open bars, complete gym and spa, tennis by night or day, scuba lessons, volleyball, water sports, free discos, golf privileges, stress therapy, yoga, aerobics galore—all included at no extra charge. If you want relief from the hubbub, you can always escape to the greener, more spacious Fiesta Americana poolside next door. The Qualton Club's 320 rooms, all with private view balconies, are luxuriously decorated in pastels and include a/c, cable TV, and phone. All-inclusive low-season rates run around $80 per person, double occupancy, about $120 high season, with wheelchair access; credit cards are accepted.

Another half-mile north, the **Hotel Krystal,** Av. de las Garzas s/n, Puerto Vallarta, Jalisco 48300, tel. 3/224-0202, tel. 800/231-9860 from the U.S. and Canada, fax 3/224-0111, website www.krystal.com.mx, is more than a hotel, it's a palmy, manicured resort-village, exactly what a Mexican Walt Disney would have built. The Krystal is one of the few Puerto Vallarta ultra-luxury resorts designed by and for Mexicans. Scores of deluxe garden bungalows, opening onto private pool/patios, are spread over its 34 beachside acres. A Porfirian bandstand stands proudly at the center, while nearby a colonial-style aqueduct gushes water into a pool at the edge of a serene spacious palm-shaded park. Guests who prefer a more lively environment can have it. Dancing goes on every night in the lobby or beside the huge, meandering beachside pool, where the music is anything but serene. The Krystal's 460 rooms and suites rent from about $170 d low season (low-season promotions as low as $100 d), $190 high; with a/c, phones, TV, 44 pools— no joke—six restaurants, and all sports.

Next door to the north, the neocolonial **Hotel Hacienda Buenaventura,** Paseo de la Marina, P.O. Box 95B, Puerto Vallarta, Jalisco 48310, tel. 3/224-6667, fax 3/224-6242, email: buenavista@pvnet.com.mx, offers a load of luxurious amenities at moderate rates. Its 150 rooms, arranged in low-rise tiers, enfold a leafy-green patio/garden, graced by a blue free-form pool and a slender, rustic *palapa.* On one side, water spills from a neo-antique aqueduct, while guests linger at the adjacent airy restaurant. The rooms are spacious, with high, hand-hewn-beam ceilings, marble floors, and rustic-chic tile and brick baths. The only drawback to all this is guests must walk a couple of short blocks to the beach. Rates run around $80 d low season, $95 d high, with a/c, phones, cable TV, some wheelchair access, and credit cards accepted.

Apartments and Condominiums— Río Cuale and South

Puerto Vallarta abounds with apartments and condominiums, mostly available for rentals of two weeks or more. A number of U.S.-based agencies specialize in the more luxurious rentals scattered all over the city: Villa de Oro Vacation Rentals, 638 Scotland Dr., Santa Rosa, CA 95409, tel. 800/638-4552, email: pvvillas @aol.com, website: www.villasdeoro.com; Villas of Mexico, P.O. Box 3730, Chico, CA 95927, tel. 800/456-3133, email: villas@villasofmexico.com, website: www.villasofmexico.com; or Condo and Villa World, 4230 Orchard Lake Rd., Suite 3, Orchard Lake, MI 48323, tel. 800/521-2980 from the U.S., tel. 800/453-8714 from Canada, email: condoinc@villaworld.com, website: www.villaworld.com.

The best-buy Puerto Vallarta apartments and condos are concentrated in the colorful Olas Altas-Conchas Chinas south-side district and are generally available only through local owners, managers, or rental agents. Among the helpful local rental agencies is **Mexi-Rent Vallarta,** the brainchild of friendly Dutch expatriate John Dommanschet, who works from his little Olas Altas neighborhood office at R. Gómez 130 across from the Hotel San Marino Plaza, tel./fax 3/222-1655, email: john@mexirent.com, website: www.mexirent.com. His rentals, largely confined to the Olas Altas neighborhood, include apartments, condos, and houses rentable by day, week, or month. High-season rates run from about $600/month up for modest studios to $1,200 and more for three-bedroom houses.

Alternative well-established south-of-Cuale rental agencies you may want to contact are Tropicasa Realty, at Pulpito 45A, corner of Olas Altas, tel./fax 3/222-6505, email: tropic @pvnet.com.mx; and Finca Sol, Aquiles Serdán 262 (next to Gutiérrez Rizo store), tel. 3/222-1606 or 3/222-0477, fax 3/222-1703, email: fincasol@fincasol.com, website: www .fincasol.com.

Other apartments are rentable directly through local managers. The following listing, by location, moving south from the Río Cuale, includes some of the best-buy Olas Altas apartments and condominiums.

Among the most economical are the top-floor studio apartments at the **Hotel Villa del Mar,** at Fco. I. Madero 440, Puerto Vallarta, Jalisco 48300, tel. 3/222-0785, a block south of the Río Cuale and four blocks uphill from Av. Insurgentes. The several apartments, which cluster around a sunny top-floor patio, are clean and thoughtfully furnished in attractive rustic brick, dark wood, and tile. A living area, with furnished kitchenette in one corner, leads to an airy, city- and hill-view private balcony. A comfortable double bed occupies an adjacent alcove. Four stories (no elevator) above an already quiet street, guests are likely to enjoy peace and tranquility here. Rents run about $40/day, $500/month high season, $30 and $400 low. Get your winter reservations in early.

Downriver several blocks, at the north foot of the Av. I. Vallarta bridge, stands the renovated **Hotel Encino-Suites Plaza del Río,** at Av. Juárez 122, Puerto Vallarta, Jalisco 48300, tel. 3/222-0051 or 3/222-0280, fax 3/222-2573, email: encino@prodigy.net.mx. The hotel lobby opens into a pleasant, tropical fountain-patio, enfolded by tiers of rooms. The suites are in the adjacent Suites Plaza del Río. Here you'll find three stories of spacious, comfortable kitchenette units. An additional bonus is the Hotel Encino's rooftop pool and sundeck, where both hotel and suite guests enjoy a panoramic view of the surrounding green jungly hills above the white-stucco-and-tile old town, spreading to the blue, mountain-rimmed bay. The approximately 25 suites rent for a daily rate of about $45 low season, $50 high; with a/c, phones, security boxes, and restaurant/bar; lower weekly and monthly rates are customarily negotiable.

Across the river, on Calle Olas Altas, from the Hotel Playa Los Arcos, walk south two short blocks to Francisca Rodríguez, then left a few steps uphill to the **Casa María Elena,** owned and operated by articulate, English-speaking María Elena Zermeño Santana. Her address is Francisca Rodríguez 163, Puerto Vallarta, Jalisco 48380, tel. 3/22201-13, fax 3/313-80, email: mariazs@prodigy.net.mx. The eight attractive fan-only brick-and-tile units stand in a four-story stack on a quiet, cobbled side street just a block and a half from the beach. The immaculate, light, and spacious units have living room with TV, bedroom, and modern kitchenettes (toaster oven and coffeemaker) and are all comfortably decorated with folk art chosen by María Elena (who owns a nearby crafts store) herself. Although the units have neither swimming pool nor phones, daily maid service and breakfast are included. High-season rates per apartment run about $62/day, $45/day when rented by the week, and $32/day when rented by the month. Corresponding low-season (May–Nov.) rates are about $43, $37, and $27. An additional discount of up to 10 percent is sometimes negotiable for rentals of three or more months. Guests also enjoy the option of three weekly hours of free Spanish lessons taught by María Elena.

One door uphill and across the street from María Elena, other attractive options are available at **Casa Andrea,** at Francisca Rodríguez 174, Puerto Vallarta, Jalisco 48380, tel./fax 3/222-1213, tel. 888/354-1089 from the U.S. or Canada, email: casaandrea@aol.com, website: www.casaandrea.com. Here, friendly, on-site owner Andrea offers 10 gorgeous one- and two-bedroom balcony apartments and a view penthouse, overlooking an invitingly tropical pool patio. The apartments themselves are immaculate, airy, and artfully decorated in whites and pastels and Andrea's tasteful selection of native crafts and paintings. Rooms include king- or queen-size beds and fully equipped, modern-standard kitchens, with use of a library, small exercise room with treadmill and weights, and a community TV down by the pool. The eight one-bedroom units rent for about $300/week low season, $450 high; the two two-bedroom/two-bath units, about $600 and $750, more for the penthouse, if available; with fans, maid service, and 10% discount for longer than a two-week stay. Children under 5 aren't allowed. For the winter, get reservations by June.

If you can't get into Casa Andrea, try **Vallarta Sun Suites,** behind Casa Andrea, on the next street south, at G†mez 169, Puerto Vallarta, Jalisco 48380, tel. 3/222-2262, fax 3/222-1626. Perched on a quiet side street, four stories of comfortably furnished new one-bedroom kitchenette apartments overlook a sunny pool patio just two blocks from the beach. Rentals run about $60/day, $1,100/month high season, $45 and $950 low season.

Two blocks toward the beach, on Amapas, between Gomez and Pulpito, **Apartments Emperador,** tel./fax 3/222-5143, fax 3/222-4689, offers plainly furnished but clean and comfortable kitchenette studio or one-bedroom apartments from about $750 per month low season, $1,100 high; with phones and a/c, but no pool nor beach facilities; credit cards accepted.

Two blocks north on beachfront Calle Malecón, stands the condo-style **Hotel Puerto Vallarta Beach,** P.O. Box 329, Puerto Vallarta, Jalisco 48300, tel. 3/22250-40, fax 3/221-76. Aptly named for its location right on popular Los Muertos Beach, the hotel has five stories of attractively furnished, tile-and-stucco kitchenette apartments offering all the ingredients for a restful beach vacation: queen-size beds, private sea-view balconies, restaurant, and rooftop pool and sundeck with panoramic beach and bay view. During low season, the spacious, one-bedroom suites rent daily for $50 with kitchenette, $45 without; during high season, $55 and $50. Depending upon occupancy, lower

weekly and monthly and low season rates may be available; amenities include cable TV, a/c, phones, and elevator.

Three blocks farther south, the path to the 63-unit condo-style **Hotel Brisas del Mar** winds uphill through its view restaurant, across its expansive pool/deck to the big white main building perched a short block below the highway. If this place weren't such a climb (although aerobicists might consider it a plus) from the beach, the builders would have sold all the units long ago. Now, however, it's owned and operated by the downhill Hotel Tropicana, whose attractive beachside facilities Brisas del Mar guests are invited to enjoy. The Brisas del Mar, Privada Abedul 10, Puerto Vallarta, Jalisco 48300, tel./fax 3/222-1800 or 3/222-1821, is quite comfortable, with light, comfortable, kitchenette suites with private balconies with a view. Most units are one-bedroom, with either one king-size bed or a double and twin combination. Rates run from about $49/night or $500/month low season to $70 and $1,000 high season, with a/c, pool, desk service, restaurant, limited wheelchair access, and credit cards accepted. Book directly or through a travel agent. Get there either by car or taxi from the highway, or by climbing the stairs from Amapas through the doorway at no. 307, labeled "Casa del Tigre."

Back down on Amapas, a half-block farther south, the 10 white designer units of the **Condominios Villa Blanca,** Amapas 349, Puerto Vallarta, Jalisco 48300, tel./fax 3/222-6190, stairstep artfully above the street. These are light, attractive, air-conditioned luxury apartments, rented out for the owners by the friendly manager Jose Luis Alvarez, whose office is at the streetfront. While the apartments vary from studios to two-bedroom units, they all have ocean views, modern kitchenettes, and rustic decorator vine-entwined palm trunks adorning the doors and walls. The best apartments occupy the upper levels; the least desirable are the pair of apartments at the bottom, where a pump buzzes continuously near the complex's small soaking pool. Rentals may be by the day, week, or month. Daily rates for studios run about $50 low season, $70 high; for a one-bedroom, $60 low, $80 high, two-bedroom, $90 and $110.

Trailer Parks and Camping

Puerto Vallarta visitors enjoy two good trailer parks, both of them owned and managed by the same family. The smallish, palm-shaded **Puerto Vallarta Trailer Park,** Francia 143, P.O. Box 141, Puerto Vallarta, Jalisco 48300, tel. 3/224-2828, is two blocks off the highway at Francia at Lucerna, a few blocks north of the *libramiento* downtown bypass fork. The 65 spaces four blocks from the beach rent for $16 per day, with one free day per week, one free week per month; with all hookups, including showers, toilets, long-distance phone access, and laundromat. Pets are okay. Luxury hotel pools and restaurants are nearby.

Much more spacious **Tacho's Trailer Park** is half a mile from Hwy. 200 on Av. Aramara, the road that branches inland across the airport highway from the cruise ship dock. Tacho's, P.O. Box 315, Puerto Vallarta, Jalisco 48300, tel. 3/224-2163, offers a large grassy yard with some palms, bananas, and other trees for shade. The 100 spaces run $12/day (one free week on a monthly rental), including all hookups and use of showers, toilets, laundry room, pool and *palapa,* and shuffleboard courts. Pads are paved, and pets are okay.

Other than the trailer parks, Puerto Vallarta has precious few campsites within the city limits. Plenty of camping possibilities exist outside the city, however. Especially inviting are the pearly little beaches, such as Las Animas, Quimixto, Caballo, and others that dot the verdant, wild coastline between Boca de Tomatlán and Yelapa. *Colectivo* water taxis regularly head for these beaches for about $3 per person from Boca de Tomatlán (see "Beaches," above). Local stores at Quimixto, Las Animas, and Boca de Tomatlán can provide water (bring water purification tablets or filter) and basic supplies. (For more camping possibilities, see "Around the Bay of Banderas," later in this chapter.)

FOOD

Puerto Vallarta is brimming with good food. Dieters beware: light or nouvelle cuisine, tasty vegetables, and bountiful salads are the exception, as in all Mexico. In the winter, when the sun-hungry vacationers crowd in, a table at even an average restaurant may require a reservation. During the low season, however, Puerto Vallarta's best eateries are easy to spot. They are the ones with the customers. (Note: If you're coming to Puerto Vallarta mainly for its gourmet offerings, avoid September and October, when a number of the best restaurants are closed.)

Stalls, Snacks, and Breakfast

Good Puerto Vallarta eating is not limited to sit-down restaurants. Many foodstalls offer wholesome, inexpensive meals and snacks to hosts of loyal repeat customers. It's hard to go wrong with hot, prepared-on-the-spot food. Each stand specializes in one type of fare—seafood, *tortas,* tacos, hot dogs—and occupies the same location daily, beginning around 6 P.M. For example, a number of them concentrate along Avenidas Consitución and Pino Suárez just south of the River Cuale; several others cluster on the side-street corners of Av. Olas Altas a few blocks away.

A number of such foodstalls have graduated to storefronts. **Rickey's Tamales,** at 325 Basilio Badillo, capitalizes on the general Mexican belief that tamales (like Chinese food and pizza in the U.S.) are hard to make and must be bought, takeout style. Big rolls of husk-wrapped, lime-soaked cornmeal are stuffed with beef, chicken, or pork, and baked—three for $2. Open Mon.–Sat. 6–10 P.M.

If you're lusting for a late-night snack, walk a few doors west toward the beach to either **Cenaduría La Jolla,** open nightly 6 P.M.–12 A.M., for great *pozole,* or neighboring **Armando's,** open Mon.–Sat. 7 P.M.–3 A.M., for a dozen styles of succulent tacos.

An exceptionally well-located late-night burrito stand operates seasonally at the nightclub crossroads of Avenidas I. Vallarta and Lázaro Cárdenas across from Mariachis Locos. Choose between burritos and *hamburguesas* in a number of styles. Open nightly until around 2 A.M.

Other tasty late-night options are available at many of the eateries along main street Av. Insurgentes, just south of the upstream Río Cuale bridge. For example, drop into the no-name *jugería* a few doors north from the Cine Bahía. Try one of the luscious *tortas de pierna,* roast leg of pork smothered in avocado on a bun, $1.75. Top it off with a banana *licuado,* with a touch of *(un poquito de)* chocolate. It's located at Insurgentes 153 and open daily 7–12 A.M.

Similar is **Tuti Fruti,** a good spot for a refreshing snack, especially while sightseeing or shopping around the *malecón.* Find it at the corner of Morelos and Corona, one block from the *malecón;* open Mon.–Sat. 8 A.M.–11 P.M. You could even eat breakfast, lunch, and dinner there, starting with juice and granola or eggs in the morning, a *torta* and a *licuado* during the afternoon, and an *hamburguesa* for an evening snack.

Some of the most colorful, untouristed places to eat in town are, paradoxically, at the tourist-mecca **Mercado Municipal** on the Río Cuale, at the Av. Insurgentes (upstream) bridge. The *fondas* tucked on the upstairs floor (climb the streetside staircase) specialize in steaming, homestyle soups, fish, meat, tacos, *moles,* and chiles rellenos. Point out your order to the cook and take a seat at the cool, river-view seating area. Open daily 7 A.M.–6 P.M.

For breakfast, **La Casa de Los Hot Cakes,** skillfully orchestrated by personable travel writer-turned-restaurateur Memo Barroso, has become a Puerto Vallarta institution at Basilio Badillo 289, between I. Vallarta and Constitución, tel. 3/22262-72. Breakfast served Tues.–Sun. 8 A.M.–2 P.M. Besides bountiful Mexican and North American breakfasts—orange juice or fruit, eggs, toast, and hash browns for about $4—Memo offers an indulgent list of pancakes. Try his nut-topped, peanut butter-filled "O. Henry" chocolate pancakes, for example. Add his bottomless cup of coffee and you'll be buzzing all day. For lighter eaters, vegetarian and less indulgent options are available.

If Casa de Hot Cakes is too crowded, you can get a reasonable facsimile at Freddy's **Tucán** restaurant (which Memo inaugurated in the 1980s) at Hotel Posada Roger, corner B. Badillo and I. Vallarta, tel. 3/22208-36. Open daily 8 A.M.–2 P.M.

Another good spot for breakfast served 7–11:30 A.M. is the airy beachfront terrace of the **Hotel Playa Los Arcos** restaurant at 380 Olas Altas. Here the ambience—tour boats arriving and leaving, the passing sidewalk scene, the swishing waves, the swaying palms—is half the fun. The other half is the food, either a hearty $7 buffet, or a briskly served à la carte choice of your heart's desire, from fruit and oatmeal to eggs, bacon, and hash browns.

Coffeehouses

Good coffee has arrived at Puerto Vallarta, where some cafes now roast from their own private sources of beans. Just a block from Los Muertos Beach, coffee and book lovers get the best of both worlds at **Page in the Sun,** corner Olas Altas and M. Dieguez, diagonally across from Hotel Playa Olas Altas. There, longtimers sip coffee and play chess while others enjoy their pick of lattes, cappuccinos, ice cream, muffins, and walls of used paperbacks and magazines. Open daily 8 A.M.–9 P.M.

Exactly one block farther up Olas Altas, at the corner of Rodríguez, take a table at the **Cafe San Ángel** and soak up the sidewalk scene. Here, you can enjoy breakfast or a sandwich or dessert and good coffee in a dozen varieties, 8 A.M.–10 P.M.

For even more relaxing atmosphere nearby, take your book or newspaper to a shady table at **Señor Book,** at the corner of R. Gómez and

a street vendor waiting for customers

Olas Altas, tel. 3/22203-24. Here, you may enjoy all espresso options, plus wines, liquors, pastries, and a very substantial library of new and used paperbacks. Open daily (except Sunday in low season) 7:30 A.M.–10:30 P.M.

For fancier offerings and upscale ambience, go to the coffeehouse of **Cafe Maximilian** on the sidewalk-front of Hotel Playa Los Arcos, at 380 Olas Altas, open daily (except Sunday in low season.)

Restaurants—Río Cuale and South

Archie's Wok, Francisca Rodríguez 130, between Av. Olas Altas and the beach, tel. 3/222-0411, is the founding member of a miniature "gourmet ghetto" that is flourishing in the Olas Altas neighborhood. The founder, now deceased, was John Huston's longtime friend and personal chef. However, Archie's wife, Cindy Alpenia, carries on the culinary mission. A large local following swears by her menu of vegetables, fish, meat, and noodles. Favorites include Thai coconut fish, barbecued ribs Hoi Sin, and spicy fried Thai noodles. Make up a party of three or four, and each order your favorite. Arrive early; there's usually a line by 7:30 P.M. for dinner. Open Mon.–Sat. 2–11 P.M.; Visa accepted. Moderate-Expensive.

One block due north, across from the Hotel Plaza San Marino, **Karpathos Taverna,** R. Gomez 110, tel. 3/22315-62, has acquired a considerable local following by creating a little corner of Greece here in Puerto Vallarta. Although the ambience comes, in part, from very correct service and the Greek folk melodies emanating from the sound system, the food—genuine Greek olives, feta cheese, rolled grape leaves, savory moussaka, spicy layered eggplant, piquant roast lamb, garlic-rubbed fish with olive oil—seems a small miracle here, half a world from the source. Open Mon.–Sat. 4–11 P.M. Moderate-Expensive.

Head back down Olas Altas to **Cafe Maximilian,** one of the latest members of the growing roll of Olas Altos gourmet gems. Here, the Austrian expatriate owner skillfully orchestrates a cadre of chefs and waiters to produce a little bit of Vienna with a hint of California cuisine. From his long list of appetizers, consider starting off with prune-stuffed mountain quail in nine-spice sauce with polenta, continue with organic salad greens in vinaigrette, and finish with scalloped *rahmschnitzel* with noodles in a cream mushroom sauce, accompanied with a Monte Xanic Baja California chenin blanc. If you have room, top everything off with Viennese apple strudel. Alas, the only thing missing at Cafe Maximilian is zither music playing softly in the background. At the Hotel Playa Los Arcos, Olas Altas 380B, tel. 3/222-5058; open daily 4–11 P.M. Reservations strongly recommended. Expensive.

Mexican food is well represented south of Cuale, by a trio of good restaurants (Tres Huastecas, Café de Olla, and Los Arbolitos, below, near the end of the restaurant section). Restaurant **Tres Huastecas'** charming, pure-blooded Huastec owner calls himself "El Querreque," while others call him the "Troubador of Puerto Vallarta." His poetry, together with sentimental Mexican country scenes, covers the walls, while everything from soft-boiled eggs and toast to frog legs and enchiladas Huastecas fills the tables. Find it at Olas Altas, corner of F. Rodríguez, tel. 3/222-4525; open daily 8 A.M.–8 P.M. Moderate.

Nearby, the **Cafe de Olla,** B. Badillo 168, tel. 3/223-1626, a few doors uphill from the Olas Altas corner, draws flocks of evening customers with its bountiful plates of scrumptious local delicacies. It serves Mexican food the way it's supposed to be, starting with enough salsa and *totopes* (chips) to make appetizers irrelevant. Your choice comes next—either chicken, ribs, and steaks from the streetfront grill—or the savory *antojitos* platters piled with tacos, tostadas, chiles rellenos, or enchiladas by themselves, or all together in its unbeatable *plato Mexicano.* Prepare by skipping lunch and arriving for an early dinner to give your tummy time to digest it all before bed. Open daily 8 A.M.–11 P.M. Budget-Moderate.

As Archie's Wok did in the Olas Altas neighborhood years ago, Memo Barroso's Casa de Los Hot Cakes has sparked a small restaurant and cafe renaissance on Basilio Badillo, now so popular it's becoming known as the "Calle de Cafes." The newest addition, **Chef Roger,** has recently moved to lower Badillo (a few doors uphill from Olas Altas, tel. 3/222-5900),from its long-time original location north of the Cuale. Arguably the best restaurant in Puerto Vallarta, Chef Roger remains among the least visible (at

180 Badillo, just uphill from the Hotel Yasmin). A legion of satisfied customers, however, is the Swiss owner/chef's best advertisement. Heated dinner plates, chilled beer and white wine glasses, candlelight, etchings hung on pastel stucco walls, guitars strumming softly, and an eclectic list of exquisitely executed continental dinner entrées keep the faithful coming year after year. Open Mon.–Sat. 6:30–11 P.M.; reservations mandatory. Expensive.

One of the Badillo originals still going strong is **Restaurant Puerto Nuevo,** at Basilio Badillo 284, tel. 3/222-6210, right across from the Casa de Hot Cakes. Some evening when you're lusting for seafood, take a table with friends and enjoy a no-nonsense gourmet's gourmet seafood feast. Completely without pretense, owner/chef Roberto Castellon brings in the customers with his ingeniously varied list of specialties. For a real party for four, try his guaranteed bottomless seafood special, served course by course, including clams, oysters, lobster, scallops, and red snapper-stuffed chiles rellenos thrown in for good measure. For dessert, he recommends either his Kahlúa cheesecake or baked ice cream. Open daily 12–11 P.M. Credit cards accepted. Moderate-Expensive.

A few doors downhill, step into the **Cafe Adobe,** at the corner of Basilio Badillo and I. Vallarta, tel. 3/222-6720, and escape from the colorful but insistent Puerto Vallarta street-bustle into the Adobe's cool, refined American Southwest ambience. You'll enjoy soft music, flowers, and white table linens while you make your choice from a short but tasty menu of soups, fettuccine, poultry, seafood, and meats. Open Wed.–Mon. 5–11 P.M., closed June, July, and August; reservations recommended. Expensive.

Noisy, smoky bus traffic mars daytime dining at Av. Basilio Badillo sidewalk cafes. Fortunately, this is not time in the evening or any time at both Cafe Adobe and Casa de Los Hot Cakes as both have inside seating.

For atmosphere, the showplace **Le Bistro** is tops, at Isla Río Cuale 16A, tel. 3/222-0283, just upstream from the Av. Insurgentes bridge, is tops. Renovations with lots of marble and tile have replaced some of the old bohemian-chic atmosphere with European-elegant. Nevertheless the relaxed, exotic ambience still remains: The river gurgles past outdoor tables, and giant-leafed plants festoon a glass ceiling, while jazz CDs play so realistically that you look in vain for the combo. Its hours are Mon.–Sat. 9 A.M.-11:30 P.M., first come, first served—reservations not accepted. Expensive.

The renovated Le Bistro has formidable competition right across the river, at **Restaurant Caruso,** owned and managed by the celebrated Brindisi-born Franco brothers. Here, the refined, airy ambience sets the tone. In the afternoon, sunlight glows warmly through a lofty glass ceiling, while overhead fans spin quietly and the river bubbles downhill just outside the open veranda. Nights, cool air flowing down the river valley swirls refreshing currents past the tables. The menu provides many choices. You might start with a savory *Insalata Caprese* (tomato, basil, and mozzarella salad); continue with *Bucatini alla Arrabiata* (with a bacon, onion, and tomato sauce) and finish with savory apple strudel for dessert. Enjoy this all with a good wine, such as a Wente California Sauvignon Blanc, or a Monte Xanic (sha-NEEK) Baja California Merlot. Restaurant Caruso is open daily noon to 11 P.M.; high season probably earlier, for breakfast. Reservations recommended, especially on weekends, at Insurgentes 109, south foot of the river bridge, tel. 3/222-2748. Expensive.

If, on the other hand, you're hungry for Chinese food, go to **Dragon Rojo,** at Insurgentes 323, uphill side, between V. Carranza and B. Badillo, tel. 3/222-0175. Here, competent chefs put out a respectable line of the usual San Francisco-style Cantonese specialties. Open daily 1–11 P.M. Moderate.

Los Arbolitos, Camino Rivera 184, tel. 3/223-1050 (bear right at the upper end of Av. Lázaro Cárdenas, way upstream along the River Cuale), remains very popular, despite its untouristed location. Here, home-style Mexican specialties reign supreme. The house pride and joy is the Mexican plate, although it serves dozens of other Mexican and international favorites. Colorful decor, second-floor river-view location, and attentive service spell plenty of satisfied customers. Open daily 8 A.M.-11 P.M. Moderate.

Your stay in Puerto Vallarta would not be complete without sunset cocktails and dinner beneath the stars at one of the Puerto Vallarta's south-of-Cuale hillside view restaurants. Of these, **Señor Chico's,** Púlpito 377, tel. 3/22235-35, remains a longtime favorite, despite its average but nicely presented food. The atmosphere—soft guitar solos, flickering candlelight, pastel-pink tablecloths, balmy night air, and the twinkling lights of the city below—is memorable. Open daily 5–11 P.M.; reservations recommended. Expensive. (Get there by turning left at Púlpito, the first left turn possible uphill past the gasoline station as you head south on Hwy. 200 out of town. After about two winding blocks, you'll see Sr. Chico's on the left as the street climaxes atop a rise.)

Restaurants North of Río Cuale

The success of up-and-coming **Restaurant Trio** at 264 Guerrero (between Hidalgo and Matamoros), two short blocks north of the Río Cuale, flows from an innovative Mediterranean menu and its cool, elegant candlelit atmosphere. Imaginative combinations of traditional ingredients, attentive service, and satisfying desserts topped off with savory espresso will keep customers coming back for years. Open noon–4 P.M. and 6 P.M.–midnight; reservations recommended, tel. 3/222-2196. Moderate-Expensive.

Within the bustle of the *malecón* restaurant row stands the longtime favorite **Las Palomas,** *malecón* at Aldama, tel. 3/222-3675. Soothing suppertime live marimba music and graceful colonial decor, all beneath a towering big-beamed ceiling, affords a restful contrast from the sidewalk hubbub just outside the door. Both the breakfasts and the lunch and dinner entrées (nearly all Mexican style) are tasty and bountiful. Open Mon.–Sat. 8 A.M.–10 P.M., Sunday 9 A.M.–5 P.M. Moderate.

If, however, you hanker for home-cooked Italian food, stop by **Rito's Baci,** tel. 3/22264-48, the labor of love of the sometimes taciturn but warmhearted owner-chef, who stays open seven days a week because his "customers would be disappointed if I closed." His establishment, as plain as Kansas in July, requires no atmosphere other than Rito himself, a member of the Mexican football league hall of fame. All of his hearty specialties, from the pestos through the pastas and the eggplant Parmesan, are handmade from traditional family recipes. Rito's Baci is located on the corner of Juárez and Ortíz de Dominguez. Open daily 1–11 P.M. Moderate.

A choice pair of romantic hillside restaurants concludes the list of north-of-Cuale dining options. Highest on the hill is the longtime favorite **Restaurant Chez Elena,** Matamoros 520, tel. 3/22201-61, on a quiet side street a few blocks above and north of the downtown church. Soft live guitar music and flickering candlelight in a colonial garden terrace set the tone, while a brief but solid Mexican-international menu, augmented by an innovative list of daily specialties, provides the food. On a typical evening, you might be able to choose between entrées such as *cochinita pibil* (Yucatecan-style shredded pork in sauce), banana leaf-wrapped Oaxacan tamales, or dorado fillet with cilantro in white sauce. Chez Elena guests often arrive early for sunset cocktails at the rooftop panoramic view bar and then continue with dinner downstairs. Open nightly 6–10 P.M.; reservations are recommended. Moderate-Expensive.

A few blocks downhill and north, the striking castle-tower of **Restaurant Cafe des Artistes** rises above the surrounding neighborhood at 740 Guadalupe Sanchez at Leona Vicario, tel. 3/22232-28. Romantics only need apply. Candlelit tables, tuxedoed servers, gently whirring ceiling fans, soothing live neoclassical melodies, and gourmet international cuisine all set a luxurious tone. You might start with your pick of soups, such as chilled cream of watercress or cream of prawn and pumpkin, continue with a salad, perhaps the smoked salmon in puff pastry with avocado pine nut dressing. For a finale, choose honey- and soy-glazed roast duck or shrimp sautéed with cheese tortellini and served with a carrot custard and a spinach-basil puree. Open Mon.–Sat. 8 A.M.–4 P.M., 7–11 P.M.; reservations recommended. Expensive.

Vegetarian Restaurants

Good macrobiotic and vegan cuisine is getting a foothold in Puerto Vallarta, in at least three locations. Downtown, off the *malecón*, you'll find **Papaya 3,** at Abasolo 169, tel. 3/222-0303 a block and a half uphill from the Hard Rock Cafe. Here, owners have succeeded with a dazzlingly varied repertoire for Puerto Vallarta's growing cadre of health-conscious visitors and locals. The list begins with dozens of creamy tropical fruit *licuados,* which they call "shakes," but which contain no ice cream, and continues through a host of salads, pastas, omelettes, sandwiches, Mexican specialties, and chicken and fish plates. The atmosphere, augmented with plants and soft music, is refined but relaxed. Moderate. (You can also enjoy the same at its second location, on upper Olas Altas, at no. 485, near the corner of Gómez, open Mon.–Sat. 8 A.M.-10:30 P.M., Sun 8 A.M.–4 P.M., tel. 3-323-1692.)

For a very worthy alternative, go to up-and-coming **Planeta Vegetariana,** downtown, near the south side of the church, at 270 Iturbide, by the corner of Hidalgo, tel. 3/222-3073. (Although I wasn't able to get there, I'm recommending it because two separate readers took the time to write and praise this place—"best food in Puerto Vallarta.")

Supermarkets, Bakeries, Organic Groceries and Produce

The king of national supermarket chains is **Comercial Mexicana,** Mexico's Kmart with groceries. The quality is generally good to excellent, and the prices match those in the U.S. and Canada. Comercial Mexicana maintains two Puerto Vallarta branches, both in the north-side suburbs: at **Plaza Marina,** Km 6.5, Hwy. 200, just before the airport, beneath the McDonald's sign, tel. 3/221-0053 or 221-0490; and three miles closer in, at **Plaza Genovese,** Km 2.5, Hwy. 200, near the John Newcombe Tennis Club, tel. 3/224-6644 or 224-5655. Both are open daily 8 A.M.–10 P.M.

Much closer to downtown is the big, locally owned **Supermarket Gutiérrez Rizo,** a remarkably well-organized dynamo of a general store at Constitución and Vallarta, just south of the Río Cuale, tel. 3/222-0222. Besides vegetables, groceries, film, socks, spermicide, and sofas, it stocks one of the largest racks of English-language magazines (some you'd be hard pressed to find back home) outside of Mexico City. Open 6:30 A.M.–10 P.M., 365 days a year.

Panadería Mungía is nearly worth the trip to Puerto Vallarta all by itself. The three branches are: downtown at Juárez and Mina; south-of-Cuale, corner Insurgentes and A. Serdán; and Francisca Rodríguez, uphill from Olas Altas, next to Hotel Alegre. Big, crisp cookies, flaky fruit tarts, hot fresh rolls, and cool cream-cakes tempt the palates of visitors, locals, and resident foreigners alike. Open Mon.–Sat. 7 A.M.–9 P.M.

Rival **Panadería Los Chatos** offers an equal-ly fine selection, also at two lo... town, at north-end Plaza Hidald... 995; and in the Hotel Zone, ac... Hotel Sheraton, Fco. Villa 359, tel. Both are open Mon.–Sat. 7 A.M.–9 ...

If you've run out of *salvado* (oat bran), stock up at the **Vida y Salud** health food store *(tienda naturista),* north end of downtown, at Av. México 1284, tel. 3/222-1652. The shelves are packed with hundreds of items, such as soy milk, vitamins, aloe vera cream, and tonics purported to cure everything from warts and gallstones to impotence. Open Mon.–Sat. 9 A.M.–2 P.M. and 4–8 P.M.

South of Cuale, health food devotees have at least two choices: **La Panza Es Primero,** at Madero 287, tel. 3/223-0090, open Mon.–Sat. 9 A.M.–9 P.M., and a competing store nearby, on Insurgentes, east side, near the corner of Badillo.

For organic produce go nearby to **Agro Gourmet,** at the south-of-Cuale corner of Basilio Badillo and Pino Suárez. Besides home-grown lettuces and other vegetables and herbs, it also offers a trove of hard-to-get cheeses, breads, ravioli, pesto, tahini, hummus, and much more.

ENTERTAINMENT AND EVENTS

Wandering Around

The *malecón,* where the sunsets seem the most beautiful in town, is a perfect place to begin the evening. Make sure you eventually make your way to the downtown central plaza by the Presidencia Municipal (City Hall). On both weekday and weekend nights, the city often sponsors free music and dance concerts beginning around 8 P.M. at the bayside **Los Arcos** amphitheater. (For current listings, see the "Calendar of Events" page of tourist newspaper *Vallarta Today.*

After the concert, join the crowds watching the impromptu antics of the *mimos* (mimes) on the amphitheater stage and the nearby street artists painting plates, watercolor country scenes, and fanciful, outer-galaxy spray-can spacescapes.

If you miss the Los Arcos concert, you can usually console yourself with a balloon, *palomitas* (popcorn), and sometimes a band concert in the plaza. If you're inconsolable, buy some peanuts, a roasted ear of sweet corn *(elote),* or a

. dog from a vendor. After that, cool down with an *agua* or *jugo* fruit juice from the *juguería* across the bayside plaza corner, or a cone of ice cream from Baskin-Robbins just north of the city hall.

A tranquil south-of-Cuale spot to cool off evenings is the **Muelle Nuevo** (New Pier) at the foot of Francisca Rodríguez (beach side of Hotel Playa Los Arcos). On a typical evening you'll find a couple dozen folks—men, women, and kids—enjoying the breeze, the swish of the surf, and, with nets or lines, trying to catch a few fish for sale or dinner.

Special Cultural Events

Puerto Vallarta residents enjoy their share of local fiestas. Preparations for **Semana Santa** (Easter week) begin in February, often with a **Carnaval** parade and dancing on Shrove Tuesday, and continue for the seven weeks before Easter. Each Friday until Easter, you might see processions of people bearing crosses filing through the downtown for special masses at neighborhood churches. This all culminates during Easter week, when Puerto Vallarta is awash with visitors, crowding the hotels, camping on the beaches, and filing in solemn processions, which finally brighten to fireworks, dancing, and food on Domingo Gloria (Easter Sunday).

The town quiets down briefly until the May **Fiesta de Mayo,** a countywide celebration of sports contests, music and dance performances, art shows, parades, and beauty pageants.

On the evening of September 15, the Plaza de Armas (City Hall plaza) fills with tipsy merrymakers, who gather to hear the mayor reaffirm Mexican independence by shouting the Grito de Dolores—"Long Live Mexico! Death to the Gachupines!"—under booming, brilliant cascades of fireworks.

Celebration again breaks out seriously during the first 12 days of December, when city groups—businesses, families, neighborhoods—try to outdo each other with music, floats, costumes, and offerings all in honor of Mexico's patron, the Virgin of Guadalupe. The revelry climaxes on December 12, when people, many in native garb to celebrate their indigenous origins, converge on the downtown church to receive the Virgin's blessing. If you miss the main December Virgin of Guadalupe fiesta, you can still

For a week, climaxing on December 12 each year, whole communities don costumes, join processions, whirl in dances, and crowd into churches, all in honor of their beloved national patron, the Virgin of Guadalupe.

enjoy a similar, but smaller-scale celebration in El Tuito (see under "Cabo Corrientes Country" in the Coast of Jalisco chapter), a month later, on the 12th of January.

Visitors who miss such real-life fiestas can still enjoy one of several local **Fiesta Mexicana** tourist shows, which are as popular with Mexican tourists as foreigners. The evening typically begins with a sumptuous buffet of salads, tacos, enchiladas, seafood, barbecued meats, and flan and pastries for dessert. Then begins a nonstop program of music and dance from all parts of Mexico: a chorus of revolutionary *soldaderas* and their Zapatista male compatriots; raven-haired señoritas in flowing, flowered Tehuantepec silk dresses; rows of dashing Guadalajaran *charros* twirling their fast-stepping *chinas poblanas* sweethearts, climaxing with enough fireworks to swab the sky red, white, and green.

The south-of-Cuale **Restaurant Iguana,** Calle Lázaro Cárdenas 311, between Insurgentes and Constitución, tel. 3/222-0105, stages a very popular and *auténtico* such show Thursday and Sunday around 7 P.M. (Sunday only in the low season, call ahead to confirm). Another safe bet is the **Hotel Krystal** show, tel. 3/224-0202, Tuesday and Saturday (Saturday only during the low season) at 7 P.M.

Other such shows are held seasonally at the **Sheraton** on Thursday, tel. 3/226-0404; the **Qualton Club** on Wednesday, tel. 3/224-4446; and the **Playa Los Arcos** on Saturday, tel. 3/222-0583.

The tariff for these shows typically runs $35 per person with open bar—except for the more modest Playa Los Arcos show, which runs about $20, drinks extra. During holidays and the high winter season reservations are generally necessary; best to book through a travel or tour desk agent.

Movies

Puerto Vallarta's former "art" movie house, the **Sala Elizabeth Taylor,** 5 de Febrero 19, just south of the River Cuale and a few doors upstream from Av. I. Vallarta, tel. 3/22206-67, has narrowed its offering to mostly hard-core erotica. The **Cine Bahía** nearby at Insurgentes 189, between Madero and Serdán, tel. 3/22217-17, however, remains a typical '50s-style small-town movie house, running a mixture of Mexican and American pop horror, comedy, and action, such as *The Perfect Storm* and *Men of Honor.* Another similar movie house on the north side of town is the **Cine Luz María,** at Av. México 227, across the street from the Pemex *gasolinera,* tel. 3/222-0705.

Live Music

Cover charges are not generally required at the hotel bars, many of which offer nightly live music and dancing. For example, the **Hotel Krystal,** tel. 3/22402-02, band plays Mexican-romantic-pop daily, 8 P.M.-12 midnight, in season, directly adjacent to the hotel reception desk. (For up-to-date listings, see the "Nightlife" page in *Puerto Vallarta Today.*

The **Hotel Westin Regina,** tel. 3/22111-00, has seasonal live guitar music nightly, 7–8 P.M., while the **Hotel Fiesta Americana,** tel. 3/22420-

10, has Mexican trio and tropical music groups (nightly 7 P.M.–1 A.M.) guaranteed to brighten the spirits of any vacationer after a hard day on the beach.

The **Hotel Playa Los Arcos,** tel. 3/222-0583, offers a combo in the *palapa* restaurant bar with a little bit of everything nightly from oldies-but-goodies to including the patrons in the act, nightly 8–10 P.M.

Other hotels with similar nightly offerings are the Sheraton, tel. 3/223-0404; the Westin Regina, tel. 3/221-1100; and the Continental Plaza, tel. 3/224-0123.

Discos

Discos open quietly around 10 P.M., begin revving up around midnight, and usually pound on till about 5 in the morning. They have dress codes requiring shoes, shirts, and long pants for men, and dresses or blouses and skirts or pants, or modest shorts for women. Often they serve only (expensive) soft drinks. Discos that cater to tourists (all of the following) generally monitor their front doors very carefully; consequently they are pleasant and, with ordinary precautions, secure places to have a good time. If you use earplugs, even the high-decibel joints needn't keep you from enjoying yourself. Listings below are grouped by Zona Hotelera (north side), *malecón,* and south-of-Cuale locations, in approximate order of increasing volume.

Zona Hotelera: In front of Hotel Krystal stands **Christine,** the showplace of Puerto Vallarta discos, tel. 3/224-0202, ext. 2000 and 2001 This disco entices customers to come and pay the $11 cover charge early (11 P.M.) to see its display of special fogs, spacy gyrating colored lights, and sophisticated woofers and tweeters, which, even when loud as usual, are supposed to leave you with minimum hearing impairment.

Malecón: Many popular *malecón* spots regularly pound out a continuous no-cover repertoire of recorded rap and rock. One of the long-time standouts, popular with all generations, is **Carlos O'Brian's,** *malecón* at Pípila, tel. 3/222-1444. High-volume recorded rock, revolutionary wall-photos, zany mobiles, zingy margaritas, and "loco" waiters often lead patrons to dance on the tables by midnight. Folks who generally shy away from loud music can still have fun at Carlos O'Brian's, since the place is big and the high-volume speakers are confined to one area.

Since most *malecón* discos are trying to imitate the **Hard Rock Cafe,** you might as well go right to the source at *malecón* at Abasolo, tel. 3/222-5532.

The **Zoo,** however, across Abasolo from the Hard Rock Cafe, tel. 3/222-4945, appears not to be imitating anyone. While animals—hippos, swooping birds, zebras, even a circulating gorilla—entertain the customers, reggae, rap, and rock thunder from overhead speakers.

South of Cuale: Longtime favorite **Cactus,** south end of I. Vallarta, tel. 3/222-6067, continues to attract youngish crowds with its super lights, sound, and whimsical Disneyland-like decor. Approximately $5 cover charge.

Newcomer **Paco Paco,** one block north at I. Vallarta, between Badillo and Carranza, is trying harder to do the same thing by charging no cover.

Malecón Cafes, Bars, and Hangouts

One of the simplest Puerto Vallarta entertainment formulas is to walk along the *malecón* until you hear the kind of music at the volume you like.

Young film buffs like the glitz and neon of **Planet Hollywood,** at the spot of former Restaurant Brazz, near the *malecón's* south end, at Morelos 518, at Galeana.

On the other hand, traditionalists enjoy Restaurant **Las Palomas,** which features live marimba music nightly, 7–9 P.M., at the corner of Aldama, tel. 3/222-3675.

Another block north, the African safari-decorated **Mogambo,** between Ortíz and Abasolo, offers low-volume live music, often piano or jazz, nightly during high season, tel. 3/222-3476.

A few blocks farther north, corner of Allende, **La Dolce Vita** entertains dinner customers with live programs, such as reggae, flamenco, or folk, 9 P.M.–midnight in season, tel. 3/22235-44.

Those who desire a refined, romantic ambience go to **Restaurant Cafe des Artistes,** tel. 3/222-3228, and take a table for dinner or a seat at the bar, where they enjoy soothing neoclassical flute-accompanied melodies nightly during high season, Friday and Saturday during low season. Find it by walking three blocks along Leona Vicario inland from the *malecón.*

South-of-Cuale Cafes, Bars, and Hangouts

The increasingly popular small entertainment district spread along I. Vallarta around the corner of L. Cárdenas has acquired a number of lively spots, among them the **Mariachis Locos** bar/restaurant. Inside, a mostly local clientele enjoys a lively nonstop mariachi show nightly from about 8 P.M. to the wee hours.

On the same side of Vallarta, half a block north, folks crowd in nightly 9 P.M.–1 A.M. at Roxy "Rythm and Blues Bar" for its unique brand of live, loud, and jazzy rock and roll.

Across the street, a block and a half north, corner of Vallarta and Carranza, the longtime favorite, friendly **Restaurant El Torito,** tel. 3/222-3784, has good ribs, reasonable prices, and seasonal live music from around 10 P.M.–midnight, bar open till around 5 A.M.

Many folks' nights wouldn't be complete without stopping in at the **Andale** Mexican pub, Olas Altas 425, tel. 3/222-1054, whose atmosphere is so amicable and lively that few even bother to watch the nonstop TV. So-so restaurant upstairs; open till around 2 A.M.

If the night is still young, continue downhill one block to the foot of Francisca Rodríguez, to beachfront restaurant **Cuates and Cuetes,** for innovative live "tropical" Latin music, beginning around 7:30 nightly, tel. 3/223-2724.

SPORTS AND RECREATION

Jogging and Walking

Puerto Vallarta's cobbled streets, high curbs (towering sometimes to six feet!), and "holey" sidewalks make for tricky walking around town. The exception is the *malecón,* which can provide a good two-mile roundtrip jog when it is not crowded. Otherwise, try the beaches or the big public sports field, Unidad Deportiva, on the airport boulevard across from the Sheraton.

Swimming, Surfing, and Boogie Boarding

While Puerto Vallarta's calm waters are generally safe for swimming, they are often too tranquil for surfing, bodysurfing, and boogie boarding. Sometimes, strong, surfable waves rise along the southern half of **Playa los Muertos.** Another notable possibility is at the mouth of the

Ameca River (north of the airport) where, during the rainy summer season, the large river flow helps create bigger than normal waves. Surfing is also common at **Bucerías** and **Punta Mita.** (For details, see under "Around the Bay of Banderas," below.)

Windsurfing and Sailboating

A small but growing nucleus of local windsurfing enthusiasts practice the sport from Puerto Vallarta's beaches. They sometimes hold a **windsurfing tournament** during the citywide Fiesta de Mayo in the first week in May.   **Sail Vallarta,** which operates from Marina Vallarta, takes parties out on sailing excursions. For more information, dial 3/221-0096. **Vallarta Adventures,** tel. 3/221-0657 does the same for $150 for two. Bargain for a discount.

Snorkeling and Scuba Diving

The biggest scuba instructor-outfitter in town is **Chico's Dive Shop,** on the *malecón* at Díaz Ordaz 770, between Pípila and Vicario, tel. 3/222-1895, fax 222-1897; open daily 9 A.M.–10 P.M. Chico's offers complete lessons, arranges and leads dive trips, and rents scuba equipment to qualified divers (bring your certificate). A beginning scuba lesson in the pool runs about $20, after which you'll be qualified to dive at Los Arcos. A day boat trip, including one 40-minute dive, costs $60 per person (two tanks, $80), gear included. Snorkelers on the same trip pay about $30. Chico's takes certified divers only to the **Marietas Islands,** the best site in the bay, for $100, including gear and two dives, and sandwiches and sodas for lunch.

Alternatively, try **Vallarta Adventures** at tel. 3/221-0657, another well-established outfit that offers scuba diving services (and much more). Or, look into small (but trying harder) Mismaloya Divers, operated by friendly Fermin (Chipol) Guzman, at Mismaloya, on the south side of the Bay, tel. 3/228-0020, email mismaloya_divers @hotmail.com. With his pair of open (but shaded) boats, Fermin offers scuba diving, starting with resort instruction and beginning dive, for $75. Open water certification usually runs about $250; certified divers get two-tank dives for about $85. You can also go fishing with him for $27/hour, equipment included. Find him, in Mismaloya, 100 yards down the dirt road to the beach, just north of the highway river bridge A.M.–6 P.M. (closed Sunday low s

Jet Skiing, Water-Skiing, and Parasailing

These are available right on the beach at a number of the northside resort-hotels, such as the Sheraton, Hotel Las Palmas, Fiesta Americana Puerto Vallarta, and Krystal.

The same sports are also seasonally available south of Cuale on Playa los Muertos, in front of the Hotels Playa Los Arcos and Tropicana.

Expect to pay about $50 per half hour for a Jet Ski personal watercraft, $75/hour for water-skiing, and $25 for a 10-minute parasailing ride.

Tennis and Golf

The eight—four outdoor clay, four indoor—courts at the friendly **John Newcombe Tennis Club,** Hotel Continental Plaza, tel. 3/224-4360, ext. 500, rent all day for about $16/hour. A sign-up board is available for players seeking partners. It also offers massage, steam baths, equipment sales and rentals, and professional lessons ($38/hour).

The **Iguana Tennis Club,** adjacent to the airport Hwy. 200, Marina side about a block north of the Isla Iguana mock lighthouse, tel. 3/221-0683, rents its three lit astroturf courts for $11 per hour. Lessons run $25/hour with a professional instructor, $11/hour with a junior instructor. Clients can also use its pool and locker rooms for small additional fees.

The several night-lit courts at the **Hotel Krystal,** tel. 3/224-0202 or 3/224-2030, rent for about $15/hour. The Krystal club also offers equipment sales, rentals, and professional lessons. Other clubs, such as the **Sheraton,** tel. 3/223-0404, and **Los Flamingos,** tel. 3/221-2525, also rent their courts to the public.

The 18-hole, par-71 **Marina Vallarta Golf Course,** tel. 3/221-0545, designed by architect Joe Finger, is one of Mexico's best. It is open to the public for $85, which includes greens fee, caddy, and cart. It's open daily 7:30 A.M. to dusk.

The green, palm-shaded 18-hole **Los Flamingos Golf Course,** at Km 145 Hwy. 200, eight miles (13 km) north of the airport, tel. 3/29802-80 or 3/29806-06, offers an attractive alternative. Open to the public daily 7 A.M.–5 P.M., the Los Flamingos services include carts ($28), caddies ($10), club rentals ($20), a pro shop, restaurant, and locker rooms. The greens fee ns about $47. Its pink shuttle bus leaves daily during the high season from the Zona Hotelera (in front of the Sheraton) at 7:30 and 10 A.M., returning twice in the afternoon, before 5 P.M. (Low season, Monday, Tuesday, and Wednesday only; call to confirm.)

Bicycling

Bike Mex offers mountain bike adventures in surrounding scenic country locations. It tailors trips from beginning to advanced levels according to individual ability and interests. More advanced trips include outback spots Yelapa and Sayulita and mountain destinations like San Sebastián, Mascota, and Talpa. Participants enjoy GT Full Suspension or Kona mountain bikes (27-gear), helmets, gloves, purified water, and bilingual guides. Drop by or call the downtown office at 361 Guerrero, tel. 3/223-1680.

Alternatively, you can contact **BBB Bobby's Bikes,** tel. 3/223-0008, which offers approximately the same services.

Horseback Riding

A pair of nearby ranches give visitors the opportunity to explore scenic tropical forest, river, and mountainside country. Options include English or Western saddles, and rides ranging from two hours to a whole day. Contact either **Rancho Ojo de Agua,** tel. 3/224-0607, or **Rancho El Charro,** tel. 3/224-0114, email: aguirre@pvnet .com.mx, or website: www.puertovallarta.com \ranchocharro\.

Adventure Tours

A number of nature-oriented tour agencies lead off-the-beaten-track Puerto Vallarta area excursions. **Vallarta Adventures** offers boat tours to the Islas Marietas wildlife sanctuary (sea turtles, manta rays, dolphins, whales, seabirds) and airplane excursions and a rugged all-day Mercedes-Benz truck ride (canyons, mountains, crystal streams, rustic villages) into the heart of Puerto Vallarta's backyard mountains. Contact a travel agent or tel. 3/221-0657 or 3/221-0658, fax 3/221-2845, email: info@vallarta-adventures.com, or website: www.vallarta-adventures.com for information and reservations.

The offerings of unusually ecologically aware **Expediciones Cielo Abierto** (Open Sky Expeditions), downtown at 339 Guerrero, two blocks north of the riverside Municipal Crafts Market, tel.3/222-3310, fax 3/223-2407, email: openair@vivamexico.com, include snorkeling around Punta Mita, hiking in the Sierra Cuale foothill jungle, birdwatching, cultural tours, dolphin encounters, and whale-watching.

Viva Tours, tel. 3/224-0410 or 3/224-8026, fax 3/224-0182, email: viva2000@prodigy.net.mx, organizes a number of relaxing adventures, including an excursion to a hot spring on the idyllic Mascota River, just half an hour from downtown Puerto Vallarta. Options include a hike or horseback ride and an overnight at a cozy, rustic Rancho Canastilla at the hot spring.

Gyms

Puerto Vallarta has a number of good exercise gyms. The best is the **European Health Spa** (say ays-PAH) at the Marina, Tennis Club Puesta del Sol, tel. 3/221-0770, offering 40 machines, complete weight sets, professional advice, aerobics workouts, and separate men's and women's facilities. Day use runs about $5.

Similar facilities and services are available at the **Hotel Qualton Club and Spa,** tel. 3/224-4446, ext. 5313, for about $10.

Sportfishing

You can hire a *panga* (outboard launch) with skipper on the beach in front of several hotels, such as Los Arcos on Playa los Muertos; the Buenaventura and Sheraton on Playa los Camarones; the Plaza Las Glorias, Las Palmas Beach, and Fiesta Americana Puerto Vallarta on Playa las Glorias; and Krystal on Playa de Oro. Expect to pay about $25/hour for a two- or three-hour trip that might net you and a few friends some jack, bonito, *toro,* or *dorado* for dinner. Ask your favorite restaurant to fix you a fish banquet with your catch.

Another good spot for *panga* rentals is near the Peines (pay-EE-nays) docks, where the fishermen keep their boats. You may be able to negotiate a good price, especially if you or a friend speaks Spanish. Access to the Peines is along the dirt road to the left of the Isla Iguana entrance (at the fake roadside lighthouse a mile north of the Marina cruise ship terminal). The fishermen, a dozen or so members of the Cooperativa de Deportes Aquaticos Bahía de Banderas, have their boats lined up along the roadside channel to the left, a few hundred yards from the highway.

At the end-of-road dock complex (the actual Peines) lie the big-game sportfishing boats that you can reserve only through agents back in town or at the hotels. Agents, such as American Express, tel. 3/223-2910, 3/223-2927, or 3/223-2955, fax 3/223-2926, customarily book reservations during high season on the big 40-foot boats. They go out mornings at 7:30 and return about seven hours later with an average of one big fish per boat. The tariff runs around $70 per person; food and drinks are available but cost extra. Big boats generally have space for 10 passengers, about half of whom can fish at any one time. If not a big sailfish or marlin, most everyone usually gets something.

Another agency that rents sportfishing boats is the **Sociedad Cooperativa Progreso Turístico,** which has 10 boats, ranging from 32 to 40 feet. Rentals run $300–400 per day for a completely outfitted boat. For more information, drop by or call the office on the north end of the *malecón* at 31 de Octubre, across the street from the Hotel Rosita, tel. 3/222-1202. Best to talk to the manager, Apolinar Arce Palomeres, who is usually there Mon.–Sat. 8 A.M.–12 P.M. and 4–8 P.M.

A number of local English-speaking captains regularly take parties out on their well-equipped sportfishing boats. **Mr. Marlin,** record-holder of the biggest marlin catch in Puerto Vallarta, acts as agent for more than 40 experienced captains. Prices begin at about $250 per boat for a full day, including bait, ice, and fishing tackle. Call 3/221-0809 at the Tennis Club Puesta del Sol (at the deli), local 16.

Alternatively, go **Fishing With Carolina** and Captain Juan, who offer sportfishing, whale-watching, and snorkeling expeditions on their fully equipped twin-engine diesel boat. For information and reservations, call Candace at 3/224-7250, cellular 044-329-229-53, or email candacepv@netmail.com.

If you'd like to enter the Puerto Vallarta **Sailfish Tournament,** held annually in November (2002 marks the 47th), call (in English) tel. 3/221-5434 or the Club de Pesca (in Spanish), tel./fax 3/223-1665; drop by the office at 874 Morelos, north end of downtown; write the Puerto Vallarta Torneo de Pez Vela (Sailfish Tournament), P.O. Box 212, Puerto Vallarta, Jalisco 48300;

or see the website www.fishvallarta.com. The registration fee runs about $400 per person, which includes the welcome dinner and the closing awards dinner. The five grand prizes usually include automobiles. The biggest sailfish caught was a 168-pounder in 1957.

At their present rate of attrition, sailfish and marlin will someday certainly disappear from Puerto Vallarta waters. Some captains and participants have fortunately seen the light and are releasing the fish after they're hooked in accordance with IFGA (International Fish and Game Association) guidelines.

Freshwater bass fishing is also an option, at lovely foothill Cajón de Peñas Reservoir (see the Coast of Jalisco chapter) on your own or by **Viva Tours,** at 439 Blv. Ascencio Medina (by the Hotel Las Palmas Beach), tel. 3/224-0410, fax 3/224-0182, email: viva2000@prodigy.net .mx. For $100 per person, you get all transportation, breakfast and lunch, fishing license, guide, and gear. The lake record is 13 pounds.

Boating

The superb 350-berth **Marina Vallarta** has all possible hookups, including certified potable water, metered 110-220-volt electricity, phone, fax, showers, toilets, laundry, dock lockers, trash collection, pump-out. Other amenities include 24-hour security, a yacht club, and complete repair yard. It is surrounded by luxurious condominiums, tennis courts, a golf course, and dozens of shops and offices. Slip rates run around $.75 per foot per day for 1–6 days, $.60 for 7–29 days, and $.50 for 30 or more days. For information, write the Marina at P.O. Box 350-B, Puerto Vallarta, Jalisco 48300, call 3/221-0275, or fax 3/221-0722.

The Marina also has a **public boat-launching ramp** where you can float your craft into the Marina's sheltered waters for about $5. If the guard isn't available to open the gate, call the marina office, tel. 3/221-0275, for entry permission. To get to the launch ramp, follow the street marked "Proa," next to the big pink and white disco, one block south of the main Marina Vallarta entrance.

Sporting Goods Stores

Given the sparse and pricey local sporting goods selection, serious sports enthusiasts should pack their own equipment to Puerto Vallarta. A few stores carry some items. Among the most reliable is **Deportes Gutiérrez Rizo,** corner of south-of-Cuale Avenidas Insurgentes and A. Serdán, tel. 3/222-2595. Although fishing gear—rods, reels, line, sinkers—is its strong suit, it also stocks a general selection including sleeping bags, inflatable boats, tarps, pack frames, wet suits, scuba tanks, and water skis. Open Mon.–Sat. 9 A.M.–2 P.M. and 5–8 P.M.

SHOPPING

Although Puerto Vallarta residents make few folk crafts themselves, they import tons of good—and some very fine—pieces from the places where they *are* made. Furthermore, Puerto Vallarta's scenic beauty has become an inspiration for a growing community of artists and discerning collectors who have opened shops filled with locally crafted sculpture, painting, and museum-grade handicrafts gathered from all over Mexico. Furthermore, resortwear needn't cost a bundle in Puerto Vallarta, where a number of small boutiques offer racks of stylish, comfortable Mexican-made items for a fraction of stateside prices.

South-of-Cuale Shopping
The couple of blocks of Av. Olas Altas and side streets around the Hotel Playa Los Arcos are alive with a welter of T-shirt and *artesanías* (crafts) stores loaded with the more common items—silver, onyx, papier-mâché, pottery—gathered from all over Mexico.

A few shops stand out, however. **Teté,** tel. 3/222-4797, owned by María Elena Zermeño and run by her daughters Olimpia and Ester, contains a treasury of unusual pre-Columbian reproductions and modern original masks, pottery, human figurines, and bark paintings. Besides such items, they also display (and if you ask, competently interpret) other pre-Columbian and modern pieces that are not for sale. Located half a block from the beach at 135 F. Rodríguez, across from Restaurant Archie's Wok; open Mon.–Sat. 10 A.M.–2 P.M. and 4–10 P.M.

Head north a few blocks to Basilio Badillo, to the corner of I. Vallarta, where you can admire the eclectic collection of designer **Patti Gallardo,** 250 B. Badillo Vallarta, tel./fax 3/222-5712 or 3/224-9658. Although Patti's creations extend

from fine art and jewelry to clothing and metal sculptures, her latest specialty is colorful handmade and designed carpets. The store is open Mon.–Fri. 10 A.M.–2 P.M. low season, and Mon.–Sat. 10 A.M.–2 P.M. and 6–10 P.M. high season.

Walk a few doors uphill and across the street, to view the varied sculpture collection at Galería Dante, at 269 B. Badillo, tel. 3/222-2477, fax 3/222-6284. Exquisite wouldn't be too strong a description of the many museum-quality pieces, ranging from neoclassic to abstract modern. Open Mon.–Sat. 10 A.M.–5 P.M.

Head west on Vallarta two blocks and take a look inside a pair of shops, **Talavera, Etc.,** and **Artesanías San Miguel** who both display selections of "Talavera"-style pottery. The label comes from the town in Spain from which the potters, who eventually settled in Puebla, Mexico, emigrated. The style, a blend of Moorish, Chinese, and Mediterranean traditions, is sometimes called "Majolica," from the island city of Majorca, an early center, where the tradition emerged and spread through the Mediterranean during the Middle Ages. Both stores are open Mon.–Sat. approximately 10 A.M.–2 P.M. and 4–7 P.M., at the corner of Lázaro Cárdenas.

Continue half a block up Lázaro Cárdenas to **Olinalá Gallery,** 274 Lázaro Cárdenas, tel.

ERIN DWYER

A Huichol ritual yarn painting depicts a pilgrim playing to the sea goddess, Aramara.

3/222-7495, Nancy and John Erickson's mini-museum of intriguing masks and fine lacquer-ware. Although their "Olinalá" name originates from the famed Mexican lacquerware village where they used to get most of their pieces, ceremonial and festival masks—devils, mermaids, goddesses, skulls, crocodiles, horses, and dozens more—from all parts of Mexico now dominate their fascinating selection. Their offerings, moreover, are priced to sell; open Mon.–Sat. 10 A.M.–2 P.M. and 5–9 P.M.

Tucked away on a quiet residential street is **Mando de Azulelos,** at Carranza 374, a few blocks uphill from Insurgentes, tel. 3/222-2675, fax 3/222-3292. It offers made-on-site tile and Talavera-style pottery at reasonable prices. Unique, however, are the custom-made tiles—round, square, oval—inscribed and fired as you choose, with which you can adorn your home entryway or facade. Open Mon.–Fri. 9 A.M.–7 P.M., Saturday 9 A.M.–2 P.M.

Shopping along the River: Mercado Municipal and Pueblo Viejo

For the more ordinary, yet attractive, Mexican handicrafts, head any day except Sunday (when most shops are closed) to the Mercado Municipal at the north end of the Av. Insurgentes bridge. Here, most shops begin with prices two to three times higher than the going rate. You should counter with a correspondingly low offer. If you don't get the price you want, always be prepared to find another seller. If your offer is fair, the shopkeeper will often give in as you begin to walk away. Theatrics, incidentally, are less than useful in bargaining, which should merely be a straightforward discussion of the merits, demerits, and price of the article in question.

The Mercado Municipal is a two-story warren of dozens upon dozens of shops filled with jewelry, leather, papier-mâché, T-shirts, and everything in between. The congestion can make the place hot; after a while, take a break at a cool river-view seat at one of the *fondas* permanent food stalls on the second floor.

One of the most unusual Mercado Municipal stalls is **Cabaña del Tío Tom,** whose menagerie of colorful papier-mâché parrots are priced a peg or two cheaper than at the tonier downtown stores.

It's time to leave when you're too tired to distinguish silver from tin and Tonalá from Tlaque-paque. Head downstream to the Pueblo Viejo complex on Calle Augustín Rodríguez between Juárez and Morelos, near the Av. I. Vallarta lower bridge. This mall, with individual stores rather than stalls, is less crowded but pricier than the Mercado Municipal. Some shopkeepers will turn their noses up if you try to bargain. If they persist, take your business elsewhere.

Downtown Shopping: Along Juárez and Morelos

A sizable fraction of Puerto Vallarta's best boutiques and arts and crafts stores lie along the six downtown blocks of Av. Juárez, beginning at the Río Cuale. The **Felix Boutique** heads the parade at Juárez 126, half a block north of the river. The friendly, outgoing owner offers reasonably priced women's resortwear of her own design. Open Mon.–Sat. 11 A.M.–2 P.M. and 4–7:30 P.M.

Galería La Indígena, Juárez 270, tel./fax 3/222-3007, in the fourth block of Juárez, features a museum of fine crafts, including Huichol yarn paintings and ceremonial paraphernalia, and religious art. Also prominent is Tarascan art from Ocumichu, Michoacán; Nahua painted coconut faces from Guerrero; a host of masks, both antique originals and new reproductions; pre-Columbian replicas; Oaxaca fanciful wooden *alebrijes* animal figures, and an entire upstairs gallery of contemporary paintings. Open Mon.–Sat. 10 A.M.–3 P.M. and 7–9 P.M.; in winter, Mon.–Sat. 10 A.M.–9 P.M.

Just across the street from Galería Indígena, at Juárez 263, arts and crafts lovers Barbara and Jean Peters collected so many Mexican handicrafts over the years they had to find a place to store their finds. **Galería Vallarta,** tel./fax 3/222-0290, a small museum of singular paintings, ceremonial masks, lampshades, art-to-wear, and more, is the result. Open Mon.–Sat. 10 A.M.–8 P.M., Sunday 10 A.M.–2 P.M.

A few doors up the street, the store of renowned **Sergio Bustamante** (who lives in Guadalajara), Juárez 275, tel. 3/222-1129, email: marcos@zonavirtual.com.mx, contains so many unique sculptures it's hard to understand how a single artist could be so prolific. (The answer: he has a factory-shop full of workers who execute his fanciful, sometimes unnerving, studies in juxtaposition.) Bustamante's more modest faces on eggs, anthropoid cats, and double-nosed clowns go for as little as $200; the largest, most flamboyant works sell for $10,000 or more. Open Mon.–Sat. 10 A.M.–9 P.M.

Back across the street, the government **Instituto de Arte Jaliscense** store, Juárez 284, tel. 3/222-1301, displays examples of nearly every Jalisco folk craft, plus popular items from other parts, such as Oaxaca *alebrijes* (ahl-BREE-hays), fanciful wooden animals. Open Mon.–Sat. 9 A.M.–9 P.M., Sun. 9 A.M.–4 P.M. Since it has a little bit of everything at relatively reasonable prices, this is a good spot for comparison-shopping.

A few blocks farther on, at the corner of Galeana, an adjacent pair of stores, the **Querubines** (Cherubs) and **La Reja** (Grillwork), display their excellent traditional merchandise—riots of papier-mâché fruit, exquisite blue pottery vases, gleaming pewter, clay trees of life, rich Oaxaca and Chiapas textiles, shiny Tlaquepaque hand-painted pottery—so artfully they are simply fun to walk through. The stores are at Juárez 501A and 501B. Queribines, tel. 3/222-2988, is open Mon.–Sat. 9 A.M.–9 P.M.; La Reja, tel. 3/222-2272, is open Mon.–Sat. 10 A.M.–2 P.M. and 4–8 P.M., winter season 10 A.M.–6 P.M.

Half a block farther north, at 533 Juárez, you'll find the **Manuel Lepe** shop, run by the family of the man who put Puerto Vallarta art on the map. His paintings and prints reflect his vision that "Puerto Vallarta is a Paradise," a sentiment to which Manuel Lepe's choirs of angels and little children still testify. Manuel Lepe was proclaimed "National Painter of Mexico" by President Echevarría not long before he died prematurely in 1982 at the age of 46.

Another half-block north, on the short block of Corona (downhill between Juárez and Morelos), are a number of interesting fine crafts stores. First is the ceramics gallery **Majolica,** 183 Corona, which uses the older name from the Mediterranean island of Majorca, where the Talavera pottery style originated before migrating to Spain and Mexico. The personable owner/manager hand-selects the pieces, all of which come from the Puebla family workshops that carry on the Talavera tradition. Her prices reflect the high demand that the Talavera style of colorful classic elegance has commanded for generations. Open Mon.–Sat. 10 A.M.–2 P.M. and 5–8 P.M.

Downhill a few doors, **Arte Mágico Huichol** displays an unusually fine collection of Huichol yarn paintings by renowned artists such as Mariano Valadéz, Hector Ortíz, and María Elena Acosta, at Corona 179, tel. 3/222-3077. Open Mon.–Sat. 10 A.M.–2 P.M. and 4–8 P.M.; winter season also open Sunday 10 A.M.–2 P.M.

Next door, at the corner of Morelos, you'll find the collection of renowned designer **Billy Moon,** Morelos 558, tel. 3/223-0169, whose best customers are interior decorators. They get their pick from choirs of fine Talavera ceramics, Tlaquepaque colored crystal balls, hand-hewn baroque furniture, sentimental Mexican paintings, and much more. Open Mon.–Sat. 10 A.M.–2 P.M. and 5–8 P.M.

Step across Morelos to **Galería Uno,** one of Puerto Vallarta's longest-established fine art galleries, at Morelos 561, tel. 3/222-0908. The collection—featuring internationally recognized artists with whom the gallery often schedules exhibition openings for the public—tends toward the large, the abstract, and the primitive. Open Mon.–Fri. 10 A.M.–8 P.M. and Saturday 10 A.M.–2 P.M.

For a similarly excellent collection, step one block north and around the uphill corner of Aldama, to **Galería Pacifico,** at Aldama 174 upstairs, tel./fax 3/222-1982 or 3/222-5502, email: gary@artmexico.com, website: www.artmexico.com. Here, in an airy upstairs showroom, personable owner Gary Thompson offers a fine collection of paintings, prints, and sculptures of Mexican artists, both renowned and up-and-coming. The mostly realistic works cover a gamut of styles and feelings, from colorful and sentimental to stark and satirical. Gary often hosts Friday meet-the-artist openings, where visitors are invited to socialize with the local artistic community. Open Mon.–Sat. 10 A.M.–2 P.M. and 5–9 P.M. Low-season hours may be shorter.

Finally, head a few blocks back south along Morelos to the **Regina Jewelry Factory,** (Fábrica de Joyería Regina)at Morelos 434, on the *malecón,* tel. 3/222-2487, for just about the broadest selection and best prices in town. Charges for the seeming acres of gold, silver, and jeweled chains, bracelets, pendants, necklaces, and earrings are usually determined simply by weight; a dollar per gram for silver. Open Mon.–Sat. 10 A.M.–10 P.M.

One more unique store, outside the downtown area, is **Ric** jewelry, which displays the gleaming one-of-a-kind master works of silver artist Erika Hult de Corral. Find them in the Villas Vallarta Shopping Center, Km 2.5, Hwy. 200, local C-8, tel. 3/224-4598, directly across the interior street from the Hotel Continental Plaza.

Department Stores
The best department stores in Puerto Vallarta are the two branches of the big **Comercial Mexicana** chain and the equally excellent local store, **Gutierrez Rizo.** For details, see "Supermarkets, Bakeries, and Organic Groceries and Produce" under "Food," preceding.

Photofinishing, Cameras, and Film
Although a number of downtown stores do one-hour developing and printing at U.S. prices, **Foto Rey,** Libertad 330, tel. 3/222-0937 (and a second branch a few blocks away, at Morelos 490) is one of the few in town that develops and prints black and whites. Open Mon.–Sat. 9 A.M.–9 P.M., Sunday 9 A.M.–3 P.M.

Right across the street, **Laboratorios Vallarta,** Libertad 335, tel. 3/222-5070, stocks the most cameras, accessories, and film of any Vallarta store: lots of Fuji and Kodak color negative (print) film in many speeds and sizes plus transparency, professional 120 rolls, and black and white. Open Mon.–Sat. 9 A.M.–9 P.M. If this store doesn't have what you need, perhaps you'll find it at its second branch, around the corner at Morelos 101.

Cameras are an import item in Mexico and consequently very expensive. Even the simplest point-and-shoot cameras cost twice as much as in the U.S. or Canada. Best bring your own.

SERVICES

Money Exchange
Banking has come to the Olas Altas district, with the branch of **Bancrecer,** on Av. Olas Altas, beach side, near B. Badillo. Hours are Mon.–Fri. 9 A.M.–5 P.M. and Saturday 10 A.M.–2 P.M. After hours, use its ATM.

Most downtown banks cluster along Juárez, near the plaza. Avoid long lines by using your card in their 24-hour ATMs for cash. One location exception is **Banco International,** just north of the Insurgentes bridge, and open the longest hours of all, Mon.–Sat. 8 A.M.–7 P.M.

National Bank of Mexico (Banamex), at the southeast corner of the town plaza, tel. 3/222-5377 or 3/222-1998, changes U.S. and Canadian cash and traveler's checks at the best rates in town. Money exchange hours (go to the special booth at 176 Zaragoza, left of the bank main entrance) are approximately Mon.–Fri. 9 A.M.–5 P.M., Saturday 9 A.M.–2 P.M.

If the lines at Banamex are too long, try **Bancomer,** two blocks north at Juárez and Mina, tel. 3/222-5050, money exchange hours approximately Mon.–Fri. 9 A.M.–5 P.M., Saturday 9 A.M.–1 P.M. or **Banco Inverlat,** across the street, tel. 3/223-1224, hours Mon.–Fri. 9 A.M.–5 P.M., Saturday 10:30 A.M.–3 P.M.

Additionally, scores of little *casas de cambio* (exchange booths) dot the old town streets, especially along the *malecón* downtown, and along Av. Olas Altas and Insurgentes south of the Río Cuale. Although they generally offer about $2 per $100 less than the banks, they compensate with long hours, often 9 A.M.–9 P.M. daily. In the big hotels, cashiers will generally exchange your money at rates comparable to the downtown exchange booths.

The local **American Express** agency cashes American Express traveler's checks and offers full member travel services, such as personal-check cashing (up to $1,000, every 21 days; bring your checkbook, your ID or passport, and your American Express card). The office is downtown, at Morelos 160, corner of Abasolo, tel. 3/223-2927, 3/223-2955 or 3/223-29101, fax 3/223-2926, one block inland from the Hard Rock Cafe. Business hours are Mon.–Fri. 9 A.M.–6 P.M., Saturday 9 A.M.–1 P.M.

Post Office, Telephone, and Internet
Puerto Vallarta has a number of branch post offices. The main *correo* is downtown, two blocks north of the central plaza, just off Juárez, at Mina 188, tel. 3/222-1888, open Mon.–Fri. 8 A.M.–4:30 P.M., Saturday 8 A.M.–noon. The branch at the Edificio Maritima (Maritime Building), near the cruise liner dock, is open Mon.–Fri. 8 A.M.–3 P.M., Saturday 9 A.M.–1 P.M., tel. 3/224-7219. The airport has lost its post office branch; deposit postcards and letters in the airport mailbox *(buzón.)*

Secure express mail, telegraph, fax, telex, and money orders *(giros)* are available at the **Mexpost** office, 584 Juárez, four blocks north of the central plaza, tel. 3/223-1360; open Mon.–Fri. 9 A.M.–9 P.M., Saturday 9 A.M.–1 P.M.

The cheapest and often most convenient telephone option is to buy a public phone card (*tarjeta de teléfono*: say tar-HAY-tah day tay-LAY-foh-noh) and use it at street telephones. They're widely available at stores, in denominations of 20, 50, and 100 pesos. Telephone card calling rates to the U.S. and Canada are much cheaper than AT&T, Sprint, and MCI. Lacking a telephone card, call from your hotel. Lacking a hotel (or if you don't like its extra charges), go to one of the many *casetas de larga distancia,* long-distance telephone offices, sprinkled all over town. For example, **Computel,** the efficient computer-assisted long-distance and public fax service, maintains a number of Puerto Vallarta offices: at Plaza Genovese, Km 2.5 airport highway, on the south side of Comercial Mexicana, tel. 3/224-7773, open daily 8 A.M.–9 P.M.; and at the Marina inner harbor, *puerto interior,* yacht basin, tel. 3/224-5561, open daily 8 A.M.–7 P.M.

A number of other offices provide *larga distancia* and public fax in the downtown area. Moving from south to north: On the north side of Plaza Lázaro Cárdenas, by the Hotel Eloisa, tel. 3/223-0850, fax 3/222-3520, open Mon.–Sat. 9 a.m–10 P.M.; or just north of the Río Cuale, at Juárez 136, below the bridge, half a block from the Hotel Encino, open Mon.–Fri. 9 A.M.–2 P.M. and 4–7 P.M., Saturday until 1:30 P.M.; or farther north by the *malecón* at Aldama 180, five blocks north of the central plaza, tel. 3/223-0199, open Mon.–Sat. 9 A.M.–8:30 P.M.

Puerto Vallarta has a number of public **internet** stores. Moving south to north: **Surf's Up,** on Olas Altas, across from the Hotel Playa Los Arcos, open 8:30 A.M.–midnight, tel. 3/223-4676, $3/hr; **The Net House and Cybercafe,** at I. Vallarta 232, open 7:00 A.M.–2 A.M., tel. 3/222-6953; and **Eclipse,** at Juárez 208, across from the Presidencia Municipal, tel. 3/222-1755.

Health, Police, and Emergencies

If you need medical advice, ask your hotel desk for assistance, or go to one of Puerto Vallarta's several good small hospital-clinics. One of the most respected is the **CMQ** (Centro Médico Quirúrgico) south of the Río Cuale at 366 Basilio Badillo, between Insurgentes and Aguacate, tel. 3/223-1919 (ground floor) or 3/223-0011 (second floor).

Right around the corner on Insurgentes, across from the gas station, is the bilingual-staffed **Hospital Medasist,** at M. M. Dieguez 358, tel./fax 3/223-0444. The hospital, which advertises that it accepts "all worldwide medical insurance for emergencies," with emergency room, lab, diagnostic equipment, and a staff of specialists, appears to be another good place to go when you're sick.

On the north side, closer to the Hotel Zone, stands the equally well-respected 24-hour hospital clinic of **Servicios Médico de la Bahía,** Km 1 on the airport boulevard across from the Sheraton, tel. 3/222-2627.

If you must have an English-speaking doctor, **IAMAT** (International Association for Medical Assistance to Travelers) has two U.S.-trained doctors in Puerto Vallarta. Contact António Sahagún Rodríguez, M.D., downtown, at Corona 234, tel. 3/222-1305, hours Mon.–Sat. 10 A.M.–1 P.M., or Alfonso Rodríguez L., M.D., at south-of-Cuale Av. B. Badillo 365, tel. 3/223-1919, hours Mon.–Fri. 6–8 P.M.

For round-the-clock prescription service, call one of the five branches of **Farmacia CMQ;** for example, south of Cuale, at B. Badillo 367, tel. 3/222-1330, 222-2941, or on the north side, at Peru 1146, tel. 3/222-1110.

A legion of loyal customers swears by the diagnostic competence of Federico López Casco, of **Farmacia Olas Altas,** Av. Olas Altas 365, two blocks south of Hotel Playa Los Arcos, tel. 3/222-2374, whom they simply know as "Freddy." Although a pharmacist and not a physician, his fans say he is a wizard at recommending remedies for their aches and pains.

For **police** emergencies, call the police headquarters; 3/222-0123, 223-2500; in case of **fire**, call the *bomberos* (fire department), at 3/224-7701.

Immigration, Customs, and Consulates

If you need an extension to your tourist card, you can get a total of 180 days at the local branch of **Instituto Nacional de Migración.**

Present your existing tourist card at the office, on the maritime terminal entrance road (cruise ship dock), next to the Pemex gas station, at street number 2755 (upstairs), tel. 3/224-7719, 3/224-7653, or 3/224-7970, open Mon.–Fri. 8 A.M.–2 P.M.

If you lose your tourist card, go to Migración with your passport or identification, and some proof of the day you arrived in Mexico, such as a copy of the original permit or your airplane ticket.

The small local **United States Consular Office** issues passports and does other essential legal work for U.S. citizens at Zaragoza 160, room 18, first floor, adjacent to the town plaza, south side, open Mon.–Fri. 10 A.M.–2 P.M. Write P.O. Box 395, Puerto Vallarta, Jalisco 48300, call 3/222-0069, or fax 3/223-0074. In an emergency after hours, call U.S. Consul General in Guadalajara, tel. 01-3/826-5553.

The **Canadian honorary consul**, tel. 3/222-5398 or 3/223-0858, fax 3/222-3517, provides similar services for Canadian citizens Mon.–Fri. 9 A.M.–5 P.M., at the same plaza-front address, room 10, first floor. In an emergency, after hours call the Canadian Embassy in Mexico City, toll-free at 01 800/706-2900.

Arts and Music Courses

The private, volunteer **Centro Cultural Vallartense** periodically sponsors theater, modern dance, painting, sculpture, aerobics, martial arts, and other courses for adults and children. From time to time it stages exhibition openings for local artists, whose works it regularly exhibits at the gallery/information center at Plaza del Arte on Isla Río Cuale. For more information, look for announcements in the "Community Corner" of *Vallarta Today,* or drop by and talk to the volunteer in charge at the Plaza del Arte gallery and information center, at the upstream end of Isla Río Cuale (see "Sights," earlier in this chapter).

Sharing the Plaza de Arte is the round **Escuela Municipal de Música** building, where, late weekday afternoons, you may hear the strains of students practicing the violin, guitar, piano, flute, and pre-Columbian instruments. Such lessons are open to the general public; apply in person during the late afternoons or early evening.

INFORMATION

Tourist Information Offices

Two tourist information offices serve Puerto Vallarta visitors. The downtown branch is on the central plaza, northeast corner (at Juárez) on the central plaza, customarily open Mon.–Fri. 8 A.M.–4 P.M., tel. 3/223-2500, extensions 230 or 232, fax extension 233. The other tourist information office, tel. 3/221-2676 and fax 3/221-2678, is in the Marina shopping plaza (marked by the big McDonald's sign), with about the same hours as the plaza branch. Both offices provide assistance, information, and dispense whatever maps, pamphlets, and copies of *Vallarta Today* and *Puerto Vallarta Lifestyles* they happen to have.

Another source of local information (in Spanish) is the Puerto Vallarta branch of the **Cámara Nacional de Comercio** (chamber of commerce), which publishes an excellent *Directorio Comercial Turístico,* a directory to everything you are likely to need in Puerto Vallarta. Find the chamber at Morelia 138, 2nd floor, tel. 3/224-2708, one block off the *libramiento* downtown bypass boulevard, four blocks from the airport highway, open Mon.–Fri. 9 A.M.–5 P.M., Saturday 9 A.M.–1 P.M.

Publications

New books in English are not particularly common in Puerto Vallarta. However, a number of small stores and stalls, such as the no-name **newsstand** at 420 Olas Altas, beach side, across from Ándale restaurant, and **Nuevo Librería Limón,** at 310 Carranza, between Vallarta and Constitución (open Mon.–Sat. 9 A.M.–2 P.M. and 4–8 P.M.), regularly sell newspapers, including Mexico City *News* and sometimes *USA Today* and the *Los Angeles Times.* Both are open daily until 9 or 10 P.M.

Supermercado Gutiérrez Rizo, corner Constitución and F. Madero, offers an excellent American magazine selection and some new paperback novels; open daily 6:30 A.M.–10 P.M. **Señor Book,** on upper Olas Altas, at Gómez, has perhaps the best English-language for-sale book collection in Puerto Vallarta.

Comercial Mexicana (see "Supermarkets, Bakeries, and Organic Groceries and Produce" above) and shops at certain big hotels—Camino

Real, Sheraton, Continental Plaza, Fiesta Americana, Melia, and Westin Regina—also stock U.S. newspapers, magazines, and paperbacks.

Vallarta Today, an unusually informative tourist daily, is handed out free at the airport and travel agencies, restaurants, and hotels all over town. Besides detailed information on hotels, restaurants, and sports, it includes a local events and meetings calendar and interesting historical, cultural, and personality feature articles. Call the newspaper if you can't find a copy, tel. 3/224-2928, fax 3/221-2255, hours Mon.–Fri. 9 A.M.–8 P.M., at Mérida 118, Colonia Versalles.

Equally excellent is *Puerto Vallarta Lifestyles,* the quarterly English-language magazine, which also features unusually detailed and accurate town maps. If you cannot find a free copy at the airport or your hotel, contact **Lifestyles** at tel.3/221-0106, Mon.–Fri. 9 A.M.–7 P.M., or at Calle Timon #1, in the Marina.

The local **public library** (actually the "DIF" federally supported library) has a small general collection, including Spanish-language reference books and a dozen shelves of English-language paperbacks, at Parque Hidalgo, one block north of the end of the *malecón,* in front of the church. Open Mon.–Fri. 8 A.M.–8 P.M., Saturday 9 A.M.–5 P.M.

A second public library, established and operated by a volunteer committee, has accumulated a sizable English and Spanish book collection, at Franscisco Villa 1001, in Colonia Los Mangos. Get there by taxi or car, several blocks along Villa, which diagonals northerly and inland at the sports field across the airport boulevard from the Hotel Sheraton. By bus, take the "Pitillal" and "biblioteca"-marked bus.

Spanish Instruction
The **University of Guadalajara Study Center for Foreigners** offers one-, two-, and four-week total immersion Spanish language instruction, including homestays with local families. For more information, visit the office, at Libertad 105 downtown or telephone 3/223-2082, fax 223-2982, email cipv@cepe.edu.mex, or see the website www.cepe.udg.mx.

Volunteer Work
A number of local volunteer clubs and groups invite visitors to their meetings and activities.

Check with the tourist information office or see the "Community Corner" listing in *Vallarta Today* for current meeting and activity details.

The **Club Internacional de la Amistad** (International Friendship Club), an all-volunteer service club, sponsors a number of health, educational, and cultural projects. It welcomes visitors to the (usually second Monday) monthly general membership meeting. For more information, see the "Community Corner" in *Vallarta Today,* call 3/222-5466, or ask at the tourist information office. One of the best ways to find out about its work is on the popular tour of Puerto Vallarta homes, which customarily begins mornings in the central plaza, near the bandstand during the Nov.–April high season. The club asks a donation of about $20 per person to further its charitable programs.

The **Ecology Group of Vallarta,** a group of local citizens willing to work for a cleaner Puerto Vallarta, welcomes visitors to its activities and regular meetings. Call Ron Walker, tel. 3/222-0897, for more information.

The **Animal Protection Association** is working to humanely reduce the number of stray and abandoned animals on Puerto Vallarta streets. For more information, see the "Community Corner" in *Vallarta Today.*

GETTING THERE AND AWAY

By Air
Several major carriers connect Puerto Vallarta by direct flights with United States and Mexican destinations.

Mexicana Airlines flights connect daily with Denver, Chicago, Mexico City, and Guadalajara. In Puerto Vallarta call 3/221-1266 or toll-free 01-800/366-5400 for reservations and 3/224-8900 for airport flight information.

Aeroméxico flights connect daily with Los Angeles, San Diego (winter-spring only), Tijuana, Guadalajara, Acapulco, León, Aguascalientes, Juárez, Monterrey, and Mexico City; for reservations and flight information, call 3/224-2777.

Alaska Airlines flights connect with Los Angeles, San Francisco, Portland, Seattle, and Anchorage; for reservations, call a local travel agent or, from Puerto Vallarta, call Alaska's U.S. direct toll-free number, tel. 001-800/426-0333.

American Airlines flights connect daily with Dallas-Ft. Worth; call 3/221-1799 or 3/221-1927, or toll-free in Mexico 01-800/904-60 reservation and information number.

Trans World Airlines charter flights connect seasonally (Dec.–April) with St. Louis; locally; call a travel agent such as American Express 3/223-2910 or 3/223-2955, or toll-free in Mexico, 01-800/238-1997 for information and reservations.

Continental Airlines flights connect daily with Houston; call 3/221-1025 or toll-free in Mexico 01-800/900-5000 for reservations.

America West Airlines flights connect with Phoenix; for reservations and information, call a travel agent, such as American Express, tel. 3/223-2910, or America West locally, at 3/321-1025, or toll-free 01-800/235-9292.

Canadian World of Vacations charter flights connect with Toronto, Winnepeg, Saskatoon, Regina, Calgary-Edmonton, and Vancouver (mostly during the winter); for information, call a travel agent, such as American Express, tel. 3/223-2910 or 3/223-2955.

Puerto Vallarta Airport Arrival and Departure

Air arrival at Puerto Vallarta (code-designated PVR, officially the Gustavo Díaz Ordaz International) Airport is generally smooth and simple. After the cursory (if any) customs check, arrivees can avail themselves of a **24-hour ATM** and **money-exchange counters,** open Mon.–Fri. 9 A.M.–8 P.M., Saturday 8 A.M.–3 P.M.; a lineup of **car rental booths** includes Budget, National, Avis, Dollar, Advantage, and Hertz. (For car-rental local telephone numbers, see "Getting Around," under "Sights" earlier in this chapter.)

Transportation to town is easiest by *colectivo* (collective taxi-vans) or *taxi especial* (individual taxi). Booths sell tickets at curbside. The *colectivo* fare runs about $4 per person to the northern hotel zone, $5 to the center of town, and $7 or more to hotels and hamlets south of town. Individual taxis run about $9, $11 and $19 for the same rides.

Taxis to more distant northern destinations, such as Rincón de Guayabitos (39 miles, 62 km) and San Blas or Tepic (100 miles, 160 km), run about $60 and $100, respectively. A much cheaper alternative is to hire a taxi from the airport to new bus terminal north of the airport, where you can continue by very frequent **Transportes Pacifico** northbound second-class bus. The Bucerías fare should run less than $1, Sayulita $2, Guayabitos about $3, and Tepic or San Blas $7 (for San Blas, go by Transportes Norte de Sonora or Transportes del Pacifico second-class and transfer at Las Varas). The buses are usually crowded; don't tempt people with a dangling open purse or a bulging wallet in your pocket.

Airport departure is as simple as arrival. Save by sharing a taxi with departing fellow hotel guests. Agree on the fare with the driver before you get in. If the driver seems too greedy (see airport arrival fares above), hail another taxi. Once at the airport, you can do last-minute shopping at a number of airport shops, or mail a letter at the airport *buzón* (mailbox).

If you've lost your tourist card, be prepared with a copy or you'll have to pay a fine unless you've gotten a duplicate through Immigration (Migración), see "Immigration, Customs, and Consulates" preceding. In any case, be sure to save enough pesos or dollars to pay your **$12 departure tax** (unless your ticket already includes it).

By Car or RV

Three road routes connect Puerto Vallarta north with Tepic and San Blas, east with Guadalajara, and south via Melaque-Barra de Navidad with Manzanillo. They are all two-lane roads, requiring plenty of caution.

To Tepic, **Mexican National Hwy. 200** is all asphalt and in good condition most of its 104 miles (167 km) from Puerto Vallarta. Traffic is ordinarily light to moderate, except for some slow going around Tepic, and over a few low passes about 20 miles north of Puerto Vallarta. Allow three hours for the southbound trip and half an hour longer in the reverse direction for the winding 3,000-foot climb to Tepic.

A shortcut connects San Blas directly with Puerto Vallarta, avoiding the oft-congested uphill route through Tepic. Heading north on Hwy. 200, at Las Varas turn off west on to Nayarit Hwy. 161 to Zacualpan and Platanitos, where the road continues through the jungle to Santa Cruz village on the Bay of Matanchén. From there you can continue along the shoreline to San Blas. In the opposite direction, heading south from San Blas, follow the signed "Puerto Vallarta" turnoff to the right (south) a few hundred yards after the Santa Cruz de Miramar junction. Allow about three hours, either direction, for the entire San Blas–Puerto Vallarta trip.

The story is similar for Mexican National Hwy. 200 along the 172 miles (276 km) to Manzanillo via Barra de Navidad (134 miles, 214 km). Trucks and a few potholes may cause slow going while climbing the 2,400-foot Sierra Cuale summit south of Puerto Vallarta, but light traffic should prevail along the other stretches. Allow about four hours to Manzanillo, three from Barra de Navidad, and the same in the opposite direction.

The Guadalajara route is a bit more complicated. From Puerto Vallarta, follow Hwy. 200 as if to Tepic, but, just before Compostela (80 miles, 129 km from Puerto Vallarta) follow the 22-mile (36-km) Guadalajara-bound toll *(cuota)* shortcut east, via Chapalilla. From Chapalilla, continue east via **Mexican National Hwy. 15** toll expressway *autopista*. Although expensive (about $20 per car, much more for motor homes) the expressway is a breeze, compared to the old, narrow, and congested *libre* Hwy. 15. Allow around five hours at the wheel for the entire 214-mile (344-km) Guadalajara–Puerto Vallarta trip, either way.

By Bus

Many bus lines run through Puerto Vallarta. The major long-distance bus action is at the new **Camionera Central** (Central Bus Station) a few miles north of the airport.

The shiny, air-conditioned complex resembles an airline terminal, with a cafeteria, juice bars, a travel agency, a long-distance telephone and fax service, luggage storage lockers, a gift shop, and a hotel reservation booth.

Mostly first- and luxury-class departure ticket counters line one long wall. First-class **Elite** (EL) line and its parent **Estrella Blanca** (EB), with other affiliated lines Turistar (TUR), Futura (FU), Transportes Norte de Sonora (TNS) and Transportes Chihuahenses (TC), tel. 3/221-0848, and 221-0850, connect the entire northwest-southeast Pacific Coast corridor. Northwesterly destinations include La Peñita (Rincón de

Guayabitos), Tepic, San Blas, Mazatlán, all the way to Nogales or Mexicali and Tijuana on the U.S. border. Other departures head north, via Tepic, Torreón and Chihuahua to Ciudad Juárez, at the U.S. border. Still others connect northeast, via Guadalajara, Aguascalientes, Zacatecas, and Saltillo, with Monterrey. In the opposite direction, departures connect with the entire southeast Pacific Coast, including Melaque, Manzanillo, Playa Azul, Lázaro Cárdenas, Ixtapa-Zihuatanejo, and Acapulco (where you can transfer to Oaxaca-bound departures.)

Transportes Pacifico, tel. 3/221-0893, offers first-class departures that also travel the northwest Pacific route, via Tepic and Mazatlán to Nogales, Mexicali, and Tijuana. Transportes Pacifico provides additional first-class connections, east with Guadalajara and Mexico City direct; and others via Guadalajara and Morelia, Michoacán, with Mexico City.

Transportes Pacifico also provides second-class daytime connections every 30 minutes, north with Tepic, stopping everywhere, notably, Bucerías, Sayulita, Guayabitos, La Peñita, Las Varas, and Compostela en route.

Affiliated lines **Autocamiones del Pacifico** and **Transportes Cihuatlán,** tel. 3/221-0021, provide many second-class and some first-class departures along the Jalisco coast. Frequent second-class connections stop at El Tuito, Tomatlán, El Super, Careyes, Melaque, Barra de Navidad, and everywhere in between. They also connect with Guadalajara by the long southern route, via Melaque, Autlán, and San Clemente (a jumping-off point for Talpa, Mascota, and San Sebastián). Primera Plus, its luxury-class line, provides a few daily express connections southeast with Manzanillo, with stops at Melaque and Barra de Navidad.

A separate luxury-class service, a subsidiary of Flecha Amarilla, also called **Primera Plus,** tel. 3/221-0095, also provides express connections, southeast, with Melaque, Barra de Navidad, Manzanillo, and Colima. Other such Primera Plus departures connect east with Guadalajara, continuing on to Aguascalientes, Irapuato, Celaya, Querétaro, and León. Affiliated line **Autobuses Costa Alegre** provides frequent second-class connections southeast along the Jalisco coast, via El Tuito, El Super, Careyes, Melaque, Barra de Navidad, and all points in between.

Additionally, **ETN (Enlaces Transportes Nacional),** tel. 3/221-0450, has first-class departures connecting east with Guadalajara and Mexico City, offering continuing connections in Guadalajara with several Michoacán destinations.

AROUND THE BAY OF BANDERAS

As a destination city, Puerto Vallarta is packed with all the services, food, and accommodations a quality resort can supply. What Puerto Vallarta often cannot offer, however, is peace and quiet.

But an out exists. The diadem of rustic retreats—fishing villages, palm-shadowed sandy beaches, diminutive resorts—that ring the Bay of Banderas can provide a day-, week-, or month-long respite from the citified tourist rush.

The Southern Arc—Mismaloya
The southern-arc beach gems of Mismaloya, Boca de Tomatlán, Las Animas, Quimixto, and Yelapa are described in the Puerto Vallarta section under "Sights."

The Northern Arc—Nuevo Vallarta, Bucerías, and Punta Mita
The northern curve of the Bay of Banderas begins as Hwy. 200 crosses the Ameca River and enters the state of Nayarit. Here clocks shift from central to mountain time; heading north, set your watch back one hour. Just after you cross over the bridge, you might want to stop at the **Nayarit tourist information office,** tel./fax 329-700-18, which regularly supplies several excellent brochures of Nayarit's interesting but mostly untouristed destinations.

NUEVO VALLARTA

The Nuevo Vallarta development, just north of the river, is Nayarit's design for a grand resort, comparable to the Zona Hotelera 10 miles south. For years, however, miles of boulevard parkways dotted with streetlights and empty cul-de-sacs remained deserted, waiting for homes, condos, and hotels that were never built. A spurt of activity in the early 1990s seemed to promise the potential of Nuevo Vallarta might someday be realized. The **Club de Playa Nuevo Vallarta,** the core of the original development, is indeed a pretty place—perfect for a relaxing beach afternoon. Get there by turning left at Av. Nuevo Vallarta about five miles (eight km) north of the airport at the Nuevo Vallarta signed monument (beach side of highway), one mile past the north end of the Ameca bridge. At the end of the 1.4-mile driveway entrance you will come to the Club de Playa, with a parking lot, small regional art and artifacts museum, pool, snack bar, and seemingly endless beach.

The miles-long beach is the main attraction. The nearly level golden white sand is perfect for beachcombing, and the water is excellent for surf fishing, swimming, bodysurfing, and boogie boarding. Beginning or intermediate surfing might be possible for those who bring their own board. Enjoy isolated beach camping during the temperate winter on the endless dune past the north end beach boulevard of Paseo Cocoteros. Bring everything, including water and a tarp for shade.

Accommodations
Adjacent to the Club de Playa is the palmy, Mediterranean-style, French-Canadian-owned **Club Oasis Marival,** which sometimes invites the public to drop in on its continuous party, which includes sports, crafts, games, and food and drink for about $50 per person, per day. If you take a room, the all-inclusive food, lodging, and activities run about $210 per day for two in low season, $270 high. Reservations are available through an agent or at the hotel, Blvd. Nuevo Vallarta, esq. Paseo Cocoteros, Nuevo Vallarta, Nayarit 63573, tel. 329/701-66, fax 329/701-60; in Mexico, call toll-free 01-800/326-00.

About three miles south of the Club Oasis Marival, a cluster of big new hotels woo vacationers with a plethora of facilities and long, vel-

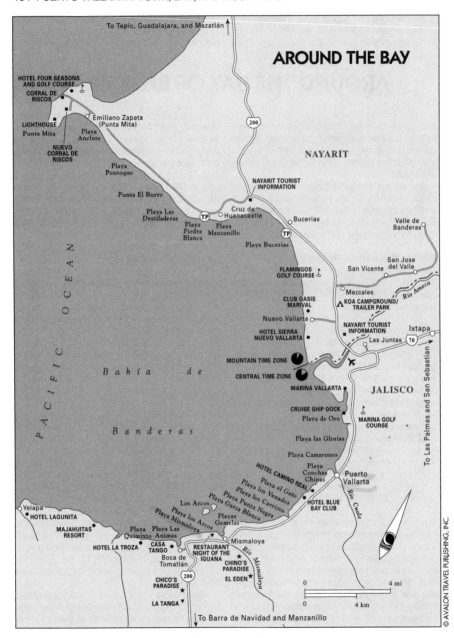

AROUND THE BAY

To Tepic, Guadalajara, and Mazatlán

HOTEL FOUR SEASONS
AND GOLF COURSE
CORRAL DE
RISCOS

LIGHTHOUSE
Punta Mita

Emiliano Zapata
(Punta Mita)

Playa
Anclote

NUEVO
CORRAL DE
RISCOS

Playa
Pontoque

NAYARIT

Punta El Burro

Playa Las
Destiladeras

Cruz de
Huanacaxtle

NAYARIT TOURIST
INFORMATION

Playa
Piedra
Blanca

Playa
Manzanillo

Bucerias

Valle de
Banderas

Playa Bucerias

FLAMINGOS
GOLF COURSE

San Vicente

San Jose
del Valle

CLUB OASIS
MARIVAL

Mezcales

Río Ameca

KOA CAMPGROUND/
TRAILER PARK

Nuevo Vallarta

HOTEL SIERRA
NUEVO VALLARTA

NAYARIT TOURIST
INFORMATION

Las Juntas

Ixtapa

70

PACIFIC OCEAN

Bahía   de

MOUNTAIN TIME ZONE

CENTRAL TIME ZONE

MARINA VALLARTA

JALISCO

Banderas

CRUISE SHIP DOCK

Playa de Oro

MARINA GOLF
COURSE

Playa las Glorias

Playa Camarones

Playa
Conchas
Chinas

Puerto
Vallarta

HOTEL CAMINO REAL

Playa el Gato

Playa los Venados

Playa los Carrizos

Playa Punta Negra

HOTEL BLUE
BAY CLUB

Río Cuale

Yelapa
HOTEL LAGUNITA

Los Arcos

Playa Garza Blanca

Playa los Arcos

Playas
Gemelas

MAJAHUITAS
RESORT

Playa Mismaloya

Playa
Quimixte

Playa Las
Animas

HOTEL LA TROZA

CASA
TANGO

Mismaloya

Boca de
Tomatlán

RESTAURANT
NIGHT OF THE
IGUANA

CHINO'S
PARADISE

Río Mismaloya

CHICO'S
PARADISE

EL EDEN

200

LA TANGA

To Barra de Navidad and Manzanillo

To Las Palmas and San Sebastian

0   4 mi

0   4 km

© AVALON TRAVEL PUBLISHING, INC.

vety beaches. The 344-room **Hotel Sierra Nuevo Vallarta** seems to be the most successful, located at Paseo de Cocoteros 19, Nuevo Vallarta, Nayarit 63732, tel. 329/713-00, fax 329/702-66. Arriving at the hotel feels like approaching a small, Elysian planet. You drive for miles past uninhabitated verdure-lined boulevards, finally pulling up to a huge, apparently deserted structure, where, inside, to your surprise, droves of relaxed, well-fed tourists are socializing in half a dozen languages. Above the reception area rises a towering, angular atrium. Nearby, a garden of lovely ceramic fruits decorates whitewashed stairs leading down to a buffet loaded with salads, fruit, poultry, fish, meats, and desserts spread on one side of an airy, guest-filled dining area. Outside are pools beneath palm trees along the beach, where crowds enjoy nightly dancing and shows. By day, guests lounge, swim, and frolic amid a varied menu of activities, from water aerobics and yoga to beach volleyball, bicycling, and kayaking.

Rates include all food, drinks, activities, and a deluxe ocean-view room with everything. They begin at about $100 s, $145 d low season, about $170 and $225 high. Children under seven stay free; there's a tariff of $25 for those from 7 to 12, and children over 12 are considered adults. If the season is right, a travel agent may be able to secure a reduced-rate package. For information and reservations, in the U.S. and Canada dial toll-free 800/515-4321,or email info@mtmcorp.com., or see the website www.hsnvr1@sidek.com.

Next door the **Allegro Resort,** Paseo de los Cocoteros 18, Nuevo Vallarta, Nayarit 63732, tel. 329/704-00, fax 706-26, offers a similar all-inclusive vacation package for about $140 s, $174 d low season, $170 and $220 high. Children under seven $40, 8–12, $60. Bargain packages may likely be available during non-peak seasons.

BUCERÍAS

The scruffy roadside clutter of Bucerías (Place of the Divers) is deceiving. Located 12 miles (19 km) north of the Puerto Vallarta airport, Bucerías (pop. 5,000) has the longest, creamiest beach on the Bay of Banderas. Local people flock there on Sunday for beach play, as well as fresh seafood from one of several *palapa* restaurants (which, however, may be mostly closed weekdays).

Bucerías, nevertheless, offers a number of options. It is basically a country town of four long streets running for three miles parallel to the beach. The town features small businesses and grocery stores and a sprinkling of local-style restaurants. Bucerías furthermore has lots of old-fashioned local color, especially in the evenings around the lively market at the south end of the business district.

The beach—seemingly endless and nearly flat, with slowly breaking waves and soft, golden-white sand—offers swimming, bodysurfing, boogie boarding, beginning and intermediate surfing, and surf fishing. Tent camping is customary beyond the edges of town, especially during the Christmas and Easter holidays.

Accommodations
At the town's serene north end is the Playas de Huanacaxtle subdivision, with big flower-decorated homes owned by rich Mexicans and North Americans. Sprinkled among the intimate, palm-shaded *retornos* (cul-de-sacs) are a number of good bungalow-style beachside lodgings. Moving southward from the north edge of town, the top accommodations begin with the **Condo-Hotel Vista Vallarta,** at Av. de los Picos s/n, Playas de Huanacaxtle, Bucerías, Nayarit 63732, tel. 329/803-61, fax 329/803-60. Here, three stories of stucco and tile apartments cluster intimately around a palm-tufted beachside pool and patio. A loyal cadre of longtime guests—mostly U.S. and Canadian retiree-couples—return year after year to enjoy the big blue pool, the *palapa* restaurant, walks along the beach, and the company of fellow vacationers. All enjoy fully furnished two-bedroom suites with dining room, kitchenette, living room, and private ocean-view balconies. Maids clean rooms daily, while downstairs, friendly, English-speaking clerks manage the desk and rent cars, boogie boards, and surfboards. High-season rates, for up to six persons per suite, run $72/nightly, $60/night monthly; bargain for a better rate during the summer-fall low season, when the place is nearly empty.

A block south, the family-style **Bungalows Princess** looks out on the blue Bay of Banderas beneath the rustling fronds of lazy coco palms.

The two-story, detached beachfront bungalows provide all the ingredients for a restful vacation for a family or group of friends. Behind the bungalows, past the swimming pools a stone's throw from the beach, a motel-style lineup of suites fills the economy needs of couples and small families. Reserve in writing or by phone at Retorno Destiladeras, Playas Huanacaxtle, Bucerías, Nayarit 63732, tel. 329/801-00 or 329/801-10, fax 329/800-68. It has a total of 36 bungalows and suites. The big bungalows (ask for a beachfront unit) rent, high season, for about $130 d; off-beach suites, about $80 d. Bargain for discounts and long-term rates, especially during low Jan.–Feb., May–June, and Sept.–Nov. months. All rooms feature TV with HBO, phone, and a/c; hotel amenities include a minimarket and two pools, and credit cards are accepted.

Continuing south, nearby **Bungalows Pico,** Av. Los Pico and Retorno Pontoque, Playas Huanacaxtle, Bucerías, Nayarit 63732, tel. 329/804-70, fax 329/801-31, shares the same palm-shadowed Bucerías beachfront. A rambling, Mexican family-style complex, Bungalows Pico clusters around a big inner pool/patio, spreading to a second motel-style bungalow tier beside a breezy beachside pool area. These units, which enjoy ocean views, are the most popular. During low season, the management offers such promotions as three nights for the price of two; discounts for long-term rentals are usually available. Bargain under all conditions.

The beachfront, three-bedroom kitchenette bungalows for up to eight run about $100; two-bedroom poolside kitchenette apartments for six cost $80. Adjacent smaller, four-person kitchenette suites run $70. Smaller non-kitchenette studios go for about $50. Corresponding low season rates run $80, $70, $60 and $40, with TV, a/c, snack restaurant, and two pools; credit cards are accepted.

About a mile away, on the opposite, or south, side of town, right across the street from the Bucerías trailer park (see below), stands popular **Bungalows Arroyo,** at 500 Lázaro Cárdenas, Bucerías, Nayarit 63732, tel. 329/802-88, fax 329/800-76. The dozen or so roomy, two-bedroom apartments are clustered beside a verdant, palmy pool and garden half a block from the beach. The units are comfortably furnished, each with king-size beds, private balcony, kitchen, and living and dining room. Units rent for about $85 a day low season, $100 high, with discounts available for monthly rentals. They're popular; get your winter reservations in months early.

Bucerías Trailer Park

Across the street from Bungalows Arroyo in a flowery, palm-shaded beachside garden is **Bucerías Trailer Park,** P.O. Box 148, Bucerías, Nayarit 63732, tel. 329/802-65, fax 329/803-00. The property was once owned by Elizabeth Taylor; the present owners, Mayo and Fred, have converted the luxurious living room of the for-

at Bucerías, on the Bay of Banderas

mer residence into a homey restaurant and social room, which they call Pira-pa. The 48 spaces rent for about $18/day or $400/month; add $1 a day for a/c power. With all hookups, showers, toilets, new blue pool, nearby boat ramp, and good drinkable well water. Get your winter reservations in early.

Rental Agent
If you can't locate your ideal Bucerías vacation retreat by yourself, try the friendly, reputable, and English-speaking real estate team of Carlos and Mina González, who rent a number of deluxe Bucerías beachfront homes and vacation apartments. Drop by their office on the highway, beach side, a few blocks south of town, or call 329/802-65, fax 329/803-00, or write them at González Real Estate, Héroes de Nacozari 128, Bucerías, Nayarit 63732.

Pie in the Sky
Even if only passing through Bucerías, don't miss Pie in the Sky, the little bakery of entrepreneurs Don and Teri Murray, who've developed a thriving business soothing the collective sweet tooth of Puerto Vallarta's expatriate and retiree colony. Their chocolate-nut cookies have to be tasted to be believed. Watch for the sign on the inland side of the highway just south of town; open Mon.–Fri. 9 A.M.–5 P.M.

PUNTA MITA COUNTRY

A few miles north of Bucerías, you might slow down after the intersection where the Punta Mita Hwy. passes over Hwy. 200 and look to see if a new Punta Mita **Nayarit tourist information office** has opened. (At this writing the old building appeared abandoned because of the new overpass construction.) If so, pick up some of the excellent brochures.

Drivers, mark your mileage at the Hwy. 200 overpass before you head west along the Punta Mita highway. Within a mile (two km), look downhill on the left and you'll see the drowsy little town of **Cruz de Huanacaxtle** above a small fishing harbor. Although the town has stores, a good cafe, a few simple lodgings, and a protected boat and yacht anchorage, it lacks a decent beach.

Playa Manzanillo and Hotel and Trailer Park Piedra Blanca
Half a mile (at around Mile 2, Km 3) farther on, a rough side road to the left leads to beautiful Playa Manzanillo and the Hotel and Trailer Park Piedra Blanca. The beach itself, a carpet of fine, golden-white coral sand, stretches along a little cove sheltered by a limestone headland—thus Piedra Blanca, "White Stone." This place was made for peaceful vacationing: snorkeling at nearby **Playa Piedra Blanca** on the opposite side of the headland; fishing from the beach, rocks, or by boat launched on the beach or hired in the Cruz de Huanacaxtle harbor; camping in RV or tent in the trailer park or adjacent open field.

The hotel is a small, friendly, family-managed resort. The best of the big comfortable suites offer upstairs ocean views. All the ingredients—a good tennis court, a shelf of used novels, and a rustic *palapa* restaurant beside an inviting beach-view pool and patio—perfect for tranquil relaxation. The 31 suites with kitchenettes and a/c rent from $45 d in the low season ($270 weekly, $840 monthly), add about 10 percent for high season; credit cards are not accepted. Reserve by writing directly to the hotel at P.O. Box 48, Bucerías, Nayarit 63732, or calling the Guadalajara agent at 3/617-6051 or faxing 3/617-6047.

The hotel also manages the trailer park in the beach-side but largely unshaded lot next door. Although trailer park residents aren't supposed to use the pool, hotel management doesn't seem to mind. This is a popular winter park, so make reservations early. The 26 spaces rent for about $15/day, $95/week, $370/month; with all hookups, showers, and toilets. Pets are allowed.

Past Piedra Blanca, the highway winds for 12 miles (19 km) to Punta Mita through the bushy green jungle country at the foot of the Sierra Vallejo, empty except for a few scattered developments and ranchos. Although new construction is beginning to block access, adventurous travelers can still follow side roads to hidden beaches for a day—or a week—of tranquil swimming, snorkeling, and beachcombing. You might want to get out and walk before your vehicle bogs down on these side roads. Campers should bring everything, including plenty of drinking water. If in doubt about anything, don't hesitate to inquire locally, or ask at the information office back at Hwy. 200.

PUNTA MITA COUNTRY

Rock coral, the limestone skeleton of living coral, becomes gradually more common on these beaches, thus tinting the water aqua and the sand white. As the highway approaches Punta Mita, the living reef offshore becomes intact and continuous.

Playa Destiladeras
A pair of ocean-side *palapa* restaurants (at Mile 5, Km 8) mark Playa Destiladeras, a beach-lover's heavenly mile of white sand. Two- to five-foot waves roll in gently, providing good conditions for bodysurfing and boogie boarding. Surfing gets better the closer you get to the end of the

headland at **Punta el Burro** (known also as Punta Veneros), where good left-breaking waves make it popular with local surfers.

The intriguing label *destiladeras* originates with the freshwater dripping from the cliffs past Punta el Burro, collecting in freshwater pools right beside the ocean. Campers who happen upon one of these pools may find their water problems solved.

**Los Veneros Beach Club and
Rancho Banderas**
About a mile past Playa Destiladeras, you'll

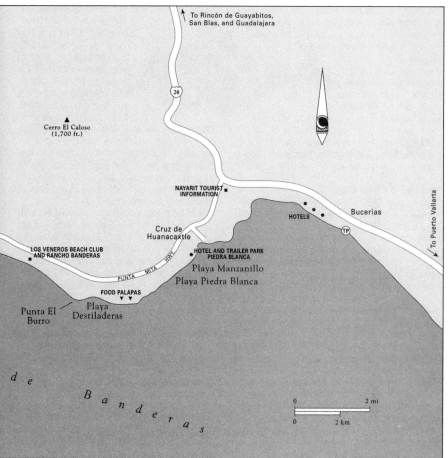

To Rincón de Guayabitos,
San Blas, and Guadalajara

Cerro El Caloso
(1,700 ft.)

NAYARIT TOURIST
INFORMATION

Bucerías

HOTELS

Cruz de
Huanacaxtle

LOS VENEROS BEACH CLUB
AND RANCHO BANDERAS

HOTEL AND TRAILER PARK
PIEDRA BLANCA

Playa Manzanillo
Playa Piedra Blanca

PUNTA MITA HWY.

FOOD PALAPAS

Punta El
Burro

Playa
Destiladeras

To Puerto Vallarta

de

Banderas

0   2 mi

0   2 km

© AVALON TRAVEL PUBLISHING, INC.

see the Los Veneros Beach Club entrance. A fee of $10 per person gets you a beach towel and entitles you to enjoy the attractive facilities, which include pools, a beach-view snack bar, and changing rooms. The half-mile-long white coral sand beach, although with waves usually too tranquil for surfing, will most likely be fine for wading, swimming, and boogie boarding. In addition, the resort rents horses and mountain bikes and furnishes guides for beach excursions or along its "archaeological" trail through the nearby tropical deciduous forest.

If you decide to stay overnight, the neighboring timeshare Rancho Banderas might be able to put you up in a deluxe suite for perhaps $100 overnight, with bargaining. For more information and reservations, call the Los Veneros Puerto Vallarta office, tel. 3/222-0305.

Restaurant Amapas

For a treat, stop in at the friendly, family-run Restaurant Amapas (Mile 8, Km 13). Homesteaded when the Punta Mita road was a mere path through the jungle, Restaurant Amapas still retains a country flavor. Ducks waddle around the yard, javelina (wild pigs) snort in their pen, and candles flicker during the evening twilight as the elderly owner recalls her now-deceased husband hunting food for the table: "We ate deer, javelina, ducks, coatimundi, rattlesnake, iguana . . . whatever we could catch." Although local hunters now provide most of the food, she and her daughter-in-law do all the cooking, and their many loyal customers still enjoy the same wild fare. The restaurant is open 9 A.M. to sunset every day.

Trouble at Punta Mita

In the early 1990s, the Mexican government concluded a deal with private interests to build the Four Seasons resort development at Corral de Riscos, at the end of the Punta Mita highway. The idyllic Corral de Riscos inlet, however, was *ejido* (communally owned) land and base of operations for the local fishing and boating cooperative, Cooperativa Corral de Riscos. In 1995 the government moved the people, under protest, into modern housing beside a new anchorage at nearby Playa Anclote. Now that the *ejido* people seem to have grudgingly accepted their new housing and harbor—they've even named their new settlement "Nuevo Corral de Riscos"—the old Corral de Riscos road has been re-opened. (See "Corral de Riscos" below.) At the highway's end, a private driveway on the right continues to the super-exclusive 18-hole golf course and 100-room Four Seasons Hotel. (See "Accommodations and Camping" below.)

Playa Anclote

Head left, downhill, at the highway's end (Mile 13, Km 21) toward Playa Anclote (Anchor Beach), which gets its name from the galleon anchor displayed at one of the beachside *palapa* restaurants. The beach itself is a broad, half-mile-long curving strand of soft, very fine, coral sand. The water is shallow for a long distance out, and the waves are gentle and long-breaking, good for beginning surfing, boogie boarding, and body-surfing.

A few hundred yards downhill from the highway, at the road "T" before the beach, stands the **Caseta Cooperativa Corral de Riscos Servicios Turisticos,** where friendly Jesús "Chuy" Casilla welcomes tourists daily 9 A.M.–6 P.M. He rents boogie boards, snorkel gear, and surfboards for about $6 per day. Chuy also arranges sportfishing launches (three-hour trip, about $75 complete) and snorkeling, wildlife viewing, and photography boat tours to the pristine offshore wildlife sanctuaries of Islas Las Marietas. During a typical half-day trip, visitors may glimpse dolphins, sea turtles, and sometimes whales, as well as visit breeding grounds for brown and blue-footed boobies, Heerman's gulls, and other birds.

When he's not working, Chuy follows his love of surfing, which he also teaches. He claims the best surfing in the Bay of Banderas is on the left-breaks off Isla del Mono, off the lighthouse point about a half mile to the west.

Half a block farther west from Chuy's place, you'll find one of Playa Anclote's best seafood restaurants, **El Dorado,** tel. 329/162-96 or 329/162-97, open daily 11 A.M. to sunset, run by friendly Benjamin López. His menu is based on meat, poultry, and the bounty of super-fresh snapper, scallops, oysters, and lobsters that local fisherfolk bring onto the beach.

Accommodations and Camping

If you decide to stay, the town of Emiliano Zapata's one hotel, the basic Hotel Punta Mita (on the left, about a quarter mile before the highway's end,) can put you up. Don't expect anything but the essentials, however. Reservations are rarely necessary.

If, however, you can afford luxury, reserve a room at the **Four Seasons Hotel.** Its airy, exquisitely appointed view rooms run about $400 low season, $500 high, with all resort amenities. For reservations in the U.S. and Canada, call 800/332-3442, or contact the hotel locally at 329/160-00, fax 329/160-60.

Tent camping is possible when not prohibited by the government because of local construction; ask at the restaurants if it's okay to camp under big trees at either end of the beach. Stores nearby and on the highway in Emiliano Zapata (commonly known as Punta Mita) back on the highway a quarter-mile east can furnish the necessities, including drinking water.

Corral de Riscos

Now that the road has been re-opened, walk or drive straight ahead through the highway-end gate. Bear left at the first fork and continue about 1.3 miles to the tennis club on the right. Turn left just before the courts and continue a few hundred yards to Corral de Riscos beach. Here you'll see an islet-enfolded aqua lagoon, bordered by a long coral-sand beach.

Two small bare-rock islands, **Isla del Mono** on the left, and **Isla de las Abandonadas** on the right, shelter the scenic lagoon. The name of the former comes from a *mono* (monkey) face people see in one of the outcroppings; the latter label springs from the legend of the fishermen who went out to sea and never returned. Las Abandonadas were their wives, who waited on the islet for years, vainly searching the horizon for their lost husbands.

Getting to Nuevo Vallarta, Bucerías, and Punta Mita

Second-class **Transportes Pacífico** buses, Insurgentes 282, tel. 322/108-93, leave the Puerto Vallarta central bus station for Tepic via Nuevo Vallarta (highway only) and Bucerías about every half hour. Small local Transportes Pacífico minibuses complete the Punta Mita roundtrip several times daily; the last bus returns from Playa Anclote at around 5:30 P.M.

Autotransportes Medina buses also complete several daily roundtrips between Playa Anclote (Restaurant El Dorado terminal) and its Puerto Vallarta station, north of the *malecón,* at 1410 Brasil, tel. 3/222-6943. Walk or hire a taxi to the terminal, or catch the bus as it heads north along the airport boulevard through the Zona Hotelera. Stops en route include Bucerías, Cruz de Huancaxtle, Piedra Blanca, and Destiladeras.

INTO THE MOUNTAINS

The **Sierra Cuale** mountains, whose foothills rise from Puerto Vallarta's downtown streets, offer unique opportunities for adventurous travelers. Exploring picturesque hidden villages, camping beside pine-shadowed lakes and streams, trekking by foot and horseback through sylvan, wildlife-rich mountain valleys by day and relaxing in comfortable small hotels and luxurious haciendas by night—all these await travelers who venture into Puerto Vallarta's backyard mountains.

San Sebastián, Mascota, and Talpa

Although these little mountain enclaves are, as the bird flies, not very far from Puerto Vallarta, they are a world apart from the coast and very distinct from each other. All are accessible directly from Puerto Vallarta by horseback, jeep (dry season only), car, bus, or light airplane charter flights.

San Sebastián is a half-forgotten former mining town, which, with a noble plaza and fine buildings, appears as it did a century and a half

ago. Some old mines, now in ruins, can still be visited, preferably in the company of local guides. Guides can also lead you on foot or horseback through verdant mountain country for day-trip explorations or to overnight campsites. There you can enjoy the sunset, relax around an evening campfire, savor the forest's quiet natural sounds, and marvel at the brilliance of a truly dark night sky.

Mascota, the hub of a rich farm valley surrounded by lush pine- and oak-forested ridges, is a departure point for outdoor excursions and explorations of idyllic villages of Yerbabuena, Cimarron Chico, and Navidad hidden nearby.

Talpa, tucked in its own lush valley, is famous throughout Mexico for its colorful village ambience. Its towering baroque basilica and surrounding plaza are magnets for hosts of visitors who flock to pay respects to the adored Virgin of Talpa, one of the renowned "Three Sisters" virgins of Mexico (see the special topic "The Three Sisters of Mexico").

SAN SEBASTIÁN

History

San Sebastián's upland valley was the heartland of the Nahuatl- (Aztec-) speaking chiefdom of Ostoticpac, which translates roughly as "hollow in the highlands." The people, known as the Texoquines, worshipped the gods of sun and fertility, cultivated corn and cotton, and extracted gold and silver from local deposits. Although the Texoquines initially accepted Christianity peaceably, they later rose in revolt, possibly in reaction to the rapacious excesses of renegade conquistador Nuño de Guzmán. Then-governor Francisco Vásquez de Coronado, reinforced with soldiers from Guadalajara, marched from the Bay of Banderas into the mountain domain of Ostoticpac, and after a bloody campaign against a determined force of 5,000 warriors, vanquished the Texoquines. The defeated people returned to their homes and fields, and for hundreds of years of Spanish-supervised peace contributed their labor to the church and *hacendados,* who grew rich from cattle, gold, and silver.

One glance around the present plaza tells you San Sebastián (pop. 1,000, elev. 5,000 feet) is unique. It is clear that proud people live here. The town's cobbled hillside plaza, lined by dignified white buildings and a straightforward steepled cathedral, and enclosing a correct Porfirian bandstand, presents a perfect picture of 19th-century gentility. Such a scene, incongruously tucked at the far end of a tortuous, dusty mountain road, requires explanation.

The "why" of San Sebastián is the same as for many Mexican mountain towns: gold and silver, from mines developed in the early 1600s and exploited at a number of local diggings on and off until the 1930s. Today, however, the gold fever has subsided and the 30,000 people afflicted by it have long departed. San Sebastián—officially San Sebastián del Oeste (Saint Sebastian of the West), to distinguish it from a host of other similarly named towns—now earns its living in other ways. In addition to the traditional corn and cattle, local folks cultivate coffee, whose red berries they harvest from the acres of bushes that flourish beneath shady mountainside pine groves.

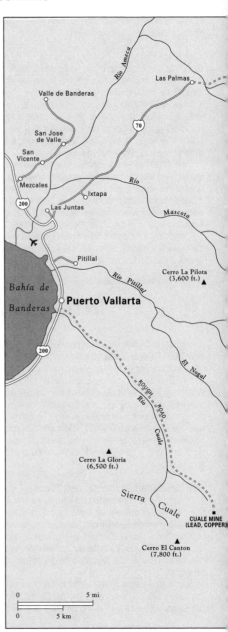

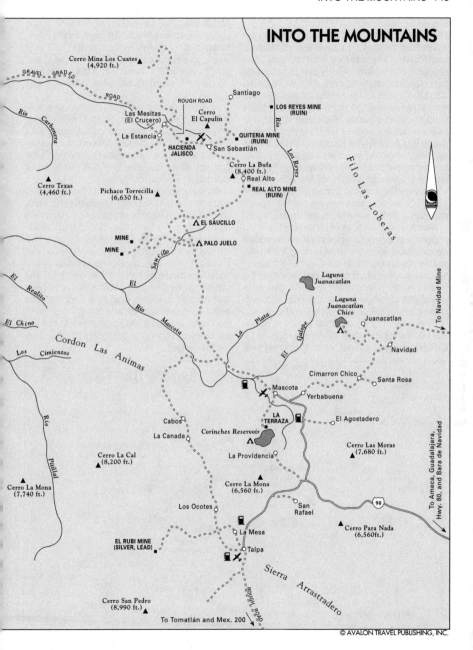

INTO THE MOUNTAINS

Cerro Mina Los Cuates (4,920 ft.)

GRAVEL GRADED ROAD

Río Carbonera

Santiago

ROUGH ROAD

LOS REYES MINE (RUIN)

Las Mesitas (El Crucero)

Cerro El Capulin

La Estancia

QUITERIA MINE (RUIN)

HACIENDA JALISCO

San Sebastián

Cerro La Bufa (8,400 ft.)

Real Alto

Cerro Texas (4,460 ft.)

Pichaco Torrecilla (6,630 ft.)

REAL ALTO MINE (RUIN)

Filo Las Loberas

EL SAUCILLO

MINE

MINE

PALO JUELO

El Saucillo

Laguna Juanacatlan

El Realito

El

Río Mascota

Laguna Juanacatlan Chico

Juanacatlan

To Navidad Mine

El Chino

La Plata

Navidad

Cordon Las Animas

Los Cimientos

El Galope

Cimarron Chico

Santa Rosa

Río Pitillal

Mascota

Yerbabuena

Cabos

LA TERRAZA

El Agostadero

La Canada

Corinches Reservoir

Cerro La Cal (8,200 ft.)

La Providencia

Cerro Las Moras (7,680 ft.)

Cerro La Mona (7,740 ft.)

Cerro La Mona (6,560 ft.)

To Ameca, Guadalajara, Hwy. 80, and Bara de Navidad

Los Ocotes

San Rafael

90

EL RUBI MINE (SILVER, LEAD)

La Mesa

Cerro Para Nada (6,560ft.)

Talpa

Cerro San Pedro (8,990 ft.)

ROUGH ROAD

Sierra Arrastradero

To Tomatlán and Mex. 200

© AVALON TRAVEL PUBLISHING, INC.

Sights

The most important sights in San Sebastián are visible from the central plaza. The road into town from Puerto Vallarta comes in on the west (sunset) side of the plaza. Far above the opposite side, the landmark mountain **La Bufa** (elev. about 8,400 feet, 2,560 meters) crowns the eastern ridge. Beyond the north edge of the plaza rises the town **church,** dedicated to San Sebastián, who is adored for his martyrdom in Rome in A.D. 288. The church, restored during the 1980s, replaced an earlier 17th-century structure destroyed in an 1868 earthquake. The main altar of the present church holds a pious, heaven-gazing image of San Sebastián dedicated in 1882. Local folks celebrate the saint's martyrdom during their major local fiesta on January 20.

Near the northeast corner of the plaza, visit the *papelería* and general store of María Francisca Perez Hernández, the unassuming local poet who wrote *La Caída de los Cedros,* lamenting the chain-sawing of old cedars that decorated the plaza before its renovation in 1984. She sells pamphlets of her poetry and the local history of chronicler-priest Gabriel Pulido Sendis.

The road angling downhill past the northwest corner of the plaza marks the route to **La Quitería mine,** the most famous local digging.

About five miles (eight km) from town, at the end of a jeep-negotiable dirt road, lie the ruins. Stripped of machinery by local people, the bare walls, gaping processing pits, and great ore tailings are all that remain of a mine that produced millions in gold and silver before closing around 1930.

Head out of town along the west (Puerto Vallarta) road; after about two downhill miles (three km), an unsigned metal gate on the right marks the driveway to **Hacienda Jalisco,** the lifelong project of American expatriate Bud Acord. Close the gate after you enter and continue another half mile to the Hacienda.

If, like many visitors, you arrive by plane, you won't be able to avoid seeing the Hacienda Jalisco, because the airstrip is on hacienda land. Bud moved into the dilapidated, 1840-era estate during the late 1960s. Although he claims he's lazy, the Hacienda Jalisco now shines with his handiwork: high-ceilinged, antique-furnished guest rooms with fireplaces and gleaming private baths. Downstairs, a kitchen and a small museum lead to a baronial *sala* and a porticoed veranda and flowery courtyard. Bud rents his guest rooms; don't miss the opportunity of staying at least one night at Hacienda Jalisco.

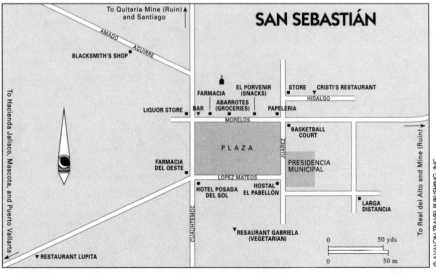

Accommodations

San Sebastián has three acceptable hotels. At the southwest corner of the plaza, the **Hotel Posada del Sol,** López Mateos 15, San Sebastián del Oeste, via Mascota, Jalisco, is distinguished by its arch-decorated high front porch. Here you can drink in the entire scene—plaza, church, mountain backdrop—by day and sleep in an 18th-century room by night. The hotel's fortunate deviation from early era furnishings is its clean rooms—accessed by huge, half-pound antique keys—with electric lights and private hot-water bathrooms. Rooms surround a homey hillside patio garden decorated with flowers and fruit trees. All of this, including the straight-laced but amiable management of mother-daughter team Chole and Margarita García, goes for about $7 s, $11 d.

A more elegant, albeit less homey, option is **Hostal El Pavellón,** at López Mateo 55, on the east end of the same plaza block. Here, you seem to be stepping into an earlier age. Past the entrance, a graceful *sala* leads to a patio/garden of fragrant orange trees surrounded by doorways opening into spacious, high-ceilinged rooms; you can easily imagine that, long ago, El Presidente once slept here. The nine rooms rent for about $16 s, $27 d, with private shower-baths and hot water.

San Sebastian's most distinguished lodging is **Hacienda Jalisco,** competently run by owner Bud Acord ("Roberto" as he's known locally) and his staff. Although the Jalisco's luxuriously rustic ambience alone is reason enough to stay, it is owner Bud Acord, with his deep, loving understanding of things Mexican, who'll most likely make your visit a memorable one. He can enlighten you about the old days on the hacienda, arrange guides for hikes or horseback excursions, or talk about the time the president of Mexico arrived virtually unannounced. Classic movie buffs are especially welcome—Bud, who comes from a longtime Hollywood family, enjoys reminiscing of days with such Hollywood chums as Humphrey Bogart, John Huston, Richard Burton, Elizabeth Taylor, and Ava Gardner.

Hacienda Jalisco's rates include a hearty breakfast and run about $37 s, $74 d, in an elegant room, with hot water shower bath. Bud insists on reservations because he's proud of the fare he serves and wants to be prepared. At

THE HACIENDA TRAIL

A Puerto Vallarta ranch organizes complete horseback package tours to and from San Sebastián, Talpa, and Mascota. Participants sign on for a week, which usually includes two or three days of guided backcountry horseback riding; exploration of San Sebastián, Mascota, or Talpa, as well as neighboring villages; camping out on the trail; enjoying local fiestas; swimming and hot-tubbing; and hearty dinners and cozy evenings at luxurious haciendas. Dr. Charles Sacamano, personable professor emeritus of plant sciences, University of Arizona, accompanies and enriches the tour with his expert commentary on trailside flora and fauna.

Tours cost about $800, including meals and lodging. For more information, contact **Rancho El Charro,** Francisco Villa 895, Fracc. Las Gaviotas, Puerto Vallarta, Jalisco 48300, tel. 3/22401-14, email: aguirre@pvnet.com.mex, website: www.puertovallarta.com.

least a week ahead of time, email Hacienda Jalisco at either ssb@pvnet.com.mx or haciendajalisco@yahoo.com. You can send a message to Hacienda Jalisco via fax 329/704-18 at the local telephone office. For more information, look at Bud's website, www.geocities.com/haciendajalisco.

Hacienda Jalisco is also a focal point for an excellent horseback tour to or from Puerto Vallarta (see the special topic "The Hacienda Trail").

Food

For store-bought food, try the limited selections of the **grocery** on the north side of the plaza, open Mon.–Sat. 8 A.M.–2 P.M. and 4–9 P.M., and the small corner produce and grocery store half a block beyond the northeast plaza corner, past the basketball court. If you're going to need lots of fresh produce, best stock up, especially during the winter season, in either Puerto Vallarta or Mascota before departure.

For restaurants, you have a treat in store at **Cristi's,** half a block past the northeast plaza corner, at 5 Hidalgo, open daily noon–8 P.M. Here, friendly community sparkplug María Cristina Dueñas probably cooks the best country Mexican fare between San Sebastián and Puerto

Vallarta. Despite being way out in the country, visitors needn't worry about the wholesomeness of Cristina's *ensalata mixta, chiles rellenos, pollo en mole,* or any of the other goodies that she prepares fresh every day.

If Cristi's is closed, a good second choice is **Restaurant Lupita,** about four blocks west of the plaza, on the left, along the Puerto Vallarta road out of town. The friendly, motherly owner cooks just what she would be cooking for her family—eggs, hot cakes, or pork chops for *desayuno,* and a four-course *comida* of soup, rice, *guisado* (savory meat of chicken stew) and dessert. Evenings, you can usually count on her hearty *pozole,* (shredded chicken or pork, over hominy in broth) with chopped onions and cabbage, and crispy *totopos* (roasted corn tortillas) on the side. Open daily 8 A.M.–9 P.M.

Third choice goes to **Gabriela's** vegetarian food, which was recommended but I didn't have a chance to check out personally. Find her place on the hillside a street or two above the plaza's south side.

Services and Information

San Sebastián's small *correo* is in the Presidencia Municipal (town hall, tel. 329/714-88 or 329/714-89), on the east side of the town plaza. The *larga distancia,* tel./fax 329/704-16, fax 329/714-08, is directly uphill and left, around the corner, a block from the Presidencia Municipal. The very basic local **Centro de Salud** (Health Clinic) is located about three blocks east, uphill, from the plaza. For minor ailments, consult the town pharmacy, *Farmacia del Oeste,* open Mon.–Sat. 9 A.M.–2 P.M. and 4–9 P.M., at the southwest plaza corner, adjacent to the Puerto Vallarta road.

For locally knowledgeable **guides,** ask Bud Acord at Hacienda Jalisco, Chole and Margarita García at Hotel Posada del Sol, or María Cristina Dueñas at Cristi's restaurant. If you have your own transportation, you can contact blacksmith Pedro González Traigos, who conducts visitors on explorations of local mines. Pedro gained his extensive practical knowledge from his father, a longtime blacksmith at the Quitería mine. A visit to Pedro's shop at Amado Aguirre 33 is worthwhile in itself; you may find him forging red-hot iron into horseshoes. Be aware he speaks little or no English. (Ask around for someone to translate.)

Getting There and Away

Charter flights provide an easy, quick connection between San Sebastián and Puerto Vallarta, especially during the wet June–Oct. season when roads may not be passable. Flying time runs about half an hour and fares are around $40 roundtrip. A well-established carrier is **Aerotaxis de la Bahía,** with up-to-date four- and six-seater passenger planes. For information and reservations call its Puerto Vallarta offfice, tel. 3/221-1990 or 3/225-0281, at the airport.

A direct **bus** connects Puerto Vallarta with San Sebastián, continuing to Mascota and Talpa. Road conditions permitting, a sturdy red ("rojo") Autotransportes Talpa Mascota Guadalajara bus departs daily at 6 A.M. from the north side of Puerto Vallarta's Parque Hidalgo a couple of blocks past the north end of the *malecón.* Check the departure schedule and buy your reserved ticket ahead of time at the little store (tel. 3/222-4816, open daily 9 A.M.–3 P.M. and 6–9 P.M.) at the corner of Argentina and Guadalupe Sánchez, two short blocks uphill, east of the bus stop. Given good road conditions, the bus arrives at the San Sebastián stop around 11 A.M., Mascota at 2 P.M., and Talpa at 4 P.M. The daily return trip follows the reverse route, departing Talpa at around 6:30 A.M., Mascota 8 A.M., San Sebastián (La Estancia) 11 A.M., arriving in Puerto Vallarta about 2 P.M. Take drinks and food; little is available en route.

Note: The minibus does not go all the way into San Sebastián, but drops off and picks up passengers at the "La Estancia" crossing, about seven miles from town. Local trucks and taxis then ferry passengers to and from town.

Driving to San Sebastián

Despite the ready air and bus access, driving your own vehicle to San Sebastián remains an attractive option for independence and flexibility. Two main road routes lead to San Sebastián. The shortest, most rugged route requires about four hours under dry conditions. A less rugged, but arduously long route heads from the Guadalajara side. From Puerto Vallarta, the 310-mile (500-km) haul starts out on Hwy. 200 north of town. Just before Compostela, cut east toward Hwy. 15 and Guadalajara. Continue on Hwy. 15 to a spot about 25 miles (40 km) before Guadalajara, where you fork right, southwest, through Tala, Ameca, and Mixtlán, arriving at the Talpa turnoff junction. Continue straight ahead to Mascota along the newly paved nine-mile (14.5-km) segment to Mascota.

Given the attraction of Mascota and nearby Talpa, this roundabout journey should be part of a leisurely several-day Talpa-Mascota-San Sebastián exploration.

After at least an overnight in Mascota, you can continue to San Sebastián. Although the route isn't paved at this writing (but may be by the time you read this) it's graveled and graded well enough that an experienced driver in a sturdy passenger car can, with caution, safely negotiate it in about three hours. At the Mascota town plaza, mark your odometer and head west along the prolongation of Av. Hidalgo, which runs past the plaza church. Fill up at the gas station—unleaded (Magna Sin) is usually available—at the edge of town (Mile 1). Continue through the lush farm valley; pass a fighting cock farm on the right (at Mile 5, Km 8), then wind gradually up an oak-studded ridge and into an intimate, green mountain valley, where (at Mile 13, Km 21) you reach an intersection. The left fork leads to some old mines, the new road continues straight ahead, while the scenic old road forks to the right. Turn right and after about two miles you pass a pair of lovely, pine-shaded creeks: the first, Palo Jueco, at about Mile 15 (Km 24), and the second, El Saucillo, about a mile farther, both good for camping. Continue, rejoining the new road (at Mile 18, Km 29), soon reaching a high, spectacular, view pass at Mile 19 (Km 30), where a right fork leads toward La Bufa peak and Real Alto village. For San Sebastián, take the left fork, winding downhill through a village at Mile 25 (Km 40). At the La Estancia fork two miles farther, follow the right branch a few miles more to Las Mesitas rancho and another fork on the right at Mile 30 (Km 48). Head right; after a bit less than three miles (five km), you reach the Hacienda Jalisco signed metal gate, on the left. Continue two miles (three km) farther to the San Sebastián town plaza at Mile 35 (Km 56).

Authorities are rapidly improving the shorter, Puerto Vallarta direct **Las Palmas route.** It may soon be completely paved. At this writing, however, it's still graveled but negotiable by an experienced driver in an ordinary passenger car: After filling up with gas—unleaded is not readily available around San Sebastián—head east from Hwy. 200 at the signed Hwy. 70 turnoff to Ixtapa and Las Palmas several kilometers north of the Puerto Vallarta airport. Continue along the excellent paved road about 15 miles (24 km) to Las Palmas. Mark your odometer just as the gravel road takes off into the foothills at the far edge of Las Palmas town. The track bumps uphill for miles, crossing sunburned ridges, threading shadowed vine-hung canyon-sides, passing a few hardscrabble ranchos. Finally you reach the signed La Estancia junction at about Mile 35 (Km 56). Turn left and continue about three miles to Las Mesitas rancho and a road fork. Turn right and continue uphill. After about three miles (five km) you reach Hacienda Jalisco's horizontal-swinging, signed gate, on the left. Another two miles (three km) brings you to the San Sebastián plaza at Mile 43 (Km 69).

MASCOTA

Mascota is a contraction of the Aztec "Mazocotlan," meaning "Place of the Deer and Pines," a translation graphically depicted by Mascota's traditional hieroglyph, which shows a profile of an antlered deer head beneath a three-limbed pine tree.

Although local gold and silver deposits drew early Spanish colonists, agriculture has proved to be the real treasure of Mascota. Its 4,300-foot (1,300-meter) altitude brings a refreshingly mild, subtropical climate and abundant moisture to nurture a bounty of oranges, lemons, avocados, apples, grapes, and sugarcane in the surrounding farm valley. Even during the dry winter months, many fields remain lush, irrigated by the Río Mascota, which eventually meanders downhill through its deep gorge to join its sister stream, the Ameca, near Puerto Vallarta.

Mascota (pop. 8,000) is the metropolis of Puerto Vallarta's mountains, offering such services as hotels, restaurants, markets, banks, doctors, and hospitals to local residents and visitors. It's the seat of the local *municipio* of the same name, which spreads beyond the Mascota Valley to a number of idyllic villages tucked away in their own remote, emerald vales.

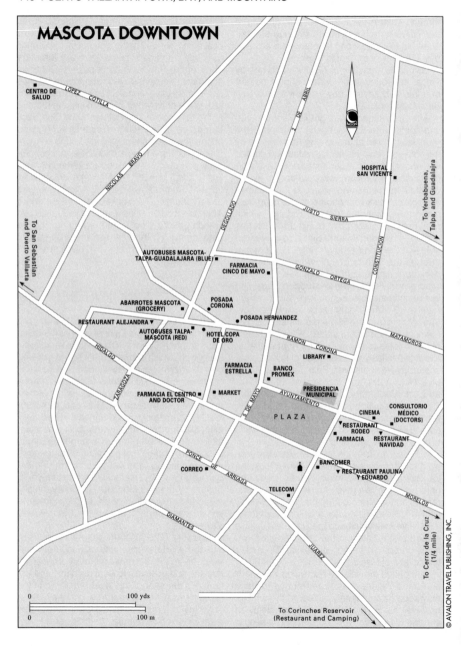

MASCOTA DOWNTOWN

CENTRO DE SALUD

LOPEZ COTILLA

NICOLAS BRAVO

2 DE ABRIL

To Yerbabuena, Talpa, and Guadalajara

HOSPITAL SAN VICENTE

JUSTO SIERRA

DEGOLLADO

CONSTITUCIÓN

To San Sebastian and Puerto Vallarta

AUTOBUSES MASCOTA-TALPA-GUADALAJARA (BLUE)

FARMACIA CINCO DE MAYO

GONZALO ORTEGA

ABARROTES MASCOTA (GROCERY)

POSADA CORONA

POSADA HERNANDEZ

MATAMOROS

RESTAURANT ALEJANDRA

AUTOBUSES TALPA-MASCOTA (RED)

HOTEL COPA DE ORO

RAMON CORONA

HIDALGO

FARMACIA ESTRELLA

BANCO PROMEX

LIBRARY

ZARAGOZA

FARMACIA EL CENTRO AND DOCTOR

MARKET

5 DE MAYO

AYUNTAMIENTO

PRESIDENCIA MUNICIPAL

CINEMA

CONSULTORIO MÉDICO (DOCTORS)

PLAZA

RESTAURANT RODEO

FARMACIA

RESTAURANT NAVIDAD

PONCE DE ARRIAGA

BANCOMER

CORREO

RESTAURANT PAULINA Y EDUARDO

TELECOM

MORELOS

DIAMANTES

JUAREZ

To Cerro de la Cruz (1/4 mile)

0   100 yds

0   100 m

To Corinches Reservoir (Restaurant and Camping)

© AVALON TRAVEL PUBLISHING, INC.

Sights

The town spreads out along roughly north-south and east-west lines from the central plaza. The Presidencia Municipal (town hall) occupies the north side of the plaza; face it and on your right streets run east, converging on Av. Justo Sierra, which at the edge of town becomes the Talpa-Guadalajara road. In the opposite direction, running from the south side of the plaza past the church, Av. Hidalgo heads west toward San Sebastián and eventually Puerto Vallarta. The town church, dedicated to the Virgen de los Dolores (Virgin of Sorrows), was begun around 1780 and not finished until 100 years later. It replaced an earlier church, built in 1649.

Looking east from the plaza you'll see the hill **Cerro de la Cruz,** site of Mascota's biggest yearly party, rising at the edge of town. On May 3, the national Día de la Cruz (Day of the Cross), nearly everyone climbs the hill for a high mass, followed by picnicking, mariachis, and evening bonfires.

Late afternoon is a good time to make the 20-minute climb to the summit, where you can enjoy the cool breeze and the sunset view. On the hilltop, look north across the green valley to see a road winding over a forested ridge. This ridge conceals Mascota's gems—the picturesque hamlets of Yerbabuena, Cimarron Chico, and Navidad.

Accommodations

A trio of good country hotels lines Calle Corona, two short blocks from the town plaza. From Banco Promex at the plaza's northwest corner, walk a block north to Corona, then west another block past Posada Hernández to the **Posada Corona** at Ramón Corona 72, Mascota, Jalisco 46900, tel. 338/602-50. Inside, past the immaculate tiled lobby, you'll probably meet the hotel's driving force, "Cuca" Díaz, whose personal mission is to make sure guests are comfortable here. When Cuca's out, her daughter Ana will do the same. Most of the hotel's 32 rooms—very clean and comfortably furnished with twin or double beds, reading lamps, ceiling fans, and hot-water shower baths—line plant-decorated upstairs corridors. Rates run about $10 s, $18 d, $25 t, except during the Talpa festivals (February 2, March 10–19, May 12, and September 10–19), when advance reservations are mandatory. Cuca and Ana are especially proud of their two new, deluxe rooms with air-conditioning that rent for $12 s, $22 d, and $28 t.

Two doors away is the similarly clean and comfortably furnished **Posada Hernández,** Ramón Corona 66, Mascota, Jalisco 46900, tel. 338/600-49. Efficiently managed by owner Esther Hernández, the hotel's 10 rooms surround a leafy, tranquil inner patio and rent for about $9 s, $14 d, $19 t.

Across the street at Ramón Corona 75, Mascota, Jalisco 46900, tel. 338/600-16, is the **Hotel Copa de Oro.** The front desk leads to an open-air interior courtyard, enclosed by ground- and upper-level room tiers. Owners have brightened up the hotel with paint, polish, and a sprinkling of new furnishings throughout. The simply furnished but clean rooms cost about $9 s, $11 d, $15 t, except during fiesta days.

Local **camping** opportunities are best at **Corinches Reservoir,** near Mascota. Here, authorities have built a fine facility, now known locally as "La Terraza." For starters, you can enjoy bass and carp dinners from a lake-view *palapa* restaurant with mariachi entertainment Saturday and Sunday afternoons. Alternatively, you can enjoy your own picnic beneath one of several airy picnic shelters, complete with car pad, useable for self-contained RV parking and camping. Launch your own boat at a good boat ramp downhill, and swim in the cool, freshwater lake to your heart's content.

Moreover, **wilderness camping** is permitted all around the reservoir's gorgeous five-mile pine- and oak-studded shoreline. Get there by car or from the Mascota Plaza, southeast corner. Follow Calle Constitución south one block. Turn left on Juárez and follow the signs about three miles (five km) to Restaurant La Terraza on the lakeshore.

The surrounding mountains offer still more wilderness camping opportunities. Pine-bordered volcanic crater Lake Juanacatlán (see under "Navidad," following), accessible from Navidad, is a good spot to set up a tent and enjoy a bit of fishing, swimming, and hiking. Additionally, west of Mascota, lovely, pine-shadowed **Palo Jueco** creek valley and nearby **El Saucillo** creek, both beside the Mascota-San Sebastián road about 15 miles (24 km) west of Mascota appear fine for a few days of pleasant camping and forest exploring. These spots are accessible either by car, (see "Driving to San Sebastián, preceding); or bus, the morning "red" (*rojo*) San Sebastián-bound bus. (See San Sebastiá "Getting There and Away," preceding.)

Food

Mascota visitors enjoy a number of dining possibilities. The fruits and vegetables are local and luscious at the town **market** on Prisciliano Sánchez at the corner of Hidalgo, a block west of the plaza. For general groceries, go to the big **Abarrotes Mascota** at the corner of Corona and Degollado, a half block west of the Posada Corona. If it doesn't have what you want, Pepe Díaz, owner of **Abarrotes Pepe,** across the street at Corona 94, tel. 338/603-74, open daily 7 A.M.–3 P.M. and 4–9 P.M., probably will.

For good breakfasts or snacks, Cuca Díaz's nephew Chole runs the **Lonchería El Cholo** on R. Corona about three doors east of the Posada Corona; open Mon.–Sat. 7 A.M.–3 P.M. and 7–10 P.M.

For a bit more serious eating, try **Restaurante Alejandra** (open 6:30 A.M.–7 P.M.), corner of Zaragoza and Corona, across Corona from Abarrotes Mascota. Alejandra, also a friend of Cuca Díaz, specializes in Mexican country cooking. Many of her satisfied customers are local ranchers who, in their cowboy hats and boots, appear as if they've just stepped out of a 1930s-genre Western.

For more refined ambience, try the **Restaurante Paulita y Eduardo,** off the southeast corner of the plaza, next to Bancomer. It's open daily 7 A.M.–9 P.M. for basic Mexican-style breakfasts, lunches, and dinners. Although the selection— eggs, *menudo,* enchiladas, chicken, roast meat, soups, tostadas—is standard country Mexican, the staff is friendly and the patio setting relaxing.

Right on the town plaza, the east side, the **Restaurant Rodeo,** open daily 8 A.M.–11 P.M., offers an airy vantage perch. Take a balcony seat and order a drink, a snack, or a full Mexican-style meal.

You're in for a treat at the **Restaurant Navidad,** where you can find out if your favorite Mexican restaurant back home is making enchiladas, quesadillas, tacos, and burritos (*burros* here) authentically. At Restaurant Navidad, they're all good and all very correct. Find it on Ayuntamiento, half a block east of the plaza's north-

east corner, across from the cinema, tel. 338/604-69, open daily 7 A.M.–11 P.M.

Entertainment and Events

Other than an occasional public dance (*baile*), bullfight (*corrida de toros*), or rodeo (*charreada*), Mascota people rely on simple diversions. You can join them in a stroll around the town plaza on any evening (especially Saturday and Sunday) or a climb to the top of **Cerro de la Cruz.** Later take in a movie at the local *cine,* on the street fronting the Presidencia Municipal, half a block east of the plaza.

Mascota life heats up during a number of regionally important **fiestas.** Fiestas Patrias kick off around September 10 with the crowning of a queen, and merrymaking continues during a week of performances, competitions, and patriotic events. On September 13, folks gather to solemnly honor the bravery of the beloved Niños Héroes; then, two days later, fireworks paint the night sky above the plaza as the crowd joins the mayor in a shouted reenactment of Father Hidalgo's Grito de Dolores.

Concurrent with the patriotic tumult, the festival of Mascota's patron, La Virgin de Dolores, continues with processions, pilgrimages, high masses, and an old-fashioned carnival to boot.

Besides participating in all of above, the nearby hamlets of Yerbabuena, Cimarron Chico, and Navidad stage their own celebrations. Yerbabuena's patron saint is the Virgin of Guadalupe, and the town honors her with native costumes, folk dances, and processions climaxing in a special mass on December 19. Neighboring Cimarron Chico celebrates its patron saint in a harvest-style fiesta, September 20–29. Navidad honors patron saints San Joaquín and Santa Ana with processions, dancing, and fireworks that climax on July 26.

Services and Information

Get the most pesos for your money at **Banco Promex,** 55 Cinco de Mayo, west side of the Presidencia Municipal, tel. 338/600-45 and 600-14, open Mon.–Fri. 9 A.M.-12:30 P.M., Sat. 10 A.M.–2 P.M.; or at **Bancomer,** on the diagonally opposite, southeast plaza corner, tel. 338/603-87 and 600-01, open Mon.–Fri. 8:30 A.M.–2 P.M., Saturday 10 A.M.–2 P.M. After hours, use the **ATM machines** at either bank.

Mascota's main health clinic is government **Centro de Salud** at R. Davalos 70, tel. 338/601-74, with three doctors on call. For serious illnesses and extraordinary diagnostic services you must travel either to Puerto Vallarta or one of the big Seguro Social Hospitals in Ameca or Tala, about 100 miles east near Guadalajara.

Alternatively, choose from either Dr. Marlin Ibarra, general surgeon; Doctora Alma D. Panduro, gynecologist; or Dr. Sergio Jiménez, general practitioner, at their *consultorio médico* on Ayuntamiento (half a block east of the plaza, across from the Restaurant Navidad.)

Additionally, you can consult with friendly, articulate Dr. Victor Díaz Arreola at his **Farmacia Estrella**, tel. 338/603-18, fax 338/602-85, on Calle Cinco de Mayo. Otherwise, for simple advice and medications, go to **Farmacia Cinco de Mayo** at Cinco de Mayo 30, two blocks north of the plaza, open Mon.–Sat. 9 A.M.–2 P.M. and 4:30–8:30 P.M., Sunday 9 A.M.–2:30 P.M.

The town *biblioteca* (library) is on Ramón Corona at the corner of Constitución, behind the Presidencia Municipal. The *correo* (post office), tel. 338/600-21, open Mon.–Fri 8 A.M.–5 P.M., Saturday 9 A.M.–1 P.M., is a block south of the plaza, behind the church, at the corner of Cinco de Mayo and Ponce de Arriaga. *Larga distancia*, public fax, and copy services are available at Farmacia Estrella, on Calle Cinco de Mayo, across from Banco Promex, at the plaza's northwest corner. Also for public fax and money orders, go to **Telecom** off the plaza's southeast corner, half a block south of Bancomer. Other long-distance telephone, fax, and copy services (open daily 8 A.M.–9 P.M.) are available at a small office on Constitución, east side of the plaza, and also at Farmacia Cinco de Mayo, two blocks north at Cinco de Mayo 30.

Getting There and Away

Aerotaxis de la Bahía, the same **charter flight** carrier that connects San Sebastián and Puerto Vallarta, also provides the quickest connection between Mascota and Puerto Vallarta, especially during the wet June–Oct. season, when the Puerto Vallarta-San Sebastián-Mascota road is sometimes impassable. Flying time runs about half an hour and fares about $50 roundtrip. The in-town ticket agent is Mariano Fabian, tel. 338/605-99, who works out of his repair shop

(walk two blocks north on Degollado, from the corner of Corona.) For more details, see "Getting There and Away" in the San Sebastián section, preceding.

Although the charter flight is quick and easy, driving will give you added mobility for exploring. During the Nov.–May dry season an experienced driver in a sturdy car can manage the roughly 80 mile (128 km) short route from Puerto Vallarta to Mascota in six hours under good conditions. Given the attraction of the San Sebastián area, you'll probably want to stop there en route for at least a day or two. For details on the Puerto Vallarta–San Sebastián leg of the drive, see "Getting There and Away" in the San Sebastián section, preceding.

Driving from San Sebastián to Mascota, zero your odometer at the San Sebastián plaza. Head west, downhill five miles to the ranch house at the "Las Mesitas" corner. Turn left, passing the ranch house on the left, toward Mascota. After three miles (Mile 8, Km 13), turn left at the "La Estancia" fork. Two miles (three km) farther, pass through a village; continue six more miles along a pine- and oak-shaded ridge to a breezy view pass at Mile 16 (Km 27). A road heads left along the summit ridge to La Bufa peak and Real Alto village. Continue downhill, where you fork left onto the old scenic road after about a mile. After another mile downhill you enter a sylvan, oak- and pine-studded valley, with a pair of good potential campsites (the first, El Saucillo Creek, at about Mile 19 (Km 31), the second, Palo Jueco Creek, about a mile later). Rejoin the main road at about Mile 22 (Km 35), continuing left (east) over a second pass at around Mile 25 (Km 40). Then coast five miles (8 km) more downhill to a fighting cock farm at around Mile 30, Km 48. Continue to the Mascota westside gas station about four miles (seven km) farther and, finally, the Mascota plaza at Mile 35 (Km 56).

Mascota has two **gas stations:** one about a mile west (San Sebastián side) of the town plaza; the other is about three miles east of town, on the Guadalajara-Talpa road. Magna Sin unleaded gasoline is customarily available at both.

During the June–Nov. rainy season the Puerto Vallarta-San Sebastián gravel road may be impassable, so drivers must go the long way around to Mascota via Highways 200 and 15.

This route is entirely paved to Mascota and requires only perseverance and an ordinary passenger car. (For details, see "Driving to San Sebastián" at the end of the San Sebastián section.)

A pair of bus lines serves Mascota. **Autotransportes Talpa Mascota Guadalajara (ATM),** known locally as the *rojo* (red) bus, connects Mascota with both Talpa and Guadalajara from the new bus station, Camionera Nueva, at the southeast edge of Guadalajara. Tickets and departures in Mascota are available from the curbside bus station at 79 Corona, tel. 338/600-93, adjacent to the Hotel Copa de Oro. A red ATM bus also runs between Puerto Vallarta, San Sebastián, Mascota, and Talpa, although poor road conditions may restrict service during the June–Nov. rainy season. For more details on this service, see "Getting There and Away" at the end of the San Sebastián section.

A separate red ATM bus also connects San Sebastián and Mascota. It starts out at "Las Mesitas" corner (five miles downhill from San Sebastián plaza, daily at 6 A.M. The return bus departs from the ATM Mascota station on Corona early afternoon, arriving at Las Mesitas at around 3 P.M.

The competing **Autobuses Mascota Talpa Guadalajara** (the "Autobus Azul," or "Blue Bus") connects Mascota with Talpa and the Guadalajara city center (old bus station, *camionera antigua*) via Ameca and the new suburban Guadalajara bus station (*Camionera Nueva.*) Tickets and departures are available at the small Mascota street-side station, tel. 338/610-07, corner of Cotilla and Zaragoza, two blocks north of Corona.

Still another option is to visit Mascota from Puerto Vallarta by guided **horseback tour.** See the special topic "The Hacienda Trail" for details.

TALPA

How a petite straw figure can bring a million visitors a year to lovely but remote little Talpa (pop. about 7,000, officially Talpa de Allende) is a mystery to those who've never heard the tale of the Virgin of Talpa. Back in the 1600s, the lit-

tle image, believed by many to be miraculous, attracted a considerable local following. The bishop of Mascota, annoyed by those in his flock who constantly trooped to Talpa to pray to the Virgin, decided to have her transported—and "jailed," some people said—to his Mascota church. But the Virgin would have none of it: the next morning she was gone, having returned to Talpa.

A few local folks brought the bishop to the outskirts of town, where they showed him small footprints in the road, heading toward Talpa. "Nonsense!" said the bishop. "The Virgin doesn't even have feet, so how could she make such footprints?" So the bishop again had the Virgin brought back to Mascota.

Determined not to be tricked again, the bishop ordered a young *campesino* to guard the Virgin at night. The Virgin, however, foiled the bishop once more. The young man dozed off, only to wake to the sound of footsteps leaving the church. The frightened young man looked up and saw that the Virgin was indeed gone; later, people found a new set of small footprints heading back toward Talpa.

The flabbergasted bishop finally relented. He left the Virgin in Talpa, where, now known as the Walking Virgin, she has remained ever since.

Sights

In the pastoral, mountain-rimmed Talpa valley, all activity centers on the town square, which spreads from the stately, steepled baroque cathedral. Inside, the beloved Virgin of Talpa, flanked by Joseph, Mary, and a pair of angels, occupies the place of high honor. The petite figure stands on her altar, dwarfed by her gleaming silk robe, golden crown, and radiant halo. The faithful, mostly poor folks from all parts of Mexico, stream in continuously—most walking, others hobbling, a few even crawling to the altar on their knees. Music often resounds through the tall sanctuary—either voices, solo or in choir, or instruments, often by mariachis playing mournful, stately melodies.

Back out in the sunshine, sample some of Talpa's other attractions. Head behind the cathedral to Talpa's excellent, church-funded **museum,** open Tues.–Sat. 10 A.M.–2:30 P.M., Sunday 8 A.M.–2:30 P.M. Two floors of expertly prepared displays begin with the basics, illustrat-

TALPA

To Tomatlán and Mex. 200

To La Rubi Mine

HOTEL PEDREGAL

RESTAURANT CAMPIÑA DEL HERRADOR

RESTAURANT LAS ARBOLEDAS

RESTAURANT LA HUERTA

PARROQUIA DE SAN JOSE

ROLLO FACTORY

ROLLO FACTORY

FARMACIA SAN MIGUEL

MARKET

PLAZA

PIZZERIA

RESTAURANT VISTA HERMOSA

POSADA OLAS ALTAS

ZARAGOZA

8. JUAREZ

23 DE JUNIO

ANAHUAC

MUSEUM

V. GUERRERO

BASILICA

HOTEL LA MISIÓN

HIDALGO

HUARACHE SHOP

HOTEL PLAZA

BANCO INTERNATIONAL

RELIGIOUS SOUVENIR STANDS

CINCO DE MAYO

RESTAURANT MOLINO ROJO

PRESIDENCIA MUNICIPAL

INDEPENDENCIA

WAY

PILGRIMAGE

To Loma Cristo Rey (View Point)

BLUE BUS

RED BUS

To Mascota, San Sebastián, and Guadalajara

50 yds

50 m

0

0

© AVALON TRAVEL PUBLISHING, INC.

ing—from a strictly Catholic point of view—the miracles and religious significance of the Virgin Mary, continuing with the three "sister" virgins of Mexico (see the special topic "The Three Sisters of Mexico") and description and documentation of a number of latter-day apparitions of the Virgin of Talpa. Upstairs, cases of the virgin's gilded vestments and other devotional objects decorate the museum's airy atrium.

After the museum, head to the **market,** downhill, at the left (east) side of the plaza. Sample the edible souvenirs: small sombreros, flowers, and baskets all fashioned of *chicle,* the basis of chewing gum. If you see a bottle filled with a yellow-or-ange liquid, it's probably *rompope* (rohm-POH-pay), eggnog laced with tequila.

When you feel like getting away from the crowd, climb **Loma Cristo Rey** (Hill to Heaven), behind and to the left of the church, for some fresh air and panoramic views of the town, valley, and mountains.

Back by the plaza, let the sweet perfume of guava fruit lead you to a *rollo* (ROH-yoh) factory.

TALPA FIESTAS

Adoration of the Virgin of Talpa climaxes four times during the year. The first, on February 2, coincides with the national festival of Candelaria. While everyone else in Mexico converges upon churches to get their plants, seeds, and candles blessed, Talpa people celebrate by blessing their beloved Virgin.

By far the biggest Talpa event occurs during the week prior to the Day of St. Joseph on March 19. A million visitors celebrate by downing tons of edible crafts, dancing in the streets, and singing mariachi serenades to the Virgin.

Merrymakers crowd in May 10–12 to celebrate the crowning of the Virgin of the Rosary, accompanied by a glittering carnival, booming fireworks, tasty regional food, and whirling folk dancers.

The prettiest and least crowded of the Talpa celebrations occurs September 10–19, concurrent with the national patriotic Fiesta de Patria. In Talpa venerable national heroes must share acclaim with the Virgin, whom people bathe, adorn with new jewelry and silks, and parade around the plaza on a flower-petal carpet.

In front of the church, cross Independencia and head left a half block. Before the corner you'll find a shop where machines crush, heat, and stir guava pulp until it thickens like candy, which are then sold in *rollos* (rolls).

Most days the Talpa plaza atmosphere is friendly and pleasantly uncrowded. The action heats up considerably, however, during the *tianguis* (tee-AHN-geese) every other Saturday, when a raft of vendors comes into town to set up their awnings and tries to hawk everything from pirated tapes and machetes to snake oil and saucepans.

The Talpa hubbub boils over during four big local fiestas—February 2, March 10–19, May 10–12, and September 10–19—when the fortunate jam hotels or sleep in tents, while everyone else makes do with the sidewalks.

Accommodations

Talpa offers good hotel choices right on the Talpa plaza. The best is the **Hotel La Misión,** corner of Hidalgo and Guerrero, Talpa de Allende, Jalisco 48200, tel. 338/502-02 or 338/500-32, behind the cathedral. The hotel's shiny, tiled lobby leads past an inviting restaurant/bar, Los Venados, to an intimate fountain and garden tucked in a sunny rear patio. Upstairs, rooms are spacious, clean, and attractively decorated in chestnut polished wood furniture and flowery bedspreads. Some of the 40 rooms have private balconies overlooking the cobbled lane below. Rentals run a very reasonable $17 s or d, except during festivals, when prices rise to about $35 d, with fans, hot water, and TV.

Another good choice is the humbler but homier family-run **Posada Olas Altas,** a block east, at Juárez 27, Talpa de Allende, Jalisco 48200, tel. 328/503-29, behind the market. Here, the 23 plainly furnished but clean rooms vary from small and private to dormitories with many beds for whole extended families. Rooms without bath (shared bathrooms down the hall) cost about $6 per double bed, rising to about $8 during fiestas; add about $2 for private bath.

Alternatively, take a look at the spic-and-span new **Hotel Plaza,** Independencia 20, Talpa de Allende, Jalisco 48200, tel. 338/500-86, directly in front of the cathedral. Here, 21 shiny white-tiled rooms with bright new furnishings occupy two stories fronting the town plaza. Guests in the street-front rooms enjoy views of the colorful cathedral plaza hubbub below. For peace and quiet, ask for a room in the rear. Rates run about $18 s or d, $24 t, with fans, TV, and hot water.

Except during fiestas, reservations are not generally necessary in Talpa hotels. If, however, you arrive when the town is crowded with pilgrims and the above hotels are filled, others will do in an emergency. Try the **Hotel Pedregal,** 23 de Junio no. 20, Talpa de Allende, Jalisco 48200, tel. 338/502-74 or 338/506-80, one block west and two blocks south, downhill, from the plaza. The 50 nondescript rooms with bath around a sunny patio rent for about $15 d, $20 t; $20 and $25 during fiestas. Fifth choice goes to the **Hotel Los Arcos,** Independencia 82, Talpa de Allende, Jalisco 48200, tel. 338/502-72, two blocks north of the plaza. The drably furnished rooms, in two tiers, surround an oft-noisy central patio and rent for about $7 per person.

Camping is customary around Talpa, especially during festivals. Privacy, however, is not. Unless you find an isolated spot a mile or so away from town, you'll probably have to cope with a flock of curious children. Try to find a spot on the far side of the river that runs south of town.

Camping prospects are much better along the pine-shaded shoreline of **Corinches Reservoir,** near Mascota, about 10 miles north. The principal amenities are a good *palapa* restaurant, space to picnic and/or set up a tent or park an RV, swimming, a boat ramp, and the *lobina* (large-mouth bass) prized by anglers. You can see Corinches Reservoir downhill south and west of the Mascota-Talpa road. Easiest access is from downtown Mascota (For access and many other details, see the Mascota "Accommodations" section, preceding.)

Food

Buy food supplies from the several groceries (especially Abarrotes Oasis, in front of the Cathedral), along main street Independencia or the town market on the plaza, west of the cathedral. As for restaurants, the steady flow of pilgrims supports several near the plaza.

For a snack, right on the plaza, the **Pizzería San Miguel** on Independencia, next to Hotel Plaza, open daily 8 A.M.–9 P.M., puts out good pizza and sandwiches, while next door, second floor, **Restaurant La Vista Hermosa** serves from a broader menu and also affords an airy, upstairs view of the plaza.

Get a bit of graceful colonial-era atmosphere with your seafood, tacos, or *hamburguesas* at the old mansion, now **El Molino Rojo** (Red Mill) restaurant. Find it, on the main street, by Banco Internacional, a block west of the plaza.

Equally serious eaters head the opposite direction, east, to the end of the main street and around the corner downhill to **Restaurant Los Arboledos,** at Juárez 1 for an airy, relaxing courtyard atmosphere. Alternatively, continue three short blocks farther (two downhill, one left) to **Restaurant Campiña del Herrador** (Branding Lot), on 23 de Junio, across the street from Hotel Pedregal, for hearty country-style breakfasts, lunches, and dinners.

Services and Information

You'll pass most of Talpa's businesses on Independencia as you enter town from the Mascota-Guadalajara direction.

For simple advice and remedies, stop by the **Farmacia San Miguel,** at Independencia 16, across the street from the plaza, tel. 338/500-85, open daily 8 A.M.–2 P.M. and 4–8 P.M.

If you're sick, visit **Doctor Daniel Zepeda,** at Reforma 4, tel. 338/500-89, one of the best physicians in town; his wife speaks English.

If you need to change money, try the **Banco Internacional,** tel. 338/501-97, open Mon.–Sat. 8 A.M.–7 P.M., or its 24-hour automated teller machine (ATM), located diagonally across from the *farmacia,* a half block west of the plaza. Across the street from the bank, at the Presidencia Municipal, you'll find both the *correo* (post office) and *Telecomunicaciones,* if you need to make a long-distance call or send a fax.

Getting There and Away

Aerotaxis de la Bahía, the same reliable local air carrier that serves San Sebastián and Mascota, also serves Talpa. Contact its local agent, taxi driver Daniel Colmenares, by calling 338/501-36, or at his taxi stand on the main street, across from Hotel Plaza. If Daniel's not there, use the phone in the taxi call box, right at curbside.

For flight tickets and information in Puerto Vallarta contact Aerotaxis de la Bahía's Puerto

Vallarta downtown agent at tel. 322/502-81, or at the airport, tel. 322/119-90. Flights take about half an hour and run about $30 per person one way.

Driving access to Talpa is similar to Mascota's. Turn at the signed junction (right from Mascota, left from Guadalajara) and continue along the good paved road another eight miles to Talpa. Unleaded gasoline is customarily available in Talpa at the Pemex *gasolinera* about a quarter mile into town, before you arrive at the town plaza.

A pair of alternate road routes access the Talpa-Mascota region from the south. From the Guadalajara-Barra de Navidad Hwy. 80, follow the signed turnoff at San Clemente. Continue 48 miles (77 km), through Ayutla and Cuatla, on paved (but sometimes potholed) roads northwest to the signed junction. There, turn left for Talpa (or continue straight ahead for Mascota and San Sebastián).

The other southern route—a rough, unpaved, and seemingly endless up-and-down backcountry adventure—heads from Hwy. 200, northeast through Tomatlán. It continues about 80 miles (130 km) via the hardscrabble hamlets of Llano Grande and La Cuesta. Figure about eight hours Tomatlán–Talpa under optimum dry conditions.

Talpa-Guadalajara buses operate from a pair of street stations along Independencia a few blocks west of the plaza. **Autotransportes Talpa Mascota Guadalajara (ATM)** *rojo* (red) first- and second-class buses connect Talpa with Guadalajara several times daily, arriving at the Camionera Nueva station in Guadalajara's southeast suburb. For Talpa departures, go to the station, tel. 338/500-15, at 56 Independencia, two blocks west of the plaza.

From its competing station directly across the street, **Transportes Mascota Talpa Guadalajara** *azul* (blue) buses, tel. 338/500-14, originate in Mascota, continue to Talpa, then Guadalajara several times daily, via the new Guadalajara suburban terminal (Camionera Nueva). There they continue to the old (Camionera Antigua) terminal near the Guadalajara city center.

Bus connection with Puerto Vallarta via Mascota and San Sebastián is made by a sturdy ATM red bus departing daily at 6:30 A.M. (road conditions permitting), via the bumpy, dusty, but very scenic Puerto Vallarta-San Sebastián-Mascota-Talpa mountain route. In Talpa, buy tickets and board the bus at the ATM red bus station. From the Puerto Vallarta end, a similar bus leaves daily around 6 A.M., from the north side of Parque Hidalgo, two blocks north of the Hotel Rosita on the malecón. Reserve your ticket ahead of time at the little store, tel. 3/222-4816, corner of Guadalupe Sánchez and Argentina, two blocks north of the plaza Hidalgo ATM red bus stop.

In the opposite, southwest direction, another minibus (which leaves between 8 and 9 A.M. from the east end of Calle 23 de Junio, past the Hotel Pedregal) connects via La Cuesta to Llano Grande village, where other buses continue to Tomatlán and coast Hwy. 200. Take water and food, and be ready for a bouncy, backcountry ride.

Still another transportation option is to visit Talpa from Puerto Vallarta by guided **horseback tour.** See the special topic "The Hacienda Trail" for details.

YERBABUENA, CIMARRON CHICO, AND NAVIDAD

Having come as far as Mascota, you'll want to spend an additional few hours poking around this idyllic trio of hamlets. Photographers should bring cameras and plenty of film. If you're driving, a single graded road safely negotiable by passenger car connects all three in a leisurely half-day, 25-mile (40-km) roundtrip from Mascota. Follow Av. Justo Sierra to the road fork at the east edge of town; the right branch heads to Talpa and Guadalajara, the left fork proceeds to Yerbabuena, Cimarron Chico, and Navidad.

If you're traveling on foot (carry water), you'll find few, if any, public buses heading to Yerbabuena, Cimarron Chico, and Navidad. You can probably catch a ride with one of the cars and trucks that often head along the road during the day. Stick out your thumb; if someone stops, offer to pay.

Yerbabuena
The latter-day renown of Yerbabuena is the labor of love of its longtime resident and official municipal historian, Father Vidal Salcedo R.:

*Yerbabuena, idyllic and enchanted little
nook,*

*You stand apart from Mascota, the noble
and lordly.*

*Whoever ventures to thee and pauses at
your door,*

*You beckon through love, both given and
received.*

That sentiment, in Spanish, heads the pamphlet that Salcedo offers visitors who arrive at his **Quinta Santa María** *minimuseo* (minimuseum) not far from the town plaza. To get there, bear east at the street past the east side of the plaza, and continue a couple of blocks until you see a tire hanging from a gigantic, spreading rubber tree.

If Salcedo is out, someone else—perhaps his nephew Hector—will offer to guide you around the flowery grounds, which bloom with the fruits of Salcedo's eclectic, unconventional tastes. Ornaments vary, from pious marble images to rusting antique farm implements. When asked why so many tires hang in the trees, nephew Hector matter-of-factly replied, "For decoration, of course."

The grounds are scattered with small one-room buildings displaying Salcedo's painstakingly gathered collections. Highlights include indigenous archaeological artifacts, working models of an ore mill and cane crusher, an ancient typewriter, religious banners and devotional objects, a fascinating coin and bill collection, and a metal step-ramp once used with Mascota's first passenger planes that now leads to an upstairs garden gazebo.

Cimarron Chico

From Yerbabuena head east again. Don't miss the antique country cemetery about a mile out of town. Next stop is Cimarron Chico (Little Wild Place), the bucolic valley and hamlet about six miles (10 km) over the next ridge. Despite its name, Cimarron Chico appears peaceful and picturesque. Adobe farmhouses, scattered about a sylvan, mountain-rimmed hollow, surround a neat village center. The town's pride and joy is its diminutive picturebook **church** at the east edge of the village.

Another don't-miss local stop is the charmingly small and tidy *abarrotería* in the middle of the village. Drop in for good fresh fruits, vegetables, and Jumex brand canned juices. Enjoy a chat with friendly proprietor and community leader Juan López Sandoval. He's a good source of local information, including homes where you might stay overnight, camping spots, and guides for horseback or hiking excursions.

Continue east, over another scenic pine-clad ridge, four miles (6.5 km) farther to Navidad. Along the way, notice the yellow lichen-daubed volcanic chimney-cliffs towering on the left halfway uphill; also note the road that forks uphill to Laguna Juanacatlán at the ridge summit a mile before Navidad.

Navidad

The town of Navidad, with a population of about 1,000, is more of a metropolis than either Cimarron Chico or Yerbabuena. It basks picturesquely on the hillside above a petite green farm valley. Hillside lanes sprinkled with tile-

Cimarron's picturebook church

roofed whitewashed houses and a venerable colonial-era steepled church, dedicated to San Joaquín and Santa Ana, complete the perfect picture.

At his store across the plaza from the church, friendly, English-speaking José Arrizon Quintero doubles as goodwill ambassador and official municipal *delegado* (county government agent). As he or any of the old-timers lounging in the shade outside his store will tell you, the short supply of *terreño* (land) is a big problem here. Young people must migrate to other parts of Mexico or the United States for jobs. The Navidad mine, still operating several miles farther east, used to employ lots of local people, but now can use only a small number of those needing jobs.

Visitors who want to stay awhile or camp nearby can try José's store and one or two local eateries for food. For lodging, check out the *casa de huéspedes* by the plaza, to the right side of the church. For a wilderness camping opportunity, ask José about **Laguna Juanacatlán,** a half-mile-long, pine-bordered volcanic crater lake. Its clear, 300-foot-deep waters are fine for swimming, kayaking, and trout and bass fishing. A larger, even more remote crater lake is accessible by trail a few miles farther on. You can reach Laguna Juanacatlán via the five-mile jeep road that leads uphill from the fork at the ridge summit of the Cimarron Chico-Navidad road.

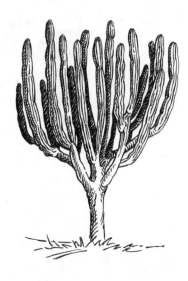

THE NAYARIT COAST

THE ROAD TO RINCÓN DE GUAYABITOS

Nayarit's long, tufted coastline is decorated by verdant mountain forests, orchard-swathed plains, and curving yellow strands of sand. Its necklace of petite, little-known beachside gems—Sayulita, Playa San Francisco, Lo de Marco, Rincón de Guayabitos, Chacala, and San Blas—offers an exceptional mix of lodging, fishing, wildlife viewing, wilderness camping, and adventure sports opportunities for those willing to follow the road an hour or two north of Puerto Vallarta.

Getting there is easy. If driving, mark your odometer as you pass the Puerto Vallarta airport so you can anticipate the small signs along Hwy. 200 that mark many turnoffs. Or take the bus, by first hiring a taxi (about $2) to the new central bus station *(Camionera Central)* a few miles north of the airport. There, ride one of the many Transportes Pacifico northbound buses. Bus travelers heading all the way to San Blas have three

options. The quickest is to ride a first-class bus (buy your ticket at the Elite counter) direct to San Blas. Barring that, ride a second-class Transportes Pacifico bus north and transfer at Las Varas (at the signed fork, marked by the *gasolinera* by Hwy. 200). There, transfer to the local navy blue-and-white bus "Transportes Noroeste de Nayarit," which leaves about five times a day between 6 A.M. and 5 P.M. and travels north on Nayarit 161 directly along the coast to San Blas. Or you can take the longer route uphill and down via Tepic. Upon arrival at the Tepic station, transfer to one of several daily San Blas-bound buses.

You can also go directly to the Nayarit coast after airport arrival by taxi; *colectivo,* if available, is cheapest. (For more details and prices, see "Transportation," under "Getting There and Away" in the Puerto Vallarta Town chapter, preceding.)

SAYULITA

Little Sayulita, 22 miles (35 km) north of the Puerto Vallarta airport, is the kind of spot romantics hanker for: a drowsy village on a palmy arc of sand, an untouristed retreat for those who enjoy the quiet pleasures and local color of Mexico. Sayulita's clean waters are fine for swimming, bodysurfing, and fishing, while stores, a few restaurants, palm-shadowed bungalows, a trailer park and campground, and a lovely bed-and-breakfast provide food and lodging.

Accommodations

Adrienne Adams, owner/manager of the bed-and-breakfast **Villa de la Buena Salud,** rents six luxurious upstairs rooms with bath from about $45 d, including breakfast for two, minimum three days. Her airy, art-draped, three-story house is located a few steps from the Sayulita beach. Although her six upper rooms are for adults only, families with children are welcome in a downstairs apartment sleeping five, with

Sayulita trailer park

kitchen, VCR, and TV, for about $80 per night. Get your winter reservations in early; Adrienne enjoys dozens of repeat customers. Adrienne's daughter Lynn, at 1754 Caliban Dr., Encinitas, CA 92024, tel. 760/942-9640, handles reservations year-round. Adrienne also takes reservations July–Oct. in California, at toll-free tel. 888/221-9247, local tel. 760/632-7716, fax 760/632-8585, email: tia@tiaadrianas.com, or by mail, at 1495 B San Elijo, Cardiff, CA 92007. She returns to Sayulita in November. You can contact her until June, by writing her at P.O. Box 5, La Peñita de Jaltemba, Nayarit 63727, or phoning her directly in Sayulita, at tel. 327/501-92. Also, take a look at Tía Adriana's website: www.tiaadrianas.com.

Nearby, the new, gorgeous *palapa*-chic **Bungalos Aurinko** ("Sun" in the Finnish language), Calle Marlin, Sayulita, Nayarit 63727, tel. 327/500-10, email: info@sayulita-vacations.com, website: www.sayulita-vacations.com, offers an excellent alternative. Labor of love of its friendly owner-builder Nazario Carranza, Aurinko glows with his handiwork: hand-crafted natural wood bedstands and dressers, rustic-chic whitewashed walls, adorned with native arts and crafts, all beneath a handsome, towering *palapa* roof, all only half a block from the beach. The four one-bedroom units rent for about $75 d, high season, $60 low. A pair of two-bedroom units go for about $100 each high, $85 low, all with modern-standard bathrooms, airy patio kitchens, and ceiling fans.

Lovely bungalows are also available beneath a drowsy beachfront palm grove, at the **Sayulita Trailer Park,** a short walk north of town. A cadre of long-time returnees enjoy 10 clean, simply but thoughtfully furnished two-bedroom bungalows with kitchen, two of them smack on the beach. Rates begin at about $50/day, $350/week, $1,200/month for two; add about $6 per extra person per day. During the two weeks before Easter and December 15–31, rates run about 20 percent higher and reservations must include a minimum seven-day stay and a 50 percent advance deposit. For reservations—for winter, get them in six months early—contact the owners, Thies and Cristina Rohlfs at Sayulita directly, at P.O. Box 11, La Peñita de Jaltemba, Nayarit 63727, tel./fax 327/502-02.

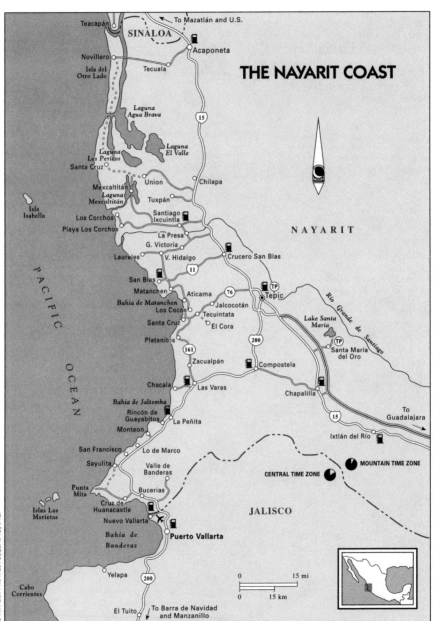

THE NAYARIT COAST

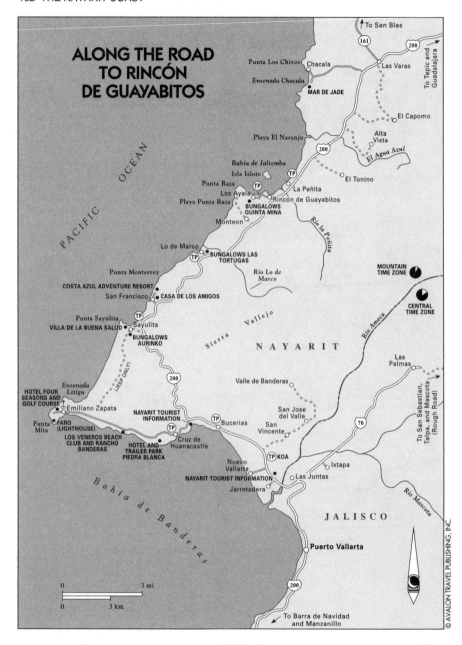

ALONG THE ROAD TO RINCÓN DE GUAYABITOS

To San Blas

PACIFIC OCEAN

Punta Los Chivos   Chacala   161   200   Las Varas
Ensenada Chacala
MAR DE JADE

To Tepic and Guadalajara

El Capomo

Playa El Naranjo   200   Alta Vista   El Agua Azul

Bahía de Jaltemba
Isla Islote   TP
Punta Raza   TP   La Peñita   El Tonino
Los Ayala   Rincón de Guayabitos
Playa Punta Raza   BUNGALOWS QUINTA MINA
Monteon   Río la Peñita

Lo de Marco   TP   BUNGALOWS LAS TORTUGAS

Punta Monterrey   Río Lo de Marco
COSTA AZUL ADVENTURE RESORT
San Francisco   CASA DE LOS AMIGOS

MOUNTAIN TIME ZONE

Sierra Vallejo   NAYARIT   CENTRAL TIME ZONE

Punta Sayulita   TP   Sayulita
VILLA DE LA BUENA SALUD   BUNGALOWS AURINKO

Río Ameca

Las Palmas

(JEEP ONLY)   200   Valle de Banderas

To San Sebastián, Talpa, and Mascota (Rough Road)

Ensenada Litigu
HOTEL FOUR SEASONS AND GOLF COURSE
Emiliano Zapata   NAYARIT TOURIST INFORMATION   TP   Bucerías
San Jose del Valle   70
Punta Mita   FARO (LIGHTHOUSE)   TP   San Vincente
LOS VENEROS BEACH CLUB AND RANCHO BANDERAS   HOTEL AND TRAILER PARK PIEDRA BLANCA   Cruz de Huanacaxtle   Ixtapa
TP   KOA
Nuevo Vallarta
NAYARIT TOURIST INFORMATION   Las Juntas
Jarretadera   Río Mascota

Bahía de Banderas   JALISCO

Puerto Vallarta   200

0   3 mi
0   3 km

To Barra de Navidad and Manzanillo

© AVALON TRAVEL PUBLISHING, INC.

RV and tent campers love the adjoining Trailer Park, in a big shady sandy lot, with about 36 hookups (some for rigs up to 40 feet) right on the beach. Guests enjoy just about everything—good clean showers and toilets, electricity, water, a bookshelf, concrete pads, dump station, pets okay—for about $15/day, or $350/month for two persons, discounts available for extended stays. Add $2 per extra person, and $2 for a/c power. Reserve through owners Thies and Cristina Rohlfs, P.O. Box 11, La Peñita de Jaltemba, Nayarit 63727, tel./fax 327/502-02.

Fourth choice in Sayulita goes to the scruffy, oft-empty **Hotel Sayulita** right on the beach. Although the owner, at the hardware store next door, asks about $17 d, $22 t, for 33 very basic rooms that surround a cavernous interior courtyard, you might be able to bargain for a better price.

Rental Agent
Drawn by the quiet pleasures of country Mexico, a number of American, Canadian, and Mexican middle-class folks have built comfortable vacation homes in and around Sayulita and are renting them out. **Propiedades Sayulita,** at Calle Delfin 9, Sayulita, Nayarit 63732, tel. 327/502-82, fax 327/501-10, email: sayulitaproperties@yahoo .com or sayulitapropiedades@pvnet.com.mx, website: www.sayulita.com, lists such properties for rental or sale.

Food
Vegetables, groceries, and baked goods are available at a pair of stores by the town plaza. Local cuisine is supplied by a good plaza taco stand weekend nights, a pair of beachfront *palapa* restaurants, and breakfast, lunch and dinner at **Restaurant Las Blancas** beach side of the plaza, tel. 327/501-71.

Sports Rentals and Tours
Propiedades Sayulita does more than sell and rent real estate. It also sells and rents snorkel gear, surfboards, kayaks, and more. Moreover, it offers guided local surfing, fishing, and kayak tours.

PLAYA SAN FRANCISCO

The idyllic beach and drowsy country ambience of the little mango-processing town of San Francisco (San Pancho, locals call it) offers yet another bundle of pleasant surprises. Exit Hwy. 200 at the road sign 25 miles (40 km) north of the Puerto Vallarta airport and continue straight through the town to the beach.

The broad, golden-white sand, enclosed by palm-tipped green headlands, extends for a half-mile on both sides of the town. Big, open ocean waves (take care—there's an undertow) pound the beach for nearly its entire length. Offshore, flocks of pelicans dive for fish while frigate birds sail overhead. At night during the rainy months, sea turtles come ashore to lay their egg clutches, which a determined group of volunteers tries to protect from poachers. Beach *palapa* restaurants provide food and drinks. If you're enticed into staying, a good hotel, an excellent bed-and-breakfast, and at least one beachside *palapa* offer accommodations.

Accommodations
A sign on the right a couple of blocks before the beach marks the bumpy road to the **Costa Azul Adventure Resort.** In-hotel activity centers around the beach and palm-shaded pool/bar/restaurant/patio. Farther afield, hotel guides take guests on kayaking, biking, surfing, and snorkeling trips and naturalist-guided horseback rides along nearby coves, beaches, and jungle trails.

The hotel itself, located at the foot of a hillside of magnificent Colima palms, offers 20 large, comfortable suites, six one-bedroom and a pair of two-bedroom villas—all with fans only—respectively, for about $90 d, $110 d, and $200 for up to six. Corresponding low-season rates run about $80, $95 and $160. Up to two children 12 and under in rooms stay free. Make reservations through the U.S. booking agent at 224 Avenida del Mar, Suite D, San Clemente, CA 92672, tel. 800/365-7613 from the U.S. and Canada, fax 949/498-6300, email: getaway @costaazul.com, website: www.costaazul.com. Reservations are strongly recommended, especially in the winter.

Back in town, American owners have rebuilt an

old side-street house, thus creating the **Hotel Los Amigos** bed-and-breakfast, seemingly perfect for those who appreciate quiet relaxation. Find it on Calle Asia, San Francisco, Nayarit 63732, tel./fax 325/841-55, website: www.losamigoshotel.com. A tiled entrance walkway guides visitors indoors, through an artfully decorated small lobby to a flowery breakfast garden patio, partially sheltered by a gracefully traditional (but water-tight) *palapa* roof. A hot tub for guests' enjoyment is tucked on one side.

Stairs lead upward to two luxuriously airy upper room stories, of six double rooms and two studio suites, all beneath yet another handsomely rustic *palapa* roof. Rooms themselves are simply but elegantly furnished with handcrafted wood furniture, wall arts and crafts, designer lamps, and colorful native-style handcrafted bedspreads. The exquisitely tiled bathrooms are fitted with gleaming modern standard wash basins, toilets, and showers. The six rooms (four with queen-size beds, two with two twins) rent for about $75 d, high season, $60 low; the two studio suites (with one queen, one twin each), go for about $95 high season, $80 low; all with ceiling fans and continental breakfast included.

Food
The growing local community of middle-class Americans, Canadians, and Mexicans and burgeoning numbers of day-trippers from Puerto Vallarta support an increasing number of respectable in-town eateries. Down on the beach, at the end of the one main street, try **Restaurant Las Palmas** for super-fresh seafood and a cooling ocean breeze beneath its shady *palapa*. Open daily 8 A.M.–8 P.M.

Back on the main street, **La Ola Rica** Restaurant and Bar offers fresh seafood and Mexican supper specialties 6–10 P.M. daily, Oct.–May.

Alternatively, you can retreat to the palm-shaded beachside ambience of **Wahoo Bar and Grill** at the Costa Azul Adventure Resort. Open daily 8 A.M.–9 P.M.

Hospital
San Francisco is host to the local **General Hospital,** tel. 325/840-77, with ambulance, emergency room, and doctors on call 24 hours. Find it off the main street, to the right (north), about a quarter-mile from the highway.

PLAYA LO DE MARCO

Follow the signed Lo de Marco (That of Marco) turnoff 31 miles (49 km) north of the Puerto Vallarta airport (or eight miles, 13 km south of Rincón de Guayabitos). Continue about a mile through the town to the *palapa* restaurants on the beach. Playa Lo de Marco is popular with Mexican families; on Sunday and holidays they dig into the fine golden sand and frolic in the gentle, rolling waves. The surf of the nearly level, very wide Playa Lo de Marco is good for most aquatic sports except surfing, snorkeling, and scuba diving. The south end has a rocky tidepool shelf, fine for bait-casting. Divers and snorkelers can rent boats to go to offshore Isla Islote.

Accommodations
The constant flow of vacationing Mexican families supports a pair of hotels on the main street, on the right, about a quarter-mile from the highway. Best by far is **Hotel Bungalows Las Tortugas,** at Luis Echevarría 28, Lo de Marco, Nayarit, tel./fax 327/500-92. The major attraction is the layout of about 20 kitchenette apartments in two stories around a broad, invitingly tropical, designer pool and patio, with kiddie pool and hot tub. Inside, the units, all with kitchenettes, are bare-bulb (bring your own lampshade), sparely but comfortably furnished, spacious, and clean. The upper apartments, with king-size beds, are more inviting than some others. Look at more than one before deciding. They rent for about $22 during the week, weekends and holidays rates may double, with TV, dishes and utensils, and fans.

If Las Tortugas is full, take a look at the very plain (bordering on drab) Bungalows Padre Nuestro, tel. 327/500-24, next door, with pool and about 20 kitchenette apartments.

Down on the beach, Lo de Marco has a superb trailer park/bungalow complex, **El Caracol,** owned and operated by German expatriate Gunter Maasan and his Mexican wife. The nine luxuriously large "little bit of Europe in the tropics" motel bungalows sleep four to six people with all the comforts of Hamburg. With a/c, fans, and complete kitchenettes, rents begin at about $45 d low season, $70 high, depending on size and amenities. Add about $10 per extra person.

The trailer park is correspondingly luxurious, with concrete-pad spaces in a palm- and banana-shaded grassy park right on the beach. With pool, all hookups, and immaculate hot-shower and toilet facilities, the 15 spaces rent for about $15 per day, $13 per day monthly, or $12 per day for two months; pets are okay. Add $5 per extra person. It's popular, so make winter reservations by September. Write P.O. Box 89, La Peñita de Jaltemba, Nayarit 63726, or call tel./fax 327/500-50, or in Guadalajara tel. 3/686-0481.

Tent, RV camping, and lodging are available at the trailer park **Pequeña Paraíso** (Little Paradise) beside the jungle headland at the south end of the beach. Here, the friendly family manager welcomes visitors to the spacious, palm-shaded beachside grove. Basic but clean apartments rent for about $27 d ($38 d with kitchenette), with hot-water showers and fans. RV spaces, with all hookups, rent for about $12/day, $300/month, with showers and toilets. Dozens of grass-carpeted, palm-shaded tent spaces rent for about $4 per person per day. Stores in town nearby can furnish basic supplies. Reserve, especially during the winter, by telephone at 327/500-89, or in writing to Parque de Trailer Pequeío Paraíso, Carretera Las Miñitas no.1938, Lo de Marco, Nayarit.

Get to the trailer parks by turning left just before the beach, at the foot of the town main street (that leads straight from the highway). Continue about another mile to El Caracol, on the right, and El Pequeño Paraíso, a hundred yards farther.

Continuing south along the Lo de Marco beach road past the trailer parks, you will soon come to two neighboring pearly sand paradises, **Playa Las Minñitas** and **Playa El Venado.** Bring your swimsuit, picnic lunch, and, if you crave isolation, camping gear.

Turtle Encampment
Be sure to stop and say a good word (*"Buenos dias"* will do) to Rogelio, who's been running the Lo de Marco beach **Campamento de Tortugas,** for several years, saving thousands of turtles from poachers. You're most likely to find him at his camp (at the foot of the town main entrance street, Luis Echevarría) during the summer-fall turtle season. He might appreciate some volunteer help, and/or a bag of food to ease his lonely but determined vigil.

RINCÓN DE GUAYABITOS AND LA PEÑITA

Rincón de Guayabitos (pop. about 3,000 permanent, maybe 8,000 in winter) lies an hour's drive north of Puerta Vallarta, at the tiny south-end rincón (wrinkle) of the broad, mountain-rimmed Bay of Jaltemba. The full name of Rincón de Guayabitos's sister town, La Peñita (Little Rock) de Jaltemba, comes from its perch on the sandy edge of the bay.

Once upon a time, Rincón de Guayabitos (or simply Guayabitos, meaning "Little Guavas") lived up to its diminutive name. During the 1970s, however, the government decided Rincón de Guayabitos would become both a resort and one of three places in the Puerto Vallarta region where foreigners could own property. Today Rincón de Guayabitos is a summer, Christmas, and Easter haven for Mexicans, and a winter retreat for Canadians and Americans weary of glitzy, pricey resorts.

SIGHTS

Getting Oriented
Guayabitos and La Peñita (pop. around 10,000) represent practically a single town. Guayabitos has the hotels and the scenic beach village ambience, while two miles north La Peñita's main street, Emiliano Zapata, bustles with stores, restaurants, a bank, and a bus station.

Guayabitos's main street, **Avenida del Sol Nuevo,** curves lazily for about a mile parallel to the beach. From the Avenida, several short streets and *andandos* (walkways) lead to a line of *retornos* (cul-de-sacs). The choicest of Guayabitos's community of small hotels, bungalow complexes, and trailer parks lie within a block of the beach.

RINCÓN DE GUAYABITOS

To La Peñita, San Blas, and Tepic

TOURIST INFORMATION

CORREO AND TELEGRAFO

R. CEDROS

CEDROS

FRUIT STANDS

MINI-SUPER JUAN DE DIOS

200

R. LAURELES

VILLAS STEFANY

VILLA DE LA BUENA VIDA

MANGLES

RESTAURANT GABY

MINI-SUPER GABY II

BUNGALOWS ANAI

JACARANDAS

To Puerto Vallarta

TRAILER PARK EL CAPITAN

Guayabitos

R. JACARANDAS

COLORINES

AV. DEL SOL NUEVO

CALLE LIRIO

PACIFIC OCEAN

Restaurant CAMPANARIO

RESTAURANT LAS ALEJANDRAS

R. TABACHINES

HOTEL POSADA LA MISION

MOCAMBO RESTAURANT

FARMACIA AND LAUNDRY

TABACHINES

HOTEL COSTA ALLEGRE

COCINA ECONOMICA DOÑA CARMEN

TRAILER PARK EL DORADO

RESTAUARNT LA CONCHA

Playa

HUANACAXTLE

HOTEL POSADA DEL SOL

TRAILER PARK OASIS

CEIBAS

POSADA REAL HOTEL AND BUNGALOWS

FISHERMAN'S PARADISE TRAILER PARK

BUNGALOWS EL RINCONCITO

TRAILER PARK AND RESTAURANT

CEIBAS

AV. GARDENIAS

VILLANUEVAS

TRAILER PARK TROPICO CABANA

MINI-SUPER GABY II

LARGA DISTANCIA

DELIA'S TRAILER PARK

HOTEL DECAMERON RINCON DE LAS PALMAS

R. PALMAS

BUNGALOWS EL DELFIN

HOTEL DECAMERON LOS COCOS

ABEL'S RESTAURANT

To Mex. 200 and Puerto Vallarta

Creek

To Los Ayala

⬛⬛⬛⬛⬛ = WALKWAY

0   0.1 mi

0   0.1 km

© AVALON TRAVEL PUBLISHING, INC.

MOON

Isla Islote

Only a few miles offshore, the rock-studded humpback of Isla Islote may be seen from every spot along the bay. A flotilla of wooden glass-bottomed launches plies the Guayabitos shoreline, ready to whisk visitors across to the island. For $15 an hour parties of up to six or eight can view fish through the boat bottom and see the colonies of nesting terns, frigate birds, and boobies on Islote's guano-plastered far side. You might see dolphins playing in your boat's wake, or perhaps a pod of whales spouting and diving nearby.

BEACHES AND ACTIVITIES

The main beach, **Playa Guayabitos-La Peñita,** curves two miles north from the rocky Guayabitos point, growing wider and steeper at La Peñita. The shallow Guayabitos cove, lined by *palapa* restaurants and dotted with boats, is a favorite of Mexican families on Sunday and holidays. They play in the one-foot surf, ride the boats, and eat barbecued fish. During busy times, the place can get polluted from the people, boats, and fishing.

Farther along toward La Peñita, the beach broadens and becomes much cleaner, with surf good for swimming, bodysurfing, and boogie boarding. Afternoon winds are often brisk enough for sailing and windsurfing, though you must bring your own equipment. Scuba and snorkeling are good near offshore Isla Islote, accessible via rental boat from Guayabitos. Local stores sell inexpensive but serviceable masks, snorkels, and fins.

A mile north of La Peñita, just past the palm-dotted headland, another long, inviting beach begins, offering good chances for beginning and intermediate surfing.

Playa los Muertos

Follow the uphill paved road to Los Ayala, and, just as it reaches its summit, curving around the Guayabitos headland, notice a dirt road forking right, downhill. It continues through a cemetery to Playa los Muertos (Beach of the Dead), where the graves come right down to the beach.

Ghosts notwithstanding, this is a scenic little sandy cove. On fair days get your fill of safe swimming, sunning on the beach, or tidepool-

ing amongst the clustered oysters and mussels and the skittering crabs. (Recently, however, the owners of houses above the beach have placed a gate across the private entrance road to discourage cars. They cannot legally bar people from the beach, so, even if you have to hire a launch to drop you off and pick you up there, Playa los Muertos is worth it.)

Playa los Ayala

Continue along the road about another mile to the once sleepy but now up-and-coming settlement and one-mile yellow strand of Playa los Ayala. Although local-style beachside *palapa* restaurants and bungalow accommodations are blossoming, the long, lovely, Los Ayalas beach retains its Sunday popularity among local families. All of the beach sports possible at Guayabitos are possible here, with the added advantage of a much cleaner beach.

Like Guayabitos, Los Ayala has its secluded south-end cove. Follow the path up the beach-end headland. Ten minutes' walk along a tropical forest trail leads you to the romantic little jungle-enfolded sand crescent called **Playa del Beso** (Beach of the Kiss). Except during holidays, for hours on end few if any people come here.

Best of Los Ayala's new accommodations is **Bungalows Quinta Mina,** Los Ayala, Nayarit 63727, tel./fax 327/411-41. This three-story stack of modern-standard kitchenette apartments enfolds an inviting beachfront pool and patio. Here, adults lounge around the small pool, while their kids frolic in a beachside kiddie pool. Upstairs, the dozen or so one-bedroom units, sleeping four, are simply but attractively furnished, with large rustic floor tiles, soft couches, white stucco walls, and shiny shower bathrooms. Low-season rentals run about $32 d, $53 for four, except holidays and *puentes* (long weekends.) Add about 20% during the winter-spring high season.

Playa Punta Raza

The road to Playa Punta Raza, while only about three miles long, requires a maneuverable high-clearance vehicle and dry weather. The reward is a long, wild beach perfect for beachcombing and camping. Bring everything, including water.

Three miles south of Guayabitos along Hwy. 200, turn off at El Monteón; pass through the village, turn right at Calle Punta Raza just before the pavement ends. Continue along the rough road through the creek and over the ridge north of town. At the summit, stop and feast your eyes on the valley view below, then continue down through the near-virgin jungle, barely scratched by a few poor cornfields. About a mile downhill from the summit, stop to see if the seasonal hillside restaurant on the right is open. This site has recently been used as headquarters for "Campo de Tortugas de Playa Punta Raza," a group of plucky volunteers who camp out on the beach trying to save endangered turtle eggs from poachers.

At the bottom of the steep grade, the track parallels the beach beneath big trees; sandy trails run through the brush to the beach—four-wheel drive and experienced sand drivers only—it's very easy to get stuck. You have two straight miles of pristine, jungle-backed sand virtually to yourself.

The beach itself slopes steeply, with the resulting close-in crashing waves and undertow. The water would be fine for splashing, but swimmers be careful. Because of the jungle hinterland, birds and other wildlife are plentiful here. Bring your insect repellent, binoculars, and identification books.

Turtles arrive periodically in late summer and fall to lay eggs here. Look for obvious tracks in the sand. The turtles attract predators—cats, iguanas, birds, and human poachers. If you find an egg nest, either report it to the volunteers or keep watch over it; your reward may be to witness the birth and return to the ocean of dozens of baby turtles.

ACCOMMODATIONS

Guayabitos Hotels

Guayabitos has more far more hotels than any other town in Nayarit, including the capital, Tepic. Competition keeps standards high and prices low. During the low season (Sept.–Dec. 15), most places are less than half full and ready to bargain. During the winter season, the livelier part of town is at the south end, where most of the foreigners, mostly Canadian and American RV folks, congregate.

Guayabitos has many lodgings that call themselves "bungalows." This generally implies a motel-type suite with kitchenette with less service, but more spacious and more suited to families than a hotel room. For long stays or if you want to save money by cooking your own meals, bungalows can provide a good option.

Perhaps the cheapest good lodging in town is the homey 32-room **Posada Real Hotel and Bungalows,** Retorno Ceibas and Andando Huanacaxtle, Rincón de Guayabitos, Nayarit 63727, tel./fax 327/401-77, built around a cobbled parking courtyard jungle of squawking parrots and shady palms, mangoes, and bamboo. The bun-

Pristine Playa Punta Raza, a few miles south of Rincón de Guayabitos, offers picnicking, fishing, camping, and wildlife viewing for prepared off-road adventurers.

galow units are on the ground floor in the courtyard; the hotel rooms are stacked in three plant-decorated tiers above the lobby in front. The 26 four-person bungalows with kitchenette rent for about $29; the 20 two-person hotel rooms rent for about $22/day year-round, with discounts possible for longer-term stays. Amenities include ceiling fans, a small pool and a kiddie pool, water slide, racquetball, and parking; credit cards are accepted.

Immediately north, across Andando Huanacaxtle, **Hotel Posada del Sol,** tel./fax 327/400-43, offers 14 tastefully furnished bungalows around a palmy garden patio, for about $35/day, $600/month.

One of the most charming off-beach Guayabitos lodgings is **Bungalows El Delfín,** managed by friendly owners Francisco and Delia Orozco at Retorno Ceibas and Andando Cocoteros, Rincón de Guayabitos, P.O. Box 12, Nayarit 63727, tel. 327/403-85. Amenities include an intimate banana- and palm-fringed pool and patio, including recliners and umbrellas for resting and reading. Chairs on the shaded porch/walkways in front of the three room-tiers invite quiet relaxation and conversation with neighbors. The spacious four-person suites are large and plainly furnished, with basic stove, refrigerator, and utensils, rear laundry porches, and big, tiled toilet-showers. The 15 bungalows with kitchenette sleep four and rent for about $37 year-round, except for holidays, with ceiling fans, pool, and parking; pets are allowed.

Right-on-the-beach **Bungalows El Rinconcito,** Retorno Ceibas s/n and Calle Ceibas, P.O. Box 19, Rincón de Guayabitos, Nayarit 63727, tel./fax 327/402-29, is one of the best buys in Guayabitos. The smallish whitewashed complex set back from the street offers large, tastefully furnished units with yellow and blue tile kitchens and solid, Spanish-style dark-wood chairs and beds. Its ocean-side patio opens to a grassy garden overlooking the surf. Three two-bedroom bungalows rent for about $46 year-round, and seven one-bedroom bungalows for about $35 year-round, with fans and parking. Discounts are generally negotiable for longer-term stays.

One of the fancier Guayabitos lodgings is the colonial-style **Hotel Posada La Misión,** Retorno Tabachines 6, Rincón de Guayabitos, Nayarit

63727, tel./fax 327/403-57, whose centerpiece is a beachside restaurant/bar/patio nestled beneath a spreading, big-leafed *hule* (rubber) tree. Extras include a luxurious shady garden veranda and an inviting azure pool and patio, thoughtfully screened off from the parking. Its rooms are high-ceilinged and comfortable except for the unimaginative bare-bulb lighting; bring your favorite bulb-clip lampshades. Doubles rent for about $25 low season, $35 high; quadruples, $32 low season and $46 high; suites sleeping six, $40 and $60. Two kitchenette bungalows go for $45 low season, $65 high. Amenities include a pool, good restaurant in front, ocean-view bar, ceiling fans, and parking; credit cards are accepted.

Travelers who play tennis and prefer an air-conditioned, modern-style lodging with all drinks, entertainment, and food included should pick the compact, pool-and-patio ambience of the **Hotel Decameron Rincón de las Palmas,** Retorno Palmas s/n at Calle Palmas, Rincón de Guayabitos, Nayarit 63727, tel. 327/401-90, fax 327/401-74, near the south end. With an airy beach-view restaurant and bar for sitting and socializing, this is a lodging for those who want company. Guests may often have a hard time *not* getting acquainted. The smallish rooms are packed in two double parallel breezeway tiers around a pool and patio above the beach. Right outside your room during the high season you will probably have your pick of around 50 sunbathing bodies to gaze at and meet. This hotel is operated by its big neighbor Hotel Decameron Los Cocos, which handles reservations (in a Bucerías office, tel. 329/811-04, fax 329/803-33), mandatory in winter. Specifically ask for Hotel Rincon de las Palmas, or you might be put in the oversize Los Cocos. The 40 rooms rent, low season, for a bargain-basement $40 per person, double occupancy, and $65 high, with all drinks, food, and in-house entertainment included, with a/c, pool, TV, tennis court, breezy sea-view restaurant and bar, and parking; credit cards are accepted.

Just as modern but more spacious is the family-oriented **Hotel Costa Alegre,** Retorno Tabachines s/n at Calle Tabachines, Rincón de Guayabitos, Nayarit 63727, tel./fax 327/402-41, 327/402-42, or 327/402-43, where the Guayabitos beach broadens out. Its pluses in-

RINCÓN DE GUAYABITOS ACCOMMODATIONS

Accommodations (area code 327, postal code 63726) are listed in increasing order of approximate high-season, double-room rates.

Posada Real Hotel and Bungalows, Retorno Ceibas s/n, tel./fax 401-77, $22

Hotel Posada del Sol, Retorno Tabachines s/n, tel./fax 400-43, $35

Hotel Posada La Misión, Retorno Tabachines 6, tel./fax 403-57, $35

Bungalows El Rinconcito, Retorno Ceibas s/n, P.O. Box 19, tel. 402-29, $35

Bungalows El Delfín, Retorno Ceibas s/n, tel. 403-85, $37

Quinta Mina, Los Ayala, postal code 63727, tel./fax 411-41, $40

Hotel Costa Alegre, Retorno Tabachines s/n, tel. 402-41 or 402-42, fax 402-43, $55

Hotel Decameron Rincón de las Palmas, Retorno Palmas s/n, tel. 401-90, fax 401-74, $65 room only, or $150 all-inclusive—all food, drinks, and entertainment for two

Bungalows Anai, Retorno Jacarandas, P.O. Box 44, tel./fax 402-45, $70

Villas Stefany, Retorno Laureles 12 Poniente, tel. 405-36 or 405-37, fax 409-63, $70

Villas de la Buena Vida, Retorno Laureles 2, P.O. Box 62, tel. 402-31, fax 407-56, website: www.villas-buenavida.com, $100

clude a big, blue pool and patio on the street side and a broad, grassy, ocean-view garden on the beach side. Although the rooms are adequate, the kitchenette bungalows are set away from the beach with no view but the back of neighboring rooms. The best choices are the several upper-tier oceanfront rooms, all with sliding glass doors leading to private sea-view balconies. Some rooms are in better repair than others; look at more than one before paying. The 30 view rooms run about $47 d low season, $55 high; the 43 kitchenette bungalows $57 and $65 d. Amenities include a/c, pool, parking, and restaurant/bar; credit cards are accepted.

Most of Guayabitos' upscale lodgings are at the north end. For peace and quiet in a luxurious tropical setting, the **Bungalows Anai,** at Calle Jacarandas and Retorno Jacarandas, P.O. Box 44, Rincón de Guayabitos, Nayarit 63727, tel./fax 327/402-45, is just about the best on the beach. The approximately 15 apartments, in two-story tiers, each with private ocean-view balcony, stand graciously to one side. They overlook a spacious, plant-bedecked garden, shaded by a magnificent grove of drowsy coconut palms. The garden leads to an ocean-view patio where a few guests read, socialize, and take in the beach-

side scene below. Inside, the two-bedroom suites are simply but thoughtfully furnished in natural wood, bamboo, and tile and come with bath, three double beds, furnished kitchen, fans, a/c, and TV. Rentals run about $45 low season, $70 high, for up to four people, one-week minimum stay.

About a block farther north, at Retorno Laureles 2, the shiny, deluxe **Villas de la Buena Vida** ranks among Guayabitos's most luxurious lodgings. About 40 tastefully appointed, ocean-view suites rise in five stories above a palm-shaded pool and patio right on the beach. For Guayabitos, the high-season asking rates are correspondingly luxurious: two-bed "villa" apartments run about $100 d high season, $80 d low; junior suites $155 and $110, master suites $165 and $135. Bargain for a discount, especially for long-term, mid-week, and low-season stays. Reserve at P.O. Box 49, Rincón de Guayabitos, Nayarit 63727, tel. 327/40-231, fax 327/40-756, website: www.villasbuenavida.com. Note: The above prices include the hefty 17% "value added" tax, which may be omitted in the rates listed on the hotel's website.

A few doors north, **Villas Steffany,** Retorno Laureles 12 Poniente, Rincón de Guayabitos, Nayarit 63727, tel. 327/405-36 and 327/405-37, fax 327/409-63, email: sales@steffanyvillas .com.mx, website: www.steffanyvillas.com.mx, offers another attractive deluxe alternative. Guests in the 34 suites enjoy private balconies overlooking a lush pool, patio, and garden and ocean vista. The apartments, simply but comfortably furnished in pastels, wood, and tile, have a living room with furnished kitchenette and one bedroom with two double beds and a bath; other extras include cable TV, telephone, and a/c. Rentals run about $70 for four year-round. Discounts are negotiable for stays of two weeks or more. There's a restaurant, pool, and lobby bar, with street parking only, and credit cards are accepted.

Guayabitos Trailer Parks
All but one of the several Guayabitos trailer parks are wall-to-wall RVs most of the winter. Some old-timers have painted and marked out their spaces for years of future occupancy. The best spaces of the bunch are all booked by mid-October. And although the longtime residents are polite enough, some of them are clannish and don't go out of their way to welcome new kids on the block.

This is fortunately not true at **Delia's,** Guayabitos's funkiest trailer park, Retorno Ceibas 4, Rincón de Guayabitos, Nayarit 63727, tel. 327/403-98. Friendly realtor/owner Delia Bond Valdez and her daughter Rosa Delia have 15 spaces, a good number of which are unfilled even during the high season. Their place, alas, is not right on the beach, nor is it as tidy as some folks would like. On the other hand, Delia offers a little store, insurance, long-distance phone service, and a small *lonchería* right next to the premises. She also rents two bungalows for about $350 a month. Spaces run about $11/night, $300/month high season, $7/night low, with all hookups, room for big rigs, showers, and toilets; pets are okay.

The rest of Guayabitos's trailer parks line up right along the beachfront. Moving from the south end, first comes **Trailer Park Tropico Cabaña,** built with boats and anglers in mind. One old-timer, a woman, the manager says, has been coming for 20 years running. It must be for the avocados—bulging, delicious three-pounders— which hang from a big shady tree. Other extras are a boat launch and storage right on the beach,

with an adjacent fish-cleaning sink and table. This is a prime, very popular spot; get your reservation in early to Retorno Las Palmas, P.O. Box 3, Rincón de Guayabitos, Nayarit 63727. The 28 cramped spaces, six 38-footers and 22 33-footers, rent for about $13/day with all hookups, discounts for longer stays, with showers, toilets, and barbecue; pets are okay.

The single Guayabitos trailer park that celebrates a traditional Christmas-eve *posada* procession is the **Trailer Park Villanuevas,** managed by friendly Lydia Villanuevas, at Retorno Ceibas s/n, P.O. Box 25, Rincón de Guayabitos, Nayarit 63727, tel. 327/403-91. Allowing for 30 spaces, including three drive-throughs, the park can still stuff in some big rigs, although room is at a premium. Shade, however, is not: lovely palms cover the entire lot. Moreover, the sea-view *palapa* restaurant is very popular with Guayabitos longtimers. Spaces go for $15/daily (or $13/day monthly), add $3/day for a/c power; with all hookups, restaurant, showers, toilets, boat ramp, and pets are allowed. Four bungalows rent for about $40 d.

Next door to the north comes **Fisherman's Paradise Trailer Park,** which is also popular as a mango-lover's paradise, Retorno Ceibas s/n, Rincón de Guayabitos, Nayarit 63727, tel. 327/400-14, fax 327/405-25. Several spreading mango trees shade the park's 33 concrete pads, and during the late spring and summer when the mangoes ripen, you'll probably be able to park under your own tree. Winter-season spaces rent for about $15/day, minimum 15-day rental (or $14 for a three-month rental), with all hookups, showers, and toilets; pets are okay.

Neighboring **Trailer Park Oasis** is among Guayabitos's most deluxe and spacious trailer parks, Retorno Ceibas s/n, Apdo. 42, Rincón de Guayabitos, Nayarit 63727. Its 19 all-concrete, partly palm-shaded spaces are wide and long enough for 40-foot rigs. Pluses include green grassy grounds, beautiful blue pool, a designer restaurant, and a luxury ocean-view *palapa* above the beach. Spaces rent for about $17/day, $15/day monthly, with all hookups, showers, toilets, fish-cleaning facility, and boat ramp; pets okay.

Residents of **Trailer Park El Dorado,** Retorno Tabachines s/n, Rincón de Guayabitos,

Nayarit 63727, tel. 327/401-52, enjoy shady, spacious, grass-carpeted spaces beneath a majestic, rustling palm grove, all the result of the tender loving care of the friendly on-site owner/manager. Other extras include a pool and recreation *palapa* across the street in **Hotel Posada Del Sol.** The 21 trailer park spaces rent for about $15/day ($14/day for a one-month stay) with all hookups, showers, and toilets; pets are allowed. Very popular; get your winter reservations in early.

Three blocks farther north along the beach, newcomer **Trailer Park El Capitán** seems to be trying harder, Retorno Jacarandas at Andando Jacarandas, Rincón de Guayabitos, Nayarit 63727, tel./fax 327/403-04. It should have no trouble acquiring a following. The majestic, rustling palm grove provides shade, the rustic *palapa* restaurant supplies food and drinks, while, a few steps nearby, the loveliest part of Playa Guayabitos brims with natural entertainments. The 14 spaces rent for $16/day (discounts for longer stays) with all hookups, showers, and toilets; larger RVs cost more. Pets are okay.

La Peñita Motel and Trailer Park
It will be good news to many longtime Mexico vacationers that **Motel Russell** remains open and ready for guests. The scene is vintage tropical Mexico—peeling paint, snoozing cats, lazy palms, and a beautiful beach with boats casually pulled onto the sand a few steps from your door—all for rock-bottom prices. Come and populate the place while octogenarian owner Mary Cárdenas Nichols is still around to tell stories about "the way things used to be." Reserve at Calle Ruben C. Jaramillo no. 24, La Peñita de Jaltemba, Nayarit, tel. 327/409-59. There are about 15 clean, spartan, one-bedroom apartments (most in need of repair) with fans for $22 d, $33 with kitchenette and refrigerator. Great fishing from the front yard, and it's two blocks from practically everything else in La Peñita. For a small fee, you may also be able to set up a tent or park your RV on one of the old beachfront trailer spaces. Get there by driving to the beach end of La Peñita's main street, Emiliano Zapata. Turn right and parallel the beach for about two blocks.

The big **Trailer Park Hotelera La Peñita,** P.O. Box 22, La Peñita, Nayarit 63727, tel. 327/409-96, enjoys a breezy ocean-view location one mile north of La Peñita; watch for the big highway sign. Its 128 grassy spaces cover a tree-dotted, breezy hillside park overlooking a golden beach and bay. Rates run $14/day, $12/day for three-month rental, with all hookups; closed June, July, and August. The many amenities include a pool, hilltop terrace club, restaurant, showers, and toilets; fine for tenting, surfing, and fishing. Get your winter reservations in early.

FOOD

Fruit Stands and Mini-Supermarkets
The farm country along Hwy. 200 north of Puerto Vallarta offers a feast of tropical fruits. Roadside stands at Guayabitos, La Peñita, and especially at Las Varas, half an hour north, offer mounds of papayas, mangoes, melons, and pineapples in season. Watch out also for more exotic species, such as the *guanabana,* which looks like a spiny mango, but whose pulpy interior looks and smells much like its Asian cousin, the jackfruit.

A number of small Guayabitos mini-supermarkets supply a little bit of everything. Try **Mini-Super Gaby II,** Retorno Ceibas across from Trailer Park Villanueva, on the south end, for vegetables, a small deli, and general groceries. Open daily 7 A.M.–2:30 P.M. and 4–7:30 P.M. Competing next door is **Mini-Super Juan de Dios,** open daily 8 A.M.–8 P.M. On the north end of Av. del Sol Nuevo, second branches of each of these, opposite the church and Hotel Peñamar, respectively, stock more, including fresh baked goods. Both are open daily, 8 A.M.–9 P.M.

For larger, fresher selections of everything, go to one of the big main-street *fruterías* or supermarkets in La Peñita, such as **Supermercado Lorena,** tel. 327/402-55, across from Bancomer, open daily 8 A.M.–2 P.M. and 4–9:30 P.M.

Restaurants
Several Guayabitos restaurants offer good food and service during the busy winter, spring, and August seasons. Hours and menus are often restricted during the midsummer and Sept.–Nov. low seasons.

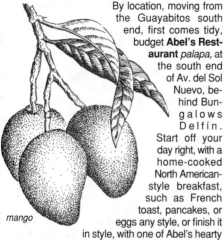

mango

By location, moving from the Guayabitos south end, first comes tidy, budget **Abel's Restaurant** *palapa,* at the south end of Av. del Sol Nuevo, behind Bungalows Delfín. Start off your day right, with a home-cooked North American-style breakfast, such as French toast, pancakes, or eggs any style, or finish it in style, with one of Abel's hearty soups, followed by a tasty meat, fish, and or chicken plates. Open daily 7 A.M.–9 P.M. in season.

Abel asked me to mention his new **Mocambo Restaurant,** three blocks north, across from rival Restaurant Las Alejandras, between Tabachines and Colorines. He promises a menu of "much more variety" than his long-standing *palapa* establishment. (Given Abel's demonstrated cooking skill, I expect his new Mocambo cuisine to rank among Guayabitos's best.) He expects to be open daily 7 A.M.–10 P.M.

Trailer Park Villanueva restaurant, at the beach-end of Andando Cocoteros, specializes in caught-in-the-bay fresh seafood at moderate prices. Breakfast here is also relaxing, sitting in the airy *palapa,* enjoying the breeze and the beach scene. Open daily 8 A.M.–9 P.M. in season.

For a refreshingly cool and refined indoor atmosphere, go to **La Concha,** Guayabitos's only air-conditioned restaurant. Here, skilled chefs specialize in tasty shrimp, fish, and chicken specialties, which patrons enjoy along with a list of good red and white Cetto-label Baja California wines. On Av. Sol Nuevo, just south of Hotel Posada del Sol, tel. 327/409-83; open daily 10 A.M.–8 P.M. Credit cards are accepted.

Right across the street, you can enjoy a homier option at the family-run **Cocina Económica Doña Carmen.** Here, dedicated cooks put out hearty tacos, enchiladas, spicy *pozole* (shredded pork roast and hominy vegetable stew), and the catch of the day at budget prices. Open every day from early morning till about 10 P.M. year-round.

Across the street, the clean, local-style **Restaurant Las Alejandras,** tel. 327/404-88, offers good breakfasts and a general Mexican-style menu; on Av. del Sol Nuevo, just north of the pharmacy, open daily in season 8 A.M.–9 P.M.

Similar good food and service is available at **Restaurant Gaby,** about two blocks north, across from Hotel Peñamar, open Mon.–Fri. 7:30 A.M.–9:30 P.M. in season.

One of Guayabitos's best, the moderately priced restaurant **Campanario** in front of the Hotel Posada la Misión, Retorno Tabachines 6 at Calle Tabachines, tel. 327/403-57, is a longtime favorite of the North American trailer colony. The menu features bountiful fresh seafood, meat, and Mexican plates at reasonable prices, open 8 A.M.–9 P.M. high season, 2–9 P.M. low; credit cards are accepted.

For a change of pace, or if your preferred Guayabitos restaurants are seasonally closed, try **Chuy's,** La Peñita's local and tourist favorite. It offers a broad, reasonably priced menu within a *típica* Mexican patio setting. Located about five blocks from Hwy. 200, on Calle Bahía Punta Mita, half a block right, off Emiliano Zapata, open daily until around 9 P.M.

SPORTS AND ENTERTAINMENT

Sports

Aquatic sports concentrate around the south end of Guayabitos beach, where launches ply the waters, offering banana (towed-tube) rides and **snorkeling** at offshore Isla Islote. Rent a **sportfishing** launch (*panga,* say PAHN-gah) along the beach. If you want to launch your own boat, ask one of the trailer parks if you can use its ramp for a fee. For more beach sports details, see "Beaches and Activities," described above under "Sights."

For **tennis,** you can rent the (daytime only) court in front of the Hotel Decameron Rincón de Las Palmas (at Guayabitos's south end) for about $4 an hour. Inquire at the hotel desk, tel. 327/401-90.

Nightlife

Although Guayabitos is a resort for those who mostly love peace and quiet, a few nightspots, findable by the noise they emanate, operate along Av. del Sol Nuevo. One of the liveliest is **Hotel Decameron Los Cocos,** the high-rise at the very south end, on Retorno Palmas, tel. 327/401-90, where a mostly Canadian and American crowd gyrates to rock most winter nights till the wee hours.

SERVICES AND INFORMATION

Nayarit State Tourism maintains an **information office,** tel. 327/406-93, hours Mon. –Fri. 9 A.M.–7 P.M., at the north end of Av. del Sol Nuevo, by the highway. If it's closed, an excellent alternative source is Jorge Castuera, the well-informed, personable, English-speaking owner of the *farmacia,* on Av. del Sol Nuevo, near the south end, corner of Tabachines.

The *correo,* tel. 327/407-17, open Mon.–Fri. 9 A.M.–1 P.M. and 3–6 P.M., and *telégrafo*, open Mon.–Fri. 8 A.M.–2 P.M., are next door. If, however, you just need stamps or a *buzón* (mailbox), they're available at Jorge Castuera's *farmacia* on Av. del Sol Nuevo at Andando Tabachines.

Another possible information source is the **travel agency,** at Km 94 on the highway, east side, about a few hundred yards north of the Guaybitos entrance, tel. 327/404-47, fax 327/404-75.

Guayabitos has no money-exchange agency, although some of the mini-supermarkets may exchange U.S. or Canadian dollars or traveler's checks. More pesos for your cash or traveler's checks are available at the **Bancomer** branch (with ATM) in La Peñita, E. Zapata 22, tel. 327/402-37; open for U.S. and Canadian money exchange, Mon.–Fri. 9 A.M.–3:30 P.M.

Although Guayabitos has no hospital, La Peñita does. For medical consultations, go to the highly recommended, small, private 24-hour **Clínica Rentería,** on Calle Valle de Acapulco in La Peñita, tel. 327/401-40, with a surgeon, gynecologist, and two general practitioners on call. Alternatively, you can drive or taxi 14 miles (22 km) south to the small general hospital in San Francisco, (known locally as

"San Pancho"). It offers X-ray, laboratory, gynecological, pediatric, and internal medicine consultations and services both during regular office hours, weekdays 10:30 A.M.–12 P.M. and 4–6 P.M., and on 24-hour emergency call, tel. 325/840-77.

For less urgent medical matters, Jorge Castuera, the well-informed, veterinarian-owner of the *farmacia,* Av. del Sol Nuevo at Tabachines, tel. 327/404-00, fax 327/404-46, can recommend medicines or put you in contact with a local doctor. Open daily except Thursday 8 A.M.–2 P.M. and 4–8 P.M. Jorge and his wife jointly run their enterprise, filling prescriptions, handling their *larga distancia* and **fax** service, selling postage stamps, and running their **laundry** on the same premises.

Another well-used Guayabitos *larga distancia* telephone office, tel. 327/403-97 or 327/403-99, fax 327/403-98, is next to Mini-Super Gaby II at south-end Retorno Ceibas, open Mon.–Sat. approximately 9 A.M.–8 P.M., Sunday 9 A.M.–12 P.M. during winter season, but it may maintain shorter hours otherwise. It also offers a shelf of mostly English used paperbacks for purchase or a two-for-one exchange.

GETTING THERE AND AWAY

Puerto Vallarta- and Tepic-bound Transportes Pacífico (TP) second-class buses routinely stop (about once every daylight hour, each direction) on the main highway entrance to Guayabitos's Av. del Sol Nuevo. Additionally, several daily first-class buses pick up Puerto Vallarta- and Tepic-bound passengers at the Transportes Pacífico station, tel. 327/400-01, at the main street highway corner in La Peñita.

Transportes Norte de Sonora (TNS) and Elite (EL) buses routinely stop at the small La Peñita station, tel. 327/400-62, just south of the main street highway corner, beach side. Northern destinations include Tepic, San Blas, Mazatlán, and the U.S. border; southern, Puerto Vallarta, Manzanillo, Zihuatanejo, and Acapulco. **Primera Plus** luxury buses en route between Puerto Vallarta and Guadalajara stop at a small station on the opposite side of the highway.

The Guayabitos coast is easily accessible by bus or taxi from the **Puerto Vallarta Interna-**

tional Airport, the busy terminal for flight connections with U.S. and Mexican destinations. Buses and taxis cover the 39-mile (62-km) distance to Guayabitos in less than an hour. For more details, see "Puerto Vallarta Airport Arrival and Departure" under "Getting There and Away" at the end of the Puerto Vallarta town chapter.

THE ROAD TO SAN BLAS

The lush 60-mile (100-km) stretch between Rincón de Guayabitos and San Blas is a Pacific Eden of flowery tropical forests and pearly, palm-shaded beaches largely unknown to the outside world. Highway 200 and the new Hwy. 161, connecting at Las Varas, lead travelers past fields of leafy tobacco, tropical orchards, mangrove-edged lagoons, vine-strewn jungle, and a string of little havens—Chacala and Mar de Jade, Platanitos, Paraíso Miramar, Casa Mañana, and Las Islitas—that add sparkle to an already inviting coastline.

PLAYA CHACALA AND MAR DE JADE

Side roads off Hwy. 200 provide exotic, close-up glimpses of Nayarit's tangled, tropical woodland, but rarely will they lead to such a delightful surprise as the green-tufted golden crescent of Playa Chacala and its diminutive neighbor, Playa Chacalilla.

Nineteen miles (31 km) north of Rincón de Guayabitos, follow the six-mile, newly paved road to the great old palm grove at Chacala. Beyond the line of rustic *palapa* seafood restaurants lies a heavenly curve of sand, enfolded on both sides by palm-tipped headlands.

A mile farther north, past Chacala village on the headland, the road ends at Chacalilla, Chacala's miniature twin. (The status of public access to Chacalilla is lately in doubt, however, due to hotel construction on the site.)

Beach Activities and Practicalities
Chacala's gentle surf is good for close-in body-surfing, boogie boarding, swimming, and beginning-to-intermediate surfing. Furthermore, the water is generally clear enough for snorkeling off the rocks on either side of the beach. If you bring your equipment, kayaking, windsurfing, and sailing are possible. Moreover, the sheltered north end cove is nearly always tranquil and safe, even for tiny tots. Fishing is so good local people make their living at it. Chacala Bay is so rich and clean that tourists eat oysters right off the rocks.

Supplied by the beachside restaurants and the stores in the village, Playa Chacala is ideal for tent or small RV camping. Now that the road is paved, motorhomes and trailers should be able to get there routinely. Chacalilla would be similarly good for camping, except new development may limit access.

Mar de Jade
The Mar de Jade, a holistic-style living center at the south end of Playa Chacala, offers unique alternatives. Laura del Valle, Mar de Jade's personable and dynamic physician/founder, has worked hard since the early 1980s building living facilities and a learning center while simultaneously establishing a local health clinic. Now, Mar de Jade offers Spanish-language and work-study programs for people who enjoy the tropics but want to do more than laze in the sun. The main thrust is interaction with local people. Spanish, for example, is the preferred language at the dinner table.

Its thatched, cool, and clean adobe and brick cabins, adjacent two-story lodging complex (with concrete floors, showers, restrooms, and good water) nestle among a flowery, palm-shaded garden of fruit trees. Additional units dot a tropical forest-view hillside nearby. Stone pathways lead to the beach-side main center, which consists of a dining room, kitchen, offices, library, and classroom overlooking the sea.

While Mar de Jade's purpose is serious, it has nothing against visitors who *do* want to laze in the sun. Mar de Jade invites travelers to make reservations (or simply drop in) and stay as long as they like, for adults from about $75/day year-round, per person double occupancy, including three hearty meals. Discounts are available for children.

The core educational program is a three-week Spanish course (fee $260 for three weeks), although it does offer one- and two-week options for those who can't stay the full three weeks. Work-study programs, such as gardening, kitchen assistant, carpentry, and maintenance can possibly be arranged. Sometimes participants join staff in local work, such as at the medical clinic or on construction projects.

For more information about the course schedule and fees, contact Mar de Jade directly in Puerto Vallarta, at tel./fax 3/222-1171 or 3/222-3524, email: info@mardejade.com, or website: www.mardejade.com.

AROUND THE BAY OF MATANCHÉN

The broad Bay of Matanchén, framed by verdant mountains, sweeps northward toward San Blas, lined with an easily accessible, pearly crescent of sand, ripe for campers and beachcombers. Village stores, seafood *palapas,* a breezy bay-view restaurant, two beachside trailer parks, and a pair of friendly, small resorts provide the amenities for a day or a month of restful adventuring.

Platanitos and Costa Custodio
About 17 miles (27 km) along Hwy. 161 north of Las Varas, orchards and fields give way to tropical forest at Punta Platanitos (Little Bananas), where a dirt road leads down to a cove lined with the *pangas* and seafood *palapas* of the Platanitos village and fishing cooperative. Local folks, drawn by the yellow sand, gentle blue waves, and superfresh seafood, have for years flocked here for Sunday outings. You can do likewise, and, if you bring your own equipment, you can also enjoy windsurfing, kayaking to nearby hidden coves, snorkeling, and fishing from headland rocks or by boat (which, most days, you can launch from the beach). Tent or RV camping appears promising (ask if it's okay: *"¿Es bueno acampar acá?"*) in the beachside shade.

If you cross the beach and continue along the dirt road that climbs uphill over the beach's westside headland, within half a mile you'll arrive at a lovely breezy ocean viewpoint, site of the **Costa Custodio** home development. Although you might want to consider buying a lot or home here

(lots about $100,000; houses about $250,000) you probably would want to rent one first.

The spot is luxuriously lovely, with a big blue meandering pool, expansive views up and down the coast, dolphins and whales sometimes swimming offshore, a pristine beach below, and a wildlife-rich mangrove lagoon, Estero Custodio, half a mile to the north. From the north side of the point you can gaze upon a long, lazy, palm-tufted beach, home ground of **campamento tortuguero,** a group of volunteers camped out to protect turtles—*carey, golfino* (olive ridley), and leatherback—and eggs from poachers. Volunteers are also reintroducing crocodiles into the lagoon. Get there by the dirt road, off of Hwy. 161, north, near Otate, between kilometer markers 21 and 22; follow the power line.

Deluxe, completely furnished villas, sleeping four to six, with maid service and use of all facilities, rent from about $1,000 per week, depending on season. For more information, contact Costa Custodio's agent at 329/229-54, email: custodi@pvnet.com.mx.

To the Bay of Matanchen and Paraíso Miramar
From Platanitos, the new road plunges into the forest, winding past great vine-draped trees and stands of cock-plumed Colima palms. If you glimpse green citrus fruit amongst the riot of leaves and flowers, you might be seeing a wild lime, or, if yellow, a guava or passion fruit dangling from its long vine. Now and then, you will pass a ponderous red-barked *papillo* tree, with its bark curling and sloughing off its great ruddy trunk and branches. The *papillo* is sometimes known as the "gringo" tree because it's always red and peeling.

The Bahía de Matanchén begins about five miles past Platanitos just about when you're first able to see it from the roadside—a spreading, shining vista of mountain, grove, and sea.

Continuing north, and downhill, you reach the end of Nayarit 161 at its intersection with the Tepic highway, Nayarit 74, near the twin villages of Santa Cruz and Miramar (total pop. about 1,000). Continue north about 1.5 km and you will pass through even tinier Playa Manzanilla village, where a small beachside sign marks the driveway to Paraíso Miramar.

PUERTO VALLARTA TO SAN BLAS

To Mexcaltitán
Campos de los Limones
Sentispac
Santiago Ixcuintla
La Presa
Rio Grande de Santiago
Bocas de Camachín
Playa Cesteo
Playa Los Corchos
Toro Mocho
Villa Juárez
Villa Hidalgo
Crucero San Blas
Laureles
Guadalupe Victoria
San Blas
SEE DETAIL
Miramar
Santa Cruz
Punta El Caballo
El Cora
El Llano
Jalotemba
Volcán San Juan (7,350 ft.)
Xalisco
El Refugio
Tepic
San Cayetano
KOALA BUNGALOWS AND TRAILER PARK
TOLL EXPRESSWAY
Lake Santa María
Punta Gorda
Platanitos
COSTA CUSTODIO
TURTLE CONSERVATION ENCAMPMENT
Otates
Emiliano Zapata
Volcán Tepetiltic (6,630 ft.)
Santa María del Oro
Tepetiltic
Lake Tepetiltic
To Guadalajara
Zacualpán
Lake San Pedro
Barra Ixtapa
Punta Los Chivos
Compostela
Chapalilla
Mazatan
Juan Escutia
TOLL
Cerro San Pedro (6,560 ft.)
Las Varas
Chacala
CASA DE LOS OBELISCOS
MAR DE JADE
Bahía de Jaltemba
Felipe Carrillo Puerto
La Peñita
Rincón de Guayabitos
Monteón
PLAYA AZUL ADVENTURE RESORT
Lo de Marcos
VILLA DE LA BUENA SALUD
San Francisco
Sayulita
Valle de Banderas
Punta de Mita
Bucerias
Islas Tres Marietas
Bahía de Banderas
Puerto Vallarta
Mismaloya
Boca de Tomatlán
Yelapa
Cabo Corrientes
El Tuito
To Tomatlán

PACIFIC OCEAN

DETAIL
Estero el Pozo
Guadalupe Victoria
Reforma Agraria
El Rey
Estero San Cristobal
Guaristemba
Marisma la Chayota
Navarrette
LIGHT-HOUSE
San Blas
La Tovara
El Espino
Las Islitas
El Camalote
Mecatan
Matanchen
Bahía Matanchen
Aticama
Los Cocos
CASA MAÑANA
PARAISO MIRAMAR
Santa Cruz
Tecuitata
Jalcocotan

0   20 mi
0   20 km

© AVALON TRAVEL PUBLISHING, INC.

The spacious, green, bay-view park is bedecked by palms and sheltered by what appears to be the grandmother of all banyan trees. On the cliff-bottom beach beneath the great tree, the surf rolls in gently, while the blue bay, crowned by jungle ridges, curves gracefully north toward San Blas.

Paraíso Miramar's owner/family, most of whom live in Tepic, and their personable, hard-working manager Porfirio Hernández, offer a little bit for everyone: six simple but clean and comfortable rooms with bath facing the bay; behind that, 12 grassy RV spaces with concrete pads and all hookups, and three kitchenette bungalows sleeping six. A small view restaurant and blue pools—swimming, kiddie, and hot tub—complete the lovely picture.

Rooms rent for about $35 d, low season, $40 high; bungalows, about $45. RV spaces go for about $14/day. For a week's stay, you customarily get one day free. If, on the other hand, you'd like to set up a tent, the shady hillside palm grove on the property's south side appears just right. Make reservations by writing Paraíso Miramar directly at Km 1.2 Carretera a San Blas, Playa La Manzanilla, Santa Cruz de Miramar, Nayarit, or calling the family at home in Tepic (in Spanish), tel./fax 325/490-30, 325/490-31, and 325/490-37.

Casa Mañana

About two and a half miles farther north (or eight miles, 13 km south of San Blas), the diminutive shoreline retreat Casa Mañana perches at the south end of breezy Los Cocos beach. Owned and managed by an Austrian man, Reinhardt, and his Mexican wife Lourdes, Casa Mañana's two double-storied tiers of rooms rise over a homey, spic-and-span, beach-view restaurant and pool deck and garden. Very popular with Europeans and North Americans seeking South-Seas tranquility on a budget, Casa Mañana offers fishing, beachcombing, hiking, and swimming right from its palm-adorned front yard. The 26 rooms rent for about $42 high season, $38 low, with a/c and ocean view, $30 low, $35 high, with a/c but no view, with one day free per week stay. Longer-stay discounts are negotiable, and winter reservations strongly recommended. For reservations, write P.O. Box 49, San Blas, Na-

yarit 63740, telephone toll-free in Mexico, 01-800/2022-79 or tel./fax 325/490-80 or 325/490-90, email reinhard@prodigy.net.mx, or visit www.casa-manana.com.

If Casa Mañana is full, try second-choice **Bungalows Marto,** on the beach side of the highway, one mile north of Casa Mañana.

From Casa Mañana, Playa los Cocos and its venerable palm grove stretches north past beachfront houses, a couple of very basic lodgings, and a sprinkling of beachside *palapa* restaurants. A "must do" among them is **Mi Restaurant,** founded by Bernie, the Austrian chef, formerly at Casa Mañana and before that, at super-plush Las Hadas resort in Manzanillo.

Continuing northward, notice that the occasionally heavy surf is gradually eroding the beach, leaving a crumbling, 10-foot embankment along a mostly rocky shore. Playa los Cocos is nevertheless balmy and beautiful enough to attract a winter RV colony to **Trailer Park Playa Amor,** which overlooks the waves, right in the middle of Playa los Cocos. Besides excellent fishing, boating, boogie boarding, swimming, and windsurfing, the park offers 30 grassy spaces for very reasonable prices. Rentals run about $10, $11, and $12 for small, medium, and large RVs respectively, with all hookups, showers, and toilets; pets are okay. Although you can expect plenty of friendly company during the winter months, reservations are not usually necessary (although you can try contact by mail: Trailer Park Playa Amor, c/o gerente Javier López, Playa los Cocos, San Blas, Nayarit 63740).

Waterfall Hikes

A number of pristine creeks tumble down boulder-strewn beds and foam over cliffs as waterfalls *(cataratas)* in the jungle above the Bay of Matanchén. Some of these are easily accessible and perfect for a day of hiking, picnicking, and swimming. Don't hesitate to ask for directions: *"¿Dónde está el camino a la catarata, por favor?"* ("Where is the path to the waterfall, please?") If you would like a guide, ask, *"¿Hay un guía, por favor?"* One (or all) of the local crowd of kids may immediately volunteer.

You can get to within walking distance of the waterfall near **Tecuitata** village either by car, taxi, or the Tepic-bound bus; it is only a few miles out of Santa Cruz along Nayarit Hwy. 74. A half-mile uphill past the village, a sign reading Balneario Nuevo Chapultepec marks a dirt road heading downhill a half-mile to a creek and a bridge. Cross over to the other side ($3 entrance fee), where you'll find a *palapa* restaurant, a hillside water slide, and a small swimming pool.

Continue upstream along the right-hand bank of the creek for a much rarer treat. Half the fun are the sylvan jungle delights—flashing butterflies, pendulous leafy vines, gurgling little cascades—along the meandering path. The other half is at the end, where the creek spurts through a verdure-framed fissure and splashes into a cool, broad pool festooned with green, giant-leafed *chalata* (taro in Hawaii, tapioca in Africa). Both the pool area and the trail have several possible campsites. Bring everything, especially your water-purification kit and insect repellent. Known locally as Arroyo Campiste, it is popular with kids and women who bring their washing.

Another waterfall, the highest in the area, near the village of **El Cora,** is harder to get to but the reward is even more spectacular. Again, on the west-east Santa Cruz-Tepic Hwy. 74, a negotiable dirt road to El Cora branches south just before Tecuitata. At road's end, after about eight km, you can park by a banana-loading platform. From here, the walk (less than an hour) cli-

maxes with a steep, rugged descent to the rippling, crystal pool at the bottom of the waterfall.

While rugged adventurers may find their own way to the waterfalls, others rely upon guides Armando S. Navarrete and Juan (Bananas) Garcia, tel. 328/504-62, founder of Grupo Ecologio in San Blas. Contact Armando at home at Sonora 179 in San Blas, Nayarit 63740.

Playa Matanchén and Las Islitas

Playa los Cocos gives way at its north end to Aticama village (a few stores and beachside *palapas*) where, northbound, the shoreline road climbs a jungle headland and swoops down to the bay once again. Past a marine sciences school, the beach, a long, palmy sand-ribbon washed by gentle rollers and frequented only by occasional anglers, curves gently northwest to the super-wide and shallow giant kiddie-pool of Playa Matanchén. A left crossroad (which marks the center of Matanchén village, pop. about 300) leads past a lineup of beachfront *palapa* restaurants to Playa las Islitas, at the bay's sheltered north cove.

The beaches of Matanchén and Las Islitas are an inseparable pair. Las Islitas is dotted by little outcroppings topped by miniature jungles of swaying palms and spreading trees. One of these is home for a colony of surfers waiting for the Big Wave, the Holy Grail of surfing. The Big Wave is one of the occasional gigantic 20-foot

Las Islitas (Little Islands) are a series of stone outcroppings that seem to float in the water just off the surfer's haven, Playa Matanchén.

breakers that rise off Playa las Islitas and carry surfers as much as a mile and a quarter (an official Guinness world record) to the soft sand of Playa Matanchén.

For camping, the intimate, protected curves of sand around Playa las Islitas are inviting. Check with local folks to see if it's okay to camp. Although few facilities exist (save a few surfing-season food *palapas*), the beachcombing, swimming, fishing from the rocks, shell-collecting, and surfing are often good even without the Big Wave. The water, however, isn't clear enough for good snorkeling. Campers should be prepared with plenty of strong insect repellent.

During surfing season (Aug.–Feb.) the Team Banana and other *palapa*-shops open up at Matanchén village and Las Islitas to rent surfboards and sell what each of them claims to be the "world's original banana bread."

Ejido de la Palma Crocodile Farm

About three miles (five km) south of Matanchén village, a sign marks a side road to a *cocodrilario* (crocodile farm). At the end of the two-mile track (trucks okay, car-negotiable with caution when dry), you'll arrive at "El Tanque," a spring-fed pond, home of the Ejido de la Palma crocodile farm. About 50 toothy crocs, large and small, snooze in the sun within several enclosures. Half the fun is the adjacent spring-fed freshwater lagoon, so crystal clear you can see half a dozen big fish wriggling beneath the surface. Nearby, ancient trees swathed in vines and orchids tower overhead, butterflies flutter past, and turtles sun themselves on mossy logs. Bring a picnic lunch, binoculars, bird book, insect repellent, and bathing suit.

SAN BLAS AND VICINITY

San Blas (pop. about 10,000) is a small town slumbering beneath a big coconut grove. No one seems to care if the clock on the crumbling plaza church remains stuck for months on end. Neither is there anyone who remembers San Blas's glory days, when it was Mexico's burgeoning Pacific military headquarters and port, with a population of 30,000. Ships from Spain's Pacific Rim colonies crowded its harbor, silks and gold filled its counting houses, and noble Spanish officers and their mantilla-graced ladies strolled the plaza on Sunday afternoon.

Times change, however. Politics and San Blas's pesky *jejenes* (hey-HEY-nays, invisible "no-see-um" biting gnats) have always conspired to deflate any temporary fortunes of San Blas. The *jejenes*' breeding ground, a vast hinterland of mangrove marshes, may paradoxically give rise to a new, prosperous San Blas. These thousands of acres of waterlogged mangrove jungle and savanna are a nursery-home for dozens of Mexico's endangered species. This rich trove is now protected by ecologically aware governments and admired (not unlike the game parks of Africa) by increasing numbers of eco-tourists.

HISTORY

Conquest and Colonization

San Blas and the neighboring, southward-curving Bay of Matanchén were reconnoitered by gold-hungry conquistador Nuño de Guzmán in May 1530. His expedition noted the protected anchorages in the bay and the Estero el Pozo adjacent to the present town. Occasionally during the 16th and 17th centuries, Spanish explorers in their galleons and the pirates lying in wait for them would drop anchor in the *estero* or the adjacent Bay of Matanchén for rendezvous, resupply, or cargo-transfer.

By the latter third of the 18th century, New Spain, reacting to the Russian and English threats in the North Pacific, launched plans for the colonization of California through a new port called San Blas.

The town was officially founded atop the hill of San Basilio in 1768. Streets were surveyed; docks were built. Old documents record that more than a hundred pioneer families received a plot of land and "a pick, an adze, an axe, a machete, a plow . . . a pair of oxen, a cow, a mule, four she-goats and a billy, four sheep, a sow, four hens and a rooster."

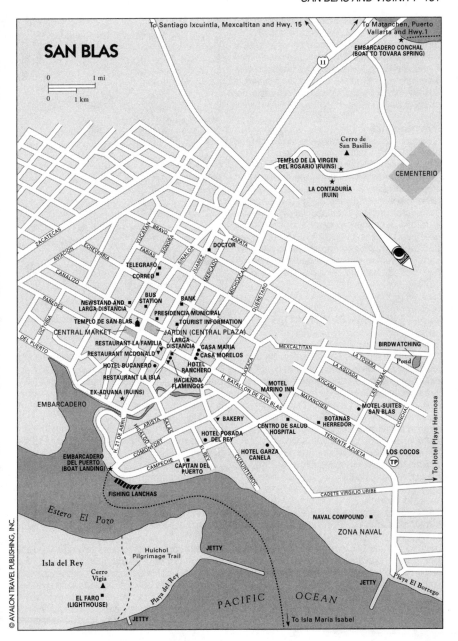

SAN BLAS

To Santiago Ixcuintla, Mexcaltitan and Hwy. 15

To Matanchen, Puerto Vallarta and Hwy.1

EMBARCADERO CONCHAL
(BOAT TO TOVARA SPRING)

0 — 1 mi
0 — 1 km

Cerro de San Basilio

TEMPLO DE LA VIRGEN DEL ROSARIO (RUINS)

CEMENTERIO

LA CONTADURÍA (RUIN)

ZACATECAS
AVIACIÓN
ECHEVERRIA
CANALIZO
PAREDES
VICTORIA
DEL PUERTO

BRAVO
YUCATAN
FARIAS
SONORA
SINALOA
JUAREZ
MERCADO
MICHOACAN
QUERETARO
ZAPATA

DOCTOR

TELEGRAFO
CORREO

NEWSTAND AND
LARGA DISTANCIA

BUS STATION

BANK

PRESIDENCIA MUNICIPAL

TEMPLO DE SAN BLAS

TOURIST INFORMATION

CENTRAL MARKET

JARDIN (CENTRAL PLAZA)

RESTAURANT LA FAMILIA

LARGA DISTANCIA

CASA MARIA

RESTAURANT MCDONALD

CASA MORELOS

HOTEL BUCANERO

HOTEL RANCHERO

RESTAURANT LA ISLA

HACIENDA FLAMINGOS

EX-ADUANA (RUINS)

MEXCALTITAN

BIRDWATCHING

Pond

LA TOVARA
LA AGUADA
LAS PALMAS
ATICAMA

MATANCHEN

OAXACA

H. BATALLON DE SAN BLAS

MOTEL MARINO INN

MOTEL-SUITES SAN BLAS

CONCHITA

To Hotel Playa Hermosa

EMBARCADERO

H. 21 DE ABRIL
ARISTA
SALAS
HIDALGO
COMONFORT
CAMPECHE
EL REY

BAKERY

CENTRO DE SALUD HOSPITAL

BOTANAS HERREDOR

TENIENTE AZUETA

LOS COCOS

TP

HOTEL POSADA DEL REY

HOTEL GARZA CANELA

CAPITAN DEL PUERTO

CUAUHTEMOC

EMBARCADERO DEL PUERTO
(BOAT LANDING)

CADETE VIRGILIO URIBE

FISHING LANCHAS

Estero El Pozo

NAVAL COMPOUND

ZONA NAVAL

Isla del Rey

Cerro Vigia

EL FARO
(LIGHTHOUSE)

Huichol Pilgrimage Trail

JETTY

Playa del Rey

JETTY

PACIFIC OCEAN

JETTY

Playa El Borrego

To Isla Maria Isabel

© AVALON TRAVEL PUBLISHING, INC.

People and animals multiplied, and soon San Blas became the seat of Spain's eastern Pacific naval command. Meanwhile, simultaneously with the founding of the town, the celebrated Father Junípero Serra set out for California with 14 missionary-brothers on *La Concepción,* a sailing vessel built on Matanchén beach just south of San Blas.

Independence
New Spain's glory, however, crumbled in the bloody 1810-21 war for independence, taking San Blas with it. In December 1810, the *insurgente* commander captured the Spanish fort atop San Basilio hill and sent 43 of its cannons to fellow rebel-priest Miguel Hidalgo to use against the loyalists around Guadalajara.

After independence, fewer and fewer ships called at San Blas; the docks fell into disrepair, and the town slipped into somnolence, then complete slumber when President Lerdo de Tejada closed San Blas to foreign commerce in 1872.

SIGHTS AND ACTIVITIES

Getting Oriented
The overlook atop the **Cerro de San Basilio** is the best spot to orient yourself to San Blas. From this breezy point, the palm-shaded grid of streets stretches to the sunset side of **El Pozo** estuary and the lighthouse-hill beyond it. Behind you, on the east, the mangrove-lined **San Cristóbal** river-estuary meanders south to the Bay of Matanchén. Along the south shore, the crystalline white line of San Blas's main beach, **Playa el Borrego** (Sheep Beach), stretches between the two estuary mouths.

Around Town
While you're atop the hill, take a look around the old *contaduria* counting house and fort (built in 1770), where riches were tallied and stored en route to Mexico City or to the Philippines and China. Several of the original great cannons still stand guard at the viewpoint like aging sentinels waiting for long-dead adversaries.

Behind and a bit downhill from the weathered stone arches of the *contaduria* stand the gaping portals and towering, moss-stained bel-

town church of San Blas

fry of the old church of **Nuestra Señora del Rosario,** built in 1769. Undamaged by war, it remained an active church until at least 1872, around the time when poet Henry W. Longfellow was inspired by the silencing and removal of its aging bells.

Downhill, historic houses and ruins dot San Blas town. The old hotels **Bucanero** and **Hacienda Flamingos** on the main street, Juárez, leading past the central plaza, preserve some of their original charm. Just across the street from the Hacienda Flamingos, you can admire the crumbling yet monumental brick colonnade of the 19th-century former **Aduana,** now replaced by a nondescript new customhouse at the estuary-foot of Av. Juárez.

At that shoreline spot, gaze across El Pozo estuary. This was both the jumping-off point for colonization of the Californias and the anchorage of the silk- and porcelain-laden Manila *galeón* and the bullion ships from the northern mines.

El Faro (lighthouse) across the estuary marks the top of **Cerro Vigia,** the southern hill-tip of

THE BELLS OF SAN BLAS

Renowned Romantic poet Henry Wadsworth Longfellow (1807-82) most likely read about San Blas during the early 1870s, just after the town's door was closed to foreign trade. With the ships gone, and not even the trickle of tourists it now enjoys, the San Blas of Longfellow's time was perhaps even dustier and quieter than it is today.

San Blas must have meant quite a lot to him. Ten years later, ill and dying, Longfellow hastened to complete "The Bells of San Blas," his very last poem, finished nine days before he passed away on March 24, 1882. Longfellow wrote of the silent bells of the old Nuestro Señora del Rosario (Our Lady of the Rosary) church, which still stands atop the Cerro San Basilio, little changed to this day.

THE BELLS OF SAN BLAS

What say the Bells of San Blas
To the ships that southward pass
From the harbor of Mazatlán?
To them it is nothing more
Than the sound of surf on the shore,—
Nothing more to master or man.

But to me, a dreamer of dreams,
To whom what is and what seems
Are often one and the same,—
The Bells of San Blas to me
Have a strange, wild melody,
And are something more than a name.

For bells are the voice of the church;
They have tones that touch and search
The hearts of young and old;
One sound to all, yet each
Lends a meaning to their speech,
And the meaning is manifold.

They are a voice of the Past,
Of an age that is fading fast,
Of a power austere and grand;
When the flag of Spain unfurled
Its folds o'er this western world,
And the Priest was lord of the land.

The chapel that once looked down
On the little seaport town
Has crumbled into the dust
And on oaken beams below
The bells swing to and fro,
And are green with mould and rust.

"Is then, the old faith dead,"
They say, "and in its stead
Is some new faith proclaimed,
That we are forced to remain

Naked to sun and rain,
Unsheltered and ashamed?

"Once in our tower aloof
We rang over wall and roof
Our warnings and our complaints;
And round about us there
The white doves filled the air,
Like the white souls of the saints.

"The saints! Ah, have they grown
Forgetful of their own?
Are they asleep, or dead,
That open to the sky
Their ruined Missions lie,
No longer tenanted?

"Oh, bring us back once more
The vanished days of yore,
When the world with faith was filled;
Bring back the fervid zeal,
The hearts of fire and steel,
The hands that believe and build.

"Then from our tower again
We will send over land and main
Our voices of command,
Like exiled kings who return
To their thrones, and the people learn
That the Priest is lord of the land!"

O Bells of San Blas, in vain
Ye call back the Past again!
The Past is deaf to your prayer;
Out of the shadows of night
The world rolls into light;
It is daybreak everywhere.

—Henry Wadsworth Longfellow

EXCURSIONS AROUND SAN BLAS

To Santiago Ixcuintla
and Mexcaltitan (signtseeing)

0   1 mi

0   1 km

Lasguna
Zoquipan

WILDLIFE VIEWING

Los
Negros

Tepiquenas

11

To Isla del Rey (birdwatching, wilderness camping, Huichol Easter ceremonies)

CORREO
PLAZA
EL POZO
(LANDING)
TOURIST
INFORMATION
San Blas

★ EL CONCHAL (LANDING)

▲ Cerro de
San Basilio
(RUINS, VIEWPOINT,
MORNING BIRDWATCHING)

Tovara Spring
(RESTAURANT,
PICNICKING,
SWIMMING)

WILDLIFE VIEWING

Rio Tovara

★ LOS AGUADAS
(LANDING)

Estero El Pozo

Camalota
Spring

★ COCODRILARIO
(CROCODILE BREEDING
STATION)

Estero San Cristobal

Playa Matanchen
(RESTAURANT, PICNICKING,
SWIMMING)

Playa Las Islitas
("THE BIG WAVE," SURFING,
RESTAURANT, PICNICKING,
SWIMMING)

To Isla Isabel (wildlife viewing
fishing, snorkeling scuba diving)

Bahia de Matanchen

To Tecuitata and El Cora
waterfall hikes, Mex. 200
and Puerto Vallarta

© AVALON TRAVEL PUBLISHING, INC.

Isla del Rey (actually a peninsula). Here, the first beacon shone during the latter third of the 18th century.

Although only a few local folks ever bother to cross over to the island, it is nevertheless an important pilgrimage site for **Huichol** people from the remote Nayarit and Jalisco mountains. Huichol have been gathering on the Isla del Rey for centuries to make offerings to Aramara, their goddess of the sea. A not-so-coincidental shrine to a Catholic virgin-saint stands on an offshore sea rock, visible from the beach-endpoint of the Huichol pilgrimage a few hundred yards beyond the lighthouse.

A large cave sacred to the Huichol at the foot of Cerro Vigia was sadly demolished by the government during the early 1970s for rock for a breakwater. Fortunately, President Salinas de Gortari (1988-94) partly compensated for the insult by deeding the sacred site to the Huichols during the early 1990s.

Two weeks before Easter, people begin arriving by the hundreds, the men decked out in flamboyant feathered hats. On the ocean beach, 10 minutes' walk straight across the island, anyone can respectfully watch them perform their rituals: elaborate marriages, feasts, and offerings of little boats laden with arrows and food, consecrated to the sea goddess to ensure good hunting and crops and many healthy children.

Hotel Playa Hermosa

For a glimpse of a relic from San Blas's recent past, head across town to the crumbling Hotel Playa Hermosa. Here, one evening in 1951, President Miguel Alemán came to dedicate San Blas's first luxury hotel. As the story goes, the *jejenes* descended and bit the President so fiercely the entire entourage cleared out before he even finished his speech. Rumors have circulated around town for years that someone's going to reopen the Playa Hermosa, but—judging from the vines creeping up the walls and the orchids blossoming on the balconies—they'd best hurry or the jungle is going to get the old place first. To get there follow H. Batallón toward the beach, turn left just after the Los Cocos Trailer Park, and continue along the jungle road for about half a mile.

La Tovara Jungle River Trip

On the downstream side of the bridge over Estero San Cristóbal, launches-for-hire will take you up the Tovara River, a side channel that winds about a mile downstream into the jungle.

The channel quickly narrows into a dark tree-tunnel, edged by great curtainlike swaths of mangrove roots. Big snowy *garza* (egrets) peer out from leafy branches; startled turtles slip off their soggy perches into the river, while big submerged roots, like gigantic pythons, bulge out of the inky water. Riots of luxuriant plants—white lilies, green ferns, red *romelia* orchids—hang from the trees and line the banks.

Finally you reach Tovara Springs, which well up from the base of a verdant cliffside. On one side, a bamboo-sheltered *palapa* restaurant serves refreshments, while on the other families picnic in a hillside pavilion. In the middle, everyone jumps in and paddles in the clear, cool water.

You can enjoy this trip either of two ways: the longer, three-hour excursion as described ($40 per boatload of six to eight) from El Conchal landing on the estuary, or the shorter version (two hours, $30 per boatload) beginning upriver at road-accessible Las Aguadas near Matanchén village. Take the hourly Matanchén bus from the San Blas central plaza. Note: Sometimes a tourist crowd draws all of the boats away from La Conchal to Las Aguadas; to go there instead, see map "Excursions Around San Blas."

The more leisurely three-hour trip allows more chances (especially in the early morning) to spot a jaguar or crocodile, or a giant boa constrictor hanging from a limb (no kidding). Many of the boatmen are very professional; if you want to view wildlife, tell them, and they'll go slower and keep a sharp lookout.

Some boatmen offer more extensive trips to less-disturbed sites deeper in the jungle. These include the Camalota spring, a branch of the Tovara River (where a local *ejido* maintains a crocodile breeding station) and the even more remote and pristine Tepiqueías, Los Negros, and Zoquipan lagoons in the San Cristóbal Estero's upper reaches.

In light of the possible wildlife-viewing rewards, trip prices are very reasonable. For example, the very knowledgeable bird specialist Oscar Partida Hernández, Comonfort 134 Pte., San Blas, Nayarit 63740, tel. 328/503-24, will

EGRETS, CORMORANTS, AND ANHINGAS

In tropical San Blas, lagoon-edge mangrove trees often appear at first glance to be laden with snow. Closer inspection, however, reveals swarms of nesting white birds. Although together they appear a white mass, individually they belong to three species of egret—*garza* in Spanish.

snowy egret

Although all may seem at home, one species is a relatively new arrival to the New World. The cattle egret, *Bubulcus ibis,* wasn't seen in North America until around 1900. The smallest of egrets, it's but one and a half feet long, with a small yellow or orange bill and blackish legs and feet. Scientists suspect the bird migrated from its native Asia or Africa, where the cattle egret has foraged amid herds of

cattle for millennia; the bird profits handsomely from the swarms of bugs attracted by cattle.

The other two members of Mexico's egret trio, the crystal-white snowy egret *(Egretta thula)* and the blue-gray great heron *(Casmerodius albus)* prefer to stalk fish and crabs in lagoons. You'll see them—especially the black-billed, two-foot-long snowy egret—poised in a pond, rock still, for what seems like a season, until—*pop!*—the sharp beak dives into the water and reappears with a luckless fish.

great heron

guide a four-person boatload to La Tovara for about $60. If Oscar is busy, call "Chencho," tel. 328/507-16, for a comparably excellent trip. More extensive options include a combined Camalota-La Tovara trip (allow four to five hours) for about $90, or Tepiqueías and Los Negros (six hours) for about $100. For each extra person, add about $8, $12, and $16, respectively, to the price of each of these options.

The San Blas tourist information office (see under "Information," below) has been organizing daily money-saving, collective high-season La Tovara boat tours for visitors. The tariff usually runs about $6 per person.

Isla Isabel

Isla Isabel is a two-mile-square offshore wildlife study area 40 miles (65 km) and three hours

cormorant

bird"—sometimes bends back into a snakelike S. The anhinga often will swim along, submerged except for its head and neck, looking every bit like a serpent slicing through the water. Cormorants frequently nest in flocks atop mangroves and seem to have either a sense of humor or no inkling of their true identity, for if you venture too close they'll start grunting like a chorus of pigs.

Cormorants and anhingas are as graceful in the water as they are clumsy on land. They plop along in the mud on their webbed feet, finally jumping to a rock or tree perch where, batlike, they unfold their wings to dry and preen them.

Although cormorants and anhingas are both about two to three feet in size, they're easily distinguishable: the anhinga generally appears in greater numbers and features arrays of silvery spots along the wings.

anhinga

The great heron's feeding habits are similar to those of its smaller cousin, and its grand six-foot wingspan and steel blue-gray hues make it easy to recognize. At a lagoon's edge, watch quietly and you might soon be rewarded with the magnificent sight of a great heron swooping down to land gracefully in the water.

Sharing the same watery feeding grounds are the Mexican (or olivaceous) cormorant *(Phalacrocorax olivaceous)* and its cousin the anhinga *(Anhinga anhinga)*. These are often confused with loons, and they do seem a bit loony. Its neck, especially that of the anhinga—also known as "darter" or "snake-

north by boat. The cone of an extinct volcano, Isla Isabel is now home to a small government station of eco-scientists and a host of nesting boobies, frigate birds, and white-tailed tropic birds. Fish and sea mammals, especially dolphins, and sometimes whales, abound in the surrounding clear waters. Although it's not a recreational area, local authorities allow serious visitors, accompanied by authorized guides, for

a few days of camping, snorkeling, scuba diving, and wildlife viewing. A primitive dormitory can accommodate several persons. Bring everything, including food and bedding. Contact English-speaking Tony Aguayo or Armando Navarrete for arrangements and prices, which typically run $150 per day for parties of up to four persons. Two- and three-day extensions run about $200 and $250, respectively. Stormy summer and fall weather limits most Isla Isabel trips to the sunnier, calmer winter-spring season. Tony and Armando's "office" is the little *palapa* to the left of the small floating boat dock at the El Pozo estuary end of Juárez. Tony can also be reached by tel. 328/503-64; Armando at home, at Sonora 179, in San Blas. Also recommended for the Isla Isabel trip is Antonio Palma, whom you can contact by inquiring at Hotel Garza Canela front desk.

Bird-Watching
Although San Blas's extensive mangrove and mountain jungle hinterlands are renowned for their birds and wildlife, rewarding bird-watching can start in the early morning right at the edge of town. Follow Calle Conchal right (southeast) one block from Suites San Blas, then left (northeast) to a small pond. With binoculars, you might get some good views of local species of cormorants, flycatchers, grebes, herons, jacanas, and motmots. A copy of Chalif and Petersen's *Field Guide to Mexican Birds* will assist in further identification.

Rewarding bird-watching is also possible on **Isla del Rey.** Bargain for a launch (from the foot of Juárez, about $2 roundtrip) across to the opposite shore. Watch for wood, clapper, and Virginia rails, and boat-billed herons near the estuary shore. Then follow the track across the island (looking for warblers and a number of species of sparrows) to the beach where you might enjoy good views of plovers, terns, Heerman's gulls, and rafts of pelicans.

Alternatively, look around the hillside cemetery and the ruins atop **Cerro de San Basilio** for good early morning views of hummingbirds, falcons, owls, and American redstarts.

You can include serious bird-watching with your boat trip through the mangrove channels branching from the **Estero San Cristóbal** and **La Tovara River.** This is especially true if you obtain the services of a wildlife-sensitive guide, such as Oscar Partida, tel. 328/503-24, "Chencho," tel. 328/507-16, or Juan "Bananas" Garcia, tel. 328/504-62.

For many more details on bird-watching and hiking around San Blas, get a copy of the booklet *Where to Find Birds in San Blas, Nayarit* by Rosalind Novick and Lan Sing Wu, at the shop at Garza Canela Hotel ($4). Or order from them

directly at 178 Myrtle Court, Arcata, CA 95521. The American Birding Association Bookstore, P.O. Box 6599, Colorado Springs, CO 80934, and the Los Angeles and Tucson Audubon Society bookstores also stock it.

Waterfall Hikes
A number of waterfalls decorate the lush jungle foothills above the Bay of Matanchén. Two of these, near Tecuitata and El Cora villages, respectively, are accessible from Hwy. 74 about 10 miles (16 km) south of San Blas. The local white bus *(autobús blanco)* will take you most of the way. It runs south to Santa Cruz every two hours 8:30 A.M.–4:30 P.M. from the downtown corner of Juárez and Paredes. See the access details under "Waterfall Hikes" in "Around the Bay of Matanchén," preceding.

While rugged adventurers may guide themselves to the waterfalls, others rely upon guides Armando Navarrette (Sonora 179, San Blas), local eco-leader Juan "Bananas" Garcia, who works out of his cafe-shop, at H. Batallón 219 (tel. 328/504-62), four blocks south of the plaza, or Lucio Rodríguez (inquire at Tourist Information, on Mercado, one block south, half a block east of the plaza).

Besides the above, Armando Navarette offers bird-watching hikes, especially around Singayta in the foothills, where birders often identify 30 or 40 species in a two-hour adventure. Such an excursion might also include a coffee plantation visit, hiking along the old royal road to Tepic, and plenty of tropical fauna and flora, including butterflies, wildflowers, and giant vines and trees, such as *ceiba, arbolde, and the peeling, red* papillo tree. Armando's fee for such a trip, lasting around five hours, runs about $12 per person, plus your own or rented transportation.

Beach Activities
San Blas's most convenient beach is **Playa el Borrego,** at the south end of Calle Cuauhtémoc about a mile south of town. With a lineup of *palapas* for food and drinks, the mile-long, broad, fine-sand beach is ripe for all beach activities except snorkeling (due to the murky water). The gradually breaking waves provide boogie boarding and intermediate surfing challenges. Bring your own equipment, as no one rents on the

beach; although Juan "Bananas" Garcia rents snorkels, surfboards, and boogie boards at his cafe-shop, at H. Battallón 219, four blocks south of the town plaza.

Shoals of shells—clams, cockles, mother-of-pearl—wash up on Borrego Beach during storms. Fishing is often good, especially when casting from the jetty and rocks at the north and south ends.

ACCOMMODATIONS

Hotels
San Blas has several hotels, none of them huge, but all with personality. They are not likely to be full even during the high winter season (unless the surf off Matanchén Beach runs high for an unusually long spell).

At the low end, the family-run *casa de huéspedes* (guesthouse) **Casa María,** tel. 328/508-20, makes a reality of the old Spanish saying, *"Mi casa es tu casa."* It is located at the corner of Canalizo and Michoacán, three blocks from the plaza. There are about eight rooms around a homey, cluttered patio, and Maria offers to do everything for the guests except give them baths (which she would probably do if someone got sick). Not too clean, but very friendly and with kitchen privileges. Rooms rent for about $10 s, $12 d, with fans, hot water showers, and dinner for $3.

Alternatively, you can try María's original guesthouse, **Casa Morelos,** operated by her daughter, Magdalena, at 108 Heróico Batallón, tel. 328/508-20, or **Hotel Ranchero** operated by her ex-husband Alfredo, right across the street. They each offer about five rooms around homey plant-filled patios for about $15 s, $18 d. María, Magdalena, and Alfredo all cooperate for the benefit of guests; if one is full, they'll probably be able to find a room next door for you.

Back in the middle of town, newly renovated **Hotel Hacienda Flamingos** lives on as a splendid reminder of old San Blas. It's located at Juárez 105, San Blas, Nayarit 63740, three blocks down Juárez from the plaza, tel. 328/504-85, email: technica@red2000.com.mx. Owners have spared little in restoring this 1863 German consulate to its original graceful condition. Now, the fountain flows once more in the tranquil, tropical inner patio, furnished with period chairs and tables and a gallery of old San Blas photos on the walls. A side door leads outside to a luxuriously spacious adjoining garden, sprinkled with recliners, a grass badminton court and a croquet set ready for service. Inside, the rooms are no less than you'd expect: Luxuriously airy and high-ceilinged, with elegantly simple decor, replete with Porfirian-era touches and wall art; with baths, gleaming with polished traditional-style fixtures. Year-round rates for the 10 rooms run about $39 s, $48 d, $60 t. For more information

San Blas's once grand former Hotel Playa Hermosa gradually returns to the earth at the lush and overgrown edge of town.

contact the owner directly, in Mazatlán at tel. 69/852-727, fax 69/851-185.

Half a block along Juárez, the **Hotel Bucanero** appears to be living up to its name at Calle Juárez 75, San Blas, Nayarit 63740, a block from the plaza, tel. 328/501-01. A stanza from the *Song of the Pirate* emblazons one wall, a big stuffed crocodile bares its teeth beside the other, and a crusty sunken anchor and cannons decorate the shady patio. Despite peeling paint the rooms retain a bit of spacious, old-world charm, with high-beamed ceilings under the ruddy roof tile. (High, circular vent windows in some rooms cannot be closed, however. Use repellent or your mosquito net.) Outside, the big pool and leafy old patio/courtyard provide plenty of nooks for daytime snoozing and socializing. A noisy nighttime (winter-spring seasonal) bar, however, keeps most guests without earplugs jumping till about midnight. The 32 rooms run, low season, about $14 s, $17 d; high season, $18 and $22, with ceiling fans and hot water.

San Blas's modern-era hotels are nearer the water. Foremost is the excellent, resort-style **Hotel Garza Canela,** Paredes 106 Sur C.P., San Blas, Nayarit 63740, tucked away at the south end of town, two blocks off H. Batallón, tel. 328/501-12, 328/503-07, or 328/504-80, fax 328/503-08, toll-free in Mexico 01-800/132-313, email: hotel@garzacanela.com, website: www.garzacanela.com. The careful manage-ment of its Vásquez family owners (Señorita Josefina Vasquez in charge) shows everywhere: manicured palm-shaded gardens, crystal-blue pool, immaculate sundeck, and centerpiece restaurant. The 60 cool, air-conditioned rooms are tiled, tastefully furnished, and squeaky clean. Rates run about $65 s, $78 d low season, $75 and $92 high, with a hearty breakfast included and credit cards accepted. The family also runs a travel agency and an outstanding crafts and gift shop on the premises.

The lively, family-operated **Hotel Posada del Rey,** Calle Campeche 10, San Blas, Nayarit 63740, tel. 328/501-23, seems to be trying hard-est. It encloses a small but inviting pool and patio beneath a top-floor viewpoint bar (and high-season-only restaurant) that bubbles with continuous soft rock and salsa tunes. Friendly owner Mike Vasquez, who splits his day between his Pato Loco everything-for-the-beach store and his hotel/bar at night, also arranges tours and fishing, snorkeling, and diving excursions to nearby coastal spots. His hotel rooms, while nothing fancy, are comfortable. Year-round asking rates for the 13 rooms are about $32 s or d, with a/c; credit cards are not accepted. Bargain for a low-season discount.

Although the facilities of the four-star **Motel Marino Pacifico Inn** look fine on paper, the place is generally unkempt. Its tattered ameni-ties—from the bare-bulb reception area and cav-

---

SAN BLAS ACCOMMODATIONS

Accommodations (area code 328, postal code 63740) are listed in increasing order of approximate high-season, double-room rates.

Casa Morelos, H. Batallón 108, tel. 508-20, $18
Hotel Ranchero, Esquina Batallón y Michoacán, tel. 508-20, $18
Casa María, Esquina Canalizo y Michoacán, tel. 508-20, $22
Hotel Bucanero, Juárez 75, tel. 501-01, $22
Hotel Posada del Rey, Campeche 10, tel. 501-23, $32
Motel-Suites San Blas, Aticama and Las Palmas, tel. 505-05, $36
Motel Marino Inn, H. Batallón s/n, tel. 503-03, $42
Hacienda Flamingos, Juárez 105, tel. 504-85, email: technica@red2000.com.mx, $48
Hotel Garza Canela, Paredes 106 Sur, tel. 501-12 or 504-80, fax 503-08, e-mail: hotel@garzacanela.com, $92

ernous upstairs disco to the mossy pool and patio and mildewy rooms—sorely need scrubbing and a modicum of care. Located at Av. H. Batallón s/n, San Blas, Nayarit 63740, tel. 328/503-03. The 60 rooms go for about $27 s or d low season, $42 high, add $5 for a/c, with private balconies; there's a seasonal restaurant, and credit cards are accepted.

In the palm-shadowed, country fringe of town not far from Playa Borrego is the **Motel-Suites San Blas,** at Calles Aticama and Las Palmas, San Blas, Nayarit 63740, tel. 328/505-05, left off H. Batallón a few blocks after the Motel Marino. Its pool, patio, playground, game room, and spacious but somewhat worn suites with kitchenettes (dishes and utensils *not* included) are nicely suited for active families. The 23 fan-only suites include 16 one-bedrooms for two adults and kids renting for about $26 low season, $36 high, and seven two-bedrooms accommodating four adults with kids for about $40 low season, $50 high; credit cards are accepted.

Trailer Park
San Blas's only trailer park, the **Los Cocos,** at H. Batallón s/n, San Blas, Nayarit 63740, is a two-minute walk from the wide, yellow sands of Playa el Borrego. Friendly management, spacious, palm-shaded grassy grounds, pull-throughs, unusually clean showers and toilet facilities, a laundry next door, fishing, and a good, air-conditioned bar with satellite TV all make this place a magnet for RVers and tenters from Mazatlán to Puerto Vallarta. The biting *jejenes* require the use of strong repellent for residents to enjoy the balmy evenings. The 100 spaces rent for about $13/day for two persons, $1 for each additional person, with all hookups. Monthly rates average $250 low season, $300 high; pets are okay.

Camping
The *jejenes* and occasional local toughs and Peeping Toms make camping on close-in Borrego Beach only a marginal possibility. However, **Isla del Rey** (across Estero El Pozo, accessible by *lancha* from the foot of Calle Juárez) presents possibilities for prepared trekker-tenters. The same is true for eco-sanctuary **Isla Isabel,** three hours by hired boat from San Blas. For those less equipped, the palm-lined strands of **Playa las Islitas, Playa Matanchén,** and **Playa**

Cocos on the Bay of Matanchén appear ripe for camping.

FOOD

Snacks, Stalls, and Market
During the mornings and early afternoons try the fruit stands, groceries, *fondas,* and *jugerías* in and around the **Central Market** (behind the plaza church). Late afternoons and evenings, many semi-permanent streetside stands around the plaza, such as the **Taquería Las Cuatas** on the corner of Canalizo and Juárez, offer tasty *antojitos* and drinks.

For sit-down snacks every day till midnight, drop in to the **Lonchería Ledmar** (also at the Canalizo-Juárez corner) for a hot *torta,* hamburger, quesadilla, tostada, or fresh-squeezed *jugo* (juice). For a change of venue, you can enjoy about the same at the **Terraza** cafe on the opposite side of the plaza.

For basic **groceries** and deli items nearby, try the plaza-front **Centro San Blas** store, corner of Juárez and H. Batallón San Blas.

Get your fresh cupcakes, cookies, and crispy *bolillos* at the **bakery** *(panadería)* at Comonfort and Cuauhtémoc, around the uptown corner from Hotel Posada del Rey, closed Sunday. You can get similar (but not quite so fresh) goodies at the small bakery outlet across from the plaza, corner of Juárez and Canalizo.

Restaurants
Family-managed **Restaurant McDonald,** 36 Juárez, half a block from the plaza, is one of the gathering places of San Blas. Its bit-of-everything menu features soups, meat, and seafood in the $5–7 range, besides a hamburger that beats no-relation U.S. McDonald's by a mile. Open daily 7 A.M.–10 P.M.

As an option, step across the street to the TV-free **Wala Wala** restaurant, for breakfast, lunch, or dinner 8 A.M.–10 P.M. daily except Sunday. Its long menu of offerings—tasty salads, pastas, seafood, and fish fillets—crisply prepared and served in a simple but clean and inviting setting, will never go out of style. Everything is good; simply pick out your favorite.

Another alternative is to step into the airy plaza-front (southeast plaza corner) **Restau-**

rant **Cocodrilo.** Here you can choose from a sandwich, or full dinner, such as a professionally prepared and served fresh fish fillet or spaghetti *a la Bolognese.* Open daily 8 A.M.–10 P.M. Moderate.

For TV with dinner, the **Restaurant La Familia** is just the place at H. Batallón between Juárez and Mercado. American movies, serape-draped walls, and colorful Mexican tile supply the ambience, while a reasonably priced seafood and meat menu furnishes the food. For dessert, step into its luminescent-decor bar next door for giant-screen American baseball or football. Open for lunch and dinner daily except Sunday. Moderate.

For a refined marine atmosphere and good fish and shrimp, both local folks and visitors choose **Restaurant La Isla,** at Mercado and Paredes, tel. 328/504-07. As ceiling fans whir overhead and a guitarist strums softly in the background, the net-draped walls display a museum-load of nautical curiosities, from antique Japanese floats and Tahitian shells to New England ship models. Open Tues.–Sun. 2–9 P.M. Moderate.

San Blas's class-act restaurant is the **El Delfín** at the Hotel Garza Canela, Cuauhtémoc 106, tel. 328/501-12. Potted tropical plants and leafy planter-dividers enhance the genteel atmosphere of this air-conditioned dining room-in-the-round. Meticulous preparation and service, bountiful breakfasts, savory dinner soups, and fresh salad, seafood, and meat entreés keep customers returning year after year. Open daily 8–10:00 A.M. and 1–9 P.M.; credit cards accepted. Moderate to expensive.

ENTERTAINMENT

Sleepy San Blas's entertainment is of the local, informal variety. Visitors content themselves with strolling the beach or riding the waves by day, and reading, watching TV, listening to mariachis, or dancing at a handful of clubs by night.

Nightlife
Owner/manager Mike McDonald works hard to keep **Mike's Place,** Juárez 36, on the second floor of his family's restaurant, the classiest club in town. He keeps the lights flashing and the small dance floor thumping with blues, Latin, and '60s rock tunes from his own guitar, accompanied by his equally excellent drum and electronic-piano partners. Listen to live music Friday, Saturday, and Sunday nights and holidays 9 P.M.–midnight. There's usually a small cover; drinks are reasonably priced.

A few other places require nothing more than your ears to find. During high season music booms out of **Botanas Herredor** (down H. Batallón, a block past the Marino Inn). The same is true seasonally at the bar at the **Hotel Bucanero,** Calle Juárez 75, tel. 328/501-01.

SPORTS AND RECREATION

Walking and Jogging
The cooling sea breeze and the soft but firm sand of **Playa Borrego** at the south end of H. Batallón make it the best place around town for a walk or jog. Arm yourself against *jejenes* with repellent and long pants, especially around sunset.

Water Sports
Although some intermediate- and beginner-level surf rolls in at Borrego Beach, nearly all of San Blas's action goes on at world-class surfing mecca Matanchén Beach. (See "Around the Bay of Matanchén," preceding.)

The mild offshore currents and gentle, undertow-free slope of Borrego Beach are nearly always safe for good swimming, bodysurfing, and boogie boarding. Conditions are often right for good windsurfing. Bring your own equipment, as no rentals are available.

Sediment-fogged water limits snorkeling and scuba diving possibilities around San Blas to the offshore eco-preserve Isla Isabel. See under "Sights and Activities" for details.

Sportfishing
Tony Aguayo and Abraham "Pipila" Murillo are highly recommended to lead big-game deep-sea fishing excursions. Tony's "office" is the *palapa* shelter to the left of the little dock at the foot of Calle Juárez. You can reach Abraham—distinguished winner of six international tournament grand prizes—at his home, Comonfort 248, tel. 328/507-19. Both Tony and Abraham regu-

larly captain big-boat excursions for tough-fighting marlin, *dorado,* and sailfish. Their fee will run about $150 for a five-hour expedition for up to three people, including boat, tackle, and bait.

On the other hand, a number of other good-eating fish are not so difficult to catch. Check with other captains, such as Antonio Palmas at the Hotel Garza Canela or one of the owners of the many craft docked by the estuary shoreline at the foot of Juárez. For perhaps $80, they'll take three or four of you for a *lancha* outing, which most likely will result in four or five hefty 10-pound snapper, mackerel, tuna, or yellowtail; afterward you can ask your favorite restaurant to cook them up for a feast.

During the last few days in May, San Blas hosts its long-running (30-plus years) **International Fishing Tournament.** The entrance fee runs around $250; prizes range from automobiles to Mercury outboards and Penn International fishing rods. For more information, contact the local tourist information office, downtown, on Juárez, across from Restaurant McDonald.

SHOPPING

San Blas visitors ordinarily spend little of their time shopping. For basics, the stalls at the **Central Market** offer good tropical fruits, meats, and staples. Hours are daily 6 A.M. until around 2 P.M.

For used clothes and a little bit of everything else, a **flea market** sometimes operates on Calle Canalizo a block past the bus station (away from the *jardín*) Saturday morning and early afternoon.

The plaza-corner store, **Comercial de San Blas,** corner of Juárez and H. Batallón, open 9 A.M.–2 P.M. and 5–9 P.M. except Sunday, offers a unique mix of everything from film developing and Hohner harmonicas to fishing poles. Hooks, sinkers, and lines are available.

Handicrafts
Although San Blas has relatively few handicrafts sources, the shop at the **Hotel Garza Canela** has one of the finest for-sale handicrafts collections in Nayarit state. Lovingly selected pieces from the famous Pacific Mexico crafts centers—

Guadalajara, Tlaquepaque, Tonalá, Pátzcuaro, Olinalá, Taxco, Oaxaca, and elsewhere—decorate the shop's cabinets, counters, and shelves.

You'll find a more pedestrian but nevertheless attractive handicraft assortment at the roadside handicrafts and beachwear shop near Playa Borrego, across the street from the naval compound.

Back downtown near the market, two or three small permanent handicrafts shops are scattered along the block (left of the church-front) of Calle Sinaloa between Paredes and H. Batallón.

SERVICES

Bank
Banamex, with a 24-hour ATM, one block east of the plaza at Juárez 36 Ote., tel. 328/500-30 or 328/500-31, exchanges U.S. traveler's checks and cash weekday mornings 8 A.M.–2 P.M. only.

Post Office, Telegraph, Telephone, and Internet
The **correo** and **telégrafo** stand side by side at Sonora and Echeverría (one block behind, one block east of the plaza church). The *correo,* tel. 328/502-95, is open Mon.–Fri. 8 A.M.–2 P.M., Saturday 8 A.M.–12 P.M.; *telégrafo,* tel. 328/501-15, is open Mon.–Fri. 8 A.M.–2 P.M.

In addition to the new long-distance public phone stands that sprinkle the town, there are a number of old-fashioned *larga distancia* stores. Most prominent is the newsstand on Juárez, on the plaza, open daily 8 A.M.–10 P.M. Its rival newsstand, on the opposite side of the plaza (on Canalizo, one block past the bus station), is trying harder, with a fax number 328/500-01, and longer hours, 8 A.M.–11 P.M. daily.

Internet access has arrived in San Blas, at the hole-in-the wall store next to Farmacia Mexicana, on the plaza, south side.

Health and Police
One of San Blas's most highly recommended **physicians** is Dr. Alejandro Davalos, available at his **Farmacia Mexicana,** tel. 328/501-22, on the plaza. Here, Dr. Davalos stocks a variety of medicines, along with a bit of everything, including film. Open daily 8:30 A.M.–1:30 P.M. and 5–9 P.M.

If you prefer a female physician, consult with general practitioner Doctora Dulce María Jácome Camarillo, at her office at Mercado 52 Pte., between Batallón and Paredes; her regular consultation hours are Mon.–Fri. 9 A.M.–1 P.M. and 4–8 P.M.

Alternatively, you can go to San Blas's respectable local hospital, the government **Centro de Salud,** at Yucatán and H. Batallón (across the street from the Motel Marino Inn), tel. 328/503-32.

For **police** emergencies, contact the headquarters on the left side behind the Presidencia Municipal (City Hall), on Canalizo, east side of the central plaza, tel. 328/500-28.

Immigration and Customs

San Blas no longer has either Migración (Immigration) or Aduana (Customs) offices. If you lose your tourist card, you'll have to go to the Secretaria de Gobernación, at Oaxaca no. 220 Sur, in Tepic, or to Migración in Puerto Vallarta. For customs matters, such as having to leave Mexico temporarily without your car, go to the Aduana in Puerto Vallarta for the necessary paperwork (see "Services and Information" in the Puerto Vallarta chapter).

INFORMATION

Tourist Information Office

The local tourist office is downtown, on Mercado, a block south and half a block east, of the plaza southeast corner. Although the officer in charge is sometimes out on business, volunteers, such as guide Lucio Rodriguez and Huichol community leader Francisco Pimentel, sometimes staff the office during the official hours, Mon.–Fri. 9 A.M.–2 P.M. and 4–7 P.M., Saturday 10 A.M.–2 P.M.

Books, News, and Magazines

English-language reading material in San Blas is as scarce as tortillas in Tokyo. The **newsstand,** on the Juárez side of the plaza, sometimes has *Time, Newsweek,* and *People* magazines. The other newsstand, on the opposite side of the plaza, a block past the bus station, tries a little harder with *Newsweek, Time, Life,* and *Cosmopolitan.*

As for English-language books, the **tourist information office,** on Mercado, one block south and half a block east of the plaza's southeast corner, has a shelf of used English and American paperbacks for sale.

GETTING THERE AND AWAY

By Car or RV

To and from Puerto Vallarta, the new Hwy. 161 cutoff at Las Varas bypasses the slow climb to Tepic, shortening the San Blas-Puerto Vallarta connection to about 94 miles (151 km), or about 2.5 hours.

From the east, Nayarit Hwy. 74 leaves Hwy. 15 at its signed "Miramar" turnoff at the northern edge of Tepic. The road winds downhill about 3,000 feet (1,000 meters) through a jungly mountain forest to shoreline **Santa Cruz** and **Miramar** villages. It continues along the **Bahía de Matanchén** shoreline to San Blas, a total of 43 miles (70 km) from Tepic. Although this route generally has more shoulder than Hwy. 11, frequent pedestrians and occasional unexpected cattle necessitate caution.

To and from the north and east, paved roads connect San Blas to main-route National Hwy. 15. From the northeast, National Hwy. 11 winds 19 miles (31 km) downhill from its junction 161 miles (260 km) south of Mazatlán and 22 miles (35 km) north of Tepic. From the turnoff (marked by a Pemex gas station), the road winds through a forest of vine-draped trees and tall palms. Go slowly; the road lacks a shoulder, and cattle or people may appear unexpectedly around any blind, grass-shrouded bend.

By Bus

From Puerto Vallarta, bus travelers have three ways to get to San Blas. Quickest is via one of the **Transportes Norte de Sonora** departures, which connect daily with San Blas. They depart from the new Puerto Vallarta bus station north of the airport; get your ticket at the Elite-Estrella Blanca desk, tel. 322/108-48.

On the other hand, many more second-class **Transportes Pacifico** buses connect Puerto Vallarta with Las Varas, on Hwy. 200, where, around 7 and 11 A.M., and 2 and 4 P.M. daily, you can transfer to a second-class **Transportes**

SAN BLAS TO MAZATLÁN

To Culiacán and U.S.A.
To Durango
15
Copala
DANIEL'S HOTEL
Mazatlán
Villa
Union
Concordia
40
El Walamo
Laguna
El Huizache
Teodoro Beltran
15
HOTEL YUACO
Rosario
Laguna
Caimanero
El Caimanero
Agua
Verde
Esquinapa
HOTEL IQ
L. Los Cerritos
L. Grande
Las Cabras
PACIFIC
L. Agua
Grande
HOTEL RANCHO LOS ANGELES
TP
15
HOTEL DENISSE
Teacapan
Río San Pedro
Río San Pedro
Acaponeta
Isla del
Otro Lado
OCEAN
HOTEL PLAYA NOVILLERO
Novillero
Tecuala

DETAIL

Union
San Andres
EMBARCADERO TICHA
Mayorquin
Higuerita
Los Patitos
Laguna
Colorados
Grande
El Mescal
San
las Pesquería
Mexcaltitán
Vicente
EMBARCADERO
de
TECOCTA
Mexcaltitán
EMBARCADERO
Las
LA BATANGA
Tuxpán
Cuatas
Las
Toluca
Gallinas
Las Tortugas
Campos de
los Limones
Sentispac

L. Agua
Brava
L. El Valle
15
Chilapa
L. Los
Pericos
Santa Cruz
Tuxpán
Mexcaltitán
La Punta
Santiago Ixcuintla
SEE DETAIL
Toro Mocho
Villa Hidalgo
Bocas de Camachin
Villa
Playa Cesteo
Juarez
Río Grande
Playa Los Corchos
de Santiago
Laureles
11
Barra Asadero
San Blas
To Puerto Vallarta

To Tepic and Puerto Vallarta

© AVALON TRAVEL PUBLISHING, INC.

0   20 mi
0   20 km

Noroeste de Nayarit navy blue and white bus, which connects with San Blas. If you're too late for that connection, continue on Transportes Pacifico to the Tepic bus station, where you might be early enough to catch the last of several daily Transportes Norte de Sonora buses that connect with San Blas.

The **San Blas bus terminal** stands adjacent to the plaza church, at Calles Sinaloa and Canalizo. First-class **Transportes Norte de Sonora (TNS),** tel. 328/500-43, buses connect more than a dozen times a day with Tepic, one continuing to Guadalajara. Additionally, a few departures connect north with Mazatlán and south

THE HUICHOL

Because the Huichol have retained more of their traditional religion than perhaps any other group of indigenous Mexicans, they offer a glimpse into the lives and beliefs of dozens of now-vanished Mesoamerican peoples.

The Huichol's natural wariness, plus their isolation in rugged mountain canyons and valleys, has saved them from the ravages of modern Mexico. Despite increased tourist, government, and mestizo contact, prosperity and better health swelled the Huichol population to around 20,000 by the late 1990s.

Although many have migrated to coastal farming towns and cities such as Tepic and Guadalajara, several thousand Huichol remain in their ancestral heartland—roughly 50 miles (80 km) northeast of Tepic as the crow flies. They cultivate corn and raise cattle on 400 *rancherías* in five municipalities not far from the winding Altengo River valley: Guadalupe Ocotán in Nayarit; and Tuxpan de Bolanos, San Sebastián Teponahuaxtlán, Santa Catarina, and San Andrés Cohamiata in Jalisco.

Although studied by a procession of researchers since Carl Lumholtz's seminal work in the 1890s, the remote Huichol and their religion remain enigmatic. As Lumholtz said, "Religion to them is a personal matter, not an institution and therefore their life is religion—from the cradle to the grave, wrapped up in symbolism."

Hints of what it means to be Huichol come from their art. Huichol art contains representations of the prototype deities—Grandfather Sun, Grandmother Earth, Brother Deer, Mother Maize—that once guided the destinies of many North American peoples. It blooms with tangible religious symbols, from green-faced Mother Earth (Tatei Urianaka) and the dripping Rain Goddess (Tatei Matiniera), to the ray-festooned Father Sun (Tayau) and the antlered folk hero Brother Kauyumari, forever battling the evil sorcerer Kieri.

The Huichol are famous for their use of the hallucinogen peyote, their bridge to the divine. The hum-

ble cactus—from which the peyote "buttons" are gathered and eaten—grows in the Huichol's Elysian land of Wirikuta, in the San Luis Potosí desert 300 miles east of their homeland, near the town of Real de Catorce.

To the Huichol, a journey to Wirikuta is a dangerous trip to heaven. Preparations go on for weeks and include innumerable prayers and ceremonies, as well as the crafting of feathered arrows, bowls, gourds, and paintings for the gods who live along the way. Only the chosen—village shamans, temple elders, those fulfilling vows or seeking visions—may make the journey. Each participant in effect becomes a god whose identity and very life are divined and protected by the shaman en route to Wirikuta.

The fertility goddess symbolically gives birth in a Huichol yarn painting.

with Puerto Vallarta. One of the Mazatlán departures continues all the way to Tijuana, at the U.S. border.

Four daily second-class navy blue and white **Transportes Noroeste de Nayarit** departures (about 6 and 8 A.M., 2 and 5 P.M.) connect south with Las Varas, via Bay of Matanchén points of Matanchén, Los Cocos, and Santa Cruz de Miramar. Other departures connect east with Tepic, north with Santiago Ixcuintla, via intermediate points of Guadalupe Victoria and Villa Hidalgo.

A local white *(autobús blanco)* bus connects San Blas with the Bay of Matanchén points of Las Aguadas, Matanchén, Aticama, Los Cocos, and Santa Cruz. It departs from the downtown corner of Paredes and Sinaloa (a block west of the church) four times daily, approximately every two hours between 8:30 A.M. and 4:30 P.M.

SANTIAGO IXCUINTLA

North of San Blas, the Nayarit coastal strip broadens into a hinterland of lush farm and marsh where, on the higher ground, rich fields of chiles, tobacco, and corn bloom and Hwy. 15 conducts a nonstop procession of traffic past the major farm towns of Ruíz, Rosamorada, and Acaponeta.

But where the coastal plain nears the sea, the pace of life slows. Roads, where they exist, wind through a vast wetland laced with mangrove channels and decorated by diminutive fishing settlements. Through this lowland, Mexico's longest river, the Río Grande de Santiago, ends its epic six-state journey downstream, past the colorful colonial town of Santiago Ixcuintla (eeks-KWIN-tlah) and its historic island-neighbor, Mexcaltitán, accessible only by boat.

On the Road

With your own wheels, Santiago Ixquintla and Mexcaltitán make an interesting off-the-beaten-track side trip from San Blas or Puerto Vallarta. The quick route is via Hwy. 15, 38 miles (60 km) north of Tepic (and 16 miles north of the Hwy. 11-Hwy. 15 junction) to the signed Santiago Ixcuintla-Mexcaltitán turnoff. Within five miles you'll be in Santiago Ixcuintla; Mexcaltitán is another 20 miles (32 km) beyond that.

Huichol shamans embellish their costumes and craft satchels full of rattles, arrows, and other ceremonial charms in preparation for their journey to their sacred peyote-land of Wirikuta.

For bus travelers, the San Blas and Tepic bus stations (see "Tepic," following) are the best jumping-off places for Santiago Ixcuintla. The regional line, navy blue-and-white Autotransportes Noroeste de Nayarit, runs a few daily buses from San Blas and Tepic to the Santiago Ixcuintla station, where you can make connections by minibus or *colectivo* (collective taxi) for Mexcaltitán.

Car travelers in the mood for a little extra adventure can (weather permitting) drive the back road that connects San Blas and Santiago Ixcuintla. The main attractions en route are the hosts of waterbirds, tobacco fields, aquaculture ponds, Huichol people in colorful local dress, and the Río Santiago, Mexico's longest river.

Directions: Mark your odometer at the

signed Guadalupe Victoria turnoff north from Hwy. 11 on the San Blas side of the Estero San Cristóbal bridge. Continue along the paved road about 10 miles (16 km) to Guadalupe Victoria village. Follow the pavement, which curves right (east) and continues another eight miles (13 km) to Villa Hidalgo. Keep going through the town; after another five miles (eight km) turn left (north) at the signed La Presa side road. Continue along the gravel track to La Presa; bear left through the village center and immediately up the river levee and across the new bridge, where you can see Santiago Ixcuintla across the river.

Orientation and Sights

The Santiago Ixquintla town plaza is a couple of blocks directly inland from the riverbank. The main town streets border the plaza: Running east-west, are 20 de Noviembre and Zaragoza, on the north and south sides, respectively; and Hidalgo and Allende, running along the east and west sides, respectively. During your stroll around the plaza, admire the pretty old church and the voluptuous Porfirian nymphs who decorate the restored bandstand. Stroll beneath the shaded porticos and the very colorful market, a block west and block north of the plaza.

Although the town's scenic appeal is considerable, the Huichol people are *the* reason to come to Santiago Ixcuintla. Several hundred Huichol families migrate seasonally (mostly December–May) from their Sierra Madre high-country homeland to work for a few dollars a day in the local tobacco fields. For many Huichol, their migration in search of money includes a serious hidden cost. In the mountains, their homes, friends, and relatives are around them, as are the familiar rituals and ceremonies they have tenaciously preserved in their centuries-long struggle against Mexicanization.

But when the Huichol come to lowland towns and cities, they often encounter the mocking laughter and hostile stares of crowds of strangers, whose Spanish language they do not understand, and whose city ways are much more alien than they appear even to foreign tourists. As strangers in a strange land, the pressure on the migrant Huichol to give up their old costumes, language, and ceremonies to become like everyone else is powerful indeed.

Centro Cultural Huichol

Be sure to reserve a portion of your time in Santiago Ixcuintla to stop by the Centro Cultural Huichol, 20 de Noviembre 452, Santiago Ixcuintla, Nayarit 63300, tel. 323/511-71, fax 323/510-06. The immediate mission of founders Mariano and Susana Valadez—he a Huichol artist and community leader, and she a U.S.-born anthropologist—is to ensure that the Huichol people endure, with their traditions intact and growing. Their instrument is the Centro Cultural Huichol—a clinic, dining hall, dormitory, library, craftsmaking shop, sale gallery, and interpretive center—which provides crucial focus and support for local migratory Huichol people.

Lately, Susana has opened another center high in the mountains in Huejuquilla, Jalisco, tel. 498/370-00, but Mariano, with the help of their daughter Angélica, continues the original mission in Santiago Ixcuintla. As well as filling vital human needs, the Huichol Cultural Center actively nurtures the vital elements of a nearly vanished heritage. This heritage belongs not only to the Huichol, but to the lost generations of indigenous peoples—Aleut, Yahi, Lacandones, and myriad others—who succumbed to European diseases and were massacred in innumerable fields, from Wounded Knee and the Valley of Mexico all the way to Tierra del Fuego.

Although they concentrate on the immediate needs of people, Mariano, Susana, and Angélica and their volunteer staff also reach out to local, national, and international communities. Their center's entry corridor, for example, is decorated with illustrated Huichol legends in Spanish, especially for Mexican visitors. An adjacent gallery exhibits a treasury of Huichol art for sale—yarn paintings, masks, jewelry, gourds, God's eyes—adorned with the colorful deities and animated heavenly motifs of the Huichol pantheon.

The Centro Cultural Huichol invites volunteers, especially those with secretarial, computer, language, and other skills, to help with projects in the center. If you don't have the time, the center also solicits donations of money and equipment (such as a good computer or two).

Get to the Centro Cultural Huichol by heading away from the river, along 20 de Noviembre, the main street that borders the central plaza. Within a mile, you'll see the Centro Cultural Huichol, no. 452, on the right.

Accommodations and Services
If you decide to stay overnight in Santiago Ixcuintla, Susana recommends the **Hotel Casino** near the plaza downtown, at Arteaga and Ocampo, Santiago Ixcuintla, Nayarit, tel./fax 323/508-50, 323/508-51, or 323/508-52. It has a respectable downstairs restaurant/bar and about 35 basic rooms around an inner parking patio for $23 d, with a/c and parking.

Santiago Ixcuintla is an important regional business center, with a number of services. Banks, all with 24-hour ATMs, include long-hours Bital (Banco Internacional), open Mon.–Sat. 8 A.M.–7 P.M., south side of the plaza, at Hidalgo and Zaragoza; Banamex at 20 de Noviembre and Hidalgo, tel. 323/500-53, open Mon.–Fri. 8 A.M.–2 P.M., Sat. 9 A.M.–2 P.M.; and Bancomer, at 20 de Noviembre and Morelos, tel. 323/505-35 or 323/503-80.

Find the *correo* (post office) at Allende 23, tel. 323/502-14, east side of the plaza. *Telecomunicaciones,* including telegraph, long-distance phone, and public fax, is available at Zaragoza Ote. 200, tel. 323/509-89.

Unleaded (Magna Sin) **gasoline** is customarily available at the Pemex station on the east-side highway (toward Hwy. 15) as you head out of town.

MEXCALTITÁN

Mexcaltitán (pop. 2,000), the "House of the Mexicans," represents much more than just a scenic little island town. Archaeological evidence indicates Mexcaltitán may actually be the legendary Aztlán (Place of the Herons) where, in 1091, the Aztecs (who called themselves the México—"MAY-shee-kah") began their generations-long migration to the Valley of Mexico.

Each year on June 28 and 29, the feast days of St. Peter and St. Paul, residents of Mexcaltitán and surrounding villages dress up in feathered headdresses and jaguar robes and breathe life into their tradition. They celebrate the opening of

Mexcaltitán is an island town, with a plan and canals reminiscent of the Aztec imperial capital Tenochtitlán.

the shrimp season by staging a grand regatta, driven by friendly competition between decorated boats carrying rival images of saints Peter and Paul.

Getting There
Mexcaltitán lies about 25 miles (32 km) by a paved, all-weather road northwest of Santiago Ixcuintla. You get to Santiago Ixcuintla either by back road from San Blas (see above) or from Hwy. 15, by the Santiago Ixcuintla turnoff 38 miles (60 km) north of Tepic. About five miles (eight km) after the turnoff, you reach the town, marked by a solitary hill on the right. Just past the hill, turn right on the main street, 20 de Noviembre, which runs by the central plaza and becomes the main westbound road out of town. Continue approximately another five miles (eight km) to the signed Mexcaltitán turnoff, where you head right. You soon pass Base Aztlán, site of the Mexican experimental rocket center; then the farmland gives way to a maze

of leafy, mangrove-edged lagoons, home to a host of cackling, preening, and fluttering waterbirds. About 15 miles (24 km) after the turnoff you reach the embarcadero (boat landing) for Mexcaltitán.

Note: Mexcaltitán is also accessible from the northeast side, by a signed turnoff from Hwy. 15, 136 miles (219 km) miles south of Mazatlán, four miles south of Chilapa village. Initially paved, the 48-km access road changes to rough gravel for its last half through the bushy, wildlife-rich wetland.

Sights

From both of the Mexcaltitán road's-end embarcaderos, boatmen ferry you across (about $1 per person for *colectivo,* $5 for private boat, each way) to Mexcaltitán island-village, some of whose inhabitants have never crossed the channel to the mainland. The town itself is not unlike many Mexican small towns, except more tranquil, due to the absence of motor vehicles.

Mexcaltitán is prepared for visitors, however. Instituto Nacional de Arqueología y Historia (INAH) has put together an excellent **museum** with several rooms of artifacts, photos, paintings, and maps describing the cultural regions of pre-Columbian Mexico; open Tues.–Sun. 10 A.M.–2 P.M., 4–7 P.M. The displays climax at the museum's centerpiece exhibit, which tells the story of the Aztecs' epic migration to the Valley of Mexico from legendary Aztlán, now believed by experts to be present-day Mexcaltitán.

Outside, the proud village **church** (step inside and admire the heroic St. Peter above the altar) and city hall preside over the central plaza, from which the town streets radiate to the broad lagoon that surrounds the town. Occasionally the rainy season water floods the streets, and folks must navigate Venice-style canals. At the watery lagoon-ends of the streets, village men set out in the late afternoon in canoes and boats for the open-ocean fishing grounds where, as night falls and kerosene lanterns are used, they attract shrimp into their nets.

Accommodations and Food

At the view-edge of the lagoon behind the museum stands Mexcaltitán's first official tourist lodging, the **Hotel Ruta Azteca.** More like a guesthouse than a hotel, it has four plain, tiled rooms with bath, some with a/c, that rent for about $12 d. For reservations, in Spanish only (have someone call the hotel for you if your Spanish is not up to par), call 323/204-26, local extension 128.

On the town plaza opposite the church stands airy **El Camarón** seafood restaurant (although the oft-noisy restaurant-bar at the south-side dock has more food).

Playa los Corchos

Beachcombers might enjoy a side trip to nearby Playa los Corchos. If, at the junction five miles (eight km) west of Santiago Ixcuintla, instead of turning off for Mexcaltitán you continue straight ahead (west) for about 15 miles (24 km), you'll arrive at Playa los Corchos. Here, waves roll in gently from a hundred yards out, leaving meringues of foam on sand speckled with little white clam shells. A few ramshackle Sunday *palapas* line the broad, wind-rippled strand.

From here, you can hike or, with care, pilot your four-wheel-drive vehicle eight km south along the beach to **Barra Asadero,** at the mouth of Río Grande de Santiago. On the sandbar and in the adjacent river estuary, many sandpipers, pelicans, gulls, and boobies gather to feast amid the summer flood deposits of driftwood troves.

TEPIC

Tepic (elev. 3,001 feet, 915 meters) basks in a lush highland valley beneath a trio of giant, slumbering volcanoes: 7,600-foot Sanganguey and 6,630-foot Tepetiltic in the east and south, and the brooding Volcán San Juan (7,350 feet, 2,240 meters) in the west. The waters that trickle from their cool green slopes have nurtured verdant valley fields and gardens for millennia. The city's name reflects its fertile surroundings; it's from the Nahuatl *tepictli,* meaning "land of corn."

Resembling a prosperous U.S. county seat, Tepic (pop. 200,000) is the Nayarit state capital and the service, manufacturing, and governmental center for the entire state. Local people flock to deposit in its banks, shop in its stores, and visit its diminutive main-street state legislature.

The **Huichol** Indians are among the many who come to trade in Tepic. The Huichol fly in from their remote mountain villages, loaded with crafts—yarn paintings, beaded masks, ceremo-

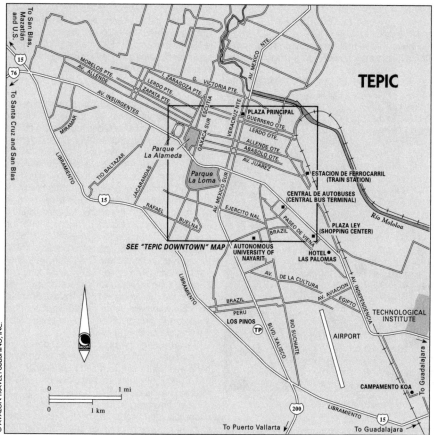

nial gourds, God's eyes—which they sell at local handicrafts stores. Tepic has thus accumulated troves of their intriguing ceremonial art, whose animal and human forms symbolize the Huichol's animistic world view. (See the special topic "The Huichol.")

Beyond the city limits, the Tepic valley offers an unusual bonus for lovers of the outdoors. About 45 minutes from town by car, sylvan mountain-rimmed lake Santa María offers comfortable bungalow lodgings and an RV park and campground, fine for a relaxing day or week of camping, hiking, swimming, kayaking, rowboating, and wildlife viewing.

HISTORY

Scholars believe that, around A.D. 1160, the valley of Tepic may have been a stopping place

Tepic's cathedral marks the center of town.

for a generation of the México (Aztecs) on their way to the Valley of Mexico. By the eve of the conquest, however, Tepic was ruled by the kingdom of Xalisco (whose capital occupied the same ground as the present-day city of Jalisco, a few miles south of Tepic).

In 1524, the expedition headed by the Great Conquistador's nephew, Francisco Cortés de San Buenaventura, explored the valley in peaceful contrast to those who followed. The renegade conquistador Nuño de Guzmán, bent on accumulating gold and *indígena* slaves, arrived in May 1530 and seized the valley in the name of King Charles V. After building a lodging house for hoped-for future immigrants, Guzmán hurried north, burning a pathway to Sinaloa. He returned a year later and founded a settlement near Tepic, which he named, pretentiously, Espíritu Santo de la Mayor España. In 1532 the king ordered his settlement's name changed to Santiago de Compostela. Today it remains Nayarit's oldest municipality, 23 miles (37 km) south of present-day Tepic.

Immigrants soon began colonizing the countryside of the sprawling new dominion of Nueva Galicia, which today includes the modern states of Jalisco, Nayarit, and Sinaloa. Guzmán managed to remain as governor until 1536, when the new viceroy, Antonio Mendoza, finally had him arrested and sent back to Spain in chains.

With Guzmán gone, Nueva Galicia began to thrive. The colonists settled down to raising cattle, wheat, and fruit; the padres founded churches, schools, and hospitals. Explorers set out for new lands: Coronado to New Mexico in 1539, Legazpi and Urdaneta across the Pacific in 1563, Vizcaíno to California and Oregon in 1602, and Father Kino to Arizona in 1687. Father Junípero Serra stayed in Tepic for several months en route to the Californias in 1767. Excitement rose in Tepic when a column of 200 Spanish dragoons came through on their way to establishing the port of San Blas in 1768.

San Blas's glory days were numbered, as were Spain's. Insurgents captured its fort cannons and sent them to defend Guadalajara in 1810, and finally the president closed the port to foreign commerce in 1872.

Now, however, trains, jet airplanes, and a seemingly interminable flow of giant diesel trucks carry mountains of produce and manufactures

JUNÍPERO SERRA: APOSTLE OF CALIFORNIA

His untiring, single-minded drive to found a string of missions and save the souls of native Californians has lifted Junípero Serra to prominence and proposed sainthood. Not long after he was born—on November 24, 1713, to illiterate parents on the Spanish island of Mallorca—he showed a fascination for books and learning. After taking his vows at the Convent of St. Francis in Palma on September 15, 1731, he changed his name to Junípero, after the beloved friend and "merry jester of God" of St. Francis Assisi.

Ordained in 1738 into the Franciscan order, Junípero soon was appointed professor of theology at the age of 30. He made up for his slight 5'2" height with a penetrating intelligence, engaging wit, and cheery disposition. Serra was popular with students, and, in 1748, when he received the missionary call, two of them—Francisco Palóu and Juan Bautista Crespi—accompanied Serra to Mexico, beginning their lifelong sojourn with him.

Serra inspired his followers by example, sometimes to the extreme. On arrival at Veracruz in December 1749, he insisted on walking the rough road all the way to Mexico City. The injuries he suffered led to a serious infection that plagued him the rest of his life. During his association with the Mexico City College of San Fernando (1750-1767), which included an extensive mission among the Pames Indians around Jalpan, in Querétaro state, he practiced self-flagellation and wore an undercoat woven with sharp bits of wire. Often he would inspire his indigenous flock during Holy Week, as he played the role of Jesus, lugging a ponderous wooden cross through the stations. Afterwards, he would humbly wash his converts' feet.

Serra's later mission to the Californias was triggered by the June 24, 1767, royal decree of King Carlos III, which expelled the Jesuit missionaries from the New World. The king's inspector general of the Indies, José de Galvez, prevailed upon Serra, at age 55, to fulfill a double agenda: organize a Franciscan mission to staff the former Jesuits' several Baja California missions, then push north and found several more in Alta California.

From the summer of 1767 to the spring of 1768, Serra paused in Guadalajara, Tepic, and San Blas with his fellow missionaries en route to the Californias. They sailed north from San Blas in March 1768.

They found the Baja California missions in disarray. The soldiers, left in custody of the missions, were running amok—raping native women, murdering their husbands, and squandering supplies. With the cooperation of military commander and governor Gaspar de Portolá, Serra managed to set things straight within a year and continue northward. On March 25, 1769, Serra, weak with fever, had two men lift him onto his mule, beginning the thousand-mile desert trek from Loreto to San Diego. On May 17 Serra's leg became so infected that Portolá insisted he return to Loreto. Serra refused. "I shall not turn back . . . I would gladly be left among the pagans if such be the will of God."

Serra, however, was always practical. He asked the mule driver's advice. "Imagine I am one of your mules with a sore on his leg. Give me the same treatment." The mule driver applied the ordinary remedy, a soothing ointment of herbs mixed with lard. Serra resumed the trip and reached San Diego, where, on July 16, 1769, he founded San Diego Mission.

The following years would see Serra laboring on, trekking by muleback up and down California, founding eight more missions, encouraging the padres whom he assigned, and teaching and caring for the welfare of the Native Americans in his charge. Given the few padres (only two per mission) and the few stores brought by the occasional supply ship from San Blas, it was a monumental, backbreaking task.

In the end, Serra's sacrifices probably shortened his life. On August 18, 1784, at his beloved headquarters mission in Carmel, Serra spent his last days with Palóu, his companion of 40 years. Palóu gave the last sacrament, and two days afterward, Serra, in pain, retraced the stations of the cross with his congregation for the last time. He died peacefully in his cell eight days later.

Whatever one believes about Spain's colonial role, the fate of the indigenous inhabitants, and sainthood, it is hard not to be awed by this compassionate, gritty little man who would not turn back.

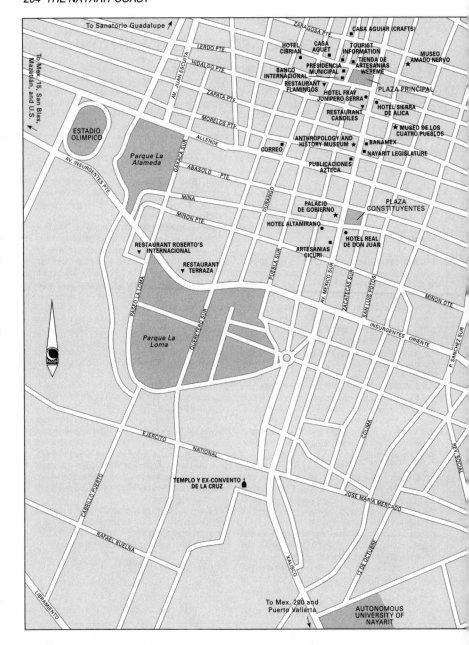

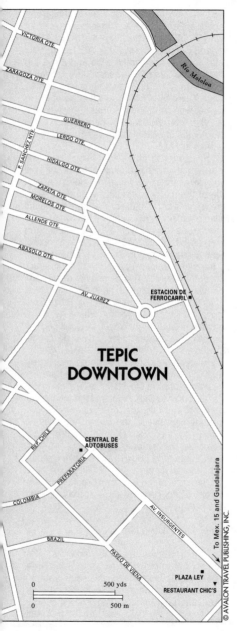

TEPIC DOWNTOWN

ESTACION DE FERROCARRIL

CENTRAL DE AUTOBUSES

PLAZA LEY

RESTAURANT CHIC'S

0   500 yds

0   500 m

To Mex. 15 and Guadalajara

© AVALON TRAVEL PUBLISHING, INC.

through Tepic to the Mexican Pacific and the United States. Commerce hums in suburban factories and in banks, stores, and shops around the plaza, where the aging colonial cathedral rises, a brooding reminder of the old days that few have time to remember.

SIGHTS

Getting Oriented
Tepic has two main plazas and two main highways. If you're only passing through, stay on the *libramiento* Hwy. 15 throughway, which efficiently conducts traffic around the city-center congestion. An interchange at the south edge of town distributes Hwy. 200 traffic approaching from Puerto Vallarta three ways: east (*libramiento* Hwy. 15 toward Guadalajara); north (*libramiento* Hwy. 15 toward San Blas, Mexcaltitán, and the U.S.), or downtown along Blvd. Xalisco. At the north end of the *libramiento,* a second interchange directs traffic either west to Santa Cruz and San Blas via Nayarit Hwy. 74 or north along Hwy. 15. Travelers enter town by either of those interchanges, which connect with the old through-town highways, east-west Av. Insurgentes and north-south Blvd. Xalisco.

Avenida México, Tepic's main north-south downtown street, angles from Blvd. Xalisco just south of big **Parque La Loma.** A few blocks farther north, it crosses Av. Insurgentes and continues downtown past the two main plazas: first Plaza Constituyentes, and then Plaza Principal, about a half mile farther north.

A Walk around Downtown
The **cathedral,** adjacent to Av. México, at the east side of the Plaza Principal, marks the center of town. Dating from 1750, the cathedral was dedicated to the Purísima Concepción (Immaculate Conception). Its twin neo-gothic bell towers rise somberly over everything else in town, while inside, cheerier white walls and neoclassic gilded arches lead toward the main altar. There, the pious, all-forgiving Virgin de la Asunción appears to soar to heaven, borne by a choir of adoring cherubs.

The workaday **Presidencia Municipal** (City-County Hall) stands on the plaza opposite the cathedral, while the **municipal tourist information office,** with many good brochures is just north of it, at the corner of Puebla and Amado Nervo. Back across the plaza, behind the cathedral and a half block to the north at 284 Zacatecas Nte., the **Museo Amado Nervo** occupies the house where the renowned poet was born on August 27, 1870. The four-room permanent exhibition displays photos, original works, a bust of Nervo, and paintings donated by artists J.L. Soto, Sofía Bassi, and Erlinda T. Fuentes. The museum is open Mon.–Fri. 9 A.M.–1 P.M. and 3–7 P.M., Saturday until 1 P.M.

Return to the plaza and join the shoppers beneath the arches in front of the Hotel Fray Junípero Serra on the plaza's south side, where a platoon of shoe shiners ply their trade.

Head around the corner, south, along Av. México. After about two blocks you will reach the venerable 18th-century former mansion that houses the **Regional Anthropology and History Museum,** Av. México 91 Nte., tel. 32/121-900, open Mon.–Sat. 9 A.M.–6 P.M. The palatial residence was built in 1762 with profits from sugar cane, cattle, and wheat. Since then, the mansion's spacious, high-ceilinged chambers have echoed with the voices of generations of occupants, including the German consul, Maximiliano Delius, during the 1880s. Now, its downstairs rooms house a changing exhibition of charming, earthy, pre-Columbian pottery artifacts from the museum's collection. These have included dancing dogs, a man scaling a fish, a boy riding a turtle, a dog with a corncob in its mouth, and a very unusual explicitly amorous couple. In an upstairs room, displays illustrate the Huichol symbolism hidden in the *cicuri* (eye of God) yarn sculptures, yarn paintings, ceremonial arrows, hats, musical instruments, and other pieces. Also upstairs, don't miss the monstrous, 15-foot stuffed crocodile, captured near San Blas and donated by ex-president Carlos Salinas de Gortari in 1989.

If you have time, cross Av. México and continue one block along Hidalgo to take a peek inside a pair of other historic homes, now serving as museums. Within the restored colonial-era house at the southwest corner of Hidalgo and Zacatecas is the **Museo de los Cuatro Pueblos** (Museum of the Four Peoples), which exhibits traditional costumes and crafts of Na-

yarit's four indigenous peoples—Huichol, Cora, Tepehuan, and Méxica. The museum is open Mon.–Fri. 9 A.M.–2 P.M. and 4–7 P.M., Saturday and Sunday 9 A.M.–2 P.M. Afterward, walk three doors farther on Hidalgo and cross the street, to the **Casa de Juan Escuita,** a colonial house furnished in original style. It's named after a Tepic-born boy who was one of Mexico's beloved six "Niños Héroes"—cadets who fell in the futile defense of Chapultepec Castle (the "Halls of Montezuma") against U.S. Marines in 1846.

Continue south along Av. México; pass the state legislature across the street on the left and, two blocks farther, on your right, along the west side of the plaza, spreads the straight-laced Spanish classical facade of the State of Nayarit **Palacio de Gobierno.** Inside, in the center, rises a cupola decorated with a 1975 collection of fiery murals by artist José Luis Soto. In a second, rear building, a long, unabashedly biased mural by the same artist portrays the historic struggles of the Mexican people against despotism, corruption, and foreign domination.

Continuing about a mile south of Plaza Constituyentes past Insurgentes, where Av. México crosses Ejército Nacional, you will find the **Templo y Ex-Convento de la Cruz de Zacate** (Church and Ex-Convent of the Cross of Grass). This venerable but lately restored monument has two claims to fame: the rooms where Father Junípero Serra stayed for several months in 1767 en route to California, and the miraculous cross that you can see in the open-air enclosure adjacent to the sanctuary. According to chroniclers, the cross-shaped patch of grass has grown for centuries (from either 1540 or 1619, depending upon the account), needing neither water nor cultivation. While you're there, pick up some of the excellent brochures at the **Nayarit State Tourism** desk at the building's front entrance.

Crater Lake Santa María

Easily accessible by car and about 45 minutes south of town, by either old Hwy. 15 or the new toll *autopista,* Laguna Santa María, tucked into an ancient volcanic caldera, offers near-perfect opportunities for outdoor relaxation. The lake itself, reachable via a good paved road, is big, blue, and rimmed by forested, wildlife-rich hills. You can hike trails through shady woods to ridgetop panoramic viewpoints. Afterwards, cool off with a swim in the lake. On another day, row a rental boat across the lake and explore hidden, tree-shaded inlets and sunny, secluded beaches. Afterwards, sit in a palm-fringed grassy park and enjoy the lake view and the orange blossom–scented evening air.

The driving force behind this seemingly too-good-to-be-true scene is Chris French, the personable owner/operator of lakeshore Koala Bungalows and Trailer Park. He's dedicated to preserving the beauty of the lake and its surroundings. It seems a miracle that, lacking any visible government protection, the lake and its forest hinterland remain lovely and pristine. The answer may lie partly in its isolation, the relatively sparse local population, and the enlightened conservation efforts of Chris and his neighbors. For accommodations and access details, see "Bungalows, Trailer Parks, and Camping," following.

ACCOMMODATIONS

Downtown Hotels
Tepic has a pair of good deluxe and several acceptable moderate downtown hotels. Starting in the north, near the Plaza Principal, the **Hotel Cibrián** is located on Amado Nervo, a block and a half behind the Presidencia Municipal, Amado Nervo 163 Pte., Tepic, Nayarit 63000, tel. 32/128-698. It offers clean, no-frills rooms with bath, ceiling fans, telephones, parking, and a pretty fair local restaurant. The Cibrián's small drawback is the noise that might filter into your room through louvered windows facing the tile (and therefore sound-reflective) hallways. Nevertheless, for the price, it's a Tepic best buy. The 46 rooms go for about $16 s, $19 d, $22 t; credit cards are not accepted.

Right on the Plaza Principal stands the five-story tower of Tepic's **Hotel Fray Junípero Serra,** Lerdo 23 Pte., Tepic, Nayarit 63000, tel. 32/122-525, fax 32/122-051. The hotel offers spacious, tastefully furnished view rooms with deluxe amenities, efficient service, convenient parking, and a cool plaza-front restaurant. The 90 rooms run a reasonable $40 s and $43 d and have satellite TV, a/c, and phones; no pool or parking, limited wheelchair access; credit cards are accepted.

On Av. México, half a block to the right (south) of the cathedral, the **Hotel Sierra de Alica** (AH-lee-kah), Av. México 180 Nte., Tepic, Nayarit 63000, tel. 32/120-325, fax 32/121-309, remains a longtime favorite of Tepic business travelers. Polished wood paneling downstairs and plain but comfortable rooms upstairs reflect the Sierra de Alica's solid unpretentiousness. The 60 rooms rent for $19 s, $25 d with fan, $32 d with a/c, satellite TV, phones, and parking; credit cards are accepted.

The **Hotel Real de Don Juan,** Av. México 105 Sur, Tepic, Nayarit 63000, tel./fax 32/161-820, 32/161-880, or 32/161-828, on Plaza Constituyentes appears to be succeeding in its efforts to become Tepic's class-act hotel. A plush, tranquil lobby and adjoining restaurant/bar matches the luxury of the king-size beds, thick carpets, marble baths, and soft pastels of the rooms. Rates for the 48 rooms are $46 s or d, with a/c, TV, parking, and limited wheelchair access; credit cards are accepted.

Nearby on Mina, half a block from the Av. México plaza corner, the **Hotel Altamirano,** Mina 19 Pte., Tepic, Nayarit 63000, tel. 32/121-377, offers basic bare-bulb rooms with bath at budget rates. The hotel, although clean, is drab. The 31 rooms with fans rent for $11 s or d; parking available.

Suburban Motels
If you prefer to stay out of the busy downtown, you have at least two good options. On the north end, three miles from the city center, try the graceful, 50-room **Hotel Bugam Villas,** Insurgentes and Libramiento Pte., Tepic, Nayarit 63000, tel./fax 32/180-225, 32/180-226, and 32/180-227. From

the lobby, the grounds extend past lovely, spreading *higuera* (native wild fig) trees to the two-story stucco and red-tile-roofed units. Inside, the rooms are clean with high ceilings, huge beds, marble shower baths, TV, a/c, and phone. The restaurant, elegant, cool, and serene within, leads outside to an airy dining veranda that overlooks a manicured shady garden. The food is appealing, professionally presented (but slowly served), and moderately priced. The only blot on this near-perfect picture is the noise—which choice of room can moderate considerably—from the trucks on the expressway nearby. Rates run $44 s or d, with parking; credit cards are accepted.

On the opposite side of town, another good choice is the motel-style **Hotel Las Palomas,** Av. Insurgentes 2100 Ote., Tepic, Nayarit 63000, tel. 32/140-239 or 32/140-948, fax 32/140-953, about two miles southeast of the city center. The two stories of double rooms and suites surround a colonial-chic pool and parking patio. The reception opens into an airy solarium restaurant, especially inviting for breakfast. The 67 clean and comfortable Spanish-style, tile-floored rooms rent for $45 s or d, with a/c, satellite TV, and phones; credit cards are accepted.

Bungalows, Trailer Parks, and Camping

On Blvd. Xalisco about a mile before the Puerto Vallarta (Hwy. 200) interchange, the **Trailer Park Los Pinos,** P.O. Box 329, Tepic, Nayarit 63000, tel. 32/131-232, offers, besides trailer and camping spaces, six large kitchenette apartments. The 25 pine-shaded concrete trailer pads, with all hookups and good drinkable well water, spread in two rows up a gradual, hillside slope. The apartments, plain but clean, well maintained, and spacious, rent for $20 year-round. Trailer spaces go for about $12/night, and camping is $6, with discounts for weekly and monthly rentals; fee includes showers and toilets.

RV and tent camping and comfortable rooms are also available at the **Koala Bungalows and Trailer Park** at the gorgeously rural, semi-tropical mountain lake Santa María (see "Sights," preceding), about 45 minutes away via Hwy. 15 southeast of Tepic. Owner Chris French maintains a tranquil, palm-studded

lakeside park, with bungalow-style rooms, houses, RV and tent sites, a snack bar, kiddie pool, small swimming pool, and rowboat rentals. For reservations, phone 32/140-509 or 32/123-772, or write P.O. Box 493, Tepic, Nayarit 63000. The four spartan but clean and comfortable garden kitchenette apartments, for up to four persons, with bath, rent from about $25 daily, $150 weekly, and $500 monthly. A small house and a larger two-bedroom house are also available for $40 and $50 per day, respectively. About 20 well-maintained shady RV sites rent for $11 daily, $60 weekly, and $200 monthly, with all hookups, toilets, and showers. Add $1 per day for a/c power. Campsites go for about $2 per adult, $1.50 per child, per night. Weekends at Koala Bungalows tend to bustle with local families; weekdays, when the few guests are middle-class European, North American, and Mexican couples, are more tranquil.

Those who yearn for even more serenity and privacy opt for one of the fully furnished semi-luxurious **view apartments,** built by Chris's daughter Hayley and her husband on the opposite side of the lake. The apartments' overall plan, on four separate levels, stair-stepping up the hillside among ancient, spreading trees, blends thoughtfully into the pristine lakeside setting. Here, all the ingredients—individual lake-vista *terrazas,* kitchenettes (bring your food), king-size beds, swimming pool—seem to come together for a perfectly tranquil weekend, week, or month of Sundays. Apartments rent for about $50/day; reserve through the same numbers and address as Koala Bungalows above.

Get there by bus or by driving, either along Hwy. 15 *libre* (non-toll) or the new toll road *(cuota autopista)* to Guadalajara, which begins at the far southeast suburb. From *libre* Hwy. 15, about 16 miles (26 km) east of Tepic, between roadside kilometer markers 194 and 195, follow the signed turnoff left (north) toward Santa María del Oro town. Keep on five more miles (eight km) to the town (pop. 3,000). Continue another five miles (eight km), winding downhill to the lake. For a breathtaking lake view, stop at the roadside viewpoint about a mile past the town. At the lakeshore, head left a few hundred yards to Koala Bungalows and Trailer Park. From the *autopista* follow the signed "Santa María del

Oro" exit. Proceed to the town and continue, winding downhill to the lake, as described above.

Laguna Santa María is directly accessible by bus from the second-class bus terminal in downtown Tepic (from the Cathedral, walk four blocks north along Av. Mexico; at Victoria, turn east a few steps to #9, at the station driveway). The relevant ticket office (*taquiila* of Transportes Noroeste de Nayarit, tel. 32/122-325) is inside at the back. Buses leave for Laguna Santa Mar three times daily, at 6 A.M., 7 A.M., and 1 P.M. On return, they depart from the lake around 9 A.M., 10 A.M., and 3 P.M.

You can also ride a long-distance Guadalajara-bound bus from the Central Camionera (Central Bus Station, on Insurgentes, southeast of the Tepic town center, see "Getting There and Away," following) to Santa María del Oro town, where you can catch a taxi, local bus, or collective van the remaining five miles downhill to the lake.

FOOD

Traffic noise and exhaust smoke sometimes sully the atmosphere in downtown restaurants. The **Hotel Fray Junípero Serra** restaurant does not suffer such a drawback, however, located in air-conditioned serenity behind its plate glass, plaza-front windows at Lerdo 23 Pte., tel. 32/122-525. Open daily 7 A.M.–9 P.M.; credit cards are accepted. Moderate to expensive.

A much humbler but colorful and relatively quiet lunch or supper spot is the downtown favorite **Lonchería Flamingos,** on Puebla Nte., half a block north behind the Presidencia Municipal, where a cadre of spirited female chefs puts out a continuous supply of steaming *tortas,* tostadas, tacos, *hamburguesas,* and *chocomiles.* The *tortas,* although tasty, are small. Best try the tostada, which is served on a huge, yummy, crunchy corn tortilla. Open daily except Wednesday, 10 A.M.–10:30 P.M. Budget.

For authentic Mexican cooking, go to Tepic's

papaya

clean, well-lighted place for tacos, **Tacos Mismaloya,** southwest plaza corner, across from the Banco Internacional. Pick from a long list of tacos in eight styles, as well as *pozole,* enchiladas, tamales, quesadillas, and much more. Open daily 8 A.M.–8 P.M.

Another popular downtown restaurant choice is the **Restaurant Altamirano,** at Av. México 109 Sur, in the big Hotel Real de Don Juan at the southeast corner of Plaza Constituyentes. Here, in a clean rustic-chic atmosphere, businesspeople lunch in the daytime, and middle- and upper-class Tepic families stop for snacks after the movies. The appetizing menu includes a host of Mexican entrées plus a number of international favorites, including spaghetti, hamburgers, omelettes, and pancakes; open Mon.–Sat. 8 A.M.–8 P.M., Sunday 8 A.M.–4 P.M. Moderate.

About a mile south of downtown, across Insurgentes from Parque La Loma, a loyal cadre of middle- and upper-class patrons keep the coffee-shop-style **Restaurant Terraza,** tel. 32/132-180, bustling morning till night. A major attraction, besides the food, is the racks of books and magazines that patrons enjoy reading, along with their good omelettes, spaghetti, and sandwiches. Open daily 7 A.M.–11 P.M. Moderate.

Tepic people enjoy a number of good suburban restaurants. On the north side of town, one of the best is the **Restaurant Higuera** at the Hotel Bugam Villas (see "Suburban Motels," above). In the southeast suburb, **Chic's,** a Mexican version of Denny's, on Av. Insurgentes, by the big Plaza Ley shopping center, about a mile and a half from downtown, tel. 32/142-810, offers a bit of everything for the travel-weary: tasty American-style specialties, air-conditioned ambience, and a mini-playground for kids around back; open Mon.–Sat. daily 7 A.M.–10:30 P.M., Sunday 7 A.M.–5 P.M. Moderate.

If Chic's is not to your liking, go into Plaza Ley nearby for about half a dozen more alternative pizzerias, *jugerías, taquerías,* and *loncherías.*

For a deluxe treat, go to **Restaurant Roberto's Internacional,** at Paseo de La Loma 472, at the corner of Av. Insurgentes, west side of La Loma park, tel. 32/132-085. Here, attentive waiters, subdued 1960s-style decor, crisp service, and good international specialties set a luxurious but relaxing tone. Open nightly until about midnight. Expensive.

SHOPPING

Its for-sale collections of Huichol art provide an excellent reason for stopping in Tepic. At least four downtown shops specialize in Huichol goods, acting as agents for more than just the commissions they receive. They have been involved with the Huichol for years, helping them preserve their religion and traditional skills in the face of expanding tourism and development. (See the special topic "The Huichol.")

Starting near the Plaza Principal, the **Casa Aguet,** on Amado Nervo, a block behind the Presidencia Municipal (look for the second-story black and white "Artesanias Huichol" sign) has an upstairs attic-museum of Huichol art. It's at 132 Amado Nervo, tel. 32/124-130; open Mon.–Sat. 9 A.M.–2 P.M. and 4–8 P.M., Sunday 9 A.M.–2 P.M. The founder's son, personable Miguel Aguet, knows the Huichol well. Moreover, he guarantees the "lowest prices in town." His copy of *Art of the Huichol Indians* furnishes authoritative explanations of the intriguing animal and human painting motifs.

The small government handicrafts store, **Tienda de Artesanías Wereme,** corner of Amado Nervo and Mérida, next to the Presidencia Municipal, open Mon.–Fri. 9 A.M.–2 P.M. and 4–7 P.M., Saturday 9 A.M.–2 P.M., stocks some Huichol and other handicrafts. The staff, however, does not appear as knowledgeable as the private merchants.

If you can manage only one stop in Tepic, make it one block north of the plaza at **Casa Aguiar,** Zaragoza 100 Pte., corner of Mérida, tel. 32/206-694, where elderly Alicia and Carmela Aguiar carry on their family tradition of Huichol crafts. There, in the parlor of their graceful old ancestral home, they offer a colorful galaxy of artifacts, both antique and new. Eerie beaded masks, venerable ceremonial hats, votive arrows, God's eyes, and huge yarn *cuadras,* blooming like Buddhist *tankas,* fill the cabinets and line the walls. Open Mon.–Sat. 10 A.M.–2 P.M. and 4–7:30 P.M.

Several blocks south on Av. México, at no. 122 Sur, just past Plaza Constituyentes and across from the Hotel Real de Don Juan, **Artesanías Cicuri,** tel. 32/123-714 or 32/121-466, names itself after the renowned *cicuri,* the "eye of God" of the Huichol. Its collection is both extensive and particularly fine, especially the beaded masks; open Mon.–Sat. 9 A.M.–2 P.M. and 4–8 P.M.

SERVICES

For best money exchange rates, go to a bank (all with ATMs), such as the main **Banamex** branch on Av. México at Zapata. It's open Mon.–Fri. 8:30 A.M.–3 P.M., Saturday 9 A.M.–2 P.M. (although money exchange hours may be shorter). If the lines at Banamex are too long, go to **Bancomer** across the street, or long-hours **Banco Internacional** on the main square next to the Presidencia Municipal (Mérida 184 Nte., open for U.S. dollar money exchange Mon.–Sat. 8:30 A.M.–7 P.M.). After hours, use a bank ATM, or try one of the many *casas de cambio* (money exchange counters) on Av. Mexico, such as the **Lidor,** just north of the Palacio de Gobierno, tel. 32/123-384; or **Mololoa,** at 53 Mexico Nte., near the corner of Morelos, open Mon.–Fri. 8:30 A.M.–2 P.M. and 4:30–6:30 P.M., Saturday 9 A.M.–2 P.M.

Tepic has two **post offices.** The main branch is downtown at Durango Nte. 27, tel. 32/120-130, corner of Morelos Pte., open Mon.–Fri. 8 A.M.–7 P.M., Saturday 8:30 A.M.–noon, about two blocks west and three blocks south of the Plaza Principal; the other is at the Central de Autobuses (Central Bus Terminal) on Av. Insurgentes about a mile east (Guadalajara direction) from downtown, open Mon.–Fri. 8 A.M.–2 P.M.

Telecomunicaciones, which provides telegraph, telephone, and public fax, likewise has both a downtown branch on Av. México, corner of Morelos, tel./fax 32/129-655, open Mon.–Fri. 8 A.M.–7 P.M., Saturday 8 A.M.–4 P.M., and a Central de Autobuses branch, tel./fax 32/132-327, open Mon.–Fri. 8 A.M.–2 P.M., Saturday 8 A.M.–noon.

If you need a doctor, contact the **Sanatorio**

Guadalupe, Juan Escuita 68 Nte., tel. 32/129-401 or 32/122-713, seven blocks west of the Plaza Principal. It has a 24-hour emergency room and a group of specialists on call. A fire-department paramedic squad is also available by calling 32/131-809.

For **police** emergencies, call the municipal *preventiva* police, tel. 32/115-765. For **fire** emergencies, call the *bomberos* (firefighters), tel. 32/131-607.

INFORMATION

Tepic's **municipal tourist information office,** tel. 32/165-523 or 32/165-661, email: turismo@tepic.gob.mx, is at the plaza principal's northwest corner, just north of the Presidencia Municipal (city hall), at the corner or Amado Nervo and Puebla. It dispenses information and a tableful of excellent brochures, many in English. Hours are 9 A.M.–8 P.M. daily.

Nayarit State Tourism offices, tel./fax 32/148-071, 32/148-072, or 32/148-073, toll-free in Mexico 800/903-92, are in the Convento de la Cruz at Av. Mexico and Calzado Ejercito, about a mile south of the Cathedral. Stop by its information booth, open Mon.–Fri. 9 A.M.–2 P.M. and 6–8 P.M., Saturday 9 A.M.–2 P.M., which stocks excellent brochures.

English-language books and magazines are scarce in Tepic. **Newsstands** beneath the plaza portals just west of the Hotel Fray Junípero Serra and the bookstore **Publicaciones Azteca** on Av. México, corner Morelos (open daily 7 A.M.–11 P.M.), tel. 32/160-811, usually have the *News* from Mexico City in the afternoon. Also, the Restaurant Terraza, tel. 32/132-180, open daily 7 A.M.–11 P.M., on Insurgentes, across from Parque La Loma, between Querétaro and Oaxaca, also generally has the *News* and a couple dozen popular American magazines, such as *Time, Newsweek,* and *National Geographic.*

GETTING THERE AND AWAY

By Car or RV

Main highways connect Tepic with Puerto Vallarta in the south, San Blas in the west, Guadalajara in the east, and Mazatlán in the north.

Two-lane Hwy. 200 from Puerto Vallarta is in good condition for its 104-mile (167-km) length. Curves, traffic, and the 3,000-foot Tepic grade, however, usually slow the northbound trip to about three hours, a bit less southbound.

A pair of routes (both about 43 miles, 70 km) connect Tepic with San Blas. The more scenic of the two takes about an hour and a half, heading south from San Blas along the Bay of Matanchén to Santa Cruz , then climbing 3,000 feet west to Tepic via Nayarit Hwy. 74. The quicker route leads west from San Blas along National Hwy. 11, climbing through the tropical forest to Hwy. 15, where four lanes guide traffic rapidly to Tepic.

To and from Mazatlán, traffic, towns, and rough spots slow progress along the 182-mile (293-km), two-lane stretch of National Hwy. 15. Expect four or five hours of driving time under good conditions.

The same is true of the winding, 141-mile (227-km) continuation of Hwy. 15 eastward over the Sierra Madre Occidental to Guadalajara. Fortunately, a *cuota autopista* (toll superhighway 15D), which begins at Tepic's southeastern edge, eliminates two hours of driving time. Allow about three hours by *autopista* and at least five hours without.

By Bus

The shiny, modern **Central Camionera** on Insurgentes Sur about a mile southeast of downtown has many services, including a **tourist information office,** left-luggage lockers, a cafeteria, a post office, long-distance telephone, and public fax. Booths *(taquillas)* offering higher class bus service are generally on the station's left (east) side; the lower class is on the right (west) side as you enter.

Transportes del Pacífico (TP), tel. 32/132-320 or 32/132-313, has many first- and second-class local departures, connecting south with Puerto Vallarta, east with Guadalajara and Mexico City, and north with Mazatlán, and the U.S. border at Tijuana and Nogales.

Estrella Blanca (EB), tel. 32/132-315, operating through its subsidiaries, provides many second-class, first-class, and super-first-class direct connections north, east, and south. First class Elite (EL) departures connect north with the U.S. border (Nogales and Tijuana) via Mazatlán, and south with Acapulco via Puerto Vallarta, Barra de Navidad, Manzanillo (with connections through Colima east to Michoacán and Mexico City), and Zihuatanejo. First-class Transportes Norte (TN) departures connect, through Guadalajara, north with Saltillo and Monterrey. Super first-class Futura (FU) connects, through Guadalajara, with Mexico City. First-class Transportes Chihuahuenses (TC) connect north with the U.S. border (Ciudad Juárez) via Aguascalientes, Zacatecas, and Torreón. Second-class Transportes Norte de Sonora (TNS) departures connect north, through Mazatlán and Nogales, Mexicali, and Tijuana, at the U.S. border.

Transportes Norte de Sonora, tel. 32/132-315, sells tickets for hourly daytime second-class connections with San Blas and with Santiago Ixcuintla, where you can continue by local bus to the Mexcaltitán embarcadero.

Besides providing many first-class connections with Guadalajara, independent **Omnibus de Mexico (OM),** tel. 32/131-323, provides a few departures that connect, via Guadalajara, north with Fresnillo, Torreón, and the U.S. border at Ciudad Juárez, and northeast with Aguascalientes, Zacatecas, Saltillo, Monterrey, and the U.S. border, at Matamoros.

By Train
The recently privatized Mexican Pacific Railway no longer offers passenger service. Until further notice, trains, which clickety-clacked along the rails for generations, connecting Guadalajara, Tepic, and the U.S. border at Nogales and Mexicali, are mere fading memories.

common bananas

INLAND TO GUADALAJARA AND LAKE CHAPALA

GUADALAJARA AND VICINITY

Puerto Vallarta residents often go to Guadalajara (pop. 3 million, elev. 5,214 feet, 1,589 meters), the capital of Jalisco, for the same reason Californians frequently go to Los Angeles: to shop and choose from big selections at correspondingly small prices.

But that's only part of the fascination. Although Guadalajarans like to think of themselves as different (calling themselves, uniquely, "Tapatíos"), their city is renowned as the "most Mexican" of cities. Crowds flock to Guadalajara to bask in its mild, springlike sunshine, savor its music, and admire its grand monuments.

HISTORY

Before Columbus
The broad Atemajac Valley, where the Guadalajara metropolis now spreads, has nurtured humans for hundreds of generations. Discovered remains date back at least 10,000 years. The Río Lerma—Mexico's longest river, which meanders across six states—has nourished Atemajac Valley cornfields for at least three millennia.

Although they built no pyramids, high cultures were occupying western Mexico by A.D. 300.

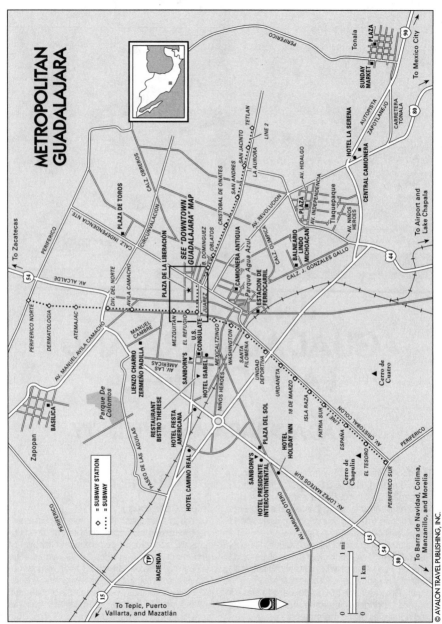

METROPOLITAN
GUADALAJARA

SEE "DOWNTOWN GUADALAJARA" MAP

= SUBWAY STATION
..... = SUBWAY

To Zacatecas

To Tepic, Puerto
Vallarta, and Mazatlán

To Mexico City

To Airport and
Lake Chapala

To Barra de Navidad, Colima,
Manzanillo, and Morelia

© AVALON TRAVEL PUBLISHING, INC.

They left sophisticated animal- and human-motif pottery in myriad bottle-shaped underground tombs of a style found in Jalisco, Nayarit, and Colima. Intriguingly, similar tombs are also found in Colombia and Ecuador.

During the next thousand years, waves of migrants swept across the Valley of Atemajac: Toltecs from the northeast; the Aztecs much later from the west. As Toltec power declined during the 13th century, the Tarascan civilization took root in Michoacán to the south and filled the power vacuum left by the Toltecs. On the eve of the Spanish conquest, semi-autonomous local chiefdoms, tributaries of the Tarascan Emperor, shared the Atemajac valley.

Conquest and Colonization

The fall of the Aztecs in 1521 and the Tarascans a few years later made the Valley of Atemajac a plum ripe for the picking. In the late 1520s, while Cortés was absent in Spain, the opportunistic Nuño de Guzmán vaulted himself to power in Mexico City on the backs of the native peoples and at the expense of Cortés's friends and relatives. Suspecting correctly that his glory days in Mexico City were numbered, Guzmán cleared out three days before Christmas 1529, at the head of a small army of adventurers seeking new conquests in western Mexico. They raped, ravaged, and burned for half a dozen years, inciting dozens of previously pacified tribes to rebellion.

Hostile Mexican attacks repeatedly foiled Guzmán's attempts to establish his western Mexico capital, which he wanted to name after his Spanish hometown, Guadalajara (from the Arabic *wad al hadjarah,* "river of stones"). Ironically, it wasn't until the year of Guzmán's death in Spain, 1542, six years after his arrest by royal authorities, that the present Guadalajara was founded. At the downtown Plaza de Los Fundadores, a panoramic bronze frieze shows cofounders Doña Beátriz de Hernández and governor Cristóbal de Oñate christening the soon-to-become-capital of the "Kingdom of Nueva Galicia."

The city grew; its now-venerable public buildings rose at the edges of sweeping plazas, from which expeditions set out to explore other lands. In 1563, Legazpi and Urdaneta sailed west to conquer the Philippines; the year 1602 saw Viz-

caíno sail for the Californias and the Pacific Northwest. In 1687 Father Kino left for 27 years of mission-building in Sonora and what would be Arizona and New Mexico; finally, during the 1760s, Father Junípero Serra and Captain Gaspar de Portola began their arduous trek to discover San Francisco Bay and found a string of California missions.

During Spain's Mexican twilight, Guadalajara was a virtual imperial city, ruling all of northwest Mexico, plus what would become California, Arizona, New Mexico, and Texas—an empire twice the size of Britain's 13 colonies.

Independence

The cry, "Death to the *gachupines,* Viva México" by insurgent priest Miguel Hidalgo ignited rebellion on September 16, 1810. Buoyed by a series of quick victories, Hidalgo advanced on Mexico City in command of a huge ragtag army. But, facing the punishing fusillades of a small but disciplined Spanish force, Hidalgo lost his nerve and decided to occupy Guadalajara instead. Loyalist General Felix Calleja pursued and routed Hidalgo's forces on the bank of the Lerma, not far east of Guadalajara. Although Hidalgo and Allende escaped, they were captured in the north a few months later. It wasn't for another dozen bloody years that others—Iturbide, Guerrero, Morelos—from other parts of Mexico realized Hidalgo's dream of independence.

Guadalajara, its domain reduced by the republican government to the new state of Jalisco, settled down to the production of corn, cattle, and tequila. The railroad came, branched north to the United States and south to the Pacific, and by 1900, Guadalajara's place as a commercial hub and Mexico's second city was secure.

Modern Guadalajara

After the bloodbath of the 1910-17 revolution, Guadalajara's growth far outpaced the country in general. From a population of around 100,000, Guadalajara ballooned to more than three million by 2000. People were drawn from the countryside by jobs in a thousand new factories, making everything from textiles and shoes to chemicals and soda pop.

Handicraft manufacture, always important in

Guadalajara, zoomed during the 1960s when waves of jet-riding tourists came, saw, and bought mountains of blown glass, leather, pottery, and metal finery.

During the 1980s, Guadalajara put on a new face while at the same time preserving the best part of its old downtown. An urban-renewal plan of visionary proportions created Plaza Tapatía—acres of shops, stores, and offices beside fountain-studded malls—incorporating Guadalajara's venerable theaters, churches, museums, and government buildings into a single grand open space.

SIGHTS

Getting Oriented

Although Guadalajara sprawls over a hundred square miles, the treasured mile-square heart of the city is easily explorable on foot. The cathedral corner of north-south Av. 16 de Septiembre and Av. Morelos marks the center of town. A few blocks south, another important artery, east-west Av. Juárez, runs above the new metro subway line through the main business district, while a few blocks east, Av. Independencia runs beneath Plaza Tapatía and past the main market to the railway station a couple of miles south.

A Walk around Old Guadalajara

The twin steeples of the **cathedral** serve as an excellent starting point to explore the city-center plazas and monuments. The cathedral, dedicated to the Virgin of the Assumption when it was begun in 1561, was finished about 30 years later. A potpourri of styles—Moorish, Gothic, Renaissance, and Classic—make up its spires, arches, and facades. Although an earthquake demolished its steeples in 1818, they were rebuilt and resurfaced with cheery canary yellow tiles in 1854.

Inside, side altars and white facades climax at the principal altar, built over a tomb containing the remains of several former clergy, including the mummified heart of renowned Bishop Cabañas. One of the main attractions is the **Virgin of Innocence,** in the small chapel just to the left of the entrance. The glass-enclosed figure contains the bones of a 12-year-old girl who was martyred in the third century, forgotten, then

SUBWAY, GUADALAJARA STYLE

Since the early 1990s, Guadalajarans have enjoyed a new underground train system, which they call simply the **Tren Ligero,** or "Light Train." It's nothing fancy, a kind of Motel 6 of subway lines—inexpensive, efficient, and reliable. A pair of intersecting lines, Linea 1 and Linea 2, carry passengers in approximately north-south and east-west directions, along a total of 15 miles (25 km) of track. The station most visitors see first is the Plaza Universidad (on line 2), accessible by staircases that descend near the city-center corner of Juárez and Colón. Look for the Denny's restaurant nearby.

Downstairs, if you want to take a ride, deposit the specified number of pesos in machines, which will give you in exchange a brass *ficha* token, good for one ride and one transfer. If you opt to transfer, you have to do it at Juárez station, the next stop west of Plaza Universidad, where lines 1 and 2 intersect. (Hint: Best begin your Guadalajara subway adventure before 9 P.M.; the Tren Ligero goes to sleep by about 11 P.M.)

rediscovered in the Vatican catacombs in 1786 and shipped to Guadalajara in 1788. The legend claims she died protecting her virginity; it is equally likely that she was martyred for refusing to recant her Christian faith.

Somewhere near the main altar you'll find either a copy of or the authentic **Virgin of Zapopan.** Between sometime in June and October 12, the tiny, adored figure will be the authentic "La Generala," as she's affectionately known; on October 12, a tumultuous crowd of worshippers escorts her back to the cathedral in Zapopan, where she remains until brought back to Guadalajara the next June.

Outside, broad plazas surround the cathedral: the **Plaza Laureles,** in front (west) of the cathedral, then moving counterclockwise, the **Plaza de Armas** to the south, **Plaza Liberación** to the east (behind), and the **Plaza de los Hombres Ilustres** to the north of the cathedral.

Across Av. Morelos, the block-square Plaza de los Hombres Ilustres is bordered by 15 sculptures of Jalisco's eminent sons. Their remains lie beneath the stone rotunda in the center; their bronze statues line the sidewalk. Right at the

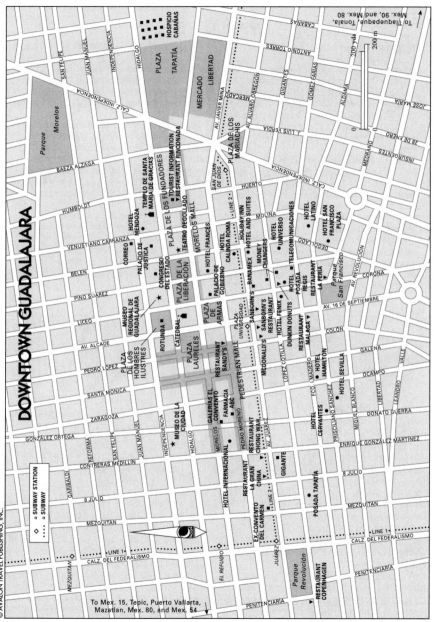

DOWNTOWN GUADALAJARA

© AVALON TRAVEL PUBLISHING, INC.

◇ = SUBWAY STATION

···· = SUBWAY

To Tlaquepaque, Tonala,
Mex. 90, and Mex. 80

0   200 m
0   200 yd

CABAÑAS

HOSPICIO
CABAÑAS

PLAZA
TAPATIA

MERCADO
LIBERTAD

Parque
Morelos

TEMPLO DE SANTA
MARIA DE GRACIAS

TOURIST INFORMATION
RESTAURANT RINCONADA

PLAZA DE LOS FUNDADORES

PLAZA DE LOS
MARIACHIS

SAN JUAN
DE DIOS

TEATRO DEGOLLADO

MORELOS MALL

HOTEL FRANCES

HOTEL
CALINDA ROMA

HOLIDAY INN

HOTEL AND SUITES

MONEY
CHANGERS

HOTEL
UNIVERSO

TELECOMUNICACIONES

HOTEL
LATINO

HOTEL SAN
FRANCISCO
PLAZA

Parque
San Francisco

HOTEL
MENDOZA

CORREO

PALACIO DE
JUSTICIA

CONGRESO
DEL ESTADO

MUSEO
REGIONAL DE
GUADALAJARA

PLAZA DE LA
LIBERACION

PALACIO DE
GOBIERNO

BANAMEX

SANBORN'S

SANBORN'S
RESTAURANT

HOTEL FENIX

DUNKIN DONUTS

RESTAURANT
MALAGA

HOTEL
POSADA
REGIS

LA FERIA
RESTAURANT

ROTUNDA

CATEDRAL

PLAZA DE LOS
HOMBRES
ILUSTRES

PLAZA
DE
ARMAS

PLAZA
UNIVERSIDAD

MCDONALD'S

HOTEL
HAMILTON

HOTEL
SEVILLA

PLAZA
LAURELES

RESTAURANT
SANDY'S

GALERIAS EL
CONVENTO

FARMACIA
ABC

MUSEO DE LA
CIUDAD

HOTEL
CERVANTES

HOTEL
INTERNACIONAL

RESTAURANT
CHONG WAH

RESTAURANT
LA GRAN
CHINA

GIGANTE

POSADA TAPATIA

EX-CONVENTO
DEL CARMEN

RESTAURANT
COPENHAGEN

Parque
Revolucion

To Mex. 15, Tepic, Puerto Vallarta,
Mazatlan, Mex. 80, and Mex. 54

CALZ. DEL FEDERALISMO

LINE 1

LINE 2

Street names visible: SAN FELIPE, JUAN MANUEL, INDEPENDENCIA, HIDALGO, CALZ. INDEPENDENCIA, BAEZA ALZAGA, HUMBOLDT, VENUSTIANO CARRANZA, BELEN, PINO SUAREZ, LICEO, AV. ALCALDE, PEDRO LOPEZ, SANTA MONICA, ZARAGOZA, GONZALEZ ORTEGA, REFORMA, GARIBALDI, CONTRERAS MEDELLIN, 8 JULIO, MEZQUITAN, MORELOS, PEDRO MORENO, AV. JUAREZ, HIDALGO, EL REFUGIO, JUAREZ, PENITENCIARIA, AV. JAVIER MINA, HUERTO, MOLINA, DEGOLLADO, CORONA, AV. REVOLUCION, AV. 16 DE SEPTIEMBRE, COLON, GALENA, OCAMPO, LIBERTAD, LEANDRO VALLE, DONATO GUERRA, ENRIQUE GONZALEZ MARTINEZ, MEZQUITAN, PENITENCIARIA, FCO. MADERO, LOPEZ COTILLA, PRISCILIANO SANCHEZ, MIGUEL BLANCO, ANTONIO TORRES, GOMEZ FARIAS, AV. ALVARO OBREGON, GIGANTES, ALDAMA, J. LUIS VERDIA, MEDRANO, 28 DE ENERO, INSURGENTES, JOSE MARIA, CALZ. INDEPENDENCIA

MARIACHIS

Mariachis, those thoroughly Mexican troubador bands, have spread from their birthplace in Jalisco throughout Mexico and into much of the United States. The name itself reveals their origin. "Mariachi" originated with the French *mariage,* or marriage. When French influence peaked during the 1864-67 reign of Maximilian, Jaliscans transposed *mariage* to "mariachi," a label they began to identify with the five-piece folk bands that played for weddings.

The original ensembles, consisting of a pair of violins, *vihuela* (large eight-stringed guitar), *jarana* (small guitar), and harp, played exclusively traditional melodies. Song titles such as "Las Moscas" (The Flies), "El Venado" (The Stag), and "La Papaya," thinly disguised their universal themes, mostly concerning love.

Although such all-string folk bands still play in Jalisco, notably in Tecalitlán and other rural areas, they've largely been replaced by droves of trumpet-driven commercial mariachis. The man who sparked the shift was probably Emilio Azcárraga Vidaurreta,

the director of radio station XEW, which began broadcasting in Mexico City in 1930. In those low-fidelity days, the subdued sound of the harp didn't broadcast well, so Azcárraga suggested the trumpet as a replacement. It was so successful the trumpet has become the signature sound of present-day mariachis.

Still, mariachis mostly do what they've always done—serenade sweethearts, play for weddings and parties, even accompany church masses. They seem to be forever strolling around town plazas on Saturday nights and Sunday afternoons, looking for jobs. Their fees, which should be agreed upon before they start, often depend on union scale per song, per serenade, or per hour.

Sometimes mariachis serve as a kind of live jukebox which, for a coin, will play your old favorite. And even if it's a slightly tired but sentimental "Mañanitas" or "Cielito Lindo," you can't help but be moved by the singing violins, bright trumpets, and soothing guitars.

corner you'll find the figure of revered Jalisco Governor Ignacio Vallarta; a few steps farther north stands the statue of José Clemente Orozco, legally blind when he executed his great works of art. (See "Jose Clemente Orozco Art Museum," following.)

Adjacent to and east of the Plaza Hombres Ilustres, the colonial building behind the lineup of horse-drawn *calandrias* housed the Seminario de San José for the six generations following its

construction in 1696. During the 1800s it served variously as a barracks and a public lecture hall, and, since 1918, it has housed the **Museo Regional de Guadalajara,** 60 Liceo, tel. 3/614-6521, open Tues.–Sun. 9 A.M.–6:30 P.M.

Inside, tiers of rooms surrounding a tree-shaded interior patio illustrate local history. Exhibits depict scenes from as early as the Big Bang and continue with a hulking mastodon skeleton and whimsical animal and human figurines recovered from the bottle-shaped tombs of Jalisco, Nayarit, and Colima. Upstairs rooms contain life-size displays of contemporary but traditional fishing methods at nearby Lake Chapala and costumes and culture of regional Cora, Huichol, Tepehuan, and México peoples.

Back outside, head east two blocks down Av. Hidalgo, paralleling the expansive Plaza Liberación behind the cathedral. On your left you will pass the baroque facades of the *congreso del estado* (state legislature) and the *palacio de justicia* (state supreme court) buildings. Ahead at the east end of the plaza rises the timeless silhouette of the **Teatro Degollado.**

The theater's classic, columned facade climaxes in an epic marble frieze, depicting the allegory of Apollo and the nine muses. Inside, the Degollado's resplendent grand salon is said to rival the gilded refinement of Milan's renowned La Scala. Overhead, its ceiling glows with Gerardo Suárez's panorama of canto IV of Dante's *Divine Comedy*, complete with its immortal cast—Julius Caesar, Homer, Virgil, Saladin—and the robed and wreathed author himself in the middle. Named for the millionaire Governor Degollado who financed its construction, the theater opened with appropriate fanfare on September 13, 1866, with a production of *Lucia de Lammermoor*, starring Angela Peralta, the renowned "Mexican Nightingale." An ever-changing menu of artists still graces the Degollado's stage. These include an excellent local folkloric ballet troupe every Sunday morning (see "Entertainment and Events," later in this chapter).

Walk behind the Degollado, where a modern bronze frieze, the **Frisa de Los Fundadores,** decorates its back side. Appropriately, a mere two blocks from the spot where the city was founded, the 68-foot sculpture shows Guadalajara's cofounders facing each other on opposite sides of a big tree. Governor Cristóbal de Oñate strikes the tree with his sword, while Doña Beátriz de Hernández holds a fighting cock, symbolizing her gritty determination (and that of dozens of fellow settlers) that Guadalajara's location should remain put.

Plaza Tapatía

Turn around and face east. The 17 acres of the Plaza Tapatía complex extend ahead for several blocks across sub-plazas, fountains, and malls. Initially wide in the foreground of Plaza de Los Fundadores, the Tapatía narrows between a double row of shiny shops and offices, then widens into a broad esplanade and continues beside a long pool/fountain that leads to the monumental, domed Hospicio Cabañas a third of a mile away. Along the Tapatía's lateral flanks, a pair of long malls—continuations of Avenidas Hidalgo and Morelos—parallel the central Paseo Degollado mall for two blocks.

The eastern end of the Morelos mall climaxes with the striking bronze *escudo* (coat of arms) of Guadalajara. Embodying the essence of the original 16th-century coat of arms authorized by Emperor Charles V, the *escudo* shows a pair of lions protecting a pine tree (with leaves, rather than needles). The lions represent the warrior's determination and discipline, and the solitary pine symbolizes noble ideals.

Continue east, to where the Plaza Tapatía widens, giving berth for the sculpture-fountain **Imolación de Quetzalcoatl,** designed and executed by Víctor Manuel Contreras in 1982. Four bronze serpent-birds, representing knowledge and the spirit of humankind, stretch toward heaven at the ends of a giant cross. In the center, a towering bronze spiral represents the unquenchable flame of Quetzalcoatl, transforming all that it touches. Locals call the sculpture the "big corkscrew," however.

At this point, Av. Independencia runs directly beneath Plaza Tapatía, past the adjacent sprawling **Mercado Libertad,** built in 1958 on the site of the traditional Guadalajara *tianguis* (open-air market), known since pre-Columbian times. Follow the elevated pedestrian walkway to explore the Libertad's produce, meat, fish, herbs, food, and handicrafts stalls.

On Independencia, just beyond the market, musicians at the **Plaza de los Mariachis** continue the second century of a tradition born when mariachi (cowboy troubadour) groups first appeared during the 1860s in Guadalajara. The musical hubbub climaxes Saturday nights and Sunday afternoons, as musicians gather, singing while they wait to be hired for serenades and parties.

Behind the long pool/fountain at the east end of Plaza Tapatía stands the domed neoclassic **Hospicio Cabañas,** the largest and one of the most remarkable colonial buildings in the Americas, designed and financed by Bishop Juan Ruiz de Cabañas; construction was complete in 1810. The purpose of the "Guadalajara House of Charity and Mercy," as the good bishop originally named it, a home for the sick, helpless, and homeless, was fulfilled for 170 years. Although still successfully serving as an orphanage during the 1970s, time had taken its toll on the Hospicio Cabañas. The city and state governments built a new orphanage in the suburbs, restored the old building, and changed its purpose. It now houses the **Instituto Cultural Cabañas,** a center for the arts at Cabañas 8, tel. 3/654-0008 or 3/654-0129. Open Tues.–Sat. 9 A.M.–8 P.M., Sunday 9 A.M.–2 P.M. Public programs include classes and films, and instrumental, chorale, and dance concerts.

Inside, seemingly endless ranks of corridors pass a host of sculpture-decorated patios. Practice rooms resound with the clatter of dancing feet and the halting strains of apprentice violins, horns, and pianos. Exhibition halls and studios of the **José Clemente Orozco Art Museum** occupy a large fraction of the rooms, while the great muralist's brooding work spreads over a corresponding fraction of the walls. Words such as dark, fiery, nihilistic, even apocalyptic, would not be too strong to describe the panoramas that Orozco executed (1938-39) in the soaring chapel beneath the central dome. On one wall, an Aztec goddess wears a necklace of human hearts; on another, armored, automaton-soldiers menace Indian captives; while in the cupola overhead, Orozco's *Man of Fire,* wreathed in flame, appears to soar into a hellishly red-hot sky.

Out-of-Downtown Sights

The former villages of Zapopan, Tlaquepaque, and Tonalá, now parts of metropolitan Guadalajara, make interesting day-trip destinations from the city center. Although local buses or your own wheels can get you there, crowds of bus commuters and congested city streets increase the desirability of the local tour option. Contact your hotel travel desk, a travel agent, or a well-equipped agency such as Panoramex, at Federalismo Sur 944, tel. 3/810-5057 or 3/810-5005, which conducts reasonably priced bilingual tours daily from the city center.

Zapopan, about six miles northwest of downtown, is famous for its soaring baroque (1730)

basilica, home of the renowned Virgin of Zapopan. The legendary image, one of the beloved "three sisters" virgins of Mexico, has enjoyed generations of popularity so enormous that it must be seen to be believed. Local folks, whenever they happen by, often stop to say a prayer (or at least make the sign of the cross as they pass) in front of the cathedral gate. Inside, the faithful crawl the length of the sanctuary to pay their respects to the diminutive blue and white figure. The adoration climaxes on October 12, when a rollicking crowd of hundreds of thousands accompanies the Virgin of Zapopan from the downtown Guadalajara cathedral home to Zapopan, where she stays from October 13 until June.

Afterward, look over the displays of Huichol Indian handicrafts in the adjacent museum-shop **Artesanías Huichola,** located on your left as you exit the basilica; open Mon.–Sat. 10 A.M.–5:30 P.M., Sunday 10 A.M.–2 P.M. Sale items

The basilica at Zapopan is the home of the miraculous Virgin of Zapopan, the fragile statue who, like her sisters the Virgins at Talpa and San Juan de los Lagos, is feted yearly by millions of faithful from all over Mexico.

include eerie beaded masks, intriguing yarn paintings, and *ojos de dios* (God's eyes) yarn sculptures. Later, browse for bargains among the handicrafts stalls in front of the basilica and in the municipal market in the adjacent plaza on the corner of Av. Hidalgo and Calle Eva Briseño.

Getting There: From downtown Guadalajara, local Zapopan-marked (on the windshield) buses depart from the south-side Camionera Antigua (Old Bus Station) on Av. Estadio, just north of Parque Agua Azul, and continue through the downtown, stopping at the corner of López Cotilla and 16 de Septiembre. By car, follow Av. Manuel Avila Camacho, which diagonals northwest for about four miles from the city center to Zapopan, marked by the old baroque arch on the left. After one block, turn left onto Av. Hidalgo, the double main street of Zapopan. Within four blocks you'll see the plaza and the basilica on the left.

Zapopan town is the *cabecera* (headquarters) of the sprawling *municipio* of Zapopan, farm and mountain hinterland, famous for **La Barranca,** the 2,000-foot-deep canyon of the Río Grande de Santiago. At the viewpoint past San Isidro, around Km 15, Saltillo Hwy. 54 north of Guadalajara, motorists stop at the viewpoint, **Mirador Dr. Atl,** to admire the canyon vista and the waterfall **Cola del Caballo** (Horse's Tail) as it plummets hundreds of feet to the river below.

Past that, a small paradise of springs decorates the lush canyonland. First, at Km 17, comes **Los Camachos,** a forest and mountain-framed *balneario* (bathing park) with pools and restaurants; a few miles farther along is the hot spring bathing complex, **Balneario Nuevo Paraíso,** at Km 24. A kilometer farther (follow the left side road from the highway about a half kilometer) you can view the **Geiseres de Ixcatan** (Ixcatan Geysers) near the village. Get there by car via Hwy. 54, the Saltillo-Zacatecas highway, which heads northward along Av. Alcalde from the city-center cathedral. Bus riders can board the "Los Camachos" bus, which leaves the Glorieta Normal (on Av. Alcalde about a mile north of the downtown cathedral) about every hour from 5 A.M. until the early afternoon. For more information about Zapopan sights, drop by the Zapopan tourist information office at Plaza Centro, Av. Vallarta 503, periférico, tel. 3/100-755, open Mon.–Sat. 9 A.M.–7:30 P.M.

THE THREE SISTERS OF MEXICO

In all of Mexico, only the Virgin of Guadalupe exceeds in adoration the all-Jalisco trio—the "Three Sister" Virgins of Talpa, Zapopan, and San Juan de los Lagos. Yearly they draw millions of humble Mexican pilgrims who bus, walk, hitchhike, or in some cases crawl, to festivals honoring the virgins. Each virgin's popularity springs from some persistent, endearing legend. The Virgin of Talpa defied a haughty bishop's efforts to cage her; the Virgin of Zapopan rescued Guadalajara from war and disaster; the Virgin of San Juan de los Lagos restored a dead child to life.

Talpa, Zapopan, and San Juan de los Lagos townsfolk have built towering basilicas to shelter and honor each virgin. Each small and fragile figurine is draped in fine silk and jewels and worshipped by a continuous stream of penitents. During a virgin festival the image is lifted aloft by a platoon of richly costumed bearers and paraded to the clamor, tumult, and cheers of a million or more of the faithful.

Even if you choose to avoid the crowds and visit Talpa, Zapopan, or San Juan de los Lagos on a nonfestival day, you'll soon see the hubbub continues. Pilgrims come and go, bands and mariachis play, and curio stands stuffed with gilded devotional goods crowd the basilica square.

Tlaquepaque and **Tonalá,** in the southeast suburbs, are among Mexico's renowned handicrafts villages. Tlaquepaque (tlah-kay-PAH-kay) (now touristy, but still interesting), about five miles from the city center, is famous for fine stoneware and blown glass; Tonalá, another five miles farther, retains plenty of sleepy, colorful country ambience. Shops abound in celebrated ceramic, brass, and papier-mâché animal figurines. The most exciting, but crowded, time to visit is during the Sunday market. (For more Tlaquepaque and Tonalá details, see "Shopping," later in this chapter.)

ACCOMMODATIONS

Downtown Hotels

Several good hotels, ranging from budget to plush, dot the center of Guadalajara, mostly in the Av. Juárez business district, a few blocks

GUADALAJARA ACCOMMODATIONS

Accommodations (telephone area code 3, postal code 44100 unless otherwise noted) are listed in increasing order of approximate high-season, double-room rates. 800 numbers are for toll-free reservations from the U.S. and Canada.

DOWNTOWN HOTELS

Hotel Hamilton, F. Madero 381, tel. 614-6726, $8

Hotel Latino, P. Sánchez 74, tel. 614-4484 or 614-6214, $16

Hotel Sevilla, P. Sánchez 413, tel. 614-9037 or 614-9354, fax 614-9172, $15

Posada Tapatía, L. Cotilla 619, tel. 614-9146, e-mail: agalmaraz@hotmail.com, $21

Hotel Posada Regis, R. Corona 171, tel. 614-8633, fax 613-3026, $25

Hotel Universo, L. Cotilla 161, tel. 613-2815, fax 613-4734, website: www.trekkersnet.com/universo, $35

Hotel San Francisco Plaza, Degollado 267, tel. 613-8954, fax 613-3257, $40

Hotel Frances, Maestranza 35, tel. 613-1190 or 613-0936, fax 658-2831, $53

Hotel Cervantes, 442 P. Sánchez, tel./fax 613-6686, 613-6846, or 613-6816, $51

Hotel Internacional, P. Moreno 570, tel. 613-0330, fax 613-2866, $55

Hotel Fénix, R. Corona 160, tel. 614-5714 or 800/465-4329, fax 613-4005, $76

Hotel Calinda Roma, Juárez 170, tel. 614-8650, fax 613-0557, $84

Hotel Mendoza, V. Carranza 16, tel. 613-4646 or 614-6752, fax 613-7310, $90

Hotel Holiday Inn Suites, Juárez 211, tel. 613-1763 or (800) 465-4329, fax 614-9766, e-mail: holiday-centro@infosel.net.mx, $100

SUBURBAN HOTELS

Hotel La Serena, Carretera Zapotlanejo 1500, tel. 600-0910, fax 600-0015, $30

Hotel Isabel, J. Guadalupe Montenegro 1572, tel./fax 826-2630, e-mail: hotelisa@jal1telmex.net.mx, $53

Hotel Casa Grande, Aeropuerto Internacional, postal code 45640, tel. 678-9099, tel./fax 678-9000, e-mail: cchica@mail.udg.mx, $150

Hotel Fiesta Americana, Aurelio Aceves 225, tel. 825-3434, 800/FIESTA1 (800/343-7821), fax 630-3725, $150

Hotel Camino Real, Av. Vallarta 5005, postal code 45040, tel. 134-2424 or 800/7CAMINO (800/722-6466), in Mexico 01-800/903-2100, fax 134-2404, e-mail: crgdlsh@webcelmex.net.mx, $180

Holiday Inn Crowne Plaza, L. Mateos Sur 2500, postal code 45050, tel. 634-1034 or 800/465-4329, fax 631-9393, e-mail: crownegd@crownegdl.com.mx, $180

---

from the cathedral and plazas. Many have parking garages; a desirable downtown option for auto travelers. Hotels farthest from the cathedral plazas are generally the most economical.

The **Posada Tapatía,** López Cotilla 619, Guadalajara, Jalisco 44100, tel. 3/614-9146, email: agalmaraz@hotmail.com, one block off Juárez, near the corner of Calle 8 Julio, is about 10 blocks from the cathedral. Its simple but gaily decorated rooms with bath are spread around a light, colorfully restored central patio. Tightly

managed by the friendly on-site owner, the Tapatía's prices are certainly right. Try for a room in the back, away from the noisy street. The 12 rooms rent for $16 s, $21 d, with fans.

Three blocks closer in, at the northeast corner of Prisciliano Sánchez and Donato Guerra, step up from the sidewalk and enter the cool, contemporary-classic interior of the **Hotel Cervantes** at 442 Prisciliano Sánchez, tel./fax 3/613-6686 and 3/613-6846. Here, everything, from the marble-and-brass lobby, the modern-chic restaurant and bar, pool, and exercise room downstairs to the big beds, plush carpets, and shiny marble baths of the rooms upstairs, seems perfect for the enjoyment of its predominately business clientele. For such refinement, rates, at about $48 s, $51 d, are surprisingly moderate; with TV, phones, parking, and a/c; credit cards are accepted.

Across the street, on Prisciliano Sánchez between Ocampo and Donato Guerra, the old standby **Hotel Sevilla**, Prisciliano Sánchez 413, Guadalajara, Jalisco 44100, tel. 3/614-9354 or 3/614-9037, fax 3/614-9172, offers basic accommodations at budget prices. Its 80 rooms, furnished in dark brown wood and rugs to match, are plain but comfortable. For more light and quiet, get an upper-story room away from the street. Amenities include a lobby with TV, parking, a hotel safe for storing valuables, and a restaurant open daily except Sunday. Rates run $14 s, $15 d, $21 t; fans and telephones included.

One block away, on Madero, the even plainer **Hotel Hamilton**, Madero 381, Guadalajara, Jalisco 44100, tel. 3/614-6726, offers a rock-bottom alternative. The 32 bare-bulb, not-so-clean rooms border on dingy; their steel doors seem to enhance the drabness more than increasing security. Store your valuables in the hotel safe. For less noise and more light, get a room in back, away from the street. Rooms rent for $8 s or d, $13 t, with fans but no parking.

Cheerier and closer in, where the pedestrian strolling mall begins on Moreno, stands the big, 110-room **Hotel Internacional**, Pedro Moreno 570, Guadalajara, Jalisco 44100, tel. 3/613-0330, fax 3/613-2866. Downstairs, a small lobby with comfortable chairs adjoins the reception area. In the tower upstairs, the 1960s-style rooms, most with city views, are clean and comfortable, but varied. Look at more than one before moving in. Try for a discount below the asking prices of $55 s or d, which are high compared to the competition. (The hotel does, however, offer a 15 percent discount for a one-week rental). Amenities include fans, some a/c, phones, TV, a cafe, and parking; credit cards are accepted.

Equally well-located but shinier, **Hotel Fénix**, Corona 160, Guadalajara, Jalisco 44100, tel. 3/614-5714, fax 3/613-4005, lies on Corona, smack in the downtown business center, a short walk from everything. The owners have managed to upgrade this rather basic small-lobby hotel into something more elaborate. The somewhat cramped result, while not unattractive, is sometimes noisy and crowded. During the day, tour groups traipse in and out past the reception desk, while at night guests crowd the adjacent lobby bar for drinks and live combo music. Upstairs the 200 air-conditioned rooms are spacious and comfortably furnished with American-standard motel amenities. Walk-in rates, which run about $76 s or d, are high for a hotel with neither pool nor parking. You might try for a better deal in advance by booking a package through a travel agent.

With the same prime location right across the street, the second-floor **Hotel Posada Regis** offers both economy and a bit of old-world charm, at Corona 171, Guadalajara, Jalisco 44100, tel. 3/614-8633 or tel./fax 3/613-3026. Its clean and comfortable high-ceilinged rooms enclose a gracious Porfirian-era indoor lobby/atrium. Evening videos, friendly atmosphere, and a good breakfast/lunch cafe provide opportunities for relaxed exchanges with other travelers. The 19 rooms cost $20 s and $25 d, with phones, fans, and optional TV, but no parking; credit cards are accepted.

Central location, comfortable though a bit worn rooms, and moderate prices explain the popularity of the nearby **Hotel Universo**, López Cotilla 161, Guadalajara, Jalisco 44100, tel. 3/613-2815, fax 3/613-4734, website www.trekkersnet.com/universo, corner of Cotilla and Degollado, just three blocks from the the Teatro Degollado. Guests enjoy renovated, carpeted, and draped air-conditioned rooms with wood furniture and ceiling-to-floor tiled bathrooms. The 137 rooms and suites rent for $33 s, $35 d, suites from about $41, with TV, phones, and parking; credit cards are accepted.

The Universo's competent owner/managers also run a pair of good-value hotels nearby. Their graceful, authentically colonial **Hotel San Francisco Plaza**, Degollado 267, Guadalajara, Jalisco 44100, tel. 3/613-8954, fax 3/613-3257, is replete with traditional charm. The reception area opens to an airy and tranquil inner patio, where big soft chairs invite you to relax amid a leafy garden of potted plants. In the evenings, the venerable arched stone corridors gleam with antique, cut-crystal lanterns. Upstairs, the rooms are no less than you would expect: most are high-ceilinged, with plenty of polished wood, handmade furniture, rustic brass lamps by the bed, and sentimental old-Mexico paintings on the walls. Each room has a phone, TV, fan, and a large, modern-standard bathroom with marble sink. You'll find an elegant restaurant with high ceilings and chandeliers downstairs in front and plenty of parking. All this for $37 s, $40 d; credit cards are accepted.

The same owners run the **Hotel Latino,** one of Guadalajara's better cheap hotels, just around the corner at Prisciliano Sánchez 74, Guadalajara, Jalisco 44100, tel. 3/614-4484 or 3/614-6214. Although it's a plain hotel with a small lobby, the Latino's guests nevertheless enjoy a modicum of amenities. The 57 rooms in four stories (no elevator) are clean, carpeted, and thoughtfully furnished, albeit a bit worn around the edges. Baths are modern-standard, with shiny-tile showers and marble sinks. Rates are certainly right, at about $12 s, $16 d, including a/c, TV, parking, and phones; credit cards are not accepted.

Guests at the nearby **Hotel Calinda Roma,** Av. Juárez 170, Guadalajara, Jalisco 44100, tel. 3/614-8650, fax 3/613-0557, enjoy luxurious amenities—plush lobby, shiny restaurant/bar, rooftop rose garden, and pool—usually available only at pricier hostelries. Owners, however, have upped the tariffs; whether they can make them stick is another question. Try bargaining for discounts below the $78 s, $84 d asking rates; with TV, phones, a/c, parking, and limited wheelchair access; credit cards are accepted. Some rooms, although clean and comfortable, are small. Look before moving in.

Across the street, the **Holiday Inn Hotel and Suites,** offers a host of luxuries, at 211 Juárez, tel. 3/613-1763, fax 3/614-9766, email: holidaycentro@infosel.net.mx. Upstairs, rooms are luxuriously appointed in soothing pastels, marble baths, plush carpets, and large beds. For all this and more, you'll pay from about $100 d, with cable TV, phones, a/c, parking, classy restaurant, but no pool; credit cards are accepted.

The three-story, authentically baroque **Hotel Frances,** Maestranza 35, Guadalajara, Jalisco 44100, tel. 3/613-1190 or 3/613-0936, fax 3/658-2831, rises among its fellow monuments on a quiet side street within sight of the Teatro Degollado. Guadalajara's first hotel, built in 1610, has been restored to its original splendor. The 40-odd rooms, all with bath, glow with polished wood, bright tile, and fancy frosted cut-glass windows. Downstairs, an elegant chandelier illuminates the dignified, plant-decorated interior patio and adjacent restaurant. However, in order to increase business, owners have installed nightly live music downstairs, which for some may not fit with the hotel's otherwise old-world ambience. Rates, however, run a very reasonable $50 s, $53 d; credit cards are accepted, fans only, and there's no parking.

The big colonial-facade **Hotel de Mendoza,** V. Carranza 16, Guadalajara, Jalisco 44100, tel. 3/613-4646, fax 3/613-7310, email: hotel@demendoza.com.mx, website: www.demendoza.com.mx, only a couple of blocks north of the Teatro Degollado, is a longtime favorite of Guadalajara repeat visitors. Refined traditional embellishments—neo-Renaissance murals and wall portraits, rich dark paneling, glittering candelabras—grace the lobby, while upstairs, carpeted halls lead to spacious, comfortable rooms furnished with tasteful dark decor, including large baths, thick towels, and many other extras. The 100 rooms and suites rent from $80 s, $90 d, with American cable TV, phones, a/c, a small pool, refined restaurant, parking, and limited wheelchair access; credit cards are accepted.

Although not in the immediate downtown area, the **Hotel Isabel,** J. Guadalupe Montenegro 1572, Guadalajara, Jalisco 44100, tel./fax 3/826-2630, email: hotelisa@telmex.net.mx, in the affluent west-side embassy neighborhood, offers a flowery garden setting at reasonable prices. The Isabel's 1960s-era amenities—comfortably furnished semi-deluxe rooms with phones, small blue pool, popular restaurant, and parking—have long attracted a loyal following of Guadalajara return visitors and local businesspeople. Buses (10 minutes to the city center) run nearby. Its 50 rooms rent for $48 s, $53 d, with ceiling fans and limited wheelchair access.

West Side Luxury Hotels

During the 1980s the Plaza del Sol, a large American-style hotel, shopping, and entertainment complex, mushroomed on west-side Av. Adolfo López Mateos. The Holiday Inn and its plush neighboring hostelries that anchor the development have drawn many of the high-ticket visitors away from the old city center to the Plaza del Sol's shiny shops, restaurants, and clubs.

The **Holiday Inn Crowne Plaza,** at Av. López Mateos Sur 2500, Guadalajara, Jalisco 45050, tel. 3/634-1034, fax 3/631-9393, a quarter-mile south on López Mateos (past the traffic circle), offers a relaxed resort setting. The rooms, most with private view balconies, rise in a 10-story tower above the pool and garden. Their luxurious furnishings, in soothing earth tones, include spacious, marble-accented baths. The 285 rooms start at about $200 s or d, with everything: spa, sauna, gym, children's area, miniature golf, tennis courts, and wheelchair access. Besides the local numbers above, you can reserve by Holiday Inn's toll-free number, 800/465-4329, in the U.S. and Canada, or by email: crownegd@crownegdl.com.mx. For more information, visit Holiday Inn's website at www.basshotels.com.

About a mile north of Plaza del Sol, the **Hotel Fiesta Americana,** Aurelio Aceves 225, Guadalajara, Jalisco 44100, tel. 3/825-3434, fax 3/630-3725, towering above Av. Vallarta, the Hwy. 15 Blvd. Ingreso, offers another luxury hotel option. From the reception area, a serene, carpeted lobby spreads beneath a lofty, light atrium. The 396 plush view rooms are furnished in pastel tones with soft couches, huge beds, and a host of luxury amenities. Rooms rent from about $150 d, with tennis courts, spa, restaurants, pool, and sundeck. For more information and reservations, from Canada and the U.S., dial toll-free 800/FIESTA1 (800/343-7821) or visit Fiesta Americana's website: www.fiestaamericana.com.mx.

Along the same boulevard, about a mile farther west, is the **Hotel Camino Real,** Av. Vallarta 5005, Guadalajara, Jalisco 45040, the graceful queen of Guadalajara luxury hotels. In contrast to its high-rise local competitors, the Camino Real spreads through a luxurious park of lawns, pools, and shady tropical verdure. Guests enjoy tastefully appointed bungalow-style units opening onto semi-private pools and patios. Rates start at $180 s or d and include cable TV, phone, four pools, tennis courts, and a nearby golf course. Reserve through its local number, tel. 3/134-2424, or from the U.S. and Canada, toll-free 800/7-CAMINO (800/722-6466), in Mexico 01-800/903-2100, fax 3/134-2404, email: crgdlsh@webcelmex.net.mx, or website: www.caminoreal.com.

Hotels La Serena and Casa Grande

Two hotels on the edge of town offer interesting bus- and air-travel-related options, respectively. For bus travelers, the big long-distance Central Camionera bus station is at Guadalajara's far southeast edge, at least 20 minutes by taxi (figure $8) from the center. Bus travelers might find it convenient to stay at the sprawling, two-pool, moderately priced modern **Hotel El Serena,** Carretera Zapotlanejo 1500, Guadalajara, Jalisco 45625, tel. 3/600-0910, fax 3/600-0015. It's adjacent to the big bus terminal and has a restaurant. Bus and truck noise, however, may be a problem. Ask for a quiet *(tranquilo)* room. The 600 tidy and comfortable rooms, all with bath, rent for about $30 s or d. Rooms vary; look at more than one before moving in.

For air travelers, the luxuriously spacious and airy **Hotel Casa Grande** just outside the airport terminal exit door, at Calle Interior, Aeropuerto Internacional Miguel Hidalgo s/n, Guadalajara, Jalisco 45640, tel./fax 3/678-9000 or 3/678-9099, email: cchica@mail.udg.mx. Rates run about $150 (ask for a discount) for a comfortable double room with TV, phone, big bed, a/c, and a pool, restaurant, and bar downstairs.

Trailer Park

Guadalajara's last surviving trailer park, the **Hacienda Trailer Park,** P.O. Box 5-494, Guadalajara, Mexico, 45000, tel. 3/627-1724 or 3/627-1843, fax 3/627-2832, is fortunately a good one. About half of the 96 spaces are occupied permanently by the rigs of Canadian and American regulars who return for their annual winter of sunny relaxation. And anyone can see why: In addition to the sparklingly healthful Guadalajara weather, the Hacienda's lavish facilities include, besides the usual concrete pad, all hookups, separate men's and women's toilets and showers, a big blue pool, patio, large clubroom with fireplace, paperback library, pool room, and a/c power. You can even throw in a golf course and Sam's Club shopping center nearby. For all this, rates run $15/day (one free day per week), $300/month, or $250/month on a yearly basis.

While summers at La Hacienda are pretty quiet, winter reservations are mandatory. Get there from four-lane Hwy. 15 about five miles (eight kilometers) west of the Guadalajara city center. If heading eastbound, from the Tepic-Puerto Vallarta direction, pull into the far right lateral lane just after crossing the *periférico* peripheral highway. After about a mile and a half (two km) from the *periférico,* turn right at the Hacienda Trailer Park sign and follow more signs another few hundred yards to the towering entrance gate. In the Hwy. 15 reverse, westbound direction, turn left at the sign about a mile (1.5 km) past Sam's Club.

FOOD

Breakfast and Snacks

Local folks flock to the acres of *fondas* (permanent foodstalls) on the second floor of the **Mercado Libertad.** Located at the east end of Plaza Tapatía; open daily about 7 A.M.–6 P.M. Hearty home-style fare, including Guadalajara's specialty, *birria*—pork, goat, or lamb in savory, spiced tomato-chicken broth—is at its safest and best here. It's hard to go wrong if you make sure your choices are hot and steaming. Market stalls, furthermore, depend on repeat customers and are generally very careful that their offerings are wholesome. Be sure to douse fresh vegetables with plenty of lime *(lima)* juice, however.

Downtown Guadalajara is not overloaded with restaurants, and many of them close early. For long-hours breakfast or supper, however, you can always rely on **Sanborn's,** which retains the 1950s' ambience and menu of its former Denny's owners. Find it right in the middle of town, at the corner of Juárez and 16 de Septiembre, open daily 7:30 A.M.–10 P.M.

For a local variation, head directly upstairs to **Restaurant Esquina** on the same corner, open 7 A.M.–10:30 P.M., or to the other **Sanborn's** across the street, open daily 7:30 A.M.–11 P.M. Besides a tranquil, refined North American-style coffee shop, it has a big gift shop upstairs and a bookstore, offering English-language paperbacks and magazines, downstairs.

For a light breakfast or a break during a hard afternoon of sightseeing, stop in at **Croissants**

Alfredo bakery, north side of Plaza Liberación (in front and east of the Teatro Degollado.) Here, a trove of luscious goodies—flaky croissants, crisp cookies, tasty tarts, and good coffee—can keep you going for hours. Open daily 8 A.M.–9:30 P.M.

If, on the other hand, you need a little break from Mexico, go to **McDonald's** for breakfast (at Juárez and Colón, one short block west of Denny's). There you can get an Egg McMuffin with ham, coffee, and hash browns for about $4 until noon daily.

Downtown Restaurants

Moving west across downtown, from the Plaza Tapatía, first comes the airy, restored Porfirian **Restaurant Rinconada,** 86 Morelos, across the plaza behind the Teatro Degollado, tel. 3/613-9914. The mostly tourist and upper-class local customers enjoy Rinconada for its good meat, fish, and fowl entrées plus the mariachis who wander in from the Plaza Mariachi nearby. By 4 P.M. many afternoons, two or three groups are filling the place with their melodies. Open Mon.–Sat. 8 A.M.–9 P.M., Sunday 1–6 P.M. Moderate to expensive.

Nearby, a pair of clean places for good local food stand out. Try **La Chata,** open daily 8 A.M.–11 P.M., on Corona, between Cotilla and Juárez, next to Bancomer. Although plenty good for breakfast, *cena* (supper) is when the cadre of female cooks come into their own. Here you can have it all: tacos, *chiles rellenos,* tostadas, enchiladas, *pozole, moles,* and a dozen other delights you've probably never heard of, all cooked the way *mamacita* used to. Budget to moderate.

One block south and one block west is the no-nonsense but worthy **Restaurant Málaga,** 16 de Septiembre 210, whose hard-working owner really does come from Málaga, Spain. The food shows it: an eclectic feast of hearty breakfasts, which include a fruit plate and good French bread; a bountiful four-course *comida corrida* for around $5; many salads, sandwiches, and desserts; and savory espresso coffee. Besides the food, customers enjoy live semi-classical piano solos, daily 2–4:30 P.M. Open Mon.–Sat. 7 A.M.–9 P.M., Sunday 8 A.M.–9 P.M. Budget to moderate.

A few blocks farther south, at Corona 291, across from Parque San Francisco, you'll find

La Fería (The Fair), tel. 3/613-7150 or 3/613-1812, which, true to its name, is a party ready to happen: ceilings hung with a rainbow of piñatas and tassels flowing in the breeze of overhead fans, and tables piled high with goodies. Here, vegetarian pretensions must be suspended temporarily, if only for time to sample the enough-in-themselves barbecued appetizers—spicy *chorizo* sausage, tacos, *ahogado* (hot dipped sandwich), ribs, and much more. Actually, vegetarians needn't go hungry—try the mixed salads, guacamole, or soups, for example. Go for it all and share a big *parrillada* specialty of the house appetizer plate with some friends. By the time the food has gone down, the next course—a mariachi concert, complete with rope tricks, singers, with maybe a juggler or magic act thrown in for good measure, will keep you entertained for hours. Open daily 1:30 P.M.–midnight. The complete show starts around 9 P.M. Moderate to expensive.

Return a few blocks west, by the Cathedral, to **Sandy's,** at mezzanine level, above the plaza, northeast corner of Colón and P. Moreno, tel. 3/614-5871. Here, snappy management, service with a flourish, and weekend evening live music make the typical, but tasty, coffee shop menu of soups, salads, meat, pasta, Mexican plates, sandwiches, and desserts seem like an occasion. Open daily 8 A.M.–10:30 P.M. Moderate.

If you're in the mood for a restful lunch or dinner, head west a few blocks to the airy interior patio of **Restaurant San Miguel,** at the northwest corner of Morelos and Donato Guerra, open Wed.–Sat. 8:30 A.M.–11 P.M., Sun.–Tues, 8:30 A.M.–6 P.M.., tel. 3/613-0809. Here, you can enjoy salad, soup (if too salty, send it back), or a full meal and take in the tranquil, traditional ambience. Around you rise the venerable arches and walls of Guadalajara's oldest convent for women, founded by the sisters of Santa Teresa de Jesús, in 1694. The old institution's topsy-turvy history mirrors that of Mexico itself. After its founding, it became the home for the Virgin of Zapopan until her present sanctuary was built decades later. In the 1860s the nuns were expelled by the liberal forces during the War of the Reforms. They were allowed to return by President Díaz in 1895, only to be pushed out by revolutionary general Venustiano Carranza in 1914. The sisters bounced back, returning after the revolution subsided in 1919, but were again expelled by President Calles during the *cristero* rebellion in 1925. Liberal but conciliatory President Lázaro Cárdenas allowed their return in 1939. Finally, the mostly aged sisters vacated their old home, this time voluntarily and for the last time, in 1977.

Continue a few blocks west along Juárez to **Restaurant La Gran China,** Juárez 590, between Martinez and 8 Julio, tel. 3/613-1447, where the Cantonese owner/chef puts out an authentic and tasty array of dishes. Despite the reality of La Gran China's crisp bok choy, succulent spareribs, and smooth savory noodles, they nevertheless seem a small miracle here, half a world away from Hong Kong. Open daily noon–10 P.M. Budget to moderate.

For a variation, try Gran China's plainer but equally authentic neighboring **Restaurant Chong Wah,** Juárez 558, half a block east, at the corner of E.G. Martinez, tel. 3/613-9950; open noon–8 P.M. Budget to moderate.

Restaurants West of Downtown

West of the immediate downtown area, about a mile from the cathedral, is **Restaurant Copenhagen 77,** one of Guadalajara's classiest institutions. Its brand of unpretentious elegance—polished 1940s decor, subdued live jazz, correct attentive service, tasty entrées—will never go out of style. It's upstairs, at 140 Z. Castellanos; follow Juárez nine blocks west of Av. 16 de Septiembre to the west end of Parque Revolución. Open Mon.–Sat. noon–midnight, Sunday 12–6 P.M.; live jazz afternoons 3–4:30 P.M. and nights 8 P.M.–midnight. Moderate to expensive.

ENTERTAINMENT AND EVENTS

Just Wandering Around

Afternoons any day, and Sunday in particular, are good for people-watching around Guadalajara's many downtown plazas. Favorite strolling grounds are the broad Plaza Tapatía west of the cathedral and, especially in the evening, the pedestrian mall-streets, such as Colón, Galeana, Morelos, and Moreno, which meander south and west from cathedral-front Plaza Laureles.

In your wanderings, don't forget to stop by the **Plaza de Los Mariachis,** just east of the Plaza Tapatía, adjacent to the Mercado Libertad

The classic façade of Teatro Degollado presides over Guadalajara's broad, airy Plaza Liberación.

and the big boulevard, Insurgentes, which runs beneath the Plaza Tapatía. Take a sidewalk table, have a drink or snack and enjoy the mariachis' sometimes soulful, sometimes bright, but always enjoyable, offerings.

If you time it right you can enjoy the concert, which the Jalisco State Band has provided since 1898, in the Plaza de Armas adjacent to the cathedral (Thursday and Sunday at 6:30 P.M.), or take in an art film at the Hospicio Cabañas (Mon.–Sat. 4, 6, and 8 P.M.). If you miss these, climb into a *calandria* (horse-drawn carriage) for a ride around town; carriages are available on Liceo between the rotunda and the history museum, just north of the cathedral, for about $15/hour.

Parque Agua Azul

Some sunny afternoon, hire a taxi (about $2 from the city center) and find out why Guadalajara families love Parque Agua Azul. The entrance is on Independencia, about a mile south of Plaza Tapatía. It's a green, shaded place where you can walk, roll, sleep, or lie on the grass. When weary of that, head for the bird park, admire the banana-beaked toucans and squawking macaws, and continue into the aviary where free-flying birds flutter overhead. Nearby, duck into the butterfly *mariposario* and enjoy the flickering rainbow hues of a host of *mariposas*. Continue to the orchids in a towering hothouse, festooned with growing blossoms and misted continuously by a rainbow of spray from the cen-

ter. Before other temptations draw you away, stop for a while at the open-air band or symphony concert in the amphitheater. The park is open Tues.–Sun. 10 A.M.–6 P.M.

Music and Dance Performances

The **Teatro Degollado** hosts world-class opera, symphony, and ballet events. While you're in the Plaza Liberación, drop by the theater box office and ask for a *lista de eventos.* You can also call (or ask your hotel desk clerk to call) the theater box office at 3/614-4773 or 3/616-4991, for reservations and information. Pick up tickets 4–7 P.M. on the day of the performance. For a very typical Mexican treat, attend one of the regular 10 A.M. Sunday University of Guadalajara folkloric ballet performances. They're immensely popular; get tickets in advance.

You can also sample the offerings of the **Instituto Cultural Cabañas,** tel. 3/618-8135 or 3/618-8132. It sponsors many events, both experimental and traditional, including folkloric ballet performances every Wednesday. For more information, ask at the Hospicio Cabañas admission desk. Open Tues.–Sun. 10 A.M.–5 P.M.

Local jazz mecca **Restaurant Copenhagen 77,** at 140 Z. Castellanos, presents Maestro Carlos de la Torre and his group nightly Mon.–Sat. 8 A.M. to midnight and afternoons 3–4:30 P.M. At the west end of Parque Revolución, about a mile west of the cathedral.

Restaurant/club **Peña Cuicalli** (House of Song) offers rock music Tuesday evenings and romantic Latin Thurs.–Sun. evenings. It's at west-side Av. Niños Héroes 1988, tel. 3/825-4690, next to the Niños Héroes monument.

For some very typically Mexican fun, plan a night out for the dinner and mariachi show at **La Fería** restaurant, at Corona 291, across from Parque San Francisco.

Fiestas

Although Guadalajarans always seem to be celebrating, the town really heats up during its three major annual festivals. Starting the second week in June, the southeast neighborhood, formerly the separate village of Tlaquepaque, hosts the **National Ceramics Fair.** Besides its celebrated stoneware, Tlaquepaque shops and stalls are stuffed with a riot of ceramics and folk crafts from all over Mexico, while cockfights, regional food, folk dances, fireworks, and mariachis fill its streets.

A few months later, the entire city, Mexican states, and foreign countries get into the **Festival of October.** For a month, everyone contributes something, from ballet performances, plays, and soccer games to selling papier-mâché parrots and sweet corn in the plazas. Concurrently, Guadalajarans celebrate the traditional **Festival of the Virgin of Zapopan.** Church plazas are awash with merrymakers enjoying food, mariachis, dances (don't miss the Dance of the Conquest), and fireworks. The merrymaking peaks on October 12, when a huge crowd conducts the Virgin from the downtown cathedral to Zapopan. The merrymakers' numbers often swell to a million faithful who escort the Virgin, accompanied by ranks of costumed saints, devils, Spanish conquistadores, and Aztec chiefs.

Dancing

The big west-side hotels are among the most reliable spots in town for dancing. Moving west from the city center, first comes the **Hotel Fiesta Americana,** about four miles along Avenidas Juárez and Vallarta, on the left side of the Minerva traffic circle. Patrons enjoy dancing both in the lobby bar nightly from about 7 P.M. and in the nightclub Caballo Negro from about 9:30 P.M. Call 3/825-3434 to double-check the times.

The **Hotel Holiday Inn Crowne Plaza,** a quarter mile past the Minerva traffic circle, features a live trio for dancing afternoons and evenings in

the lobby bar La Cantera (happy hour 5–8 P.M.), and another trio Thurs.–Sat. from about 9 P.M. at the Bar La Fiesta. Additionally, its Da Vinci disco booms away seasonally from about 9 P.M. Call 3/634-1034 for confirmation.

On the same boulevard, about a mile farther west, the relaxed tropical garden ambience of the **Hotel Camino Real** probably offers Guadalajara's most romantic setting for dancing and dining. Call 3/134-2424 to verify live music programs and times.

Bullfights and Rodeos

Winter is the main season for **corridas de toros,** or bullfights. The bulls charge and the crowds roar *"Olé"* (oh-LAY) Sunday afternoons at the Guadalajara Plaza de Toros (bullring), on Calz. Independencia about two miles north of the Mercado Libertad.

Local associations of *charros* (gentleman cowboys) stage rodeolike Sunday **charreadas** at Guadalajara *lienzos charro* (rodeo rings). Oft-used Guadalajara rodeo rings include Lienzo Charro de Jalisco, 477 Calz. Las Palmas, tel. 3/619-3232, just beyond the southeast side of Parque Agua Azul. Watch for posters, or ask at your hotel desk or the tourist information office, tel. 3/688-1600, for *corrida de toros* and *charreada* details and dates.

The Tequila Express

Ride the tourist train to the town of Tequila, an hour's ride west of Guadalajara, for a tour of the tequila liquor factory. Included are viewing of the blue *agave* harvesting process, a Mexican buffet, and a folkloric show, including dances, mariachis, a roping exhibition, and handicrafts. Buy tickets for the 10 A.M.–6 P.M. Saturday-only tour at the Guadalajara Chamber of Commerce, tel. 3/880-9015 or 3/122-7020, at the corner of Vallarta and Niño Obrero, west of downtown. Tariffs run $52 per adult; kids $32, children under six free.

Entertainment and Events Listings

For many more entertainment ideas, pick up the events schedule at the Hospicio de Cabañas, behind the long pool/fountain at the east end of Plaza Tapatía, or the tourist information office, in the Plaza Tapatía, on Paseo Morelos, the mall-extension of Av. Morelos, behind the Teatro De-

CHARREADAS

The many Jalisco lovers of *charrera*, the sport of horsemanship, enjoy a long-venerated tradition. Boys and girls, coached by their parents, practice riding skills from the time they learn to mount a horse. Privileged young people become noble *charros* or *charras* or *"coronelas"*—gentleman cowboys and cowgirls—whose equestrian habits follow old aristocratic Spanish fashion, complete with broad sombrero, brocaded suit or dress, and silver spurs.

The years of long preparation culminate in the *charreada,* which entire communities anticipate with relish. Although superficially similar to an Arizona rodeo, a Jalisco *charreada* differs substantially. The festivities take place in a *lienzo charro,* literally, the passageway through which the bulls, horses, and other animals run from the corral to the ring. First comes the *cala de caballo,* a test of the horse and rider. The *charros* or *charras* must gallop full speed across the ring and make the horse stop on a dime. Next is the *piales de lienzo,* a roping exhibition during which an untamed horse must be halted and held by having its feet roped. Other bold performances include *jineteo de toro* (bull riding and throwing) and the super-hazardous *paso de la muerte,* in which a rider tries to jump upon an untamed bronco from his or her own galloping mount. *Charreadas* often end in a flourish with the *escaramuza charra,* a spectacular show of riding skill by *charras* in full, colorful dress.

charra

gollado at Morelos 102. Another good source of entertaining events is the weekly English-language Guadalajara **Reporter.** If you can't find a newsstand copy, call the office, at Duque de Rivas 254, Guadalajara, tel. 3/615-2177.

SPORTS

Walking, Jogging, and Exercise Gyms
Walkers and joggers enjoy several spots around Guadalajara. Close in, the **Plaza Liberación** behind the cathedral provides a traffic-free (although concrete) jogging and walking space. Avoid the crowds with morning workouts. If you prefer grass underfoot, try **Parque Agua Azul** (entrance $3) on Calz. Independencia about a mile south of the Libertad Market. An even better jogging-walking space is the **Parque de los Colomos**—hundreds of acres of greenery, laced by special jogging trails—four miles northwest from the center, before Zapopan; take a taxi or bus 51C, which begins at the old bus terminal, near Parque Agua Azul, and continues along Av. 16 de Septiembre, through downtown Guadalajara.

Guadalajara has a number of exercise gyms with the usual machines, plus hot tubs and steam rooms. For example, try the big **World Gym** fitness center, with a battery of weight machines, indoor pool, squash courts, mixed aerobics area, 250-meter jogging track, and women-only weights area. It's at JesÚs Garcia 804, corner of Miguel Angel de Quevedo, tel. 3/640-0576, beside the Cinema Charlie Chaplin.

Tennis, Golf, and Swimming
Although Guadalajara has few, if any, public tennis courts, the west-side Hotel Camino Real, Av. Vallarta 5005, tel. 3/134-2424, rents its tennis courts to the public, by appointment, for about $10 per hour. Also, the Hotels Fiesta Americana, Aurelio Aceves 225, Glorieta Minerva, tel. 3/825-3434, and the Holiday Inn, Av. López Mateos Sur 2500, tel. 3/634-1034, have courts for guests.

The 18-hole **Burgos del Bosque Golf Club** welcomes nonmembers from dawn to dusk Tues.–Sunday. Greens fee runs $50 Tues.–Fri. and $60 Saturday and Sunday. Clubs and carts rent for about $14 and $23; a caddy will cost about $12. Get there via Chapala Hwy. 44, the south-of-town extension of Calz. J. Gonzales Gallo. The golf course is at Km 6.5, past the edge of town, near Parque Montenegro.

Nearly all the luxury hotels have swimming pools. One of the prettiest (but unheated) pools perches atop the moderately priced Hotel Calinda Roma in the heart of town (corner Juárez and Degollado).

If your hotel doesn't have a pool, try the **World Gym** (above), or go to the very popular public pool and picnic ground at Balneario Lindo Michoacán, Rio Barco 1614, corner Calz. J. Gonzalez Gallo, tel. 3/635-9399. Find it about two miles along Gallo southeast of Parque Agua Azul. Open daily 10 A.M.–5 P.M.; entrance about $4 adults, $2 kids.

Farther out but even prettier are the canyon-country *balnearios* **Los Camachos** and **Nuevo Paraíso** on Hwy. 54 north toward Saltillo. (For more details, see "Out-of-Downtown Sights," earlier in this section.)

SHOPPING

Downtown

The sprawling **Mercado Libertad,** at the east end of Plaza Tapatía, has several specialty areas distributed through two main sections. Most of the handicrafts are in the eastern, upper half. While some stalls carry guitars and sombreros, leather predominates—in jackets, belts, saddles, and the most huaraches you'll ever see under one roof. Here, bargaining *es la costumbre*. Competition, furthermore, gives buyers the advantage. If the seller refuses your reasonable offer, simply turning in the direction of another stall will often bring him to his senses. The upper floor also houses an acre of foodstalls, many of them excellent.

A central courtyard leads past a lineup of bird-sellers and their caged charges to the Mercado Libertad's lower half, where produce, meat, and spice stalls fill the floor. (Photographers, note the photogenic view of the produce floor from the balcony above.) Downstairs, don't miss browsing intriguing spice and *yerba* (herb) stalls, which feature mounds of curious dried plants, gathered from the wild, often by village *curanderos* (traditional healers). Before you leave, be sure to look over the piñatas, which make colorful, unusual gifts.

Of the few downtown handicrafts shops, a pair stand out. Right near the city center, try the **Galerias El Convento** complex, in a big restored mansion, on Donato Guerra, corner of Morelos, four blocks west of the Cathedral front, between Morelos and Pedro Moreno. Inside, a sprinkling of shops offer fine arts and handicrafts, from leather furniture and Tlaquepaque glass to Baroque religious antiques and fine silver. Stop for a restful drink or meal at the Restaurant San Miguel (See "Downtown Restaurants," preceding).

You might also find what you're looking for at the government **Casa de Artesanías Agua Azul,** by Parque Agua Azul. Here, you can choose from virtually everything—brilliant stoneware, handsome gold and silver jewelry, and endearing ceramic, brass, and papier-mâché animals—short of actually going to Tonalá, Tlaquepaque, and Taxco. Find it at Calz. Gonzales Gallo 20, next to Parque Agua Azul (off of Independencia); hours are Mon.–Sat. 10 A.M.–7 P.M., Sunday 10 A.M.–2 P.M.

Two other promising, but less extensive, downtown handicrafts sources in the Plaza Tapatía vicinity are at the **tourist information office** at Morelos 102, and the native vendors in the adjacent alley, called Rincón del Diablo.

Tlaquepaque

Tlaquepaque was once a sleepy village of potters miles from Guadalajara. Attracted by the quiet of the country, rich families built palatial homes during the 19th century. Now, entrepreneurs have moved in and converted them into upscale restaurants, art galleries, and showrooms, stuffed with quality Tonalá and Tlaquepaque ceramics, glass, metalwork, and papier-mâché.

In spite of having been swallowed by the city, Tlaquepaque still has the feel and look of a small colonial town, with its cathedral and central square leading westward onto the mansion-decorated main street, now mall, Av. Independencia.

Mercado Libertad's exterior patio provides a cool, shady break from Guadalajara shopping chores.

Although generally pricier than Tonalá, Tlaquepaque still has bargains. Proceed by finding the base prices at the more ordinary crafts stores in the side streets that branch off of the main mall-street Independencia. Then, price out the showier, upscale merchandise in the galleries along Independencia itself. For super-fine examples of Tlaquepaque and Tonalá crafts, be sure to stop by the **Museo Regional de Cerámica y Arte Popular,** 237 Independencia, open Tues.–Sat. 10 A.M.–6 P.M., Sun. 10 A.M.–3 P.M.

From the *museo,* cross the street to the **Sergio Bustamante** store, tel. 3/639-5519, upscale outlet for the famous sculptor's arresting, whimsical studies in juxtaposition. Bustamante supervises an entire Guadalajara studio-factory of artists who put out hundreds of one-of-a-kind variations on a few human, animal, and vegetable themes. Prices seem to depend mainly on size; rings and bracelets may go for as little as $200, while a two-foot humanoid chicken may run $2,000. Don't miss the restroom. Open Mon.–Sat 10 A.M.–7 P.M., Sun. 10 A.M.–2 P.M.

Next to Bustamante, at 232 Independencia, **La Rosa Cristal** is one of the few spots where (until 2 P.M. daily) visitors may get a chance to see glassblowers practicing their time-honored Tlaquepaque craft. Although the glassblowers do not actually work in the store, ask them to show you (before about 1 P.M.) to the nearby location where they do. The results of their work—clutches of giant red, green, blue, and silver glass balls—are hard to forget. Open Mon.–Sat. 10

A.M.–7 P.M., Sunday 10 A.M.–2 P.M.

Not far west, at the intersection of Independencia and Alfarareros (Potters), a pair of regally restored former mansions, now galleries, enjoy a dignified retirement facing each other on opposite sides of the street. **La Casa Canela,** Independencia 258, tel. 3/657-1343, takes pride in its museum-quality religious art, furniture, paper flowers, pottery, blown glass, and classic, blue-on-white Tlaquepaque stoneware. Open Mon.–Fri. 10 A.M.–2 P.M. and 3–7 P.M., Saturday 10 A.M.–6 P.M., Sunday 11 A.M.–3 P.M. Across the street, **Antigua de Mexico,** Independencia 255, tel. 3/635-3402, specializes in baroque gilt wood antiques and reproductions, being one of the few studios in Mexico to manufacture fine 17th century-style furniture. Open Mon.–Fri. 10 A.M.–2 P.M. and 3–7 P.M., Saturday 10 A.M.–6 P.M.

Getting to Tlaquepaque: Taxi (about $15 roundtrip) or ride the usually crowded city bus 275 (look for "Tlaquepaque" scrawled on the front window), from stops (such as at Madero) along downtown Av. 16 de Septiembre. By car, from the center of town, drive Av. Revolución southeast about four miles to the Niños Héroes traffic circle. From Av. Niños Héroes, the first right off the traffic circle, continue about a mile to the west end of Av. Independencia, on the left.

Tonalá
About five miles past Tlaquepaque, Tonalá perches at Guadalajara's country edge. When

the Spanish arrived in the 1520s, Tonalá was dominant among the small kingdoms of the Atemajac Valley. Tonalá's widow-queen and her royal court were adorned by the glittering handiwork of an honored class of silver and gold crafters. Although the Spaniards carted off the valuables, the tradition of Tonalá craftsmanship remains today. To the visitor, everyone in Tonalá seems to making something. Tonalá family patios are piled with their specialties, whether it be pottery, stoneware, brass, or papier-mâché.

Right at the source, bargains couldn't be better. Dozens of shops dot the few blocks around Tonalá's central plaza corner at Av. Hidalgo (north-south) and Av. Juárez (east-west). For super-bargaining opportunities and *mucho* holiday excitement and color, visit the Thursday and Sunday *tianguis* (market), which spreads along the tree-lined *periférico* highway about four blocks west of the Tonalá plaza.

Under any circumstances, make the **Museo Tonallan** your first stop, at Ramón Corona 75, near the corner of Constitución, about two blocks east and two blocks north of the town plaza; open Mon.–Sat. approx. 9 A.M.–2 P.M. and 4–6 P.M. Although it was only recently organized, the museum staff members plan to install exhibits tracing the origins of local crafts in a historical context, working up to modern popular handicrafts. They also plan to eventually have artisans working at the site.

After the museum, go back down Constitución to Hidalgo, where several shops stand out. Moving south along Hidalgo toward the town plaza from Constitución, **Artesanías Garay,** Hidalgo 86, one of several *fábrica* (factory) shops that retail directly, offers a host of Tonalá motifs. The shop is especially proud of its fine floral-design stoneware. Open Mon.–Sat. 10 A.M.–3 P.M. and 4–7 P.M., Sunday 10 A.M.–3 P.M.; credit cards are accepted.

El Bazar de Sermel, Hidalgo 67, tel. 3/683-0010, diagonally across the street, has stretched the Tonalá papier-mâché tradition to the ultimate. Stop in and pick out the life-size flamingo, pony, giraffe, or zebra you've always wanted for your living room. Open Mon.–Fri. 9 A.M.–6:30 P.M., Saturday 9 A.M.–2 P.M., Sunday 10 A.M.–3 P.M.

La Mexicanía, at 13 Hidalgo, tel. 3/683-0152, corner of the plaza, offers an interesting eclectic assortment, both from Tonalá and other parts of Mexico. These include Huichol Indian yarn paintings and God's eyes, painted tin Christmas decorations from Oaxaca, and Guanajuato papier-mâché clowns. Open Mon.–Sat. 10 A.M.–7 P.M.

Around the corner, a few steps west on Juárez, **Artesanías Nuño,** Juárez 59, tel. 3/683-0011, displays a fetching menagerie, including parrots, monkeys, flamingos, and toucans, in papier-mâché, brass, and ceramics. Open Mon.–Sat. 10 A.M.–7 P.M., Sunday 10 A.M.–5 P.M.; bargain for very reasonable buys.

Continue south past the Juárez plaza corner (where Hidalgo becomes Madero) one block, to **La Antigua Tonalá,** Madero 50, tel. 3/683-0200. There you'll find a storeful of hand-hewn tables, chairs, and chests all complete with the Tonalá stoneware place settings to go with them. Open Mon.–Sat. 10 A.M.–7 P.M., Sunday 10 A.M.–3 P.M.; they ship.

Getting to Tonalá: Taxi (about $20 roundtrip) or ride the oft-crowded city bus 275 (look for "Tonalá" scrawled on the windshield) from the stops, such as the corner of Madero, on downtown Av. 16 de Septiembre. By car, drive Av. Revolución about six miles southeast of the city center to the big Plaza Camichines interchange. Continue ahead along the Carretera Tonalá *libre* (free) branch; avoid forking onto the Hwy. 90 Carretera Zaplotanejo *cuota* toll road. The Carretera Tonalá continues due east for about three more miles, passing under the Carretera Zaplotanejo. Continue across the arterial *periférico* (peripheral highway); three blocks farther turn left and within a few blocks you'll be at the Tonalá central plaza.

Photo, Grocery, and Department Stores

The several branches of the **Laboratorios Julio** chain offer quick photofinishing and a big stock of photo supplies and film, including professional 120 transparency and negative rolls. Its big downtown branch is at Colón 125 between Juárez and Cotilla, tel. 3/614-2850; open Mon.–Sat. 10 A.M.–8 P.M., Sunday 10 A.M.–6 P.M. Its west-side store, at Av. Americas 425, corner of Manuel Acuña, tel. 3/616-8286, is open daily 8 A.M.–9 P.M.

For convenient, all-in-one shopping, including groceries, try **Gigante,** downtown on Juárez, corner of Martínez, tel. 3/613-8638. Open daily 8 A.M.–10 P.M. For even more under one air-conditioned roof, try the big **Comercial Mexicana** at Plaza del Sol, Av. Lípez Mateos Sur 2077. Open daily 9 A.M.–9 P.M.

SERVICES AND INFORMATION

Money Exchange
Change more types of money (U.S., Canadian, German, Japanese, French, Italian, and Swiss) for the best rates at the downtown streetfront **Banamex** office and ATM (Juárez, corner of Corona, open Mon.–Fri. 9 A.M.–5 P.M.). After hours, go to one of the dozens of *casas de cambio* (money changers) nearby, a block east of Banamex, on Cotilla between Maestranza and Corona.

The Guadalajara **American Express** branch is on the west side, at Plaza Los Arcos, Av. Vallarta 2440, about three miles west of the city center, tel. 3/818-2323, fax 3/616-7665. It provides both travel-agency and member financial services, including personal-check and traveler's-check cashing, Mon.–Fri. 9 A.M.–6 P.M., Saturday 9 A.M.–1 P.M.

Consulates
The **U.S. Consulate** is at Progreso 175 (between Cotillo and Libertad) about a mile west of the town center; open Mon.–Fri. 8 A.M.–4:30 P.M., tel. 3/825-2020 and 3/825-2031. The **Canadian Consulate** is in the Hotel Fiesta Americana at Aurelio Aceves 225, local 31, near the intersection of Av. López Mateos and Av. Vallarta, tel. 3/615-6215; open Mon.–Fri. 8:30 A.M.–2 P.M. and 3–5 P.M.

Consular agents from many other countries maintain Guadalajara offices. Consult the local Yellow Pages, under *"Embajadas, Legaciones y Consulados."*

Health, Police, and Emergencies
If you need a doctor, the **Hospital Mexico Americano,** Colomos 2110, tel. 3/641-3141, ambulance emergency 3/642-7152, has specialists on call. For ordinary medications, one of the best sources is the Guadalajara chain, **Farmacia ABC,** with many branches. You'll find one downtown at 518 P. Moreno between M. Ocampo and D. Guerra, tel. 3/614-2950, open daily 8 A.M.–9 P.M.

For **police** emergencies, call the radio patrol (dial 060) or the police headquarters at 3/617-6060. In case of **fire,** call the *servicio bomberos* fire station at 3/619-5241 or 3/619-0794.

Post Office, Telephone, Public Fax, and Internet
The downtown Guadalajara Post Office is two blocks west of the Teatro Degollado, just past the Hotel Mendoza, at Independencia and V. Carranza. **Telecomunicaciones** offers public telephone and fax in the city center, at Degollado and Madero, below the city *juzgado* "hoosegow" (jail), Mon.–Fri. 8 A.M.–6 P.M., Saturday 9 A.M.–2 P.M.

Connect with the Internet at travel agency Ramos Ramírez (at the street entrance of Hotel Internacional), at Pedro Moreno 570, five blocks west of the cathedral; call ahead, at tel. 3/613-7318.

Tourist Information Office
The main Guadalajara tourist information office is in the Plaza Tapatía, on Paseo Morelos, the mall-extension of Av. Morelos, behind the Teatro Degollado, at Morelos 102, tel. 3/668-1600 or 3/668-1601, fax 3/668-1686; open Mon.–Fri. 9 A.M.–7:30 P.M. and Sat.–Sun. 9 A.M.–1 P.M. For lots of online information, visit the website: www.visita.jalisco.gob.mx.

Publications
Among the best Guadalajara sources of English-language magazines is **Sanborn's,** a North American-style gift, book, and coffee shop chain. It's located downtown, corner Juárez and 16 de Septiembre, open 7:30 A.M.–11 P.M.; at Plaza Vallarta, Av. Vallarta 1600, open 7–1 A.M.; and Plaza del Sol, 2718 López Mateos Sur, open 7–1 A.M.

You can usually get the excellent *News* from Mexico City at one of the newsstands edging the Plaza Laureles, across from the cathedral.

While you're downtown, if you see a copy of the informative local weekly, the ***Colony Reporter,*** buy it. Its pages will be stuffed with valuable items for visitors, including local events calendars, restaurant and performance reviews, meaty feature articles on local customs and excursions, and entertainment, restaurant, hotel, and rental listings. (If you can't find one, call the

Reporter, tel. 3/615-2177, to find out where you can get a copy.)

Additionally, suburban southwest-side **Librería Sandi,** at Tepeyac 718, Colonia Chapalita, Guadalajara, tel. 3/121-0863, open 9:30 A.M.–2:30 P.M. and 3:30–7 P.M. has one of the best selections of English-language books and magazines in the Guadalajara area.

Language and Cultural Courses

The University of Guadalajara's **Centro de Estudios Para Extranjeros** (Study Center for Foreigners) conducts an ongoing program of cultural studies for visitors. Besides formal language, history, and art instruction, students may also opt for live-in arrangements with local families. Write the center at Tomás S. V. Gómez 125, P.O. Box 1-2130, Guadalajara, Jalisco 44100, or call tel. 3/616-4399 or 3/616-4382, fax 3/616-4013, or email: cepe@corp.udg.mx.

GETTING THERE AND AWAY

By Air

Several air carriers connect the **Guadalajara Airport** (officially, the Miguel Hidalgo International Airport, code-designated GDL) with many U.S. and Mexican destinations.

Mexicana Airlines flights, reservations tel. 3/678-7676, arrivals and departures tel. 3/688-5775, connect frequently with U.S. destinations of Los Angeles, San Francisco, San Jose, Oakland, Las Vegas, and Chicago, and Mexican destinations of Puerto Vallarta, Tijuana, Mexicali, Hermosillo, Mexico City, and Cancún.

Aeroméxico flights, reservations, arrivals and departures tel. 3/669-0202, connect frequently with U.S. destinations of Los Angeles, Phoenix, Atlanta, and New York, and Mexican destinations of Puerto Vallarta, Acapulco, Culiacán, Monterrey, Tijuana, and Mexico City.

Aerocalifornia, reservations tel. 3/616-2525, flight information tel. 3/688-5514, connects with U.S. destinations of Los Angeles and Tucson, and Mexican destinations of Tijuana, Mazatlán, La Paz, Los Cabos, Culiacán, Los Mochis, Durango, Monterrey, Puebla, and Mexico City.

Other carriers include: **American Airlines,** reservations toll-free in Mexico, tel. 91-800/362-70 or local 3/616-4090, which connects daily with Los Angeles and Dallas; **Delta Air Lines,** reservations toll-free in Mexico, tel. 01-800/902-2100, or local 3/630-3530, which connects several times daily with Los Angeles; **Continental Airlines,** reservations toll-free in Mexico, tel. 01-800/900-5000, local reservations, 3/647-4251, which connects twice daily with Houston; and **America West Airlines,** tel. 800/235-9292, which connects seasonally with Phoenix. For information and reservations contact a travel agent, such as American Express, tel. 3/818-2323 or 3/818-2325.

Airport arrival is simplified by a money exchange counter (daytime hours only) and banks with ATMs inside the terminal (Serfin) and just outside the terminal door (Bital). Many car rental agencies maintain booths: Avis, tel. 3/678-0502; Alamo, tel. 3/613-5551 or 3/613-5560, email: alamogdl@ibm.net; Arrasa, tel. 3/615-0522; Budget, tel. 3/613-0027 or 3/613-0286; Dollar, 3/688-6319; Hertz, tel. 3/688-5633 or 3/688-6080; National, tel. 3/614-7175 or 3/614-7994, email: nationalcar@1cabonet.com.mx; Optima, tel. 3/688-5532 or 3/812-0437; Ohama, tel. 3/614-6902; and Thrifty, 3/825-5080, ext. 121.

Ground transportation is likewise well organized for shuttling arrivees the 12 miles (19 km) along Chapala Hwy. 44 into town. Tickets for *colectivos* (shared VW van taxis, about $9 for one, $11 for two persons) and *taxis especiales* (individual taxis, $12 for one to four persons) are sold at a booth just outside the terminal door. No public buses serve the Guadalajara airport.

Many simple and economical card-operated public telephones are also available; buy telephone cards at the snack bar by the far right-hand terminal exit. Also you'll find a newsstand (lobby floor), bookstore (upstairs), and many crafts and gift shops convenient for last-minute business and purchases.

Airport departure is equally simple, as long as you save enough for your international departure tax of $19 ($12 federal tax, $7 local), unless it's already included in your ticket. A post office, a (securemail) Mexpost office, and *telecomunicaciones* office (telegraph, fax, long-distance phone) are inside the terminal, right of the entrance as you enter). A public telephone and fax office operates mid-terminal, by the car rental counters.

By Car or RV

Four major routes connect Guadalajara to the rest of the Puerto Vallarta region. From **Tepic-Compostela-Puerto Vallarta** in the west, federal Hwy. 15 winds about 141 miles (227 km) over the Sierra Madre Occidental crest. The new *cuota* (toll) expressway, although expensive ($30 for a car, RVs more), greatly increases safety, decreases wear and tear, and cuts the Guadalajara-Tepic driving time to three hours. The *libre* (free) route, by contrast, has two oft-congested lanes that twist steeply up and down the high pass and bump through towns. For safety, allow around five hours to and from Tepic.

To and from Puerto Vallarta, bypass Tepic via the toll *corta* (cutoff) that connects Hwy. 15 (at Chapalilla) with Hwy. 200 (at Compostela). Figure on four hours total if you use the entire toll expressway (about $20), six hours if you don't.

From Barra de Navidad in the southwest, traffic curves and climbs smoothly along two-lane Hwy. 80 for the 190 miles (306 km) to Guadalajara. Allow around five hours.

An easier road connection with Barra de Navidad runs through Manzanillo along *autopistas* (superhighways) 200, 110, and 54 D. Easy grades allow a leisurely 55 mph (90 km/hour) most of the way for this 192-mile (311-km) trip. Allow about four hours from Manzanillo; add another hour for the additional smooth (follow the Manzanillo town toll bypass) 38 miles (61 km) of Hwy. 200 to or from Barra de Navidad.

From Lake Chapala in the south, the four level, straight lanes of Hwy. 44 whisk traffic safely the 33 miles (53 km) to Guadalajara in about 45 minutes.

By Bus

The long-distance Guadalajara *camionera central* (central bus terminal) is at least 20 minutes by taxi (about $8) from the city center. The huge modern complex sprawls past the southeast-sector intersection of the old Tonalá Hwy. (Carretera Antigua Tonalá) and the new Zaplotanejo Autopista (Freeway) Hwy. 90. The *camionera central* is sandwiched between the two highways. Tell your taxi driver which bus line you want or where you want to go, and he'll drop you at one of the terminal's seven *modulos* (buildings). For arrival and departure convenience, you might consider staying at the adja-

cent, moderately priced Hotel La Serena.

Each of the *modulos* is self-contained, with restrooms, cafeteria or snack bar, stores offering snack foods (but few fruits or veggies), bottled drinks, common medicines and drugs, and handicrafts. Additionally, *modulos* 1, 3, and 7 have public long-distance telephone and fax service.

Dozens of competing bus lines offer departures. The current king of the heap is **Estrella Blanca,** a holding company that operates a host of subsidiaries, notably Elite, Turistar, Futura, Transportes del Norte, Transportes Norte de Sonora, and Transportes Chihuahenses. Second-largest and trying harder is **Flecha Amarilla,** which offers "Servicios Coordinados" through several subsidiaries. Trying even harder are the biggest independents: Omnibus de Mexico, Enlaces Terrestres Nacionals ("National Ground Network"), Transportes Pacífico, and Autobuses del Occidente, all of whom would very much like to be your bus company.

To northwest **Pacific Coast** destinations, go to either *modulo* 3 or 4. Take first-class **Elite,** tel. 3/600-0601, via Tepic and Mazatlán, to the U.S. border at Nogales, Mexicali, and Tijuana. Alternatively, ride first-class Transportes Pacífico, tel. 3/600-0211, for the same northwest Pacific destinations as Elite. For southwest Pacific Coast destinations, go by **Transportes Pacífico,** either first-class, tel. 3/600-0601, *modulo* 3, or second-class, tel. 3/600-0450, *modulo* 4, for the small southwest Nayarit coastal towns and villages, such as Las Varas, La Peñita, and Rincón de Guayabitos, en route to Puerto Vallarta. Moreover, you can ride second-class **Transportes Norte de Sonora** west and northwest, tel. 3/679-0463, *modulo* 4, to smaller northern Nayarit and Sinaloa towns, such as Tepic, San Blas, Santiago Ixcuintla-Mexcaltitán, Acaponeta-Novillero, and Escuinapa-Teacapan.

Additionally, in *modulo* 3, second-class **Autotransportes Guadalajara-Talpa-Mascota,** tel. 3/600-0098, offers connections to the non-touristed western Jalisco mountain towns of **Talpa and Mascota,** where you can connect on to Puerto Vallarta by the rugged super-scenic backcountry route via the antique mining village of San Sebastián.

For far southern Pacific destinations of **Zihuatanejo, Acapulco, and the Oaxaca coast** you can go one of two ways: Direct to Acapulco by

Futura (*modulo* 3) east, then south, all in one day, bypassing Mexico City (one or two buses per day). Alternatively, go less directly via Elite (*modulo 3*) west to Tepic or Puerto Vallarta (or by a **Flecha Amarilla** affiliate, *modulo* 1, south to Tecomán), where you must transfer to a Zihuatanejo-Acapulco southbound Elite bus. This may necessitate an overnight in either Tepic, Puerto Vallarta, or Tecomán and at least two days traveling (along the scenic, untouristed Pacific route, however), depending upon connections. Finally, in Acapulco, connections will be available southeast to the Oaxaca coast.

If you're bound southeast directly to the city of **Oaxaca,** go conveniently by Futura (*modulo* 3) to Mexico City Norte (North) station, where you transfer, via ADO (Autobuses del Oriente), southeast direct to Oaxaca City.

Also at *modulo* 4 allied lines Autocamiones del Pacífico and Transportes Cihuatlán, tel. 3/600-0076 (second-class), tel. 3/600-0598 (first class), together offer service south along scenic mountain Hwy. 80 to the Pacific via Autlán to **Melaque, Barra de Navidad and Manzanillo.**

For eastern to southern destinations in **Jalisco, Guanajuato, Aguascalientes, Michoacán, and Colima,** go to either *modulos* 1 or 2. In *modulo* 2, ride first-class **ETN,** tel. 3/600-0501, east to Celaya, León, and Aguascalientes, or west and southwest to Uruapan, Morelia, Colima, Manzanillo, and Puerto Vallarta. Also in *modulo* 1, Flecha Amarilla subsidiary lines, tel. 3/600-0052, offer service to a swarm of northeast destinations, including León, Guanajuato, and San Miguel de la Allende, and southeast and south to Uruapan, Morelia, Puerto Vallarta, Manzanillo, Barra de Navidad, and untouristed villages—El Super, Tomatlán, and El Tuito—on the Jalisco coast. Also, from *modulo* 2, **Autobuses del Occidente,** tel. 3/600-0055, offers departures southeast to Michoacán destinations of Zamora, Zitácuaro, Quiroga, Pátzcuaro, and Uruapan. Additionally, **Autotransportes Sur de Jalisco** first- and second-class buses offer southern departures, via old Hwy. 54 or *autopista* 54 D, via Sayula, Ciudad Guzman, Tecomán, and Cuyutlán, to Manzanillo.

In *modulo* 5, small independent **Linea Azul** tel. 3/679-0453, offers departures northeast, via Tampico, to the U.S. border, at Matamoros and Reynosa.

Omnibus de Mexico, tel. 3/600-0184 or 3/600-0469, dominates *Modulo* 6, offering broad service in mostly north and northeast directions: to the U.S. border at Juárez via Zacatecas, Saltillo, Durango, Torreón, Fresnillo, and Chihuahua; and northeast, via Tampico, to the U.S. border at Reynosa and Matamoros.

The Estrella Blanca subsidiary lines operating out of *modulo* 7 also mostly offer connections north. Ride first-class **Transportes Chihuahuenses,** tel. 3/679-0404, via San Juan de los Lagos, Zacatecas, Torreon, Chihuahua, and Juárez; luxury-class Turistar, tel. 3/679-0404, along the same routes as Transportes Chihuahuenses; or first-class **Transportes del Norte,** tel. 3/679-0404, via San Juan de los Lagos, Zacatecas, Saltillo, Monterrey, and Matamoros, at the U.S. border.

For many other subsidiary regional destinations, buses arrive and depart from the **camionera antigua** (old bus terminal), at the end of Estadio, off Calz. Independencia downtown. For Lake Chapala, ride one of several daily departures of the second-class red and white Autotransportes Guadalajara-Chapala buses. For Talpa, Mascota, and San Sebastián in the western Jalisco mountains, go by the red second-class Auto Transportes Guadalajara-Talpa-Mascota, tel. 3/619-0708.

By Train
Passenger rail service to and from Guadalajara has been stopped by the privatization of the Mexican Railways' Pacific route. Unless future government subsidies offset private losses, Pacific passenger trains will have gone the way of buggy whips and Stanley Steamers.

LAKE CHAPALA: CHAPALA AND AJIJIC

The folks who live around shallow Lake Chapala, Mexico's largest lake, pride themselves on their lake's brilliant sunsets, its quiet country ambience, and its famously temperate weather. Formed by gigantic earth movements millions of years ago, the lake originally spread far beyond its present cucumber-shaped 50- by 20-mile (80- by 30-km) basin south of Guadalajara.

Now, rounded, gentle mountains shelter the sprinkling of small towns and villages that decorate the shoreline. Chapala's sleepy, rural southern lakeside contrasts with the northern shore, which has become both a favored holiday retreat for well-to-do Guadalajara families and home to a sizable colony of American and Canadian retirees. The 10-mile procession of petite, picturesque towns—Chapala, Chula Vista, San Antonio, La Floresta, Ajijic, San Juan Cosala, and others—scattered along the northern shore have collectively become known as the "Chapala Riviera." Here, a stream of visitors and an abundance of resident talent and resources sustain good restaurants and hotels as well as fine shops that offer the works of an accomplished community of artisans and artists.

HISTORY

Bands of hunter-gatherers, attracted by the lake basin's trove of fish, game, and wild fruits and grains, may have occupied Lake Chapala's shores as early as 10,000 B.C. Interestingly, they probably used the strategy of driving wild animals into the lake, where they could be subdued more easily. The Regional Museum of Guadalajara displays remains of a number of species, such as antelope, camel, horse, and a very complete mammoth, all unearthed at likely hunting grounds near the prehistoric lakeshore.

Recorded history began for Lake Chapala during the 1400s when a tribe known as the "Cocas," after victorious campaigns against Purépecha (Tarascans) of Michoacán, established themselves at Cutzatlán (now San Juan Cosala) on Chapala's northwest shore. Under King Xitomatl, Cutzatlán flourished. A flurry of new towns, such as Axixic (now Ajijic), Xilotepec

(now Jocotepec), and later Chapala (around 1500), was established.

The Spanish, in the person of Captain Alonso de Avalos and a platoon of soldiers, arrived in the early 1520s. Impressed by the Spanish armor, guns, and horses, the Cocas offered little resistance. Franciscan padres arrived soon afterwards, baptized the Cocas's chief Andrés Carlos and, not insignificantly, named their new Ajijic church San Andrés.

It was not long before Ajijic and Chapala, the Lake Chapala Riviera's best-known towns, began to assume their present characters. The curative springs around Ajijic (in Nahuatl "the place where water overflows") have long attracted travelers and settlers to the lakeshore. Spanish colonists arrived early, in 1530, when the Saenz family was awarded rights of *encomienda* to the labor of the local people. Their establishment, the Hacienda de Cuije, prospered, manufacturing *mescal* liquor for generations. During the 1910 revolution, the local campesinos divided its holdings into a number of small *ejidos* that tried several schemes, including coffee production and gold refining, with mixed results. In 1938, new managers converted the old main house into a hotel, the Posada Ajijic, which now lives on as a picturesque, elegant lakeshore restaurant.

In contrast to Ajijic, the origin of the name "Chapala" remains an intriguing mystery. Every scholar seems to have a different explanation. It's tempting to believe that the name has something to do with grasshoppers, which the Aztecs called *chapulín*. Another possibility stems from the name Chapa, a local chief at the time of the conquest. The name also might originate with *chapalac,* which translates as "wet place." On the other hand, the word *chapaltlán* (place of many pots) provides the most intriguing explanation of all. It seems that warriors of the Coca tribe used to sanctify themselves by ritually splattering the blood of their vanquished battlefield victims on themselves. Later, as a ceremonial substitute for their own bodies, they sprinkled the victims' blood on small clay jars and figurines, which they tossed into the water at the Chapala lakefront as offerings to their lake god. Fishing

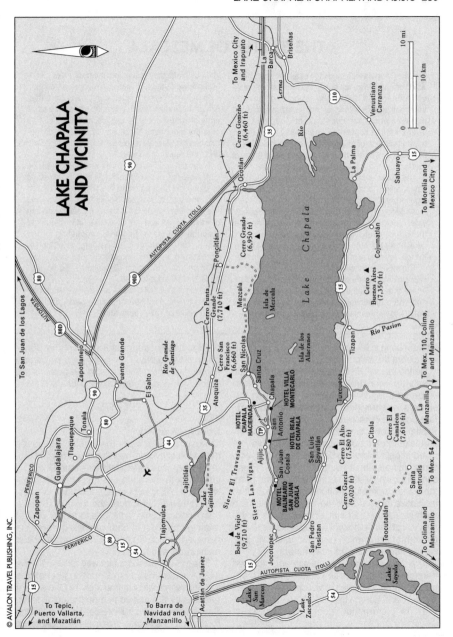

LAKE CHAPALA
AND VICINITY

© AVALON TRAVEL PUBLISHING, INC.

THE BATTLE OF MEZCALA

Lake Chapala was the stage of a renowned heroic drama played out during the Mexican war of independence (1810-21). The struggle centered on the small, half-mile-long island of Mezcala, located mid-lake about six miles east of Chapala town. There, for four continuous years 1812-16, a determined battalion of *insurgente* guerrillas held off the best the royal Spanish army and navy could throw at them.

The rebels' principal players were Marcos Castellanos, a fiery local priest; and José Santana, an indigenous village leader who by heroic example eventually became the rebel commander. On the Spanish side, General José de la Cruz directed the several thousand royalist soldiers deployed around the lakeshore; his subordinate officer, José Navarro, led the day-to-day campaign against the insurgents.

The rebels—a thousand armed men, plus women and children—retreated to the island in late 1812. There they fortified their island with walls, ditches, and sharp underwater stakes. By day, they grew fruits and vegetables and manufactured their own

shot; by night, they resupplied themselves at friendly shoreline farms and raided lakeshore garrisons.

In June 1813, both sides were ready for battle. Royalist commanders, having accumulated a small army of troops, acres of supplies, and boats carried over the mountains all the way from San Blas, demanded the Mezcala rebels surrender. "Let blood run first," the rebels answered.

Blood did run, freely, for three years. Hundreds on both sides fell, as the tide of battle swept from island to shore and back again. In late 1816, many rebels, suffering from a two-year blockade, were sick and starving. General de la Cruz was meanwhile weary of wasting lives and resources in a futile attempt to dislodge the rebels. Santana, negotiating for the rebels, bargained for a full pardon, including repaired farms, supplies, and seeds for his men, and a good church position for Castellanos. To his surprise, de la Cruz accepted.

In November 1816 the rebels left the island, inspiring others to fight on for the *independencia* they finally achieved five years later.

nets still bring in little ceramic human forms or animals from the lakebottom.

During the twilight decade of President Porfirio Díaz's 34-year rule, Lake Chapala began to surge as a tourist destination. Many rich foreigners, encouraged by government *laissez-faire* policies, were living in Mexico. One of them, Septimus Crow, came and developed hot springs and lakeshore land around Chapala town. He raved about Chapala to his wealthy friends, who came and also built sumptuous homes. President Díaz, who visited in 1904 and several years thereafter, opened the floodgates. Dozens of millionaire families soon moved to Chapala. One such was Alberto Braniff, of the famous airline family. In 1906 he bought a fancy lakeshore Victorian mansion, which remains gracefully preserved as the El Cazador restaurant.

The fame of Lake Chapala spread. Improved transportation—first trains, then cars and airplanes—brought droves of visitors from the U.S., Canada, and Europe by the 1940s. Soon, Ajijic—with its picturesque cobbled lanes, quiet lakeshore ambience, and bargain prices—enticed a steady stream of American and Canadian retirees to stay. Their lovely restored colonial homes and bougainvillea-adorned gardens still grace Ajijic and its surroundings today.

SIGHTS

Getting Oriented

Chapala and Ajijic are the Chapala Riviera's most-visited towns. Chapala (pop. about 10,000), at the Hwy. 23 freeway terminus from Guadalajara, is both the main business center and a weekend picnic spot for Guadalajara families. Ajijic (ah-HEE-heek, pop. about 5,000), by contrast, is the scenic, artistic, and tourist center, retaining the best of both worlds—picturesque rustic ambience *and* good, reasonably priced restaurants and hotels.

The paved lakeshore highway runs about five miles west to Ajijic from Chapala, through the tranquil retirement communities of Chula Vista (marked by the golf course on the uphill side), San Antonio, and La Floresta. From Ajijic, the route continues another five miles past lakeshore vineyards and gardens to San Juan Cosala village and hot springs resort. About five miles farther on, you reach Jocotepec, the lake's west-end commercial center, just before arriving at the Morelia-Guadalajara Hwy. 15 junction.

On the opposite, eastern side of Chapala town, the lakeshore is much less developed. The road, which runs east as Paseo Corona from the Chapala lakefront, is paved for about five miles to San Nicolas (pop. about 1,000). After that, it changes to gravel, passing small inlets and tiny isolated cliffbottom beaches en route to sleepy Mezcala (12 miles, 19 km, 30 minutes from Chapala).

Chapala Town Bypass

Drivers who want to avoid Chapala town traffic do so via the *libramiento* (bypass road) that forks from Hwy. 23 two miles uphill from Chapala. The *libramiento* continues for four miles, joining the lakeshore highway about a mile east of the center of Ajijic.

Getting Around

Generally light traffic makes your **automobile** the most convenient way to explore Lake Chapala. Car rentals are available either directly at the Guadalajara airport (Hertz, Avis, Budget, Optima and more, see the airport section, under

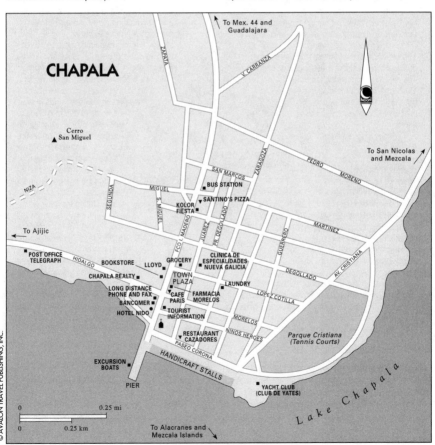

OF WHITEFISH AND WATER HYACINTHS

On the scale of geologic time, lakes are momentary features of the landscape. Mother Nature, having created lakes in the first place, immediately sets out to drain them, evaporate them, or pack them with silt. Plants encroach on their shores until, finally, they're filled and forgotten. Such natural forces are particularly consequential for a shallow lake, such as Lake Chapala, which, although large in area, is only about 15 feet deep.

In recent years nature has not intruded upon Lake Chapala nearly as much as people have. Factories, towns, and farms are demanding an ever-greater share of the lake's most significant source, the Río Lerma, which trickles through four states before entering Lake Chapala's eastern end. Without care, it may simply dry up.

Most of the same upstream culprits who demand more water are also major polluters. The resulting contamination does double harm, both shrinking the fish population and increasing the plague of water hyacinth plants.

The delicious whitefish (pescado blanco), which comprises a number of species of the genus Chirostoma, once flourished in both Lake Chapala and Lake Pátzcuaro in Michoacán. But, as at Pátzcuaro, the Chapala whitefish catch has declined steadily since the 1960s, when yearly hauls in excess of 2,000 tons were routine.

The water hyacinth, Eichornia crassipes, a native of South America, was introduced into Lake Chapala long ago for the beauty of its purple blossoms and brilliant green leaves. It has since burgeoned into a three-pronged menace. Besides blocking the navigation of fishing boats, canoes, and tourist launches on great swaths of the lake's surface, the hyacinth kills fish by decreasing water oxygen and encourages mosquitoes and other disease carriers to breed beneath its floating mass.

The water hyacinth, or lirio as it's known locally, has defied attempts at eradication. Authorities gave up trying to kill it with chemicals; a more benign solution involved the introduction of manatees, which officials hoped would make quick work of the hyacinth. Unfortunately, hungry local fisherfolk made quicker work of the manatees. In recent years a few mechanical harvesters have operated on the lake, pathetically scratching away at the nightmarishly swelling vegetable expanse.

Huge floating hyacinth beds, which appear as solid green fields when viewed near the shore, cover areas varying from as little as a few percent to as much as a fifth of the lake's surface. For a few weeks, as westerly winds prevail, the lioro beds drift and clog the western shore, only to reverse direction after the winds change, a few weeks or months later.

While whitefish fingerlings from a government lakeshore hatchery are repopulating the lake, whitefish from commercial ponds reduce the pressure on the lake fishery. Meanwhile, government eco-scientists are studying both the lioro and the whitefish at a local laboratory. And if the Consortio Nacional de Agua, a four-state Lake Chapala blue-ribbon commission, continues to move effectively to manage water use and curb pollution, Lake Chapala may yet find its way back to health.

KAREN McKINLEY

"Getting There and Away," preceding) or through a Chapala travel agent such as Viajes Vikingo, tel. 3/765-3292, fax 3/765-3494.

Red and white local **minibuses** run frequently from curbside across from the Chapala bus station (about six blocks uphill from the lake, along main street Francisco I. Madero). Most frequent is the westbound bus, which heads along the lakeshore to San Juan Cosala and back via Ajijic, and which will stop anywhere along the road. Other lakeshore destinations (departing from inside the terminal) include Jocotepec every half hour 5 A.M.–8:30 P.M., and San Nicolas eastbound every half hour 7 A.M.–7 P.M.

A Walk around Chapala Town

Start your Chapala walk beneath the great shady trees in the old town **plaza,** three blocks from the lakefront, on main street Av. Francisco I. Madero. Stroll toward the lake, a block and a half, to the town **church.** Although dedicated to St. Francis of Assisi when founded in 1538, the church wasn't completed for more than 200 years. Inside rest the venerated remains of Padre Miguel de Bolonia, one of the pioneer local Franciscan missionaries. He was probably instrumental in building the 16th-century former hermitage (now merely a crumbling foundation) on Cerro San Miguel, the hill that rises just west of town. A white summit cross marks the spot.

Continue across lakefront Paseo Corona, past the curio stands, to the municipal **pier.** In good times, the adjacent anchorage is free of *lirio* (water hyacinths). Otherwise, boaters must frequently chop a navigation path through the thick green vegetable carpet. From the pier, a number of excursions are possible, from a one-hour ride along the lakeshore to extended lake and island tours. These could include a two-hour visit to Scorpion Island (Isla Alacranes), with its regional-food restaurants and bird-watching; or to Mezcala Island (Isla Presidio) with its ruins and bird-watching, for four hours. Rental rates run about $15 hourly per boat while running, $10 hourly while waiting. For Mezcala Island (see the special topic "The Battle of Mezcala") bring food and drinks; none are available on the island, which is a national monument.

If you continue east a quarter mile, past the curio stands lining the lakefront walkway, you'll reach spreading green **Parque Cristiania,** one of Mexico's most complete public parks. Appropriately built for the droves of Sunday visitors, Cristiania has a children's playground, a picnic area, good public tennis courts, and a big swimming pool, all usable for modest fees.

Head back west along lakefront boulevard Paseo Corona, where, a block before the church, you'll see the big Victorian **Braniff Mansion,** now the Restaurant Cazaderos, corner of Degollado, open daily 8 A.M.–5 P.M.. Drop in for lunch or a drink and relax and enjoy the passing scene from the mansion veranda. Later, step inside and admire what amounts to an informal museum of Porfiriana, from the original silk wall-paper to patriarch Alberto Braniff's white-bearded portrait (which bears an uncanny resemblance to revolutionary President Venustiano Carranza).

For a bit more nostalgia, step into the towering lobby/atrium of the turn-of-the-20th-century **Hotel Nido** at Madero 20, across from the church. Although the years have taken their toll, the present owners have succeeded in preserving a bit of the traditional elegance from the old days when President Díaz would visit. For added historical interest, step into the halls bordering the lobby and enjoy the antique photos of old Chapala scenes.

From the downtown traffic intersection and signal on Madero, a block uphill from the church, Av. Hidalgo heads west along the lakeshore toward Ajijic. Follow it about six blocks to view an inextricably connected pair of Chapala fixtures, one as famous as the other is notorious. The famous one is the spreading, parklike **Hotel Villa Montecarlo,** adjacent to the lake. Facilities inside, which the public can enjoy for a fee of about $8 per day, include flowery green lakeview grounds, tennis courts, picnic areas, and pools, one of which is fed by a natural underground hot spring.

The subterranean hot water gathers along an earth fault that runs from the adjacent hillside, beneath the highway and hotel grounds. Earth movement along the fault causes the notorious 50-yard-long rough "hump" in the highway adjacent to the hotel. The pesky mound defies all attempts to alter its growth, which must be scraped off regularly to keep the road passable. Citizens of Chapala, irritated by hump-caused traffic jams, have long petitioned local government for a solution. Engineers, after many proposals, have widened the road and installed underground drains. Hopefully, this will not upset the natural balance and interfere with the hot spring for which the Hotel Villa Montecarlo was built in the first place.

Exploring Ajijic

Continue west by car or bus, about five miles along the lakeshore highway. Past La Floresta, marked by a shady stretch of great trees overarching the highway, an old church tower poking above the left-side neighborhood identifies Ajijic. Its main street is Colón, which runs downhill toward the lake, on the left, just after Danny's restaurant.

A good first stop would be **Ajijic Fine Arts Center** (Centro de Bellas Artes de Ajijic, CABA) at 43 Colón. It's a community center as much as a gallery, where artists and interested local folks gather for classes (painting, graphics, photography, ceramics, sculpture) and exhibits, coffee, and conversation Tues.–Sun. 10 A.M.–5 P.M., tel. 3/766-1920. (Try the heavenly rear-garden restaurant for a tranquil light lunch or refreshment, open Tues.–Thurs. 8 A.M.–4 P.M. and Fri.–Sun. 8 A.M.–8 P.M.)

Continue downhill a half block to the Ajijic town **plaza** and take a look inside the old (circa 1540) chapel of the Virgin of Santiago on the north (uphill) edge of the plaza. From the opposite side of the plaza, head east one block to the baroque parish **church of San Andrés,** founded during the mid-1500s and completed in 1749. For nine days during Ajijic's late-November **Fiesta of San Andrés,** the church's spreading front courtyard and surrounding streets overflow with food stands, carnival rides, pitchpenny games, fireworks, and folk dancing. Moreover, Ajijic's **Semana Santa** (pre-Easter week) celebration at this same spot is becoming renowned for its elaborately costumed, three-day reenactment of Jesus's trial and crucifixion.

From the church-front, head downhill along Castellanos; after two blocks, turn right at 16 de Septiembre. Not far, on your left, will be the **Neill James Library,** open Mon.–Sat. 10 A.M.–2 P.M., and the lovely garden it shares with the adjacent Spanish-language library, open Mon.–Sat. 10:30 A.M.–1 P.M. and 4–6 P.M. The garden is a delight for quiet contemplation. Before you leave, look over the notices of local performances, exhibits, and fiestas on the walkway bulletin board between the two buildings.

Continue half a block west along 16 de Septiembre to the corner of Morelos, where you'll enjoy browsing through the excellent **arts and crafts shops** clustered here.

Note: Although Morelos has a different name, it is actually the downhill continuation of Colón. The reason is Ajijic streets change names midtown. Streets that run parallel to the lakeshore change names at the Colón-Morelos line. Streets that run perpendicular to the lakeshore change names at the Constitución-Ocampo line.

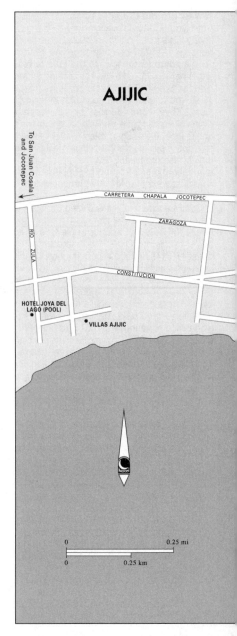

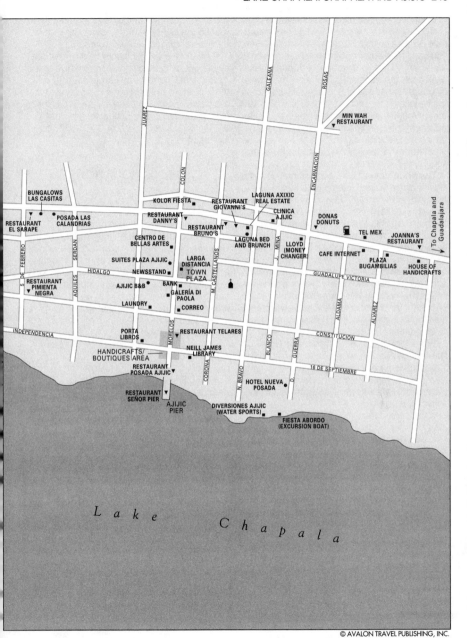

GALEANA

ROSAS

JUAREZ

COLON

ENCARNACION

MIN WAH
RESTAURANT

To Chapala and
Guadalajara

BUNGALOWS
LAS CASITAS

POSADA LAS
CALANDRIAS

RESTAURANT
EL SARAPE

KOLOR FIESTA

RESTAURANT
GIOVANNI'S

LAGUNA AXIXIC
REAL ESTATE

CLINICA
AJIJIC

DONAS
DONUTS

TEL MEX

JOANNA'S
RESTAURANT

RESTAURANT
DANNY'S

RESTAURANT
BRUNO'S

LAGUNA BED
AND BRUNCH

LLOYD
(MONEY
CHANGER)

CAFE INTERNET

PLAZA
BUGAMBILIAS

HOUSE OF
HANDICRAFTS

CENTRO DE
BELLAS ARTES

SERDAN

5 DE FEBRERO

SUITES PLAZA AJIJIC

NEWSSTAND

LARGA
DISTANCIA

TOWN
PLAZA

MINA

M. CASTELLANOS

GUADALUPE VICTORIA

ALDAMA

ALVAREZ

HIDALGO

AQUILES

RESTAURANT
PIMIENTA
NEGRA

AJIJIC B&B

BANK

GALERIA DI
PAOLA

LAUNDRY

CORREO

INDEPENDENCIA

PORTA
LIBROS

MORELOS

RESTAURANT TELARES

CONSTITUCION

BLANCO

GUERRA

HANDICRAFTS/
BOUTIQUES AREA

NEILL JAMES
LIBRARY

16 DE SEPTIEMBRE

RESTAURANT
POSADA AJIJIC

CORONA

N. BRAVO

HOTEL NUEVA
POSADA

D

RESTAURANT
SEÑOR PIER

AJIJIC
PIER

DIVERSIONES AJIJIC
(WATER SPORTS)

FIESTA ABORDO
(EXCURSION BOAT)

Lake   Chapala

Continue another block downhill to the Ajijic lakeshore, where the petite **Señor Pier restaurant** perches on the dock above the water. Here, you can relax, enjoy a refreshment, and take in the scene. Late afternoons, a gentle breeze often cools the lakeshore. Overhead, great white clouds billow above blue mountains bordering the far lakeshore. On the beach by the pier, fishermen mend their nets, while at the beach's uphill edge, a few *indígena* women in native costumes weave their colorful wares beneath the great trees that shelter the **Restaurant Posada Ajijic.**

The restaurant is the present incarnation of the Hacienda de Cuije, founded here by the Saenz family in 1530. In 1938, Englishman Nigel Millet turned the building into a hotel, the Posada Ajijic. By the 1970s, the Posada Ajijic was attracting a loyal clientele, which included a number of artists, writers, and film stars such as Elizabeth Taylor and Charles Bronson. New owners, the Eager family of Vancouver, Canada, took over in 1975 and stayed until 1990, when they moved to another hotel nearby. The current proprietors, who operate it as a restaurant exclusively, remodeled the Posada Ajijic to its present state of rustic elegance.

For a look at the new showplace **Hotel La Nueva Posada,** which the Eager family built in 1990, stroll four blocks east (left as you face the lake). Their gorgeous neo-colonial creation at the foot of Donato Guerra spreads from its inti- mate, art-decorated lobby through an airy, romantic terrace restaurant, climaxing in a verdant, semitropical lake-view garden.

If you time your Ajijic arrival right (winter only), you might be able to join an informative tour of Ajijic's lovely homes and gardens. Local volunteers conduct the programs regularly and give the donations (customarily, about $10 per person) to the Jocotepec School for the Deaf. Call 3/766-0589, 3/766-0652, or 3/766-0376 for information.

ACCOMMODATIONS

The Chapala Riviera offers a wide range of lodgings, from luxury lake-view hotels and friendly motel complexes to intimate bed and breakfasts and a good trailer park. Although both Ajijic and Chapala have plenty of colorful old-Mexico atmosphere, Ajijic is quieter and more charming, and consequently has most of the better lodgings. Rates depend strongly upon availability and season; the lodging figures given below approximate winter high-season rates. Summer low-season (May–Oct.) prices will generally be 10–30 percent lower.

Ajijic Hotels
By location, starting on the highway and moving downhill, first comes the **Posada Las Calandrias,** about four blocks west of Danny's restau-

Fishing canoes wait on the Lake Chapala shoreline at Ajijic.

LAKE CHAPALA ACCOMMODATIONS

Accommodations (telephone area code 3) are listed in increasing order of approximate high-season, double-room rates.

AJIJIC HOTELS (POSTAL CODE 45920)

Posada Las Calandrias, Carretera Chapala-Jocotepec no. 8 Poniente, P.O. Box 76, tel. 766-1052, $28
Bungalows Las Casitas, Carretera Chapala-Jocotepec Poniente no. 20, tel. 766-1145, $32
Laguna Bed and Brunch, Carretera Chapala-Ajijic 24 Oriente, tel. 766-1174, fax 766-1188, e-mail: laguna@laguna.com.mx, $35
Ajijic Plaza Suites, Colón 33, P.O. Box 555, tel. 766-0383, e-mail: ajijic@infosel.net.mx, $40
Los Artistas Constitución 105, tel. 766-1027, fax 766-1762, e-mail: artistas@laguna.com.mx., $52
Ajijic B&B, Hidalgo 22, tel. 766-2377, fax 766-2331, $60
Hotel La Nueva Posada, Donato Guerra 9, tel. 766-1444 or 766-1344, $60
Hotel Real de Chapala, Paseo del Prado 20, tel. 766-0007 or 766-0014, fax 766-0025, $70
Villas Ajijic, Linda Vista 14, Fracc. Tío Domingo, tel. 766-0983, $80

CHAPALA HOTELS (POSTAL CODE 45900)

Hotel Chapala Haciendas, Km 40, Carretera Guadalajara-Chapala, tel. 765-2720, $25
Hotel Nido, Fco. Madero 202, tel.765-2116, $25
Hotel Villa Montecarlo, Hidalgo 296, tel. 765-2120 or 765-2024, fax 765-3366, $56

SAN JUAN COSALA (POSTAL CODE 45800)

Motel Balneario, San Juan Cosala, P.O. Box 181, Chapala, tel./fax 761-0302 or 761-0222, $48

---

rant at Carretera Chapala-Jocotepec No. 8 Poniente, P.O. Box 76, Ajijic, Jalisco 45920, tel. 3/766-1052. Many folks with cars and RVs like the motel-style setup and the reunions with fellow Ajijic longtimers. The 25 clean, comfortably furnished but not fancy one- and two-bedroom apartments include living room, kitchen, ceiling fans, and plenty of daily company around a blue pool and sundeck adjacent to the parking lot. By night, residents relax on their front porches, enjoying the balmy evenings visiting and playing cards; later some might stroll down the street together for dinner at a favorite restaurant. One-bedroom apartments rent, in high winter season, for about $28 per day, $180 per week, or $700 per month; two-bedrooms for $43 per day, $270 per week, or $900 per month. All rentals include fans, TV, and daily maid service. Get your winter season (Nov.–April) reservations in early.

If you can't get in at Las Calandrias, try the neighboring **Bungalows Las Casitas,** one door to the west at Carretera Chapala-Jocotepec no. 20 Poniente, Ajijic, Jalisco 45920, tel. 3/766-1145. Here, as next door, about two dozen sim-

ply but comfortably furnished apartments surround a pool and sundeck by the parking lot. The friendly winter residents are mainly North American retirees. One-bedroom units rent for $32 per day, $150 per week, and $430 per month; two-bedrooms run half again as much. Discounts are generally available during May–July and Sept.–Nov. low seasons. All have kitchens, living rooms, ceiling fans, maid service, and satellite TV.

On the highway, only a couple of blocks from the town center, the Laguna Real Estate office marks the location of its **Laguna Bed and Brunch.** Reserve through Laguna Real Estate, Carretera Chapala-Ajijic 24 Oriente, Ajijic, Jalisco 45920, tel. 3/766-1174, fax 3/766-1188, email: laguna@laguna.com.mx. Four comfortable rooms with bath, an adjacent cheery breakfast room/living room/lobby, and a partially shaded outside patio keep a steady stream of satisfied customers returning year-round. Extras are king-size beds, a shelf of thick used paperbacks, and sofas for reading and socializing. Hearty breakfasts are included with lodgings. Rooms rent for

$35 s or d high season, about $30 d low season. By day, you can make Inquiries or access Laguna Bed and Brunch through the real estate office or by telephone. With your key, you can get in anytime through the residential entrance at Zaragoza 29 Oriente, behind the real estate office, one block downhill from the highway.

Nearby on Colón by the plaza, close to everything, is **Ajijic Plaza Suites,** Colón 33, P.O. Box 555, Ajijic, Jalisco 45920, tel. 3/766-0383, fax 3/766-2331, email: ajijic@infosel.net.mx. The small, sometimes busy lobby leads to a sunny, apartment-lined inner patio. Inside, the new owners have spruced up the 12 one-bedroom units with tasteful, colorful Mexican-style decor. Rentals run about $35 s, $40 d, including breakfast, phone, maid service, optional satellite TV, and limited wheelchair access; credit cards are accepted.

Around the downhill corner, at Hidalgo 22, the new **Ajijic B&B,** tel. 3/766-2377, fax 3/766-2331, email: ajijic@infosel.net.mx, attracts a cadre of loyal returnees. The front entry leads you into an inviting fountain courtyard, past breakfast tables set beneath a shady side portico to a manicured tropical garden, with the six rooms set artfully to one side. Inside, they are lovingly decorated in earth tones and pastels, embellished with flowers hand-painted on the walls, and hung with original oils and watercolors. Rooms include ceiling fans, king-size beds, modern-standard decorator bathrooms, telephones, and large-screen TVs. Rates run $60 s or d, including full breakfast. Make reservations early, especially during the winter.

Arguably Ajijic's loveliest accommodation is **Los Artistas,** on the east side of town, at Constitución 105, Ajijic, Jalisco 45920, tel. 3/766-1027, fax 3/766-1762, email: artistas@laguna.com.mx. Owners Kent Edwards and Linda Brown's lovingly tended accommodations are arranged around the edge of a flowery rear garden. Rooms, some with king-size beds, all with attractively tiled and fitted baths, are artfully furnished with weavings, paintings, and sculpture. Rooms vary; if possible, take a peek before picking. Rates range $52–70 d, including breakfast and parking. Reserve early, especially for the winter season. Find it about five blocks east of main street Colón.

Nearby, downhill, stands Ajijic's newish **Hotel La Nueva Posada,** on the east-side lakeshore at Donato Guerra 9, P.O. Box 30, Ajijic, Jalisco 45920, tel. 3/766-1444, fax 3/766-1344, email: posada@laguna.com.mx, is so lovely, prospective winter guests need reservations far in advance. Its Canadian family/owners have spared little in embellishing the hotel's colonial-style decor. Past the lobby, an elegant but comfortable bar provides nightly piano entertainment, and a romantic, airy terrace-restaurant leads to a verdant, semitropical lake-view garden. The 17 rooms vary from poolside rooms to upstairs view suites. All are immaculate and tastefully decorated in colonial style, with original watercolors and native crafts. Rooms rent, year-round, for $50 s, $60 d, $66 t, add about $5 for view, including full breakfast, ceiling fans, and parking. Bargain for a low-season or long-term discount; credit cards are accepted (although you get a 10 percent discount if you pay cash).

Two more deluxe accommodations occupy lakeshore spots on opposite ends of town. The Universidad Autonoma de Guadalajara owns one, the plush **Hotel Real de Chapala,** Paseo del Prado 20, Ajijic, Jalisco 45920, tel. 3/766-0007 or 3/766-0014, fax 3/766-0025, in the choice La Floresta subdivision just east of Ajijic. Except for Christmas and Easter holidays and weekends, the hotel is minimally occupied, and consequently very quiet. Its lavish facilities—a spreading lakefront park, big blue pool, night-lit tennis courts, volleyball, soccer field, billiard room, Ping-Pong, and bars and restaurants—are often unused. Weekends are more lively; guests, mostly middle- and upper-class Guadalajarans, enjoy seasonal live combo music Friday and Saturday evenings, and mariachis and folkloric dance on Sunday. The 86 spacious, luxurious rooms and suites (40 of which have lake and mountain views) rent for about $70 s or d, with ceiling fans, queen-size beds, satellite TV, parking, and limited wheelchair access. Credit cards are accepted.

The condo-style **Villas Ajijic,** in the quiet lakeshore neighborhood on the opposite side of town, offers an entirely different luxury option, at Linda Vista 14, Fracc. Tío Domingo, Ajijic, Jalisco 45920, tel. 3/766-0983. The attractive, two-story, tile-and-stucco apartments cluster around a manicured inner garden leading to an adjoining pool and kiddie play area by the beach, which is, unfortunately, often clogged with water hyacinths. The units themselves are spacious, Spanish-style apartments with two bedrooms, dining room, living room, bar, view balcony in upstairs units, and modern-standard kitchens. They rent for $80 per day or $1,000 per month high season, about $55 per day and $850 per month low season, with hotel-style desk manager, maid service, satellite TV, and telephone. Get there via the lakeshore highway, about a mile west of the Ajijic town center. Turn left, downhill, at the Hotel Danza del Sol sign at Río Bravo Street. After two blocks, turn left at the Coronado Resort sign at Ocampo; after one block, turn right at the second Ajijic Resort sign. One block farther, turn left at the Villas Ajijic sign.

Chapala Hotels

Swimmers discouraged by the prospect of diving into shallow, brown Lake Chapala have an alternative in the blue pool and sunny patio of the budget **Hotel Nido,** Av. Fco. Madero 202, Chapala, Jalisco 45900, tel. 3/765-2116. For sentimentalists, the hotel retains a bit of its old-world charm. An airy atrium rises above its graceful restaurant/lobby, which leads to alcoves and halls decorated with photos of old Chapala scenes. The hotel is right in the middle of Chapala's colorful downtown, a block from the lakeshore pier, near restaurants, stores, and transportation. However, its approximately 30 simply furnished but clean and comfortable rooms vary considerably. For maximum quiet, get one in the hotel's rear or side wings, away from the street. Rooms rent for about $22 s, $25 d, with bath and parking.

About six blocks west along Chapala's main lakeshore street, **Hotel Villa Montecarlo** basks in palmy, lake-view grounds at Hidalgo 296, Chapala, Jalisco 45900, tel./fax 3/765-2120 or 3/765-2024, fax 3/533-66. The site, originally developed because of its hot spring, is now owned and operated by the University of Guadalajara. The natural setting—lush green lawns overlooking the lake's mountain- and cloud-framed expanse—sets the tone. When not gazing at the view, guests can soak in the natural warm pool, cool off in another, play some tennis, or enjoy a drink at the bar or a meal in the restaurant. The double-story, motel-style lodging tiers occupy only one side of the grounds and consequently avoid cluttering the views. The rooms, furnished in 1960s semi-deluxe style, open to airy balconies, many with lake vistas. They rent for about $35 s or d, with ceiling fans, parking, and many extras, but no phones or TV.

Guests at the **Hotel Chapala Haciendas,** by contrast, enjoy a high hillside setting, five minutes' drive uphill from the lakeshore at Km 40, Carretera Guadalajara-Chapala, tel. 3/765-2720. Its lush country lakeview location, inviting pool and patio, friendly family management, and reasonable prices explain the Chapala Hacienda's continuing popularity with both North American and Mexican vacationers. Breakfast, sunrise view, piano-bar, and live oldies-but-goodies music Wednesday and Saturday are popular traditions in the hotel's homey restaurant. The 20 rooms, in rows facing a flower garden and panoramic lake views, are simply but attractively furnished, with rustic high-beamed rattan ceilings. Rentals run $20 s, $25 d, with discounts for long-term stays. (If you're planning on using the pool, check to see if it's being maintained; sometimes it becomes green.)

San Juan Cosala Hot Spring Resort

San Juan Cosala, on the lakeshore eight miles (13 km) west of Chapala, has long been famous for its therapeutic hot springs. The major hotel is the **Motel Balneario San Juan Cosala,** whose complex of several big blue pools and a water slide is a weekend and holiday magnet for Mexican families. Contact the motel at P.O. Box 181, Chapala, Jalisco 45900, tel./fax 3/761-0302 or 3/761-0222. Although the main pools and facilities are open to the public for a fee of $6 adults and $3 kids, the hotel reserves some pools and gardens for hotel guests only. Other hotel amenities include hot tub, massage, natural vapor sauna, and volleyball, basketball, and tennis courts. The rooms, while not luxurious, are comfortably furnished with two double beds and have airy, private garden patios, which, from the second floor, have lake views. If you prefer peace and quiet, best to book your stay during the calm midweek period. The approximately 50 rooms rent for $40 s, $48 d, breakfast included.

Trailer Park

The long-established **Pal Trailer Park,** on the Chapala lakeshore highway three miles west of

Chapala, just past the Chula Vista golf course and tennis courts, amounts to a mini-village, with many year-round residents. Write for reservations at P.O. Box 84, Chapala, Jalisco 45900, tel. 3/766-1447, fax 766-0040, email: lloyd@lloyd.com.mx, website: www.southmex .com/palresort.html. Its host of deluxe extras include a heated swimming pool, separate children's pool, satellite TV hookup, recreation room and barbecue area, pure water system, laundromat, night security guard, and clean, separate toilets and showers for men and women. Its 110 large (40- by 30-foot) spaces, each with terrace, rent for $14 per day, $90 per week, $320 per month, or about $3,000 per year, with all hookups, including 30-amp electric power. Tent camping is permitted, but for two or three days only.

Long-Term Rentals and Home Exchanges
A number of agents rent Chapala-area apartments, houses, and condos. Among the busiest is **Coldwell Banker-Chapala Realty,** in downtown Chapala, Hidalgo 223, Chapala, Jalisco 45900, tel. 3/765-2877 or 3/765-3676, fax 3/765-3528, email: chapala@infosel.net.mx, website: www.chapala.com. **Ajijic Real Estate,** at Colón 1, Ajijic, tel. 3/766-1716, fax 3/766-0967, email: rentals@infosel.net.mx does about the same. Also, check the local newspaper *Ojo de Agua* classifieds and the bulletin board at the Ajijic post office, a block downhill from the town plaza, or the Neill James library, a block downhill and a block east from the post office. (If you can't find a copy of *Ojo de Agua,* drop by the Coldwell Banker-Chapala Realty office in Chapala, at Av. Hidalgo 223, or telephone 3/765-3676 or 3/756-2877, fax 3/765-3528, or email: oljodellago@laguna.com.mx.

FOOD

Breakfast and Snacks
In Ajijic, all roads seem to lead to **Danny's Restaurant** on the lakeshore highway at Colón, open Mon.–Sat. 8 A.M.–5 P.M., Sunday 8 A.M.–1 P.M., tel. 3/776-2222. Hot breakfasts (eggs, hash browns, and toast, $3), hamburgers, Mexican specialties, bottomless cups of coffee, and plenty of friendly conversation long ago ensured Danny's local following.

Alternatively, you can try **Evies,** for good coffee and American breakfast, at 21 Hidalgo, half a block west of the Ajijic plaza, open daily except Wed., 8 A.M.–4 P.M.

Two Ajijic bed and breakfasts offer both breakfast and a Sunday brunch to the public. The **Laguna Bed and Brunch** offers a country breakfast Mon.–Sat. 8–11 A.M. This includes several entrée choices plus fruit, rolls, apple-bran muffins, and coffee or tea for about $2. On Sunday, local folks crowd in for its even heartier brunch, offered 8 A.M.–noon, for about $4. Reservations are required, tel. 3/766-1174. Goodies include all of the above plus old-fashioned tummy-fillers such as beef pot pies, mashed potatoes, and vegetables; or enchiladas, rice, and refried beans. Get there from the highway, through Laguna Real Estate, or through Laguna Bed and Brunch's front door, a block downhill from the highway, at Zaragoza 29 near the corner of Galeana.

The **Ajijic B&B,** farther down the hill at 22 Hidalgo, half a block west of the town plaza, offers a similarly popular Sunday brunch 11 A.M.–4 P.M. Be sure to phone or fax ahead, tel. 3/766-2377, fax 3/766-2331, for reservations.

In Chapala, **Cafe Paris,** right in the center of town on Madero, corner of Hidalgo, open daily 9 A.M.–9 P.M., enjoys similar renown. Good service, tasty offerings—breakfasts, soups, salads, sandwiches, Mexican plates, beer, wine, and cafe espresso—and shady sidewalk tables attract a loyal local and North American clientele.

Another relaxing spot in Chapala is **Restaurant Los Cazadores,** open daily 8 A.M.–5 P.M., in the distinguished old Braniff Mansion on lakeshore Av. R. Corona, a block behind the church. Here you can enjoy the lakefront scene over a leisurely breakfast or lunch on the airy front veranda. Before you leave, step inside for a look at the collection of polished Porfiriana that adorns the mansion's venerable silk-covered walls.

Homier but just as enjoyable is **Che Mary,** where regulars flock for bountiful, very reasonably priced breakfasts, lunches, and dinners in an inviting, airy palapa setting. It's open daily 8 A.M.–10 P.M., on Madero, across the street and about two blocks uphill from the Chapala town plaza.

The baked offerings of **Santino's Pizza,** in Chapala (Madero 467A, two blocks up the street from the plaza), tel. 3/775-2360, are equally good on location or delivered; open daily 1–10 P.M.

Ajijic Restaurants

The resident brigade of discriminating diners has led to the unusually high standards of Ajijic's successful restaurants. Starting on the highway, east side, and moving downhill toward the lake, first comes **Joanna's Restaurant,** tel. 3/766-0437, whose bona fide claim of "authentic German cuisine" seems a marvel, two continents and an ocean away from Luneborg where Joanna was born. But remarkable it is—from the *Gemischecter Fruhling Salat* (with *Hausdressing*) through the *Reibekuche* (potato pancakes) and *Mandel Forelle* rainbow trout, to the finale of scrumptious apple strudel. Find Joanna's at 118 A Blv. La Floresta, three blocks east of the gas station, in a suburban house, set back from the north side of the street; open Tues.–Thurs. 1–8 P.M., Fri.–Sun 1–9 P.M. Moderate-Expensive.

Two blocks west, plain good food at very reasonable prices draws a flock of local Americans and Canadians to coffee shop-style **Salvador's,** at 88 Carretera Oriente, highway-front of the Plaza Bugambilias shopping center, tel. 3/776-2301. Besides a very familiar American-style breakfast, lunch, and dinner menu, owner Salvador also offers a big $5 Sunday brunch and specialties of the day, such as roast beef, lasagna, and stuffed rainbow trout, all for around $5. Open Mon.–Fri. 7 A.M.–8 P.M., Sunday 7 A.M.–5 P.M., closed Saturday. Budget.

Next comes **La Trattoria de Giovanni** (or, locally, just Giovanni's), a spacious (but dark in the daytime) restaurant/bar, also on the highway, lake side, at the corner of Galeana, tel. 3/766-1733. Here, friends and family gather for a good time. The happy mixture of folks—kids, retirees, Mexicans, Americans, Canadians—is both a cause and effect of the amiable atmosphere. The food—pizzas, pastas, salads, fish, chicken, steaks—is crisply served and tasty. Desserts, which include carrot cake and apple, chocolate, or banana cream pie, are a specialty. Open Mon.–Sat. noon–10 P.M., Sunday noon–8 P.M. Moderate.

Next door, the friendly owner/chef of **Restaurant Bruno's,** tel. 3/766-1674, is so skilled that he has to open only a few hours per day (12:30–3 P.M. and 6–8 P.M.) to be successful. Bruno, who also sometimes waits on tables, puts out an innovative repertoire of mostly Italian- and Chinese-style dishes at lunchtime, and good old reliables such as barbecued ribs or chicken for dinner. He buys his food fresh daily, and in quantities calculated so that nothing will be left over. By 3 P.M. on a busy day, he begins to run out of food. Arrive early for a full choice. Recently, Bruno has been cooking on weekends only. Check when you call for reservations. Moderate.

Diners seeking elegance enjoy a number of good Ajijic options. For the food, many Ajijic regulars pick **Telares,** downhill about two blocks below the Ajijic town plaza, tel. 3/766-0428. Patrons have a choice of seating, either in the sunny central patio/garden or in the shady surrounding veranda. Likewise they have plenty of choice in the long menu of tasty appetizers, soups and salads, and expertly prepared continental-style meat, seafood, and pasta entrées. Open Sun.–Thurs. noon–9 P.M., Fri.–Sat. noon–10:30 P.M. Reservations strongly recommended.

Soft lighting, live background piano melodies, and an airy stone-arched dining room terrace set the romantic tone of the **Hotel La Nueva Posada** restaurant, tel. 3/766-1444 or 3/766-1344. The menu of mesquite-broiled fish, chicken, ribs, and steaks garnished with delicious broiled vegetables provides the successful conclusion. The hotel is at 9 Donato Guerra, by the east-side lakefront. Open daily 8 A.M.–9 P.M., reservations recommended.

For a relaxing lakeshore lunch or sunset dinner, try the landmark **Restaurant Posada Ajijic** at the foot of Colón, tel. 3/766-1430. Once a hacienda, later a hotel, the Posada Ajijic restaurant now rests in comfortable old age beneath a grove of spreading lakeshore eucalyptus trees. Inside the dining room, furnished in colonial-style leather and wood, spreads beneath rustic beamed ceilings to lake-view windows. Service is crisp, and the soups, salads, sandwiches, and entrées (chicken, fish, steak) are tasty and professionally presented. Open Mon.–Thurs. noon–9 P.M., Fri.–Sat. noon–1 A.M., Sunday noon–9 P.M. Recorded dance music Fri.–Sun. evenings.

Local Ajijic folks recommend a number of

Campesinos, in hundreds of yearly village fiestas, turn out in Moro (Moor) masks (above) and costumes to do mock battle with their neighbors, dressed up as 15th-century Spaniards, in the "Dance of the Moors and Christians."

other restaurants, too numerous to describe in detail. They include: **Min Wah,** for good Chinese cooking, at Callejon del Tepala 6, (from landmark Lloyd's Financial on the highway, go about three blocks uphill), tel. 3/766-0686, open daily 11 A.M.–9 P.M.; **Pimienta Negra,** featuring Lebanese-Middle Eastern food, on Ocampo, about three blocks west of the Ajijic Plaza, open Tues.–Thurs. noon–8 P.M., Fri.–Sat. noon–9 P.M., Sunday noon–6 P.M.; **El Sarape,** for good Mexican cooking, Tex-Mex and Arizona-Mex style, with salad bar, west-side Ajijic, on the highway, just west of Bungalows Las Casitas, tel. 3/766-1599, open daily 11 A.M.–8:30 P.M.; and **Restaurant Diana de Italia,** for perfect *pasta al dente* and a good Sunday brunch (11:30 A.M.–3 P.M.), in San Antonio (midway between Ajijic and Chapala), at Independencia #124, a few blocks downhill from the highway, tel. 3/766-0097.

Groceries

In Ajijic, smart shoppers go to **Super El Torito** for a wide selection of fresh veggies, fruit, meat, groceries, and a small but good English-language newsstand. It's open daily 7:30 A.M.–9 P.M., at Plaza Bugambilias, on the highway, east side, tel. 3/766-2202. **Super Lake,** tel. 3/766-0174, midway between Ajijic and Chapala, enjoys equal popularity. It offers a wide choice of groceries, vegetables, and fruits, plus many frozen foods, a deli, and a soda fountain. Also available are magazines and newspapers, including the Mexico City *News, USA Today,* and the informative local monthly, *El Ojo del Lago.* It's open daily 8 A.M.–8 P.M. in San Antonio, on the lake side of the highway.

In downtown Chapala, although you can get most of the basic groceries at **Surtidora Ribera,** (open Mon.–Sat. 8 A.M.–8:30 p.m., Sunday 8 A.M.–3 P.M.), on the north (uphill) side of the town plaza, you'll have to go to the nearby town market, west side of the plaza, for fresh fruits and vegetables.

ENTERTAINMENT AND EVENTS

Nightlife

As many locals do, start off your Lake Chapala evening in proper style by enjoying the sunset (5:30–6:30 P.M. in the winter, an hour later in summer). An excellent spot to ensure that you don't miss something spectacular is the Ajijic pier at the foot of Colón. The Chapala Pier offers a similarly panoramic prospect.

Evening lake cruises offer another possibility. While at the Chapala pier, ask the boatmen about a *crucero de puesta del sol* (sunset cruise). In Ajijic, seasonal onboard parties *(fiestas a bordo)* leave by lake cruiser from the beach, foot of Donato Guerra by the Hotel La Nueva Posada, on weekends around 12 and 4 P.M. Additional special cruises, when passengers can enjoy both the sunset and the full moon shimmering on the lake, depart at around 4 P.M. from the same point on dates when the moon is full.

Furthermore, Chapala romantics sometimes organize horseback *lunadas* (moonlight rides) to a campfire-lit viewpoint in the hills above Ajijic. Dates depend on the full moon. Watch for an announcement in the "Mark Your Calendar" section of the local newspaper, *El Ojo del Lago* (get a copy at its Chapala office, tel. 3/765-3676), or check with the tourist information office in Chapala.

A major exception to the generally quiet nights around Ajijic and Chapala occurs at the Ajijic **Hotel La Nueva Posada** bar, with live piano happy hour Tues.–Thurs. 7–10 P.M., and music for dancing, Fri. and Sat. 8–11 P.M. Find it at the lakeshore, foot of Donato Guerra, four blocks east, two blocks downhill from the central plaza, tel. 3/766-1444.

Subdued and very appropriate for dinner is the live music that **Las Telares** restaurant, tel. 3/766-0428, two blocks downhill from the Ajijic plaza, customarily offers Saturday and Sunday 7–9 P.M.

Hotel Chapala Haciendas, tel. 3/765-2720, a five-minute drive uphill from downtown Chapala along the highway to Guadalajara, entertains patrons with Armando's piano-guitar-drum combo Wednesday and Saturday.

For more entertainment suggestions such as concerts, plays, and art exhibitions, see the informative "Lakeside Living" and "Mark Your Calendar" sections in the widely available English-language monthly, *El Ojo del Lago.*

Fiestas

Occasional local festivals quicken the ordinarily drowsy pace of Lake Chapala life. Jocotepec, at the lake's west end, kicks off the year in early January with the two-week fiesta of **El Señor del Monte**. The fiesta's origin is local—an image of Jesus on the Cross, originally carved from the branches of a *guaje* tree, is believed miraculous because it was seen either glowing or burning (depending on which account you believe). Nevertheless, folks make plenty of the legend, with a swirl of events including masses, processions, bullfights, and cockfights, all accompanied by a continuous carnival and fair. The celebration climaxes on the third Sunday of January, when downtown is awash with merrymakers thrilling to the boom, roar, and flash of a grand fireworks display.

The local North American community joins in the party, usually in early February, with a big for-charity **Chili Cookoff** on the beach by the Ajijic pier. Events include "Las Vegas Lounge" gambling tables; a "Mexican Night" with music, dancing, and a "Miss Chili Cookoff" pageant; and, finally, chili judging and awards, with plenty left over for everyone. For schedule and entry information, contact *El Ojo del Lago* newspaper, P.O. Box 279, Chapala, Jalisco 45900, tel. 3/765-3676 or 3/765-2877, fax 3/765-3528, email: ojodellago@laguna.com.mx.

Merrymaking continues with **Carnaval** (Mardi Gras) dancing and parades before Ash Wednesday, the first day of Lent, usually in late February. On several subsequent Fridays, rockets boom high over town and village streets, as image-bearing processions converge for special masses at local churches. This all culminates in **Semana Santa** festivities, notably in Ajijic, where local people, in full costume, reenact Jesus's ordeal.

The hubbub resumes in Chapala around October 4, with the climax of the fiesta of the town patron, **San Francisco.** Townsfolk dance, join processions, watch fireworks, ride the Ferris wheel, and pitch pesos. Later, party animals can enjoy more of the same during Ajijic's **Fiesta of San Andrés** during the last nine days of November.

SPORTS AND RECREATION

Jogging and Gyms

The breezy Lake Chapala shore is the best spot for a stroll or a jog. Best to get out early or late and avoid the heat of the day. In Ajijic, try the beach by the pier (foot of Colón), where several hundred yards of level, open sand invite relaxing walking, and running. In Chapala, the lakefront boardwalk or the grassy perimeter of Parque Cristiania on lakefront Av. R. Corona, a few hundred yards east of the church, offers similar opportunities. Alternatively, you might join company with the many local folks who bike, jog, and walk along the paved bicycle path *(pista)* that parallels the Chapala-Ajijic highway.

A few Chapala and Ajijic gyms, such as the **Ann Claus Gym,** tel. 3/766-2260 (on the highway, in the Bugambilias shopping plaza , second floor), offer machines and low-impact aerobics classes.

Swimming

Although Lake Chapala's shallowness (which keeps bottom mud stirred up) and hyacinth-clogged shorelines make it uninviting, hotel pools remain an option. In Chapala, both the lakeshore Hotel Nido and the uphill Hotel Chapala Haciendas have inviting, medium-size, but unheated pools. Most luxurious, however, is the big lake-view pool at the Hotel Villa Montecarlo, whose palmy grounds and natural hot spring are open for public day use. Cost is about $8 per adult; call ahead, tel. 3/76521-20, to see if the big pool is open.

In Ajijic, an equally luxurious swimming possibility exists at the beautiful lakefront pool at the Hotel Real de Chapala, where, for the price of a poolside lunch, you can enjoy a swim. Although a similar prospect exists at the nearby Hotel La Nueva Posada, a better swimming opportunity is available at the Balneario Motel San Juan Cosala hot spring resort, where spring-fed lake-view pools are available for public use, $6 per day per adult, $3 children.

Probably the best local lap swimming ($3 per person) spot is at the **Hotel Joya del Lago,** on Calle Río Zula, on the far west side of town. Get there by taxi, car, or foot about one mile west of Ajijic town center. (From the highway, turn toward the lake, at the Hotel Danza del Sol sign and continue about three long blocks downhill, to Hotel Joya del Lago, on the right.)

Water Sports and Boat Launching

Although winds and currents often push mats of pesky water hyacinths on to Lake Chapala beaches, lake access is possible at certain times and locations. If so, nothing else will stop you from floating your kayak, or your sailboard, on the lake.

If you want to launch your own boat, ask the Club de Yates (YAH-tays) de Chapala if you can rent its boat ramp (although in recent years, the lake level has been so low that boaters can launch right on the beach in Ajijic). You can find

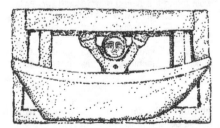

carving of a pre-Columbian boat

the club on lakefront Paseo Corona, across from Cristiania Park, about a quarter-mile from the Chapala pier, tel. 3/765-2276.

Golf, Tennis, and Horseback Riding

Local enthusiasts enjoy a pair of nine-hole golf courses. The **Chula Vista Country Club,** tel. 3/765-2515, greens carpet the intimate valley that spreads uphill from the highway, midway between Chapala and Ajijic. Play starts daily at 8 A.M.; the last round begins at 3 P.M. The nine-hole greens fee runs $22 weekdays, $32 weekends, plus caddy, $6. A clubhouse bar and restaurant serves food and refreshments. Golfers enjoy similarly good conditions at the nine-hole **Chapala Country Club,** tel. 3/763-5736, overlooking the lake near San Nicolas, about five miles (eight km) east of Chapala.

Private tennis courts are available at the Chula Vista Country Club, tel. 3/765-2515, $3 per hour; the Hotel Villa Montecarlo in Chapala, tel. 3/765-2120, $6 per day; and the Hotel Real de Chapala, tel. 3/766-0007, in Ajijic (night-lit), $8 per hour. Even cheaper public tennis courts are available at Parque Cristiania in Chapala.

Guided horseback rides and rental horses ($5 per hour) are available daily at the corner of Avenidas Camino Real and Camino del Lago, in La Floresta subdivision, a block west of the Hotel Real de Chapala.

SHOPPING

Handicrafts and Clothes

For the more common, but attractive, handicrafts, try the stalls that line the lakefront walkway, beginning at the Chapala pier. Look for good bargains in Oaxaca wool weavings, Jocotepec serapes, Tonalá pottery and papier-mâché, Guadalajara huaraches, Paracho (Michoacán) guitars, Santa Clara del Cobre (Michoacán) copperware, and dozens more colorful items brought from all over Mexico.

In Ajijic, you have at least a couple of close-to-the-source handicrafts options: the woven art of a number of indigenous women at lakeshore and the Jalisco State **Casa de las Artesanias** (House of Handicrafts), tel. 3/766-0548, open Mon.–Fri. 10 A.M.–6 P.M., Saturday 10 A.M.–4 P.M., Sunday 10 A.M.–2 P.M. Watch for the sign on the highway as you're entering from Chapala, just after the big white roadside sculpture on the left. Inside, a host of Jalisco handicrafts—shiny Tlaquepaque red and blue glass and fine painted stoneware, fanciful painted pottery figures, cute papier-mâché and pottery animals from Tonalá, charming nativity sets, bright paper flowers—fill the gallery.

Ajijic's well-to-do resident expatriate community has nurtured local arts and crafts activity. Products of Chapala area artists and artisans, combined with national sources, make up a number of unusually fine selections in several Ajijic shops and boutiques. A good place to start is **Centro de Bellas Artes de Ajijic,** at 43 Colón, tel. 3/766-1920, open Tues.–Sun. 10 A.M.–5 P.M., a block and a half downhill from the highway. As much a community art center as a store, it offers many sensitively executed paintings and photographs by local artists. Don't miss the tranquil, verdant sculpture garden and cafe in the rear.

Downhill two blocks, on the east side, just uphill from the post office, don't neglect to step into the **Galería de Paolo,** tel. 3/766-1010, fax 3/766-2572, labor of love of owner-photographer María de Paola Blum. Here, you can peruse downstairs and upstairs and be entertained by her eclectic gallery of carefully chosen sculptures, paintings, photos, handicrafts, and artistic odds and ends. Open Mon.–Sat. 10 A.M.–3 P.M. and Sunday 11 A.M.–2 P.M.

More interesting Ajijic shops cluster another block downhill, near the corner of Morelos (Colón's downhill continuation) and 16 de Septiembre. Among the best is **Mi México,** the labor of love of its expatriate owners, at Morelos 8, corner of 16 de Septiembre, tel. 3/766-0133. Their collection seems to include a little bit of everything handmade—paintings, jewelry, Guadalajara resortwear, block-printed cottons, Javan batiks—from all over Mexico and the world. Open Mon.–Sat. 10 A.M.–2 P.M. and 3–6 P.M., Sunday 11 A.M.–3 P.M.

Ready-to-wear clothes are a specialty of **Opus Boutique,** across the street, at Morelos 15, tel. 3/766-1790, email: loiscugi@laguna.com.mx. The inventory blooms with attractive, comfortable resortwear—dresses, slacks, skirts, blouses—and some Indonesian batiks, jewelry, and small paintings. Open Mon.–Sat. 10 A.M.–6 P.M., Sunday 11 A.M.–3 P.M.

Directly across the street downhill, **La Flor de la Laguna,** 17 Morelos, tel. 3/766-1037, offers a bright kaleidoscope of Mexican handicrafts. Its assortment includes glistening papier-mâché parrots, a rogue's gallery of masks, and fetching menagerie of nativity sets, yarn dolls, and much more in leather, wood, brass, copper, and cotton. Open Mon.–Sat. 10 A.M.–6 P.M., Sunday 10 A.M.–2 P.M.

On the same side of Morelos, a few doors uphill, is **Calipso,** whose eclectic, attractively arranged wares fill two intimate, adjacent rooms. You'll find it at Morelos 7 and 7B, open Monday and Wed.–Sat. 10:30 A.M.–2 P.M. and 3:30–6:30 P.M., and Sunday 11 A.M.–4 P.M. Calipso specializes in unusual resortwear—dresses, skirts, blouses—in striking bright and dark hues, plus some pieces of tie-dyed art-to-wear, bright clay dolls, colorful wooden horses, silver jewelry, leather purses, and more.

Continue next door to **Ángel Cantor** ("Singing Angel"), at Morelos 13, tel. 3/766-0717. Here, a galaxy of selected all-Mexico handicrafts includes ceramic masks, antique photo postcards, fine Tlaquepaque stoneware, shiny Oaxaca metal-framed mirrors, and a pile of attractive baskets. Open Mon.–Sat. 10 A.M.–7 P.M., Sunday 10 a.m.–5 P.M.

Continue west along the prolongation of 16 de Septiembre (which has changed to Independencia) half a block from the Morelos corner, to **Porta Libros,** another labor of love (at Independencia 7). Here, a library of used books, mostly old paperbacks, and new magazines, fills several small rooms.

After a hard day perusing so many shops, you might want to take a break. You have at least three good possibilities. Off the town plaza, on Hidalgo, half a block west of the bank, you'll find **Evie's** restaurant, open Mon.–Sat. 8 A.M.–4 P.M., Sunday 8 A.M.–3 P.M., closed Wednesday, whose friendly owners' specialties are house-roasted coffee, home-baked fruit pies, and gourmet soups and sandwiches. Next, two blocks downhill from the town plaza is **Las Telares** restaurant, right among the shops, at Morelos 6, open from noon daily. Lastly, try the **Restaurant Posada Ajijic,** open daily at noon, at the foot of Coló.

Finally, be sure to take a look at the attractive hand-woven art—wool rugs, serapes, blankets, and more—that a number of indigenous Oaxaca and Chiapas women make and sell, adjacent to the Restaurant Posada Ajijic.

Photofinishing, Cameras, and Film
The best local photo services are available in downtown Chapala, at **Foto Centro** on Madero, corner of Romero, two blocks uphill from the town plaza, tel. 3/765-4874, open Mon.–Sat. 9 A.M.–7 P.M., Sunday 9 A.M.–2 P.M. Besides the usual color print films, its relatively broad film stock includes professional 120 Ektacolor and Fujicolor, black-and-white, and both Ektachrome and Fujichrome 35 mm transparency films. Foto Centro additionally offers some point-and-shoot cameras and common photo accessories. Services, besides color negative, transparency, and black-and-white developing and printing, include enlargements, photo identity cards, and camera repairs.

In Ajijic, you'll find a smaller branch of Foto Centro on the uphill side of the highway, across from Danny's Restaurant, open Mon.–Sat. 9 A.M.–2:30 P.M. and 4:30–7 P.M.. It offers developing services and a small stock of popular film, point-and-shoot cameras, and supplies.

SERVICES

Money Exchange
In both Chapala and Ajijic, bank-rate money exchange, traveler's checks, and prompt service in English are available at **Lloyd's.** In Chapala, go to Madero 232, across from the town plaza, tel. 3/765-2149 and 3/765-3598; in Ajijic, it's on the highway, east side of the town center, across the street from the gas station, tel. 3/766-3110. Lloyd's, moreover, offers a number of financial and investment services. Both branches are open Mon.–Fri. 9 A.M.–5 P.M.

Conventional **banks,** all with ATMs, are well represented in Chapala, all located near the corner of Hidalgo (the Ajijic highway) and main street Madero. They have longer than usual money-changing hours. Moving uphill, first comes Banco Internacional, tel. 3/765-4110, open Mon.–Fri. 8 A.M.–7 P.M. Two doors farther is Bancomer, tel. 3/765-4515, open Mon.–Fri. 8:30 A.M.–4:30 P.M. After bank hours, use the banks' **automated teller machines,** or the small **casas**

de cambio change money until about 7 P.M. around the corner from Bancomer.

In Ajijic, change your American or Canadian cash or traveler's checks at plaza-front **Banco Promex,** corner of Hidalgo and Colón, tel. 3/766-2300, open Mon.–Fri. 8:30 A.M.–4 P.M., Saturday 10 A.M.–2:00 P.M. After hours, use the bank's ATM or go to the hole-in-the-wall **casa de cambio** at 28 Colón, on the plaza, tel. 3/766-2213, open Mon.–Sat. 8:30 A.M.–5 P.M., Saturday 8:30 A.M.–4 P.M.

Post, Telecommunications, and Internet
Both the Chapala town **correo** and **telecomunicaciones** are on lakeshore Av. Hidalgo, about three blocks west of Madero. The correo (downstairs, in back) is open Mon.–Fri. 9 A.M.–3 P.M., while the telecomunicaciones (upstairs, in front) is open Mon.–Fri. 9 A.M.–2 P.M.

In Ajijic, the small correo is at Colón and Constitución, one block downhill from the plaza; it's open Mon.–Fri. 8 A.M.–2 P.M., and (sometimes) Saturday 9 A.M.–1 P.M.

Computel booths, at both the Chapala (tel. 3/765-4951) and Ajijic (tel. 3/766-2028) town plazas, provide long distance and fax service Mon.–Sat. 8 A.M.–9 P.M., Sunday 8 A.M.–8 P.M. Long distance phone, fax, Xerox copies, and Internet connection (for a steep $6 per hour) are available at **Centro de Copiado de Chapala,** at the center of town, corner of Madero and Hidalgo, fax 3/765-3311, open Mon.–Sat. 9 A.M.–6 P.M.

Internet connection ($4 per hour) is available in Ajijic at **Cafe Internet,** on the highway east side of town, across from Tel Mex telephone office.

You can have everything—express mail, fax, long-distance phone, message center, mailbox, copies, office services, and even a San Diego, California, P.O. box—at **Mailboxes, Etc.** on the highway in San Antonio, halfway between Ajijic and Chapala at Carretera Chapala-Jocotepec 144, San Antonio Tlayacapan, Jalisco, tel. 3/766-0647, fax 3/766-0775.

Health, Police, and Emergencies
Both Chapala and Ajijic have well-equipped small private hospitals, with 24-hour ambulance service and English-speaking specialists available for both regular and emergency consultations. Among the most highly recommended is the

Núcleo Médico y Dental de Especialidades de Chapala on the highway in San Antonio, halfway between Chapala and Ajijic, tel. 3/765-4805. Also in Ajijic you can go to the **Clínica Ajijic** on the highway, no. 33 Oriente, four blocks east of Colón, tel. 3/766-0662 or 3/766-0500.

If you get sick in Chapala, contact your hotel desk or the **Clínica de Especialidades Nueva Galicia,** at Juárez 563A, tel. 3/765-2400, around the northeast plaza corner. Here, general practitioner Doctora Adela Macias Vengas and gynecologist Dr. Felipe de JesÚs Ochoa offer services, on-call 24 hours.

If you prefer homeopathic treatment, go to **Farmacia Abejita** (Little Bee), next to the above doctors' office, at Juárez 559, corner of L. Cotilla, no phone.

For medicines and routine advice, the best-supplied Chapala-area pharmacy is **Hector's Farmacia Morelos** at 421 Madero, south corner of the plaza, tel. 3/765-4002, open 8 A.M.–1 P.M. and 3–8 P.M., except Sunday and Thursday, 8 A.M.–3 P.M. In Ajijic, get your medicines and drugs from **Farmacia Cristina,** at Plaza Bugambilias, on the highway, about six blocks west of the town center, tel. 3/766-1501, open daily 8 A.M.–9 P.M.

For **police emergencies** in Chapala, call or go to the police station on Madero, near the town plaza, tel. 3/765-2851. In Ajijic, contact the police at the Presidencia Municipal town hall, on Colón by the plaza, tel. 3/766-1760.

Consulates
The U.S. Consul in Guadalajara, Progreso 175, Guadalajara, about a mile west of the city center, open Mon.–Fri. 8 A.M.–4:30 P.M., tel. 3/825-2020 or 3/825-2031, periodically visits the Chapala area. The visitation schedule is customarily posted on one of the bulletin boards at the Ajijic library at 16 de Septiembre.

In an emergency, call the Canadian consul in Guadalajara, at the Hotel Fiesta Americana, tel. 3/615-6215.

Travel and Real Estate Agents
Travel and real estate agents can provide many services and are also often willing sources of information. One of the most friendly local travel agencies is **Caminos Camelot,** run by the husband-and-wife team of Karl and Anne Roettger in

San Antonio, midway between Chapala and Ajijic, at Carretera Chapala-Ajijic 133A, San Antonio Tlayacapan, tel. 3/766-0268, fax 3/766-1058.

Also highly recommended are **Chapala Realty,** at Hidalgo 223, tel. 3/765-2877, fax 3/765-3528; and **Laguna Real Estate** in Ajijic, on the highway, tel. 3/766-1174, fax 3/766-1188, email: laguna@laguna.com.mx.

Handicrafts and Fine Arts Courses
Jalisco State **Casa de las Artesanias** (House of Handicrafts) offers pottery, painting, weaving, and other courses in handicrafts. For more information call 3/766-0548, or drop into its Ajijic gallery, open Mon.–Fri. 10 A.M.–6 P.M., Saturday 10 A.M.–4 P.M., Sunday 10 A.M.–2 P.M., on the highway as you're entering from Chapala, just after the big white roadside sculpture on the left.

The **Centro de Bellas Artes de Ajijic** (Fine Arts Center of Ajijic) offers painting, sculpture, ceramics, and photography classes. Ask for details at 43 Colón, Ajijic, tel. 3/766-1920, open Tues.–Sun. 10 A.M.–5 P.M., a block and a half downhill from the highway.

INFORMATION

Tourist Information Office
The small Chapala office of Jalisco state tourism is downtown, near the lakefront, across the street from the Hotel Nido, at Madero 407, upper level. During regular hours, Mon.–Fri. 9 A.M.–6 P.M., Saturday 9 A.M.–1 P.M., the staff will answer questions and give out brochures and maps.

Publications
The best local bookstore is **Libros y Revistas de Chapala** across from the plaza at Madero 230; open daily 9 A.M.–7:30 P.M. Its extensive stock includes racks of English paperback books and dozens of American popular magazines and newspapers, such as *USA Today* and the *Los Angeles Times.* It also has many Mexico maps and some guidebooks. In Ajijic, the small newsstand by the plaza, at Colón 29, open daily 9 A.M.–2 P.M. and 3–6 P.M., offers a very limited assortment of American newspapers and magazines.

While in Chapala, be sure to pick up a copy of the superb local monthly *El Ojo del Lago.* Its lively pages are packed with details of local exhibits, performances, and events; pithy articles of Mexican lore and nearby places to visit; and even interesting advertisements. If you can't find a copy, drop by the office at Av. Hidalgo 223, at Coldwell Banker-Chapala Realty, tel. 3/765-3676, fax 3/765-3528, or email: ojodellago@laguna.com.mx.

The **Neill James Library,** a good work of the charitable Lake Chapala Society, stands in its flowery showplace garden two blocks downhill from the Ajijic town plaza on Calle 16 de Septiembre, a block east of main street Colón; open Mon.–Sat. 10 A.M.–2 P.M. Its broad all-English loan collection includes many shelves of classic and contemporary literature, donated by Ajijic residents. The Society also maintains the adjacent Spanish-language children's library, open Mon.–Sat. 10:30 A.M.–1 P.M. and 4–6 P.M. In the corridor between the two buildings, an informative bulletin board and community calendar details local cultural, civic, and social events.

The Lake Chapala Society

The Lake Chapala Society, a volunteer civic organization, welcomes visitors for coffee and conversation Mon.–Fri. 10 A.M.–2 P.M. at its El Patio coffee shop and its Video Club movies, Mon.–Sat. 10 a.m.–2 P.M., at the Neill James Library, on Calle 16 de Septiembre, Ajijic.

Amigos del Lago

Conservation-minded local citizens have banded together to form Amigos del Lago, "Friends of the Lake." They advise and monitor government efforts to restore Lake Chapala and sponsor educational projects, such as lakeshore trash cleanup and tree-planting. For more information, contact articulate and bilingual Aurora Michel, one of the organization's friendly sparkplugs (and Chapala manager of Lloyd Financial) at Fco. Madero 232, tel. 3/765-2149 and 3/765-3598, or at home at 3/766-3111.

GETTING THERE AND AWAY

By Air

Chapala is accessible directly from many U.S. gateways, via the Guadalajara airport, just 21 miles (33 km) north of the lake. For flight and airport details, see "Getting There and Away" in the Guadalajara section, preceding.

By Car or RV

The town of Chapala is about 33 miles (53 km) by the federal Hwy. 44 south of the Guadalajara city center—less than an hour. The road connections with major Puerto Vallarta region destinations are the same as those from Guadalajara except for minor adjustments. (See "By Car or RV" in the Guadalajara section, preceding.)

If you're connecting with Lake Chapala directly to or from Tepic or Puerto Vallarta, use the Guadalajara *periférico* (peripheral city-center bypass). This links the Chapala Hwy. 44 directly with the west-side Tepic-Puerto Vallarta leg of Hwy. 15.

To or from southern destinations of Barra de Navidad, Colima, and Manzanillo, route yourself south of Guadalajara, along the lake's northwest shore, via Hwy. 15's Jocotepec-Acatlán de Juárez leg. Around Acatlán de Juárez, pay close attention to turn-off signs. They'll guide your connection from Hwy. 54 D *cuota autopista* (toll freeway) (Colima and Manzanillo) or two-lane Hwy. 80 (Barra de Navidad).

By Bus

The main Lake Chapala bus station is in Chapala downtown on Madero at M. Martínez, about three blocks uphill from the town plaza. The red and white second-class buses of **Autotransportes Guadalajara-Chapala,** tel. 3/765-2212, connect about every half hour with the Guadalajara downtown old terminal (Camionera Antigua) until about 8:30 P.M., and every half hour until about 8:30 P.M. with the new suburban Guadalajara Camionera Central. Other red and white departures connect about every half hour with both Jocotepec and San Nicolas, and every hour with Mezcala.

THE COAST OF JALISCO

THE ROAD TO BARRA DE NAVIDAD

The country between Puerto Vallarta and Barra de Navidad is a landscape ripe for travelers who enjoy getting away from the tourist track. Development has barely begun to penetrate its vast tracts of mountainous jungle, tangled thorny scrub, and pine-clad summit forests. Footprints rarely mark miles of its curving, golden beaches.

Fortunately, everyone who travels south of Puerto Vallarta doesn't have to be a Daniel Boone. The coastal strip within a few miles of the highway has acquired some comforts—stores, trailer parks, campgrounds, hotels, and a scattering of small resorts—enough to become well known to Guadalajara people as the Costa Alegre, the Happy Coast.

This modicum of amenities makes it easy for all visitors to enjoy what local people have for years: plenty of sun, fresh seafood, clear blue water, and sandy beaches, some of which stretch for miles, while others are tucked away in little rocky coves like pearls in an oyster.

Heading Out

If you're driving, note your odometer mileage (or reset it to zero) as you pass the Pemex gas station at Km 214 on Hwy. 200 at the south edge of Puerto Vallarta. In the open southern country, mileage and roadside kilometer markers are a useful way to remember where your little paradise is hidden.

If you're not driving, simply hop onto one of the many southbound Autocamiones del Pacífico or Transportes Cihuatlán second-class buses just before they pass at the south-end gas station. Let the driver know a few minutes beforehand where along the road you want to get off.

CHICO'S PARADISE

The last outpost on the Puerto Vallarta tour-bus circuit is Chico's Paradise, 13 miles (22 km, at Km 192) from the south edge of Puerto Vallarta in the lush jungle country. Here, the clear, cool Río Tuito cascades over a collection of smooth, friendly granite boulders. Chico's restaurant is a big multilevel *palapa* that overlooks the entire beautiful scene—deep green pools for swimming, flat warm rocks for sunning, and gurgling gentle waterfalls for splashing. Although a few homesteads and a humbler rival restaurant, Indian Paradise, dot the streamside nearby, the original Chico's still dominates, although its reputation rests mainly on the beauty of the setting rather than the quality of its rather expensive menu.

La Tanga bar and restaurant offers a similarly airy (but not quite so scenic) *palapa* set-

ting about a mile upstream from Chico's, at more reasonable prices. After a refreshment, stroll along the shady stream bank and drink in the beautiful scene.

The forest-perfumed breezes, the gurgling, crystal stream, and the friendly, relaxed ambience are perfect for shedding the cares of the world. Although there are no formal lodgings, a number of potential camping spots border the river, both up- and downstream. Stores at either the nearby upstream villagev or Boca de Tomatlán, three miles downhill, can provide supplies.

Adventurers can hire local guides (ask at La Tanga) for horseback rides along the river and overnight treks into the green, jungly **Sierra Lagunillas** that rises on both sides of the river. If you're quiet and aware, you may be rewarded with views of chattering parrots, dozing iguanas, feisty javelinas (wild pigs), clownish *tejones*

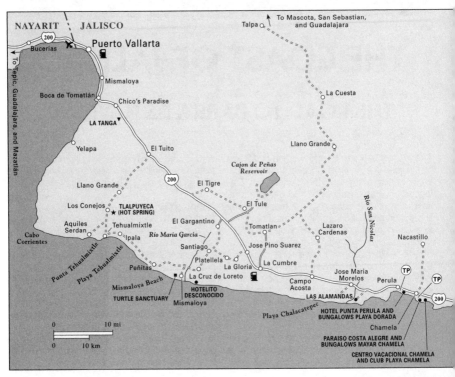

(coatimundis), and wary *gatos montaña* (wildcats). If you're especially lucky, you might even get a glimpse of the fabled *tigre* (jaguar).

CABO CORRIENTES COUNTRY

El Tuito

The town of El Tuito, at Km 170 (27 miles, 44 km, from Puerto Vallarta), appears from the highway as nothing more than a bus stop. It doesn't even have a gas station. Most visitors pass by without even giving a second glance. This is a pity, because El Tuito (pop. 3,000) is a friendly little colonial-era town that spreads along a long main street to a pretty square about a mile from the highway.

El Tuito enjoys at least two claims to fame: besides being the mescal capital of western Jalisco, it's the jumping-off spot for the seldom-visited coastal hinterland of Cabo Corrientes, the southernmost lip of the Bay of Banderas. This is pioneer country, a land of wild beaches and sylvan forests, unpenetrated by electricity, phone, and paved roads. Wild creatures still abound: turtles come ashore to lay their eggs, hawks soar, parrots swarm, and the faraway scream of the jaguar can yet be heard in the night.

The rush for the **raicilla,** as local connoisseurs call El Tuito mescal, begins on Saturday when men crowd into town and begin upending bottles around noon, without even bothering to sit down. For a given individual, this cannot last too long, so the fallen are continually replaced by fresh arrivals all weekend.

Although El Tuito is famous for the *raicilla,* it is not the source. *Raicilla* comes from the sweet sap of the maguey plants, a close relative of the cactuslike century plant, which blooms once

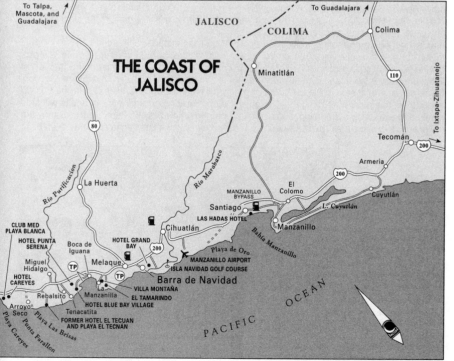

then dies. The *ejido* (cooperative farm) of Ci-catan (see-kah-TAHN), six miles out along the dirt road as you head to the coast west of town, cultivates the maguey.

Along the Road to Aquiles Serdán

You can get to the coast with or without your own wheels. If you're driving, it should be a strong, high-clearance vehicle (pickup, jeep, very maneuverable RV, or VW van) filled with gas; if you're not driving, trucks and VW taxi-vans (combis or *colectivos*) make daily trips. Their destinations include the coastal hamlet of Aquiles Serdán, the storied fishing cove of Tehualmixtle, and the farming village of Ipala beside the wide Bahía de Tehualmixtle. Fare runs a few dollars per person; inquire at the Hwy. 200 crossing or the west end of the El Tuito central plaza.

Getting there along the bumpy, rutted, some-times steep 23-mile (37-km) dirt track is half the fun of Aquiles Serdán (pop. 200). About six miles (10 km) from Hwy. 200, you'll pass through the lands of the mescal cooperative, Cicatan, marked only by a crumbling whitewash-and-thatch house in front of a tiny school on the right. On the left, you'll soon glimpse a field of maguey in the distance. A few dozen families (who live in the hills past the far side of the field) quietly go about their business of tending their maguey plants and extracting, fermenting, and distilling the precious sap into their renowned *raicilla*.

The road dips up and down the rest of the way, over sylvan hillsides dotted with oak *(rob-les),* through intimate stream valleys perfect for parking an RV or setting up a tent, and past the hardscrabble rancho-hamlets of Llano Grande (Broad Plain, 14 miles, 22 km), with stores, *comedores* (places to eat) and a *Centro de Salud* (health center), and Los Conejos (The Rabbits, 19 miles, 30 km).

You can't get lost, because there's only one route until a few miles past Los Conejos, where a fork (23 miles, 37 km) marks your approach to Aquiles Serdán. The left branch continues south to Maito and Tehualmixtle. A mile and a half to the north along the right branch you will arrive at the Río Tecolotlán. Aquiles Serdán stands on the far bank, across 100 yards of watery sand. Fortunately the riverbed road is concrete-bot-tomed, and (if it's in good repair, which it wasn't at this writing) you can drive right across the streambed any time other than after a storm. If you can't drive across, roll up your pant legs and walk across, like most of the local folks do.

Aquiles Serdán

The Aquiles Serdán villagers see so few out-siders that you will become their attraction of the week. Wave and say *hola,* buy a *refresco,* stroll around town, and, after a while, the kids will stop crowding around and the adults will stop staring when they've found out you, too, are human. By that time, someone may even have

At Chico's Paradise, fragrant mountain air and the murmur of the river splashing over friendly rocks invites relaxation.

invited you into their tree-branch-walled, clean dirt-floor house for some hot fish-fillet tacos, fresh tomatoes, and beans. Accept, of course.

Aquiles Serdán basks above the lily-edged river lagoon, which during the June–Oct. rainy season usually breaks through the beach-sand-bar and drains directly into the surf half a mile below the town. During the dry season, the lagoon wanders lazily up the coast for a few miles. In any case, the white-sand beach is accessible only by boat, which you can borrow or hire at the village.

If you do, you'll have miles of untouched white sand and surf all to yourself for days of camping, beachcombing, shell collecting, surf fishing, wildlife viewing, and, if the waves permit, swimming, surfing, boogie boarding, and snorkeling. The town's two stores can provide your necessities.

Back at the fork (23 miles, 37 km from the highway) continue along the left branch about two miles through Maito (pop. 100), which has two stores. A right fork just after Maito leads half a mile to **Playa Maito**, a surf fishing and beachcombers' paradise, where you could either park your RV or tent on the beach or stay at a new but still rough small beachfront hotel with "water and a washing machine" (bring all your food) for about $10 per night.

Tehualmixtle

Back on the main road, you arrive at another fork (at 26 miles, 42 km). The right branch goes steeply up and then down a rough track to the right, which soon levels out on the cliff above the idyllic fishing cove of Tehualmixtle. Here, a headland shelters a blue nook, where a few launches float, tethered and protected from the open sea. To one side, swells wash over a submerged wreck, while an ancient, moss-stained warehouse crumbles above a rocky little beach. At the end of the road downhill, a pair of beachside *palapas* invite visitors with drinks and fresh-out-of-the-water oysters, lobster, *dorado,* and red snapper.

Candelario, owner/operator of the right-side *palapa,* is the moving force behind this pocket-size paradise. After your repast, and a couple more bottles of beer for good measure, he might tell you his version of the history of this coast—of legends of sunken galleons, or of the days when the old warehouse stored cocaine for legal ship-ment to the United States, when Coca-Cola got its name from the cocaine, which, generations ago, was added to produce "the pause that refreshes."

Nowadays, however, Tehualmixtle serves as a resting point for occasional sailboaters, travelers, fisherfolk, and those who enjoy the rewards of clear-water snorkeling and scuba diving around the sunken shrimp trawler and the rocky shoreline nearby. Several level spots beside the cove invite camping or RV parking. Candelario will gladly supply you with your stomach's delight of choice seafood and drinks.

Furthermore, Candelario and his family, led by his friendly, outgoing English-speaking daughter Gaby, have built a small **hotel.** They offer four clean, simply furnished rooms with shiny white bathrooms, view windows, and ceiling fans. Asking rates are about $22 s, $27 d, $32 t. Additionally, they rent out a comfortable view bungalow sleeping five, fine for groups, with a kitchenette, good bathroom, and ceiling fans for $37 nightly, discount for one-week stay. Reserve by telephone at 3/228-0117 (in Spanish) with Candelario's daughter Evangelina Joya, in El Tuito.

Exploring Tehualmixtle and Vicinity: For those who stay a few days, Candelario offers his services as **guide** for equipped snorkelers and scuba divers to investigate nearby sites, especially the submerged wreck right offshore. Farther afield, he also can lead parties inland a few miles, by foot or horseback, to hot spring **Tlapuyeca,** where, years ago, a French company operated a logging concession.

Southeast of Tehualmixtle

Returning back up the road above the cove, glimpse southward toward the azure Bay of Tehualmixtle washing the white-sand ribbon of the Playa de Tehualmixtle. The village of **Ipala,** three miles down the road, is supply headquarters (unleaded gasoline available) for the occasional visitors drawn by the good fishing, surfing, beachcombing, and camping prospects of the Playa de Tehualmixtle. Being on the open ocean, its waves are usually rough, especially in the afternoon. Only experienced swimmers who can judge undertow and surf should think of swimming here.

From Ipala (29 miles, 47 km), you can either retrace your path back to the highway at El Tuito, or continue down the coast (where the road gets rougher before it gets better) through the hamlet and beach of **Peñitas** (36 miles, 58 km; a few stores, restaurants), past **Mismaloya** (46 miles, 74 km), site of a University of Guadalajara turtle-hatching station. To get there, turn right onto the dirt trail just before the concrete bridge over the broad Río María Garcia.

From Mismaloya, return to the bridge, continue over the river three miles farther, and you will soon be back to the 20th century at **Cruz de Loreto** (49 miles, 79 km; many stores, sidewalks, electric lights, and phones).

After all the backcountry hard traveling, treat yourself to a few nights at luxury eco-resort **Hotelito Desconocido** (inquire locally for directions, or follow the signs west to the hotel, at the lagoon and beach nearby); reservations are strongly recommended. For more details, see Special Topic "Splendid Isolation" in the Puerto Vallarta town chapter.

Alternatively, from Cruz de Loreto, you can head directly to Hwy. 200 (10 miles via Santiago and El Gargantino) at the highway Km 133 marker, just 23 miles (37 km) south of where you started at El Tuito.

CAJÓN DE LAS PEÑAS RESERVOIR

The lush farms of the Cabo Corrientes region owe much of their success to the Cajón de Peñas dam, whose waters enable farmers to profit from a year-round growing season. An added bonus is the recreation—boating, fishing, swimming, camping, and hiking—the big blue lake behind the dam makes possible.

With a car, the reservoir is easy to reach. Trucks and cars are frequent, so hikers can easily thumb rides. At Hwy. 200 Km 131, about a mile south of the Cruz de Loreto turnoff, head left (east) at a signed, paved road. After about five miles the road turns to gravel. Continue another four miles to a road fork atop a complex of three rock-fill dams, separated by a hill. The left road continues over the smaller two dams to a dead end. The right fork leads to a sign reading Puerto Vallarta Bass Club and a left fork just before the largest dam. Turn left and continue downhill to **La Lobina,** a humble family-run restaurant *palapa* and boat landing. The friendly husband-wife team maintains their little outpost in hopes of serving the trickle of mostly holiday and weekend visitors. Besides their children, who help with chores, their little settlement consists of two parrots, a brood of turkeys, and a flock of chickens that flies into the nearby forest to roost at night. Their cooking, based mostly upon freshly caught *lobina* (large-mouth bass) is basic but wholesome. Their parking lot above the lake has room for a number of self-contained RVs, while the forested knoll nearby might serve for tent camping. They offer their boat for lake sightseeing and fishing excursions for about $15 an hour.

Cajón de las Peñas Reservoir is a favorite lobina *(bass) fishing ground.*

Otherwise, you could swim, kayak, or launch your own motorboat right from the lakeshore below the restaurant.

Head back, turn left at the uphill fork and continue over the larger dam, counterclockwise around the forested, sloping lakeshore. Within about two miles (three kilometers) you'll arrive at the boat-cooperative village, where several downscale *palapa* restaurants and boat landings provide food and recreational services for visitors. For a fee (ask at one of the restaurants, *"¿Hay una tarifa para acampar?"*—"Is there a fee to camp?"), you can usually set up a tent or park your RV under a nearby lakeside tree.

PLAYA CHALACATEPEC

Playa Chalacatepec (chah-lah-kah-tay-PEK) lazes in the tropical sun just nine and a half kilometers from the highway at Km 88. Remarkably few people know of its charms except a handful of local youths, a few fisherfolk, and occasional families who come on Sunday outings.

Playa Chalacatepec, with three distinct parts, has something for everyone: on the south side, a wild, arrow-straight, miles-long strand with crashing open-ocean breakers; in the middle, a low, wave-tossed, rocky point; and on the north, a long, tranquil, curving fine-sand beach.

The north beach, shielded by the point, has gently rolling breakers good for surfing, body-surfing, and safe swimming. Shells seasonally carpet its gradual white slope, and visitors have even left a pair of *palapa* shelters. These seem ready-made for camping by night and barbecuing fish by day with all of the driftwood lying around for the taking.

The point, Punta Chalacatepec, which separates the two beaches, is good for pole fishing on its surf-washed flanks and tidepooling in its rocky crevices.

Folks with RVs can pull off and park either along the approach road just above the beach or along tracks (beware of soft spots) downhill in the tall acacia scrub that borders the sand.

One of the few natural amenities that Playa Chalacatepec lacks is drinking water, however. Bring your own from the town back on the highway.

Getting There

Just as you're entering little José María Morelos (pop. 2,000), a hundred feet past the Km 88 marker, turn toward the beach at the corner. (If you're planning to camp, best stock up with water and groceries at the stores in the town down the road, south.)

The road, although steep in spots, is negotiable by passenger cars in good condition and small-to-medium RVs. Owners of big rigs should do a test run. On foot, the road is an easy two-hour hike—much of which probably won't be necessary because of the many passing farm pickups.

Mark your odometer at the highway. Continue over brushy hills and past fields and pastures, until Mile 5.2 (Km 8.4) where the road forks sharply right. You take the left track and pass a gate (close it after yourself). Atop the dune, glimpse the mangrove lagoon (bring kayak or rubber boat for wildlife-watching) in the distance to the left. Downhill, at Mile 6 (Km 9.7), you will be at Playa Chalacatepec.

LAS ALAMANDAS

After roughing it at Playa Chalacatepec, you can be pampered in the luxurious isolation of Las Alamandas, a deluxe 1,500-acre retreat a few miles down the road.

The small sign at Km 83 gives no hint of the pleasant surprises that Las Alamandas conceals behind its guarded gate. Solitude and elegant simplicity seem to have been the driving concepts in the mind of Isabel Goldsmith when she acquired control of the property in the late 1980s. Although born into wealth (her grandfather was the late tin tycoon Antenor Patiño, who developed Manzanillo's renowned Las Hadas; her father, the late multimillionaire Sir James Goldsmith, who bought the small kingdom her family now owns at Cuitzmala, 25 miles south), she was not idle. Isabel converted her dream of paradise—a small, luxuriously isolated resort on an idyllic beach in Puerto Vallarta's sylvan coastal hinterland—into reality. Now, her guests (22 maximum) enjoy accommodations that range from luxuriously simple studios to villas that sleep six. Activities include a health club, tennis, horseback riding, bicycling, fishing, and lagoon and river excursions.

Daily rates begin at about $350 low season, $450 high for garden-view studios, to beachfront villas for about $900 low, $1,400 high; all with full breakfast. Three meals, prepared to your order, cost about $200 additional per day per person. For more information and reservations, call its agents, from U.S. and Canada, tel. 888/882-9616, or contact Las Alamandas in Mexico directly, at Quémaro, Km. 83 Carretera Puerto Vallarta-Barra de Navidad, Jalisco 48854, tel. 328/555-00, fax 328/550-27, email info@las-ala-mandas.com, website: www.las-alamandas.com. Don't arrive unannounced; the guard will not let you through the gate unless you have reservation in hand or have made an appointment.

CHAMELA BAY

Most longtime visitors know Jalisco's Costa Alegre through Barra de Navidad and two big, beautiful, beach-lined bays: Tenacatita and Chamela. Tranquil Bahía de Chamela, the most northerly of the two, is broad, blue, dotted with islands, and lined by a strip of fine, honey-yellow sand.

Stretching five miles south from the sheltering Punta Rivas headland near Perula village, Chamela Bay is open but calm. A chain of intriguingly labeled rocky *islitas,* such as Cocinas (Kitchens), Negrita (Little Black One), and Pajarera (Place of Birds), scatter the strong Pacific swells into gentle billows by the time they roll onto the beaches.

Besides its natural amenities, Chamela Bay has three bungalow-complexes, one mentionable motel, two trailer parks, and an unusual "camping club." The focal point of this low-key resort area is the Km 72 highway corner (88 miles, 142 km, from Puerto Vallarta; 46 miles, 74 km, to Barra de Navidad). This spot, marked "Chamela" on many maps, is known simply as **"El Super"** by local people. Though the supermarket and neighboring bank have closed and are filled with the owner's antique car collection, El Super, nevertheless, lives on in the minds of the local folks.

Beaches and Activities
Chamela Bay's beaches are variations on one continuous strip of sand, from Playa Rosadas in the south through Playa Chamela in the middle to Playas Fortuna and Perula at the north end.

Curving behind the sheltering headland, **Playa Perula** is the broadest and most tranquil beach of Chamela Bay. It is best for children and a snap for boat launching, swimming, and fishing from the rocks nearby. A dozen *pangas* usually line the water's edge, ready to take visitors on fishing excursions (figure $15 per hour, after bargaining) and snorkeling around the offshore islets. A line of seafood *palapas* provides the food and drinks for the fisherfolk and mostly Mexican families who know and enjoy this scenic little village/cove.

Playas Fortuna, Chamela, and Rosada: Heading south, the beach gradually changes character. The surf roughens, the slope steepens, and the sand narrows from around 200 feet at Perula to perhaps 100 feet at the south end of the bay. Civilization also thins out. The dusty village of stores, small eateries, vacation homes, and beachfront *palapa* restaurants that line Playa Fortuna give way to farmland and scattered houses at Playa Chamela. Two miles farther on, grassy dunes above trackless sand line Playa Rosada.

The gradually varying vigor of the waves and the isolation of the beach determine the place where you can indulge your own favorite pastimes: For bodysurfing and boogie boarding, Rosada and Chamela are best; and while windsurfing is usually possible anywhere on Chamela Bay, it will be best beyond the tranquil waves at La Fortuna. For surf fishing, try casting beyond the vigorous, breaking billows of Rosada. And Rosada, being the most isolated, will be the place where you'll most likely find that shell-collection treasure you've been wishing for.

The five-mile curving strand of Chamela Bay is perfect for a morning hike from Rosada Beach. To get there, ride a Transportes Cihuatlán second-class bus to around the Km 65 marker, where a dirt road heads a half-mile to the beach. With the sun comfortably at your back, you can walk all the way to Perula if you want, stopping for refreshments at any one of several *palapas* along the way.

The firm sand of Chamela Bay beaches is likewise good for jogging, even for bicycling, provided you don't mind cleaning the sand out of the gears afterwards.

El Super Accommodations

Three accommodations serve travelers near the El Super corner: an emergency-only motel on the highway, bungalows, and a "camping club." The owners of the "camping club," **Paraíso Costa Alegre,** who live in Guadalajara, don't call it a campground because, curiously, in the past their policy has been, instead of allowing campers to use their own tents, to rent out one of their stuffy, concrete, tent-shaped constructions. Unfortunately these have fallen out of repair and are unusable, so they may have to let people put up their own tents after all. It's worth asking about it, for Paraíso Costa Alegre would be a beautiful tent camping spot, where the beach and bay set the mood: soft, golden sand, island-silhouetted sunsets, tranquil surf, abundant birds and fish, sometimes whales and dolphins, and occasionally great manta rays leap from the water offshore.

Even without your own tent you can still enjoy staying in the outdoors by renting one of Paraíso Costa Alegre's several recently renovated open-air oceanfront Swiss Family Robinson-style cabañas, each with a cooking and eating area and toilet and shower downstairs, and a pair of thatch-roofed bedrooms with soft floor-sleeping pads upstairs.

In addition, you could rent one of the 15 shady spaces in its **trailer park** with all hookups, right next to the communal showers and toilet. Moreover, the lovely, palm-shadowed complex has two tall, elaborate *palapa* restaurant/bars, a minimarket, drinkable water, hot water, communal showers, toilets, and a laundry.

A minor drawback to all this, besides there being no pool, are the somewhat steep rates: the open-air cabanas go for the same price as a moderate hotel room: about $35 for four, $25 for one or two; the trailer spaces go for about $15 per day or $400 per month. Tent camping, if allowed, will probably go for about $7 a day. These prices, however, are subject to bargaining and discounts any time other than peak holidays. For reservations and more information write Paraíso Costa Alegre at Km 72, Carretera 200, Barra de Navidad a Puerto Vallarta, Chamela, Jalisco, or call 328/552-47.

Right across the lane from Paraíso Costa Alegre stands the **Bungalows Mayar Chamela,** Km 72, Carretera Puerto Vallarta, Chamela, Jalisco, tel. 328/552-52. The 18 spacious kitch-enette-bungalows with fans (no a/c) surround an attractive inner garden and a palmy, banana-fringed pool and patio. Although the blue meandering pool and palmy grounds are very inviting, the bungalows themselves have suffered from neglect in the past. Look inside three or four and make sure that everything is in working order before moving in. If so, the bungalows' pool and garden setting and the long, lovely Chamela beach just a block away might be perfect for a week or month of tranquil relaxation. If you're passing through, it might be worthwhile to take a look. Rentals run $22 d, $40 for four; monthly discounts are available. For reservations, write or fax the owner, Gabriel Yañez G., at Obregón 1425 S.L., Guadalajara, Jalisco, tel. 3/644-0044, fax 3/643-9318. Note: The summer-fall season is pretty empty on the Chamela Bay beaches. Consequently, food is scarce around Paraíso Costa Alegre and Bungalows Mayar Chamela. Meals, however, are available at the restaurant at the El Super corner, and a few groceries at small stores along the highway nearby, or in San Mateo a mile south.

Perula Hotels and Trailer Parks

At Km 76, a sign marks a dirt road to Playas Fortuna and Perula. About two miles downhill, right on the beach, you can't miss the bright yellow stucco **Hotel, Bungalows and Trailer Park Playa Dorada,** Perula, Km 76, Carretera 200 Melaque-Puerto Vallarta, Jalisco 48854, tel. 328/551-32, fax 328/551-33. More a motel than bungalows, its three tiers of very plain rooms and suites with kitchenettes are nearly empty except on weekends and Mexican holidays.

Playa Dorada's two saving graces, however, are the beach, which curves gracefully to the scenic little fishing nook of Perula, and the motel's inviting palm-shaded pool and patio. The best-located rooms are on the top floor, overlooking the ocean. Eighteen plain rooms sleeping two or three rent for about $25; 18 kitchenette units sleeping four go for about $40, all with parking. Although a 20 percent discount for weekly rentals is routinely available, you might be able to bargain for an even better deal any time other than peak holidays.

Folks who take one of the dozen trailer spaces in the bare lot across the street are welcome to lounge all day beneath the palms of the pool

SAVING TURTLES

Sea turtles were once common on Puerto Vallarta beaches. Times have changed, however. Now a determined corps of volunteers literally camps out on isolated beaches, trying to save the turtles from extinction. This is a tricky business, because their poacher opponents are invariably poor, determined, and often armed. Since turtle tracks lead right to the eggs, the trick is to get there before the poachers. The turtle-savers dig up the eggs and hatch them themselves, or bury them in secret locations where the eggs hopefully will hatch unmolested. The reward—the sight of hundreds of new

hawksbill turtle

hatchlings returning to the sea—is worth the pain for this new generation of Mexican eco-activists.

Once featured on a thousand restaurant menus from Puerto Angel to Mazatlán, turtle meat, soup, and eggs are now illegal commodities. Though not extinct, Pacific Mexico's three main sea turtle species—green, hawksbill, and leatherback—have dwindled to a tiny fraction of their previous numbers.

The **green turtle** *(Chelonia mydas),* known locally as *tortuga verde* or *caguama,* is named for the

green turtle

and patio. Spaces rent for about $10, with all hookups, and with luxurious, brand-new showers and toilets. Add about $2/day for a/c power.

It's easy to miss the low-profile **Hotel Punta Perula,** just one block inland from the Bungalows Playa Dorada, at Perula, Km 76, Carretera 200, Melaque-Puerto Vallarta, Jalisco 48854, tel. 328/550-20. This homey place seems like a scene from Old Mexico, with a rustic white stucco tier of rooms enclosing a spacious green garden and venerable tufted grove. Its 14 clean, gracefully decorated, colonial-style, fan-equipped rooms go for about $20 d, except for Christmas and Easter holidays. Bargain for lower, long-term rates. (Being out of Old Mexico, it has no pool, of course.)

A few blocks north of the Hotel Playa Dorada is the downscale **Punta Perula Trailer Park,** Perula, Km 76, Carretera, Puerto Vallarta, Jalisco 48854. The spare facilities include about 16 usable but shadeless spaces right on the beach, with all hookups, a fish-cleaning sink, and showers and toilets. Punta Perula Trailer Park resi-

dents enjoy stores nearby, good fishing, and a lovely beach for a front yard. Rates are low, but indefinite—one of the residents said he was paying a monthly rate that amounted to about $6 a day.

Centro Vacacional Chamela and Club Playa Chamela

Four miles south of El Super, at Rosada Beach, sharing the same luscious Chamela Bay strand, is the **Centro Vacacional Chamela,** a teachers' vacation retreat that rents its unoccupied units to the general public. The building is a modern, two-story apartment house with a well-maintained pool and patio. An outdoor *palapa* stands by the pool and another open room invites cards and conversation. The units themselves are large, bright, and airy one-bedrooms, sleeping four, with sea views and kitchens. They rent for about $40, drop-in only. Call 328/552-24 or arrive before about 4 P.M., when the manager is usually around to check things before going home for the night. On nonholiday weekdays the place is often nearly empty. Have a look by color of its fat. Although officially threatened, the prolific green turtle remains relatively numerous. Females can return to shore up to eight times during the year, depositing 500 eggs in a single season. When not mating or migrating, the vegetarian greens can be spotted most often in lagoons and bays, especially the Bay of Banderas, nipping at seaweed with their beaks. Adults, usually three or four feet long and weighing 100–200 pounds, are easily identified out of water by the four big plates on either side of their

leatherback turtle

shells. Green turtle meat was once prized as the main ingredient of turtle soup.

The endangered **hawksbill** *(Eretmochelys imbricata)* has vanished from many Pacific Mexico beaches. Known locally as the *tortuga carey,* it was the source of both meat and the lovely translucent tortoiseshell that has been supplanted largely by plastic. Adult *careys,* among the smaller of sea turtles, run two to three feet in length and weigh 30–100 pounds. Their usually brown shells are readily identified by shingle-like overlapping scales. During late summer and fall, females come ashore to lay clutches of eggs (around 100) in the sand. *Careys,* although preferring fish, mollusks, and shellfish, will eat most anything, including seaweed. When attacked, *careys* can be plucky fighters, inflicting bites with their eagle-sharp hawksbills.

You'll be fortunate indeed if you glimpse the rare **leatherback** *(Dermochelys coriacea),* the world's largest turtle. "Experts" know so little about the leatherback, or *tortuga de cuero,* it's impossible to determine just how endangered it is. Tales are told of fisherfolk netting seven- or eight-foot leatherbacks weighing nearly a ton apiece. If you see even a small one you'll recognize it immediately by its back of smooth, tough skin, creased with several lengthwise ridges.

following the upper of two side roads at the big "47" sign near the Km 66 marker. Within a few hundred yards you'll be there. Ask one of the teachers to explain the significance of "47."

If the teachers' retreat is full, try next door at the **Club Playa Chamela,** perhaps the most downscale timeshare in Mexico, if not the world. The manager said that, for a one-time fee of about $1,200, you can get one idyllic week for each of 20 years there. In the meantime, while the units are being sold, the owner is renting them out. All 12 of the pink and blue, bare-bulb cottages have two bedrooms, a kitchenette, and small living room. Although plainly furnished, they're reasonably clean and have ceiling fans and hot water. Outside, beyond a shady palm grove, is a blue pool, a *palapa* sometimes-restaurant, and a long, pristine, sunset-view beach. The asking rate is about $32/day, $300/week, or $700/month. Try bargaining for a better price anytime other than the popular Christmas, Easter, and August seasons. Contact the manager, Martin Palafox, directly at tel. 328/551-11, or

owner Jose A. Santana Soto at tel. 333/434-061, for information and reservations.

Camping

For RVs, the best spots are the trailer parks at **Paraíso Costa Alegre,** the **Hotel, Bungalows and Trailer Park Playa Dorada,** and **Punta Perula Trailer Park** (see above).

If you can walk in, you can probably set up a tent anywhere along the bay you like. One of the best places would be the grassy dune along pristine Playa Rosada a few hundred yards north of the Centro Vacacional (Km 66; see above). Water is available from the manager (offer to pay) at the Centro Vacacional.

Playa Negrita, the pristine little sand crescent that marks the southern end of Chamela Bay, offers still another picnic or camping possibility. Get there by following the dirt road angling downhill from the highway at the south end of the bridge between Km 63 and Km 64. Turn left at the Chamela village stores beneath the bridge, continue about two miles, bearing left to the end of the road, where the *palapa* of an old restaurant stands at beachside. This is the southernmost of two islet-protected coves flanking the low Punta Negro headland. With clear, tranquil waters and golden-sand beaches, both coves are great for fishing from the rocks, snorkeling, windsurfing, and swimming. The south-end beach is unoccupied and has plenty of room for tenting and RV parking; a house sits back from the north-end beach about a quarter-mile away on the far side of the point. If you want to camp around there, ask if it's okay: *"¿Está bien acampar acá?"*

Food

Groceries are available at stores near the **El Super** corner (Km 72) or in the villages of **Perula** (on the beach, turn off at Km 76), **San Mateo** (Km 70), and **Chamela** (walk north along the beach, or follow the side road, downhill, at the south end of the bridge between Km 64 and 63).

Hearty country Mexican food, hospitality, and snack groceries are available at the **Tejeban** truck stop/restaurant at the El Super corner; open daily from breakfast time until 10–11 P.M. Two popular local roadside seafood spots are the **La Viuda** (The Widow, Km 64), and **Don Lupe Mariscos** (Km 63), on opposite ends of the Río Chamela bridge. They both have their own divers who go out daily for fresh fish ($5), octopus *(pulpo)* ($5), conch, clams, oysters, and lobster ($8). Open daily 8 A.M. until around 9 P.M.

Services, Information, and Emergencies

The closest **bank** is 34 miles north at Tomatlán (turnoff at La Cumbre, at Km 116). *Casetas de larga distancia* operate at the Tejeban restaurant at El Super corner, daily 8 A.M.–9 P.M., and at Pueblo Careyes, the village behind the soccer field at Km 52.

Until someone re-opens the **Pemex** *gasolinera* at El Super, the closest unleaded Magna Sin gas is 27 miles north at La Cumbre (Km 116) or 50 miles (80 km) south at Melaque (Km 0).

If you get sick, the closest health clinic is in Perula (Km 76, one block north of the town plaza, no phone, but a pharmacy) or at Pueblo Careyes at Km 52 (medical consultations daily 8 A.M.–2 P.M.; doctor on call around the clock in emergencies).

Local special **police,** known as the Policia Auxiliar del Estado, are stationed in a pink roadside house at Km 46, and also in the house above the road at Km 43. The local *preventiva* (municipal police) are at the El Super corner.

HOTEL CAREYES

The Hotel Careyes, one of the little-known gems of the Pacific Coast of Mexico, is really two hotels in one. After Christmas and before Easter it brims with well-to-do Mexican families letting their hair down. The rest of the year the hotel is

Hotel Careyes, a two-hour drive south of Puerto Vallarta, remains a hidden gem among Pacific Mexico boutique hotels.

a tranquil, tropical retreat basking at the edge of a pristine, craggy cove.

The natural scene sets the tone: a majestic palm grove opens onto a petite sandy beach set between rocky cliffs. Offshore, the water, deep and crystal clear, is home for dozens of kinds of fish. Overhead, hawks and frigate birds soar, pelicans dive, and boobies and terns skim the waves. At night nearby, turtles carry out their ancient ritual by silently depositing their precious eggs on nearby beaches where they were born.

As if not to be outdone by nature, the hotel itself is an elegant, tropical retreat. A platoon of gardeners manicure lush spreading grounds that lead to gate and reception area. Past the desk, tiers of ochre-hued Mediterranean lodgings enfold an elegant inner courtyard where a blue pool meanders beneath majestic, rustling palms. At night, the grounds glimmer softly with lamps. They illuminate the tufted grove, light the path to a secluded beach, and lead the way up through the cactus-sprinkled hillside thorn forest to a romantic restaurant high above the bay.

Hotel Activities

Hotel guests enjoy a plethora of sports facilities, including tennis courts, riding stables, and a polo field. Aquatic activities include snorkeling, scuba diving, kayaking, sailing, and deep-sea fishing. Boats are additionally available for picnic-excursions to nearby hidden beaches, wildlife-viewing, and observing turtle nesting in season. A luxury spa with view pampers guests with massage, facials, sauna, hot tub, and exercise machines. Evenings, live music brightens the cocktail and dinner hours at the elegant beach-view restaurant/bar.

The hotel was named for *carey* (kah-RAY), the native word for an endangered species of sea turtle that used to lay eggs on the little beach of Careyitos that fronts the hotel. Saving the turtles at nearby Playa Teopa, accessible only through hotel property, has now become a major hotel mission. Guards do, however, allow access to serious outside visitors during hatching times; follow the dirt road between Km 49 and 50 to gate and beach; no camping, please. Check with the hotel desk for information and permission.

Hotel Information

For reservations and more information, contact the hotel directly at tel. 335/100-00, fax 335/101-00, or through its booking agents, toll-free in Mexico tel. 01-800/021-7526, email careyes @ghmmexico.com. The luxurious rooms and suites, depending on location and size, run between approximately $225 d and $400 d, low season; $250–450 d high. Ocean-view suites with private hot tub run $500 d low season and $550 d high; all accommodations have a/c, TV, and direct-dial phones. Additional hotel facilities and services include fiber-optic telecommunications, a children's activity center, 100-person meeting room, several shops and boutiques, library, movie theater, babysitters, heliport, private landing strip, boutiques, shops, and many business services.

Getting There

The Hotel Careyes is a few minutes' drive down a cobbled entrance road (bear left all the way) at Km 53.5 (100 miles, 161 km, from Puerto Vallarta; 34 miles, 55 km from Barra de Navidad; and 52 miles, 84 km from the Manzanillo International Airport).

CLUB MED PLAYA BLANCA

The Club Med Playa Blanca basks at the opposite corner of the same little bay as the Hotel Careyes. Club Med's youngish (mostly 25–45, kids under 12 not allowed) guests enjoy an extensive sports menu, including trampoline, scuba diving, snorkeling, a climbing wall, kayaking, racquetball, volleyball, sailing, and more. Action centers around Playa Blanca, the resort's luxuriously intimate little sand crescent, tucked beneath cactus-decorated tropical headlands. Above the beach, a verdant, tufted grove shades a platoon of reclining vacationers. From there, garden walkways lead past the pool, disco, bars, and restaurants to a hillside colony of 320 luxurious a/c view cabanas.

All meals, drinks, and activities (except for outside tours and deep-sea fishing) are included in a single package price. Rates run approximately $120 per person per day, one-week minimum, (open approximately November through April only). Add a one-time $50 per person "membership" fee. For information and reservations call locally 335/100-01, 335/100-02, or 335/100-03, fax 335/100-04, or from the U.S. and Canada, call 800/CLUBMED (800/258-2633).

Get there via the same Km 53.5 side road as the Hotel Careyes. Bear right and follow signs about a mile to the gate. For security reasons, Club Med Playa Blanca doesn't take kindly to outsiders. If you simply want to look around, be sure to arrive with an appointment.

PLAYA CAREYES AND CUITZMALA

At Km 52, just south of a small bridge and a bus stop, a dirt road leads to the lovely honey-tinted crescent of Playa Careyes. Here, a car-accessible track (be careful for soft spots) continues along the dune, where you could enjoy a day or week of beach camping. Beyond the often powerful waves (swim with caution), the intimate, headland-framed bay brims with outdoor possibilities. Birdwatching and wildlife viewing can be quite rewarding; notice the herons, egrets, and cormorants in the lagoon just south of the dune. Fishing is good either from the beach, by boat (launch from the sheltered north end), or the rocks on either side. Water is generally clear for snorkeling and, beyond the waves, good for either kayaking or windsurfing. If you have no boat, no problem, for the local fishing cooperative (boats beached by the food *palapa* at north end) would be happy to take you on a fishing trip. Figure about $20 per hour, with bargaining. Afterwards, they might even cook up the catch for a big afternoon dinner at their tree-shaded *palapa*. Nearby Pueblo Careyes (behind the soccer field at Km 52) has a store, a **Centro de Salud** (Health Center), and *larga distancia.*

Access to the neighboring **Playa Teopa** is, by contrast, carefully guarded. The worthy reason is to save the hatchlings of the remaining *carey* turtles (see the special topic "Saving Turtles") who still come ashore during the late summer and fall to lay eggs. For a closer look at Playa Teopa, you could walk south along the dune-top track, although guards might eventually stop you. They will let you through (entry gate on dirt road between Km 49 and 50) if you get official permission at the desk of the Hotel Careyes.

The pristine tropical deciduous woodlands that stretch for miles around Km 45 are no accident. They are preserved as part of the **Fideicomiso Cuitzmala** (Cuitzmala Trust), the local kingdom of beach, headland, and forest held by the family of late multimillionaire Sir James Goldsmith. Local officials, many of who were not privy to Sir James's grand design (which includes a sprawling sea-view mansion complex), say that a team of biologists are conducting research on the property. A ranch complex, accessible through a gate at Km 45, is Fideicomiso Cuitzmala's most obvious highway-visible landmark.

PLAYA LAS BRISAS

For a tranquil day, overnight, or weeklong beach camping adventure consider Playa las Brisas, a few miles by the dirt road (turnoff sign near Km 36) through the village of Arroyo Seco.

About two miles long, Playa las Brisas has two distinct sections: first comes a very broad, white sandy strand decorated by pink-blossomed verbena and pounded by wild, open-ocean waves. For shady tent camping or RV parking, a regal coconut grove lines the beach. Before you set up, however, you should offer a little rent to the owner/caretaker, who may soon show up on a horse. Don't be alarmed by his machete; it's for husking and cutting fallen coconuts.

To see the other half of Playa las Brisas, continue along the road past the little beachside vacation home subdivision (with a seasonal store and snack bar). You will soon reach an open-ocean beach and headland, backed by a big, level, grassy dune, perfect for tent or RV camping. Take care not to get stuck in soft spots, however.

The headland borders the El Tecuán Lagoon, part of the Rancho El Tecuán, whose hilltop hotel you can see on the far side of the lagoon. The lagoon is an unusually rich fish and wildlife habitat; see "Hotel El Tecuán" following, for details.

Getting There

You reach the village of Arroyo Seco, where stores can furnish supplies, 2.3 miles (3.7 km) from the highway at Km 36. At the central plaza, turn left, then immediately right at the Conasupo rural store, then left again, heading up the steep

Besides its luxurious resort facilities, the Hotel El Tecuán presides over acres of lagoon, forest, and beach ripe for exploring.

dirt road. In the valley on the other side, bear right at the fork at the mango grove, and within another mile you will be in the majestic beach-bordering palm grove.

FORMER HOTEL AND PLAYA EL TECUÁN

Little was spared in perching the Hotel El Tecuán above its small kingdom of beach, lagoon, and palm-brushed rangeland. It was to be the centerpiece of a sprawling vacationland, with marina, golf course, and hundreds of houses and condos. Although those plans have yet to materialize, the hotel, unoccupied and for sale, still stands proudly, with an ambience more like an African safari lodge than a Mexican beach resort.

Masculinity bulges out of its architecture. Its corridors are lined with massive, polished tree trunks, fixed by brawny master joints to thick, hand-hewn mahogany beams. The view restaurant was patterned after the midships of a Manila Galleon, complete with a pair of varnished tree-trunk masts reaching into the inky darkness of the night sky above. If the restaurant could only sway, the illusion would have been complete.

Wildlife Viewing, Hiking, and Jogging
It is perhaps fortunate the former hotel and its surroundings, part of the big **Rancho Tecuán,**

may never be developed into a residential community. Being private, public access has always been limited, so the Rancho has become a de facto habitat-refuge for the rapidly diminishing local animal population. Wildcats, ocelots, small crocodiles, snakes, and turtles hunt in the mangroves edging the lagoon and the tangled forest that climbs the surrounding hills. The lagoon itself nurtures hosts of waterbirds and shoals of *robalo* (snook) and *pargo* (snapper).

At this writing, visitors were still being allowed to pass along the entrance road and enjoy wildlife-viewing opportunities. If such visitors tread softly, clean up after themselves, start no fires and refrain from fishing or hunting, present owners may continue to allow access. This would be ideal, because wildlife-viewing opportunities are superb. First, simply walk along the lagoonfront below the hotel hilltop, where big white herons and egrets perch and preen in the mangroves. Don't forget your binoculars, sun hat, mosquito repellent, telephoto camera, and identification book. Try launching your own rowboat, canoe, or inflatable raft for an even more rewarding outing.

The environs offer plenty of jogging and walking opportunities. For starters, stroll along the lagoonside entrance road and back (3 miles, 4.8 km) or south along the beach to the Río Purificación and back (4 miles, 6.4 km). Take water, mosquito repellent, sunscreen, a hat, and something to carry your beachcombing treasures in.

Tecuán Beach

The focal point of the long, wild, white-sand Playa El Tecuán is at the north end, where, at low tide, the lagoon's waters stream into the sea. Platoons of waterbirds—giant brown herons, snowy egrets, and squads of pelicans, ibises, and grebes—stalk and dive for fish trapped in the shallow, rushing current.

On the beach nearby, the sand curves southward beneath a rocky point, where the waves strew rainbow carpets of limpet, clam, and snail shells. There the billows rise sharply, angling shoreward, often with good intermediate and advanced surfing breaks. Casual swimmers beware; the surf is much too powerful for safety.

Getting There

The former Hotel El Tecuán is six miles (10 km) along a paved entrance road marked by a white lighthouse at Km 33 (112 miles, 181 km, from Puerto Vallarta; 22 miles, 35 km, from Barra de Navidad.

PLAYA TENACATITA

Imagine an ideal tropical paradise: free camping on a long curve of clean white sand, right next to a lovely little coral-bottomed cove, with all the beer you can drink and all the fresh seafood you can eat. That describes Tenacatita, a place that old Mexican Pacific hands refer to with a sigh: Tenacatitaaaahhh . . .

Folks usually begin to arrive sometime in November; by Christmas, some years, there's only room for walk-ins. Which anyone who can walk can do: carry in your tent and set it up in one of the many RV-inaccessible spots.

Tenacatita visitors enjoy three distinct beaches: the main one, Playa Tenacatita; the little one, Playa Mora; and Playa la Boca, a breezy, palm-bordered sand ribbon stretching just over three kilometers north to the *boca* (mouth) of the Río Purificación.

Playa Tenacatita's strand of fine white sand curves from the north end of Punta Tenacatita along a long, tall packed dune to **Punta Hermanos,** a total of about two miles. The dune is where most visitors—nearly all Americans and Canadians—park their RVs. The water is clear with gentle waves, fine for swimming and windsurfing. Being so calm, it's easy to launch a boat for fishing—common catches are *huachinango* (red snapper) and *cabrilla* (sea bass)—especially at the very calm north end.

The sheltered north cove is where a village of *palapas* has grown to service the winter camping population. One of the veteran establishments is **El Puercillo,** run by longtimer José Bautista. He and several other neighbors take groups out in his launches ($80 total per half-day, bring your own beer) for offshore fishing trips and excursions.

Playa Tenacatita's superb fishing, snorkeling, diving, wildlife viewing, and beachcombing attract a community of winter RV campers.

Trouble at Tenacatita

Tenacatita is headed for changes, however. The federal government has made a deal with private interests to develop a hotel at Tenacatita. The trouble began when the fifty-odd squatter-operators of the Tenacatita *palapas* refused to leave. One night in November 1991, after giving the squatters plenty of warning, federal soldiers and police burned and smashed the *palapas*. Nevertheless, the squatters, backed by the Rebalsito *ejido*, the traditional owner of Tenacatita, have vowed to have their day in court. Despite further destruction by an earthquake and 10-foot tidal wave in October 1995, the squatters have tenaciously rebuilt their *palapas*.

Lately, government authorities have adopted a friendlier attitude toward the beach community. The hotel plans, so far not realized, have been scaled back to a low-profile, eco-friendly development, something like Hotelito Desconocido, north at Cruz de Loreto. (See the Special Topic "Splendid Isolation" in the Puerto Vallarta town chapter.)

Playas Mora and La Boca

Jewel of jewels Playa Mora is accessible by a steep, but short, uphill dirt road running north from Playa Tenacatita, past the *palapas*. Playa Mora itself is salt-and-pepper, black sand dotted with white coral, washed by water sometimes as smooth as glass. Just 50 feet from the beach the reef begins. Corals, like heads of cauliflower, some brown, some green, and some dead white, swarm with fish: iridescent blue, yellow-striped, yellow-tailed, some silvery, and others brown as rocks. (Careful: Moray eels like to hide in rock crannies, and they bite. Don't stick your hand anywhere you can't see.)

If you get to Playa Mora by December you may be early enough to snag one of the roughly dozen car-accessible camping spots. If not, plenty of tent camping spaces accessible on foot exist; also, a few abandoned *palapa* thatched huts are usually waiting to be resurrected.

Playa la Boca is the overflow campground for Tenacatita. It's not as popular because of its rough surf and steep beach. Its isolation and vigorous surf, however, make Playa la Boca the best for driftwood, beachcombing, shells, and surf fishing.

Wildlife Viewing

Tenacatita's hinterland is a spreading, wildlife-rich mangrove marsh. From a landing behind the Tenacatita dune, you can float a boat, rubber raft, or canoe for a wildlife-viewing excursion. Local guides also furnish boats and lead trips from the same spot. Take your hat, binoculars, camera, telephoto lens, and plenty of repellent.

Tenacatita Bugs

That same marshland is the source for swarms of mosquitoes and *jejenes,* "no-see-um" biting gnats, especially around sunset. At that time no sane person at Tenacatita should be outdoors without having slathered on some good repellent.

Food, Services, and Information

The village of **El Rebalsito,** on the Hwy. 200-Tenacatita road, a mile and a half back from the beach, is Tenacatita's supply and service center. It has two or three fair *abarroterías* (groceries) that carry meat and vegetables. Best of all these is friendly **Minisuper "La Morenita,"** on the highway, with a little bit of everything and a long-distance telephone/fax, 335/152-24.

Additional services include a *gasolinera* that dispenses gasoline from drums, a water *purificadora* that sells drinking water retail, and even a bus stop. A single Transportes Cihuatlán bus makes one run a day between El Rebalsito and Manzanillo, leaving El Rebalsito at the crack of dawn (inquire locally) and returning from the Manzanillo central bus station around 3 P.M., arriving at El Rebasito around 6 P.M.

If you want a diversion from the fare of Tenacatita's seafood *palapas* and El Rebalsito's single restaurant, you can drive or thumb a ride seven miles (11 km) to **Restaurant Yoly** at roadside Miguel Hidalgo village (Km 30 on Hwy. 200) for some country-style enchiladas, tacos, *chiles rellenos,* tostadas, and beans. Open daily 7 A.M.–8 P.M.

Getting There

Leave Hwy. 200 at the big Tenacatita sign and interchange (at Km 27) half a mile south of the big Río Purificación bridge. El Rebalsito is 3.7 miles (six km), Tenacatita 5.4 miles (8.7 km), by a good paved road.

HOTEL BLUE BAY VILLAGE

Despite new owners, who have changed its name to Hotel Blue Bay Village, the former Hotel Los Angeles Locos (which had nothing to do with crazy people from Los Angeles) lives on in minds of local people. Once upon a time, a rich family built an airstrip and a mansion by a lovely little beach on pristine Tenacatita Bay and began coming for vacations by private plane. The local people, who couldn't fathom why their rich neighbors would go to so much trouble and expense to come to such an out-of-the-way place, dubbed them *los angeles locos,* the "crazy angels," because they always seemed to be flying.

The beach is still lovely and Tenacatita Bay, curving around Punta Hermanos south from Tenacatita Beach, is still pristine. Now the Hotel Blue Bay Village makes it possible for droves of sun-seeking vacationers to enjoy it en masse.

Continuous music, open bar, plentiful buffets, and endless activities set the tone at Blue Bay Village—the kind of place for folks who want a hassle-free week of fun in the sun. The guests are typically working-age couples and singles, mostly Mexicans during the summer, Canadians and some Americans during the winter. Very few children seem to be among the guests, although they are welcome.

Hotel Activities

Although all sports and lessons—including tennis, snorkeling, sailing, windsurfing, horseback riding, volleyball, aerobics, exercises, water-skiing—plus dancing, disco, and games cost nothing extra, guests can, if they want, do nothing but soak up the sun. Hotel Blue Bay Village simply provides the options.

A relaxed attitude will probably allow you to enjoy yourself the most. Don't try to eat, drink, and do too much in order to make sure you get your money's worth. If you do, you're liable to arrive back home in need of a vacation.

Although people don't come to the tropics to stay inside, Blue Bay Village's rooms are quite comfortable—completely private, in pastels and white, air-conditioned, each with cable TV, phone, and private balcony overlooking either the ocean or palmy pool and patio.

Hotel Information

For information and reservations, contact a travel agent or the hotel at Km 20, Carretera Federal No. 200, Melaque, Jalisco, tel./fax 335/150-20, toll-free in Mexico 01 800/713-3020, email: lal@bluebayresorts.com, website: www.bluebayresorts.com. From the U.S. and Canada, telephone toll-free 800/BLUEBAY (800/258-3229). High-season rates for the 201 rooms and suites run about $155 per person per day, double occupancy, $115 low season. Two children under 12 with parent go free. For a bigger, better junior suite, add about $22 per room; prices include everything except transportation.

Getting There

The Hotel Blue Bay Village is about four miles (six km) off Hwy. 200 along a signed cobbled entrance road near the Km 20 marker (120 miles, 194 km, from Puerto Vallarta; 14 miles, 23 km, from Barra de Navidad; and 32 miles, 51 km, from the Manzanillo International Airport).

If you want to simply look around the resort, don't drive up to the gate unannounced. The guard won't let you through. Instead, call ahead and make an appointment for a "tour." After your guided look-see, you have to either sign up or mosey along. The hotel doesn't accept day guests.

Hotel Punta Serena

Part of the Blue Bay development, but separate in concept and location is Punta Serena, tel. 335/150-13, from the U.S. and Canada 800/551-2558, fax 335/150-13, email: info@puntaserena .com, website: www.puntaserena.com, perched on a breezy hilltop overlooking the entire broad sweep of Tenacatita Bay. Here, the idea is a holistic summit meditation retreat, for lovers of contemplation and tranquility. Activities—sauna, ocean-view hot tub, native Mexican *temazcal,* yoga, drumming, martial arts, gym, and more—centers on the main hilltop reception-restaurant-pool-patio building.

Paths radiate out to the tile-roofed lodging units, spread over the palmy summit-park like a garden of giant mushrooms. The units themselves are designer spartan, in white and blue, with modern baths, luxuriously high ceilings, and broad ocean vistas from view balconies.

The 70 rooms, all with a/c, rent for the same as

Hotel Blue Bay, about $155 per person low season, $115 high, with all in-house food and activities included.

Directions and address are identical to Hotel Blue Bay above. Turn right at the signed Punta Serena entrance driveway before heading downhill to Hotel Blue Bay.

PLAYA BOCA DE IGUANAS

Plumy Playa Boca de Iguanas curves for six miles along the tranquil inner recess of the Bay of Tenacatita. The cavernous former Hotel Bahía Tenacatita, which slumbered for years beneath the grove, is being reclaimed by the jungle and the animals that live in the nearby mangrove marsh.

The beach, however, is as enjoyable as ever: wide, level, with firm white sand, good for hiking, jogging, and beachcombing. Offshore, the gently rolling waves are equally fine for bodysurfing and boogie boarding. Beds of oysters, free for those who dive for them, lie a few hundred feet offshore. A rocky outcropping at the north end invites fishing and snorkeling while the calm water beyond the breakers invites windsurfing. Bring your own equipment.

Accommodations

First choice goes to **Camping Trailer Park Boca Beach,** with about 50 camping and RV spaces shaded beneath a majestic, rustling grove at Km 16.5 Carretera Melaque-Puerto Vallarta, P.O. Box 18, Melaque, Jalisco 48987, tel. 338/103-93, fax 338/103-42, email: bocabeach@correoweb.com.mx. In 10 years, friendly owners Michel and Bertha Billot (he's French, she's Mexican) have built up their little paradise, surviving hurricanes and a 1995 tidal wave by trying harder. Their essentials are in place: electricity, water, showers, toilets, and about 40 spaces with sewer hookups. Much of their five acres is undeveloped and would be fine for tent campers who prefer privacy with the convenience of fresh water, a small store, and congenial company at tables beneath a rustic *palapa.* Rates run about $15/day for motor home, trailer, van, or camper, with discounts for weekly or monthly rentals. Add $2 for a/c power. Camping runs about $5 per day per group.

The original local pocket paradise, **Camping and Trailer Park Boca de Iguanas,** Km 16.5, Carretera Melaque-Puerto Vallarta, P.O. Box 93, Melaque, Jalisco 48987, seems to be succeeding where the old hotel down the beach failed. Instead of fighting the jungle, the manager is trying to coexist with it. A big crocodile lives in the mangrove-lined lotus marsh at the edge of the trailer park.

"When the crocodile gets too close to my ducks," the manager says, "I drive him back into the mangrove where he belongs. This end of the mangrove is ours, the other side is his."

The trailer park offers 40 sandy, shaded (but smallish) spaces for tents and RVs, including electricity, well water for showering, flushing, and laundry, bottled water for drinking, and a dump station. The manager runs a minimarket that supplies the necessities for a relaxed week or month on the beach. A loyal cadre of American and Canadian regulars stay here all winter. The trailer park includes a genuinely funky kitchenette bungalow that sleeps four for $28/day. Reserve by mail, generally necessary only during Christmas or Easter week. Rates run about $7 per RV.

A third-choice lodging, the nearby **Hotel and Campamento Entre Palmeras,** offers six plain rooms with fans for one to four persons for about $20. The grounds feature much tent or RV camping space, electricity, showers, toilets, a simple restaurant, and a big, funky swimming pool. Its location, closer to the mangrove marsh and farther from the beach, is buggier, however.

Get to Playa Boca de Iguanas by following the signed paved road at Km 17 for 1.5 miles, 2.4 km.

PLAYA LA MANZANILLA

The little fishing town of La Manzanilla (pop. 2,000) drowses at the opposite end of the same long, curving strip of sand that begins at the Boca de Iguanas trailer parks. Here the beach, Playa la Manzanilla, is as broad and flat and the waves are as gentle, but the sand is several shades darker. Probably no better fishing exists on the entire Costa Alegre than at La Manzanilla. A dozen seafood *palapas* on the beach manage to stay open by virtue of a trickle of foreign visitors and local weekend and holiday patronage.

A fine new addition to La Manzanilla accommodations is the beautiful new **Posada Tonalá,** life project of kindly owner-builder Alfonso Torres López. You must, at least, come and look at his handiwork: the graceful teak *(granadillo)* stairway, the vines cascading on one side of the airy lobby, all topped by a uniquely lovely overhead *palapa* roof.

Señor López retired from his auto parts business in Guadalajara and returned to realize his life-long dream, to contribute to his hometown. His rooms are immaculate and spacious, with modern shower baths and plenty of attractive tile, as well as handsome, dark, hand-carved furniture and colorful, handmade bedspreads. All this, year-round, for only $32 s or d, $43 t, with fans. Reserve at Posada Tonalá, María Asunción 75, La Manzanilla, Jalisco, tel./fax 335/154-74. Find it on the town's main street, about three blocks past the edge of town.

For an equally pleasurable but completely different experience, stay at private, secluded **Villa Montaña,** on the hillside above and behind the town. For more information and reservations, contact Dan, owner-operator of Outland Adventures, P.O. Box 16343, Seattle, WA 98116, tel./fax 206/932-7012, website: www.choice1 .com. (Look for Outland Adventures under "Special Tours and Study Options" in the introductory On the Road chapter.)

A handful of more basic hotels also accommodates guests. At **Hotel Posada del Cazador** (The Hunter), visitors enjoy friendly husband-wife management, a lobby for sitting and socializing, a shelf of used paperback novels, and a long-distance telephone. Find it on the main street on the left, as you enter town, at María Asunción 183, La Manzanilla, Jalisco 48988, tel./fax 335/150-00. It has seven plain but clean rooms for $7 s, $9 d low season, $14 and $17 high. Kitchenette suites sleeping four rent for $30 low, $38 high; a larger suite, sleeping eight, $40 low, $50 high, all with fans and hot-water showers.

On the opposite, even sleepier country edge of town, the **Hotel Puesta de Sol** (Sunset), Calle Playa Blanca 94, La Manzanilla, Jalisco, tel. 335/150-33, offers 17 basic rooms around a cool, leafy central patio. Rates run about $8 s, $17 d, $22 t, with discounts for longer-term rentals.

Get to La Manzanilla by following the signed paved road at Km 13 for one mile. The Hotel Cazador is on the left, one block after you turn left onto the main beachfront street. The Hotel Puesta de Sol is a quarter-mile farther along; bear right past the town plaza for a few blocks along the beachfront street, Calle Playa Blanca.

CLUB EL TAMARINDO

The Costa Alegre's newest big development, Club El Tamarindo, occupies the lush, green peninsula that forms the southernmost point of Tenacatita Bay. Plans project a giant jungle country club, based on sales of about a hundred parcels averaging 20 acres apiece. Owners will have access to extensive resort facilities, including golf course, tennis courts, hotel, restaurants, heliport, skeet range, equestrian paths, beach club, and small marina. Plans apparently include owner commitment to leaving a sizable fraction of the present forest in its original, pristine state.

Nearly all of the resort facilities have been installed, including the golf course, tennis courts, heliport, boat dock, restaurant, and hotel. Accommodations, at the **Hotel El Tamarindo,** tel. 335/150-32 or 335/150-52, toll-free in Mexico, tel. 01-800/021-7526, fax 335/150-70, email: tamarindo@ghmmexico.com, website: www .ghmhotels.com, are in airy, white-stucco and tile, super-deluxe jungle-edge housekeeping villas. Rates for the several lodgings run between about $400 and $650 d per day.

Get there via the signed side road at Km 8, five miles north of Melaque. After about two miles of winding through the sylvan tropical forest, you arrive at the gate, where you must have either a reservation in hand or a prior appointment before the guard will let you through.

BARRA DE NAVIDAD, MELAQUE, AND VICINITY

The little country beach town of Barra de Navidad, Jalisco (pop. 5,000), whose name literally means "Bar of Christmas," has unexpectedly few saloons. In this case, "Bar" has nothing to do with alcohol; it refers to the sandbar upon which the town is built. That lowly spit of sand forms the southern perimeter of the blue Bay of Navidad, which arcs to Barra de Navidad's twin town of San Patricio Melaque (pop. 10,000), a few miles to the west.

Barra and San Patricio Melaque, locally known as "Melaque" (may-LAH-kay), are twin, but distinct, towns. Barra has the cobbled, shady lanes and friendly country ambience; Melaque is the metropolis of the two, with most of the stores and services.

HISTORY

The sandbar is called "Navidad" because the Viceroy Antonio de Mendoza, the first and arguably the best viceroy Mexico ever had, disembarked there on December 25, 1540. The occasion was auspicious for two reasons. Besides being Christmas Day, Don Antonio had arrived to personally put down a bloody rebellion raging through western Mexico that threatened to burn New Spain off the map. Unfortunately for the thousands of native people who were torched, hung, or beheaded during the brutal campaign, Don Antonio's prayers on that day were soon answered. The rebellion was smothered, and the lowly sandbar was remembered as Barra de Navidad from that time forward.

A generation later, Barra de Navidad became the springboard for King Philip's efforts to make the Pacific a Spanish lake. Shipyards built on the bar launched the vessels that carried the expedition of conquistador Miguel López de Legazpi and Father André de Urdaneta in search of God and gold in the Philippines. Urdaneta came back a hero one year later, in 1565, having discovered the northern circle route, whose favorable easterly winds propelled a dozen sub-

sequent generations of the fabled treasure-laden Manila Galleon home to Mexico.

By 1600, however, the Manila Galleon was landing in Acapulco, with its much quicker land access to the capital to transport their priceless Asian cargoes. Barra de Navidad went to sleep and didn't wake up for more than three centuries.

Now Barra de Navidad only slumbers occasionally. The townsfolk welcome crowds of beachgoing Mexican families during national holidays, and a steady procession of North American and European budget vacationers during the winter.

SIGHTS

Exploring Barra and Melaque

Most Barra hotels and restaurants lie on one oceanfront street named, uncommonly, after a conquistador, Miguel López de Legazpi. Barra's other main street, Veracruz, one short block inland, has most of the businesses, groceries, and small, family-run eateries.

Head south along Legazpi toward the steep Cerro San Francisco in the distance and you will soon be on the palm-lined walkway that runs atop the famous sandbar of Barra. On the right, ocean side, the Playa Barra de Navidad arcs northwest to the hotels of Melaque, which spread like white pebbles along the far end of the strand. The great blue water expanse beyond the beach, framed at both ends by jagged, rocky sea stacks, is the **Bahía de Navidad.**

Opposite the ocean, on the other side of the bar, spreads the tranquil, mangrove-bordered expanse of the **Laguna de Navidad,** which forms the border with the state of Colima, whose mountains (including nearby Cerro San Francisco) loom beyond it. The lagoon's calm appearance is deceiving, for it is really an *estero* (estuary), an arm of the sea, which ebbs and flows through the channel beyond the rock jetty at the end of the sandbar. Because of this natural

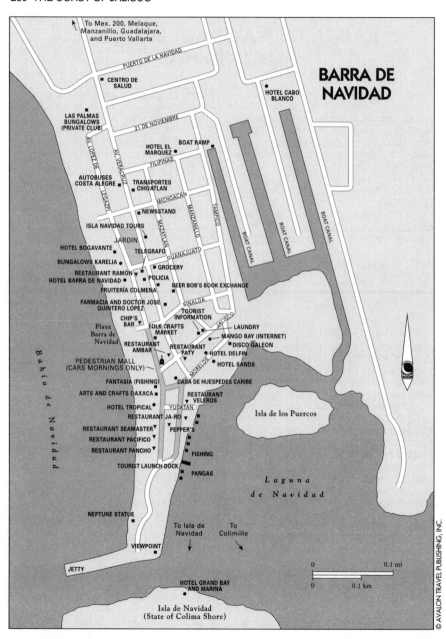

To Mex. 200, Melaque, Manzanillo, Guadalajara, and Puerto Vallarta

PUERTO DE LA NAVIDAD

CENTRO DE SALUD

HOTEL CABO BLANCO

BARRA DE NAVIDAD

LAS PALMAS BUNGALOWS (PRIVATE CLUB)

21 DE NOVIEMBRE

AV. LOPEZ DE LEGAZPI

AV. VERACRUZ

HOTEL EL MARQUEZ

BOAT RAMP

FILIPINAS

AUTOBUSES COSTA ALEGRE

TRANSPORTES CIHUATLAN

MICHOACAN

MANZANILLO

TAMPICO

NEWSSTAND

MAZATLAN

ISLA NAVIDAD TOURS

JARDIN

HOTEL BOGAVANTE

TELEGRAFO

GUANAJUATO

BUNGALOWS KARELIA

GROCERY

RESTAURANT RAMÓN

POLICIA

HOTEL BARRA DE NAVIDAD

FRUITERÍA COLMENA

BEER BOB'S BOOK EXCHANGE

FARMACIA AND DOCTOR JOSÉ QUINTERO LOPEZ

SINALOA

TOURIST INFORMATION

CHIP'S BAR

Playa Barra de Navidad

FOLK CRAFTS MARKET

JALISCO

LAUNDRY

MANGO BAY (INTERNET)

RESTAURANT AMBAR

RESTAURANT PATY

DISCO GALEON

HOTEL DELFIN

PEDESTRIAN MALL (CARS MORNINGS ONLY)

MORELOS

HOTEL SANDS

Bahía de Navidad

FANTASIA (FISHING)

CASA DE HUESPEDES CARIBE

ARTS AND CRAFTS OAXACA

RESTAURANT VELEROS

Isla de los Puercos

HOTEL TROPICAL

YUCATAN

RESTAURANT JA-RO

RESTAURANT SEAMASTER

PEPPER'S

RESTAURANT PACIFICO

RESTAURANT PANCHO

FISHING

TOURIST LAUNCH DOCK

PANGAS

Laguna de Navidad

NEPTUNE STATUE

To Isla de Navidad

To Colimilla

VIEWPOINT

JETTY

HOTEL GRAND BAY AND MARINA

Isla de Navidad (State of Colima Shore)

0   0.1 mi

0   0.1 km

© AVALON TRAVEL PUBLISHING, INC.

flushing action, local folks still dump fishing waste into the Laguna de Navidad. Fortunately, new sewage plants route human waste away from the lagoon, so with care, you can usually swim safely in its inviting waters. Do not, however, venture too close to the lagoon-mouth beyond the jetty or you may get swept out to sea by the strong outgoing current.

On the sandbar's lagoon side, a *panga* (fishing launch) mooring and passenger dock hum with daytime activity. From the dock, launches ferry loads of passengers for less than half a dollar to the Colima shore, which is known as **Isla de Navidad,** where the marina and hotel development has risen across the lagoon. Back in the center of town, **minibuses** enter town along Veracruz, turn left at Sinaloa, by the crafts market, and head in the opposite direction, out of town, along Mazatlán, Veracruz, and Hwy. 200, three miles (4.8 km) to Melaque.

The once-distinct villages of San Patricio and Melaque now spread as one along the Bay of Navidad's sandy northwest shore. The business district, still known locally as San Patricio (from the highway, follow a small "San Patricio" sign two blocks toward the beach), centers around a plaza, market, and church bordering the main shopping street López Mateos.

Continue two blocks to beachfront Calle Gómez Farías, where a lineup of hotels, eateries, and shops cater to the vacation trade. From there, the curving strand extends toward the quiet Melaque west end, where *palapas* line a glassy, sheltered blue cove. Here, a rainbow of colored *pangas* perch upon the sand, sailboats rock gently offshore, pelicans preen and dive, and people enjoy snacks, beer, and the cooling breeze in the deep shade beneath the *palapas.*

Beaches and Activities

Although a continuous strand of medium-fine golden sand joins Barra with Melaque, it changes character and names along its gentle, five-mile arc. At Barra de Navidad, where it's called **Playa de Navidad,** the beach is narrow and steep, and the waves are sometimes very rough. Those powerful swells often provide good intermediate surfing breaks adjacent to the jetty. Fishing by line or pole is also popular from the jetty rocks.

Most mornings are calm enough to make the surf safe for swimming and splashing, which, along with the fresh seafood of beachside *palapa* restaurants, make Barra a popular Sunday and holiday picnic-ground for local Mexican families. The relatively large number of folks walking the beach unfortunately makes for slim pickings for shell collectors and beachcombers.

For a cooling midday break from the sun, drop in to the restaurant of the Hotel Tropical at the south end of Legazpi and enjoy the bay view, the swish of the waves, and the fresh breeze streaming through the lobby.

As the beach curves northwesterly toward Melaque, the restaurants and hotels give way to dunes and pasture. At the outskirts of Melaque, civilization resumes, and the broad beach, now called **Playa Melaque,** curves gently to the west.

Continuing past the town center, a lineup of rustic *palapas* and *pangas* pulled up on the sand decorate the tranquil west-end cove, which is sheltered from the open sea behind a tier of craggy sea stacks. Here, the water clears, making for good fishing from the rocks.

Colimilla and Isla de Navidad

A boat trip across the lagoon for super-fresh seafood at the palm-studded village of Colimilla is a primary Barra pastime. While you sit enjoying a moderately priced oyster cocktail, *ceviche,* or broiled whole-fish dinner, gaze out on the mangrove-enfolded glassy expanse of the Laguna de Navidad. Far away, a canoe may drift silently, while white herons quietly stalk their prey. Now and then a launch will glide in and deposit its load of visitors, or a fisherman will head out to sea.

One of the most pleasant Colimilla vantage spots is the **Restaurant Susana,** whose broad *palapa* extends out into the lagoon; open daily 8 A.M.–8 P.M. Take mosquito repellent, especially if you're staying for dinner. Launches routinely ferry as many as six passengers to Colimilla from the Barra lagoonside docks for about $5 roundtrip. Tell them when you want to return, and they'll pick you up.

From the same Barra lagoonside dock, launches also shuttle passengers for $.50 roundtrip across the lagoon to Isla de Navidad and its new Hotel Grand Bay marina, vacation home development, and golf course.

the view from
Restaurant Pelícanos,
on the beach at
Melaque's north end

Playa de Cocos

A trip to wild, breezy Playa de Cocos, hidden just behind the Cerro San Francisco headland south of Barra, makes an interesting afternoon outing, especially when combined with the trip to Colimilla. A wide, golden sand beach curves miles southward, starting beneath a cactus-dotted jungly headland. The beach, although broad, is steep, with strong shorebreakers. Although swimming is hazardous, fishing off the rocks and beachcombing are the delights here. A feast of driftwood and multicolored shells—olives, small conches, purple-striated clams—litters the sand, especially on an intimate, spectacular hidden cove, reachable by scampering past the waves.

There are two ways to get to Playa de Cocos. Through Colimilla, walk uphill to the road above the La Colimilla restaurants. Head left (east) for about a quarter-mile. Turn right at the palm-lined boulevard and continue along the golf course about a mile and a quarter to the beach beneath the tip of the Cerro San Francisco headland.

You can also taxi or drive there by turning off Hwy. 200 at the Ejido La Culebra (or Isla Navidad) sign as the highway cuts through the hills at Km 51 a few miles south of Barra. Mark your odometer at the turnoff. Follow the road about three miles (4.8 km) to a bridge, where you enter the state of Colima. From there the road curves right, paralleling the beach. After about two more miles (3.2 km), you pass through the golf course gate. After winding through the golf course another mile, fork left at the intersecting boulevard and traffic circle at the north edge of the golf course. Continue another mile to the end of the road and beach.

Playa Coastecomate

Playa de Cocos has its exact opposite in Playa Coastecomate (kooah-stay-koh-MAH-tay), tucked behind the ridge rising beyond the northwest edge of Melaque. The dark, fine-sand beach arcs along a cove on the rampart-rimmed big blue **Bahía de Coastecomate.** Its very gentle waves and clear waters make for excellent swimming, windsurfing, snorkeling, and fishing from the beach itself or the rocks beneath the adjacent cliffs. A number of *palapa* restaurants along the beach serve seafood and drinks.

The Coastecomate beachside village itself, home for a number of local fisherfolk and a few North Americans in permanently parked RVs, has a collection of oft-empty bungalows on the hillside, a small store, and about three times as many chickens as people.

To get there, drive, taxi, or bus via the local minibus or Transportes Cihuatlán to the signed Melaque turnoff from Hwy. 200. There, a dirt side road marked Hotel Real Costa Sur heads northwest into the hills, winding for two miles (3.2 km) over the ridge through pasture and jungle woodland to the village. If you're walking, allow an hour and take your sun hat, insect repellent, and water.

Barra-Melaque Hike

You can do this four-mile stroll either way, but starting from Barra in the morning, with the sun behind you, the sky and the ocean will be at their bluest and best. Take insect repellent, sunscreen, and a hat. At either end, enjoy lunch at one of the seaside restaurants. At the Melaque end you can continue walking north to the cove on the far side of town. The trail beneath the cliff leads to spectacular wave-tossed tidepools and rugged sea rocks at the tip of the bay. At the Barra end, you can hire a launch to Colimilla. End your day leisurely by taxiing or busing back from the bus station at either end.

Bird-Watching and Wildlife Viewing

The wildlife-rich upper reaches of the Laguna de Navidad stretch for miles and are only a boat ride away. Besides the ordinary varieties of egrets, terns, herons, pelicans, frigate birds, boobies, ducks, and geese, patient bird-watchers can sometimes snare rainbow flash-views of exotic parrots and bright tanagers and orioles.

As for other creatures, quiet, persistent observers are sometimes rewarded with mangrove-edge views of turtles, constrictors, crocodiles, coatimundis, raccoons, skunks, deer, wild pigs, ocelots, wildcats, and, very rarely, a jaguar. The sensitivity and experience of your boatman/guide is, of course, crucial to the success of any nature outing. Ask at the dock-office of the **Sociedad Cooperativos de Servicios Turístico,** 40 Av. Veracruz on the lagoon front. You might also ask Tracy Ross at Crazy Cactus (on Jalisco, next door to the church, near the corner of Veracruz) to recommend a good guide, or even a complete wildlife-viewing excursion.

ACCOMMODATIONS

Barra Hotels

Whether on the beach or not, all Barra Hotels (except the world-class Hotel Grand Bay) fall in the budget or moderate categories. One of the best, the family-run **Hotel Sands,** offers a bit of class at moderate rates at Morelos 24, Barra de Navidad, Jalisco 48987, tel./fax 335/550-18. Two tiers of rooms enclose an inner courtyard lined with comfortable sitting areas opening into a lush green garden of leafy vines and graceful coconut palms.

A side-corridor leads past a small zoo of spider monkeys, raccoons, and squawking macaws to a view of Barra's colorful lineup of fishing launches. On the other side, past the swim-up bar, a big curving pool and outer patio spreads to the placid edge of the mangrove-bordered Laguna de Navidad. The pool-bar (happy hour daily 4–6 P.M., winter season) and the sitting areas afford inviting places to meet other travelers. The rooms, all with fans (but with sporadic hot water in some rooms—check before moving in) are clean and furnished with dark varnished wood and tile. Light sleepers should wear earplugs or book a room in the wing farthest from the disco down the street, whose music thumps away until around 2 A.M. most nights during the high season. Its 43 rooms and bungalows rent from $42 d low season, $60 high (bargain for a better rate); bungalows sleeping four with kitchenette run $103 low season, $150 high. Credit cards (with a six-percent surcharge) are accepted, and parking is available.

Although neither rare nor endangered, the blue-footed booby is nevertheless uncommon and therefore keenly anticipated by birdwatchers along the Nayarit-Jalisco coast.

BARRA AND MELAQUE ACCOMMODATIONS

A ccommodations (area code 335) are listed in increasing order of approximate high-season, double-room rates.

BARRA HOTELS (POSTAL CODE 48987)

Casa de Huéspedes Caribe, Sonora 15, tel. 559-52, $19

Hotel Delfín, Morelos 23, tel. 550-68, fax 560-20, $33

Hotel Bogavante, Legazpi s/n, tel. 553-84, fax 561-20, $46

Hotel Tropical, Legazpi 96, tel. 550-20, fax 551-49, $60

Hotel Sands, Morelos 24, tel./fax 550-18, $60

Bungalows Karelia, Legazpi s/n, tel. 557-48, $70

Hotel Barra de Navidad, Legazpi 250, tel. 551-22, fax 553-03, $75

Hotel Cabo Blanco, P.O. Box 31, tel. 551-03 or 551-36, fax 564-94, $100

Hotel Grand Bay, P.O. Box 20, tel. 550-50, fax 560-71, $325

MELAQUE HOTELS (POSTAL CODE 48980)

Hotel Santa María, Abel Salgado 85, P.O. Box 188, tel. 556-77, fax 555-53, $17

Hotel de Legazpi, Av. de las Palmas s/n, P.O. Box 88, tel./fax 553-97, $33

Posada Pablo de Tarso, Gómez Farías 408, tel. 551-17, fax 552-68, $35

Hotel Villas Camino del Mar, P.O. Box 6, tel. 552-07, fax 554-98, e-mail: skennedy@ciber.net.mx, $46

Bungalows Azteca, P.O. Box 57, tel./fax 551-50, $52

Bungalows Mallorca, Abel Salgado 133, P.O. Box 157, tel. 552-19, $52

Hotel Club Náutico, Gómez Farías 1A, tel. 557-70 or 557-66, fax 552-39, $56

Hotel Real Costa Sur, P.O. Box 12, tel./fax 550-85, $70

Across the street, its loyal international clientele swears by the German family-operated **Hotel Delfín,** Morelos 23, Barra de Navidad, Jalisco 48987, tel. 335/550-68, fax 335/560-20. Its four stories of tile-floored, balcony-corridor rooms (where curtains, unfortunately, must be drawn for privacy) are the cleanest and coziest of Barra's moderate hotels. The Delfín's tour de force, however, is the cheery patio buffet where guests linger over the breakfast offered every morning ($3–5, open daily 8:30–10:30 A.M.) to all comers. Overnight guests, like those of the Sands, must put up with the moderate nighttime noise of the disco half a block away. For maximum sun and privacy take one of the top-floor rooms, many of which enjoy lagoon views. The Delfín's 30 rooms rent for $27 d low season, $33 high; with fans, small pool, and parking; credit cards are accepted.

One block away and a notch down the economic scale is **Casa de Huéspedes Caribe,** Sonora 15, Barra de Navidad, Jalisco 48987, tel. 335/559-52, tucked along a side street. The owner, Maximino Oregon, offers 11 clean, plain rooms, all with bath and hot water, to a devoted following of long-term customers. Amenities include a secure front door (which Maximino personally locks every night), a homey downstairs garden sitting area, and more chairs and a hammock for snoozing on an upstairs porch. Rates run $14 s, $19 d, and $22 t in rooms with twin, double, or both types of beds.

The longtime **Hotel Tropical,** near the "bar" end of Legazpi, at Av. L. de Legazpi 96, Barra de Navidad, Jalisco 48987, sustained serious damage in the October 9, 1995, earthquake. Alas, at this writing, it is not yet open, but repairs appear largely completed. It seems as if it will be an improved version of the old hotel. In previous editions, I wrote: "guests in many of its renovated oceanfront tiers of comfortable, high-ceilinged rooms enjoy luxuriously private ocean-view balconies. Downstairs, the natural air-conditioning of an ocean breeze often floods the sea-view lobby-restaurant." The 57 rooms will probably rent for about rent for about $40 s, $60 d, with fans and a tiny pool; credit cards are accepted. For reservations, write, or, if the phone numbers remain the same, call 335/550-20 or fax 335/551-49.

Sharing the same beachfront by the town plaza a few blocks away, the white stucco three-story **Hotel Barra de Navidad** encloses a cool, leafy interior courtyard at Av. L. de Legazpi 250, Barra de Navidad, Jalisco 48987, tel. 335/551-22, fax 335/553-03. Guests in the seaside upper two floors of comfortable (but not deluxe) rooms enjoy palm-fringed ocean vistas from private balconies. An inviting pool and patio on one side and a dependable upstairs restaurant complete the picture. High-season rates for the 57 rooms run a pricey $65 s, $75 d, $78 t high season, $53, $60, $66 low. Ask for one of the sunnier, more scenic ocean-side rooms, with a/c. Credit cards are accepted.

The friendly ambience and homey beachside porch of the **Hotel Bogavante** keep a steady stream of mostly North American and European travelers returning year after year to Av. L. de Legazpi s/n, Barra de Navidad, Jalisco 48987, tel. 335/553-84, fax 335/561-20. Eight of its 14 rooms are spacious kitchenette suites, especially handy for groups and families weary of the hassles and expense of eating out. The rooms rent for about $38 s, $46 d, $50 t high season, $32 s, $38 d, and $42 t low season. The kitchenette units run about $50 low season, $60 high. Monthly rates available; with fans, but no pool.

Bungalows Karelia, the Bogavante's downscale twin lodging next door, shares the same pleasant beachside porch, Av. L. de Legazpi s/n, Barra de Navidad, Jalisco 48987, tel. 335/557-84. All the Karelia's rentals are kitchenette bungalows, satisfactory for many young families and travelers who don't mind cleaning up a bit. The 10 bungalows with fans rent for a pricey $70 high season, $57 low; bargain for a cheaper rate or long-term discount.

Hint: If considering a beachside room in one of the several Barra oceanfront hotels, listen to the waves before you move in. They may be loud enough to interfere with your sleep. If so, use earplugs or switch to a streetside room or a hotel on the lagoon.

Barra's original deluxe lodging is the peach-hued, stucco-and-tile, four-star **Hotel Cabo Blanco,** P.O. Box 31, Barra de Navidad, Jalisco 48987, tel. 335/551-03, 335/551-36, or 335/551-82, fax 335/564-94. The 125-room complex anchors the vacation home development along the three marina-canals that extend from the lagoon to about five blocks inland from the town. Within its manicured garden-grounds, Hotel Cabo Blanco offers night-lit tennis courts, restaurants, bars, two pools, kiddie pools, and deluxe sportfishing yachts-for-hire. The deluxe, pastel-decorated rooms run about $100 d high season, $70 d low, all with a/c, cable TV, and phones; with a folkloric dance show, many water sports, and credit cards accepted. Bring your repellent; during late afternoon and evening mosquitoes and gnats from the nearby mangroves seem to especially enjoy the Cabo Blanco's posh ambience.

Barra's plushest accommodation is the class-act **Hotel Grand Bay,** P.O. Box 20, Barra de Navidad, Jalisco 48987, tel. 335/550-50, fax 335/560-71, a short boat ride across the lagoon. Builders spared little expense to create the appearance of a *gran epoch* resort. The 198 rooms are elaborately furnished in marble floors, French provincial furniture and jade-hued Italian marble bathroom sinks. Accommodations run from spacious "superior" rooms for $325 d high season, $200 d low, and master suites ($700 high, $500 low) through grand four-room executive suites that include their own steam rooms, from $2,300. With all conveniences, including three pools, three elegant restaurants, tennis, volleyball, children's club, marina, and golf course. **Note:** Security is tight at Hotel Grand Bay. Guards at the lagoon-side boat dock only allow entrance to guests and prospective guests. If you want to look around, you have to be accompanied by an in-house guide. Call the desk beforehand for an appointment.

Melaque Hotels

Melaque has a swarm of hotels and bungalows, many of them poorly designed and indifferently managed. They scratch along, nearly empty except during the Christmas and Easter holiday deluges when Mexican middle-class families

MELAQUE

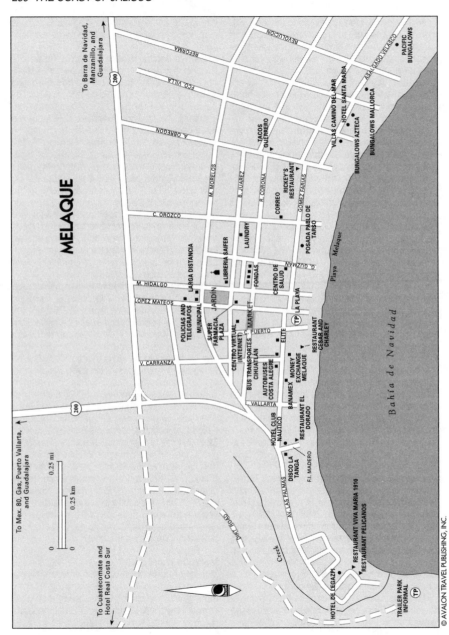

To Barra de Navidad, Manzanillo, and Guadalajara

To Mex. 80, Gas, Puerto Vallarta, and Guadalajara

To Cuastecomate and Hotel Real Costa Sur

0.25 mi

0.25 km

REVOLUCION

REFORMA

FCO. VILLA

A. OBREGON

M. MORELOS

B. JUAREZ

R. CORONA

C. OROZCO

M. HIDALGO

LOPEZ MATEOS

V. CARRANZA

L. VALLARTA

F.I. MADERO

AV. LAS PALMAS

DR. ROJO

Creek

PACIFIC BUNGALOWS

ASACADO VELASCO

HOTEL SANTA MARIA

VILLAS CAMINO DEL MAR

BUNGALOWS AZTECA

BUNGALOWS MALLORCA

TACOS GUERRERO

RICKEY'S RESTAURANT

CORREO

GOMEZ FARIAS

POSADA PABLO DE TARSO

G. GUZMAN

LIBRERIA SAIFER

LAUNDRY

FONDAS

CENTRO DE SALUD

LARGA DISTANCIA

Playa Melaque

LA PLAYA

JARDIN

POLICIAS AND TELEGRAFOS

MUNICIPAL

SUPER FARMACIA PLAZA

CENTRO VIRTUAL (INTERNET)

MARKET

P. PUERTO

ELITE

RESTAURANT CESAR AND CHARLEY

BUS TRANSPORTES CIHUATLAN

AUTOBUSES COSTA ALEGRE

BANAMEX MONEY EXCHANGE MELAQUE

HOTEL CLUB NAUTICO

RESTAURANT EL DORADO

DISCO LA TANGA

RESTAURANT VIVA MARIA 1910

RESTAURANT PELICANOS

HOTEL DE LEGAZPI

TRAILER PARK INFORMAL

Bahía de Navidad

© AVALON TRAVEL PUBLISHING, INC.

must accept anything to stay at the beach. There are, nevertheless, several bright exceptions, which can be conveniently divided into "South" and "North of Town" groups:

Hotels South of Town: Classy in its unique way is the **Villas Camino del Mar,** whose owner doesn't believe in advertising. A few signs in the humble beach neighborhood about a quarter-mile on the Barra side of the Melaque town center furnishes the only clue that this gem of a lodging hides among the Melaque dross at Calle Francisco Villa, corner Abel Salgado, P.O. Box 6, San Patricio-Melaque, Jalisco 48980, tel. 335/552-07, fax 335/554-98, email: skennedy @ciber.net.mx. (Note: Recently, owners have added an annex across the street, which, although inviting, is not as attractive as the original building. Specifically ask for a room in the original building in your written or faxed reservation request.) A five-story white stucco monument draped with fluted, neoclassic columns and hanging pedestals, the original Villas Camino del Mar hotel offers a lodging assortment from simple double rooms through deluxe suites with kitchenettes to a rambling penthouse. The upper three levels have sweeping ocean views, while the lower two overlook an elegant blue pool and patio bar and shady beachside palm grove. The clientele is split between Mexican middle-class families who come for weekends all year around, and quiet Canadian and American couples who come to soak up the winter sun for weeks and months on end. Reserve early, especially for the winter. Year-round rates for the 37 rooms and suites run as little as $46 ($42 per day weekly, $30 monthly) for comfortable ocean-view doubles; $72 ($65 weekly, $47 monthly) for one-bedroom kitchenette suites, and $105 ($95 weekly, $70 monthly) for deluxe two-bedroom, two-bath suites with kitchen; all with fans only.

If the Camino del Mar is full or not to your liking, you can choose from a trio of acceptable lodgings around the corner that share the same golden sunset-view strand. The plainer but priced-right **Hotel Santa María** offers 46 rooms and kitchenette apartments with bath, close enough to the water for the waves to lull guests to sleep at Abel Salgado 85, P.O. Box 188, San Patricio-Melaque, Jalisco 48980, tel. 335/556-77, fax 335/555-53. Rooms, popular with budget-conscious Canadians and Americans in winter,

are arranged in a pair of motel-style stucco tiers around an invitingly green inner patio. Units vary; upper rooms are brighter, so look at a few before you move in. All-season prices for the spartan but generally tidy rooms begin at about $17 d per day, $110/week, $350/month, with fans, but no pool.

Right next door, the sky-blue and white **Bungalows Azteca** auto court-style cottages line both sides of a cobbled driveway courtyard garden that spreads to a lazy beachfront patio. The 14 spacious kitchenette cottages, in small (one-bedroom) or large (three-bedroom) versions, are plainly furnished but clean. The nine one-bedroom units rent, high season, for about $53/day, $170/week, $500/month; the four three-bedrooms rent for about $130/day, $450/week, $1400/month. Expect a low-season discount of about 25 percent. Send your reservation request to P.O. Box 57, San Patricio-Melaque, Jalisco 48980, or tel./fax 335/551-50 in Melaque, or 3/825-5118, fax 3/826-1191 in Guadalajara. Get your reservation in early, especially for the winter.

Less than a block away, the open, parklike grounds, spacious blue pool, and beachside palm garden of the **Bungalows Mallorca** invite unhurried outdoor relaxation. Its stacked, Motel 6-style layout, now draped with tropical greenery, has aged gracefully. Here, groups and families used to providing their own atmosphere find the kitchens and spacious (but dark) rooms of the Bungalows Mallorca appealing. The 24 two-bedroom bungalows with a/c and TV rent for about $57 d, 20% discount for a one-month rental. A pair of beachside units with hot tubs and view balconies rent for about $68. Reserve directly, at Abel Salgado 133, Colonia Villa Obregón, P.O. Box 157, San Patricio-Melaque, Jalisco 48980, tel. 335/552-19.

Closer toward town is the well-kept, colonial-chic **Posada Pablo de Tarso,** Av. Gómez Farías 408, San Patricio-Melaque, Jalisco 48980, tel. 335/551-17, fax 335/552-68, named after the apostle Paul of Tarsus. This unique label, along with the many classy details, including art-decorated walls, hand-carved bedsteads and doors, and a flowery beachside pool and patio, reflect an unusual degree of care and devotion. The only drawback lies in the motel-style corridor layout, which requires guests to pull the dark drapes for privacy. High season rates for the 27 rooms and bungalows begin at about $35 d; a kitchen raises the tariff to about $53 d, with fans or a/c, TV, and phones. You can also reserve through the owner in Guadalajara, at tel. 3/616-4850, or tel./fax 3/616-6688 or 3/615-1426.

Hotels North of Town: If you prefer hotel high-rise ambience with privacy, a sea-view balcony, and a disco next door, you can have it right on the beach at the in-town **Hotel Club Náutico**, Av. Gómez Farías 1A, San Patricio-Melaque, Jalisco 48980, tel. 335/557-70 or 335/557-66, fax 335/552-39. The 40 deluxe rooms, in blue, pastels, and white, angle toward the ocean in sunset-view tiers above a smallish pool and patio. The upper-floor rooms nearest the beach are likely to be quieter with the best views. The hotel also has a good beachside restaurant whose huge *palapa* both captures the cool afternoon sea breeze and frames the blue waters of the Bay of Navidad. The hotel's main drawback is lack of space, being sandwiched into a long, narrow beachfront lot. Rentals run about $36 s, $56 d high season, $32 s, $51 d low; with a/c, TV, phones, and restaurant/bar; credit cards are accepted.

In contrast, the friendly, downscale-modern, white stucco **Hotel de Legazpi** in the drowsy beach-end neighborhood nearby offers a more personal and tranquil ambience, at P.O. Box 88, San Patricio-Melaque, Jalisco 48980, tel./fax 335/553-97. A number of the hotel's spacious, clean, and comfortable front-side rooms have balconies with palmy ocean and sunset views. Downstairs, guests enjoy use of a homey restaurant and a rear-court pool and patio. The hotel's beachside entrance leads through a jungly front garden straight to the idyllic Melaque west-end sand crescent. Here, good times bloom among an informal club of longtime winter returnees beneath the *palapas* of the popular Pelícanos and Viva María restaurants. The hotel's 16 fan-only rooms (two with kitchenette) rent for $29 s, $29 d, $33 t low season, $32, $32, $36 high.

The five-star **Hotel Real (Royal) Costa Sur** on Playa Coastecomate a few miles north offers a local resort alternative at P.O. Box 12, San Patricio-Melaque, Jalisco 48980, tel./fax 335/550-85. The hotel's low-rise view guest cabañas spread like a giant mushroom garden in the jungly palm-forest hillside above the beach. Patrons—mostly Canadians and Americans in winter, Mexicans in summer and holidays—enjoy deluxe air-conditioned view rooms with cable TV, tennis courts, sailing, windsurfing, pedalboats, snorkeling, volleyball, and a broad pool and sundeck right on the beach. Rooms run about $70 d high season, $55 d low. During times of low occupancy the hotel may accept day guests for a set fee. (Note: a reader complained that she got sick from musty mildew in her room here. Although new management seems competent and seems to have corrected such problems, be sure to choose a clean, satisfactorily ventilated room before moving in.)

Apartments, Houses, and Long-Term Rentals

If you're planning on a stay longer than a few weeks, you'll get more for your money if you can find a long-term house or apartment rental. Peggy Ross, at Crazy Cactus store in Barra (on Jalisco, corner of Veracruz, next to Restaurant Ambar) specializes in finding local rentals for visitors. Drop by, or write several weeks in advance, at Tienda Crazy Cactus, Calle Jalisco, esquina Veracruz, Barra de Navidad, Jalisco 48987.

Trailer Parks and Camping

Barra-Melaque has one formal trailer park, **La Playa**, right on the beach in downtown Melaque at P.O. Box 59, Av. Gómez Farías 250, San Patricio-Melaque, Jalisco 48980, tel. 335/550-65. Although the park is a bit cramped and mostly shadeless, longtimers nevertheless get their winter reservations in early for the choice beach spaces. The better-than-average facilities include a small store, fish-cleaning sinks, showers, toilets, and all hookups. The water is brackish—drink bottled. Boat launching is usually easy on the sheltered beach nearby; otherwise, use the ramp at the Hotel Cabo Blanco, tel. 335/550-22, one block east, past the adjacent boat canal. The Trailer Park La Playa's 45 spaces rent for about $15/day, $300/month.

Scores of winter returnees enjoy Melaque's **informal RV-trailer park-campground** with room for about 50 rigs and tents. The cliff-bottom lot spreads above a calm rocky cove, ripe for swimming, snorkeling, and windsurfing. Other extras include super fishing and a sweeping view of the entire Bay of Navidad. All spaces are usually filled by Christmas and remain that way until March. The people are friendly, the price is certainly right, and the beer and water trucks arrive regularly throughout the winter season. Please dump your waste in sanitary facilities while staying here; continued pollution of the cove by irresponsible occupants has led to complaints, which may force local authorities to close the campground. Get there by the dirt road that splits left, toward the bay, about two blocks west (toward Coastecomate), from the Hwy. 200 intersection at Melaque's northwest edge.

Wilderness campers will enjoy **Playa de Cocos,** a miles-long golden sand beach, accessible by launch from Barra to Colimilla, or by road the long way around. Playa de Cocos has an intimate hidden sandy cove, perfect for an overnight or a few barefoot days of birdwatching, shell collecting, beachcombing, and dreaming around your driftwood campfire. The restaurants at the village of Colimilla or the stores (by launch across the lagoon) in Barra are available for

Churros, *foot-long doughnuts, are still a favorite everywhere in Mexico.*

food and water. Mosquitoes come out around sunset. Bring plenty of good repellent and a mosquito-proof tent.

FOOD

Breakfast, Snacks, and Stalls
An excellent way to start your Barra day is at the intimate *palapa*-shaded patio of the **Hotel Delfín,** Av. Morelos 23, tel. 335/700-68. While you dish yourself fruit and pour your coffee from its little countertop buffet, the cook fixes your choice of breakfast options, from savory eggs and omelettes to French toast and luscious, tender banana pancakes; a complete breakfast costs $3–5, daily 8:30–10:30 A.M.

In Melaque, the restaurant at Club Náutico and *palapa* Restaurant Pelícanos are also good places to start your day.

Also, plenty of good daytime eating in Melaque goes on at the lineup of small, permanent *fondas* (foodstalls) in the alley that runs south from Av. Hidalgo, half a block toward the beach from the southwest plaza corner. You can't go wrong with *fonda* food, as long as it's made right in front of you and served piping hot.

For evening light meals and snacks, Barra has plenty of options. Here, families seem to fall into two categories: those who sell food to sidewalk passersby, and those who enjoy their offerings. The three blocks of Av. Veracruz from Morelos to the city *jardín* (park) are dotted with tables that residents nightly load with hearty, economical food offerings, from tacos *de lengua* (tongue) and pork tamales to *pozole Guadalajara* and *chiles rellenos.* The wholesomeness of their menus is evidenced by their devoted followings of longtime neighbor and tourist customers.

On the other hand, you can enjoy the strictly North American fare—hamburgers, salads, sandwiches, malts—of Tessa's Malt Shop, between the Barra church and Cafe Ambar.

Restaurants
One local family has built their sidewalk culinary skills into a thriving Barra storefront business, the **Restaurant Paty,** at the corner of Veracruz and Jalisco, tel. 335/707-43. They offer the traditional menu of Mexican *antojitos*—tacos, quesadillas, tostadas—plus roast beef, chicken, and very tasty

pozole soup. Open daily 8 A.M.–11 P.M. Budget. For a variation on the same theme, try **Restaurant Chela,** across the street, on the corner.

Restaurant Ambar, Veracruz 101A, corner Jalisco, one of Barra's most refined eateries, stands beneath a luxuriously airy upstairs *palapa* diagonally across from the Paty. The unusual menu features lighter fare—eggs, fish, whole-wheat *(harina integral)* tortillas, and bread. Besides a large selection of sweet and savory crepes, it also serves a number of seafood and vegetable salads and Mexican plates, including scrumptious *chiles rellenos.* The wine list, which features the good Baja California Cetto label, is the best in town. Open daily, in season, 8 A.M.–noon for breakfast, 5–10 P.M. for dinner; American Express accepted. Moderate.

Among Barra's best eateries is the **Restaurant Ramon,** tel. 335/564-85, tucked beneath its tall *palapa* at 260 Legazpi, across the street from the Hotel Barra de Navidad. Completely unpretentious and making the most of the usual list of international and Mexican specialties, friendly owner/chef Ramon and his hardworking staff continue to build their already sizable following. Choose whatever you like—chicken, fish, *chiles rellenos,* guacamole, spaghetti—and you'll most likely be pleased. Meals include gratis salsa and chips to start, hearty portions, and often a healthy side of cooked veggies on your plate. Open daily 7 A.M.–11 P.M. Moderate.

One of Barra's most entertainingly scenic restaurants is **Veleros,** right on the lagoon at Veracruz 64, tel. 335/558-38. If you happen to visit Barra during the full moon, don't miss watching its shimmering reflection from the restaurant *palapa* as it rises over the mangrove-bordered expanse. An additional Veleros bonus is the fascinating darting, swirling school of fish attracted by the spotlight shining on the water. Finally comes the food, which you can select from a menu of carefully prepared and served shrimp, lobster, octopus, chicken, and steak entrees. The brochettes are especially popular. Open daily noon–10 P.M.; credit cards are accepted. Moderate.

Nearby, half a block south, a relative newcomer on the Barra lagoon-front is **Jarro,** the brain-child of personable restaurateur Raoul Canet, who built his original Jalapeños in Manzanillo from a solid formula of savory, authentically Mexican-style specialties, professionally served and invitingly presented. Here in Barra, his beachfront *palapa* branch seems destined for similar success. Closed September and October.

For change of scene, try **Restaurant Seamaster,** one block away, on the beach side of the sandbar, where guests enjoy a refreshing sea breeze every afternoon and a happy-hour sunset every evening at López de Legazpi 140. Besides super-fresh seafood selections, it features savory barbecued chicken and rib plates. Open daily 8 A.M.–11 P.M. Moderate.

Restaurant Pancho, three doors away at Legazpi 53, is one of Barra's original *palapas,* which old-timers can remember from the days when *all* Barra restaurants were *palapas.* The original Pancho, who has seen lots of changes in the old sandbar in his 70-odd years, still oversees the operation daily 8 A.M.–8 P.M. Moderate.

Melaque has a scattering of good beach-side restaurants. **Restaurant El Dorado,** under the big beachside *palapa* in front of the Hotel Club Náutico, provides a cool breezy place to enjoy the beach scene during breakfast or lunch at Calle Gómez Farías 1A, tel. 335/557-70. Service is crisp and the specialties are carefully prepared. Open daily 8 A.M.–11 P.M.; credit cards are accepted. Moderate to expensive.

Restaurant Pelícanos, a beach *palapa* on the tranquil cove about five blocks northwest of the town-center, remains one of Melaque's most enduring institutions. Although the picture-perfect shoreline and the social scene are half the attraction here, the restaurant nevertheless ensures its popularity with respectable hamburgers and very fresh fish. Open daily 8 A.M.–10 P.M. Moderate.

Viva María 1910 next door accomplishes about the same by specializing in good Mexican-style food. The restaurant's name is in honor of the thousands of unsung "Marías," *soldaderas* who fought and died along with their men during the Revolution of 1910-17.

Although it's not on the beachfront, **Restaurant Ricardo's,** in the rustic-chic *palapa* on the east-side corner of Obregón and Gómez Farías, is earning a reputation as Melaque's up and coming restaurant of choice. Especially recommended for breakfast, open daily 8 A.M.–10 P.M.

SPORTS AND RECREATION

Swimming, Surfing, and Boogie Boarding

The roughest surf on the Bahía de Navidad shoreline is closer to Barra, the most tranquil closest to Melaque. Swimming is consequently best and safest toward the Melaque end, while, in contrast, the only good surfing spot is where the waves rise and roll in beside the Barra jetty. Bodysurfing and boogie boarding are best somewhere in between. At least one shop in Barra—Crazy Cactus on Jalisco, corner of Veracruz, next to (and below) upstairs Restaurant Ambar—rents surfboards and boogie boards.

Sailing and Windsurfing

Sailing and windsurfing are best near the Melaque end of the Bay of Navidad and in the Bay of Coastecomate nearby. Bring your own equipment, however; none is available locally.

Snorkeling and Scuba Diving

Local snorkeling is often good, especially at Playa Tenacatita several miles north. The Crazy Cactus beach shop, near the corner of Jalisco and Veracruz, next to Restaurant Ambar, organizes snorkeling excursions.

Although no commercial dive shops operate out of Barra or Melaque, Susan Dearing, the very professional Manzanillo-based instructor, outfits and leads dives in the Barra-Melaque area. Susan, a veteran certified YMCA-method instructor with a record of many hundreds of accident-free guided dives and her partner, NAUI-certified instructor Carlos Cuellar, can be contacted at P.O. Box 295, Santiago, Colima 28860, tel./fax 333/306-42, cellular tel. 335/803-27, email: scubamex@bay.net.mx.

Tennis and Golf

The Hotel Cabo Blanco tennis courts, tel. 335/551-82 or 335/551-03, fax 335/564-94, are customarily open for public rental for about $5 per hour. Call ahead to check. Lessons may also be available. The Hotel Costa Sur, tel. 335/550-85, has tennis courts for guests and day members.

The plumy, breezy 18-hole **Isla de Navidad Golf Course** is available to the public for a fee of around $70 per person. Get there by regular launch from the Barra launch dock on the lagoon (to the Casa Club landing, about $5 roundtrip). By car, turn right from Hwy. 200 at the Ejido La Culebra (or Isla de Navidad) sign as the highway cuts through the hills at Km 51 a few miles south of Barra. Follow the road about three miles (4.8 km) to a bridge, where the road curves right, paralleling the beach. After about two more miles (3.2 km), you pass through the golf course gate. After winding through the golf course another mile (1.6 km), turn right at the traffic circle at the north edge of the golf course. Continue another mile (1.6 km), between the golf course and the adjacent hillside, to the big golf clubhouse on the right.

Sportfishing

Big-game fishing boat rentals are available from friendly Captain Eduardo Castellos, at his shop, **Fantasia,** on Legazpi, corner of Jalisco, diagonally across from the church, at López de Legazpi 213, Barra de Navidad, Jalisco 48987, tel./fax 335/568-24, email: pati2.1@prodigy.net.mx. Eduardo has three boats: a launch and two medium-sized craft, one with cabin and toilet. His all-day fee runs about $160 (six hours, three people fishing) for the *lancha* and $300 for the biggest boat (six hours, four people fishing) complete with bait, tackle, and soft drinks.

The captains of the Barra Boat Cooperative **Sociedad Cooperativa de Servicios Turístico** routinely take parties on successful marlin and swordfish hunts for about $22 per hour, including bait and tackle. Their lagoonside office-dock is at Av. Veracruz 40.

There are many other fish in the sea besides deep-sea marlin and swordfish, both of which often make tough eating. Half-day trips arranged through Fantasia, the Sociedad Cooperativa de Servicios Turístico, or others will typically net a number of large dorado, albacore, snapper, or other delicious eating fish. Local restaurants will generally cook up a banquet for you and your friends if you give them the extra fish caught during such an outing.

If you'd like to enter one of a pair of annual Barra de Navidad **International Fishing Tournaments** (billfish, tuna, and *dorado* in January and May) and father and son/daughter tournament in August, contact Eduardo Castellos (above) or the tourist information office (following) for information.

Boat Launching

If you plan on mounting your own fishing expedition, you can do it from the Barra boat-launching ramp at the end of Av. Filipinas near the Hotel Cabo Blanco. The fee—about $10 per day—covers parking your boat in the canal and is payable to boatkeeper José Miguel, whose headquarters is inside the boatyard adjacent to the ramp, Mon.–Fri. 8 A.M.–4 P.M.; if he's not there, ask at the Hotel Cabo Blanco desk, tel. 335/551-82 or 335/551-03, one block east, toward the beach, past the adjacent boat canal.

Sports Equipment Sales and Rentals

Barra's sport shop, **Crazy Cactus,** run by friendly, English-speaking Tracy Ross, offers rental surfboards, boogie boards, bicycles, and snorkels, masks, and fins. It's on Jalisco, corner of Veracruz, next to (and below) upstairs Restaurant Ambar.

ENTERTAINMENT AND EVENTS

Most entertainments in Barra and Melaque are informal and local. *Corridas de toros* (bullfights) are occasionally held during the winter-spring season at the bullring on Hwy. 200 across from the Barra turnoff. Local *vaqueros* (cowboys) sometimes display their pluck in spirited *charreadas* (Mexican-style rodeos) in neighboring country villages. Check with your hotel desk or the Barra tourist information office, near the east end of Jalisco, at no. 67, across the street from the Terraza upstairs bar, tel./fax 335/551-00, for details.

The big local festival occurs in Melaque during the St. Patrick's Day week of March 10–17. Events include blessing of the local fishing fleet, folk dancing, cake eating, and boxing matches.

Nightlife

Folks enjoy the Bahía de Navidad sunset colors nightly during the happy hours at Restaurant Seamaster, Hotel Tropical (if it's open), or Sunset Restaurant-bar (across Legazpi from the church).

The same is true at the beachside Restaurant Dorado at Hotel Club Náutico in Melaque, north end of main street Gómez Farías. You can prepare for this during the afternoons (December, January, and February mostly) at the very congenial 4–6 P.M. happy hour around the swim-up bar at Barra's Hotel Sands.

Lovers of pure tranquility, on the other hand, enjoy the breeze and sunset view from the end of Barra's rock jetty.

After dinner, huge speakers begin thumping away, lights flash, and the fogs ooze from the ceilings around 10 P.M. at disco **El Galeón** of the Hotel Sands, tel. 335/551-48 (young local crowd), and **La Tanga,** tel. 335/554-72, across the street from Hotel Club Náutico, north end of beachfront street Gómez Farías (entrance $7, mixed young and older, local and tourist crowd). Hours vary seasonally; call for details.

SERVICES AND SHOPPING

Money Exchange

Barra has no bank, but Melaque does: **Banamex,** with ATM, across the street and half a block north of the main bus station, is open Mon.–Fri. 9 A.M.–2 P.M. for traveler's checks, and until 3 P.M. for cash. Barra's official *casa de cambio,* at Veracruz 214, just north of the plaza, changes both American and Canadian dollars and offers long-distance telephone service; open Mon.–Sat. 9 A.M.–2 P.M. and 4–7 P.M., Sunday 9 A.M.–2 P.M. With even longer hours, the **Liquoría Barra de Navidad,** on Legazpi, across from the Hotel Barra de Navidad, exchanges both Canadian and American traveler's checks and cash; open daily 8:30 A.M.–11 P.M.

After bank hours in Melaque, use the Banamex ATM, or go to **Money Exchange Melaque,** Gómez Farías 27A, across from the bus terminal, tel. 335/553-43. It exchanges both American and Canadian traveler's checks and cash Mon.–Sat. 9 A.M.–2 P.M. and 4–7 P.M., Sunday 9 A.M.–2 P.M. The tariff, however, often amounts to a steep three dollars per 100 above bank rate.

Post Office, Telephone, Telegraph, and Internet

Barra and Melaque each have a small **post of-**

fice (correo) and a **telégrafo.** The Barra post office is unfortunately far from the town center. From the plaza, head north along Veracruz, continue three blocks past the health clinic, to Calle Nueva España; go right three blocks to the correo on the right, open Mon.–Fri. 8 A.M.–3 P.M., Saturday 9 A.M.–1 P.M. The Melaque post office is three blocks south of the plaza, at 13 Clemente Orozco, between G. Farías and Corona, a block and a half from the beach, tel. 335/552-30. Open Mon.–Fri. 8 A.M.–3 P.M., Saturday 9 A.M.–1 P.M.

The Barra **telégrafo,** which handles money orders, is right at the Av. Veracruz corner of the jardín, tel. 335/552-62; open Mon.–Fri. 9 A.M.–3 P.M. The Melaque telégrafo does the same on Av. López Mateos, behind the delegación municipal (municipal agency), northeast corner of the plaza.

In Barra, at the plaza-front municipal agency office, you may use the 24-hour public **larga distancia** telephone. Another long distance telephone office, tel./fax 335/556-25, is at Mini-super Hawaii, on Legazpi, across from the Hotel Tropical, open daily, except holidays, noon–11 P.M. In Melaque, go to the long-distance telephone office on the jardín northeast corner, at the intersection of Morelos and Hidalgo.

For Internet connection in Barra, go to **Mango Bay** Internet cafe, at 70 Jalisco, across the street from turismo. In Melaque, you have a pair of Internet choices: **Ciber@Net** across from the bus terminal on Gómez Farías, interior hall, next to the money exchange; open Mon.–Sat. 9 A.M.–2:30 P.M. and 4–8 P.M., and **Centro Virtual** in the Melaque market, opposite the food stalls, half a block toward the beach from the Plaza, cellular tel. 335/376-97; open Mon.–Sat. 9 A.M.–2 P.M. and 4–10 P.M.

Health

In Barra, the government **Centro de Salud** (health clinic), corner Veracruz and Puerto de La Navidad, four blocks from the town square, tel. 335/562-20, has a doctor 24 hours a day. The Melaque Centro de Salud, Calle Gordiano Guzman 10, tel. 335/550-80, off main beach-side street Gómez Farías two blocks from the trailer park, offers access to a doctor 24 hours a day.

In a medical emergency, dial local number 335/523-00 for a Red Cross (Cruz Roja) **ambu-**lance to whisk you to the well-equipped hospitals in Manzanillo.

For routine consultations, a number of Barra and Melaque doctors and pharmacists are available long hours at their own pharmacies. For example, in Melaque, go to Dr. Juan Manuel Aragon, at the **Super Farmacia Plaza,** on López Mateos, northwest corner of the town plaza, tel. 335/551-67.

Police

The Barra police, tel. 335/553-99, are on 24-hour duty at the city office at 179 Veracruz, adjacent to the jardín.

For the Melaque police, either call 335/550-80, or go to the headquarters behind the plaza-front delegación municipal (municipal agency) at the plaza corner of L. Mateos and Morelos.

Travel Agent

For airplane tickets, fishing trips, tours, and other arrangements in Barra, contact friendly Sandra Kosonoy of **Nayah Hibiba Tours** travel agency, at Veracruz 204A (between Sinaloa and Guanajuato), tel./fax 335/556-67. Open daily 9 A.M.–8 P.M.

Grocery Stores

There are no large markets, traditional or modern, in Barra or Melaque. However, a number of good mini-supers and fruterías stock basic supplies. In Barra, your best bet for fruits and vegetables is frutería **La Colmena,** east side of Veracruz, three doors south of the plaza, open daily until around 9 P.M. Three doors north, corner of Veracruz and Guanajuato, the **Mini-super Costa Alegre** stocks basic groceries.

In Melaque, nearly all grocery and fruit shopping takes place at several good stores on main street López Mateos, which runs away from the beach past the west side of the central plaza.

Laundries

Barra and Melaque visitors enjoy the services of a number of lavanderías. In Barra, try **Lavandería Jardín,** at Jalisco 69, next to turismo, open Mon.–Fri. 9 A.M.–2 P.M. and 4–7 P.M., Saturday 9 A.M.–noon. In Melaque, step one block east (parallel to beach) along Juarez from the plaza, to **Lavandería Francis.**

Handicrafts

While Melaque has many stores crammed with humdrum commercial tourist curios, Barra has a few interestingly authentic sources. For example, a number of Nahua-speaking families from Guerrero operate small individual shops on Legazpi. One shop, **Artesanías Nahua** (NAH-waht), run by Oligario Ramírez, at the northeast corner of Sinaloa and Legazpi, is a small museum of delightful folk crafts, made mostly by *indígena* country craftspeople. Pick what you like from among hundreds—lustrous lacquerware trays from Olinalá, winsome painted pottery cats, rabbits, and fish, a battalion of wooden mini-armadillos, and glossy dark-wood swordfish from Sonora. Do bargain, but gently.

You can pick from an equally attractive selection across the street, at **Arts and Crafts of Oaxaca,** across Legazpi from the church. Besides a fetching collection of priced-to-sell Oaxacan *alebrijes* (crazy wooden animals), *tapetes* (wool rugs), and masks, you'll also find a host of papier-mâché and pottery from Tlaquepaque and Tonalá, *sombreros* from Zitácuaro in Michoacán, and much more.

Barra's small **folk-crafts market,** on Legazpi, corner of Sinaloa, behind the church, is open daily during the high season, from about 9 A.M. to 6 P.M. The vendors, many indigenous, offer handmade items from their own locales, which range along the Pacific from Sinaloa and Nayarit in the north to Guerrero and Oaxaca in the south. The Jalisco items especially—such as sculptures of human figures in local dress, and papier-mâché parrots—can be bargained to prices significantly below Puerto Vallarta levels. Don't bargain too hard, however. Many of these folks, far from their country villages, are strangers in a strange land. Their sometimes-meager earnings often support entire extended families back home.

INFORMATION

Tourist Information Office

The small Barra-Melaque regional office of the Jalisco Department of Tourism is tucked in a little office near the east end of Jalisco, at no. 67, across the street from the Terraza upstairs bar, which is on the east end of the south end of Ve-

racruz. Staff distributes maps and literature and answers questions during office hours (Mon.–Fri. 9 A.M.–5 P.M., tel./fax 335/551-00). The office is a good source of information about local civic and ecological issues and organizations.

Books, Newspapers, and Magazines

The Barra **newsstand,** open daily 7 A.M.–10 P.M., at the corner of Veracruz and Michoacán, customarily stocks the Mexico City *News,* which usually arrives by 4 P.M.

Perhaps the best English-language lending library in all of the Mexican Pacific is **Beer Bob's Book Exchange** on a Barra back street, 61 Mazatlán, near Sinaloa. Thousands of vintage paperbacks, free for borrowing or exchange, fill the shelves. Chief librarian and Scrabble devotee Bob (actually Robert Baham, retired counselor for the California Youth Authority) manages his little gem of an establishment just for the fun of it. It is not a store, he says; just drop your old titles in the box and take away the equivalent from his well-organized collection. If you have nothing to exchange, simply return whatever you borrow before you leave town.

In Melaque, the **Librería Saifer,** open Mon.–Sat. 2–11 P.M. and Sunday 6–11 P.M., on the central plaza, southwest corner, by the church, also stocks the *News.*

Ecology Groups

The informal community **Grupo Ecobana** accomplishes ecological improvement through practical examples, which include beach-cleaning sessions with schoolchildren and camping out at secluded local beaches in order to discourage turtle egg poachers. For more information, contact the Tourist Information Office, in Barra, at Jalisco 67, open Mon.–Fri. 9 A.M.– 5 P.M.

The University of Guadalajara also runs the local **Centro Estudios Ecologíos de la Costa,** which, through research, education, and direct action, is trying to preserve local animal and plant species and habitats. Now and then you may spot one of its white vans on the highway or around town. At the wheel might be the director, Enrique Godinez Domínguez, one of whose better-known efforts is the turtle-hatching station at Mismaloya, about 72 miles (115 km) north of Barra, near Cruz de Loreto. The local headquarters is in Melaque at V. Gómez Farías 82, tel. 335/563-30, fax 335/563-31, across from the Hotel Pablo de Tarso in Melaque.

GETTING THERE AND AWAY

By Air
Barra de Navidad is air-accessible either through **Puerto Vallarta Airport** (see "Getting There and Away" in the Puerto Vallarta chapter) or the **Manzanillo Airport,** only 19 miles (30 km) south of Barra-Melaque. While the Puerto Vallarta connection has the advantage of many more flights, transfers to the south coast are time-consuming. If you can afford it, the quickest option from Puerto Vallarta is to rent a car. Alternatively, ride a local bus or hire a taxi from the airport to the new central bus station, north of the airport. There, catch a bus, preferably **Autocamiones del Pacífico,** tel. 322/100-21, or its luxury service **Primera Plus,** tel. 3/221-0095, to Barra-Melaque (three hours).

On the other hand, arrival via the Manzanillo airport, half an hour from Barra-Melaque, is much more direct, provided that good connections are obtainable through the relatively few carriers that serve the airport.

Manzanillo Airport Flights
Aerocalifornia Airlines flights connect with Los Angeles and Mexico City. For local reservations and flight information, call 333/ 414-14.

America West Airlines flights connect with Phoenix during the winter-spring season. For local reservations and flight information, call 333/411-40.

Aeroméxico Airlines' subsidiary carrier **Aerolitoral** flights connect Manzanillo airport with Guadalajara (where many U.S. connections are available). For reservations in Barra and Melaque, contact a travel agent, such as **Nayah Habiba Tours,** at Veracruz 204A, tel./fax 335/556-67; or for flight information, contact Aeroméxico's Manzanillo office, tel. 333/412-26.

Mexicana Airlines flights connect daily with Mexico City, where many U.S. connections are available. For reservations and flight information, contact its airport office, tel. 333/323-23, or the national toll-free number, 01-800/502-2000 or 01-800/501-9900.

Canada 3000 charter flights connect with Toronto, Calgary-Edmonton, and Vancouver during the winter-spring season. Contact a travel agent for information and reservations.

Airport Arrival and Departure
For an international destination, the **Manzanillo airport** (officially the Playa de Oro International Airport, code ZLO) facilities are rather sparse. Although a few shops, snack stands, an upstairs restaurant, and a *buzón* (mailbox) just inside the front entrance provide some essentials, the terminal has neither money exchange, hotel booking, nor tourist information booths. Consequently, you should arrive with a day's worth of pesos and a hotel reservation. If not, you'll be at the mercy of taxi drivers who love to collect fat commissions on your first-night hotel tariff. Upon departure, be sure to save enough cash to pay the approximate $12 **departure tax,** (if your ticket doesn't already include it.)

After the usually rapid immigration and customs checks, independent arrivees have their choice of a car rental (see below) or taxi tickets from a booth just outside the arrival gate. *Colectivos* head for Barra de Navidad and other northern points seasonally only. Taxis, however, will take three passengers to Barra, Melaque, or Hotel Real Coastecomate for about $25 total or to Hotel Blue Bay Village, $42; to hotels Club Med Playa Blanca and Careyes, $60; Chamela-El Super, $65; or Las Alamandas, $90. *Colectivo* tickets run about $6 per person to any Manzanillo hotel, while a *taxi especial* runs about $15.

No public buses service the Manzanillo airport. Strong, mobile travelers on tight budgets could save pesos by hitching or hiking the three miles to Hwy. 200 and flagging down one of the frequent north or southbound second-class buses (fare about $2 to Barra or Manzanillo). Don't try it at night, however.

As for airport **car rentals,** you have a choice of **National,** tel. 333/306-11, fax 333/311-40; **Hertz,** tel. 333/331-41, 333/331-42, or 333/331-43; and **Budget** tel./fax 333/314-45. Hint: Unless you don't mind paying upwards of $50 per day, shop around for your car rental by calling the car rentals' U.S. and Canada toll-free numbers at home *before* you leave (see the chart "Car Rental 800 Numbers" in the On The Road chapter).

By Car or RV

Three highway routes access Barra de Navidad: from the north via Puerto Vallarta, from the south via Manzanillo, and from the northeast via Guadalajara.

From Puerto Vallarta, **Mexican National Hwy. 200** is all asphalt and in good condition (except for some potholes), along its 134-mile (216-km) stretch to Barra de Navidad. Traffic is generally light, but it may slow a bit as the highway climbs the 2,400-foot Sierra Cuale summit near El Tuito south of Puerto Vallarta, but the light traffic and good road make passing safely possible. Allow about three hours for this very scenic trip.

From Manzanillo, the 38-mile (61-km) stretch of Hwy. 200 is nearly all countryside and all level. It's a snap in under an hour.

The same is not true of the winding, 181-mile (291-km) route between Barra de Navidad and Guadalajara. From Plaza del Sol at the center of Guadalajara, follow the signs for Colima that lead along the four-lane combined **Mexican National Highways 15, 54, and 80** heading southwest. Nineteen miles (30 km) from the city center, as Hwy. 15 splits right for Morelia and Mexico City, continue straight ahead, following the signs for Colima and Barra de Navidad. Very soon, follow the Hwy. 80 right fork for Barra de Navidad. Two miles farther, Hwy. 54 branches left to Colima; take the right branch, Hwy. 80, to Barra de Navidad. From there, the narrow, two-lane road continues through a dozen little towns, over mountain grades, and around curves for another 160 miles (258 km) to Melaque and Barra de Navidad. To be safe, allow about six hours' driving time uphill to Guadalajara, five hours in the opposite direction.

A longer but quicker and easier Barra de Navidad-Guadalajara road connection runs through Manzanillo along *autopistas* (superhighways) 54D (start out as described above, but southwest of Guadalajara, continue straight ahead on 54 D toward Colima, instead of turning right on to Hwy. 80 for Barra). Continue via 110 past Colima and 200 (via the Manzanillo *cuota* toll town bypass). Easy grades allow a leisurely 55 mph (90 km/hour) most of the way for this 192-mile (311-km) trip. Allow about four and a half hours, either direction.

By Bus

Various regional bus lines cooperate in connecting Barra and Melaque north with Puerto Vallarta; south with Cihuatlán, Manzanillo, Colima, Playa Azul, Zihuatanejo, and Acapulco; and northeast with Guadalajara, via Hwy. 80. They arrive and leave so often (about every half-hour during the day) from the little Barra de Navidad station, on Av. Veracruz a block and a half past the central plaza, tel. 335/552-65, that they're practically indistinguishable.

Of the various companies, affiliated lines **Transportes Cihuatlán and Autocamiones del Pacífico** provide the most options: super-first-class "Primera Plus" buses connect (several per day) with Guadalajara, Manzanillo, and Puerto Vallarta. In addition to this, they offer at least a dozen second-class buses per day in all three directions. These often stop anywhere along the road if passengers wave them down.

Another small line, **Autobuses Costa Alegre,** now affiliated with bus giant Flecha Amarilla, provides similar services, including a different "Primera Plus" luxury-class service to Manzanillo, Puerto Vallarta, Guadalajara, and León, out of its separate little station at Veracruz 269, across and half a block up the street, tel. 335/561-11.

The buses that stop in Barra also stop in Melaque; all Autocamiones del Pacífico and Transportes Cihuatlán buses stop at the Melaque main terminal, **Central de Autobuses** on Gómez Farías at V. Carranza, tel. 335/550-03; open 24 hours daily.

Flecha Amarilla maintains its own fancy new a/c station across the street, tel. 335/561-10, where you can ride its luxury-class **Primera Plus** buses, in addition to regular second-class Autobuses Costas Alegre, north to Puerto Vallarta, south to Manzanillo, and with recently expanded service, to Guadalajara and León.

However, one line, **Elite (EL),** does not stop in Barra. It maintains its own little Melaque station a block south of the main station, across from the Melaque Trailer Park, at Gómez Farias 257, tel. 335/551-77. From there, Elite connects by first-class express north (two daily departures) all the way to Puerto Vallarta, Mazatlán, and Tijuana, and south (two daily departures) to Manzanillo, Zihuatanejo, and Acapulco.

Note: All Barra de Navidad and Melaque bus departures are *salidas de paso,* meaning they originate somewhere else. Although seating can-not be ascertained until the bus arrives, seats are generally available, except during super-crowded Christmas and Easter holidays.

INTERNET RESOURCES

A number of websites may be helpful in preparing for your Mexico trip.

Mexico in General

www.visitmexico.com The official website of the public-private Mexico Tourism Board; a good general site for official information, such as entry requirements. It has lots of summarily informative sub-headings, not unlike an abbreviated guidebook. If you can't find what you want here, call its toll-free information number 800/4-MEXICO.

www.mexconnect.com A very good work in progress; with dozens upon dozens of sub-headings and links, especially helpful for folks thinking of working, living, or retiring in Mexico.

www.amtave.com This is the website of the Mexican Association of Adventure and Ecotourism. Lists contact addresses, telephones and email addresses of dozens of ecotourism operators in nearly all Mexican states.

www.go2mexico.com An aspiring commercial site that covers the Pacific Mexico destinations of Mazatláan, Puerto Vallarta, Ixtapa-Zihuatanejo, Acapulco, Huatulco, Oaxaca, Guadalajara, and Manzanillo (including current weather reports.) However, several of these destinations are very incomplete at this writing. A work in progress, potentially good if completed.

www.mexicodesconocido.com The site of the excellent magazine *Mexico Desconocido* ("Undiscovered Mexico"), which mostly features stories of unusual and off-the-beaten-track destinations. Presently the site covers only a few locations; hopefully it will expand in the future.

www.travel.state.gov The U.S. State Department information website. Lots of subheadings and links of varying completeness. (For example, the subheading listing medical care available worldwide, listed only about a dozen doctors and hospitals.) Other links, however, had plenty of solid information, especially consular advice, such as travel advisories or accessing U.S. citizens arrested overseas. Didn't seem to contain many specifics on Mexico, however.

DESTINATIONS

Jalisco In General

www.jalisco.com Fair site (at this writing not updated for nearly two years) but potentially very helpful if it had more detailed sub-headings and more links. Some links, such as connections to state government offices, might be useful.

Puerto Vallarta

puertovallarta.net Wow! All you need to prepare for your Puerto Vallarta trip. Contains a wealth of details in dozens of competently linked sub-headings, such as hotels, both humble and grand, car rentals, adventure tours, and on and on. Nearly every tourism service provider in Puerto Vallarta seems to be on board.

virtualvallarta.com The relatively new website of *Vallarta Lifestyles* magazine. May eventually become strong like its parent magazine in things upscale, such as boutiques, expensive restaurants, and condo sales and rentals.

Guadaljara and Lake Chapala

www.vivegdl.com.mx Official site of joint Guadalajara area tourism offices. English translation available. Extensive, but contains only neutral summary information of limited usefulness. For example, it lists lots of hotels, according to categories, with phone, fax, email addresses, and services available, but no prices, photos, or link for reservations as most commercial sites do. It has a current events listing daily that would be handy if you were in Guadalajara at the time you logged on.

www.chapala.com The website of the excellent monthly Chapala-area newspaper, *El Ojo del Agua*. Doesn't contain the entire newspaper—only the (good, however) monthly lead articles per edition, archived back about three years to the beginning of publication.

GLOSSARY

Many of the following words have a social-historical meaning;
others you will not find in the usual English-Spanish dictionary.

abarrotería—grocery store

alcalde—mayor or municipal judge

alfarería—pottery

andando—walkway or strolling path

antojitos—native Mexican snacks, such as tamales, *chiles rellenos,* tacos, and enchiladas

artesanías—handicrafts, as distinguished from *artesanio,* a person who makes handicrafts

audiencia—one of the royal executive-judicial panels sent to rule Mexico during the 16th century

ayuntamiento—either the town council or the building where it meets

bienes raices—literally "good roots," but popularly, real estate

birria—goat, pork, or lamb stew, in spiced tomato broth, especially typical of Jalisco

boleto—ticket, boarding pass

cabercera—head town of a municipal district, or headquarters in general

cabrón—literally a cuckold, but more commonly, bastard, rat, or S.O.B.; sometimes used affectionately

cacique—chief or boss

calandria—early 1800s-style horse-drawn carriage, common in Guadalajara

camionera—bus station

campesino—country person; farm worker

canasta—basket of woven reeds, with handle

casa de huéspedes—guesthouse, usually operated in a family home

caballero—literally, "horseman," but popularly, gentleman

caudillo—dictator or political chief

charro, charra—gentleman cowboy or cowgirl

chingar—literally, "to rape," but also the universal Spanish "f" word, the equivalent of "screw" in English

churrigueresque—Spanish baroque architectural style incorporated into many Mexican colonial churches, named after José Churriguera (1665–1725)

científicos—literally, scientists, but applied to President Porfirio Díaz's technocratic advisers

cofradia—Catholic fraternal service association, either male or female, mainly in charge of financing and organizing religious festivals

colectivo—a shared public taxi or minibus that picks up and deposits passengers along a designated route

colegio—preparatory school or junior college

colonia—suburban subdivision/satellite of a larger city

Conasupo—government store that sells basic foods at subsidized prices

correo—post office

criollo—person of all-Spanish descent born in the New World

cuadra—Huichol yarn painting, usually rectangular

Cuaresma—Lent

curandero(a)—indigenous medicine man or woman

damas—ladies, as in "ladies room"

Domingo de Ramos—Palm Sunday

ejido—a constitutional, government-sponsored form of community, with shared land ownership and cooperative decision making

encomienda—colonial award of tribute from a designated indigenous district

estación ferrocarril—railroad station

farmacia—pharmacy or drugstore

finca—farm

fonda—foodstall or small restaurant, often in a traditional market complex

fraccionamiento—city sector or subdivision

fuero—the former right of clergy to be tried in separate ecclesiastical courts

gachupín—"one who wear spurs"; a derogatory term for a Spanish-born colonial

gasolinera—gasoline station

gente de razón—"people of reason"; whites and mestizos in colonial Mexico

gringo—once-derogatory but now commonly used term for North American whites

grito—impassioned cry, as in Hidalgo's Grito de Dolores

hacienda—large landed estate; also the government treasury

hidalgo—nobleman; called honorifically by "Don" or "Doña"

indígena—indigenous or aboriginal inhabitant of all-native descent who speaks his or her native tongue. Commonly, but incorrectly, an Indian *(indio)*

jejenes—"no-see-um" biting gnats, especially around San Blas, Nayarit

judiciales—the federal or state "judicial" or investigative police, best known to motorists for their highway checkpoint inspections

jugería—stall or small restaurant providing a large array of squeezed vegetable and fruit *jugos* (juices)

juzgado—the "hoosegow," or jail

larga distancia—long-distance telephone service, or the *caseta* (booth) where it's provided

licencado—academic degree (abbrev. Lic.) approximately equivalent to a bachelor's degree

lonchería—small lunch counter, usually serving juices, sandwiches, and *antojitos* (Mexican snacks)

machismo; macho—exaggerated sense of maleness; person who holds such a sense of himself

mestizo—person of mixed native-European descent

mescal—alcoholic beverage distilled from the fermented hearts of maguey (century plant)

milpa—native farm plot, usually of corn, squash and beans.

mordida—slang for bribe; literally "little bite"

palapa—thatched-roof structure, often open and shading a restaurant

panga—outboard launch *(lancha)*

papier-mâché—the craft of glued, multilayered paper sculpture, especially in Tonalá, Jalisco, where creations resemble fine pottery or lacquerware

Pemex—acronym for Petróleos Mexicanos, the national oil corporation

peninsulares—the Spanish-born ruling colonial elite

peón—a poor wage-earner, usually a country native

piñata—papier-mâché decoration, usually in animal or human form, filled with treats and broken open during a fiesta

plan—political manifesto, usually by a leader or group consolidating or seeking power

Porfiriato—the 34-year (1876–1910) ruling period of President-dictator Porfirio Díaz

pozole—stew, of hominy in broth, usually topped by shredded pork, cabbage, and diced onion

preventiva—municipal police

presidencia municipal—the headquarters, like a U.S. city or county hall, of a Mexican *municipio,* county-like local governmental unit

pronunciamiento—declaration of rebellion by an insurgent leader

puta—whore, bitch, or slut

pueblo—town or people

quinta—a villa or country house

quinto—the royal "one-fifth" tax on treasure and precious metals

retorno—cul-de-sac

rurales—former federal country police force created to fight bandidos

Semana Santa—pre-Easter holy week

taxi especial—private taxi, as distinguished from *taxi colectivo,* or collective taxi

telégrafo—telegraph office, lately converting to high-tech **telecomunicaciones,** or *telecom,* offering telegraph, telephone, and public fax services

vaquero—cowboy

vecinidad—neighborhood

yanqui—Yankee

zócalo—town plaza or central square

PRONUNCIATION GUIDE

Your Puerto Vallarta adventure will be more fun if you use a little Spanish. Mexican folks, although they may smile at your funny accent, will appreciate your halting efforts to break the ice and transform yourself from a foreigner to a potential friend.

Spanish commonly uses 30 letters—the familiar English 26, plus four straightforward additions: ch, ll, ñ, and rr, which are explained in "Consonants," below.

Vowels

Once you learn them, Spanish pronunciation rules—in contrast to English—don't change. Spanish vowels generally sound softer than in English. (Note: The capitalized syllables below receive stronger accents.)

Pronounce *a* like ah, as in hah: *agua* AH-gooah (water), *pan* PAHN (bread), and *casa* CAH-sah (house).

Pronounce *e* like ay, as in may: *mesa* MAY-sah (table), *tela* TAY-lah (cloth), and *de* DAY (of, from).

Pronounce *i* like ee, as in need: *diez* dee-AYZ (ten), *comida* ko-MEE-dah (meal), and *fin* FEEN (end).

Pronounce *o* like oh, as in go: *peso* PAY-soh (weight), *ocho* OH-choh (eight), and *poco* POH-koh (a bit).

Pronounce *u* like oo, as in cool: *uno* OO-noh (one), *cuarto* KOOAHR-toh (room), and *usted* oos-TAYD (you).

Accent

The rule for accent, the relative stress given to syllables within a given word, is straightforward. If a word ends in a vowel, an n, or an s, accent the next-to-last syllable; if not, accent the last syllable.

Pronounce *gracias* GRAH-seeahs (thank you), *orden* OHR-dayn (order), and *carretera* kah-ray-TAY-rah (highway).

Otherwise, accent the last syllable: *venir* vay-NEER (to come), *ferrocarril* fay-roh-cah-REEL (railroad), and *edad* ay-DAHD (age).

For practice, apply the accent ("vowel, n, or s") rule for the vowel-pronunciation examples above. Try to accent the words correctly without looking at the "answers" to the right.

Exceptions to the accent rule are always marked with an accent sign: (á, é,í, ó, or ú), such as *teléfono* tay-LAY-foh-noh (telephone), *jabón* hah-BON (soap), and *rápido* RAH-pee-doh (rapid).

Consonants

Seventeen Spanish consonants, *b, d, f, k, l, m, n, p, q, s, t, v, w, x, y, z,* and *ch,* are pronounced almost as in English; *h* occurs, but is silent—not pronounced at all.

As for the remaining seven *(c, g, j, ll, ñ, r, and rr)* consonants, pronounce *c* "hard," like k as in keep: *cuarto* KOOAR-toh (room), Tepic tay-PEEK (capital of Nayarit state). Exception: Before *e* or *i,* pronounce *c* "soft," like an English s, as in sit: *cerveza* sayr-VAY-sah (beer), *encima* ayn-SEE-mah (atop).

Before *a, o, u,* or a consonant, pronounce *g* "hard," as in gift: *gato* GAH-toh (cat), *hago* AH-goh (I do, make). Otherwise, pronounce g like h as in hat: *giro* HEE-roh (money order), *gente* HAYN-tay (people).

Pronounce *j* like an English h, as in has: *Jueves* HOOAY-vays (Thursday), *mejor* may-HOR (better).

Pronounce *ll* like y, as in yes: *toalla* toh-AH-yah (towel), *ellos* AY-yohs (they, them).

Pronounce *ñ* like ny, as in canyon: *año* AH-nyo (year), *señor* SAY-nyor (Mr., sir).

The Spanish *r* is lightly trilled, with tongue at the roof of your mouth like the British r in very ("vehdy"). Pronounce *r* like a very light English d, as in ready: *pero* PAY-doh (but), *tres* TDAYS (three), *cuatro* KOOAH-tdoh (four).

Pronounce *rr* like a Spanish r, but with much more emphasis and trill. Let your tongue flap. Practice with *burro* (donkey), *carretera* (highway), and Carrillo (proper name), then really let go with *ferrocarril* (railroad).

SH-SPANISH PHRASEBOOK

e route to learning Spanish in Mexico is to refuse to speak English.
ourself (instead of watching the in-flight movie) with a basic word list
a pocket notebook. Use it to speak Spanish wherever you go.

Basic and Courteous

Courtesy is very important to Mexican people. They will appreciate your use of basic expressions. (Note: The upside-down Spanish question mark merely warns the reader of the query in advance.)

Hello—*Hola*
How are you?—*¿Cómo está usted?*
Very well, thank you.—*Muy bien, gracias.*
okay, good—*bueno*
not okay, bad—*malo, feo*
and you?—*¿y usted?*
(Note: Pronounce *"y,"* the Spanish "and," like the English "ee," as in "keep.")
Thank you very much.—*Muchas gracias.*
please—*por favor*
You're welcome.—*De nada.*
Just a moment, please.—*Momentito, por favor.*
How do you say . . . in Spanish?—*¿Cómo se dice . . . en español?*
Excuse me, please (when you're trying to get attention).—*Disculpe* or *Excúseme, con permiso.*
Excuse me (when you've made a boo-boo).—*Lo siento.*
good morning—*buenos días*
good afternoon—*buenas tardes*
good evening—*buenas noches*
Sir (Mr.), Ma'am (Mrs.), Miss—*Señor, Señora, Señorita*
What is your name?—*¿Cómo se llama usted?*
Pleased to meet you.—*Con mucho gusto.*
My name is . . .—*Me llamo . . .*
Would you like . . . ?—*¿Quisiera usted . . . ?*
Let's go to . . .—*Vámonos a . . .*
I would like to introduce my . . .—*Quisiera presentar mi . . .*
wife—*esposa*
husband—*esposo*
friend—*amigo* (male), *amiga* (female)
sweetheart—*novio* (male), *novia* (female)
son, daughter—*hijo, hija*
brother, sister—*hermano, hermana*
father, mother—*padre, madre*
See you later (again).—*Hasta luego (la vista).*
goodbye—*adiós*
yes, no—*sí, no*
I, you, he, she—*yo, usted, él, ella*
we, you (pl.), they—*nosotros, ustedes, ellos*
Do you speak English?—*¿Habla usted inglés?*

Getting Around

If I could use only two Spanish phrases, I would choose *"Disculpe (dee-SKOOL-pay),"* followed by *"¿Dónde está . . . ?"*

Where is . . . ?—*¿Dónde está . . . ?*
the bus station—*la terminal autobús*
the bus stop—*la parada autobús*
the taxi stand—*el sitio taxi*
the train station—*la terminal ferrocarril*
the airport—*el aeropuerto*
the boat—*la barca*
the bathroom, toilet—*el baño, sanitorio*
men's, women's—*el baño de hombres, de mujeres*
the entrance, exit—*la entrada, la salida*
the pharmacy—*la farmacia*
the bank—*el banco*
the police, police officer—*la policía*
the supermarket—*el supermercado*
the grocery store—*la abarrotería*
the laundry—*la lavandería*
the stationery (book) store—*la papelería (librería)*
the hardware store—*la ferretería*
the (long distance) telephone—*el teléfono (larga distancia)*
the post office—*el correo*
the ticket office—*la oficina boletos*
a hotel—*un hotel*
a cafe, a restaurant—*una café, un restaurante*
Where (Which) is the way to . . . ?—*¿Dónde (Cuál) está el camino a . . . ?*
How far to . . . ?—*¿Qué tan lejos a . . . ?*
How many blocks?—*¿Cuántos cuadras?*
(very) near, far—*(muy) cerca, lejos*

to, toward—*a*
by, through—*por*
from—*de*
the right, the left—*la derecha, la izquierda*
straight ahead—*derecho, directo*
in front—*en frente*
beside—*a lado*
behind—*atrás*
the corner—*la esquina*
the stoplight—*la semáforo*
a turn—*una vuelta*
right here—*aquí*
somewhere around here—*acá*
right there—*allí*
somewhere around there—*allá*
street, boulevard, highway—*calle, bólevar, carretera*
bridge, toll—*puente, cuota*
address—*dirección*
north, south—*norte, sur*
east, west—*oriente (este), poniente (oeste)*

Doing Things

Verbs are the key to getting along in Spanish. They employ mostly predictable forms and come in three classes, which end in ar, er, and ir, respectively:

to buy—*comprar*
I buy, you (he, she, it) buys—*compro, compra*
we buy, you (they) buy—*compramos, compran*

to eat—*comer*
I eat, you (he, she, it) eats—*como, come*
we eat, you (they) eat—*comemos, comen*

to climb—*subir*
I climb, you (he, she, it) climbs—*subo, sube*
we climb, you (they) climb—*subimos, suben*

Got the idea? Here are more (with irregularities marked in bold).

to do or make—*hacer*
I do or make, you (he she, it) does or makes—**hago**, *hace*
we do or make, you (they) do or make—*hacemos, hacen*

to go—*ir*
I go, you (he, she, it) goes: **voy, va**

we go, you (they) go: **vamos, van**

to love—*amar*
to swim—*nadar*
to walk—*andar*
to work—*trabajar*
to want—*desear, querer*
to read—*leer*
to write—*escribir*
to repair—*reparar*
to arrive—*llegar*
to stay (remain)—*quedar*
to stay (lodge)—*hospedar*
to look at—*mirar*
to look for—*buscar*
to give—*dar* (regular except for **doy**, I give)
to have—*tener* (irregular but important: **tengo, tiene**, tenemos, **tienen**)
to come—*venir* (similarly irregular: *vengo, viene, venimos, vienen*)

Spanish has two forms of "to be." Use *estar* when speaking of location: "I am at home." *"**Estoy** en casa."* Use *ser* for state of being: "I am a doctor." *"**Soy** una doctora."* Estar is regular except for **estoy**, I am. Ser is very irregular:

to be—*ser*
I am, you (he, she, it) is—*soy, es*
we are, you (they) are—*somos, son*

At the Station and on the Bus

I'd like a ticket to . . .—*Quisiera un boleto a . . .*
first (second) class—*primera (segunda) clase*
roundtrip—*ida y vuelta*
how much?—*¿cuánto?*
reservation—*reservación*
reserved seat—*asiento reservado*
seat number . . .—*número del asiento . . .*
baggage—*equipaje*
Where is this bus going?—*¿Dónde va este autobús?*
What's the name of this place?—*¿Cómo se llama este lugar?*
Stop here, please.—*Pare aquí, por favor.*

Eating Out

A *restaurante* (rays-tah-oo-RAHN-tay) generally implies a fairly fancy joint, with prices to match. The food and atmosphere, however, may be more to your liking at other types of eateries (in approximate order of price): *comedor, café, fonda, lonchería, jugería, taquería.*

I'm hungry (thirsty).—*Tengo hambre (sed).*
menu—*lista, menú*
order—*orden*
soft drink—*refresco*
coffee, cream—*café, crema*
tea—*té*
sugar—*azúcar*
drinking water—*agua pura, agua potable*
bottled carbonated water—*agua mineral*
bottled uncarbonated water—*agua sin gas*
glass—*vaso*
beer—*cerveza*
dark—*obscura*
draft—*de barril*
wine—*vino*
white, red—*blanco, tinto*
dry, sweet—*seco, dulce*
cheese—*queso*
snack—*antojo, botana*
daily lunch special—*comida corrida*
fried—*frito*
roasted—*asada*
barbecue, barbecued—*barbacoa, al carbón*
breakfast—*desayuno*
eggs—*huevos*
boiled—*tibios*
scrambled—*revueltos*
bread—*pan*
roll—*bolillo*
sweet roll—*pan dulce*
toast—*pan tostada*
oatmeal—*avena*
bacon, ham—*tocino, jamón*
salad—*ensalada*
lettuce—*lechuga*
carrot—*zanahoria*
tomato—*tomate*
oil—*aceite*
vinegar—*vinagre*
lime—*limón*
mayonnaise—*mayonesa*
fruit—*fruta*
mango—*mango*
watermelon—*sandía*
papaya—*papaya*
banana—*plátano*
apple—*manzana*
orange—*naranja*

fish—*pescado*
shrimp—*camarones*
oysters—*ostiones*
clams—*almejas*
octopus—*pulpo*
squid—*calamare*
meat (without)—*carne (sin)*
chicken—*pollo*
pork—*puerco*
beef, steak—*res, biftec*
the check—*la cuenta*

At the Hotel
In Puerto Vallarta region resorts, finding a reasonably priced hotel room presents no problem except during the high-occupancy weeks after Christmas and before Easter.

Is there . . . ?—*¿Hay . . . ?*
an (inexpensive) hotel—*un hotel (económico)*
an inn—*una posada*
a guesthouse—*una casa de huéspedes*
a single (double) room—*un cuarto sencillo (doble)*
with bath—*con baño*
shower—*ducha*
hot water—*agua caliente*
fan—*abanico, ventilador*
air-conditioned—*aire acondicionado*
double bed—*cama matrimonial*
twin beds—*camas gemelas*
How much for the room?—*¿Cuánto cuesta el cuarto?*
dining room—*comedor*
key—*llave*
towels—*toallas*
manager—*gerente*
soap—*jabón*
toilet paper—*papel higiénico*
swimming pool—*alberca, piscina*
the bill, please—*la cuenta, por favor*

At the Bank
El banco's often-long lines, short hours, and minuscule advantage in exchange rate make a nearby private *casa de cambio* a very handy alternative:

money—*dinero*
money-exchange bureau—*casa de cambio*
I would like to exchange traveler's checks.—

Quisiera cambiar cheques de viajero.
What is the exchange rate?—*¿Cuál es el cambio?*
How much is the commission?—*¿Cuánto cuesta el comisión?*
Do you accept credit cards?—*¿Aceptan tarjetas de crédito?*
money order—*giro*
teller's window—*caja*
signature—*firma*

Shopping

Es la costumbre—it is the custom—in Mexico that the first price is never the last. Bargaining often transforms shopping from a perfunctory chore into an open-ended adventure. Bargain with humor, and be prepared to walk away if the price is not right.

How much does it cost?—*¿Cuánto cuesta?*
too much—*demasiado*
expensive, cheap—*caro, barato (económico)*
too expensive, too cheap—*demasiado caro, demasiado barato*
more, less—*más, menos*
small, big—*chico, grande*
good, bad—*bueno, malo*
smaller, smallest—*más chico, el más chico*
larger, largest—*más grande, el más grande*
cheaper, cheapest—*más barato, el más barato*
What is your final price?—*¿Cuál es su último precio?*
Just right!—*¡Perfecto!*

Telephone, Post Office

In smaller Mexican towns, long-distance connections must be made at a central long-distance office, where people sometimes can sit, have coffee or a *refresco,* and socialize while waiting for their *larga distancia* to come through.

long-distance telephone—*teléfono larga distancia*
I would like to call . . .—*Quisiera llamar a . . .*
station to station—*a quien contesta*
person to person—*persona a persona*
credit card—*tarjeta de crédito*
post office—*correo*
general delivery—*lista de correo*
letter—*carta*
stamp—*estampilla*

postcard—*tarjeta*
aerogram—*aerograma*
air mail—*correo aero*
registered—*registrado*
money order—*giro*
package, box—*paquete, caja*
string, tape—*cuerda, cinta*

Formalities

Though many experienced travelers find Mexico among the most exotic of destinations (more so than either India or Japan), crossing the border remains relatively easy.

border—*frontera*
customs—*aduana*
immigration—*migración*
tourist card—*tarjeta de turista*
inspection—*inspección, revisión*
passport—*pasaporte*
profession—*profesión*
marital status—*estado civil*
single—*soltero*
married, divorced—*casado, divorciado*
widowed—*viudado*
insurance—*seguros*
title—*título*
driver's license—*licencia de manejar*
fishing, hunting, gun license—*licencia de pescar, cazar, armas*

At the Pharmacy, Doctor, Hospital

For a third-world country, Mexico provides good health care. Even small Puerto Vallarta regional towns have a basic hospital or clinic.

Help me please.—*Ayúdeme por favor.*
I am ill.—*Estoy enfermo.*
Call a doctor.—*Llame un doctor.*
Take me to . . .—*Lleveme a . . .*
hospital—*hospital, sanatorio*
drugstore—*farmacia*
pain—*dolor*
fever—*fiebre*
headache—*dolor de cabeza*
stomache ache—*dolor de estómago*
burn—*quemadura*
cramp—*calambre*
nausea—*náusea*
vomiting—*vomitar*
medicine—*medicina*

antibiotic—*antibiótico*
pill, tablet—*pastilla*
aspirin—*aspirina*
ointment, cream—*pomada, crema*
bandage—*venda*
cotton—*algodón*
sanitary napkins (use brand name)
birth control pills—*pastillas contraceptivos*
contraceptive foam—*espuma contraceptiva*
diaphragm (best carry an extra)
condoms—*contraceptivas*
toothbrush—*cepilla dental*
dental floss (bring an extra supply)
toothpaste—*crema dental*
dentist—*dentista*
toothache—*dolor demuelas*

At the Gas Station

Some Mexican gas station attendants are experts at shortchanging you in both money and gasoline. If you don't have a locking gas cap, either insist on pumping the gas yourself, or make certain the pump is zeroed before the attendant begins pumping. Furthermore, the kids who hang around gas stations are notoriously light fingered. Stow every loose item—cameras, purses, binoculars—out of sight *before* you pull into the *gasolinera.*

gas station—*gasolinera*
gasoline—*gasolina*
leaded, unleaded—*plomo, sin plomo*
full, please—*lleno, por favor*
gas cap—*tapón*
tire—*llanta*
tire repair shop—*vulcanizadora*
air—*aire*
water—*agua*
oil (change)—*aceite (cambio)*
grease—*grasa*
My . . . doesn't work.—*Mi . . . no sirve.*
battery—*batería*
radiator—*radiador*
alternator, generator—*alternador, generador*
tow truck—*grúa*
repair shop—*taller mecánico*
tune-up—*afinación*
auto parts store—*refaccionería*

Numbers and Time

zero—*cero*

one—*uno*
two—*dos*
three—*tres*
four—*cuatro*
five—*cinco*
six—*seis*
seven—*siete*
eight—*ocho*
nine—*nueve*
10—*diez*
11—*once*
12—*doce*
13—*trece*
14—*catorce*
15—*quince*
16—*dieciseis*
17—*diecisiete*
18—*dieciocho*
19—*diecinueve*
20—*veinte*
21—*veinte y uno,* or *veintiuno*
30—*treinta*
40—*cuarenta*
50—*cincuenta*
60—*sesenta*
70—*setenta*
80—*ochenta*
90—*noventa*
100—*ciento*
101—*ciento y uno,* or *cientiuno*
200—*doscientos*
500—*quinientos*
1,000—*mil*
10,000—*diez mil*
100,000—*cien mil*
1,000,000—*millón*
one-half—*medio*
one-third—*un tercio*
one-fourth—*un quarto*

What time is it?—*¿Qué hora es?*
It's one o'clock.—*Es la una.*
It's three in the afternoon.—*Son las tres de la tarde.*
It's 4 A.M.—*Son las cuatro de la mañana.*
six-thirty—*seis y media*
a quarter till eleven—*un cuarto antes de las once*
a quarter past five—*un cuarto pasada las cinco*

Monday—*lunes*
Tuesday—*martes*

Wednesday—*miércoles*
Thursday—*jueves*
Friday—*viernes*
Saturday—*sábado*
Sunday—*domingo*

January—*enero*
February—*febrero*
March—*marzo*
April—*abril*
May—*mayo*
June—*junio*
July—*julio*
August—*agosto*
September—*septiembre*
October—*octubre*
November—*noviembre*
December—*diciembre*

last Sunday—*domingo pasado*
next December—*diciembre próximo*
yesterday—*ayer*
tomorrow—*mañana*
an hour—*una hora*
a week—*una semana*
a month—*un mes*
a week ago—*hace una semana*
after—*después*
before—*antes*

SUGGESTED READING

Some of these books are informative, others are entertaining, and all of them will increase your understanding of Mexico. Some are easier to find in Mexico than at home, and vice versa. Take a few along on your trip. If you find others that are especially noteworthy, let us know. Happy reading.

HISTORY

Calderón de la Barca, Fanny. *Life in Mexico, with New Material from the Author's Journals.* New York: Doubleday, 1966. Edited by H.T. and M.H. Fisher. An update of the brilliant, humorous, and celebrated original 1913 book by the Scottish wife of the Spanish ambassador to Mexico.

Casasola, Gustavo. *Seis Siglos de Historia Gráfica de Mexico* (Six Centuries of Mexican Graphic History). Mexico City: Editorial Gustavo Casasola, 1978. Six fascinating volumes of Mexican history in pictures, from 1325 to the present.

Collis, Maurice. *Cortés and Montezuma.* New York: New Directions Publishing Corp., 1999. A reprint of a 1954 classic piece of well-researched storytelling. Collis traces Cort*s's conquest of Mexico through the defeat of his chief opponent, Aztec Emperor Montezuma. He uses contemporary eyewitnesses—notably Bernal Díaz de Castillo—to re-vivify one of histories greatest dramas.

Cortés, Hernán. *Letters From Mexico.* Translated by Anthony Pagden. New Haven: Yale University Press, 1986. Cortés's five long letters to his king, in which he describes contemporary Mexico in fascinating detail, including, notably, the remarkably sophisticated life of the Aztecs at the time of the conquest.

Díaz del Castillo, Bernal. *The True Story of the Conquest of Mexico.* Translated by Albert Idell. Garden City: Doubleday, 1956. A soldier's still-fresh tale of the conquest from the Spanish viewpoint.

Garfias, Luis. *The Mexican Revolution.* Mexico City: Panorama Editorial, 1985. A concise

Mexican version of the 1910–1917 Mexican revolution, the crucible of present-day Mexico.

Gugliotta, Bobette. *Women of Mexico.* Encino, CA: Floricanto Press, 1989. Lively legends, tales and biographies of remarkable Mexican women, from Zapotec princesses to Independence heroines.

León-Portilla, Miguel. *The Broken Spears: The Aztec Account of the Conquest of Mexico.* New York: Beacon Press, 1962. Provides an interesting contrast to Díaz del Castillo's account.

Meyer, Michael, and William Sherman. *The Course of Mexican History.* New York: Oxford University Press, 1991. An insightful, 700-plus-page college textbook in paperback. A bargain, especially if you can get it used.

Novas, Himilce. *Everything You Need to Know About Latino History.* New York: Plume Books (Penguin Group), 1994. Chicanos, Latin rhythm, La Raza, the Treaty of Guadalupe Hidalgo, and much more, interpreted from an authoritative Latino point of view.

Reed, John. *Insurgent Mexico.* New York: International Publisher's Co., 1994. Republication of 1914 original. Fast-moving, but not unbiased, description of the 1910 Mexican revolution by the journalist famed for his reporting of the subsequent 1917 Russian revolution. Reed, memorialized by the Soviets, was resurrected in the 1981 film biography *Reds.*

Ridley, Jasper. *Maximilian and Juárez.* New York: Ticknor and Fields, 1999. This authoritative historical biography breathes new life into one of Mexico's great ironic tragedies, a drama that pitted the native Zapotec "Lincoln of Mexico" against the dreamy, idealistic Archduke Maximilian of Austria-Hungary. Despite their common liberal ideas, they were drawn into a bloody no-quarter struggle that set the Old World against the New, ending in Maximilian's execution, insanity of his wife, and the emergence of the United States as a power to be reckoned with in world affairs.

Ruíz, Ramon Eduardo. *Triumphs and Tragedy: A History of the Mexican People.* New York: W.W. Norton, Inc., 1992. A pithy, anecdote-filled history of Mexico from an authoritative Mexican-American perspective.

Simpson, Lesley Bird. *Many Mexicos.* Berkeley: The University of California Press, 1962. A much-reprinted, fascinating broad-brush version of Mexican history.

UNIQUE GUIDE AND TIP BOOKS

American Automobile Association. *Mexico Travelbook.* Heathrow, FL: 1995. Published by the American Automobile Association, offices at 1000 AAA Drive, Heathrow, FL 32746-5063. Short sweet summaries of major Mexican tourist destinations and sights. Also includes information on fiestas, accommodations, restaurants, and a wealth of information relevant to car travel in Mexico. Available in bookstores, or free to AAA members at affiliate offices.

Burton, Tony. *Western Mexico, A Traveller's Treasury.* Guadalajara: Editorial Agata (Juan Manuel 316, Guadalajara 44100). A well-researched and lovingly written and illustrated guide to dozens of fascinating places to visit, both well-known and out of the way, in Michoacán, Jalisco, and Nayarit.

Church, Mike and Terry. *Traveler's Guide to Mexican Camping.* Kirkland, WA: Rolling Homes Press, P.O. Box 2099, Kirkland, WA 98083-2099. This is an unusually thorough guide to trailer parks all over Mexico, with much coverage of the Pacific Coast in general and the Puerto Vallarta Region in particular. Detailed maps guide you accurately to each trailer park cited, and clear descriptions tell you what to expect. The book also provides very helpful information on car travel in Mexico, including details of insurance, border crossing, highway safety, car repairs, and much more.

Franz, Carl. *The People's Guide to Mexico.* Santa Fe, NM: John Muir Publications, 11th edition, 1998. An entertaining and insightful A to Z general guide to the joys and pitfalls of independent economy travel in Mexico.

Freedman, Jacqueline, and Susan Gerstein. *Traveling Like Everybody Else.* Brooklyn NY: Lambda Publishing, Inc. Your handicap needn't keep you at home. This book was out of print at press time, but libraries may have copies.

Graham, Scott. *Handle With Care.* Chicago: The Noble Press, 1991. Should you accept a meal from a family who lives in a grass house? This insightful guide answers this and hundreds of other tough questions for persons who want to travel responsibly in the third world.

Howells, John, and Don Merwin. *Choose Mexico.* Oakland, CA: Gateway Books (distributed by Publishers Group West, Berkeley, CA). A pair of experienced Mexico residents provide a wealth of astute counsel about the important questions—health, finance, home ownership, work, driving, legalities—of long-term travel, residence, and retirement in Mexico. Includes specific sections on Puerto Vallarta, Guadalajara, and Lake Chapala.

Jeffries, Nan. *Adventuring With Children.* San Francisco: Foghorn Press, 1992. This unusually detailed book starts where most travel-with-children books end. It contains, besides a wealth of information and practical strategies for general travel with children, specific chapters on how you can adventure—trek, kayak, river-raft, camp, bicycle, and much more—successfully with the kids in tow.

Rogers, Steve, and Tina Rosa. *The Shopper's Guide to Mexico.* Santa Fe, NM: John Muir Publications. A well-written guide to shopping in Mexico, with emphasis on handicrafts.

Contains inventory details and locations of out-of-the-ordinary shops in towns and cities all over Mexico, including much on the Pacific centers, especially Puerto Vallarta, greater Guadalajara, Mazatlán, Pátzcuaro, and Oaxaca.

Stillman, Alan Eric. *Kwikpoint.* Alexandria, VA: GAIA Communications, P.O. Box 238, Alexandria, VA 22313-0238, email: kwikpoint@his .com. Eight dollars by cash or check gets you a super handy, durable color fold-out of pictures to point to when you need something in a foreign country. The pictures, such as a frying pan with fire under it (for "fried"), a compass (for "Which direction?"), a red lobster, and a cauliflower, are imaginative and unmistakable, anywhere between Puerto Vallarta and Pakistan or San Blas and Santander.

Weisbroth, Ericka, and Eric Ellman. *Bicycling Mexico.* New York: Hunter, 1990. These intrepid adventurers describe bike trips from Puerto Vallarta to Acapulco, coastal and highland Oaxaca, and highland Jalisco and Michoacán.

Werner, David. *Where There Is No Doctor.* Palo Alto, CA: Hesperian Foundation (P.O. Box 1692, Palo Alto, CA 94302). How to keep well in the backcountry.

FICTION

Bowen, David, and Ascencio, Juan A. *Pyramids of Glass.* San Antonio: Corona Publishing Co., 1994. Two dozen-odd stories that lead the reader along a month-long journey through the bedrooms, the barracks, the cafes, and streets of present-day Mexico.

Doerr, Harriet. *Consider This, Señor.* New York: Harcourt Brace, 1993. Four expatriates tough it out in a Mexican small town, adapting to the excesses—blazing sun, driving rain, vast, untrammeled landscapes—meanwhile interacting with the local folks while the local folks observe them, with a mixture of fascination and tolerance.

Fuentes, Carlos. *Where the Air Is Clear.* New York: Farrar, Straus and Giroux, 1971. The seminal work of Mexico's celebrated novelist.

Fuentes, Carlos. *The Years With Laura Díaz* New York: Farrar, Straus, and Giroux, 2000. A panorama of Mexico from Independence to the 21st century, through the eyes of one woman, Laura Díaz, and her great-grandson, the author. As one reviewer said, that she " ...as a Mexican woman, would like to celebrate Carlos Fuentes; it is worthy of applause that a man who has seen, observed, analyzed and criticized the great occurrences of the century now has a woman, Laura Díaz, speak for him." Translated by Alfred MacAdam.

Jennings, Gary. *Aztec.* New York: Atheneum, 1980. Beautifully researched and written monumental tale of lust, compassion, love, and death in pre-conquest Mexico.

Peters, Daniel. *The Luck of Huemac.* New York: Random House, 1981. An Aztec noble family's tale—of war, famine, sorcery, heroism, treachery, love, and finally disaster and death—in the Valley of Mexico.

Porter, Katherine Ann. *The Collected Stories.* New York: Delacorte, 1970.

Rulfo, Juan. *The Burning Plain.* Austin: University of Texas Press, 1967. Stories of people torn between the old and new in Mexico.

Traven, B. *The Treasure of the Sierra Madre.* New York: Hill and Wang, 1967. Campesinos, *federales,* gringos, and *indígenas* all figure in this modern morality tale set in Mexico's rugged outback. The most famous of the mysterious author's many novels of oppression and justice set in Mexico's jungles.

Villaseñor, Victor. *Rain of Gold.* New York: Delta Books (Bantam, Doubleday, and Dell), 1991. The moving, best-selling epic of the author's family's gritty travails. From humble rural beginnings in the Copper Canyon, they flee revolution and certain death, struggling through parched northern deserts to sprawling border refugee camps. From there they migrate to relative safety and an eventual modicum of happiness in Southern California.

PEOPLE AND CULTURE

Berrin, Kathleen. *The Art of the Huichol Indians.* Lovely, large photographs and text by a symposium of experts provide a good interpretive introduction to Huichol art and culture.

Castillo, Ana. *Goddess of the Americas.* New York, Riverhead Books, 1996. Here, a noted author has selected from the works of seven interpreters about Mesoameriacan female deities; and whose visions range as far and wide as Sex Goddess, the Broken-Hearted, the Subversive, and the Warrior Queen.

Lewis, Oscar. *Children of Sanchez.* New York: Random House, 1961. Poverty and strength in the Mexican underclass, sympathetically described and interpreted by renowned sociologist Lewis.

Medina, Sylvia López. *Cantora.* New York: Ballantine Books, 1992. Fascinated by the stories of her grandmother, aunt, and mother, the author seeks her own center by discovering a past that she thought she wanted to forget.

Meyerhoff, Barbara. *Peyote Hunt: the Sacred Journey of the Huichol Indians.* Ithaca: Cornell University Press, 1974. A description and interpretation of the Huichol's religious use of mind-bending natural hallucinogens.

Palmer, Colin A. *Slaves of the White God.* Cambridge: Harvard University Press. A scholarly study of why and how Spanish authorities imported African slaves into America and how they were used afterwards. Replete with poignant details, taken from Spanish and Mexican archives, describing how the Africans struggled from bondage to eventual freedom.

Riding, Alan. *Distant Neighbors: A Portrait of the Mexicans.* New York: Random House Vintage Books. Rare insights into Mexico and Mexicans.

Toor, Frances. *A Treasury of Mexican Folkways.* New York: Crown Books, 1947, reprinted by Bonanaza, 1985. An illustrated encyclopedia of vanishing Mexicana—costumes, religion, fiestas, burial practices, customs, legends—compiled during the celebrated author's 35 years' residence in Mexico.

Wauchope, Robert, ed. *Handbook of Middle American Indians.* Vols. 7 and 8. Austin: University of Texas Press, 1969. Authoritative surveys of important Indian-speaking groups in northern and central (vol. 8) and southern (vol. 7) Mexico.

FLORA AND FAUNA

Goodson, Gar. *Fishes of the Pacific Coast.* Stanford, CA: Stanford University Press, 1988. Over 500 beautifully detailed color drawings highlight this pocket version of all you ever wanted to know about the ocean's fishes (including common Spanish names) from Alaska to Peru.

Leopold, Starker. *Wildlife of Mexico.* Berkeley: University of California Press. Classic, illustrated layperson's survey of common Mexican mammals and birds.

Mason, Jr., Charles T., and Patricia B. Mason. *Handbook of Mexican Roadside Flora.* Tucson: University of Arizona Press, 1987. Authoritative identification guide, with line illustrations, of all the plants you're likely to see in the Puerto Vallarta region.

Morris, Percy A. *A Field Guide to Pacific Coast Shells.* Boston: Houghton Mifflin. The complete beachcomber's Pacific shell guide.

Novick, Rosalind, and Lan Sing Wu. *Where to Find Birds in San Blas, Nayarit.* Order through the authors at 178 Myrtle Court, Arcata, CA 95521, tel. 707/822-0790.

Pesman, M. Walter. *Meet Flora Mexicana.* Delightful anecdotes and illustrations of hundreds of common Mexican plants. Published around 1960, now out of print.

Peterson, Roger Tory, and Edward L. Chalif. *Field Guide to Mexican Birds.* Boston: Houghton Mifflin. With hundreds of Peterson's crisp color drawings, this is a must for serious birders and vacationers interested in the life that teems in the Puerto Vallarta region's beaches, jungles, lakes, and lagoons.

Wright, N. Pelham. *A Guide to Mexican Mammals and Reptiles.* Mexico City: Minutiae Mexicana, 1989. Pocket-edition lore, history, descriptions, and pictures of commonly seen Mexican animals.

ART, ARCHITECTURE, AND CRAFTS

Baird, Joseph. *The Churches of Mexico.* Berkeley: University of California Press. Mexican colonial architecture and art, illustrated and interpreted.

Cordrey, Donald, and Dorothy Cordrey. *Mexican Indian Costumes.* Austin: University of Texas Press, 1968. A lovingly photographed, written, and illustrated classic on Mexican Indians and their dress, emphasizing textiles.

Covarrubias, Miguel. *Indian Art of Mexico and Central America.* New York: Knopf, 1957. A timeless work by the renowned interpreter of *indígena* art and design.

Martínez Penaloza, Porfirio. *Popular Arts of Mexico.* Mexico City: Editorial Panorama, 1981. An excellent, authoritative, pocket-sized exposition of Mexican art.

Sayer, Chloë. *Arts and Crafts of Mexico.* San Francisco: Chronicle Books, 1990. All you ever wanted to know about your favorite Mexican crafts, from papier-mâché to pottery and toys and Taxco silver. Beautifully illustrated by traditional etchings and David Lavender's crisp black-and-white and color photographs.

ACCOMMODATIONS INDEX

TRAILER PARKS

RESTAURANT INDEX

INDEX

FISH/FISHING

GALLERIES

---

permits: boat 39; car 75–76
personal watercraft: 36; Puerto Vallarta 121; *see also specific place*
pesos: 76–77; devaluation of 23
pets: 75
peyote: 196
pine-oak forest: 5–7
pines: Chihuahua 5; Chinese 5; Montezuma 7; *pino triste* (sad pine) 5
Platanitos: 176
Playa Anclote: 140
Playa Boca de Iguanas: 277
Playa Borrego: 192
Playa Camarones: 98
Playa Careyes: 272
Playa Chacala: 175
Playa Chacalilla: 175
Playa Chalacatepec: 265
Playa Chamela: 266
Playa Coastecomate: 282
Playa Cocos: 191
Playa de Cocos: 282, 289
Playa del Beso: 167
Playa de Navidad: 281
Playa de Oro: 98
Playa Destiladeras: 138
Playa de Tehualmixtle: 263
Playa el Borrego: 182, 188–189
Playa El Gato: 96
Playa El Tecuán: 273, 274
Playa El Venado: 165
Playa Fortuna: 266
Playa Garza Blanca: 96
Playa Gemelas: 96
Playa Guayabitos-La Peñita: 167
Playa La Boca: 275
Playa La Manzanilla: 277–278
Playa Las Brisas: 272
Playa Las Glorias: 98
Playa las Islitas: 179–180, 191
Playa Lo de Marco: 164–165
Playa los Ayala: 167
Playa Los Carrizos: 96
Playa los Cocos: 178, 179
Playa los Corchos: 200
Playa los Muertos (Puerto Vallarta): 95–96
Playa los Muertos (Rincón de Guayabitos): 167
Playa Los Tules: 98
Playa Los Venados: 96
Playa Maito: 263
Playa Manzanillo: 137

Playa Matanchén: 179–180, 191
Playa Melaque: 281
Playa Mora: 275
Playa Negrita: 269–270
Playa Nuevo Vallarta: 133
Playa Perula: 266
Playa Piedra Blanca: 137
Playa Punta Negra: 96
Playa Punta Raza: 167–168
Playa Rosada: 266
Playa San Francisco: 163–164
Playa Sas Minñitas: 165
Playas Conchas Chinas: 96
Playa Tenacatita: 274–275
Playa Teopa: 272
Plaza de Armas: 216
Plaza de los Hombres Ilustres: 216–218
Plaza de los Mariachis: 219, 227–228
Plaza del Sol: 224–225
Plaza John Huston: 94
Plaza Laureles: 216
Plaza Liberación: 216
Plaza Tapatía: 216, 219–220
poisonous lizards: 9
police: 84; *see also specific place*
pompano: 10
population: 28–31
Porfiriato, the, revolution, stabilization: 18–21
Porfirio Díaz, Don: 18–19
postal service: 80; *see also specific place*
pottery: 48–49
PRD (Partido Revolucionario Democratico): 27
Presidencia Municipal: 205–206
PRI (Institutional Revolutionary Party): 21–24, 27
Princess Vallarta: 98–99
Princess Yelapa: 98–99
publications: *see* Information *section of specific place*
Puerto Vallarta: 88–133
Punta el Burro: 138
Punta Hermanos: 274
Punta Mita (Emiliano Zapata): 137–141
Punta Veneros: 138

QR
Quetzalcoatl: 11–12
Quimixto: 97
Quinta Santa María: 157
raicilla: 261–262
Rancho Tecuán: 273

ABOUT THE AUTHOR

In the early 1980s, the lure of travel drew Bruce Whipperman away from a 20-year career of teaching physics. The occasion was a trip to Kenya, which included a total solar eclipse and a safari. He hasn't stopped traveling since.

With his family grown, he has been free to let the world's wild, beautiful corners draw him on: to the ice-clawed Karakoram, the Gobi Desert's trellised oases, the pink palaces of Rajasthan, Japan's green wine country, Bali's emerald terraces, and now, the Puerto Vallarta region's golden beaches, wildlife-rich mangrove wetlands, and flower-festooned mountain valleys.

Bruce has always pursued his travel career for the fun of it. He started with slide shows and photo gifts for friends. Others wanted his photos, so he began selling them. Once, stranded in Ethiopia, he began to write. A dozen years later, after scores of magazine and newspaper feature stories, *Moon Handbooks: Pacific Mexico* became his first book. For him, travel writing heightens his awareness and focuses his own travel experiences. He always remembers what a Nepali Sherpa once said: "Many people come, looking, looking; few people come, see."

Travel, after all, is for returning home, and that coziest of journeys always brings a tired but happy Bruce back to his friends, son, daughter, and wife Linda in Oakland, California.

Bruce invites *Moon Handbooks: Puerto Vallarta's* readers likewise to "come see"—and discover and enjoy—Puerto Vallarta's delights with a fresh eye and renewed compassion.

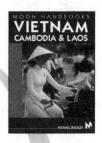

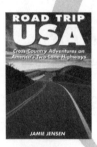